WITHDRAWN

MOTIVATION, BEHAVIOR, AND EMOTIONAL HEALTH
an Everyman's Interpretation

Donald MacKay Wonderly
PSI Associates, Inc.
Twinsburg, Ohio

Lanham • New York • London

Copyright © 1991 by

University Press of America®, Inc.
4720 Boston Way
Lanham, Maryland 20706

3 Henrietta Street
London WC2E 8LU England

All rights reserved
Printed in the United States of America
British Cataloging in Publication Information Available

Library of Congress Cataloging-in-Publication Data

Wonderly, Donald MacKay, 1920-
Motivation, behavior, and emotional health : an everyman's interpretation / Donald MacKay Wonderly.
p. cm.
Includes bibliographical references and index.
1. Motivation (Psychology) 2. Human behavior.
3. Mental health. 4. Psychology and philosophy.
5. Psychobiology. I. Title.
BF503.W66   1991
153.8—dc20   91-23927 CIP

ISBN 0-8191-8383-0 (hardcover, alk. paper)
ISBN 0-8191-8384-9 (pbk., alk. paper)

 The paper used in this publication meets the minimum requirements of American National Standard for Information Sciences—Permanence of Paper for Printed Library Materials, ANSI Z39.48–1984.

Dedication

To the Memory of Arthur Koestler
(1905-1983)

In 1963 I came across a book entitled *The Act of Creation*. I was so deeply impressed by the insights of a man with whose works I had, until then, been quite unfamiliar, that I immediately sought other examples of his writing. By the time I had completed *The Sleepwalkers*, and *Darkness at Noon*, I had joined the many thousands of devotees of Arthur Koestler. Whether in fictionalized accounts of bizarre human behavior, in straight historical reporting, or in essays on a wide variety of topics, Koestler stood head and shoulders above most of his contemporaries. He was described as "a writer unequalled in his generation for the extraordinary breadth of his genius.... His literary output [was] witness to his many sided imagination, to his intellectual power, and to his extraordinary literary prowess."[1] He was occasionally referred to as a "gadfly," but his sting was intended to provoke intellectual exchange. His pen made issues come to life. Scientists of every discipline have quoted him. They continue to remark on the ideas that he disseminated in lectures, seminars, and symposia around the world, over a period of 40 odd years.

The thinking of those of us who participated in the development of the motivational scheme presented here has been significantly influenced by many of Koestler's ideas, particularly regarding the Janus faced nature of living creatures, and especially of human beings. My brief contact with him a few years prior to his untimely death provided moments that I shall never forget. He was a kind and accommodating host, as well as a fascinating conversationalist, in any of a variety of European languages. Our loss is Valhalla's gain.

---

1. Harris (1984), p. 10

Acknowledgements

The material presented in this text is based on experiences with a decade of classes comprised of an exceptional group of students who contributed heavily to every aspect of the work (which accounts for the use of the "royal" *we* throughout the text). Our relationship was always more than that of teacher to pupil. It was rather, an ongoing series of struggles with every concept that came to the floor. The result was an intense, personal, often loving, relationship that has endured in many cases across the years.

It is, of course, impossible to adequately credit each individual. Thus we must risk the indignation of some, by naming only a few of those whose insights seem to have been most influential. Dr. Joel Kupfersmid, who had difficulty with spelling (we were concerned that he may not be able to spell PhD!) coined the acronym PSI (Prevention Systems Intervention), which identified both the training model and the professional organization that grew out of it. He also collaborated on some 15 publications. Dr. Mike Connelly read and reread, coming up again and again with an unexpected inconsistency. Dr. Steve Rosenberg, now president of PSI Associates, an organization that was founded on the principles developed here, went from being an excellent student, to a trusted colleague, to a best friend over two decades. Dr. Jeanne Simpson was her own special case. Never satisfied with an unclear concept, she refused to surrender until a point was ironed out. Jeanne could make the sun shine with her smile, while she attacked a dubious contention with gritted teeth. Dr. Linda Carter brought a breath of fresh air to the proceedings—and to the preparation of this text—with her brilliant, creative, and penetrating analysis of complex issues.

Dr. Kathleen McNamara was perhaps our conscience, pointing out the need for recognizing the unique contribution of females in every professional field, while preparing endless examples of gourmet cuisine that belied her feminist leanings. Dr's. Joanne Deak, Nancy Nazzario, Tom Wrenn, Dennis Pinciotti, and Steve Jessie all made critical contributions. To these, and all of the other students involved, a most humble thanks is extended.

The task of editing—cutting, fitting, deleting, modifying, harassing, complaining, and on rare occasion expressing satisfaction—fell to Dr. Caven Mcloughlin, without whose persistent effort, the work would never have been completed. His sincere commitment, punctuated by a demand for continual exertion, provided the essential motivational element.

A special expression of gratitude is due to Laura Guerreiro-Ramos whose skill as a compositor, and patience with my organizational innocence, cannot be overestimated.

Contents

DEDICATION III

ACKNOWLEDGEMENTS V

ILLUSTRATIONS XIII

PREFACE XV

1   **CONCEPTIONS OF LIFE** 1
    METASCIENCE 3
      Finalism 3
      Vitalism 7
      Phenomenology and Existentialism 9
    SCIENCE: MECHANISTIC REDUCTIONISM 13
      Evolution 19
      Organicism 27
      The Dilemma 28
    SUMMARY 31
    CHAPTER NOTES 35

2   **HOLONIC NATURE OF EXISTENCE** 39
    SUBSTANCE: THE WORLD OF PRE-EXISTENTIAL BEING 40
    EXISTENCE: THE WORLD OF PERCEPTUAL CHARACTERISTICS 42
    REALITY 45
    MEANING 50
    THE HOLON 55
    SYSTEMS CONCEPTS 61
    SUMMARY 64
    CHAPTER NOTES 65

3   **LIFE: A HOLARCHIC CONTINGENCY** 69
    EMERGENCE 73
    THE HOLARCHY 75
    BIOCHEMICAL ELEMENTS 78
    THE CHICKEN OR THE EGG? 79
    THE PLAN AND THE PATTERN 84

  THE PHENOTYPE AS AGENT 87
  SUMMARY 95
  CHAPTER NOTES 97

4 PURPOSE 101
  BIOLOGICAL INTERPRETATIONS 105
  PHILOSOPHIC AND SCIENTIFIC POSITIONS 109
  EVIDENCE IN PLANT AND ANIMAL BEHAVIOR 112
  PURPOSE DEFINED 114
  THE IMMEDIATE TARGET 116
  DELIBERATE SYSTEMS 119
  THE ULTIMATE GOAL 121
  THE MECHANICS OF PURPOSE 123
  SUMMARY 125
  CHAPTER NOTES 127

5 EPISTEMOLOGY 129
  THE CYBERNETIC PROCESS IN LIVING BEINGS 134
  EPISTEMICS OF LIFE 138
    Drive 140
    Perception 142
    Learning 146
    Intelligence 148
  SUMMARY 149
  CHAPTER NOTES 151

6 MIND 153
  COGNITION 163
  CONCEPTION 165
  AFFECT 166
  BELIEF 168
  MENTAL LEARNING 179
  MENTAL INTELLIGENCE 185
  HIGHER MENTAL PROCESSES 187
  SUMMARY 189
  CHAPTER NOTES 191

7 MIND: INFORMATION CHANNELS 193
  DESIRE 193
  THE NEGATIVE ASPECT 194

TYPES OF DESIRE 197
   Assertive Desires 198
      Hunger 199
      Sex 200
      Potency 202
      Stimulation 203
      Power 205
   Protective Desires 206
      Integrity 207
      Safety 207
      Appestats 208
   Transcendent Desires 208
NEEDS 210
   Desire/Need Interaction 211
PERCEPTION AND MIND 214
SUMMARY 219
CHAPTER NOTES 221

8 MENTAL COMPONENTS 223
FACT 225
   TRUTH 229
   Proof 229
MEASUREMENT 230
   Judgment 231
   Reason 234
   Evaluation 235
      Aesthetics 236
      Morality 238
SUMMARY 249
CHAPTER NOTES 251

9 EMOTION 255
THE EMOTIONAL EXPERIENCE 261
POSITIVE EMOTIONS 266
NEGATIVE EMOTIONS 268
PARAMETERS OF EMOTION 276
   Attitudes 276
      Love 276
      Hope 279
      Wish 280

  Excitation 283
 Summary 283
 Chapter Notes 287

10 Conflict, Control, & the Emergent Self 289
 Parameters of the Self 289
 Emotion and the Self 296
 The Problem of Identity 300
  Analytic Dynamisms and the Self *303*
  Belief and the Self 304
   The Continuity of the Self 306
   The Self as Independent 307
 Summary 310
 Chapter Notes 311

11 Motivation I: Theoretical Concepts 313
 The Holarchic Model 314
 Problems of Interpretation 318
  Applied Behavioral Interpretations 321
 Consciousness 327
  The Psychoanalytic View 328
   The Unconscious 328
   The Preconscious 331
   The Superego 332
 The Holarchic View of Nonconscious States 334
 Summary 341
 Chapter Notes 343

12 Motivation 2: Cognate Factors 347
 Desires as Limited 347
 Morality and Behavior 350
  The Oedipus Complex *351*
 Reason and Behavior 354
 Freedom and the Dominant Emotion 356
 Determinism and Responsibility 363
 The Role of Aggression 366
  Hostility 373
  Sadism 373
 Summary 375
 Chapter Notes 377

13 BEHAVIOR 379
    NETWANT/NETCOST 380
    THE DELIBERATIVE SEQUENCE 381
    BEHAVIOR CLASSES 383
    INSTINCTIVE KNOWLEDGE AND INSTINCTIVE BEHAVIOR 385
    LEARNED BEHAVIOR 393
    CHARACTERISTICS OF BEHAVIOR 396
    THE BEHAVIORAL EVENT 399
    SUMMARY 401
    CHAPTER NOTES 403

14 EMOTIONAL HEALTH AND THE COUNSELING PROCESS 405
    MENTAL HEALTH 406
    THE HOLARCHIC MODEL OF EMOTIONAL HEALTH 406
    DEFENSE MECHANISMS 412
    DEFENSE AS BELIEF 415
    EMOTIONAL MALADJUSTMENT 421
    COUNSELING 425
        Clienthood 425
        Diagnostic Principles 426
        Intervention Caveats 427
    SETTING THE STAGE 428
        Counselor Characteristics 431
    THE COUNSELING PROCESS 432
        The Therapeutic Theater 434
        The Case of Madeline G. 436
    SUMMARY 440
    CHAPTER NOTES 443

15 BEHAVIOR/BELIEF ALTERATION 445
    EMOTIONAL ELEMENTS 446
    BEHAVIOR ELEMENTS 447
    THE BEHAVIOR ADJUSTMENT PARADIGM 448
    THE DIAGNOSTIC PROCESS 453
    EMPLOYING THE BEHAVIOR ADJUSTMENT PARADIGM 457
        Assessing Emotional States 458
        Behavior Alteration 460
        Deviant Behavior Types 461
    DIAGNOSIS/TREATMENT EXAMPLES 462
    SUMMARY 473

CHAPTER NOTES 475

16 PRIMARY PREVENTION - A LOOK TO THE FUTURE 477
    PSI - PREVENTION SYSTEMS INTERVENTION 479
    INEFFECTIVE PRACTICES 479
    THE ROLE OF THE SCHOOL 481
        Responsibility 482
        The Right to Decide 483
            Children's Rights 483
            Professional Rights 484
            Parent's Rights 486
            The School Board's Role 487
        Coherence 487
        Quality 488
    THE IMPACT OF SCHISMATIC BELIEFS 489
        The Natural Rights Dilemma 491
            The Historical Perspective 493
            The Right to Self Indulgence 495
            The Right to Equal Treatment 497
        The Fact/Value Dichotomy 498
        An Alternative Approach 499
        Knowledge as Learned 499
        The Holarchic Position Restated 500
    DEVELOPMENTAL CONCEPTS 503
        The Nature of Discipline 503
        The Role of Work 505
        The Development of Responsibility 508
    SUMMARY 510
    CHAPTER NOTES 511

EPILOGUE 517

GLOSSARY 519

REFERENCES 525

INDEX 545

Illustrations

TABLES
- 2.1 Inorganic Holon Chain 59
- 3.1 Organic Holon Chain 75
- 6.1 Action/Reaction/Consequence/Interpretation 173
- 7.1 Desire Types 198
- 7.2 Pre-mind/Mind Signal Systems 216
- 9.1 Positive Emotional Terms 267
- 10.1 The Emergent Self 297
- 13.1 The Behavioral Progression 400

FIGURES
- 3.1 Genotype/Environment Interaction 86
- 5.1 Pre-mind Information Processing System 139
- 6.1 Pre-mind/Mental Knowledge 177
- 6.2 Response Patterns 181
- 6.3 Learning Holon Chain: A Soccer Example 184
- 7.1 Arousal Levels for Classes of Desire 212
- 8.1 Experience/Activity Sequence 226
- 8.2 Estimation and Evaluation Standards 233
- 9.1 Wish/Hope and Rain Potential 281
- 9.2 Wish/Hope Paradigm 282
- 10.1 Identification and Behavior Continua 294
- 11.1 The Holarchic Motivation Model 318
- 11.2 The Eye of Consciousness 335
- 11.3 Psychoanalytic Mental Model 336
- 11.4 Holarchic Mental Model 338
- 12.1 Characteristics of Aggression, Hostility, and Sadism 374
- 14.1 Emotional Health and Behavior Potential 408
- 15.1 The Behavior/Adjustment Paradigm 449
- 15.2 The BAP and Alcohol Abuse 470
- 16.1 Work, Discipline, and Responsibility 506

Preface

There is, today, no agreement concerning the nature of positive emotional health in spite of the dedicated attention of workers in such fields as medicine, psychology, and social work. No behavior patterns have been identified as singularly associated with the acquisition of emotional health, and there is little evidence that specific programs can guarantee its maintenance.

Research is being conducted worldwide in an effort to find methods for improving the emotional health of children and adults. It is carried out in schools, universities, mental health clinics, and even prisons and neighborhood hangouts. Funded by federal, state, and local grants; by foundations and by individual philanthropy, the research is marked by confusion and doubt, semantic disagreement, and mutual antipathy between adherents of conflicting views. Most seriously, such studies have provided no clear direction—either in terms of what is sought or how the problem may be effectively addressed.

Research projects are based on a variety of theories of personality development and methodology which are divergent enough to suggest that some must surely be in error. This is due, in part, to disagreement on the very meaning of the concept *emotional health*, and on what degree of adjustment is optimal. Hebb's mid-twentieth century contention that little is known about "mental hygiene," or how to influence it, remains valid today.

In attacking the problem, much current emphasis is being placed on a preventive approach through such avenues as community psychology, revised interpretations of the role of the school, a new focus on the potential contributions of sociological analyses due to the maturity of ecological study, and a number of recent ethological findings. Their potential contribution is, however, vitiated by a reluctance to condone intervention prior to the emergence of symptoms that preventive approaches demand. It is one thing to treat water sources with chemical agents when the bacillus which carries typhoid fever can be isolated. It is entirely another matter to expect communities to support programs designed to have an impact on future generations, especially when the variables under study are so poorly understood.

Attempts to interpret the role of humankind in our vast and incomprehensible universe have been manifested in the writings of many thinkers in different ways at different times. In the first 15 centuries of Christianity, philosophers stressed the primacy of God and eternity. In spite of the cogency of much of their argument, the perennial appeal to an omniscient being destroyed their credibility. The inductive (scientific) approach, which calls for a rejection of prophecy as well as for the repudiation of introspective accounts of human behavior, has become so ensconced that much invaluable information has been discarded.

As the perspective of this text was being developed and the contributions of early thinkers were considered, it became obvious that the wheel of thought has been reinvented not once but many times. The extent to which so many insights have been forgotten or ignored is explicable only as a modern overreaction based on an arrant conviction that empirical science holds the only keys to true knowledge. In the rush to rat research, little attention has been paid to yesterday's wisdom. Koestler stated that "as a result of their divorce, neither faith nor science is able to satisfy man's intellectual curiosity. In the divided house both inhabitants lead a thwarted existence."[1]

Theories concerning such topics as ethics and epistemology are, of course, tentative in nature, and in 2,000 years of analysis little consensus has been reached. A myriad of hypotheses have been developed including those which see humans as a special kind of animal, as ethology suggests; those which view human life as a unique creation, as finalism insists; and those which reduce human behavior to a complex, but essentially mechanical reaction, as behaviorism proposes. Angel, animal, or machine? No compromise seems acceptable.

Twentieth Century thinkers have taken tremendous strides toward the elimination of essentialist and rationalist conceptualizations. William James asserted that essentialist notions are vacuous; Ayer considered the positing of an intuitive sense an example of metaphysical nonsense; Nagel found the invoking of purpose unnecessarily teleological; and Waddington would be amused that anyone might cling to a vitalistic interpretation that has been characterized by most biologists as thoroughly obsolete.

A careful study of these many interpretations has led to the conclusion that all are, in some regard, wanting. This is not because of the arrogance of the pragmatic-humanist-existential contention that humans are essentially the creators of their own universe. Such a view has considerable logical merit. Neither is it because of the narrow cognitive perspective of the analytic-positivist-empiricist conviction that legitimate propositions must be subject to sensory validation. Hume's charge that any book which does not contain statements about facts or relations between ideas should be committed to the flames, and Russell's claim that "what science cannot discover, mankind cannot know" are impressive sentiments, girded by volumes of evidence.

Our rejection of such claims is based on the discovery that each of these purveyors of a "new truth" which discards the eternal, and proclaims the contingency of human life, assumes some moral, as well as intellectual superiority. Each, in fact, employs the very form of knowledge that is being denied in justifying the acceptance of his own "enlightened" philosophy.

Berkeley's appeal to an omniperceptive God was a frank effort to explain the paradox that grew out of the logical conclusion of his argument, and rightly so, since his epistemology might otherwise have limited knowledge to human perception. For this he has been widely criticized. However, James was equally presumptuous in his contention that the creation of truth in the universe adds both to human "dignity and responsibility." What strange terms to defend pragmatically! Even the toughest minded empiricist leans heavily on some intellectual *intuition* in arguing that his position *should* be accepted if people are to "fulfill their obligations."

The new evolutionary ethic, embraced by so many biologists, would make sense if it followed the harsh but inescapable conclusions of Nietzchian analysis. Instead, it offers a bastardization which attempts to reconcile the mechanistic implications of Mendelian genetics with a philosophy that defends such concepts as that of inalienable human rights—which is inimical with an honest interpretation of Neo-Darwinian principles.

Behaviorists disdain the naive assumption that a chicken crosses the street because it "wants" to. With scientific hauteur, they explain, with some annoyance, that such concepts as desire and emotion are not fit subjects for scientific analysis. However, in substituting such terms as *deprivation* and *satiation*, the behaviorist deals in the same type of reification despite an insistence that behavior is the only legitimate focus of study.

Skinner suggested that theory is unnecessary—that the datum should be allowed to speak for itself.[2] If the pigeon pecks, it may be assumed that reinforcement has occurred. The evidence of human and animal self-sacrifice, which suggests a self transcendent presence, is ignored or attributed to some type of environmental reinforcement. In behavioral terms, the non-active individual cannot be described psychologically; guilt and aggression are considered only behavioral concomitants. An approach to emotional health based on such a viewpoint is apt to be severely handicapped, since, if the purpose of deliberate action is to achieve an affective state which is peculiar to some idiosyncratic need, its redirection toward a goal selected by the manipulator may be wholly inappropriate.

Motivation for challenging some of the tenets of the so-called "scientific" approach is based on the urgency of the issue, and some distress concerning the rate at which the nature of the problem is apt to be recognized. It took thousands of years to locate the nervous center in the head; 400 years to discover that Copernicus was deceived; and 200 years for science to recover from Newton's pessimistic aerodynamic theory. Evidence of a more rapid recovery from the pronouncements of extremist hypothesists is seen in the less than one century it has taken to put Freudian psychology into a more reasonable perspective. We can only hope that the oversimplification of human activity which behavioral technology and similarly myopic views of humankind propose will be ameliorated even more rapidly. Science is enjoined to seek explanation in the facts. But the facts are mute.

If the emotional health of a nation's citizenry is to be significantly improved, it is essential that programs be based on an interpretation of emotion, motivation and behavior that takes into account *all* of the contributing agencies. To do this, the sterile data provided by sheer perceptual observation and cognitive manipulation must be transcended. Explanations that synthesize and extrapolate, or even posit causal agents that cannot be counted, weighed, or poked, must not be rudely dismissed. The capacity to understand must not be stifled by a set of rules that eliminates our most effective weapons.

In this text we will propose an emotional health model based on a philosophical and psychological interpretation of human behavioral motivation which departs from traditional approaches in certain aspects while retaining elements that seem meaningful. The model is predicated on the thesis that at least part of the reason for the current state of affairs is that educational and mental health institutions have been developed on the basis of misleading assumptions about the causes of behavior. The result has been the development of practices which are at best inefficient and at worst destructive. Popular assumptions regarding human behavior are challenged as inimical, in many instances, with respected scientific principles and, in others, with sound logical conclusion.

An interpretation of human activity is presented in a language which may offend purists, but which, hopefully, will be acceptable to those who do not tremble at the thought that human behavior is functional, emotions are purposive, and decisions are based in part on moral as well as rational judgment.

This position is based in part on Koestler's holonic model; an approach that bridges holism and reductionism.[3] The contention is that all existents and especially humans, must be understood both in their role as independent agents and in their subordination as parts of more comprehensive entities. Koestler's interpretation of the basis for the human proclivity for conspecific destruction, which is based heavily on MacLean's work with reptilian brains shall, however, be denied.[4] Learning, rather than emotion-control will be offered as a more appropriate approach to the amelioration of problems of emotional adjustment.

Teleological explanations are anathema to Twentieth Century thinkers. Cybernetics and reductionist positivism have provided a refuge from the necessity of assuming final causes in the acts of any form of life although such speculators have had difficulty in accounting for any of its vital phenomena. Furthermore, certain terms employed by philosophers have become so derogated by those for whom the scientific approach has come to represent the only respectable avenue to understanding behavior, that it is difficult to clarify a position in a way that is placating to all. In spite of this, an attempt shall be made to offer some explanation for the position taken in this text in a philosophic context, although emphasis is placed not on the logical, but on the pragmatic aspect of the argument.

Among the many alternative interpretations of human existence, one shall be employed here that accepts the constraint that personal, social and cultural behavior do not lend themselves to deductive-nomological or "covering law" explanations.[5]

No set of principles can be offered from which may be predicted with precision that, given a set of antecedent conditions, a unique structure, function, or behavior will ensue. We believe, however that historical and functional descriptions based on processes developed in simpler forms of life, offer a promising technique with which to understand motivation, adjustment, and sources of debilitation. This is not to deny that humans are unique in some respects, nor even that mechanistic and finalistic explanations may be adequate at some level. However, neither polar extreme appears sufficiently comprehensive to provide a thorough account of human behavior.

We posit an interpretation of life that calls for the acceptance of emergent properties, with the implicit assumption that this phenomenon plays a significant role in the universe. The logical adequacy of the precisely opposite view is, however, appreciated. The cosmic urge may be toward a state of total entropy. Only an infinitesimal fraction of all that exists is negentropic over time, and the patterns of equal distribution are as magnificent as those of the irregularity that life introduces.

Perhaps life is an embarrassment to the universal design. The elements certainly mount a continuous, and often successful, assault against the various forms in which life is manifested. Whole species have been obliterated by unanticipated climatic alteration. Humans have not learned to avoid the devastation of earthquake, or the insidious affect of cosmic rays, and all known organic forms live out their existence within a trivial envelope of space on an ordinary planet in a disinterested solar system.

Such a view is by no means uncommon. Freud's death wish, Schopenhauer's pessimism, Sartre's nihilism, and the many philosophies which exalt non-existence are constant reminders that to see life as positive represents only one of many possible viewpoints. But the position we present is not defended simply on the ground that it brings hope. Rather, we believe it to be as logically sound as others, and that it provides an efficacious framework on which to develop emotional health programs.

This may seem a most audacious posture. However, the urge to respond to what in many instances seems unwarranted is compelling. And to question those whose pronouncements affect the welfare of humankind is a responsibility rather than a privilege. As Thomas Mann's Herr Settembrini described the obligation to criticize, "You *should* judge—to that end you have been given your eyes and your understanding."[6]

1. Koestler (1959), p. 537
2. Skinner (1961)
3. Koestler (1967)
4. MacLean (1969)
5. Hempel (1965)
6. Mann (1967), p. 65

─────────── *Chapter 1* ───────────
Conceptions of Life

Divergent philosophies have evolved in the attempt to unravel the enigma that is life. Each theory provides useful but limited data and each suffers from an insistence on rejecting conceptualizations not totally consonant with its own basic tenets.

Reductionists disavow as fanciful and mysterious the vitalist contention that life is irreducible to the principles of chemistry and physics, while phenomenologists abjure the sterility of the allegations of molecular biologists. Evolutionists and creationists stalk each other as enemies of "truth" and purveyors of unsupportable claims. No compromise is considered.

A view of life is proposed here that includes elements of both holistic and organismic theoretical positions. Data from genetics, biology, ethology, and related disciplines which are accepted as valid by a significant representation of the scientific community have been incorporated in order to provide a more heuristic approach.

The annals of speculation concerning the nature of life are marked by philosophic and psychological convictions that have stifled progress toward the development of programs for optimizing mental health. Problems associated with discriminating between the living and the nonliving have resulted in an unprofitable polarization.

Reductionist scientists tolerate as muddle-headed those humanists who maintain that concepts such as innate desire and motivation are essential to an understanding of human behavior. In much the same manner, the sterile approach of the laboratory-minded is derided by theologians, phenomenologists, and assorted mystics as explaining everything but life.

Rationalist and empiricist, pragmatist and essentialist, each has developed a body of knowledge which purports to explain existence. Each has assumed that those whose views are not in accord can be proven to be in error. Disagreement regarding concepts such as freedom, determinism, and purpose is based on the assumption that opposing positions are necessarily mutually exclusive and probably exhaustive.

But this is a great mischief. Purpose, for example, may be described in a variety of ways, one of which shall be developed in this text. Other concepts shall also be considered as embracing more possible definitions than either scientist or metaphysicist allows. Terms like *accidental*, *contingent*, and *uncaused* are only possible synonyms for the word "free," and purpose may be characterized in such a way as to remove the stigma of final cause which has been perennially attached to it.

Conflicting views of life are described in this chapter. Our intention is not to prove that one of the options is "correct." Rather, it is to show that some seem highly unlikely, while others appear at best minimally competent to describe the essential attributes of the flowing, striving phenomenon that characterizes the living process. Although human life is of central concern, it will be necessary to deal with many levels of organic existence in order to provide a compelling interpretation.

We propose a theoretical model which we hope to be of sufficient persuasion that it may represent a foundation on which a program of psychological intervention can be constructed. In order to do so as efficiently as possible, philosophic postures will be accepted without discussion where there is reason to believe that a significant part of the scholarly community finds them acceptable. However, in some instances this is not possible, and an attempt will be made to justify the adopted approach.

There is a peculiar mind-set that characterizes people of all levels of education and intellect that causes them to define the living as either a trivial peculiarity of physicochemical action, or the result of deliberate (divine?) intervention. Such elections produce the paradox of benevolent, reductionist biologists and pea-hybridizing monks. Each class of scholars either ignores the inconsistency of their own behavior or explains it with arguments that are inconsistent with their philosophic commitment.

Students of the life process can be classified as belonging to one of several schools, although many philosophers have modified their positions as their thoughts matured. In the attempt to attend to each of the many proposed interpretations, one is apt to be buried under an avalanche of such terms as materialism, causalism, determinism, organicism, and positivism. In order to reduce the number of distractors, and in the interest of brevity, composite values are described here along a continuum of belief regarding the nature of organic and inorganic existence.

CONCEPTIONS OF LIFE

Irreconcilable positions include: That which sees life as different from non-life and humans as a unique form (finalism); that which separates life from non-life on the basis of attributes that are peculiar to the living (vitalism); and that which sees all matter, organic and inorganic, as reducible to common elements (reductionism).

Our position is based on the proposition that life cannot be adequately explained by principles employed either in the physical sciences or through metaphysical speculation. Although chemistry and physics are essential to an understanding of the mechanics by which living forms carry out their functions, problems arise when an attempt is made to explain the dynamic interrelationship that obtains among individuals, species, and ecological systems.

Thus, a biology which seeks an explanation for behavior through a reductive approach faces insurmountable problems. It is essential that living forms be understood and expressed in terms that include both their part and whole aspects. This requires an acceptance of species, gene pools, populations, etc., as influential entities which cannot be accounted for under strict evolutionary principles, although many biologists claim to have shown how this may be accomplished.

Metascience

Finalism

In the infancy of human intellectual development—perhaps preceding the conviction that life has unique qualities—a sense of spirit captured imaginations. This capacity to conjure up fictitious beings, which was accompanied by feelings of dread and awe, led to the positing of a relationship between temporally bound existents and an eternal presence. During that period, inorganic entities were often worshipped as gods. Souls were believed to exist in every object. Over time, a special relationship to a creator became limited; first to all that lives, and, ultimately, exclusively to the human race.

Finalists appeal to the introspective. They believe that the relationship between humans and God is known through revelation, a sense that is as powerful as any of the others, and superior in that it is not subject to the fallibility associated with perceptual distortion. It is highly probable that the revulsion felt by reductionist scientists for any form of vitalism, and especially finalist versions, is due to the extremist convictions of those now described as "creationists."

Creationism is not, of course, an exotic Twentieth Century phenomenon expressed only in fundamentalist ministries. It is the vestige of an era that has lasted for thousands of years. Its principal tenets are that the human being is a special creation of God, that all forms of life have remained essentially the same from the beginning of time, and, for extremists, that the earth is no more than a few thousand years old.

But such beliefs are far more than mere superstition. They are, to a great extent, based on efforts to analyze and interpret the Bible and other sacred works which were, until relatively recently, the principal source of information regarding human history.

Furthermore, prior to the eighteenth century most of the finest thinkers accepted such notions as valid. Just as with today's scientists, they vested their faith in the efforts of recognized scholars and those whose obligation it was to search out and disseminate "truth." Such opinion makers were, unfortunately, no more free from the influence of the mysterious than were the people whom they counseled. Miraculous events were believed to represent believable occurrences—elements of the natural world—a world in which the commands and activity of a God or gods were accepted as beyond the ken of human thinkers.

Finalism was evident in the earliest and most profound philosophic speculation. Plato not only suggested the presence of a soul that is peculiar to life, but presaged the view that individuals are bound to species in his contention that it is the soul's nature to continue to exist beyond the life of the individual. Aristotle, although demonstrably wrong in reserving self-movement to the living, expanded Plato's notion of the soul, which he saw as representing the actualization of biological potential. He, too, offered an hierarchical interpretation of existence. He believed form and matter to be complementary aspects of all existents, with form representing the system and matter the individual. Form may be interpreted as that which is common or universal, and matter as that which is peculiarly individual or unique and which constantly strives to become form. Aristotle was, to this extent, suggesting that matter possesses the potential to *become* while form is eternally (if latently) present. This represented another hint of the relationship between the individual and a superordinate existence, since it implied that reality includes more than the immediately present.

Aristotle represented the finalist position when he suggested a first cause or unmoved mover in order to explain change in the universe. "The fact that the universe exhibits not only an eternal fixed, formal structure but also an everlasting process of constant movement and change...[can] not be taken for granted."[1] Aristotle's explanation came in the form of pure actuality, an essence which could cause change without taking part in it, and which represented a parameter of existence in which all the lesser characteristics coincided.

The Thomist view, coming on the crest of a millennium of argument for a personal God and the promise of salvation, was based on Aristotelian principles, with the addition of such explanatory concepts as the inclusivity of God's self. Imperfection in humans and the world represents evil, Aquinas contended, reflecting the Augustinian plaint, "for any part which harmonizeth not with its whole, is offensive."[2]

Here again, the individual was recognized as being part of a more comprehensive existence and an awareness is seen of the opposition between the appetites and self-transcendent demands that is so often emotionally destructive. Aquinas' interest was, of course, in the human as God's ultimate and unique creation. Reductionism was unacceptable. Human life was not only seen as different from nonlife, but as different from all other biological forms.

Thomism represents the classic form of finalism. Body functions are seen as determined by a principle which is (finally) for the good of the individual. All behavior should be directed toward ultimate morality. Human impulses are, in fact, said to be directed toward the highest good—with evil representing merely an error in decision.

This form of finalism demands an assayer—a paragon against which to assess behavior—and the soul in humans is presumed to represent the vehicle through which divine intervention occurs. It makes possible behavior with a dimension not found in lower animals. Specifically, it introduces a paradigm for living into the world of human beings, a measure of perfection which is revealed through moral intuition.

The conviction of the special status of humans is widely supported on the grounds of the evidence in much human behavior. Among all animals only one appears to possess a sense of morality, the capacity to reflect, to speak, to abstract, to conceptualize, to base action on reason. That animal is the human being, who in these things is unique. But beyond this, human life is seen by finalists to be the cause and the reason for existence.

Chardin stated,: "Man, the centre of perspective, is at the same time the *centre of construction* of the universe."[3] To which Dobzhansky added, "[Man] is so much unlike any other biological species that his evolution cannot be adequately understood in terms of only those causative factors which are operating in the biological world outside the human kind."[4] Bugental, in a more specific denial of the relevance of cross species analogies, insisted that the humanist "disavows as inadequate and even misleading, descriptions of human functioning and experience based wholly or in large part on subhuman species."[5]

Finalism is essentially a theistic doctrine. However, many scholastic philosophers were mechanists, with the distinction between interpretations being that while some saw divine intervention as beyond mechanics, others—Cartesians, for example—believed that the physical-mechanical universe represents the manifestation of an eternal plan. In Cartesian philosophy God's role is limited to setting the existential process in motion.

This form of deism has been questioned as representing an attempt to reduce the significance of the prime mover. "He would have liked, in all his philosophy," said Pascal of Descartes, "to be able to do without God; but he could not help making God give a fillip, to set the world in motion; after that he can do without God."[6] Thus, mechanism was viewed by many as inimical with a dynamic interpretation of life.

For the finalist, the truth of the proposition that humans have a moral and intellectual sense is known intuitively, and forms the basis on which people are motivated and their responsibility defined. Such issues are not fit subjects for scientific study. The basic and essentially unanswerable argument of those who have insisted on a final cause is embodied in the classic question: How a watch, without a watchmaker? The "watch" on which the finalist focuses is the human being.

It is not difficult to appreciate the conviction with which such beliefs are held. People have been shown to have practiced some form of worship in every community, in all parts of the world, as far back as human remains have been discovered. Theologians claim that such worship grows from the fact that humans are God's special creatures. God is not discovered through logical analysis, but through intuitive or emotional experience. Such a view receives little respect from the scientifically oriented.

Although the relationship need not be extended beyond that between the individual and some more comprehensive structure, it is worth more than a passing glance. The notions of God or gods, of eternal life, and of salvation, may well be explained as representing an input into that structure of knowledge which carries the message of the individual/species relationship, or of the inescapable bond between each biologic entity and its genetic line, family, or other transcendent existence.

Since such messages are imparted to all forms of life, this view may appear to reduce the human's pre-eminence. However, if human nature is to be understood, evidence must not be ignored simply because it does not show it in an attractive light. More importantly, humans are not demeaned by the argument that they are, in their behavior, not unlike other animals. Such a view need represent no more than the observation that some organizational plan operates according to a set of consistent laws which are evident in all forms of life. In Cartesian fashion, it suggests only that the plan for the propagation of living beings is carried out in much the same way at all levels.

Many explanations for belief in a superior being have been offered. Sinnott provided a social view:

> This exalted opinion of his [man's] position has not been simply an expression of his vanity and egotism. It was vitally necessary. From it he drew courage and comfort in times of tribulation. Without this conviction of his worth and this belief in his relationship to the Divine, it is doubtful whether man would have been able to survive the ordeals of his eventful history. A sense of his own significance has constantly reassured him.[7]

This explanation makes the experience of believing in eternity a valuable asset, and thus perhaps consistent with evolutionary theory in that those who "drew courage and comfort," from the belief would be more apt to survive. As with all such evolutionary explanations, however, it fails to account for many of the behaviors associated with such beliefs.

The similar occurrence in different parts of the world of methods that provide "reassurance" cannot be overlooked. The sacrifice of humans in obeisance, and many other such activities, suggest a relationship to something which transcends individuals and for which they give their life when it is deemed necessary.

J. S. Huxley offered a biological account:

> In the biological view, the other animals have not been created to serve man's

needs, but man has evolved in such a way that he has been able to eliminate some competing types, to enslave others by domestication, and to modify physical and biological conditions over the larger part of the earth's land area. The theological view was not true in detail or in many of its implications; but it had a solid biological basis.[8]

The basis, for Huxley, was the fact of the human's capacity to rule and to destroy. Such biological support, however, is hardly the kind that would appeal to theologians.

Scientists have provided a myriad of explanations for finalistic interpretations. All are based on the value of such belief to the individual who can, of course, be seen and touched. The sense of the supernatural is said to persist because of what it does for the individual. Although such interpretations, in their practicality and appeal to the obvious, however, fail to account for family, population, and species priority and the ecological juggling act.

Vitalism

Not all of those who consider life unique can be considered finalists. Many assume only that living beings possess a quality that is "nonmechanical, nonmaterial, nonchemical,"[9] although their interest has tended to focus on the human situation, and often with at least a quasi-finalistic orientation.

Intuitionists, following Bergson, posited an *elan vital* that is not manifested in nonliving entities, and which has a monitoring function that directs individuals toward ultimate goals. Insofar as this force typifies all living things it is a potentially useful concept. However, vitalism has been anathematized because of the use of terms that suggest extra-natural forces. Hilgard, for example, pointed out that "vitalism lingers on among those who believed in spiritualism."[10] This type of definition, including such esoteric terms as "psychoid," suggests the influence of some alien force. However, to the extent that a nonmaterial entity is involved, why should there be such concern? Physicists have a warehouse of such "entities"—and they, too, call them forces.

The use of the adjective "vital" need represent no more than the recognition of the unique behavior of organic elements as they serve the needs of more comprehensive entities. In essence, this should be no more enigmatic than the action of a compass as it "seeks" the magnetic pole. The distinction is that the pole can be located with geographic coordinates, while in life, the mother lode resides in a spatiotemporal existence of immense complexity.

Recognition of an urge to exist in living beings is found in Schopenhauer's "will to live" and Nietzsche's more specific "will to power." Somehow, the living manifest a constant willingness to do battle with the forces of nature, although such activity is seen alternatively as an evil tendency to be overcome by death or as an attractive positive experience in which the strong individual revels. In each case, however, the individual is seen as invested with a blind, driving, directional force.

Although not always insisting on the special relevance of humans, vitalists offer many powerful arguments in their opposition to mechanism. First, it is claimed that the organization of living forms is so tenuous and impermanent that, unless principles of existence beyond those related to the inorganic are involved, its endurance cannot be explained. Living forms are composed of the weakest molecular structure known. They are subject to rapid decomposition, prone to injury, dependent on sharply limited thermal conditions and circumscribed amounts of oxygen, hydrogen, water vapor, and other environmental elements. They could not survive without some organizational dynamic that is not found in other forms of existence.

Secondly, life persists in spite of the consistent battle which must be waged against destruction and decay. This struggle does not characterize nonlife. Holocaust, cataclysm, predation, and interpersonal conflict mark the daily fare of all living things. Yet populations and species tend to survive and grow over long periods, and even the individual has a remarkable ability to recover from battle damage and the ravages of disease. Beyond this, growth patterns appear to follow definite developmental lines. Margalef, in discussing changing life phenomena, stated, "The important point is that it is an orderly and *directed* [italics added] change. Unmistakable trends that permit prediction can be recognized."[11]

A third peculiarity of life is found in the activity of living individuals which seem often to be directed toward the endurance of their type. This, the vitalist claims, cannot be explained without invoking some unique principle. Animals at all levels die to protect each other and the species in general. Mothers protecting their young, chimpanzees warning the herd of danger, the killdeer feigning injury to ward off attackers, and heroic sacrifice on battlefields all represent activity peculiar to living things. Such activity makes difficult a total acceptance of the naturalist, reductionist position in biology.

Eisely put his speculations so impressively that they will be repeated here at some length:

> Darwin, in one of his less guarded moments, had spoken hopefully of the possibility that life had emerged from inorganic matter in some "warm little pond." From that day to this biologists have poured, analyzed, minced and shredded recalcitrant protoplasm in a fruitless attempt to create life from nonliving matter.
>
> A hundred years ago men spoke optimistically about solving the secret.... Periodically there were claims that the emergence of life from matter had been observed, but in every case the observer proved to be self-deluded. With the failure of these many efforts science was left in the somewhat embarrassing position of having to postulate theories of living origins which it could not demonstrate.[12]

Eisely thus presented the position of the vitalists who appeal to the unique in biological forms, as evidence that life cannot be reduced to chemical or physical equations. The physical sciences, they claim, are not competent to explain behavior on the same principles as those employed to describe inert matter.

It has been pointed out that some vitalists have chosen to elevate humans to special status. The majority of those who consider themselves life-scientists, however, specifically deny that humans are any more than a highly developed animal. Engel stated; "Over all stands the law of nature, governing every form of life, man not least; and man must therefore seek to play the part allotted to him in the whole complex pattern."[13] For Smith, "man is just another bit of biology, and therefore much of the animal kingdom is entirely relevant to his body, to his mechanism of sperm transfer, to his sex ratio, to his brain, to his sense of smell."[14] Morris is pithier, contending that, in spite of the complexity of our behavior patterns, "*Homo sapiens* has remained a naked ape nevertheless."[15] Each of these views is based on an interpretation of biological existence as different from the nonbiological, without assuming any oracular contribution.

The extreme enthusiasm of some vitalistically oriented scientists has been sharply criticized. Ethologists, in their attempt to draw analogies between human and animal behavior have advanced their position with a vigor that Rose described as *Chimpomorphia*—the attempt to reduce human behavior to animal explanation. He contended that:

> No serious examination of either human history or of contemporary sociology could bear out the sort of sweeping generalizations about human aggressiveness, sexuality or the territorial imperative suggested by some of these chimpomorphic ethologists' wilder extrapolations. The parallels do not hold.[16]

The criticism is sound. However, the argument of this text is that the commonality shared by humans and many animals is the emergence of consciousness and of affect in the form of desire, emotion, etc. As to how desires are met, instinctive knowledge and learned techniques are so dependent on different complexity levels and social and cultural influence that it is unnecessary to draw the conclusions that Rose and others find so distasteful. It is more important that similarities not be discounted.

Phenomenology and Existentialism

The apparent freedom of choice and comparative independence of humans provide additional evidence for the argument that they are essentially different from lower forms. In many of the arguments for the uniqueness of humans, however, one senses a passionate anxiety—a basic need to discover this ultimacy. A commonly employed approach is to attack essentialist, mechanistic interpretations of human behavior which are believed to both oversimplify its nature and improperly separate or fractionate existence.

Leading the assault is a group including humanists, phenomenologists, and some existentialists. They are by no means all finalists in the usual sense of the word. However, the position is vitalistic in the sense that it denies mechanism or essentialism as capable of explaining the special human condition. Every individual is seen as a center of existence with the unique contribution of each essential to an understanding of the world.

Early phenomenologists, such as Brentano, Heidigger, and Husserl focused on the absurdity of attempts to understand the world except through the acceptance of the essentiality of each observer. They concentrated on the conscious state which includes among its realities not only the perceived, but the broad range of cognitive and affective experiences.

Wild, following this view, complained that philosophy has become sterile because it ignores the existent individual in its attempt to describe reality. He was discouraged that the metaphysics of essentialism does not allow that existence is other than essence:

> Thus it can give no intelligible account of the difference between noetic and real existence, between the potential and the actual, between the active and the passive. It can shed no light on either the nature of human freedom or on that free mode of existing which distinguishes a person from a thing.[17]

Binswanger, following Heidegger's concept of existence as *being-in-the-world*, saw pre-transcendental psychology as suffering from "the fatal defect...[of separating] world into subject and object."[18] This separation, he believed, allows for an explanation of existence which does not include the critical role of experiencing humans. Such a view is consistent with modern physics with its insistence on the vital role of the observer in any experience. May summarized the existentialist attempt to overcome this problem. He explained that, *"existentialism...is the endeavor to understand man by cutting below the cleavage between subject and object."*[19] Each of these views focuses on the essential contribution of the existing individual to an understanding of human life.

Sartre presented an atheistic form of existentialism in his view that the human is inherently a free, choice-making animal. He contended that the ethics of humans are situational, their nature is to be dynamic and creative, their goal is nothingness, and their weakness is in attempting to alter or justify this scheme.[20] Although Sartre's extremism is rejected by many members of the existential school, his description of humans as dynamic and essential to an understanding of *being* is characteristic of the position.

Our concern with this version of existentialism, as with mechanism, is based on the fact that it, once again, poses a view of the *individual* as logically prior. It is precisely what Sartre saw as desirable that so often causes difficulty in human adjustment, namely the separation or independence of the individual, and the resulting potential for alienation. In the effort to allow for human existence as a critical aspect of experience, it implicitly denigrates other existents.

The argument that a *species* or a gene pool struggles to survive must be denied under such a philosophy since it would suggest that the species has a dasein of its own, and it is only in the human individual that the existentialist ultimately defines *being*. Much has been written to deny this allegation. May believed that it is erroneous to assume that existentialists deny the significance of the world around them. "*World is the structure of meaningful relationships in which a person exists.*"[21] Nevertheless, in practice, all radiates around the sentient being.

Existentialists claim that most scientific approaches to human life are based on an attempt at rational objectivity. They deny that reality can be understood through the cognitive process. They do not view humans as merely subjects, but rather as experiencing totalities, related to "a reality *underlying both subjectivity and objectivity.*"[22] They insist that truth cannot be a basis for understanding reality; that one may know truth without being able to relate to reality. Although this seems a reasonable position, there seems little merit in positing a reality that minimizes the relationship between the individual and humankind.

When the existentialist describes existence, it is always in terms of an emerging individual. Merleau-Ponty criticized science as being hypocritical in its claim that all existents are *things* which would deny the reality of consciousness. Sartre concurred in this view because he believed that the mode of being of consciousness is precisely a being for self. Kierkegaard claimed that, "the self of man is a relationship that is related to itself."[23] May stated the position most clearly:

> To the extent that my sense of existence is authentic, it is precisely *not* what others have told me that I should be, but is the one Archimedes' point I have to stand on from which to judge what parents and other authorities demand...the sense of one's own existence...is in basis not the product of social forces...it always presupposes *Eigenwelt*, the "own" world.[24]

Such statements present a persistent denial that authenticity comes from without. If it appears that May takes the environmental aspect into account, consider that even when *eigenwelt* is defined as a relating of the individual to the world, it is referred to as "a grasping of what something in the world...*means to me* [italics added]."[25] I am the ultimate referent.

Existentialists believe that there is strong empirical evidence for the view that reality is limited to human interpretation. May suggested that the more individuals are interested in a situation the better will be their perception. This is true if reality is thought of as relational. A situation about which one has great concern can be described in greater detail by that individual than by any casual observer. Perception psychologists have demonstrated that affect hunger can sharpen attention to relevant objects. A common example of this is seen in the behavior of lovers, whose heightened mutual sensitivity makes possible a form of non-verbal communication that depends on an acute perceptual exchange.

However, no one who has studied distortions of fact (e.g., as in opposing viewpoints about an auto accident) can deny that perceptions become altered when the perceivers are not in emotional synchrony. *It is in just such cases that the distinction between truth and reality becomes an issue.* The individual who is emotionally involved is least apt to be capable of making "objective" interpretations. Existentialists insist that they are dealing with being and, thus, that their position has ontological verity. Truth (what is) and reality (what exists) are offered by different schools as representing the same concept. The difference lies in the Hegelian notion that existence is not dependent on the observer, and the existential insistence that it is.

Mathematical propositions such as $E = mc^2$ express truths that for existentialists are unreal except when considered by people. The fact that the square root of four is two is *true* but not *real*.[26] Its reality is no more than the perceived phenomenon. On the other hand, the fact that humans are mortal is as real as it is true. Reality, for the existentialist refers to the actualizing of potential, a notion as old as philosophic thought. The problem of whether potentiality is as real as actuality remains. Existentialism cannot be charged with totally denying the relationship between humans, and their species. However, in insisting that humans cannot be understood through dissection, it puts such intense emphasis on their being *as individuals* that there is a tendency to minimize their potential contribution as parts or instances.

May made this rejection of communal man explicit as he decries the contemporary American tendency for people to define themselves by their economic position and the "mass collectivist trends and widespread conformist tendencies in our culture."[27] But the alienated often represent those very individuals who have rejected the relationship between themselves and society in the pursuit of personal freedom. Unfortunately, the freedom they seek is also a snare, which they do not recognize because they overlook the obligation and responsibility that existentialism imposes on those who adhere to its tenets.

In all existentialist comment there is a plea for special consideration of the human animal. Chardin introduced the term *hominization* to describe reflective behavior, which he felt is an exclusively human attribute. "Admittedly the animal knows. *But it cannot know that it knows*: That is quite certain."[28] Such an argument is, of course, highly speculative. It makes assumptions about the nature of subhuman cognitive and affective processes which are difficult to validate. There is, in fact, considerable evidence that animals do know about their knowledge and react to their own presence. Who has not known a dog who at some time acted in such a way that there was an *appearance* of "shame" on violating a family rule? (Behaviorists would, of course, see such a statement as representing the extremity of anthropomorphism. However, one need not assume an advanced intellectual capacity to interpret the animals action as manifesting some emotional state other than fear, for example, which apparently is accepted as a possible feeling state among lower animals.)

There is no room for compromise between those who view humans as a class of animal and those who are repulsed by the comparison. The essentialist-reductionist explanation is totally absurd from the viewpoint of the existentialist. Koestler provided an incisive summary of the position when, in a lucid account of the pitfalls of behavioral learning theory in psychology, he concluded: "For the anthropomorphic view of the rat, American psychology [has] substituted a rattomorphic view of man."[29] This is reflected in the widespread view of system theorists that S-R models of human nature are so unrealistic as to be potentially dangerous.[30] For such individuals, the existential conceptualization of human uniqueness is so compelling that efforts to reduce behavior to its mechanistic minimum are considered to be without merit.

Science: Mechanistic Reductionism

As the task of understanding the world was pursued, scholars came slowly to realize that many events could be more efficiently explained when cast in the form of relationships that embraced commonalities. They noted further that it was often possible to explain data in one domain by extending and modifying postulates from another. Through this process, a set of beliefs was developed that made possible predictions far superior to those based on an appeal to the supernatural in explaining the phenomenon of life.

Empedocles (490-435 B.C.) saw life as no more than a special combination of the four elements (air, fire, water, earth), with love and strife added. His was a primitive attempt to explain the apparent difference between organic and inorganic matter by clinging to the stability of the elements then known, while subtly inserting a few novel concepts. Democritus (460-390 B.C.) was explicitly opposed to a life/non-life distinction, asserting that all qualitative variations in the universe result from differing arrangements of the ubiquitous atom. In the 2,500 years that followed, a persistent attempt has been made to demonstrate that this approach is ineluctable and that all is reducible to a modicum of elements and equations.

Early thinkers approached the problem of existential nature as resolvable through rational inquiry. Mathematical demonstration and logical deduction flowing from self-evident truths were believed the keys to true knowledge. However, during the past several centuries this view has been criticized by empiricists, who, while allowing the need for reasoning, arguing that any claim to understanding the world must come from experience. Newton's celebrated *hypotheses non fingo*, by which he castigated those who drew conclusions from rational rather than experiential sources, heralded an era which has seen the experiment promulgated as the only appropriate method of gaining knowledge.[31] To establish the legitimacy of reductionist contention a plethora of research methods have been developed. Data collection and recording seem to provide an objective, inductive approach to knowledge which seem to make possible efficient, honest communication and the development of a solid foundation on which to erect new models and to substantiate existing paradigms.

This integration of reductionist thinking with inductive practice is called *science*, which is today essentially logical, positivistic, determinism. The method has been adopted by all of the physical sciences including those which seek to explain the peculiarities of organic existence. Strictly speaking, the positivist position, a branch of scientific empiricism or physicalism, assumes that descriptive terms employed in science must have counterparts in observable properties of entities. The *verification principle*, a cornerstone of the position, reduces meaning to only that which is subject to observation. Thus, a statement such as "There is a God" is considered vacuous since no observation would be sufficient to prove or disprove it.

This principle has contributed to the rejection of introspective data as well as, for some, to the elimination of internal "states" as useful in the effort to identify causes of behavior. Unfortunately, no observation seems available that could, prove or disprove the verification theory. Just as are the assertions of the mentalists it criticizes, it is not subject to verification as the warranted standard.[32]

The implication of positivistic philosophy is that the sciences must share common principles since what is observable must follow ultimately discernible "basic" rules whether the subject matter is biological, chemical, or physical. Many philosophers, however, have taken the position that there is no set of laws presently known, and perhaps that none may ever be discovered, which may be applied across sister sciences. In spite of this, biologists have developed theories in accordance with the tenets of chemistry and physics. Plant growth, food assimilation, and fermentation are explained in terms of chemical characteristics. Energy conservation is considered a physical phenomenon—no more than a predictable constant. Abiogenesis, discarded as impossible by nineteenth century medical science, which retained some allegiance to the notion that life was unique, is considered today in terms of *when* it shall be accomplished rather than *whether*.

Life is seen as a chemical machine—different only in that it is capable of producing duplicates of itself. Even the separate contributions of the sexes is a mechanical process. Support for the reductionist view has been provided in many research laboratories, and biology is moving closer to physics in the descriptors it employs. Such accomplishments as the synthesizing of urea and parthenogenesis in humans have provided continued and growing support for those who claim that all is reducible to certain common elements, with life being no more than a feature of unusual perversity. Research in genetics has provided the most dramatic showcase for the argument that life can be completely understood as a chemical phenomenon. Drosophila, sweet pea, and man are assumed to represent manifestations of chromosomal action that follows classical law. The helixes of Pauling and Crick and the central dogma (DNA —> RNA —> Protein) are orderly, mechanical processes which require no purpose, nor ultimate goal, in order to be understood.

Some of the contentions of reductionists are impervious to attack and, thus,

CONCEPTIONS OF LIFE 15

themselves violate the principle that there must be some observation which would invalidate the position. For example, any apparent violation of mechanical law is said to represent a failure of comprehension—of not having accounted for all of the contributing variables. Introducing psychic principles is said merely to complicate the problem without providing a superior explanation.

It is argued that although at any time, within any specific level of the development of any science, it may be proper to state that one (e.g., biology) is not reducible directly to another (e.g., mechanics), at some future time the development of each discipline shall reach the point that such a reduction is possible. Or it may be feasible to restate postulates in such a way that the relationship is revealed.

Nagel believed that "if the laws of [organic] chemistry...cannot be systematically deduced from one theory of atomic structure, they may be deducible from an alternate set of assumptions."[33] And:

> It is an elementary blunder to claim that, because some one physicochemical theory (or some class of such theories) is not competent to explain certain vital phenomena, it is *in principle* impossible to construct and establish a mechanistic theory that can do so.[34]

Nagel contended that, with patience, existence will be understood in terms that bring the several positions together, and some way of describing organic nature will be discovered which meets the objection raised by those who cannot accept its being equated with the inorganic. Reductionists are sure that this will eventually occur. "The history of biology," said Bertalanffy, "is [marked by] the refutation of vitalism."[35]

This argument is a remarkable example of the scientific predisposition. Since more is known today than was known yesterday, and since each new bit of information leads in the same direction, all shall eventually be known. Biologists are most anxious to reduce the equations of life to physical principles. This in spite of the fact that a significant group of biological physicists has serious reservations. Bohm, for example, said, "We do not at present know whether the new order that must underlie current physical laws will be significant in biology or not.... Just when physics is...moving away from mechanism, biology and psychology are moving closer to it."[36] Thorpe pointed out that:

> It has come about that though the basic world of the physicist is even more mysterious and non-concrete than ever before, the world of living things has seemed (until very recently) more than ever a world of mechanical models, of chemical and physical models.[37]

Nevertheless many powerful arguments are offered to support the contentions of the scientific community. Consider the following:

- *Inorganic material, of which organic individuals are composed, must itself possess the potential for living.* Life appears when the proper catalytic agents are present. When it does appear, it must follow principles that are potential, and thus, in some sense, present, in preorganic nature. But the combining of elements results in emergent dynamisms even in the inorganic world. Liquidity is peculiar to hydrogen and oxygen only when they are combined in certain proportions under specific conditions. To make the argument that hydrogen possesses the potential for liquidity does not alter the uniqueness of the liquid state.

Several efforts have been made to show that this concept of "emergent" properties is fallacious. Hofstadter[38] said that it is absurd to believe that the properties of water cannot be derived from the properties of the elements when completely analyzed. He is correct in his argument, but wrong in its implication. The fact that the liquid state is predictable in no way alters the fact that it is unique or emergent. To predict with perfect accuracy that an individual will act differently when influenced by alcohol is not to deny that in an inebriated state a different personality emerges. An entire existential philosophy presses the claim that potentiality cannot be, in any sense, predicated on actuality. (Emergence, as applied to such concepts as *awareness* poses other problems which shall be addressed in Chapter 3.)

- *The manifestations of living entities, are no more remarkable than those found in many types of inert matter.* Crystalline forms, even those of snowflakes, are of as much wonder as human intelligence. Thus, it is argued, the incredible complexity of the human structure, and even of human thought, cannot be offered as evidence of the uniqueness of life. *The issue, however, is not one of complexity but of unique organization.* Although organic as well as inorganic compounds combine and decay in similar manner, there is neither any evidence that a snowflake ever sacrificed itself to the blizzard it represented, nor that a stone suffered from melancholia.

- *Mechanism, in its deterministic aspect, provides an adequate basis for prediction.* Vitalistic principles and finalistic purposes are believed to be unproductive predictors since they are not couched in contemporaneous causes, and are thus not subject to scientific inquiry. However, *no mechanistic explanation has as yet been provided which predicts behavior with any high degree of accuracy.* Furthermore, the equating of prediction and understanding is presumptuous. Cancer and auto accidents rates are predicted with considerable precision. Understanding either phenomenon is far more complicated.

Mechanistic arguments form the basis for the general belief in reductionism—which insists that apparently irreconcilable differences will eventually succumb to parsimony. Arguments based on deduction are passe. Reason should follow experience, which provides the only dependable data. The employment of mechanisms such as "instinct" to explain behavior are considered equivalent to the invoking

CONCEPTIONS OF LIFE 17

of demons which lurk within the individual, pushing and pulling strings to cause activity.

Such explanations are seen as providing convenient, but purely mythical, agents. J. S. Huxley, for example, attacked vitalists on the ground that their definition of life is equivalent to explaining the steam engine's motion by invoking an "elan locomotive" principle.[39] This clever analogy delights the scientifically-oriented who see in it the ultimate rebuttal to those who suppose that some mysterious power must be called into account to explain the action of living beings.

Huxley and his followers are, however, victims of a more subtle, but no less devastating, hoax. When the principle of gravitation is proposed as a superior explanation for the interaction of mass, to the assumption of a spirit within objects which causes them to repel or attract, how far have we come from positing a ghost in the machine? Gravitation is, itself, a mysterious force, no less romantic than that of the *vis vitalis*. It is, in fact, current opinion that gravity has no separate existence but represents no more than a peculiarity of the space/time continuum. Koestler and many others have pointed out that scientists in the twentieth century employ far more incredulous concepts than do the metaphysicists they deride.[40] And Barnett added, "there is no mystery of the physical world which does not point to a mystery beyond itself."[41]

Reductionists carry on the argument. Beck claimed that "nothing has been observed empirically that forces us to believe any one thing about the basic nature of life." And, regarding hypotheses about the nature of life, "none has been capable of definite testing."[42] Finally, he asserted, "whatever quality one would like to consider as a minimal requirement or a diagnostic trait of life, that quality can be found present in objects that we all agree are not living and absent in objects that everyone knows are living."[43]

Simon, one of a diminishing number of objectionists, explained that "biologists are committed to attempting to explain the phenomenon of life in terms of its non-living [elements].... The property of being alive...is simply not treated as a logical primitive in biological science."[44] An example of this practice is observed in the contention of Schroedinger who, although admitting that a new type of physical law must be discovered to account for life, proposed that "the new principle that is involved is a genuinely *physical one* [italics added]."[45] Nothing, he felt, is subject to any non-physically reducible principle.

The goal of science is, of course, to analyze forces in the attempt to maximize prediction. It is the heuristic value of an explanation that recommends it. Furthermore, when it is possible to replace a "spirit" as a cause with conditions that provide for duplication, replication, etc., there is no doubt that scientific approaches are superior. But the price of such reduction in the case of biological activity is, in many instances, the loss of its significance. Because the human intellect is sufficiently powerful to extract increasingly subtle characteristics of existential elements, there is an implicit assumption that some day all mystery will be eradicated. And the retreat from teleological explanation—where faith is substituted for reason—is understandable.

But science is invested with its own phantasmagoria. Material and formal causes may be more satisfying to reason than the notion of future control over the present, but they are no less enigmatic. Caprice is no more puzzling as a causal agent than the principle of "efficient" cause (Hume surely made this clear), and "causal" laws themselves are assumed by many to merely describe observed or inferred action. Furthermore, scientists are often at a loss to cope with the interpretations provided in their own tests. Asked to explain the nature of corpuscular existence, Schroedinger remarked, "I ought to confess honestly that I am almost as little prepared to answer that as to tell where Sancho Panza's second donkey came from."[46] But he was obviously ready to abjure such mysterious explanations as implied by a concept that suggested a unique role for biological entities!

The notions of replicability or persistence cannot be invoked as evidence of superiority of the scientific approach. Phantom manipulators may be substituted for thermodynamic laws with little loss of predictive power. Nor can the paradox be evaded by showing that particular relationships can be found in all forms of existent. Handler attempted to reduce the significance of life by pointing out that conservation of energy is "valid also in a living guinea pig."[47] He did not deal with the question of how energy conservation is dealt with in living creatures, and/or what end it serves. This is a prime example of the erroneous assumption that questions related to *how* an entity performs can be satisfactorily substituted for the question *why*. (Which is not to propose that a purposive statement itself solves the mystery of the reason for such action.)

Scientists consider questions dealing with ethics, beauty, etc., beyond the realm of investigation and thus not within their province. They, of course, mean beyond investigation according to their rules, which are dictated today by the postulates of neo-positivism, thus limiting the capacity for inquiry. Positivism, is itself subject to criticism as blocking progress toward the exercise of thought. Ouspensky lamented that "a Chinese wall of 'positivistic' sciences and methods is built up around free investigation. Everything rising above this wall is condemned as *unscientific*."[48]

The social sciences, latest to join the parade, have applied the tools of the physical sciences wherever possible. The credo, "whatever exists, exists in some quantity," has been extended to include qualities as diverse as paranoia and sex appeal. The piquancy of such an approach resides in its potentiality for reducing all things to a common denominator. It is an appeal to the elegance of simplicity that delights the mathematical mind.

There are occasional objections raised to such parochialism, and there has recently been some movement away from the glorification of objectivity. Psychologists who propose the legitimacy of behavioral elements that cannot be seen, scholars who express doubt about the ability of technology to solve human problems, and preachers who bemoan the loss of a relationship with the eternal, all challenge the ultimacy of physicochemical interpretations. The reaction of offended scientists is predictable. They are repulsed by such regression. Jones, in expressing his distress at these challenges, stated:

> Maybe we are seeing, in the modern rejection of "irrelevant" science, a hint of that ancient retreat from the rigor and neutrality of objective truths to the consolation of private gratifications and ideologies, which over the centuries sapped the creative impetus of the first science research institute, and finally scattered its rubble in the city streets.[49]

In answer to the question of why the common person rejects many contemporary scientific findings such as the value of fluoridation, Mausner & Mausner suggested that one reason may be "the Zeitgeist, a suspicion of scientists, the fear of conspiracy."[50] Why, they ask, do we have so little faith [sic] in the value of the scientific endeavor?

But faith in science does not necessarily quicken the senses and open the eyes to greater truths. In fact, the passionate scholar often embraces convictions with as much zeal as a Baptist preacher. Margalef stated that, "acquired information [often] is subsequently used to close the door to a further inflow of information."[51] Perhaps Pascal summarized it most elegantly in his concern that science attempts to explain morality as an adaptive contingency: "The knowledge of external things will not console me for my ignorance of ethics in time of affliction, but the science of morals will always console me for my ignorance of external knowledge."[52] Amen.

Evolution

The outstanding example of mechanist supremacy in the biological sciences is the acceptance of the evolutionary explanation of life as a happenstance of self-duplicating molecular units. Mayr claimed that "the theory of evolution is quite rightly called the greatest unifying theory in biology."[53] And there is little question that the theory provides the best explanation for the emergence of life that is currently available.

Evidence from paleontological, geological, morphological, anthropological, embryonic, and other studies, marshalled by Darwin, supported by Lyell, Wallace, and many others, and brilliantly expounded by T. E. Huxley, overwhelmed clerics in the last third of the eighteenth century in a series of often acerbic exchanges. Since that dramatic confrontation, evidence has continued to provide verification for what is today a monumental theoretical structure, which has been girded by a continual series of impressive supportive data in spite of its problem with explaining such phenomena as self-sacrifice.

Evolutionist theory is believed to meet all of the primary logical requirements of sound theory building. It is said to provide a simple unifying idea, to be logically consistent internally, subject to falsification, and "clearly limited by explicitly stated boundary conditions so that it is clear whether or not any particular data are or are not relevant to [its] verification."[54]

Today, the principal objections to the acceptance of evolutionist data are raised by those who proclaim that the theory is ungodly. "Satan himself is the originator of the concept of evolution."[55] They also argue against various types of evidence. "Because the vast majority of mutations are lethal or cause impairment...it follows that mutations are not useful as supporting evidence for the general evolution model."[56] Such dissent comes from an extreme fundamentalist group of individuals who refer to themselves as "creation scientists," and whose arguments center around a literal acceptance or a very narrow interpretation of the book of Genesis. The parent body, the Creation Research Society is, however, considered by many biologists to represent a "dishonest and thoroughly corrupt enterprise."[57]

The evolutionist position includes several essential points. First, those features of an individual which are useful in the struggle to exist are most apt to be transmitted to the next generation. This is based on the assumption that the most able will produce a disproportionate share of offspring. Second, no characteristic which is not immediately useful will survive. Any skill or ability which does not provide some advantage during the sexually active lifetime of the (total) individual possessing it will disappear over time (which is one explanation for the nonrecurrence of ineffective or disabling mutations). Third, the continuing stream of life, death, and new birth are the controlling factors. Only through expression in a phenotype is the survival law obeyed.

There is general agreement that during the earliest era of life there were fewer, less complex, organisms. Whether "Adam" was predated by individuals whose structure provided superior adaptability to climatic conditions matters not. Unless there was a simultaneous eruption of organic beings (certainly not an impossibility), there was at least *once* at some *place* a "being" that had the capacity to replicate itself. (Such an individual, of course, *had to* duplicate itself if conditions were propitious; it was not a matter of choice.) Whatever the mechanics, the "idea" or model of the original individual was passed on to subsequent organisms that possessed, to a great extent, characteristics identical to those of their progenitors. Building on this assumption, evolutionists have provided a case supported by evidence from many disciplines.

Acceptance of evolutionist claims and their reductionist implications has not come without considerable resistance from respectable members of the scientific community. Dobzhansky, in 1970, pointed out that "the general principles of biological theory are widely, but not universally, accepted among present day biologists."[58] And Waddington added, "even the most doctrinaire reductionist cannot tell biologists just what they have to reduce their system to."[59] However, by the early 1980s such concerns had been largely overcome.

Gould, for example, stated, "well, evolution is a theory.... [But] it is also a fact.... Facts don't go away when scientists debate rival theories to explain them."[60] And Root-Bernstein added, "There is no *scientific* need for a new theory to replace evolution."[61] Mayr, in fact, argued that since biologists agree on evolution, "it is rather puzzling that so many nonbiologists...still refuse to accept the Darwinian explanation."[62] For these and many others, the theory has been satisfactorily proven.

There remains a persistent minority of biologists such as Ambrose who contended that experiments designed to support evolutionist theory "have not been performed."[63] His criticism was more pointed. "The theory of evolution...has been singularly lacking from this point of view,"[63] after which he quoted Medawar as complaining that "the biologist has no alternative but to accept the theory of evolution."[63] Most such concerns are based, not on a denial of the general theory, but with problems regarding the evidence.

As to the issue of falsification, Bertalanffy and others had argued that no evidence could refute the evolutionist interpretation. Any unusual occurrence, they believed, could be encompassed under some argument based on ultimate reduction to random mutation.[64] Rosen concurred, contending that Darwinian arguments could be used to explain any evolutionary history and accused it of being as slippery a conceptualization as that of the creationists.[65]

Evolutionists today claim that falsification is quite possible. Gould, for example, said, "I can envision observation and experiments that would disprove any evolutionary theory I know [sic].... Unbeatable systems are dogma, not science."[66] (As a matter of fact, since sound theory requires only that falsification be *possible*, the discovery of a 500 million year old mammalian fossil would surely be embarrassing—perhaps fatal—to evolutionist argument.)

A similarly persistent issue involves the discovery of transitional states—the existence of intermediate forms of species—which would provide support for the notion of gradual change. Darwin proposed that new species develop in remote places, then spread to replace earlier types which should have left fossils at every level.[67] The argument has not been entirely convincing. Bertalanffy stated, "we find no evidence either in the living world of today or of past geological epochs for a continuous transition,"[68] concluding that, "Like a Tibetan prayer-wheel, selection theory murmurs untiringly: Everything is useful."[69]

Once again explanations are provided. Gould pointed out that, "preserved transitions are not common, and should not be according to our understanding of evolution...but they are not wanting.... Non-mammalian jawbones are reduced, step by step...until they become tiny nubbins."[70] There is, further, he claimed, extensive evidence of evolution in action. "It ranges from countless experiments on change in nearly everything about fruit flies...to the famous British moth that turned black when industrial soot darkened the trees on which they rest."[71] And Roger Cuffey, a well known paleontologist, stated that he was "appalled that many otherwise well-informed persons have repeated the grossly misinformed assertion that transitional fossils do not exist."[72] After which he provided an extensive list of examples. Still the challenges go on. Ambrose questioned the adequacy of the neo-Darwinian explanation on several grounds, "firstly because a large proportion of mutations give rise to 'neutral genes' not affected by natural selection, and secondly because paleontological evidence indicates that in most cases new species appear to arise comparatively suddenly."[73]

Simon added the caveat that if natural selection is to be considered a deductive principle "it is necessary to assume that all population changes can be seen as a consequence of natural selection, and must be produced by that mechanism and that mechanism alone."[74]

Creationists and other critics have allowed that changes *within* a species may occur, but that such modifications do not make the evolutionist's case. What *they* require as evidence would be examples of species that stand in a continuous line with none of the "gaps" that they insist have always been discovered. And this may be a somewhat vulnerable point. Gould, in a less than impressive response, argued that phylogenetic leaps from species to species must be accepted on the basis of inference, "but are no less secure for that reason...[since]...all historical sciences rest on inference, and evolution is no different from geology, cosmology, or human history in that respect."[75]

Underlying everything that modern biology stands for is the attempt to remove the mystery that surrounds life. Vitalistic arguments are countered with explanations that require no cabalistic interpretation. Creationist claims are destroyed with evidence that stands the most rigorous examination. However, in the pursuit of objectivity and the elimination of spectres, the limitations of reductive explanations are often overlooked.

J. S. Huxley stated that "If we repudiate creationism, divine or vitalistic guidance...we must...invoke natural selection...[which] achieves its results by giving probability to otherwise highly improbable combinations."[76] Is natural selection, in its violation of the rules of probability, non-mysterious? Without direction? Totally contingent? The espousers of the evolutionary position explain the occurrence on the basis of an improbable but conceivable series of contingencies. A most popular explanation attributes it to "the natural origin of complex molecules capable of influencing or directing the synthesis of units like themselves."[77] The staggering implications of the positing of such events does not seem to be fully appreciated.

From a neo-Darwinian standpoint, natural selection, gene flow (allele changes based on immigration and emigration of population members) and random genetic choice, account for most change in evolving populations. Mutations and genetic drift (chance fluctuation among alleles) play only a subsidiary role. The foundation for this view rests on the principle that the most capable members of a species are most apt to survive and reproduce, and on the speculation that environmental impact on the phenotype provides no direct input into the evolution of genotypes. Thus, the evolution of species which appears so obviously to be occurring is supported by a theory which has been accused of being either tautological (survival of the fittest) or incapable of accounting for evolution (fortuitous genotypic development).

CONCEPTIONS OF LIFE 23

The tautology resides in the meaning of "survival" and "fittest." Since survival is environment specific, and appropriate fitness varies, with environment, "fitness" may lose all of its meaning except as defining any form of life that survives. Bohm pointed out that until one includes some notion of harmony, viability, or similar principle, "the notion of survival [is] a mere tautological statement that those forms of life that continue indefinitely to produce offspring...are the ones that will survive."[78] Mayr contended, by way of response, that what Darwin really said was that, "it is the possession of certain characteristics which determines evolutionary success and that such characteristics have, at least in part, a genetic basis."[79]

More significant is the concept of fortuitous genotypic development. In its degenerate form it would require that change in the system be recognized as random, with individual profit taking precedence. And it could not be argued that any *progress* has occurred since progress can be shown to reduce to a value judgment. It is only when terms such as family, species, population, or survival value, which are directional and "mysterious" are applied, that the story of evolution can account for the full range of biologic activity. Evolutionists have argued that they can accommodate the notion of progress since it need mean no more than that sequential change is observed to occur. Thus, evolutionists reduce *progress* to *progression*, a highly questionable semantic leap. (Darwin's own account viewed man as far "superior" to his progenitors, although he denied the significance of the fact.)

The argument that a particular genetic combination has persisted because of the happenstance of a preservative mating is delusive, since such a condition need not result in evolution at all. Very simple organisms have remained intact for eons. Each change has meant risk and, in many instances, destruction. To ask why this occurred would invite an answer invested with direction and perhaps even purpose. Fortuitous change should, at best, have resulted in individuals with the protection of the self always having first (or ultimate) priority, which is simply not the case. Instead, many characteristics which are potentially destructive to the individual have persisted, with risk-taking, creativity, and others found in greatest abundance among the most highly developed organisms.

Other concerns remain. Consider the argument that to be transmitted a characteristic must be useful to survival. The appearance of selectively neutral elements (such as the existence of millions of hemoglobin variants among humans) has been mentioned. Beyond this, the moral sense, the aesthetic sense, the facility to perform complex mathematical tasks, or the ability to sing would appear to have little immediate survival value for individuals. Darwin's explanation was that civilized nations are replacing barbarians all over the world. "And they succeed mainly, though not exclusively, through their arts, which are products of the intellect. It is, therefore, highly probable that with mankind the intellectual faculties have been mainly and gradually perfected through natural selection."[80]

Many arguments have been offered as giving credence to this view in spite of its contradiction in Darwin's own statement that "disuse...will often have reduced organs when rendered useless under changed habits or conditions of life."[81] In the case of such a skill as artistic competence, the individual would have to make such use of it as to gain preferential survival. But, of course, so too would many generations of offspring.

Such an appeal to the persistent reappearance and use of the beautiful in controlling the environment is suspect. Because of the conviction that the aesthetic sense helped humans to overcome their enemies, the logic that suggests it would disappear unless it provided the individual with an immediately improved probability of survival, and unless it occurred with sufficient regularity to overcome the tendency to regress, is not satisfactorily refuted.

Social groupings are equally difficult to understand. In what manner does a culture act to enhance survival? Acculturation is clearly of benefit to a society, a population, or a species, and in many ways to its individual members. However, in some instances the individual suffers from the relationship. How can this be accounted for? Evolutionists speak either of species or individual goals as the situation demands, although in so doing they destroy their argument for genetic transference based on successful individual survival. Allee and others define society as any group of individuals sufficiently integrated so that natural selection can act on the group as a unit.[82] This, however, provides no support for evolutionist argument since genes are transported by individuals. Thus, it must be some *social* gene that is the decision-maker.

Species evolution, in the sense of improved ability to cope with varying environments, while exploring more effective life styles, occurs because of the advent of increasingly creative and exploratory types. But at the same time, especially among humans, relatively "useless" individuals are preserved. Thus, group behavior does not even move toward its *own* survival in all cases. The practice of protecting the weak against the powerful cannot be shown to profit the group, if group survival is the issue. To understand it, one must look beyond the simple notion of survival of the fittest (individual). Some further principles must be operating. Somehow individuals and groups are related in a way that transcends either as an independent entity.

Nietzsche contended that Darwinism was refuted on the grounds that the adjustment to the environment which the theory calls for is not observed in any form of sub-human life. Rather, there is a continual struggle to overcome the environment including one's neighbors—often even one's immediate family. Individuals who survive are apt to be those who do not merely adapt, but who search for new and better solutions (thus, of course, risking their individual existence). For this reason, Nietzsche complained that existing cultures are destructive and unworthy. He saw Christianity as an ungodly creed destined to destroy the human race by protecting those individuals which in other forms of life are discarded. If the species is to develop, why does a culture preserve the unfit?

Edmund Wilson, the father of sociobiology, suggested that this is one of the most disturbing qualities of social behavior. In deciding whom to protect and whom to destroy, "the individual is forced to make imperfect choices based on irreconcilable loyalties—between the 'rights' and 'duties' of self and those of family, tribe, and other units of selection."[83] Nietzsche saw no problem. He considered the preservation of the weak a "sublime abortion," accusing the human race of cultivating "a wizened, almost ludicrous type, a herd-animal, a creature compounded of good will, sickliness, and mediocrity."[84] The evidence supports Nietzsche. The well-being of living *types* in most species takes precedence over the preservation of biological individuals. Fitness, then, should be applied to characteristics which have value beyond the individual. But this would be an unlikely occurrence if Mendelian principles operate precisely as they are defined.

In spite of such problems, there is the onerous practice of presenting evolution as though it made an understanding of the concept of life quite simple—almost a trivial matter. Cairns-Smith, apparently in seriousness, said that, "a primitive organism... should be quite easy to make—if we know what to do. First we should try to think of any practical physicochemical system capable of indefinite Darwinian evolution."[85] His intention was to make the point that neither nucleic acid nor any other organic polymer is essential, but his conclusion is a gross oversimplification, and one based on the typical reductionist contention that in the final analysis solutions are bound to be quite elementary. Although that may be so, research to date is far from identifying such simple explanatory principles.

The evolutionist suggestion that life began in some "warm little pond" remains conjectural. Salisbury believed that with odds of 1 in 10^{600} against, the DNA molecule could not have arisen fortuitously.[86] Wigner argued that from a quantum-mechanics viewpoint the probability of the occurrence of self reproducing entities is zero.[87] And Hoyle claimed that "in accepting the 'primeval soup theory' of the origin of life, scientists have replaced the religious mysteries which shrouded the question with equally mysterious scientific dogmas."[88]

Supporters of the evolutionist argument have proposed a continual reappraisal of the conditions under which stable or organic compounds came into being. The general premise has maintained its vitality. Wald, in fact, demonstrated the influence of the evolutionist argument in the face of the difficulty in proving the validity of the position as it deals with the first chance occurrence of a living entity:

> One has only to contemplate the magnitude of this task [these interactions in appropriate amounts and proportions] to concede that the spontaneous generation of a living organism is impossible. Yet here we are—as a result, I believe, of spontaneous generation.[89]

Although such an admission might be expected to engender a degree of humility, an annoying "elitism" has been developed which has alienated many who may otherwise be supportive. The tendency of the biologically sophisticated to close their ranks against objections is as devastating in biology as are the demands of a priesthood that the prognostications of the Delphian oracle be accepted. This is perhaps an inevitable result of efforts to reduce the study of life to the mechanics and the chemistry of its constituent parts. The true scientist does not allow the "passions, propensities, and aversions" that Hume described to play any part in scientific determinations. Analysis is dispassionate and findings are accepted without prejudice, which, (it is believed) separates the scientist from the uninitiated—perhaps justifying a certain sense of superiority!

In other aspects a similar insularity is observed. Since a naturalist posture, which requires the acceptance of an indifferent world, represents the philosophic basis of science, and since the life sciences seek scientific respectability, biologists have stated their theses in terms that parallel those of physics and chemistry. Mead insisted that "the theory of evolution, offering as it does a purely naturalistic explanation of biological phenomena, appears to eliminate the need for Purpose or the Creative Will in the universe."[90] This view, which has consistently gained evidential support and thus favor among biologists, has struck what may well be a fatal blow at belief in divine causation and the eternal existence of the human species.

The denial of a divine creator is not, however, true for all biologists. Some even claim a finalist allegiance. Kenneth Miller, an acknowledged evolutionist, said, "I am a creationist (I'm a Roman Catholic) and so is every scientist who professes a religious belief."[91] Opposed are those such as Halstead, who maintained, "I personally do not see how the concept of evolution can be made consistent with that of creation by a personal god, or indeed any sort of god."[92]

This text is based neither on a defense of theologic orthodoxy nor on the assumption of a "creative will." However, we will present an argument for the existence of purpose and other such concepts as characteristics of, and unique to, living entities, and this is antithetical to the conclusions drawn by reductionist biologists. It is their contention that "the realm of nature is unbroken in its inclusive extent, and man...is no less subject to its laws...his actions are as strictly controlled by cause and effect as anything else in the Universe."[93] Emergent functions and relationships are, however, so obvious as to be undeniable.

As for many of the contributions of evolutionism there is little reason for disagreement. Natural selection is as sound a premise as science may propose, in spite of the attacks mounted by creationists. The sociopolitical convictions of these authors make their literary efforts suspect, and their arguments border on the absurd. Asimov contended that "however much the creationist leaders might hammer away at their 'scientific' and 'philosophical' points, they would be helpless and a laughing stock if that were all they had."[94] On the other hand, however, as Sir John Eccles succinctly stated, "A kind of religion, Darwinism, is being foisted on us...but for me it fails as a complete and satisfactory explanation for my personal existence. For me there is a profound mystery in existence."[95] This Nobel Laureate was not attacking evolutionism as a science, but the travesty of attempting to eschew the "mysterious" aspect of life.

Nor will the legitimacy of the evolutionist position be challenged here. It will, in fact, be the basis for much of the ensuing argument. However, the relationship, among phenotype, family, and genotype as well as among individuals, their relatives, their communities, and their species must be understood in such a manner as to legitimize altruistic behavior. It is important that we look beyond the weary argument that in the final analysis people always look out first for themselves.

Organicism

Toward the middle of the twentieth century, a point of view regarding the appropriate way to understand existence began to take root in the scientific community. It represented an outgrowth of the principle of *holism* introduced by Smuts, which suggests that atomistic interpretations are incompetent to describe the functions of complex structures.[96] Holism has not fared well as a theory probably because of its non-reductive nature. Further, it was not believed sufficiently heuristic to provide a vehicle for research, and was thus not subject to validation. By the 1950s, however, some of the flavor of the holistic notion began to show up in a variety of disciplines. From gestalt principles in psychology, to systems theory in mathematics and mechanics, a framework for other disciplines was provided that calls for the rejection of both vitalist and mechanist claims.

Analytic arguments are felt to collapse in the face of evidence that *wholes* are, in part, responsible for the configurations observed in their *parts*. Vitalism is refuted on the ground that the priority of wholes requires neither a divinity nor any unique quality that separates life from the inorganic. Thus, organismic thinkers find vitalism inane (being grounded in needlessly mysterious principles) and mechanism inappropriately focused.

Organismic theory has been rapidly adopted by personality theorists since it provides possible explanations for many behaviors that are difficult to understand when viewed in isolation. Actions heretofore described as based on unconscious mechanisms can, perhaps, be better explained in terms of their service to existing systems. It appears that conflicting views of life might be reconciled under the umbrella of a philosophic stance which can accommodate both. This, however, would mandate the acceptance of the fact that realities are peculiar to the level of existence at which they occur, an issue to be considered in Chapter 2.

An excellent example of this can be found in the work of Polanyi, who attempted to demonstrate that many of life's processes are irreducible. He suggested that living beings, as well as machines, share performance characteristics that cannot be understood in physicochemical terms. Weiss argued that principles inherent in organized structures "show that to reduce this hierarchy to ultimate particulars is to wipe out the very sight of it. [Careful analysis] proves this ideal to be both false and destructive."[97] Polanyi took a similar position, claiming that each existent is subject to "boundary conditions" which determine its significance. In terms of this model, a machine is comprised of *parts* which represent a "lower" boundary and a *function* or "higher" boundary, and nothing inherent in the parts can predict the function of the machine.

This argument is, of course, neither new nor particularly subtle. Koestler quoted a variety of scientists who refer to the emergence of levels of organization "whose properties *cannot be reduced to, nor predicted from, the lower level.*"[98] But this is true for every aspect of existence that may be considered. Language as a form of communication exemplifies this. Polanyi drew the following conclusion:

> You cannot derive a vocabulary from phonetics; you cannot derive grammar from a vocabulary; a correct use of grammar does not account for good style; and a good style does not supply the content of a piece of prose.[99]

In the case of the DNA code, which provides the individual with, for example, the structure essential for sight, Polanyi confessed that a serious problem is involved. How does the experience of *seeing* arise from a physical structure? How can a lower order faculty (in this instance the visual apparatus) account for the appearance of a higher order of existence? "It is as if the faculty of vision were to be made intelligible to a person born blind by a chapter of sense physiology." He suggested that DNA does not determine, but rather *evokes*, the higher level.[99]

This evocation begs the question of the reason for, or the purpose behind, the emergence of such a capacity, but it does speak again to the concept of emergent qualities, and the interdependence as well as the independence of levels of existence. A "systems approach" seems, for many, the only intelligible technique for the study of human behavior.

The Dilemma

Each interpretation of life has something to offer. Each is inadequate alone. Unfortunately, elements are, in many instances, so diametrically opposed that no eclectic approach seem viable. In the case of the reductionist view, the failing lies in the attempt to provide physicochemical explanations for the goal-seeking and adaptive behavior of biological organisms. It suffers from the "nothing-but" fallacy developed by MacKay, which represents the attempt to explain an entity as being no more than (nothing but) the sum of its parts—allowing for no synergistic effect.[100] Wolman, commenting on the attempt, suggested that "reductionism is probably an infantile disease common to all young sciences."[101]

Reductionist philosophy is also beset by an arrogance which, in many instances, is not justified. Medicine, once the province of faith healers and assorted charm dispensers, is today believed to be based on solid scientific evidence. Superstition is presumably replaced by knowledge. But to what extent? Magill, in a presidential address to the American Association of Immunologists, said "medical science has not explained infections...it has merely substituted 'microbes' for 'evil spirits'."[102]

Adherents to the mechanistic interpretation are challenged, not only by vitalists,

CONCEPTIONS OF LIFE 29

but by the theoretical speculation of modern physicists, who deny the adequacy of mechanistic explanation. Quantum and quark theories, the uncertainty principle, and complementarity theory, to name a few relatively recent hypotheses, have led to disillusionment with the physicist's ability to explain matter.

Feynman suggested, "it [quantum physics] is a terrible mix-up, and you might say it's a hopeless mess physics has got itself worked into" though it is "much smaller than the mess [it was in] ten years ago."[103] Regarding gravitation he added, "not only have we no experiments with which to check a quantum theory of gravitation, we also have no reasonable theory."[103] As to its application to the living, Matson observed that "The mechanist viewpoint has been found to be inadequate for the full comprehension of inorganic matter and natural events; it is a fortiori inadequate for the understanding of human nature and human events."[104]

Ouspensky much earlier had said that positivist thinking will ultimately be required to repudiate its own foundations. "Then all the world will see before it the colossus with feet of clay, or rather without any feet at all, but with a formidable misty body, hanging in the air."[105] Positivist writers themselves have had second thoughts about their positions. Ayer, a logical positivist whose book *Language Truth and Logic*,[106] was the foundation for the celebrated *verification theory* of the proof of propositions, agreed some 40 years later that "the book is extremely vulnerable to minute criticism...my use of the verification principle led me into error."[107] Analytic procedures and every effort to discover common principles represent an extremely valuable undertaking. Such processes, however, are limited in their potential for explaining the enigmas of life, and its adherents often appear to suffer from a severe myopia when alternative explanations are offered.

Finalists are equally unable to present a compelling argument. They insist on a closed system of reality with some specific "ultimate" goal of behavior that is as limiting at the upper extreme as is contingency at the lower. To conceptualize an ultimate end would be difficult—to recognize one, impossible. Of course, the finalist does not suggest that such a concept is arrived at through intellectual analysis, but by a revelatory experience not subject to rational investigation. There does appear to be some need to explain life in terms other than those employed by reductionists. However, the insistence on a basic difference between humans and lower animals, the positing of a soul especially for humans, and the allegation that a unique relationship holds between humans and a personal God which has occupied the attention of philosophers for several thousands of years do not seem justified by the evidence.

No aspect of the finalist position is convincing. On the basis of reason, it is argued that the existence of the world demands a "prime mover." For many finalists, the presence of a moral sense is evidence of the existence of a deity and of each individual's responsibility to a supreme being. (Atheistic existentialists counter that people are responsible ultimately only to themselves. But they have merely replaced an ethereal supremacy with one of flesh and blood.) Most difficult to accept is the notion of a personal God who is ministered to by a divine court. This powerful

Superbeing is believed to define the goals toward which humans should aspire. Attractive as the prospect of eternal life may be, such an explanation represents only the substitution of a place (heaven) and a person (God) for a condition (the existence of life over time) and the sense of unity held by people who share common nationalities, races, or ethnic beliefs.

The intellectual aspect of finalist interpretations rests largely on the necessity for explaining life's propensity for resisting the descent into equilibrium or decay which characterizes the inorganic. The "watchmaker" alluded to earlier is the divinity (in most recent times the personal God) who provides the spark for a phenomenon unaccounted for by the principles of physics. Recent discoveries, however, have made possible a solution which does not violate the laws of entropy. Prigogine, for example, received a Nobel prize for his work with open systems or "dissipative structures." Highly technical in nature, the model proposes that "under specific circumstances and in certain local areas, the organization of energy can increase rather than run downward."[108] That is, in a universe which is for the most part moving in the direction of equilibrium or "heat death," in some situations matter may be so organized that it will "interact with [its] environment, feed on it and dump [its] waste back into the general downhill flow."[108]

The implication of the theory is considered optimistic in view of the fact that "man retains an opportunity—at least in theory—to cope with entropy by means of scientific breakthroughs that may occur next in, say, genetic engineering."[109] This, of course, would not be an optimistic interpretation for finalists since it would substitute human genius for God's benevolence.

The valuable contribution of finalist philosophy resides in its insistence that a moral sense exists, and in the stressing of self denial in those situations which require it. Social obligation, community interest, and respect for the dignity of life can be shown to provide an essential ingredient in the development of a positive emotional state. And beyond all else is the brazen fact that billions of people accept some form of deistic relationship. It would seem safe to propose that if the number of people alive today were to be represented by the number 100, the totality of all thoroughly atheistic individuals could be counted on one finger, with sufficient joints remaining to beckon a heavenly host.

Existential thinkers are concerned with the role of the individual, but among the many existential writers, one comes across such radically diverse formulae for human behavior that it is difficult to find a common denominator. In explaining the Christian principle of loving thy neighbor, Kierkegaard said that it is the intention of Christianity to strip humans of their selfishness.[110] And such selflessness, he suggested, is good and desirable. Furthermore, Kierkegaard argued that the Good, without any condition, qualification, or compromise, is absolutely the only thing that individuals may and should will.[111] In contrast is the position of those like Sartre who denigrated the Christian relationship and claims regarding the existence of an ultimate good. Without God Sartre proclaimed: "There can no longer be any good, *a priori*, since

CONCEPTIONS OF LIFE   31

there is no infinite and perfect consciousness to think it. It is nowhere written that 'the good' exists."[112]

Summary

Somewhere in the vague never-never land that separates these polarizations is the human animal. Feeble in physical dependence, potent in creative power, humble in the sensing of a relationship to some superior entity, arrogant in the notion of self superiority, unique in the potential for using talents to create a heaven on earth, and adamant in the practice of inventing a hell instead, humans are emergent and thus, to some extent, unpredictable beings. Science cannot account for their presence, nor anticipate their future. Theological speculation is similarly impotent.

The most viable interpretation of life seems to lie in some variant of the organismic and certain elements of the vitalist position, although, as we have stated, neither is satisfactory in itself. Organismic philosophy leans toward reductionism in its scientific conceptualizations. Life is seen as an "energy system" which should lend itself to research and perhaps ultimately to physicochemical explanation. In this sense, it is anti-vitalistic. However, the holistic interpretation does not adequately account for the functional significance of parts and instances. Once again, Koestler provided a trenchant insight. "'A rose is a rose is a rose' may be regarded as a holistic statement, but it tells us no more about the rose than the formulae of its chemical constituents."[113]

The performance of any entity at any time involves both part and whole relationships. This is particularly significant where mental processing is concerned. When the whole simply replaces the part as the appropriate focus of study, a critical element is lost. Just as each existent stands in a part/whole relationship with some superordinate existent, it also interacts in a whole/part sense with its own subordinates. In the highest organisms, and especially in humans, the interface between part and whole creates conflict, which is the central issue in personality theory. The wholeness inherent in "parts" must not be overlooked when behavior is interpreted. That principle is a major focus of our text. As to vitalism, when lines are drawn between philosophic positions, this interpretation represents the general class which includes finalists, existentialists, etc., on the ground that they share the conviction that a unique force is invested in the living.

We pointed out that reductionist philosophy—and the scientific community in general—resist vitalistic interpretations since they seem to suggest divine intervention as the source of the vital force. Unfortunately, the entire field of life-science is charged with the creationist interpretation, in spite of the denials we have mentioned. Molecular biologists, in their attempt at scientific purity, do not care *what* comprises the vitalist position, *who* presents it, or *what they have to say*. Their aloofness is clearly understandable. Polanyi said,

There is evidence of irreducible principles...in the sentience that we ourselves experience and that we observe indirectly in higher animals. Most biologists set aside these matters as unprofitable considerations.[114]

They do more. They contend that such irreducibility and the presence of affective states are offered as evidence only because they excite the desire to see humans as unique. This, the mechanistic biologist believes, makes it a purely emotional philosophy. But it is inaccurate to assume that those who accept such principles are swayed only by passion. "It is quite possible to be a vitalist on the basis of intellectual appeal, as is proved by the existence of a hardy minority of biologists holding this position."[115]

Vitalism could perhaps, become more "intellectually appealing" if its adherents avoided the use of supernatural explanation, and contended only that organizational states observed in the living require the application of principles that exceed those of classical physics and chemistry. It does not seem necessary to invest individuals with psychic power, but rather to accept the presence of organizational and behavioral characteristics not observed in the inorganic. These unique elements bind the individual to systems of life which are organismic in character, and which introduce relationships that may provide more satisfactory predictive power. This is the appropriate goal of a text on motivational processes.

By accepting elements of holistic theory, without ignoring the many aspects of evolutionist explanation that have stood the test of scientific scrutiny, a model of human behavior and related emotional health will be developed in ensuing chapters. Many of the interpretations may be distressing to those of an atomistic or finalist persuasion. But there is no way to placate those who insist on interpreting human behavior in terms of "God's will," or those who see life as an insignificant happenstance.

It is equally unfortunate that scientific parochialism demands acceptance of the notion that the thorough analysis of inorganic substance will ultimately be sufficient to account for all of life's characteristics. The result has been the creation of a most embarrassing closet queen. Every text in genetics and biology is crowded with vitalist terms, their use being excused as "essential to communication." Progress, adaptation, fitness, etc., occur with dreadful regularity. But such terms are absent from books on chemistry, physics, and mathematics. Their presence in the truly "soft" science of biology belies a subtle awareness of unmentionable principles.

Szent-Gyorgyi stated that he had sought higher organizing principles that lead the living system toward improvement and adaptation. But, he confessed, "I know this is biological heresy." In reviewing the biologist's stance over the past several decades, he concluded, "If someone ventured to call our knowledge inadequate, we scornfully dismissed him as a 'vitalist'."[116] Such rejection is equally powerful today.

The geneticist/biologists' claim that a humanist position can be held while adhering to a mechanical view of the meaninglessness—the triviality—of human beings, is precarious. Morality is explained as a selfish adaptive technique and sacrifice as genetically efficient. Biologists cling to feelings which they deny have any purpose, and when they give credence to the genetic plan, it is done without accepting the mysteriousness and uniqueness of a rule or idea that violates thermodynamic law in so many of its manifestations.

How could it happen, they ask, that there could emerge a form of existence with spirit, with direction, and with a sense of its own precious nature from a lifeless, purposeless, wandering universe? *But such an existence has appeared!* And although in its composition it retains many of its physicochemical properties, novel principles have been introduced that cannot be ignored. An understanding of life can never be achieved unless purpose, belief, and similar concepts are recognized as legitimate and dynamic characteristics, unique to the living. Biologists, philosophers, chemists, physicists, and social scientists must recognize that their contributions to an understanding of the human species are hampered by their rigid insistence on beginning on Page Two of the Book of Life.

Chapter Notes

1. Aristotle in Fuller (1955), p. 180
2. Augustine (1937), pp. 39-40
3. Chardin (1965), p. 33
4. Dobzhansky (1956), p. 6
5. Bugental (1967), p. 9
6. Pascal in Bishop, (1936), p. 275
7. Sinnott (1958), p. 15
8. Huxley, J. S. (1970), p. 240
9. Mead (1959), p. 116
10. Hilgard (1987), p. 375
11. Margalef (1968), p. 27
12. Eisley (1946), pp. 199-200
13. Engel (1965), p. 192
14. Smith, A. (1968), p. 1
15. Morris, D. (1967), p. 9
16. Rose (1973), pp. 281-282
17. Wild (1966), p. 18
18. Binswanger (1958), p. 193
19. May (1958b), p. 11
20. Sartre (1947)
21. May (1958b), p. 58
22. *Ibid.*, p. 14
23. Kierkegaard (1944), p. 146
24. May (1958a), p. 45
25. *Ibid.*, p. 63
26. Reality demands some spatio-temporal location—some place in time at which the equation is expressed.
27. May (1958b), p. 40
28. Chardin (1965), p. 165
29. Koestler (1963), p. 560
30. In spite of such comments, however, behavioral models of humanity persist. The urge to reduce behavior to complete predictability is compelling.
31. Christianson (1984): Newton spent the greatest part of his life seeking the "experimentum crucis" for every claim to knowledge that he advanced. He borrowed the term from Robert Hooke but perhaps adhered to its tenets more firmly than any scientific scholar before his day.
32. Logical positivism, also known as "scientific empiricism" is not as consistent a philosophy as is often assumed. Hesse described it as "a recurrent phenomenon in the history of science...where it quickly develops from a search for a firm grounding in knowledge to a skepticism about all knowledge, and thence to the revival of metaphysics in one form or another." (1986, p. 69).
33. Nagel (1961), p. 311
34. *Ibid,* p. 438. Once again, a remarkable proposition. The contention that the failure of extant theories does not prove that no mechanistic theory can be developed is of a class of arguments that can be made by anyone who is convinced of the ultimacy of their position (e.g., the creationists).
35. Bertalanffy (1952), p. 8
36. Bohm (1969a), p. 34
37. Thorpe (1978), p. 5
38. Hofstadter (1981). Hofstadter was puzzled that people insist on believing that "a living being is greater than the sum of its parts" (p. 144). His thesis was that if the parts were fully understood,

properties of the whole could be anticipated.
39. Huxley, J. S. (1942)
40. Koestler (1972b)
41. Barnett (1948), p. 109
42. Beck (1961), p. 140
43. *Ibid.*, p. 201
44. Simon (1971), p. 180
45. Schrodinger (1962), p. 81
46. Schrodinger (1953), p. 7
47. Handler (1970), p. 4
48. Ouspensky (1970), p. 305
49. Jones (1972), p. 53
50. Mausner & Mausner (1955), p. 7
51. Margalef (1968), p. 29
52. Pascal in Kegan Paul (1899), p. 84
53. Mayr (1970), p. 1
54. Root-Bernstein (1984), p. 65
55. Morris, H. M. (1974), p. 75
56. Moore, J. N. (1973), pp. 25-26
57. Ruse (1984), p. 331
58. Dobzhansky (1970b), p. 29
59. Waddington (1968d), p. 103
60. Gould (1984), p. 118
61. Root-Bernstein (1984), p. 71
62. Mayr (1976), P. 44
63. Ambrose (1982), p. 124
64. Bertalanffy (1952)
65. Rosen (1985), pp. 80-81
66. Gould (1984), p. 120
67. Adherents of a recently developed school of biological thought called "cladistics" even question any claim made from fossil discoveries. They contend that only inferences—not proof—can ever be inferred from such findings. President of the group, S. Farris said: "Fossils are just a bunch of bones at different times at different levels. [Ancestry is] something you fill in with your mind" adding "you don't have to presuppose evolution to do cladistics" (1985, p. 81).
68. Bertalanffy (1952), p. 95
69. *Ibid.*, p. 92
70. Gould (1984), p. 122. Furthermore, the notion of gradual change is challenged by Gould and others who want to substitute the notion of "punctuated equilibrium". This explanation contends that after long periods of little or no change, new features appear with dramatic suddenness.
71. *Ibid.*, p. 121
72. Cuffey (1984), p. 256
73. Ambrose (1982), p. 131
74. Simon (1971), p. 61. This criticism is not limited to creationists. The confirmed secularist Lewontin of Harvard said that Darwinists are telling "just so" stories, and that natural selection as a method of life on earth should be relegated here to the [explanation] of last resort" (1985). Eldredge added that the so-called transitional states appear to represent a trend occurring within species (1985). And, Stanley proposed that the record of fossils "has never been in accord with gradualism" (1981, p. 71).
75. Gould (1984), p. 121
76. Huxley, J. S. (1942), pp. 473-474
77. Simpson (1967), p. 16
78. Bohm (1969b), p. 45
79. Mayr (1976), p. 13
80. Darwin (1970a), p. 265

81. Darwin (1970b), p. 81
82. Allee (1951)
83. Wilson E. O. (1975), p. 129
84. Nietzsche (1955), p. 72
85. Cairns-Smith (1968), p. 66. Recently, Cairns-Smith has proposed a "Dual-Origin" theory of the beginning of life. He contends that clay or silicon crystals, which have existed for millions of years, demonstrate a kind of metabolism because they attract ions and continually sheer off as they become too large. At some point, he suggests that they may have started to produce organic compounds *"in order to help themselves to survive and multiply."* (Casti, 1989, p. 113). Ultimately the organic compounds took over because they reproduced more rapidly than the crystal "life" that had created them.
86. Salisbury (1971), pp. 335-338
87. Wigner (1961), pp. 231-238
88. Hoyle & Wickramsinghe (1978), p. 26
89. Wald (1979), p. 48
90. Mead (1959), p. 113
91. Miller, K. R. (1984), p. 21
92. Halstead (1984), p. 240
93. Mead (1959), p. 80
94. Asimov (1981), p. 90
95. Eccles (1967), pp. 25-26
96. Smuts (1926)
97. Weiss, P. (1969), p. 9
98. Koestler (1978), p. 32
99. Polanyi (1968), p. 1311
100. MacKay (1952)
101. Wolman (1973), p. 33
102. Magill (1954), p. 35
103. Feynman (1985), pp. 148-149
104. Matson (1966), p. 139
105. Ouspensky (1970), p. 210
106. Ayer (1946)
107. Ayer (1987), p. 34
108. Prigogine (1980), p. 17. At a conference on Artificial Life (Santa Fe, New Mexico, Feb. 5-9, 1990), a large group of physicists, biologists, and other scientists concurred with the notion that there is "a tendency of complex dynamic systems to fall into an ordered state without any selective pressures whatever." (Science, March 30, 1990, p. 30.) However, their conclusions are based on "abstract mathematical and computational models" (ibid. p. 30).
109. *Ibid.*, p. 18
110. Kierkegaard (1944)
111. Kierkegaard (1941)
112. Sartre (1955), p. 128
113. Koestler (1978), p. 26
114. Polanyi (1968), p. 1310
115. Mead (1959), p. 119
116. Szent-Gyorgyi (1972), p. xxx

―――――――― *Chapter 2* ――――――――
Holonic Nature of Existence

The existential world is a product of the interaction between primordial substance and perceptual experience. Entities are simultaneously *parts* or *instances* of more inclusive existents and *wholes* with their own contributory elements. The term *holon* was coined by Arthur Koestler to describe this dual nature of all existents. It is introduced here as the basis for the motivational scheme to be developed.

Reality may be ascribed to the focus of perceptual experience along the existential hierarchy, while *meaning* represents the relationship between an entity and some transcendent existence.

Species, *populations*, and *gene pools* are legitimate realities—dynamic systems—that provide a focus of meaning for their constituent instances. As systems they bridge the whole/part dichotomies of which they are comprised, thus providing a vehicle for protracted existence. These organic systems differ critically from their inorganic counterparts in that the survival and growth of parts is subservient to that of the wholes they represent.

In order to characterize the relationship between humans and simpler forms of life, and to determine the extent to which comparisons are appropriate, several ontological problems shall be considered. It must be demonstrated that existence cannot be understood as residing exclusively in either the physical instance or in the idea it represents. Although the principle applies to all existential forms, our focus shall be on the organic. The first problem with understanding the nature of being comes from the use of the term *existence*. This term is sometimes employed to define all that is actually or potentially real or existent, and at other times only to describe matter as it is organized (i.e., in its form as mass or energy), the interactive aspects of being, or simply that which is perceived or experienced. Many modern physicists propose, in fact, that the only legitimate existence may well be the events occasioned by the interaction of particles which in themselves are no more than symbols.

The term substance has also been used in a variety of ways, ranging from the classic use, where essence and substance were jointly employed to describe pre-existential being, to scholastic usage, which included both the non-existent as well as that which is incapable of existing, as representing some substratum of being that may possess essence. A clarification of the distinction between these two concepts is essential to a complete description of our model.

Substance: The World of Pre-existential Being

Substance has generally referred to the primary nature of that-which-is or the fabric of which *essence* represents the attributes. The ultimate nature of being—should there be one—is not at issue. (Zukav pointed out that "according to the Everett-Wheeler-Graham theory, the development of the Schrodinger wave equation generates an endlessly proliferating number of *different branches of reality*."[1]) The reference here is, however, to whatever pre-exists as an entailment of existence—or existences. Substance, which is probably an unknowable (certainly an unperceivable) form of being, shall be employed to mean that which some philosophers suggest "really is," the *sine qua non* of that which appears or is perceived. Runes proposed that "The nature of substance is that it exists in itself, independently from another being. While accidents [quantity, quality, etc.] are in another, substance is in itself."[2] This interpretation follows that of Leibnitz and Spinoza who believed that an underlying substratum of reality must exist on the basis of the observation of so many predicates that are palpably related to a common subject. Perhaps in some sense *energy/mass* or virtually massless particles may be a loose equivalent.

Essence shall be used to define the characteristics of substance which determine its nature independently of whether it is "labelled" or even recognized by sentient beings. It refers to the laws to which substance itself is subject. It provides substance with *identity*. Although Aristotle assumed that substance is comprised only of things, those "things" shall, in this text, include the many entities without physical co-extension (specifically, those substances which at the existential level include, gene pools, populations, and species).

Aristotelian philosophers—on the contention that only individual entities are generated—believed that substance is a characteristic of discrete entities. Platonists, on the other hand, assumed that primitive reality could only be found in those universals which are common to collectives. Following such philosophic beginnings, it would seem that the study of substance, would be the appropriate subject matter of philosophic discourse. However, this is not the case. Most ontological theory is based on existential analysis, a distinction which has not in all instances been clearly articulated. Berkeley, for example, argued that without properties, qualities, and attributes substance is without being—but he was actually dealing with *existence*, a quite different concept.

The "ontological argument" of Anselm provides another example of the confusion of concepts. Anselm made the case that since God is perfect, he must exist, for whatever is greatest and exists has one characteristic more than that which is (may be considered) greatest and does not exist.[3] (God existing only as an idea would be imperfect in lacking one characteristic essential to being greatest.) Leibnitz offered a parallel argument, claiming that since the predicate "exists" is contained in the subject "God," God's existence is *necessary*.[4] He concluded from this that it would be a contradiction in terms to deny the existence of God. Unfortunately, Anselm's analysis was based on the notion of "greatest," a comparative term which is meaningless in the pre-existential world. In like manner, Leibnitz appealed to such concepts as *necessary* and *perfection* which are peculiar to existence, rather than to substance.

The attributes of substance are of prime importance, although the selection of units or levels of essence on which to focus is an arbitrary matter. Identity is no more the quality of any one (bit of) substance, than of the totality of all that has essence.

Attributes currently believed to have such universal application (as essence) include the physical forces today assumed to be four: strong and weak nuclear, electromagnetic, and gravitational. Chemical interaction (though reducible) characterizes specific performance at various levels of substantive aggregation. Entropy and other regular change may be involved. Essences include dynamic interaction, where performance in one substance bears on that of another, as well as static or non-interactive attributes. In Chapter 4, a "fifth force," *Purpose*, which characterizes certain relationships unique to biology, will be introduced.[5]

Essence, though describing physical/chemical and sometimes biological relationships, is without spatial or temporal referent. Such concepts as time, distance, size, measurement, and summation, are all without application pre-existentially. There is no before or after, larger or smaller, some, all, or any other such relational descriptor. Twoness, for example, cannot be shown to be a characteristic of either member of existentially summed essences. There is neither any meaning, identification, nor other attribute which binds elements together in any directional sense, where inorganic elements are involved. Most importantly, neither chance nor probability may be ascribed. Such concepts are unique to the mental process, which is, itself, a characteristic of the existential world.

If a substance were to be fractured by a lightning bolt, its state of being afterward (i.e., its essence) would not be one of "halfness." Nor is any measurement taken of an object an attribute of the substance. The notion that entity "A" is larger than entity "B" is not a description of substantial, but only of existential being.

A further critical peculiarity of pre-existential being is that substances cannot be located some*where*. No such substratum of being can be posited. Since comparison is meaningless it is inappropriate to assume that substance requires discriminant essence in the way that "redness," for example, an existential quality, requires "nonredness" for its existence. The result is that a finite world of substance is conceivable.

The error in presuming a paradox comes from the assumption of the primal postulate common to monistic philosophic argument. Feibleman provided an example of the claim: "Whatever has been, is, or will be in existence, and whatever is or could be in essence, is part of a single inclusive whole."[6] His interpretation is insupportable in that there is no more warrant for claiming the essential being of the "whole" than there is for supposing that any less inclusive element is ultimate. *Partness* and *wholeness* have no meaning in the pre-existential world since subordinance is not involved. Elements of a system may interact dynamically, but the separate substances have no characteristic which identifies them as parts or instances.

Because the aggregate of what is (pre-existentially), is related only in the ways stated and does not exist at some place, it is not necessary to deal with the problem of what there is where substance is not. Another of Feibleman's statements is further illustrative of the ostensive paradox:

> Every unity implies limits and a boundary.... The signs of integrity are limits.... A totality of this sort would have to include everything, and there could be nothing outside the boundary, and yet there can be no boundary without something outside; so then how can anything have and not have limits and a boundary.[6]

Here the error lies in the assumption that substance has a spatial referent. It is on the basis of this untenable assertion that the antimony is inappropriately created. Dualist arguments face the same problem. The very notion of multiplicity, which assumes the legitimacy of "someness," does not characterize substance.

Existence: The World of Perceptual Characteristics

Epistemology, as it relates to the world of substance, refers to the discovery or revelation of that which has pre-existential being. Substance cannot be known directly. To be known it must be clothed in characteristics that can be intercepted by a knower. In the case of existence, knowledge refers to the capacity to recognize attributes that are elemental, and to impose descriptive characteristics onto them. Perception does not relate to *substance* but to *existence*, and idealist and phenomenological philosophy concern themselves only with the world as organized by mind.

HOLONIC NATURE OF EXISTENCE

The term *perception* is intended here to include all forms of awareness, or sentience, including impressions generated by the senses (e.g., vision and hearing), and those aroused as affect (e.g., desire and emotion). A strong case could be made for the inclusion of plants and even inorganic substances as "creating" existents in terms of their ability to be influenced by an underlying substance. However, our concern is to focus on the universe as it is experienced by humans.

To exist is to partake in an interactive experience with other beings capable of such an experience. It is thus a contingent, but nonetheless valid, phenomenon. For phenomenologists, it is the "underlying" substance that is no more than a contingency, with reality being limited to the experienced phenomenon. The key to the interpretation offered here is that one must choose whether to assume that the world is *created* or *encountered* when it is observed.

In the case of inorganic matter and simple biological beings, the experience may be no more than a reaction to physical, chemical, gravitational or other forces. As for the mentally endowed, the experience is recognized or created in terms of psychological categories. (In an extremely rough sense, it may be suggested that the photons that are reflected when an object is illuminated come into existence as visual perceptual experiences only when their wave lengths are between roughly .00004 and .00007 centimeters.)

No claim is made regarding the nature of the relationship of existence to substance except for the contention that what exists must be based on some pre-incarnate "stuff" that makes it possible. It is exclusively in this, the phenomenal world, that descriptive properties reside.

All such definitions are conventional, providing simply a basis for discussion. They are not presumed to represent the "true" meaning of each term but rather one possible interpretation, and particularly one that mirrors ordinary experience. To quote Barnett:

> The whole march of science toward the unification of concepts—the reduction of all matter to elements...the reduction of "forces" to the single concept of "energy," and then the reduction of matter *and* energy to a single basic quantity—leads still to the unknown.[7]

As indicated above, many who accept quantum mechanics presume that entities may not exist at all! The physical world may be no more than "a web of relationships between elements."[8] It is proposed that elementary particles, considered in classical physics to occupy a region in space, may well represent no more than *tendencies* to happen or exist. Powerful as its principles are, quantum mechanics remains admittedly a theory and, at its limit, proposes only to describe subatomic existence.

Our concern is with the world *as it is experienced* and as macrolevel entities interact, which is consistent with Ashby's suggestion regarding the indeterminacy of subatomic activity. He proposed that although atoms may behave in an indeterminate way "we shall assume...that the *significant* unit is determinate...so that only the average property of many atoms is significant."[9]

It is possible, here, to reconsider the ostensible difference between idealist and nominalist or realist positions. Each can be seen to be correct in one sense, incorrect in another, the problem being that they do not deal with the same level of being. Dogmatic idealists (e.g., Berkeley) are correct in their claim that perception is a necessary aspect of existence, but this ignores the contribution of pre-existential substance. The realist, or critical idealist (e.g., Kant) is correct in claiming legitimate being for the unperceived, but his reality refers only to the level of substance.

A formula may be employed to describe the situation. Substance (A), interacting with perception (B) results in existential being (C) or (A+B). Modern physical equations, based essentially on Heisenberg's principle, assume that the observation of an entity is necessarily influenced by the act of observing. Heisenberg contended that "we have to accept the fact that the very act of perceiving a thing changes it, and that we, the observers, are in a very real sense part of the experiment—there is no clockwork that ticks away regardless of whether we look at it or not."[10] But there is something ticking away; the substantial underpinning of existence.

Because of the unique role of existential being in the world, it is extremely difficult to provide a model. However, imagine a machine that sorts a collection of indefinable substances, painting some red and some blue according to an unknown and unknowable principle (e.g., weight, size, age, solidity). It would be considered appropriate to say that the observed entities existed by virtue of, among other things, their color. Assuming, further, that no other characteristic of the substance could be discerned, it would be proper to state that the existence of the entity was a function of, in part, a capacity of the perceiver. However, the "what" that was red would retain its legitimacy as pre-existential substance.

And here may be a clue to the ostensible paradox that quantum mechanics—though it has been consistently and precisely correct—poses. Consider the following proposition:

> Each step toward an understanding of the nature of the physical universe has resulted in the discovery of elements with a smaller number of characteristics. Perhaps at the level of the photon existential characteristics are almost nil. *Perhaps the entity being described approaches the level of mere substance.*

Should that be the case, the vexing problem of superluminal speed (shown by Bell to be an ineluctable consequence of the acceptance of quantum theory) would disappear.[11] The substances being referenced have no such parameter as location or speed, and thus cannot be measured with existential tools. Hawking speaks of *virtual* particles which "unlike 'real' particles...cannot be detected by a particle detector."[12] However, he said, "we know they exist...because they do have a measurable effect."[12] More importantly, Hawking said that "at the time of the big bang itself, the universe is thought to have had zero size, and so to have been infinitely hot."[13] A further step in the direction of sheer substance.

Reality

Words like "team," "race," and "bouquet" appear to violate a common (nominalist) interpretation of existence which reduces reality to only those things which appear to be physically connected. Thus, human *individuals* are believed to exist. They represent examples of *entities* which may be defined as *corporeal existents*. A debating team, however, in nominalist philosophy is not an existent at all. Its illusory existence is dependent exclusively on the individuals of which it is comprised.

The controversy surrounding such terms stems from a perennial argument over the status of universals. Although philosophic speculation in this area is considered outmoded by many scientists, the failure to resolve the conflict has resulted in the acceptance of absurd pronouncements. The problem centers on the disagreement regarding the existential priority of particulars (nominalism) or classes (realism). Whether a physical object or its class is an objective (real) existent has been the subject of continual harangue.

The argument extends beyond physics into the realm of ethics. The sophist position (predating Sartre by some 2,500 years) rested on the assumption that individuals are the measure of their own morality. Only individuals can determine the nature of the *right* and the *good* since such concepts have no existence separate from the acts of people. This view limited existence to particulars. In the same sense that atomistic physics had been developed by Leucippus, particularist philosophy was cultivated by the Aristotelian school. "Values" and other collective terms were described as mere constructs invented in order to classify. One outcome of this position was the situational ethic which saw the stronger privileged to subjugate the weaker and to impose their own ideas of justice.

Socratic-Platonic adherents, on the other hand, claimed that despite the apparent ultimacy of each particular, analysis would reveal commonalities which have a prior existence. Such common features, they insisted, are more permanent and dependable than their unstable manifestations in the particular and, therefore, have a greater claim to ultimate reality.

The *idea* of a square is not subject to change, modification, or decay. It is eternal and perfect, while the squares that individuals produce are transient, imperfect approximations. They last only briefly and for this reason cannot claim existential verity. Thus, ostensibly irreconcilable points of view have been developed. For one school, only material things have true existence. For the other, reality resides in the form which transitory, material things approach or exemplify.

It is assumed by particularists that it is possible to distinguish between that which is real (a particular object) and that which is a construct or universal. A real thing can be seen, heard, touched, tasted, felt, or otherwise recognized as having quiddity.

Particularists use a broad interpretation of that which exists. "A particular's parts may be constantly changing, as with a flame, and it need not be solid (shadows, rainbows, clouds...) can all be particulars."[14] However, a particular "must be identifiable and distinguished from other particulars."[14] That is, it must have an immediate impact on the sense organs as a tangible and discrete entity.

The universe, a particularist would say, is comprised of *things* (i.e., entities) which are real, while generic classifications are constructed by humans to identify commonalities among these realities. Although the controversy may not appear relevant to the views of reductionist biologists, the distinction drawn between a red chair and the concept of redness bears a striking resemblance to that drawn between a species member and its parent population.

By such reasoning, a planet is considered real while a solar system represents only a configuration that is posited because of a recognized relationship between such real things as a sun and certain other entities. A galaxy is also unreal. It is comprised of (unreal) star systems, which are comprised of such (real) things as suns and planets.

But what is a planet? Is it something other than its rivers, mountains, and valleys? If not, it is simply another construct that has been created to describe the collection of real things of which it is comprised. Suppose that a planet loses some part through celestial explosion. Is it still a planet? If so, it must be something more than the sum of its parts. How much of its consistency must it lose before it stops being a planet? Unless some such point can be identified, it appears that the planet is as "unreal" as the solar system to which it belongs.

Furthermore, different planets are composed of different aggregations of matter. How, then, can they qualify as the same *thing*? The same question can be asked about a (real) person. If a man loses a leg, is he still a person? Does not such a claim suggest that the existent derives its meaning from some source that exceeds its accumulated parts (i.e., some such unreality as humankind)? Answers to such questions have been posed for millennia.

Consider a tea service. The nominalist philosopher or biologist would claim that what really exists are cups and saucers, which are collectively *called* a tea service, but which may equally well be *called* a coffee set. But, may someone not call a cup a glass? The nominalist would argue that in this instance it is only a matter of employing a name not ordinarily applied to existents with such qualities.

Suppose that the cup were shaped thus ▜ and were made of glass. If the handle were removed ▌ would it become a glass? And if it were broken down to a half-inch lip ▬ would it then become another entity—perhaps an ashtray? The particularist argument is that whatever it is called, it remains a real thing. But, when further dismembered, it begins to lose its identity as an ashtray. When is it no longer an ashtray, but merely some collection of glass that in another form was called an ashtray? Perhaps reality is the glass particles of which the ashtray (a construct based on the accident of the form of the glass) is made. The same thing could be done with the glass particles, each of which is a compound. Where is the ultimate reality? What

HOLONIC NATURE OF EXISTENCE   47

truly exists? For the nominalist, each entity would exist, albeit in different forms so long as it was a unitary entity.

If a collection of beads is placed in a circle, it could be argued that the beads are real and the circle an (unreal) construct. Now a piece of chain is added to the collection. Still there exists only a collection of real things. However, if the beads are strung on the chain, a "real" thing (a bead chain) apparently emerges. Is reality created by the way in which the parts are ordered? What happens if the beads are suspended so that they do not touch the chain? Is the bead chain no longer real?

Similar analyses can be developed, with varied interpretations. For the particularist, a bee is real. A swarm is a construct. What, then, exists when all their bodies touch? Unlike the case of the touching beads, it is somehow felt that the bees remain real while the mass they represent has not become a thing simply because of the conjunction of bodies. Is this because the bees are each a living thing? Apparently not, because the same conclusion would be drawn if two of the beads had been simply touching (in which case the resultant duo would not be reified).

There are, in fact, many instances of organisms living in such a manner that their totality bears a separate name. The Portuguese man-of-war, or jellyfish, is an excellent example. Here a colony of differentiated polyps provide specific services to the system in which they participate. Is the man-of-war real? Does it become real when the individuals (parts) come into contact? This may be one key to the confusion. What does *touching* mean? Contemporary physics sees molecular existence as largely void, with submicroscopic parts out of contact with each other, except by some form of electromagnetic influence. For the particularist to extend reality to include all that is mutually attractive would be too presumptuous.

But what does the relative emptiness of space suggest? How is reality dependent on the peculiarity of the perceptual process? Consider what individuals would "see" if they viewed the world from several different vantage points. Physicists in the recent past assumed that the atom contains a "shell" of electrons. The shell was not assumed to be a form of matter, but represented merely an orbit or the introduction of a temporal or spatial parameter as essential to understanding the phenomenon. However, the tendency to assume the existence of such a "shell" is evident. In describing atomic existence, many texts describe the properties as "in the atom" which indicates the extent to which such interpretations persist.[15]

Suppose that an individual of microscopic size were to sit on a proton and gaze out at the world. Such an individual would see no such shell, but would rather observe a universe of empty space with tiny objects whirling about at a great distance.[16] For this subatomic observer, the proton would seem real, and the atom and anything beyond, a mere construct.

At the other extreme, particularist super beings, who required an electron microscope equivalent to observe the human race, would complain that in trying to see the entity "people," it was necessary to disturb it. ("It" being the sub-microscopic particles with the peculiar property of violating thermodynamic law because of some negentropic quality.) They may even consider the possibility that anti-matter was involved. However, they would not doubt the reality of this pervasive entity. Furthermore, if time moved rapidly enough within their framework, they would observe their specimen growing and changing and might even suggest some metamorphic characteristic which apparently served a function in the preservation of the organism. New individuals would sporadically come into being, with others disappearing. Thus, our observers may speak of "virtual" entities that spring into and out of existence in some statistical ratio.[17]

Perhaps they would assume that although there was an obvious systemic need being served by the behaviors of the individual parts, such a relationship was simply a characteristic of this form of substance. It would seem imprudent, however, to suggest that a similar relationship should be inferred regarding interactions among super beings like themselves. It would seem more accurate, in their view, to argue for the existential priority of *real* super-individuals, as against the notion of some superbeinghood (a mere construct) that controlled individuals' actions.

How unfortunate that the accident of size and the viewpoint of the observer so influence notions of reality! Physical connectedness provides no clue to ultimate reality since the appropriate level at which to define the nexus cannot be established. The size and discriminatory capacity of sensory organs do not provide the requisite information.[18]

What we have presented here represents a vertical view of existence; a momentary glimpse of the universe. This representation illuminates the difficulty with accepting the assumption that existential reality must be understood as particularistic, in that reality requires physical connectedness.

When the horizontal or temporal factor is considered, the more extended existence and the dynamic influence of ostensibly non-connected entities (gene pools, populations, or species) mandate the acceptance of these beings as equally entitled (or not) to reality status. Geneticists agree that differentiation in the development of parts persists only where the whole profits from the mutation. A variation in any part will not persist unless the total organism finds it useful. This reduces the special significance of the part, and points up the necessity for accepting reality at a higher level of existence.[19]

In challenging the particularist view of existence, the position of those who deny reality to an instance (i.e., strict realists) cannot be ignored. They propose that reality is to be found only in the eternal forms to which specific instances aspire. The "class" is believed to exist at the level of *substance* prior to its manifestation.

But what reality could be ascribed to an eternally memberless class? Must its nature not be manifested in some instance? Is not every imperfect effort at producing a square mirrored by some eternal form? If so, the number of such perfect forms is infinite. Beyond this, the eternal form would be completely specified by each entity––since every instance of a construction is unique in some manner.

Taking each position into account, consider performing semantic surgery on an

HOLONIC NATURE OF EXISTENCE

entity. If an apple is cut in half, there appear to be two entities. Each is, in one sense, a whole thing, but each is meaningless until it is related to something beyond itself (in this case, most immediately, a complete apple), in which relationship it is but a part. Is there any longer an apple once the division has been made? Where is it? The argument becomes increasingly confusing and unnecessarily complex. The distinction between the half-apple as substance—and as existent— clouds the picture.

However, there remains the question: At what point does an existent qualify as *real*? Should it be assumed that this occurs whenever any collection adopts a form that can be recognized as having some meaningful organization? This would make organization the critical factor and would support the realist's interpretation of reality. In the case of a whole animal, the integrating factor could be a nervous system "with permanent topographical relations between the elements."[20]

In an entity such as a bee colony, the organization might be non-physical. "Obviously, the secret is in the intercommunication of its members."[20] Thus, some characteristic which unites or organizes would be involved. Such a definition, being realistic in form, would have to face the problem of manifestation. Form, or organization, represents a collection of *something* into a particular pattern. This something may be material or immaterial, but if it is to provide a referent it must possess some palpable or otherwise discernible quality, and that would identify it as real.

This view would define reality at the level immediately below a specified existent at any point. For example, in the case of a solar system, reality would be expressed by its planets. For the planet, reality would mean that of which it was "ultimately" comprised. Similarly, the solar system would represent one of the "real" parts of which the galaxy (or organization) is comprised. Such an interpretation would make reality contingent on the focused aspect of an existent. As a whole, an entity would be an unreal construct; as a part, a real existent. But this supports the particularist contention!

The dilemma need not persist. Existence is dependent on perception or other mental process. Substance is not. The problem lies in attempting to reduce one to the other. And, it is complicated by the practice of confusing concepts like "species" with those such as "love." The first refers to the existential point at which one chooses to focus. The second refers to an attribute which exists as a generalized term, used to describe a feeling state that resides in individuals or groups. It is with terms such as these, including such universals as morality, justice, and patriotism, that reductionists have had the most difficulty. The summary view is that such words are no more than appellations applied to collections of certain forms of behavior.

Morality, for example, may be seen as a descriptor for behavior in one directed toward the welfare of another. Justice is similarly behaviorally circumscribed. Pears offered a telling argument in support of this view to the effect that appealing to universals to justify the use of a label (e.g., redness) is circular; "that what is being done is to recognize a similarity with another particular."[21]

If such an interpretation is valid, what is the nature of that which Socrates and thousands of subsequent thinkers have sought as they attempted to isolate specific behavioral manifestations? It may seem simple enough to explain the statement "his action was based on compassion," with the thesis that compassion describes only a (physically based) feeling state, and even that the moral superiority of the action was learned. However, this does not diminish the propensity of the thought to initiate action. More importantly, what is the nature of the difference between concepts? What distinguishes *compassionate* from *aggressive* behavior?

There seems a more reasonable way to deal with the problem. A terminology shall be proposed here which may provide a more heuristic approach. The problem of what should be correctly defined as "real" seems beyond resolution since each proponent makes different demands on the term. However, it may be possible to communicate more effectively by recognizing what students of such phenomena appear to be saying. Thus, a definition of reality shall be proposed which purports only to provide a foundation on which to erect a series of relationships. No ultimacy is intended—nor needed.

On the premise that all existents—whether particulars or universals—are complex, reality may best be understood as describing any existent as it represents the summation of some organization of parts and/or instances. To be real means *to be at the sentient focus along the hierarchy of existence*. It is to be in an existential state; to be actively interactive; to influence and/or be influenced by other existents; to participate in the exchange of information.

Reality is a relational term. The specification of a focal point implies the necessary existence of lower and higher order realities. To possess the quality of "realness" requires the inclusion of those elements of which the existent is comprised, and each of these is real in terms of further analysis.

Meaning

Existents are, perforce, meaningful. The meaning of an existent resides in its relationship to superordinate existents, which in turn derive their meaning from similar relationships. For any existent, reality refers to analyzability (to be "comprised of") while meaning describes a relationship to some whole (to be "a..."). The term "whole" is employed to avoid any implication of necessary dynamic interaction.[22]

Existential being refers to an instant along the spatio-temporal flow of becoming. A planet is real in that it has parts—meaningful both in its relationship to planethood and to the solar system. Because being is transient, both reality and meaning also fluctuate.

The biological individual may be described as a protoplasmic being. This is an analytic definition. But, protoplasm represents only a vehicle. It must be related to something beyond itself if its meaning is to be revealed. It cannot be understood through analysis any more than gravitation could be explained by dealing solely with separate entities (i.e., existential elements) that are gravitationally related. Protoplasm may be analyzed as *a colloidal system comprised of chemical compounds*. How many of these compounds must be specified before the meaning of protoplasm is revealed? How far would it be necessary to go in order to explain what function, if any, it serves?

Compare the former analysis with the statement: *Protoplasm is a part of the material of which all plants and animals are composed.* The latter statement identifies protoplasm in a meaningful way. In the previous statement, the terms colloid, system, and chemical must all be defined in their relationship to some class if they are themselves to be meaningful. Analysis makes possible the discernment of the *unique* characteristics of protoplasm since other chemical compounds exist. However, the relationship of each part to some class or whole must be identified before the entity becomes meaningful. This is true for all existents.[23]

The term "meaning," of course, has many applications. However, stipulative or denotative interpretations are not at issue. The question, for example, of what the *word* "stone" means deals only with what arbitrary referent is intended by the label. The existential question of what *that-entity-labeled-stone* means is, on the other hand, a vital concern of this text. At issue is the status of individuals and the source of their meaning.

Meaning as the designation or defining of a being has a long history of philosophic speculation. Analytic philosophers, notably G. E. Moore, proposed that "definition is enumeration of the simple parts [and] the *real* meaning and *real* nature of a thing are identical to one another."[24] Moore's concern with definitional meaning was associated with his moral philosophy which has come under serious attack in recent years. The concern here is with his ignoring of the fact that in order to be meaningful the entity, or its parts, must be related to some more general whole. In defining a horse, Moore said, "It is composed in a certain manner: that it has four legs, a head, a heart, a liver, etc., etc., all of them arranged in definite relations to one another."[25]

But each of these elements is both a member of a class which performs a function (e.g., the class of *legs*) and a part of an entity which possesses other parts (e.g., a leg is part of a horse, a person, a dog). Both classes and entities participate in part/whole relationships as members in an ascending hierarchy. If an entity or a class had no superordinate referent, it would be meaningless. If it had no parts, it would be unreal. Scientific study is continually directed toward analyzing matter in greater detail to determine its "nature or tendencies." Some are even convinced that through this process they may ultimately find its meaning.

Such analysis, valuable as it is, can, however, only reveal constituent parts which will either mirror actions of elements already known, or introduce components that are meaningless until referential classes are provided. Examples are found in every area of scientific interest. Consider the following: "The proton is the nucleus of the commonest and lightest kind of hydrogen atom."[26] What would be understood of this statement by a person who did not comprehend the notion of "nucleus" or "hydrogen atom?" There is, of course, no requirement that a concept be thoroughly understood, but merely that there be some sense of what the referent represents.

More puzzling, perhaps, is the attempt to find meaning in an entity without a class referent. An obvious example would be the idea of "universe" or "world." One may define the universe, as the collection of all things, or the totality of all that exists. Such a definition enumerates the parts but does not indicate what the totality means. For example, it includes "people" but this term is defined only by synonymous terms such as "human beings." No meaning resides in such explanations.

There is a widely observed practice, discussed earlier, of positing a being (God) to whom the universe belongs, and who, in this relationship, invests the world with meaning. Such a being would, itself, be meaningless—or would participate in an infinite regress of "watchmaker makers," since the meaning of an existent resides only in its relationship to some superordinate existence. Its manifestation (as real) is no more than a function of its parts or instances. To be fully explained or defined, an entity must be related to a more inclusive existent, while at the same time it must be expressed as a configuration of its own parts or instances. Many modern physicists employ this interpretation. Stapp says that the world represents a series of elemental interactions "whose meanings arise wholly from their relationship to the whole."[8]

The term "existent" is employed here to identify all forms of perceived being, including *entities* (corporeal existents) but also behaviors, ideas, situations, events, relationships, etc., which are existentially legitimate in spite of the fact that they may have no spatial referents. Also included are such spatially bound existentials as force-fields and other influential elements that pre-exist as substance.[27]

Perceived configurations are limiting forms, often transitory, so that the same existent may appear in many guises. Furthermore, an individual may be related to many classes. Similarly, a class may have different constituent parts. Consider the following, in which the same "whole" is, in each instance, comprised of different parts:

```
                        0              o            x
Triangle              0   0           o  o         x  x
```

Below, the same "parts" comprise different "wholes."

```
                     x  x                          x
Square               x  x         Diamond        x   x
                                                   x
```

It is because of this characteristic of existents that it is essential to recognize meaning to be a relational term. No existent has meaning in itself, but rather many

HOLONIC NATURE OF EXISTENCE   53

meanings as it relates to a variety of superordinates. A diamond, for example, is a beautiful object, an extremely hard substance, and a source of equity. The complete specification of the meaning of an entity (e.g., an individual) would require that all relationships be identified, and it is the lack of thoroughness in psychological studies that contributes to many of the failures in schemes of personality and mental health interpretation. It would, of course, be impossible to describe all of the many meanings of an existent, and definitions must be limited somewhere. However, too often even the first approximations have been lacking, and the individual has not been related to any more general class.

We have pointed out that since protoplasm is an entity, its meaning can be determined by relating it to some more complex entity such as a plant, while the plant must, in turn, be related to a superordinate existent such as a population or species if it is to have meaning. The first relationship is commonly expressed. The second is often overlooked, although most biologists have tacitly alluded to the relationship in their statements that species survive through their expression in individuals and that species are parts of ecologic communities. Such statements suggest a legitimate existence and, in fact, the priority of species, kingdoms, and other levels of living existence.

Mayr rejected typological or essentialist accounts of reality because they "make genuine evolutionary thinking well-nigh impossible."[28] His solution to the posited dilemma was to distinguish species from nominalist or idealist categorization in terms of their composition. Species, he said, are uniquely real in that their elements are relational. The genetic interdependence of members of a biologic community requires that the totality be recognized as real. With this, there is no argument. However, Mayr's own writing reveals a continual confusion of "realities." Consider the following:

Bessey had considered species to be purely mental concepts. He argued that only individuals are produced by nature and that "species are without actual (real) existence."[29] Mayr disagreed—or seemed to. First, he differentiated between a population and a species in that a population represents any group of individuals in a given location that may interbreed. In 1959, he stated that, "only the individuals of which the populations are composed have reality."[30] However, in 1970, he stated that species "consist of populations and...have reality and an internal genetic cohesion owing to the historically evolved genetic program that is shared by all members of the species."[31] Thus, he implied that "real" individuals comprise populations (mere statistical abstractions?) but also make up "real" species whose reality is dependent on the fact that they represent protected gene pools! By 1976, Mayr had again refocused his interpretation. At that point, he considered a species "a group of [real?] populations."[32]

In spite of having distinguished species from populations by designating the latter as manifested in local interbreeding groups, while the former encompasses all individuals that comprise a reproductively isolated group, Mayr stated that a species "is a Mendelian population that has its own devices...to protect it from harmful gene flow from other gene pools.... If only a single population existed in the entire world, it would be meaningless to call it a species."[33] But what if only one population of a particular species survived? Would it become real at that instant?

Certainly a difference between population and species can be demonstrated, but a more useful definition may be employed. Each of these entities—species and population—possesses the characteristics of reality, in being analyzable, and of meaning, in their relationship to some whole. Each, furthermore, is characterized by being comprised of interrelated elements.

As to other "realities," among biological phenomena, any reading of Wilson,[34] Dawkins,[35] or DeVore,[36] would reveal an acceptance of the gene as "real" in spite of the puzzle that such an existent poses. Is this reality a transient existence that flows through temporary structures? Does the structure as well as the prototype endure?

By definition, a gene is a chromosomal vehicle for the transmission of hereditary characteristics. Although most descriptions consider the gene to be a physical existent found within each individual, there is some issue as to what it is that lives across generations. Either the gene is a form of matter that is essentially indestructible, or it is only the pattern or idea that survives physical death. Either DNA is an eternal substance or its constituency changes while its features remain (relatively) constant.[37]

Genes that reside in somatic cells obviously do not survive, but what of those in germ cells? Genetics presents a garbled account of the distinction between the organic element which is a gene (and, thus, is itself a phenotype) and the pattern, plan, or rule that guides its formation. The gene is called a blueprint; but a blueprint is a carrier of an idea.

Ideas or laws are common to all scientific explanation. The combining of hydrogen and oxygen includes both material elements and a particular rule. The fact that the rule is only recognized by inference does not eliminate its contribution. A house is constructed of a plan as it interacts with local material. The role played by the plan is not reducible to the blueprint that carries it, but may be equally well represented by any number of physical materials.

When the acceptance of the legitimacy of the plan as real is accomplished, the unique vitality of genetic existence is revealed. Reproduction is a physical fact, observed in some forms in the non-living—but the reproductive plan of the living is unique. Biologists are loath to deal with this issue, in spite of their willingness to make such statements as "the population...is the proving ground of new genes and of novel gene combinations."[38] Surely the population is as purely ideational as a gene. It has, in fact, a less specific material manifestation! (Mayr, himself, has—at times—denied its reality.)

Consider these further examples: "our natural unwillingness to admit that one species has given birth to other and distinct species...."[39] "It [life] invents a highly developed nervous system and therewith pain."[40] "If...any species should produce a

HOLONIC NATURE OF EXISTENCE   55

variety having slightly increased powers of preserving existence...."[41] "It [natural selection] brings into existence real novelties.... Moreover, these genotypes...are harmonious."[42] "Mother Nature...insists that everything is secondary to survival, not of the individual but of the species."[43] And, finally, "Almost all taxonomists and field naturalists and evolutionists consider the species as being a real biologic unit, having definite and provable objective existence."[44]

Although in each of these statements reference is made to some entity that transcends the phenotype, most do not accept this external being as existentially valid in the same sense that it is ascribed to the biological individual. To allude continuously to such things as *life*, the *species*, or *biomass*, and then to deny that they have any credible existence apart from their instances is difficult to understand. In the case of Dobzhansky's statement that "natural selection brings into existence," the inference is either that the outcome is *as if* chance had acted, or that some more general existence than the individual is involved.

The view of existence which allows for the legitimacy of universals and reference to species reality is as old as the written word. Two thousand years ago, Marcus Aurelius wrote: "Thou has existed as a part. Thou shalt disappear in that which produced thee; but rather thou shalt be received back into its seminal principle by transmutation."[45] And, of course, Hindu and many other finalist philosophies are extreme in their insistence on the reality of the human species, though as finalists they consider all species eternal.

In view of the evidence of continual interaction and interdependence, it appears that life cannot be understood either when viewed as exclusively individual or species specific but only in a sense which includes both. The function of the corporeal gene is incomprehensible except as part of some general plan. Our focus is on the relationship between individuals and their species, with existential, if transient, legitimacy afforded to each. Molecular biologists, have, by contrast, attempted to explain life by reducing it to the physical elements of particularist philosophy.

The Holon

Our position regarding part/whole relationships is a variant of organismic philosophy (although that doctrine is expressed in many ways and under diverse labels). The principal postulate is that no existent can be fully described through analysis alone. Meaning represents the relationship between the focused datum, and some more inclusive existence, thus requiring that both aspects be considered.

Differences of opinion on this issue are rife. Although the relationship between part and whole is commonly accepted, there is little agreement on the chronology of the relationship. Do parts combine to create wholes? Do wholes control the action of their parts? Or are the contributions of each aspect essentially equal?

Theorists in biology commonly describe organic existence as beginning at some sub-atomic corporeal level and culminating in physical beings. Existence is presented as an expanding growing experience; a directional, synthetic process with all wholes having parts, but apparently not necessarily *being* parts. Again and again, this unidirectionality of being creeps into the thinking and writing of such theorists. Existence is believed to *start* infinitesimally and to *proceed* to the infinite. Perhaps this vectored interpretation springs from the conviction of the "big bang" theory of an exploding universe.

But wholes are no more necessarily the outcome or result of their parts than parts are the product of their wholes. The contingent nature of many wholes—where some catalytic occurrence apparently causes a new event—represents directionality only from an observer's viewpoint. When water evaporates, the parts (hydrogen and oxygen) may be equally well considered to be contingent.

Bohm's suggestion that the structure of existence has an ordered nature is a typical example of the directional interpretation.

> Let us consider the structure of a house. One begins with the bricks, which are similar in size and shape but different in position and orientation. The similarity of these differences of the bricks leads to the order of the wall. The wall in turn becomes an element of a higher order, in such a way that the similar differences in the walls make the rooms. Likewise, the similar differences of the rooms make the house, those of the houses the streets, those of the streets the city, etc.... It is clear that the principle...is universal.[46]

Although the analogy is appropriate, his "wall" is both comprised of bricks, and contributes to the room *at the same time and without exception* and cannot be completely explained by either aspect alone. It is defined (i.e., it has meaning) in relation to the room and is manifested (as real) in the bricks with which it is built. Bohm was surely aware of this, but his exposition does not clarify it. Lange's remarks from his theory of systems behavior make an unequivocal case for directionality:

> Wholes can never remain in the changeless state; they must change constantly. The changes, however, show a definite direction; in other words: they represent *a process of development*. In the course of development, individual wholes combine into more complex systems, into wholes "of higher order" which exhibit new properties and new modes of action hitherto not encountered. Thus, in the course of dialectical development, *new properties* (new "qualities") and new modes of action [new laws of behavior] come into being.[47]

To the concept of spatial direction, Wiener added a temporal dimension. "The individual is an arrow pointed through time in one way, and the race is equally directed from the past into the future."[48] All such viewpoints suggest growth from the smaller to the larger, from today until tomorrow, from the simple to the complex.

HOLONIC NATURE OF EXISTENCE   57

But no such existential vector exists.[49] Entropy and negentropy are mutually and constantly operative. Fusion and fission occur sequentially. At the level of mind, this periodicity is reflected in the description of an existent at any moment, with mental dissection and combining essential to its identification. Whether the ultimate state of the universe will be one of total entropy, the observed cosmos provides considerable evidence of at least pockets of resistance to decay—life being not the least of the examples.

Communication is hampered by the lack of convenient terms for expressing an interpretation of existence which is hierarchical but non-directional. Gerard suggested the term *org*, saying: "I have found the word *org* convenient for those material systems or entities which are individuals at a given level but are composed of subordinate units, lower level orgs, and which serve as units in superordinate individuals; higher level orgs."[50]

Koestler coined a term which seems better suited to fill this void and it shall be adopted here. In his concern about the dual aspect of each individual in the hierarchy of living forms, he stated:

> To talk of sub-wholes (or sub-assemblies, sub-structures, sub-skills, sub-systems) is awkward and tedious. It seems preferable to coin a new term to designate those nodes on the hierarchic tree which behave partly as wholes or wholly as parts, according to the way you look at them. The term I would propose is "holon" from the Greek *holos* = whole, with the suffix *on* which, as in prot*on* or neut*on*, suggests a particle or part.[51]

We shall employ the term *holon*, as Koestler later suggested, to describe *all* existents at *all* levels, since they are neither whole nor part in an absolute sense—but always an aggregate of parts or individuals in one sense and parts or instances of larger wholes in another.[52]

This is a departure from Gerard's position, in that all meaningful existents are considered to possess both these qualities, and the relationship is not limited to only those whose relationships are dynamic. There is some awkwardness in the term holon. It would seem more accurate to say that existents are *holonic*. This usage is in itself subject to misinterpretation since it suggests that existents have a holonic parameter such as that of extension or color. But that is not the case. Partness and wholeness, like meaning and purpose, are relational terms. No entity is endowed exclusively with partness. Rather its relationship to some whole qualifies it as such. Partness and wholeness are not aspects of substance but describe relationships between existents.

There are critical differences in the manner that elements at various levels relate to each other. Where an entity functions subordinately (bears the part aspect of the relationship), it possesses parameters peculiar to that role. In its whole aspect, it functions differently. In systemic organizations those elements functioning as parts retain their integrity over shorter periods than does the system itself. Conversely, systems as such outlive their specific manifestations.

Table 2.1 exemplifies a holon chain classification in inorganic matter. A galaxy, for example, is comprised of star systems and is an instance of a galactic cluster. A planet is a part of a star system which includes stars, meteors, etc. For grammatical purposes we shall employ the terms holon, part, whole, etc. However, in each instance the word refers to a relationship between the entity and some correspondent at another level.

Some wholes are extremely ephemeral aggregations, while others are relatively permanent. In the case of life, (in general) the novelty of combinations of elements provides for the increasing potency of the whole. This represents the creative aspect of existence. The potential residing in the metamorphosing existent provides for many syntheses. Creativity in living beings may best be viewed as a phenotypic expression of potential for species development. The holonic view mandates the acceptance of an infinite existential universe. Just as the substantial world is finite, the existential world is not. *This is where the paradox resides.*

The condition of infinite, temporal, and spatial extension is based on the nature of each level of existence. In order to have a whole aspect, the individual must also be part of (i.e., be holonic). To exist, to be capable of having parts, is by definition to belong to some greater whole. For example, a fingernail is part of a hand; but to have that part, the hand must be definable, once again in terms of its relationship to some superordinate existent.

The possibility that life on Earth is not an upper limit but rather merely a spoke in a larger wheel is not only logically sound, but is consistent with current speculation about the relative significance of Earth as compared to other celestial bodies. The problem with both reductionist and finalist views becomes apparent. Finalists, who deal always with existence, attempt to cap the holonic chain with a Godhead. But such a being, since it must exist in a relational sense to all else, including something superordinate, could not represent an omniprevalent existent.

Reductionists make a similar error at the opposite extreme. In the search for ultimates at the level of indivisibility, they assume physics to represent the "simplest" level, with biology and other sciences being reducible to that fulcrum. However, since partness is also infinite, there is no reason to accept the path that physicists propose. The fact that an entity is altered in form below some minimal level does not indicate that a "smallest" has been reached. In fact, to insist that the minimum size of some entity has been reached when it changes form, is to accept some form of emergence, which reductionists deny.

It is quite conceivable (and highly probable) that biological roots do not all pass through the realm of physics. The two sciences may come together at some "lower" level, or never at all, the nature of infinity being what it is. The characterization of the universe as infinite does not collide with the relativistic theory of a curvature that bends space back onto itself. The possibility of a moebus-shaped world does not alter

Table 2.1

Inorganic Holon Chain

Item	Examples of Systemic Relationships	Examples of Non-dynamic Relationships
Galaxy	Instance re: galactic cluster Whole re: star system, meteor, galactic dust, etc.	Instance re: all galaxies
Star system	Part re: galaxy Whole re: planet, moon, etc.	Instance re: all star systems
Planet	Part re: star system Whole re: stone, lake, etc.	Part re: all cold bodies
Lake	Part re: planet Whole re: water, lake bed, etc.	Part re: all topographic features
Water	Part re: lake Whole re: hydrogen, oxygen molecules, etc.	Part re: all compounds
Oxygen molecule	Part re: water Whole re: its atoms, etc.	Instances re: all types of molecule

its divisibility into parts and wholes, and infinity in such a case may reflect no more than the two dimensional spherical surface that may be traversed endlessly.

Although an entity at any holonic level may appear to behave as an individual, its action may be more properly described as a "summation" of the behaviors of its parts or instances (each subordinately dependent) which are manifested in the response. When for example, individuals behave by lifting their arms, they do so through the action of certain parts (such as the arm muscles), each of which represents the sum of its parts. This interpretation is significant in assessing the position of those who describe behavior as a reaction by a *specific* entity to environmental manipulation. The conclusion that this is even a roughly invariant response must be challenged, as the complexity and diversity available in the simplest reflex action is appreciated.

The terms that we have used shall be more specifically defined since they are so ambiguous that they have tended to mislead not only readers but writers of philosophy as well. Once again we must point out that they are offered only as labels with which to identify relationships between elements at various levels of existence. While the holonic conceptualization refers both to corporeal and noncorporeal entities, the following examples refer essentially to physically discernible entities since it is in the realm of such existence that most arguments have been developed.

The term *whole* shall identify a holon in its classificatory or total sense. A stone, a human, a baseball team, or a stellar constellation can be considered a whole when the focus is on its totality, and its relationship to its members. A critical characteristic of a whole is its ultimacy in that aspect. It is a limiting form as in the case of whole numbers. Measurements only approach reality, but one (1), in the sense of one unit, is "exact." In spite of its evanescence, a whole is at any stated time complete. Similarly, a legislature or a country is as complete as it can become. A whole is only such relative to its parts or instances. The term *part* shall be used when the individuals comprising the whole are dissimilar from the whole itself. The kidney is a part of an animal. A planet is part of the solar system.

The term *instance* shall be used for individuals when the whole refers to a collection of similar individuals. Species and populations are comprised of instances which are those living things of which the totality is composed. This term is ordinarily used when there is no physical connection. Instances need not be identical. This does not affect the way in which the term is used. The instances of a rock pile are rocks of a great range of size and perhaps even of type. The only qualification is that they can be identified for some purpose as rocks. The fact that in some cases the instances are interdependent does not alter the legitimacy of the whole they represent.

The term *individual* will be used to refer to both parts and instances in order to avoid awkward construction. Thus, a rock (as an instance) or a kidney (as a part) may be referred to as an individual. The most troublesome case will be that in which the term is applied to a person or animal since usage represents such existents as wholes. The term, individual, however, does serve as a reminder of the incompleteness of the biologic entity—of the fact that a thorough understanding of a person, involves more than an analysis of that individual's parts.

The part/instance issue is of critical importance in the understanding of noncontiguous entities. In discussing the problem with accepting the reality of, for example, a species—because it is comprised of nonproximate instances—we suggested that wholes with coterminal "parts" are easier to recognize as being real. However, in every case, parts are themselves comprised of instances. The heart, a recognized "part" of the body, is constructed of millions of cells (instances of the class of such cells), many of which are widely separated from each other.

Here is further evidence of the problem with the particularist interpretation. If partness describes an existential relationship it must refer only to situations in which there is functional interaction. Planets are parts of the solar system because they have an impact on the totality. By contrast, their identification as instances of the order of planets is a classificatory scheme based on the recognition of similarities that is another type of creation of mind. In this sense, the relationship to planethood is a parameter of each planet, and again part of the confusion lies in the failure to make this distinction. Nominalists concern themselves essentially with labels such as "redness" or "justice," but the practice of using such denotations as "humankind" or "species" as existentials exemplifies the same principle.

Platonic ideals may be considered as only figments of the imagination unless the eternal idea of a square, for example, exerts an influence on any attempt to draw one. And this may be a way to save the theory. However, it should not be necessary to do so since idealists can defend their view by referring to existing horses as imperfect representatives of the class of horses (i.e., the species "horse") which represents a legitimate part/whole relationship. This does not indicate that all of the classificatory labels that may be applied lack influence. To the extent that classifications cause interaction between existential levels they represent one of the marvels of life. Part/whole relationships can be created!

Consider the labelling of an individual as a Catholic, an American, or a fisherman. Each categorization has an effect on the members of the class as they act in accordance with the accoutrements of their designation, and on the totality as its "instances" perform. The view of such classifications as *parts* of individuals shall be developed in Chapter 4. However, the casual application of a label to a class is not equivalent to the describing of a functional relationship. To equate the existence of a species, which represents the relationship between a person and that "whole," and that between a teacup and all teacups, would be erroneous.

This analysis is offered to support the claim for the dynamic nature of the relationship between a species and its genetically controlled members. In each case there is a mutually entailing relationship between individuals and a superordinate existent. This reciprocal transaction identifies the aggregation as a system, a concept that represents a critical factor in the evolution of increasingly insulated gene pools.

Systems Concepts

General systems theorists have attempted to account for life in thermodynamic terms through the concept of the open system. They substitute the notion of feedback, for purpose. This represents a holistic interpretation since systems are seen as being within larger systems, ad infinitum.

The term, *system*, however, is defined in many ways. Rapaport suggested that it is "A whole which functions as a whole by virtue of the interdependence of its parts."[53] Flake-Hobson, Robinson, and Skeen, said "a system is defined as a set of parts (subsystems) and the interactions or relationships among those parts."[54] Gray, Duhl, and Rizzo proposed that systems theory "provides a new type of science based on organismic and open models in which humanistic values are a necessary part."[55]

Such an interpretation would provide for a wedding of organicismic and humanistic interests.

Berrien, from a sociological standpoint, defined a system as "a set of components, interacting with each other, and a boundary which selects both the kind and rate of flow of inputs and outputs to and from the system."[56] DeGreen suggested that organisms have much in common with systems. "Both organisms and systems consist of wholes that transcend the sum of the dynamically interacting parts."[57]

Thus, there is something in systems theory for everyone. But each interpretation assumes that a system can be defined at a single existential level. Such interpretations are, however, inconsistent with the organismic philosophy they represent. A system must represent parts, individuals, and wholes to which they are related. Humans as individuals, and *homo sapiens* as a species, exist in a dynamic relationship which may be defined as systemic. The misinterpretation of this characteristic is perhaps the most serious impediment to understanding the nature of a system, *which is unique in its capacity for bridging holonic levels of existence.*

This aspect of a *system* must be appreciated. As an entity, a system must, *in toto*, be comprised of both parts and some whole, and its function at each level must include each constituent. If an organization such as a corporation makes use of a quality control system, that entity, in its part or whole sense alone, cannot faithfully represent its systemic nature. The system is further unique in that even when it is comprised of organic members (as in a team of employees functioning systemically), if one wishes to reference the totality of that system the ordinary priority of whole over part does not apply. The system loses its integrity when any effort is made to separate the two elements.

In those cases where a modification in either part or whole has an impact on the activity or continued existence of the other the relationship may be considered dynamic. A planet is a dynamic *part* of the solar system. It is also an *instance* of the whole "planets." Only to the extent that a change in one planet affected the collection of planets *per se* could a systemic relationship be assumed. There must be some characteristic of the whole that exerts a controlling influence on its parts. Gravitational attraction may be an example among inorganic systems.

The failure to distinguish between systems and wholes related in a non-systemic manner has resulted in objections to generalizing systemic relationships to all things. Bertalanffy cautioned against overinterpretation since "superficial [systems] analogies...are useless in science and harmful in their practical consequences."[58] Miles stated that there is a "tendency to go 'over-organismic,' reifying the organization into some kind of gigantic person, or [at] least organism."[59] The problem is that collective terms are used in many cases to describe a summation of individuals related at the whim of the observer.

Although a part may be related to many wholes in a non-dynamic relationship, system membership is often involved. A teacup, for example, is an instance of the whole "cups," but when it functions as a teacup it is carrying tea in the service of some

HOLONIC NATURE OF EXISTENCE 63

individual (whole) who exerts control over it. The dynamism referred to in such cases is the subordination of the part (teacup) to some whole (human).

The problem of understanding systemic relationships is most apt to arise in the case of *instances* where the relationship is obscure—since parts often have a more obvious systemic relationship to some whole. Furthermore, since instances are in some ways related systemically, and in others non-systemically (as in the case of the teacups and teacuphood), there is a tendency to ignore the systemic relationship where it does exist. It is easy to confuse "people," in the systemic sense (where genetic influence is involved in their actions), with "people" in the collective (non-systemic) sense that people are, for example, sentient beings.

Three classes of system may be identified: Natural inorganic systems, natural organic systems, and deliberate systems. *Natural inorganic systems* are those in which relationships are described in the language of chemistry and physics, and where the dynamism is a force field. Parts and wholes are of equal significance and neither can claim prior existential value except through reference to some external source. A solar system, interacting molecules, and magnetic attraction between elements are examples of natural inorganic systems. Such systemic interaction is a characteristic of substance, but the specification "part" or "whole" is only existentially applicable.

In *natural organic systems*, the relationship between part and whole is directional, in the sense that the interests of the part are subordinate to those of the whole. There is evidence that to some extent the part functions to enhance the whole. Such systems represent all forms of life at the levels of ecosystem, species, population, individual, organ, cell, organelle, etc. Here *for the only time in nature* directionality of function is involved. This does not suggest existential priority (a person is as legitimate an existent as a species) but a unique, whole-directed relationship. The systemic aspect refers to the unification of the individual with some totality. The relationship may not hold at the level of substance, since the "parts" (individuals) as well as the "wholes" at each holonic level lose their relational identity pre-existentially. A third class, *deliberate systems*, shall be described in Chapter 4, where the concept of purpose is introduced.

One of the properties of systems is their tendency to resist entropy. The interlocking dependency of parts creates a natural barrier to the forces of decay. However, in the case of inorganic systems, disorganization is not avoided; it is only delayed. By contrast, organic systems, being open (through continually drawing energy from the environment), are capable of persisting in what appears to be a relatively permanent negentropic condition. This position was proposed by neo-Darwinists to explain the paradox of living systems violating the second law of thermodynamics. It has received considerable support from biologists who theorize that through genetic mutation, the greater complexity of organisms provides for continued stability.

Seed bearing and the reproductive practice in plants are clear evidence of interaction between levels of organic existence. At the level of animal life, sacrificial activity provides a more tangible clue to the existence of a compelling part/whole relationship.

Most relevant to this text, the species/individual relationship is identified as a system because of the dynamic relationship between the individuals and the whole, in spite of the fact that the population or species as an existent undergoes constant alteration. The distinction between various types of system is essential to an understanding of human behavior. It bears on the meaning of purpose, morality, mental health and the concept of meaning itself. One of the most significant characteristics of living beings is, in fact, the systemic organization of individuals, whether as members of well defined populations or of more ambiguously integrated species.

Summary

A critical issue in the development of the relationship between individuals and their parent gene pools or species, concerns our contention regarding the legitimate *reality* and thus the influence of these collective entities. Idealists are correct in their insistence on the role that perception plays in defining existents, but fail to account for the contribution of substance. Realists are accurate in assuming pre-existential being, but do not accept the limitation that observer characteristics play in the determination of what exists.

In all of nature, the *meaning* of entities resides in their relationship with superordinate entities—be that relationship dynamic or not—while their reality is expressed in the parts and/or instances of which they are comprised. Such interaction is a function of their status as realities. The influence of such existents is a highly significant element in the evaluation of human adjustment as individuals attempt to adapt to the demands of those systems with which they are involved. One is, at the same time, a father, a son, a Hindu, an existentialist, a Republican, a teacher, and an environmentalist, as well as a friend, a lover, and an advocate. Each of these relationships makes demands for allegiance, and support—sometimes in situations that require the denial of one's responsibility as conflicts occur.

Systems have the unique characteristic of bridging several levels of existence. This factor removes them a step further from their substantive underpinning. An understanding of their impact on behavior and its emotional concomitants provides an additional tool in the information gathering process. Organic systems, which are the concern of this text, differ from the inorganic in that they have a *directional* focus. The interests of parts and instances are subservient to those of the wholes they manifest.

Chapter Notes

1. Zukav (1979), p. 83. Wheeler and his colleagues refer to this view as the *Many Worlds* interpretation of quantum physics.
2. Runes (1962), p. 305. Kant's noumena, or "ding-an-sich" would apparently represent something of the nature of substance as it is defined here, being external to experience and only deducible from observed phenomena.
3. Anselm (1965)
4. Leibnitz cited in Copleston (1963). Leibnitz contended that God, being necessary, must exist. "For if the necessary being is possible, He exists" (p. 325). This interpretation supposed the ability of a perceiver to apprehend the substance that is God.
5. Perhaps purpose represents a Sixth force, since physicists in the 1980s appear to have discovered a force that is "a medium range force that [is] repulsive but much weaker than ordinary gravity," and that varies in terms of the nature of the material acted upon (Thomsen, 1987, p. 212.) The force, dubbed "hypercharge" apparently repels protons and neutrons from one another, which would cause substances to respond differently according to their mass. Begley proposed that it could "come from...a fifth force in nature" (Begley, 1986, January 20, p. 64)
6. Feibleman (1968), pp. 190-191
7. Barnett (1948), p. 65
8. Stapp (1971), p. 1303
9. Ashby (1960), p. 9
10. Heisenberg (1958)
11. Bell, cited in Zukav, (1979). Bell's contention was based on the necessity of accepting superliminal speed for photons. "Local causes," a *sine qua non* of modern physics, cannot account for the instantaneous common reaction of widely separated paired photons to stimulation of one of them. However, "the superluminal communication explanation had one drawback. It was impossible." (p. 282).
12. Hawking (1988), p. 69. These virtual particles cannot be properly assigned a location in space— —perhaps even in time—nor can any assumption be made about how rapidly they get from "place" to "place." It is simply inappropriate to make *any* assumption about such beings, except in terms of their effects.
13. *Ibid.*, p. 117
14. Lacey (1976), p. 288
15. Armstrong & King (1970). They say: "electrons occupy [some level of] the atomic shell" (p. 390). The notion of the atom as a closed system was shown by Spruch (1974). Young added "Gone now is the simple billiard ball atom. In its place we have a sort of electrically neutral *struc-*

ture with easily detachable electrons on its surface" (1965, p. 56). Either they assume a continuous entity or accept the reality of a *structure* whose "shell" is comprised of discontinuous electron activity. Similarly, when Feinberg said that "atoms...have a finite size" (1977, p. 7), he obviously referenced something that he accepted as real. Many authors write as if such an entity as an atom had a discernible spatio-temporal location.

16. Current thinking is that no such whirling objects may exist. Rather there are probabilities of such existence at any specified location. However, this indeterminacy concept has not yet been proven to the satisfaction of all physicists.
17. Actuarial figures on birth and death expectancies are certainly of sufficient reliability to support such an interpretation. Who knows—perhaps "virtual" particles that jump in and out of existence are the equivalent in inanimate nature of the origin and cessation of the life of organic beings!
18. Quantum physics, both the Copenhagen and "many worlds" interpretations, accept the essentiality of including the influence of the observer in any experimental undertaking. Many experiments have been carried out and more are in process which consistently support this contention. However, all such studies deal with subatomic elements, and the translation to the middle-space world of human perception is highly questionable.
19. This anticipates the concept that genetic variation occurs when the totality profits. It exemplifies the problem of determining the focus of the performance of parts, as well as the larger problem of which entities have part-like qualities.
20. Wiener (1948) p. 182
21. Pears cited in Flew (1984), p. 360
22. The term *reality*, as it relates to meaning, is not intended to refer to the possession of substantial identity, but only to being comprised of parts and/or instances; to the capacity for analysis. It should be clear that the manifestations referred to are existential, not substantial elements. By this definition, reality is limited to the existential world. Substance, being beyond the capacity to be perceived, carries no qualification as real or unreal. This does not affect the potential for reducing existentials to substances as a rational matter.
23. In no instance can meaning be derived from the parts or instances of the focused entity.
24. Moore, G. E., in Soghoian (1979), p. 10
25. Moore (1903), p. 8
26. Darrow (1952), p. 48
27. Their "pre-existence" is deduced from the fact that an expressed function must be grounded in

some *unique* substantial base.
28. Mayr (1970), p. 4
29. Bessey (1908), p 517
30. Mayr (1959), p. 2
31. Mayr (1970), p. 12. Here he was in agreement with Dobzhansky who said that a species is "a supraindividual biological integration." Regarding humanity, Mayr added, "The species is not an invention of the taxonomist but a biological (as well as sociological and existential) reality" (p. 358).
32. Mayr (1976), p. 492. He thus denied Bessey's claim that species are "mental concepts and nothing more" (p. 517). He pointed out that Linnaeus had believed species to be real and that it had been one of the tragedies of the history of biology in the Darwinian era that "one must either believe in evolution...and then have to deny the existence of species except as purely subjective, arbitrary figments of the imagination...or believe in the sharp delineation of species but think that this necessitates the denying of evolution" (p. 494). Mayr had evidently finally accepted species reality, but in a context that could embrace evolutionary theory. Shortly afterward he defined evolution as "change in the diversity and adaptation of *populations* [italics added] of organisms." (Mayr, 1978, p. 47.)
33. Mayr (1970), pp. 13-14
34. Wilson, E.O. (1975)
35. Dawkins (1976)
36. DeVore (1977). Each of these sociobiologists considers genetic inheritance to be the focus of all behavior. However, they presume that germ and somatic cells have different life spans—with somatic genes decaying along with the rest of the (gamete controlled) individual.
37. In the 1980's, certain cells were discovered that seem to live an inordinately long time. However, there is little reason to believe that their existence is "eternal."
38. Mayr (1970), p. 83
39. Darwin (1897), p. 430
40. Bertalanffy (1952), p. 108
41. Wallace (1895), p. 28
42. Dobzhansky (1970a), p. 145
43. Smith (1968), p. 37
44. Funk (1963), p. 2332
45. Aurelius (1937), p. 214
46. Bohm (1969b), p. 22
47. Lange (1965), pp. 1-2
48. Wiener (1948), pp. 47-48
49. The issue of whether existence is different as viewed from the past or the future has many adherents. The fact that in matrix mathematics such concepts as commutability (i.e., $4 \times 5 = 5 \times 4$) do not hold, and the discovery that many subatomic processes seem irreversible has led to the supposition that the world has a fixed past but a future determined not by chance but by the choices exhibited by observers. Gribbin pointed out that time flows only in one direction because "the radiation emitted by an atom now

is going to be absorbed by other atoms later on. This is only possible because most of these other atoms are in their ground state, which means that the future of the universe is cold" (1984, pp. 189-190). Since the ground state of an atom represents the lowest level at which electrons can be added, in terms of the atomic number of the nucleus, the "cold" universe can accept the emitted radiation, and this is irreversible.
50. Gerard (1957), p. 430
51. Koestler (1963), p. 48
52. Koestler used the term "holon" in several ways. In *Janus*, however, he made the point that "each member of this (living) hierarchy on whatever level is a sub-whole or "holon" in its own right." (1978, p. 27). This was essential to his later concern that such sub-units have varying degrees of autonomy as well as subservience.
53. Rapaport (1968), p. xviii
54. Flake-Hobson, Robinson, and Skeen (1983), p. 36
55. Gray, Duhl & Rizzo (1969), p. xix
56. Berrien (1968), p. 32
57. DeGreen (1970), p. 20
58. Bertalanffy (1968), p. 81
59. Miles (1965), p. 1

Chapter 3
Life: A Holarchic Contingency

Life is best understood as the manifestation of genotypes or gene pools in phenotypes, which are produced by the interaction of genetic templates and environmental contingency. This hierarchical network is unique in that the autonomous characteristics of the parts or instances shield the totality from decay.

Phenotypes are products of the interaction of gene pool elements and environmental happenstance. They serve as agents of the parent species. Thus, the impetus to behavior includes a drive or desire to act in the interest of transcendent levels in many forms of life.

This view differs from that of molecular biologists who tend to view life as focused in cells or molecules. Although living beings are said to differ from the inorganic in terms of function, structure, and complexity, most biological definitions center on the primacy of the individual.

In this chapter we shall depict life in such a way as to both account for self-oriented activity and to legitimize altruism while maintaining most Neo-Darwinian principles. Any such process is constrained by the amount of dependable evidence and rests heavily on an interpretation of observed behavior and related events. What is critical is an appreciation of the complexity of developing life and the relationship between individuals and the species or gene pools they manifest. As we pointed out earlier, no form of deductive or "covering-law" explanation can be provided. This does not, however, preclude the possibility of providing a meaningful account of the life process.

The method employed in this text will be essentially historical-functional. While the evolution of the cerebrum could not have been precisely predicted, its appearance represents evidence of the functional nature of orders of life. Such occurrences have been observed persistently in the development of species, as well as in the idiosyncratic characteristics of individuals. Structures seem to develop as they meet some need that improves adaptability.

Life is characterized by resistance to entropy and continued existence over time through the interaction of cell and cell group, genotype and phenotype, species and ecosystem, etc. It would be meaningless to apply the term *life* to any individual as if it had significance at some specific level, since all forms of life are defined in terms of more comprehensive existents and manifested in the form of instances or parts. To "be alive" is to possess metabolic characteristics that, under appropriate circumstances, can be activated. Thus, life cannot be understood by analyzing individuals. In a strict sense the individual is not an instance of life, but of an extant species or gene pool. The temporal factor must be considered—and this is a formidable task.

Consider the persistent "sameness" of the living individual as body parts undergo constant change. The living self is what persists from birth until death. No moment in that progression characterizes the totality. Suppose that an attempt were made to define a meal (e.g. a dinner) by focusing on one aspect, such as the appetizer, or the entree. No description of such a single segment could describe the meal *in toto*. This necessary temporal aspect represents a form of *symmetry*, with the focus of activity of each living creature being centered on the spatio-temporality that is life.

The tendency toward preservation and growth that is ascribed to the living is based on a universally observed phenomenon. The characteristics of life have the same status as descriptive terms such as gravitation, differing only in the subtlety of their manifestation and their unique occurrence in the domain of the living. Life in an individual organism represents *the phenotypic expression of genotypic existence as modified by the environment.* Each living creature is the resultant of these two essential contributions in a state of tenuous equilibrium. However, the temporally unbounded nature of life precludes the conclusion that any such moment (even as extensive as the life of an individual—or of a species) is a plenary sample of the totality. This represents a departure from orthodox views of either realist or idealist.

It is not intended that a force called "life" be posited as residing in certain things. The definition merely provides a criterion by which existents can be identified as "being alive" or not. The assumption of this stance precludes acceptance of the position that all existents can be explained under the same set of principles. As the liquidity of water at particular temperatures represents an existential state not characterized by its constituent elements, human behavior cannot be assessed by the most thorough analysis of the liver or the teeth.

LIFE: A HOLARCHIC CONTINGENCY   71

The discrimination between the organic and the inorganic that we propose has been questioned by theorists of every discipline. Zukav asserted that "the distinction between organic and inorganic is a conceptual prejudice,"[1] basing his argument on the contention that organicity may be assumed whenever an entity can be shown to respond to processed information. However, the concept of "processing" is appropriately restricted to functions performed by organic entities, where maintenance and growth interests are served. The fact that a "process" occurs when, for example, elements combine, does not legitimize the contention that the entities are "processing" information, which assumes deliberation—or at least a goal. And even in the holonic interpretation, the direction is only a vector associated with function. Wholes are not always assumed to be generated by the parts or instances of which they are comprised.

Biologists have developed interpretations of life based on the study of such concepts as metabolism, irritability, and reproductive capacity. Waddington, for example, suggested that life is unique due to the mere fact that it engages in the evolutionary process.[2] Others have provided a variety of possibly critical distinctions between life and nonlife. Smith differentiated on the grounds of complexity in that living beings possess many parts (such as organs) which ensure survival.[3] Pattee stated that "living matter has distinguished itself from nonliving matter by its ability to achieve greater reliability in its molecular hereditary storage and transmission processes than is obtainable in any thermodynamic or classical system."[4] By reliability," he was referring to a system which can be depended on to guarantee the production of sufficient mutations to avoid entropic decay.[5]

Weisz proposed that the basic distinction between life and nonlife can be described in terms of structure and function. "The essence of 'living' lies in characteristic activities, or processes, or functions."[6] The need to perform the function demands the presence of an organism:

> Accordingly, the essence of "organism" lies in characteristic building materials and building patterns, or *structures*.... A "living organism," therefore, is what it is by virtue of its functions, which endow it with the property of life, and its structures, which make possible the execution of the life-sustaining functions.[7]

Bohm stated more specifically that:

> What is *basic to all* life is a genetic process, in which changes in the genotype are *always* fortuitously related to the experiences of the phenotype and in which these changes will survive *only* if they are favorable to continued propagation of offspring in the existing environment.[8]

Waddington was most precise. "Of course the final answers to biological problems must, ultimately, be in molecular terms. What, other than molecules, is there for biological systems to be constructed out of?"[9] In all instances biological "answers" are based on an admixture of information gleaned from genetic studies and inferences based on evolutionist theory. But each interpretation limits the uniqueness of life to certain structures or functional characteristics. Oparin, for example, saw the step from nonlife to life as representing only the emergence of novel permutations of primitive material stating that "the only difference between living and nonliving matter is one of organization."[10] Schrodinger agreed, contending that life should be defined in terms of the shape and organization of the molecular structures.[11] Democritus revisited!

Mayr emphasized the distinction between life and non-life in his attempt to show the necessity for indeterminacy in biology. He suggested that "when two entities are combined at a higher level of integration, not all the properties of the new entity are necessarily a logical or predictable consequence of the properties of the components."[12] Once again, however, the argument is couched in terms which suggest that all existence is unidirectional. The emphasis is on a one-way process in nature, with wholes being the product of parts. The interpretation of life developed in this text involves the assumption that *only in the instance of organic existence* is directionality involved, and that parts and instances are, in many cases, created by wholes.

Unlike non-life forms, which are subject to all of the elements with no pattern except decomposition or temporary combination with similar senseless structures, living existents appear to exert control over the environment, and over their constituent parts and/or instances. Beyond this, living forms manifest a dynamic survival pattern which is expressed in some optimal state. This is accomplished in hierarchical order with each ascendant level having an existence which supersedes those elements that manifest its reality. The activity displayed by an individual is, in part, determined by a growth vector of some gene pool or species of which it is an expression. The process is revealed in the evolutionary continuum, being thus a *homeorhetic* occurrence.[13]

In presuming that life manifests a hierarchical control system, that its characteristics are uniquely dynamic, and that it is irreducible to the principles of chemistry and physics, we seek to disassociate ourselves from the posture of those evolutionists who seek parsimony at any cost. Our position is, however, intended only to serve as a point of departure and makes no presumption of ultimacy. It is, in fact, posed as a tentative model, being thus consistent with the hypotheses proposed by many reputable biologists. Waddington, in spite of the quality of his research, considered some of his interpretations "wildly speculative."[14] Dawkins deemed his own account of life's origin to be conjectural, (although he assumed it to be "probably not too far from the truth"[15]).

This raises the question of the level at which life becomes distinguishable from inert matter. Chardin called the cell "a decisive step in the progress of consciousness," and therefore the point at which life can be distinguished from non-life.[16]

LIFE: A HOLARCHIC CONTINGENCY 73

This is, of course, only a convenient fiction based on an awkward use of the term *conscious* and is no more than an arbitrary starting point. Although many biologists agree with his view, there is reason to challenge such an interpretation.

Biologists, in general, (e.g., Dawkins), consider the cell the smallest living unit; the basic *living* unit of organization. When one considers the current biological position—that the controlling elements of heredity are genes, the logical conclusion to be drawn is that the (apparently) non-living gene directs the activity of all living matter.[17] It would seem more reasonable to avoid such issues (e.g., is the heart or the brain "alive"?) and to define the process of living without focusing on a "proper" starting point. The critical issue is the distinction to be made between organic and inorganic existential levels.

Emergence

The issue of emergence, dealt with so often in this and other texts, need not be interpreted as a peculiarity of the living. The relevant question is whether the emergent properties observed in life are unique. The contention here is that they are. But defending the notion of emergence does not placate those on either side of the issue.

Reductionists deny emergence because it presumes that characteristics of the so-called *emergent* cannot be traced to the entities of which they are comprised, and is thus inconsistent with the orderly universe that they seek. Their view is challenged by many biologists. Mayr argued that "it makes no sense to say that biological evolution [can] be reduced to physical laws."[18] Its processes, he said are meaningful "only at the level of complexity of specific [living] systems."[18] Ruse took a more strident position. "Anyone who says that life and its problems is just a set of molecules is either a fool or a liar."[19] Unfortunately, finalists are equally disturbed, because if emergent properties can be shown to arise out of their constituent parts there would seem no need to posit a transcendent being. Emergence seems an embarrassment to everyone.

The distinction that we wish to draw is between characteristics such as liquidity, where hydrogen and oxygen are appropriately combined (which may be ceded to the reductionists), and such qualities as vision and hearing which defy reductionist explanation. Physiological analysis may trace physical and chemical activity from the stimulus producing entity to the corresponding sensitized portion of the brain. However, researchers can never, in that manner, explain the leap from *stimulation* to *conscious awareness*. There is no sound in the auditory canal, the eustachian tube, or in the auditory centers of the brain, though there may be physical vibration. The trip from auricle to cochlea is taken in tomb-like silence. There is no sound *anywhere*, until it is *heard*. These are the characteristics of the living that we will consider emergent in the sense of their irreducibility.

This situation is viewed with such alarm by extreme positivists that they deny that consciousness (the arena of sense experience) exists at all. Koestler quoted "eminent" neurologists at a symposium on the brain as saying "the existence of something called consciousness is [only] a venerable *hypothesis*" and "although we cannot get along without the concept of consciousness, actually *there is no such thing* [italics added]."[20] The issue of consciousness as an aspect of mind will be discussed in Chapter 6.

We are focusing here on organic existence which, although it follows the same general pattern as the inorganic in its holonic nature, exhibits a variety of additional characteristics including sensitivity, metabolic and catabolic processes, and procreation.[21] More importantly, our hypothesis is that life differs from nonlife in the unique dynamism that characterizes the relationship between individuals and wholes with which they are related. Organic existence cannot be completely understood through reductionist principles, since the substances they study include no such inherent characteristics. Carbon, for example, an element of all organic substance, is not itself "organic." Furthermore, the relationship between interacting levels of life manifests a directedness that does not characterize inorganic holon chains.

Table 3.1 demonstrates a holon chain in organic matter. Here the interrelations are far more complex than with the inorganic, but the principle is the same. Holon chains which include organic and inorganic entities in dynamic relationships have been exemplified. Many such configurations could be developed. In each instance the relationship must meet the condition that the whole has some impact on its elements.

In the case of organic systems there is a potential for conflict based on the difference between the function of an existent as a part and as a whole. A species which is a food provider for other species will tend to develop techniques for avoiding that fate. This represents an example of species "assertive" interests which conflict with obligation to the whole. Among humans there is, similarly, a conflict between behavior which directs environmental opportunity toward personal profit and that which is performed for others' welfare.

This description of life stresses the necessity of maintaining a balance between demands for growth and independence and the sense of belonging or transcendence that all individuals recognize in some form and which operates on living beings from a distance—the "distance" of the individual from the gene pool it manifests. The result of this priority of transcendent levels of living existents—where the individual is possessed of an affective system—is the potential for emotional distress. It is futile to attempt to treat such disturbances without recognizing the unavoidable impact of feeling states based on the subservient, (as well as the independent) aspect of each individual. If scientific analysis should one day reveal that inorganic entities share the directional characteristics claimed here as being unique to the living, the value of programs designed to optimize the emotional health of human beings shall not be diminished.

Table 3.1

Organic Holon Chain

Item	Examples of Systemic Relationships	Examples of Non-dynamic Relationships
Ecologic community	Instance re: life Whole re: species	Instance re: community
Species	Instance re: ecologic community Whole re: person	Part re: kingdom
Person	Instance re: species Whole re: leukocyte	Instance re: all corporeal substances
Leukocyte	Part re: person Whole re: mitochondria	Instance re: all leukocytes
Mitochondria	Part re: leukocyte Whole re: protein molecule	Instance re: all mitochondria
Protein molecule	Part re: mitochondria Whole re: mononucleotides	Instance re: all protein

The Holarchy

One of the principal characteristics of life is the ability to temper the impact of environmental caprice. While nonliving entities are subject to the influence of physico-chemical forces, living holons intercept and challenge such threats. Although inorganic matter drifts toward entropy, living beings consistently overcome decay as hierarchies are "ascended." The stone, assailed by wind and water, gradually loses its identity as its parts become configured in a less ordered fashion.

By contrast, living systems approach states of extreme improbability. This is accomplished through a reproductive process which causes wholes (e.g., species) to extend their duration beyond that of any specific parts and to spread existence over time by expression through replication, which limits decay to disposable instances.

Thus, species persists although individuals reproduce and die. Ecologic communities have an even longer life cycle and outlive the species which contribute to their existence. Thousands of species have disappeared from the earth but the communities to which they contributed have persisted. The biomass has survived for millions of years with ecologic communities being replaced by adaptively superior interacting species. And the life process is, itself, even more enduring.

The procedure by which life carries out its remarkable scheme is based on a technique of differentiation and specialization which insulates higher levels through more efficient function at lower levels. The term *holarchy*, coined by Koestler, describes this phenomenon. He proposed that it replace the term hierarchy which, though appropriate to a description of inorganic relationships, does not reflect the independence that characterizes the function of lower level echelons of organic existence. While hierarchy "conveys the impression of a rigid, authoritarian structure [a holarchy] consists of autonomous, self-governing holons with varying degrees of flexibility."[22]

This view identifies an element of freedom in parts and instances which increases the probability of survival and growth (while representing a risk to adjustment in the most sophisticated forms of life). The holarchic schema is the basis for the emotional health model that will be developed in this text. The paradigm describes humans not only in their simultaneous part/whole existence, but as possessing the greatest potential for focusing on their partness.

Organic holons are less durable than inorganic entities. Cells that make up the body are more fragile than comparable inorganic atomic configurations. Bodies that comprise a species are extremely delicate as compared to quarry stones, and the species certainly exists more tenuously than an entity such as a solar system. Such fragility is compensated for, however, by docility or capacity for modification.

A second conservational characteristic is the development of increasingly intricate systems as shown in the organic holon chain (Table 3.1). Clearly, the complexity of an ecologic community provides it with greater resistance to destruction than that of an individual or a species. Such a community can withstand the loss of many more of its characteristics without itself being destroyed.

It is this preservative characteristic of complex systems which challenges the tendency of evolutionist biologists to see life as developing from individual entities to aggregations of individuals, which makes possible a philosophy such as the survival of the fittest; where reproductive advantage is based on the superiority of individuals. Although increasing complexity does characterize larger systems, two serious objections can be made regarding the view that this could occur as an attempt at enhanced survival by individual phenotypes—that is, were the phenotype the ultimate existent.

First, the same hierarchy characterizes the inorganic. Thus, it represents no more than the organizational structure of all existence. Unless some unique relationship is involved, there is no reason to separate the living from the nonliving along this

LIFE: A HOLARCHIC CONTINGENCY

dimension. Rivers, planets, and solar systems provide as orderly a procession of complexity as do forms of life.

Second, if life developed according to strict evolutionary principles the relationship between systemic parts and wholes would be reversed. Although each living creature may attempt to improve its potential vitality by combining with other forms, its value or significance as an individual would exceed that of the group in which it participated. The purpose in combining would be to enhance each individual and *not* to create a system directed toward the dilatation of some "super" existence.

However, as activity at each level of existence is studied, we observe that from the lowest divisible living form each individual ordinarily acts partly to enhance the survival of some whole to which it belongs, directly or mediately. In most instances the whole to which the individual is related exerts systemic control (e.g., as in the genetically based reproductive capacity). When the need for survival and growth arises at any level, individuals at lower levels are often sacrificed. If the individual were existentially "prior," this would represent either developmental error or an indefensible tyranny. Rather, the dynamism which characterizes developing life forms is more accurately explained in terms of individuals being in many ways subject or subservient to the needs of transcendent wholes.

This interpretation is at variance with the usual description of the evolutionary process, in that individuals are not viewed here as expressing only their potential for personal existence. On the contrary, the viability of natural organic systems is improved through the influence that, as wholes, they exert over their constituent parts and instances. This includes both the maximizing of the "health" of the parts and the destruction of any part as needed for development of the whole. The former is a result of the fact that the whole is not independent of its parts in their interaction and is no more "healthy" than are its constituents. The very reality of a whole was shown earlier to be no more than the focus of the interaction of its parts and/or instances. (A species or gene pool devoid of any instances would not, in fact, qualify as *real*.)

The fact that instances survive and perform at the discretion of wholes is not obvious in all cases. It does, however, occur regularly at all levels—although it should be clear that such a relationship requires no deliberation, being simply a characteristic of the dynamic part-whole relationship. The species does not "decide" who or what should survive.

A more accurate interpretation of evolutionary development would be related to the increasing control over the environment exerted by the biomass. In explaining the Descent of Man, all of the interactions at each existential level should be considered as they contribute to the *totality* of life. This can be recognized in the relationship between every assemblage of organic tissue as well as between ecologic systems.

From the time an entity that practiced self-replication emerged (i.e., that imposed its form on environmental material), a new relationship existed. Directional force obtained. The survival and growth of the idea (life) is vested in every instance and at every level, although, as we shall discuss, the obligation is extended in most cases almost exclusively to members of the protected gene pool, which limits the immediate recognition of constituency to its phenotypes. The whole persists across time as parts and instances reproduce. This characteristic, most difficult to accommodate, requires further explanation.

Biochemical Elements

The first billion years of life on earth left no fossil evidence. However, extrapolation from known data support the premise that the earliest form of organic existence represented the amalgamation of a variety of protein and other molecules in such a way as to resist decay. This was accomplished on the basis of a peculiar capacity of certain molecules (nucleic acids) to store and transmit what came ultimately to be the genetic code, although, as Handler stated: "At the present time there is no satisfactory hypothesis to explain the evolution of the protein synthesizing mechanism."[23] And again, stressing the primitive state of biological knowledge of beginnings, "any discussion of this question is necessarily speculative."[24]

Wald proposed that two factors were involved in the evolutionary process. First, competition for energy sources led to the earliest expression of the Darwinian principle of the survival of the fittest. The strongest individual was victorious in the search for sustenance. Secondly (reflecting Oparin's earlier suggestion), the attainment of some physical size may have resulted in an unstable condition and an inevitable breaking down of the entity into less complex components. "A growing colloidal particle may reach a point at which it becomes unstable and breaks down into smaller particles, each of which grows and redivides."[25] Although the molecules that comprise these colloids are phenotypes they are the carriers and reproductive agents of their genotypic sponsors. Thus, the "sameness" or identity of the constitution of each separate redividing particle.

At some point in the process the cell came into existence. This entity, still considered to be the principal element in the structure of each living organism (if not the first form of life) is comprised of a nucleus which contains the DNA/RNA. These in turn control the formation of the cytoplasm, the remainder of the cell and are the source of energy that is essential to the function of the nucleus. This relationship requires that "molecules must enter into intricate designs and connections; they must eventually form a self repairing, self constructing dynamic machine."[26] The question of whether primitive cells (Oparin referred to them as "protobionts") represented the first form of life remains shrouded in mystery.[27] These microscopic single celled structures, (similar to what are today's bacteria) are, however, assumed to have been "alive."

Dawkins' proposal that smaller molecular units that come in close proximity to larger chains "with an affinity for their own kind" will stick there, seems a poor argument for assuming that such activity represented life.[28] But perhaps the fixing of such a point is not essential to appreciating the nature of the cell as a living entity.

Whether or not the virus is alive, challenging as the question may be, does not appear to be critical to an understanding of human behavior.[29]

Whatever the process, it is clear that from the nucleus emanates the direction and control of cellular action while the cytoplasm under such direction provides all of the supportive protoplasmic elements. As the individual develops, various cell groups come to specialize in the production of organs which function interactively, resulting in a phenotype which comprises the totality of interacting organs. Thus, mice as well as oak trees represent the sum of all of the specialized functions of their constituent parts.

The extent to which such parts are the product of adaptive mutations, or of symbiotic interactions is difficult to determine.[30] In any event, it can be argued that at least the total host profits from the arrangement. (There has been some literature on the possibility that the host in such a relationship is merely the home and food source for its symbiont,[31] but this is an unsupportable fiction. Cattle may be understood to provide beef and milk in return for being fed, but there is little question about whether the cattle rancher exists to provide the corn.) The probability that the nuclear material of the total organism will be carried forward through the reproductive cycle is the significant issue—regardless of the manner in which the sub-units come to play their contributory roles.

The Chicken or the Egg?

Simon proposed that "preorganismic molecules may have been formed from simple molecules [and] the basic biochemical molecules...can be produced by electrical discharge.... These molecules are presumed to have formed the constituents of a 'primeval soup.'"[32] With that as background, he concluded:

> It would have to have been at this stage that there appeared the mechanism of reproduction and replication of long chain molecules. The final stage in the origin of life on earth would then consist of the formation of the simplest organisms through biochemical and structural transformation of these elements, leading to the development of internally organized systems.[32]

Simon surely made it all seem simple. No mystery here! But, unfortunately, no explanation either. To say that their "appeared" mechanisms of reproduction is to provide no elucidation.

Beck provided a more detailed account of the earliest steps in the creation of life, and especially of the first colonization. Like Simon, he offered only a highly conjectural account of the stages between the formation of protein molecules and the ultimate evolution of the cell. He did offer an explanation of the development from the fission occurring in the first cells to the fusion of later organism, proposing that the technique was developed to provide security to cells that came together by chance.

His interpretation, however, calls for even more (unnecessarily) mysterious and unreasonable occurrences.

Lake made the summary statement that "all living things evolved from a single celled organism that had a penchant for living in boiling sulphur springs."[33] He added that "whatever else they were, they were probably heat loving sulphur breathing bacteria."[33] Cairns-Smith, however, offered the hypothesis that avoided the need to presume a "primeval soup." He proposed that clay crystals may have been the first duplicating elements to emerge. As "naked genes" they could have produced elaborate environments for themselves (i.e., phenotypes) which, over time, may have produced superior replacement genes, ultimately leading to what may have represented the earliest life form. As to the originals, he pointed out that "[they] would have been pretty unimpressive, and not, I think, alive."[34]

In spite of these varied interpretations confidence in the general theory of evolving life remains at a high level. Stebbins and Ayala note that molecular biologists present a picture of *impelled* variation in evolving DNA, which would rule out chance, while traditionalists insist that chance governs both the initial genetic variant and its establishment in a population. However, they agree that "(although) the synthetic theory of the 21st Century will differ from the one developed a few decades ago...the process...will be one of evolution, rather than upheaval."[35] Weinberg goes further. "Biology in 1985 is dramatically different than its antecedents only 10 years ago.... The new technology [molecular biology] has made it possible to change critical elements of the biological blueprint at will, and in so doing to create versions of life that were never anticipated by natural evolution."[36]

But what *is* "natural evolution?" Van Valen said that it may not represent adaptation at all, in the sense of meeting the demands of the "niches" in the environment. Since the environment is continuously decaying, "natural selection operates essentially to enable the organisms to *maintain* their state of adaptation."[37] What then of Weinberg's new versions?

And while biologists develop esoteric theories regarding the future of genetic manipulation, there remains a perennial problem—the nature of the evolutionary process itself—the *focus* of the evolutionary progression. May reminds us that "strictly speaking, ecological systems do not evolve.... Natural selection acts almost invariably on one individual or a group of related individuals. Populations...cannot be regarded as units subject to Darwinian evolution."[38] If we are to find biologists closing ranks over the next several decades their task appears more monumental than many of their adherents suggest.

Since it is critical to an understanding of our argument, a detailed quote from Beck's text following his account of the formation of individual cells follows:

> The next evolutionary step toward greater complexity of form was the establishment by individual cells of cell colonies. While clearly not multicellular organisms, the colonies were considerably more than casual get togethers

LIFE: A HOLARCHIC CONTINGENCY 81

of random cells. Although the first such grouping probably happened by chance, its survival value for the participants quickly gave significance to the arrangement, thus converting a chance distribution into one of meaningful order. The problem was: If a group of cells should discover each other and find that living together is exceedingly beneficial for one and all, how would it be possible to transmit this confidential information to the offspring so long as each member cell continues to multiply by solitary fission? There could be no way except to appoint a keeper of the plan, a specialized cell that could somehow retain within its structure the coded pattern of colony structure.[39]

This is followed by the statement that "at this point, the individual cells had cast their lots; thenceforth they could live better lives, but only if they lived with each other."[40] Such an interpretation raises serious questions.

First is the assumption that living together provided "survival value." How? From predators? One of the principle arguments of evolutionists for the survival of the earliest cells was that predation was not at issue and no other survival threat can be shown to have been thus alleviated. Second, it supposes that the cells "discovered each other," "appointed a keeper of the plan," and performed other activities quite foreign to any known in the inorganic world—a world that Beck denied as being in any way significantly different. Third, and most important, it maintains the focus of activity on the welfare of each *individual*.[41]

Consider an alternative chronology, beginning as Beck and others have, with the appearance of the earliest self-maintaining organic cell. The continued existence of such an entity would require that its constituent parts function in such a manner as to prioritize the well-being of the totality.[42] To understand this, we must again stress the notion of whole organisms as *emergent systems*, with ineluctable synergistic relationships with their parts and instances. The principle is by no means implausible, in spite of the many objections to its acceptance. Fuller pointed out that:

> Chemists discovered that they had to recognize synergy because they found out that every time they tried to isolate an element...the isolated parts and their separate behaviors never explained the associated behaviors at all.... They had to deal with the wholes in order to be able to discover the group proclivities as well as integrated characteristics of parts.[43]

Fuller was, of course, referring to the field of chemistry. However, in a similar manner, to understand an organism, one must appreciate that some central nucleus––somehow genetic in nature—is served by cytoplastic elements in even the most primitive creatures. Thus, for example, protozoa and sperm cells possess flagella that provide for locomotion, as well as, in some species, feeding and other tactile functions.

This does not require the assumption of some mysterious relationship or the manifestation of a divine plan. It does no more than describe a set of conditions that are physically—as well as logically—essential to the persistence of the total cell over time, individually as well as serially. It does, however, call for another look at the nature of the plan that is encoded.

At some later stage, when size and/or other consideration led to the splitting of the cell into *attached* daughter or sister cells, each with its own nucleus, the fission would not alter the necessity that each half function to serve the totality. Independent activity could well be destructive. The existent served would, of course, be not only the parent cell, but, through replication and reproduction, all of the family of individuals that followed and which represented the life form peculiar to the first cell.

The most difficult aspect to accept, and the reason for our inclusion of Chapter 2, is that when the progeny of the original entity that had been created by the process of fission separated from each other (i.e., became instances), *there was no difference in the role that they played relative to their precursor.* Each cell in the colony was organized just as it had been when it was joined. Each reproduced and otherwise functioned in such a way that the totality *measured across time as well as space* was enhanced to the limit of the capacity of the instances to perform their innately determined functions.

This interpretation is quite opposite to that proposed by Beck. The coming-together of individual cells as described in this account represented rather a *re*-union of inherently commonly focused instances. Such a "get-together" followed, rather than preceded the practice of replication. *Reproduction preceded motility.*

If many cells evolved approximately simultaneously, interaction between colonies may well have occurred, and if the parent cells were essentially the same, reproduction and other functions may have served the more general existence represented by the progenitor cells. The central issue is that shared activity occurred not only—and perhaps not at all—because of its value to the individual, but because of the organizational state of each entity as it served the life form that it manifested.

The continual reproduction of organic life led to the existence of many idiosyncratic groupings as varied genetic accident and environmental data coincided. Over time, protected gene pools developed. Such existents as phyla, species, and populations, developed as subsets of an enduring reality.

It is somewhat misleading to depict this continuity of growth and change as a tree-of-life whose leaves and branches represent emergent, independent existence. A more appropriate analogy would be of a tree whose roots (i.e., parts) explore the earth for the purpose of meeting the needs of the total plant, which retains its identity and superordinacy. The fact that novel rhizomes emerge may be of great survival value both to themselves and the tree, but they never cease to be a part of the totality.

Life persists, expands, flourishes. Its parts and instances change as opportunity presents itself. But the unity *was* and *is*. This is not metaphysical conjecture. It is an inevitable conclusion, based on a conceptualization of the origin and continuity of life that is as reasonable as any biological treatise.

This interpretation accounts for the apparent paradox of the emergence of new species. The crossbreeding of plants and animals does not result in the creation of an individual without a species, nor does the process of natural selection alter anything but life's *expression*. The procedure is no different than that which takes place when an individual grows, gains weight, and otherwise, matures. The person is a total entity from the moment of conception—only the manifestation is modified. The individual becomes more complex. Differentiation represents only the sophistication of the totality.

In the case of a species, there is a temporal evolutionary process which results from the continuing recombinations and occasional mutations from within the gene pool. The meaning of an individual derives from some extant species or gene pool. The reality of such an entity, (i.e., the species), may seem tenuous, unstable, fluctuating, and in fact, quite different from the relatively constant individual. But the term *relative* may provide the explanation.

- Is the identity of the individual constant?
- Do not cells and thus organs undergo constant replacement?
- Is not the adult, in some sense, the same person as the child, although no drop of blood is identical?

Stability across change accounts for the continued existence of the total individual. But the idea of an individual without a species seems much more acceptable than that of a species without a member. It seems credible to assume that new individuals precede their species and thus should not be viewed as subject to (part of) it. However, another example may help to demonstrate the propriety of this ostensibly inappropriately posited relationship.

We pointed out that at the moment of conception, the child (as embryo) begins to "be." This anomaly does not seem distressing. But who or what is it that is called "child?" Is it not simply the act of focusing on a level of existence which is the sum of its parts? How does the name that is applied to this collection differ from the name that is applied at higher levels of existence? Recalling the inaccuracy of interpretations of existence that are based on the spatial contiguity of parts, the same kind of assumptions regarding reality in the individual are made as for the species (e.g., organization of parts).

This explanation is based on both the logical similarity and the available empirical evidence. Although the child did not exist prior to conception, its parts perform to its ends according to some pre-existing plan. A parallel statement for the species/individual relationship can be made. The species "emerges" as a unique individual is born. Just as the foot or hand has no existential priority, neither has the individual person.

In order to narrow the scope of this discussion and because the ultimate focus of this text is on humankind, we have chosen to study only the selected level of the systemic relationship between protoplasmic organisms and their species. We will attempt to trace the hierarchy of increasing capacity for seeking and utilizing more adaptive techniques. However, the following discussion does not represent a chronology of development but rather a logical analysis of any contemporaneous state of affairs. To assume that all of this happened precisely as evolutionists suggest would be to lose the special flavor of species control over individuals that we wish to emphasize.

The Plan and the Pattern

Consider first the nature of the phenotype—the physical manifestation of the species idea. The gene pool, carrier of the plan, delivers into the universe through its phenotypal agents (parents) a pattern for a life form. This pattern is impressed on environmental material which limits the extent and the manner in which it is expressed. Both the pattern and the contingent environment are limiting factors. The resultant of this interaction is the phenotype.

The phenotype is an entity whose potential is circumscribed on either side prior to its issuance. Born as an instance of the gene pool it represents and comprised of the environment that it must overcome, in its simplest form, it is almost totally dependent. However, even at this level there are built-in techniques for challenging oblivion. Given the proper chemical and physical conditions it will reproduce. Being without the capacity to react differentially to varied forms of stimulation it will act in accordance with the genetic plan. At this stage the control of such action is totally determined by genotypic structure as it interacts with the environment and is expressed in the form of an urge or drive.

The matter which fills out the phenotype is not homogeneous. What the genetic plan calls for is some organization of matter that can fulfill a function. To some extent this is accomplished by the genetically determined transmutation of substances (e.g., the creation of chlorophyll from local material). However, there remains considerable individuality in the substances employed and the contributions of microlevel parts. The concepts of freedom and determinism are related to this phenomenon. Specifically, although the gene is responsible for some fixed macrolevel characteristic, it does not account for the variability in the parts. Here there seems to be a statistical or random characteristic.

The genotype represents the potential of an individual that resides in the genes. It is "the totality of genetic factors [not the genes!] that make up the genetic constitution of an individual."[44] It will be useful, though not thoroughly accurate, to consider the genotype as the constant, timeless representative of a species or gene pool. The phenotype represents life biologically expressed, changing in response to the environment and having a shorter temporal existence than more complex existents.

The simplest cells, and plants of most varieties, represent life forms in which all or almost all reactive modes are built into the individual as invariant (i.e., as fully genotypically determined). Little or no learning is possible and the same stimulus constellation produces essentially the same reaction within structural limitations and, in some cases, in the internal balance or state of the organism. In higher animals such activities are referred to as *reflexive* or *taxic*. The individual at this primitive level seems to be doing little more than transporting existence from one point in time to another, with some general class of existence superseding its own. The species or gene pool has a more extended existence with living and dying organisms representing its instances, just as the parts of the organism itself continuously generate and decay.

Although biologists do not take the position that wholes control the parts of which they are comprised, it is this aspect of the relationship on which we will focus attention. That biological forms exist by virtue of their interacting parts is easily understood. More subtle is the systemic relationship between living organisms and some whole, especially when the individuals (instances) appear to function as independent totalities.

In plant life this dependence of the individual can be demonstrated. Most plants are unable to locomote and none are believed to possess an emotional component. To consider them to be individuals seems somehow unfitting. They appear to be no more than specimens of some more complex existence. In a highly developed plant, such as a daisy, there is a capacity to react to photoelectric stimulation; to take nourishment from soil, water, and air; and to reproduce. What the daisy does not demonstrate is the capacity to learn or to care. It is incapable of evaluating various potential responses or of modifying its activity accordingly. Nonetheless, although daisies die, daisyhood persists. Although the individual is relatively non-aggressive, without defense, and limited in its ability to communicate, the essence of the species survives and, under optimal conditions, prospers.

Genetic instructions include signals that result in metabolic and procreative activity. In many cases, especially at the level of affective life, there is also a signal which, under certain conditions, forces or recommends inhibiting and even self-destructive actions. The incontrovertible evidence of self-denying actions would appear to obviate any interpretation of life that views the individual as ultimate. Such sacrificial action is observed at every level of organic existence (although exceptions are found at each level as well).

The process is charted in Figure 3.1. The environment referred to includes the inorganic world, individuals of the same as well as different types, and the interaction among all such factors. Improved capacity as an expression of evolutionary action remains conjectural. It is included here only as highly probable.

Epigenetic space refers to that place and time in which the pattern is being impressed on local material. During this phase many of the phenotypal possibilities fail to materialize. Those that do succeed will at some later time carry the message to a rendezvous which may result in the birth of another generation of that species, and in some instances to the birth of new species.

In the case of simple organisms, the reproductive method and the relatively small

Figure 3.1

Genotype/Environment Interaction

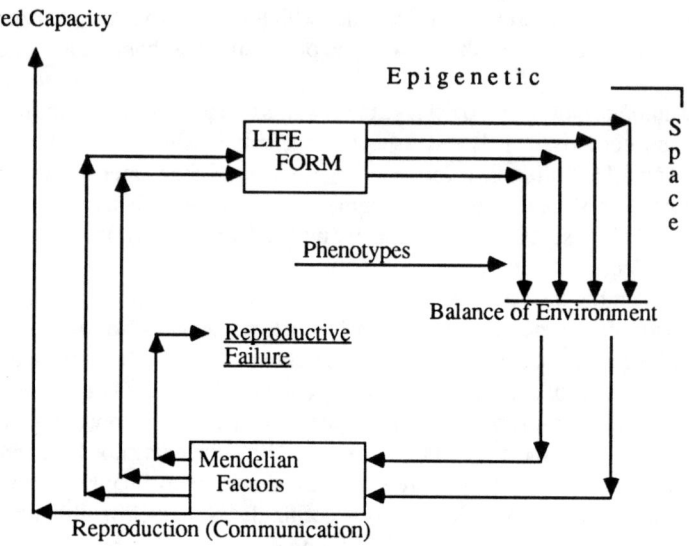

number of genetic combinations limit the potentiality for effective mutation. At this level, with the capacity for reaction limited to very few types of stimulation, little can happen. For example, the ability of a plant to respond to a greater range of photoelectric stimulation would have relatively little additional survival value. As a result, such mutations—though potentially advantageous—tend to regress. With animal life complexity becomes greater and meaningful variance can be anticipated. But even here advantageous variation is believed to occur only rarely.

Protozoa, the simplest form of animal life, have apparently existed from almost the dawn of life, with little if any, modification. One may be tempted to credit the amoeba with some "decision-making" capacity as it flows along a surface and seems to select a meal from among the flagellate prey which surround it. However, the protozoan reacts to stimulation with a relatively rigid response. It is this commonality that has been referred to as being determined in the genotype. There has been recent speculation that such responses are less fixed than was once claimed, but concern here is only with the relative lack of opportunity for choice-making in the individual. Many characteristics can be identified that are clearly inherited. The capacity for reproduction, for example, is obviously not a "skill" that the individual learns.

In more complex life forms it is often difficult to discriminate between activities that are based on exclusively genetic decisions and those that are influenced by phenotypic experience. Psychologists are in wide disagreement regarding which aspects of human behavior are based on learning, often confusing factors that are innate (e.g., capacity to feel pain) with those that are experientially derived (i.e., knowledge of that-which-causes-pain).

At the peak of the evolutionary cycle there would be no challenge to the claim that the body parts of each individual represent the energy and material basis for the perpetuation and welfare of that individual. But are they designed to serve the interest of any existence beyond? Can it be argued that the action of the extra-nuclear portion of the body may function to serve a more general existence? And may that more general being transcend the family gene line that sociobiologists suggest? It is the premise of this text that the species or protected gene pool represents that transcendent existence as it relates to many types of organism. In fact, such generalization of responsibility transcends species lines in the case of human and certain other life forms. What follows represents a possible explanation for the commonly observed occurrence of activity carried out in the interest of others.

The Phenotype as Agent

It is necessary, first, to consider the structural and functional elements that must be represented in an entity activated by a system of signals or "triggers." In the case of living tissue such elements are constructed and monitored by genetic command. (For the purposes of this section only determinants of function and not those of such characteristics as shape, size, and color, are considered.)

While the procedure involved in the positing of such information through the action of the DNA/RNA chain is accepted by geneticists, the critical focus of the action of such cells, cell groups, organs, or individuals that respond to such commands has yet to be thoroughly analyzed. And it is this essential prerequisite of any functional entity that must be taken into account. (The principle applies not only to the special case of biological substance but to any entity, organic or not, that performs a function.)

Entities that perform in ways that serve the survival and procreation potential of total individuals, and thus the gene pools to which they are related as instances, may be described as *agents*. At all levels of life, parts as well as instances often perform in such a way as to enhance higher integrative structures, and may appropriately be considered to perform agential functions. In this sense they act no differently than do inanimate objects that serve some end beyond that which profits the performing entity. This subordinate aspect of any entity is a characteristic of its partness or of its role as an instance. In its whole aspect the organic existent is *always* a recipient, *never* a provider of such services. That is, the whole never functions to serve *its* parts or instances, except to its own ultimate profit.

In order to carry out their role agents must possess specific response repertoires. There must be some prescribed type of activity which they are capable of performing when activated. Thus, a radio has a repertoire that includes the dissemination of sound, but not of sight, nor is any locomotion involved. In the biologic domain the heart pumps blood but is not competent to provide oxygen nor purification, while blood corpuscles have a variety of specific responses available and each performs only within a fixed category.

Second, an agent must have the equipment—physical, chemical, or even psychological—to perform its function. The toy vehicle, designed to traverse the floor, must possess wheels or tracks. If it is to climb a wall some suction device must be incorporated. The biological organ must have muscle tissue if it is to contract and expand, bronchi if it is to accommodate air transfer, and other equipment for each specialized function.[45]

Third, an agent must be sensitive to a particular signal or trigger mechanism. Remote radio signals are sometimes employed to activate television sets and other appliances. Such signals may themselves be auditory, where sound waves trip an activator; thermal, as in heat sensitive units; or perhaps tactual, where an operators touch initiates a desired response.

In biological entities genetically based instructions are believed to provide the triggers that activate, and often sustain, the functions of the various cells, cell groups, and organs. But who or what is to be the recipient or beneficiary of such processes? Here may be discovered the factor that has caused so much controversy about the relationship between individuals and their kin groups, their subspecies and other extra-individual entities.

The crux of the problem lies in the failure to attend to the evidence regarding what or who profits from the action of various body parts. Clearly, each element, cell group or organ serves some structure (or function) immediately above it in the holonic chain. The pancreatic exudation stimulated by the passage of food through the intestine emulsifies fats and converts starch to sugar. The total individual only profits indirectly. Most importantly, the function of most parts or instances is not geared exclusively to some predetermined whole. Rather, responses are made to wholes of a recognizable *type*.

Once again, the principle involved can be observed by considering the function of mechanical devices. The remote television control does not open a garage door, nor does the door opener trigger the television set. Each is coded to activate or influence a specific type of entity. Thus, although the television operator will not open a garage door, it will operate any television set similarly coded. In sum, the focus of action of any holonic part may range from serving only one specific whole, to the providing of a useful function to a broad range of similarly constructed wholes.

Consider the biological parallel. From grafted roses, through blood transfusions, to organ transplant—the evidence is clear. Parts or instances are coded to perform not only for that entity to which they originally belong but often to the same part of any entity with recognizably similar characteristics. Knowledge in the part must be such that it can respond to information generated by a range of comparable entities. This characteristic, furthermore, requires no assumption that the generality of response is deliberately established.

Blood typing in humans is, of course, an example of a coding difference, and the rejection of organs indicates that a biological "fit" can not always be assured. However, efforts to employ mechanical and even animal hearts to prolong the life of the desperately ill demonstrates an awareness of the principle. The agential function of many parts is such that they may be employed to serve the needs of any sufficiently similar individual.

There remains one issue—one critical requirement. The part or instance, beyond possessing the required repertoire, having the equipment essential to carrying out its function and being sensitive to the triggering mechanism, must be capable of recognizing the entity that it is to serve. The activating signal does not, in all cases, identify the target.

The worker bee may be aroused by a signal that emanates from a condition peculiar to the queen of the hive. Here the signal includes the object of the action. Only the queen's interests will be served. Such a plan allows for many stereotyped—–though sometimes functionally useless—actions. The turtle whose eggs have been removed from the nest will continue to cover the empty nest with sand. In this case, the response is independent of the presence of the appropriate target. The knowledge of what action to take is genetically fixed. It is not based on what the animal observes, and the action is peculiar to that situation.

However, in many instances the target is imprecisely specified. Much of the action of blood cell types is of a generalized nature. The oxidation process is not directed toward use by any particular organ; that occurs only when an appropriate recipient is discerned. It has, in fact, become commonplace for geneticists to say that suitable developmental activity occurs only when a gene "recognizes" a particular state of affairs.

In a simple organism such as a plant, when a new stem is grafted onto a root system the passage of liquid up the stem occurs when the pertinent cells identify the target. Phagocytes digest bacteria when they recognize, or become aware of, the presence of *any* collection of such entities. This awareness or recognition cannot be equated with, but runs parallel to, that experienced in the conscious state. It refers to the capacity of an entity to respond to information that identifies another; an individual or group to be served.

At higher levels of life individuals of many species respond to environmental and/or internal cues by performing instinctive behaviors,[46] including in some instances activities which are destructive to the agent. Such performances have in many cases perplexed neo-Darwinian biologists. Cairnes-Smith and many other sociobiologists have proposed that genetic commonality (shared genes) explains the paradox. Unfortunately, such presumptions have led to serious misinterpretation.

Following such reasoning, in fact, the mystery of extra-individual control would be greater. How does the individual selectively recognize its counterpart in another? How is the distinction from perceptually similar others made? It is far more likely that the signal for action is triggered by some observed phenomenon which identifies the target, and in this case the target would have to possess some similarity of class or type (e.g., that which characterizes a queen bee).

Grene proposed that the endurance of a gene pool be understood as "the survival of a type, a mode of living, an order of orders.... That is the only judgment that can fill in the tautology of survival-for-survival-for-survival."[47] But that judgment would reify the extra-individual, as is proposed here, and such notions are not consistent with most current biological thinking. Thom, for example, argued for a "purely local determinism," based in part on the fact that "every point in an embryo is at a small distance from a cellular nucleus, which contains, in vertical form at least, all the necessary information for the local realization of the plan of the individual."[48] He surely would not like to have to deal with "types" or "orders of orders." Grene did allow that "a clock needs its clockwork," but she argued that nothing about "time" can be discerned from the workings of physics or chemistry.[49] Nor can the identification of the focus of an action!

We pointed out that the target of the activity of cells and cell groups is on the immediately higher holonic entity. Indirectly, however, still higher levels are served. This proceeds from specialized organs to total "bodies" that support germ cells, more indirectly to the gene pool, and at the highest level extra-species life forms. This house-that-Jack-built sequence is a holarchic phenomenon which must be appreciated, particularly as it describes the relationship between a specific "body" and other individuals.

Dawkins offered a colorful but misleading description, making the case that genes survive many generations of individuals:

> They swarm in huge colonies safe inside gigantic lumbering robots, sealed off from the outside world, communicating with it by tortuous indirect routes, manipulating it by remote control. They are in you and in me; they created us, body and mind; and their preservation is the ultimate rationale for our experience. They have come a long way, those replicators. Now they go by the name of genes, and we are their survival machines.[50]

Here is an example of the confusion between the genotype or pattern and the gene itself—the phenotypal expression of that plan. Wilson, erring in similar fashion, added:

> The hypothalamic-limbic complex of a highly social species, such as man, "knows" or more precisely it has been programmed to perform as if it knows, that its underlying genes will be proliferated maximally only if it orchestrates behavioral responses that bring into play an efficient mixture of personal

survival...in blends designed not to promote the happiness and survival of the individual, but to favor the maximum transmission of the controlling genes.[51]

Such statements exemplify several of the common sociobiologist problems. First, of course, is the hint of value judgments and decision making in the qualifying clause "only if." Equally serious is the practice of confusing entities with ideas, a problem that has crept into biological thinking throughout the post Darwinian era. What Dawkins described as "in you and me" is *not* what survives. What survives is the plan or model. And this requires a review of the problem of existence—of particulars and universals.

If a child wishes to draw a red wagon he may choose a red crayon. If it were to be lost he may purchase another. Redness would reside in each. As the child grew, he may, over time, own many red crayons. The persistent element would *not* be the crayon (gene equivalent) but the color (gene *pool* equivalent). The gene pool is not a collection of genes but a reservoir of genetic characteristics.

Imagine a vat containing a great quantity of cubes of varying colors. From it a sample is ladled. It may be mixed with a second, similar, ladle—with a sample of that mix again extracted. If this were done continuously, a variety of color mixes would continually arise, though the cubes were different. The gene pool represents the color that persists through mixing, *not* the cubes that transport it.

At issue here may be the question: If there were no genes, would there be a gene pool? (Were there no objects, would there be redness?) The obvious answer, alluded to earlier is *no*! Which may seem to relegate gene pools to secondary status. However, just as objects must have attributes in order to *exist*, so must genes (as phenotypes). But does this not mean that they are created by the interaction of perception with substance as was proposed in Chapter 2?

While the answer to this question is *yes*, a closer inspection of the nature of existence will reveal that it is dependent on a substantive underpinning that cannot be described. To contend that gene pools without genes, or for that matter genes without gene pools, could not exist is not to deny the legitimacy of the *being* of either. This is not a semantic issue. It is, rather, the recognition of both the limitation of the existential world to its being perceived, and the temerity of the contention that nothing can *be* unless it is perceived.

In essence, the emergence of the first gene carried with it certain characteristics which were mirrored in its progeny. Unlike a parameter such as color, this characteristic included a capacity to control the nature of future genes, though not the phenotypes they fostered since the accidental environment also plays a part. (This is no more mysterious than a characteristic such as magnetism in that items possessing that feature will attract entities of a particular type.)

Furthermore, in spite of the fact that those genes that are located in the germ cells may pass intact into new bodies (at least for a period of time), their somatic sisters die along with the rest of the "mortal body." Although in many parts of the body there is an ongoing reproductive process that provides for the replacement of destroyed cells, not only do somatic genes die with individual cells, but the span of their life––even collectively—is only that of the individual whose body they pervade.

Such an arrangement is not particularly difficult to understand. During the development of the zygote, germ cells are not specialized to perform metabolic or irritability functions. Rather they are differentiated only with respect to reproductive capacity; and when reproduction occurs, they pass on into the body of a new individual. By contrast, somatic cells are differentiated for various specialized functions, become directly involved in the activity of the body, and ultimately they and/or their progeny, die along with their host.

As the forms that individuals take become more sophisticated, and as capacities are relevant to survival, the ability to "recognize" environmental cues that identify relevant entities becomes more acute. With the emergence of such phenomena as visual and auditory perception and consciousness, objects at a distance can be discerned in ways that both profit the individual (where, for example, food, sexual mates, and dangerous situations are identifiable) and indirectly profit the gene pool (where the target of behavior is generalized to individuals external to the perceiving agent). The gene pool, of course, also profits whenever the individual functions successfully.

This is the most subtle aspect of the behavioral process. It involves the interaction of cognitive processing of perceptual material and the affect aroused by the products of such processing. It is peculiar in its expression to various types and developmental levels of life in terms of the nature of the capacity to recognize particular characteristics in others. Organs (parts) and instances, such as blood cells, are only aware of the target of their actions through kinaesthetic and other senses that require physical interaction. This is also true of many animal phenotypes. But the fact that one organism is aware of the presence of another does not entail any empathic relationship.

Most fish and many other forms of animal life show little or no interest in caring for their young, for the welfare of others, or any such "altruistic" action. However, they do recognize food, mates, and danger. Fish are attuned to situations which optimize continued personal existence. In a great variety of living creatures, from the praying mantis to the alligator, not only is there evidence that the biological self is often the exclusive concern of the individual, but the destruction of same species individuals—even the "murder" of a sex partner, and the eating of offspring—is commonly observed.

Such conspecific aggression occurs because the failure to develop recognition skills has not been an evolutionary problem. Insects that lay thousands, and oysters that lay millions, of eggs survive as species without need for the advantage brought by protecting others of the same type. The killing of the male by a female mantis may be based on a mutational error, but such behavior, at least in part, results, from the fact that the male's survival is not advantageous to the endurance of germ plasm, or the extinction of the species could be anticipated. However, in many forms of life, the protection of others has proved advantageous. Bee and ant colonies have already been mentioned. But even more essential, as in the case of most mammals, has been an ability to recognize others—particularly in that form of life where offspring are helpless.

Here is evidence of profit to the germ cells of those individuals that do extend their concern to the welfare of others. Further, the term "itself" must itself be properly understood. It represents both the ability to recognize the target of a solicitous action, an affective state which invests it with positive potential and the capacity to relate such action to all other possible behaviors. The affectively endowed individual, unlike instinctively programmed organisms, must put the welfare of others in perspective as its personal survival is taken into consideration. The critical point is that serving the interest of others represents no essential difference from serving the physical self. Each form of activity is based on a response to the genetically inscribed signal system as it relates to various species of life. The anxiety created by the awareness of self will be detailed in Chapter 10.

This interpretation of all forms of activity, as performed by agents, makes so-called "self"-directed functions no more than a special case of all activity. The self being served is *not* ultimately the biological entity—the total phenotype—but its germ plasm. All such activity abets the continued existence of "another." Thus Waddington's claim that "we perceive only what is good for us to perceive"[52] and "we know what it is good for us to know, and it is good for us to know what we know"[52] is highly misleading. By "know" he apparently meant "perceive" but clearly much of what is perceived serves not the perceiver but some transcendent entity. His "we" seems to refer to us as cytoplasmic, transient beings, and this is quite inaccurate.

J. Maynard Smith suggested that "an organism...is composed of organs...which ensure the survival and/or reproduction of their possessor."[53] And, "it should be possible to demonstrate 'teleological' effects whereby a succession of mutations occur which are individually non-adaptive; but which, together adapt the organisms to a new environment."[54] This is a much more accurate position in that it points up the role of the organ as agent; here, the total individual is recognized as an agent of the gene pool.

There is no rationale for accepting the notion that individuals "naturally" recognize what is good for themselves but do not similarly recognize the positive nature of behaviors carried out in the interest of others. The individual as an agent is programmed to serve a type rather than an individual, although in those forms of life where recognition is limited or lacking, only the biological entity itself is served by its behavior.

The focus of bodily activity is often assumed to be the brain. But the brain and the perceptual organs are merely agents of the germ plasm, as are all other bodily organs. They are only intermediate steps—functionaries—with their focus on the germ plasm and, in the case of human and many lower forms of life, on the needs of other individuals recognized as similar. The preservation of the central nervous system itself is pertinent only as it exists to serve the gene pool.

The code to which the perceptual system is geared includes those who are perceived to be the same. The signal that ostensibly says to care for *this* individual in fact says care for individuals *like* this. The response focus generalizes to similar types, though such things as pain sensors tend toward a more immediate focus. This is no more than an inevitable characteristic of the human biologic system. Much behavior is performed to serve classes rather than individuals.

This interpretation offers both an explanation for the source of altruistic or moral action, and reduces it to contingencies of the perceptual process. Self-sacrifice in the service of others is based on an interpretation of others as entities-to-be-served. The significant factor is that such affective reactions (altruistic feelings) are not, as the sociobiologist contends, ultimately in the interest of the biological self, or even of the kin line. It is essential that an emotional health program be based on a recognition of the distinction.

The behavior that is observed, in many instances, seems to focus on the individual to the exclusion of others, even where a moral sense is assumed to exist. Such activity is a contingency of holarchic existence. Although the ultimate goal is the preservation of higher levels of life, parts and instances are "free" to make choices that may profit the immediate self at cost to others. This is a form of perversion that the advantage of freedom of action must accept as an unavoidable spin-off. It is a violation of the general "directedness" of action by sentient holons.

To consider self-centeredness perverse may seem peculiar if the ultimate goal is reproductive advantage to the individual. However, perversion itself must be defined as interpreted by those who make use of the term. Individuals avoid acting "selfishly" because of an affective reaction that informs of the value of others. That information grows out of the capacity of the individual to recognize the object of abetting action as being more than the perceiving individual. It is based on the nature of the code built into brain cells of various kinds.

For those forms of life for which there is no profit in extending care beyond the self, the final recipient of agential function—excepting reproductive activity—is the performing individual. This is not to suggest that individual "parts" (e.g., body organs) could not serve others, but only that the total individual cannot perceive of similar organs as having equivalence. The characteristics of the cognitive/affective system are such that recognition does not occur.

As to those types of life that do profit from such recognition (e.g., animals whose young are born relatively helpless, as well as insects where whole individuals are specialized), the goal of activity transcends the physical self. In some animals that may include only the newborn by a parent, but in many forms of life such recognition extends to other members of a "family" or "tribe." Among humans, the capacity to relate to others extends well beyond species limits, to include not only other animal life forms, but even that of plants—a sense of life's "preciousness" becomes universal. Speculative as this interpretation may be, it is not based solely on an attempt to provide a reasonable alternative but, as we will show, on a considerable amount of evidence to be found in the behavior of human and other forms of life.

Summary

Life began as a self-maintaining organic entity which passed on to its progeny, not only the capacity for self preservation, but a proclivity for functioning in the interest of the preservation of the class of entities that it represented. To appreciate the role that each individual plays in the life process the concept of *agency* was introduced. Phenotypes at every level of living existence, serve the needs of higher echelons. They do so on the basis of instinctive and/or learned perceptual acuity. This dual responsibility—serving biological self and others—has led to the potential for emotional conflict.

The holarchic interpretation of life provides the basis for an understanding of the struggle between assertive, protective, and transcendent desires. Decisions must be made that pit one against another. Positive adjustment requires that these opposing demands be reconciled. The purpose of this text is to introduce programmatic possibilities for reducing the conflict and for improving the general level of emotional health.

Chapter Notes

1. Zukav (1979), p. 47
2. Waddington (1968a)
3. Smith, J. M. (1969)
4. Pattee (1968), p. 78
5. One of the problems with the Darwinian interpretation is the difficulty of accounting for sufficient species enhancing chance occurrences (mutations, etc.) to avoid regression. The usual technique is to couch assumptions in magnaterms—the immense time across which evolution unfolded, and the compelling evidence that it has occurred.
6. Weisz (1967), p. 17
7. *Ibid.*, p. 71
8. Bohm (1969a), p. 41
9. Waddington (1968b), p. 104
10. Oparin (1953), p. vii
11. Schrodinger cited in Augros & Stanciu (1986), p. 33
12. Mayr (1968), p. 53
13. Waddington (1968b) introduced the term *homeorhesis* to describe this phenomenon. "The thing that is being held constant is not a single parameter but is a time-extended course of change, that is to say, a trajectory...i.e., stabilized flow rather than stabilized state" (p. 12). Evolutionary development seems to follow such a "stabilized flow."
14. Waddington (1968a), p. 29
15. Dawkins (1976), p. 126
16. Chardin (1965), p. 88
17. Dawkins (1976)
18. Mayr (1978), p. 47
19. Ruse (1985), p. 321. Many philosophers of science see the acceptance of emergence of any kind as a potential stifling of scientific inquiry. They propose instead, that life and mind be considered emergent, only in the sense that "no explanation in terms of micro-structure theories is available at present for large classes of phenomena studied in biology and psychology." Hempel & Oppenheim, cited in Feigl & Brodbeck (1953) pp. 336-337.
20. Koestler (1981), pp. 102-103
21. While many inorganic substances appear to display some of these characteristics (and "clever" researchers delight in pointing them out), only the living exhibit all of them.
22. Koestler (1978), p. 34
23. Handler (1970), p. 187
24. *Ibid.*, p. 186
25. Wald (1979), p. 53
26. *Ibid.*, p. 52
27. Oparin (1953); Oparin proposed that coazervate droplets (the concentrate of organic substance) represented the first entities with a "degree of individuality". It was in this sense that he assumed such primary organisms were alive. The antiquity of his interpretation (1938) does not detract from its significance.
28. Dawkins (1976), p. 12. Dawkins has suggested that these small

molecular units or "building blocks" would arrange themselves in a sequence that faithfully copied the replicator, ultimately forming as stable a chain as did the original.
29. Pauling & Pauling (1975). The Paulings pointed out that the virus has neither eggs nor seeds, cannot replicate itself outside the living cell, and can do no more, in fact, than catalyze a chemical reaction which results in synthesizing molecules with clone-like characteristics. They believed that the virus is hardly worth consideration as a form of life.
30. The problem of mutations, particularly as representing a source of *random* change will not be dealt with here. However, it has been challenged as operative by a variety of individuals. Harvard biologists have shown that certain bacteria create new genes within their bodies that assist in the process of adapting to new environments. The significance of such findings lies not in their Lamarckian hints, but that at every level living creatures seem to *try* to survive and grow (Cairns, Overbaugh & Miller, 1988, September 5).
31. Thomas (1974)
32. Simon (1971), p. 163
33. Lake in Weiss, R. (1988), p. 38
34. Cairns-Smith (1985), p. 96
35. Stebbins and Ayala (1985), p. 82
36. Weinberg (1985), p. 48
37. Van Valen in Lewontin (1978), p. 230
38. May (1978), p. 160
39. Beck (1961), p. 272
40. *Ibid.*, p. 273
41. Although Beck did refer to the species retaining advantages of specialization, his thesis would provide for profit as no more than a spin-off. He used the term as a collective noun, as particularists assert.
42. The reference here is not necessarily to the first entity that may appropriately be referred to as "alive," but to the first entity so organized as to have the capacity for metabolism, reproduction etc., and thus to be considered as possessing a primitive "self." It is highly probable that many such entities appeared at approximately the same time—certainly during the same era. The discussion here, focuses on one such entity in the interest of describing the process as simply as possibly. The critical factor is that the notion of the parts serving a genetically organized totality is consistent with every biological treatise.
43. Fuller (1975), p. 4
44. Mayr (1970), p. 417
45. The repertoire may not be functional in the case of weak or diseased muscles, or similar debilitating condition.
46. Instinctive behavior, or activity carried out on the basis of an information chain which includes both stimulus and response patterns, independently of learning, is detailed in Chapter 12.

47. Grene (1969), p. 67
48. Thom (1968), p. 41
49. Grene (1969), p. 68
50. Dawkins (1976), p. 21
51. Wilson, E. O. (1975), p. 4
52. Waddington (1969), p. 3
53. Smith, J. M. (1969), p. 82
54. *Ibid.*, p. 85

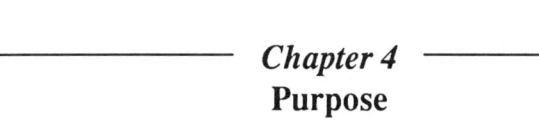
Chapter 4
Purpose

Purpose, which is unique to the living, describes the subservient role of parts and instances as they act in the interest of transcendental existents. It was born into the universe at the moment that one (organic) entity used another (organic or not) to its own ends. Evidence for the existence of this emergent force is observed in every form of organic existence. No presumption of divine intervention is necessary—the relationship represents only an inherent characteristic of living systems.

In spite of the evidence in human and animal behavior, biologists and other scientists have provided alternative explanations for behavior that purport to eliminate the need to accept final causes. Their formulae are, however, incompetent to purge this ineluctable force of its influence on human behavior.

Purpose, as a guiding factor, creates increasing pressure on living beings, as the intellect becomes more powerful, and the potential for decision making arises. Emotional health is significantly influenced by the conflicting signals generated by the many elements of this incredibly complex system.

Among the many concepts that raise the hackles of positivist oriented scientists, none exceeds the scorn that is heaped on the notion of *purpose*. The very suggestion of purpose is viewed in many circles as specious; unnecessary to an understanding of behavior or any other form of activity. In a determined effort to reduce behavior to a scientifically respectable concept, the teleological interpretation has been dropped as superfluous by the physicist, the biologist, and many psychologists.

Schlick proposed that the term purpose "should really be banished from biology right from the start."[1] He then, in the tradition of Nagel and his fellow logicians, defined purpose as "no doubt...a concept derived from human action [that is] nothing but the anticipated outcome of our action."[1] Elliot echoed this sentiment contending that among those who are not highly cultivated there is a "passionate conviction" that the universe is working out some plan associated with the welfare of humankind.[2] Having carefully constructed such straw men, philosophers neatly destroy each argument based on the definitions *they* have proposed. The same science that suffers from an addiction to evolutionism, which in its narrow focus fails to account for life's "other-directedness," spawns these miracles of self-evident literature that purport to eradicate ineluctable concepts.

The notion of purpose is, however, not simply a product of the imaginations of prehistoric speculators who proposed that God created the universe in the service of human interest. (Even Aristotle's final cause claimed only to describe the natural development, and the possible end state of material entities.) Rather, the concept of purpose grew out of the regular observation of action that failed to serve its initiator in both conscious and unconscious arenas. And here the term describes a demonstrably legitimate occurrence.

Those "seekers after truth" who mock the medieval clergyman who proposed that the grooves in a melon were so placed by God to provide for the appropriate division of the parts among family members, fasten on such bizarre claims; convictions that grew out of simple attempts to explain wondrous occurrences. To generalize from such anomalies to all discussion of purposeful action is, however, contentious.

The convictions that color the thinking of the vast majority in all of the so-called "hard" sciences are intense. It is inconceivable, they state, that the behavior of any entity can be caused by some future goal. This would be tantamount to saying that some mysterious force "pulled" the individual along a fixed path or one of a limited number of fixed paths. They argue that even if there were such an agent, it would perform through techniques that operate contemporaneously, in which form it would be subject to scientific inquiry.

It is both amusing and instructive to note the care with which molecular biologists affirm their allegiance to evolutionary theory by stating most vigorously that they reject purpose as heresy, although their writings include extensive reference to such a concept. Waddington argued that "in itself [natural selection] is of course no more purposive than is the process of formation of inter-atomic chemical bonds."[3] However, in establishing a series of meetings to discuss theoretical biology, he stated that the sponsoring group "has felt that it is its *duty* [italics added]" to explore possibilities for formulating concepts around which the discipline may grow.[4] Excepting that by duty he meant legal responsibility, how did he avoid the sense of purpose that the word duty implies?

Koestler, in commenting on the uncertainty principle in physics, made an impressive point:

> An example of the *hubris* of contemporary science is the rigorous banishment of the word "purpose" from its vocabulary.... Yet, if causality has broken down and events are not rigidly governed by the pushes and pressures of the past, may they not be influenced in some manner by the "pull" of the future?... It betrays a great lack of imagination to believe that the concept of "purpose" must necessarily be associated with some anthropomorphic deity.[5]

The first problem posed by those who reject purpose is that it places the initiation of such acts in the future. A purposeful act, it is argued, must predict an outcome— —plan an occurrence that it currently appreciates. Although premeditation is commonly observed in the behavior of humans, it is audacious, they claim, to ascribe teleological action to life in general. Dobzhansky risked a compromise:

> Explanations in terms of adaptedness or teleology are not only appropriate but indeed necessary in biology, whereas they are meaningless in the nonliving world, [however, he insisted] adaptedness is neither devised nor planned by any external conscious agent.... Rather, it has evolved and is being maintained and often improved [*sic*] by natural selection.[6]

The question that concerns us here is not whether purpose exists, but what is meant by the term, and whether relationships can be discovered which bear out the meaningfulness of a particular definition. Runes stated, "Purpose [is] an ideally or imaginatively envisaged plan or end of action."[7] Wiener added that it is "the thought in the present, of an end or aim, in the future."[8] Both interpretations place the concept in the mental sphere, since it must be imagined. Although these definitions are too restrictive, they point to the necessity of including some superordinate existence, which is the argument of these chapters.

Kant's caveat must be considered. He denied that anything may exist for the purpose of another, and that the described relationship exists only in the mind. His contention was that mental processes are so organized that the individual must begin with elements in a relationship and synthesize these factors. The result, he maintained, is the appearance that the parts cause the whole. It was his belief that since efficient causes are directional, the whole cannot be construed as the cause of its parts. Rather, the two must stand in a relationship that is determined by one's mental organization.

Although Kant conceded that biological nature does seem to show ostensibly purposive relationships, he warned against accepting the teleological explanation as ultimate. He was opposed to any dogmatic assertion that there is a purpose behind phenomena—but agreed that events occur *as if* there were.[9] Furthermore, he denied that purpose is a *real* attribute of nature, but that it does seem an irresistible hypothesis—a heuristic principle.[10] Can it be that all that is assumed to represent purpose is the result of limitations of the mental process? Perhaps all behavior is no more than an automatic response to environmental stimuli. Surely, many psychologists would applaud such an interpretation.

Many rather subtle efforts have been made to find a niche for action that seems to represent evidence of purpose through the introduction of more prosaic terms. Teleotamy (the end state to which all matter is directed as in the cessation of action when an object hits the ground) and teleonomy (behavior that owes its goal directedness to the operation of a program) are exemplars. In each instance the object is to provide an explanation that avoids intentionality. Such processes must be shown to be essentially mechanical.

The tendency to view purposeful behavior as reducible to mechanical relationships is understandable. Observing causal relationships in nature, the principles were applied to machine building. As machines became more complex, the similarity between the activity of living things and the machines that humans invented was noted. In describing this parallelism, living things were characterized as machine-like. For some strange reason this seemed more appropriate than saying that machines are, in some respects, like living things. This would have been equally descriptive and certainly more accurate. Hatt exemplified the usual expression of this homology:

> When I say that there is a pervasive *imago machinae* for speaking of man, I am referring not only to the affinity between the human brain and the electronic brain, but also to the development of the electronic brain from the mechanical computer, to the relationship between the mechanical computer and the machine model of the entire universe, and to the development of the machine model from the displacement of the teleological by mechanical explanation in the sixteenth century.[11]

The human brain is not seen as the model, nor indeed does it seem that living organisms have characteristics that are imitated by machines. Instead, the discovery that the world was governed by mechanical causes made possible the escape from teleology. Humans behavior is to be understood in terms of their machinelike characteristics!

Machines differ from living things in many ways, and an understanding of these differences is essential. Assuming the definition of machine to include its relationship to a task or goal, the activity involved is always "rational." The function which the machine performs is based on expedience and efficiency in producing what some*one* wants produced, which is similar to the way in which the most primitive organisms appear to function. In living beings, however, reasoning is simply one of many techniques which individuals employ in striving for what they want, and this aspect of human existence (desire) is noncognitive, being interrelated with other informational systems which shall be specified in later chapters.

Biological Interpretations

Biologists are concerned with the many strange ways in which populations appear to preserve themselves. In some instances, modification in living and reproductive styles seems to follow a statistical path with only some unspecified members apt to be affected. The size of a population is a function of available food supplies and other factors. This is, of course, understandable without appealing to a willingness on the part of certain members of the group to die for others, but in many cases the decision to die is not an issue. The question is whether to be born at all!

At the lowest levels, organisms are to a great extent at the mercy of the environment. Extreme differences in the characteristics of populations result from climatic and other changes that are not subject to individual or species control. However, more adaptive animals are not so affected.

> Population is determined by interactions either among its members or with other species of competitors, predators, or parasites. The simplest scheme is a self-regulating population; when the numbers are high the population decreases and when the numbers are low the population increases.[12]

This is certainly a scheme, but it is far from simple. Whose scheme, and to what end? Why do populations rise and fall around some mysterious mean? If the authors merely intended to note the occurrence of such statistical facts, the term *self*-regulating is inappropriate. If the reference is to some ecological balance, although the causes become more difficult to pinpoint, it may still be possible to consider it accidental. However, when the arguments of biologists who have studied the mechanics of population control are considered, it is more difficult to accept the "contingent" explanation as satisfactory.

Christian, for example, related glandular dysfunction to food availability. When there is not enough to eat, glands will not react properly in all cases and there will be fewer offspring.[13] However, although in the first generation the size of the population will be reduced, the improved quality of the offspring should, in a few generations, again cause over-population. Since just those with better glands survive and reproduce, this should ultimately act against the group through over-production, creating more—but weaker—individuals.

Of course, the argument can be made that the accident of food availability is the regulator and evolution (the contingent growth and improvement of *individuals*) could represent an adequate explanation. Another phenomenon has been studied, however, which suggests that, in addition to environmental impact, some more general existent affects the activity of individuals—what biologists alternately call the population, species, system, or organization.

Wynne-Edwards hypothesized that group activities among some insects, such as swarming and dancing, are designed to feed back to the individual the need of the colony to reduce its number.[14] Such an interpretation may be correct, but what is the source of the signal? The individual cannot appreciate the value of reducing the population. In this case the probability of ever *becoming* is influenced by factors which optimize population or species survival. In such cases, evidence of movement toward qualitative superiority is obvious, since though an excess of progeny would not necessarily be fatal to the species, it may result in inferior individuals.

The principle of survival of the fittest suggests that many be produced and the strongest survive. If genetic signals limit the number that are born, how can such activity be accounted for by Darwinian principles? Grobstein referred to the behavior of the biomass which "is capable of adjusting in order to maintain itself,"[15] and "is director of the nonliving and utilizes the nonliving to suit its needs."[16] Directs? Utilizes? Either these terms are merely employed to dramatize his point or he is suggesting control by an existence *beyond the individual.*

These aggregations represent populations of similar individuals. The relationship is with a community comprising those of like kind. In systems of other types similar activity is observed. Within the animal body, threat of invasion calls forth the destruction of leukocytes in the process of preserving the individual. Here is an example of systemic interaction where the members are not at the same existential level. The system which is preserved is not a collection of like individuals but some supra-individual for which the leukocytes serve an agential function. In this case, feedback passes "through" a gene pool and influences individuals several levels lower in the hierarchy.

Ecological balance represents a third variation. It refers to the behavior of mutually dependent organisms where the system which directs is less visible than in the case of the leukocytes. Whole species live and die in response to some prior demand at a more complex level. Grobstein stated that the biomass develops by "capturing and internalizing the environment and by manipulating and rearranging it externally."[16] Symbiotic and parasitic relationships are effective only so long as the ecosystem is preserved.

In each form of life, a systematic, dependable subordination of each level of existence to that of which it is a part obtains. How can the disciples of contingency report that development is directional and controlled by such a mysterious agent as the biomass? How can they avoid the implication of their own writing—that life is unexplainable as residing exclusively in particular biological instances, and that functions at every level can be shown to serve a transcendent existential level?

Many explanations have been offered for the directional nature of activity in living things. One that would seem to call for little stretch of the scientific imagination is based on a unique characteristic of the living mentioned earlier. "New" individuals are not additions to, or replicas of, but are *part* of the parent:

> A gene enters into some set of chemical reactions with materials in its surroundings; the outcome of these reactions is the appearance of two genes in the place of one. In other words, a gene synthesizes a copy of itself from nongenic materials.[17]

And this copy is an extension of the life it manifests rather than simply a duplicate.

Genes, therefore, belong to, are part of, represent, stand for, *are*, in a sense, extensions of the parent genes. Nongenic material is employed in a way that enhances survival and growth. But what is it that the process ultimately serves? Certainly not the contingent corporeal matter! In point of fact, the reverse is more nearly true. By contrast, inert matter does not reproduce itself, catalytically or otherwise, in any way that characterizes the bonding observed in living tissue. No such dynamism as is represented by genes has been discovered. It has no inherent function relative to the enhancement of any whole to which it is related. No *purpose* can be discerned.

It is perhaps difficult to recognize purposeful relationships in primitive forms of life. At the simplest levels of organic existence, actions/reactions of an individual may be described as no more than mechanical responses to environmental opportunity. Changes in a species over time can be shown to be merely the result of selective breeding discriminating in favor of particular types. The organism relates most directly to its surroundings, with its genetic inheritance being an accident of time and place. This interpretation seems sufficient to destroy any requirement for the positing of purpose.

Such reductionist explanations of biological phenomena grow from particularist philosophy. According to the atomistic argument described earlier, the individual is the only reality. Populations are mere statistical occurrences of the many possible combinations of elements. Evolution represents only the fact that higher level organisms evolved because they were capable of metabolizing the bodies of simpler organisms.

But consider some of their statements. Huxley, though denying purpose in the universe, concluded that if humans do not increase knowledge and intensity of feeling, "we cannot hope that we are in the main line of evolutionary progress."[18] No purpose, he contended, but *hope*! While denying that any nonmechanistic force controls living things, he posited "hope" in the particular. But why *hope* for anything unless it has some ultimacy? Would it not be equally sound to hope for the destruction of all human life? Wilson suggested that "to maintain the species indefinitely we are compelled to drive toward total knowledge."[19] Of course, if pressed, he might say that his claim is related merely to the mechanics of the situation and that it really does not matter whether or not it is done....

Mayr, in his definition of purpose, stated that "[only] an individual who...has been 'programmed' can act purposefully."[20] This is a thoroughly mechanistic view which he emphasized by pointing out that "historical processes, however, can *not* act purposefully.... The word *purpose* is singularly inapplicable to evolutionary change."[21] That is, purpose is a useful term only in the limited internal sense of local program. His argument, however, was vitiated when he stated immediately afterward:

> Natural selection *does its best* [italics added] to favour the production of codes guaranteeing behavior that increases fitness...a behavior programme that allows for appropriate learning and the improvement of behavior reactions by various types of feedback gives greater likelihood of survival than a programme that lacks these properties.[22]

But why should survival be of importance, and why should selection favor certain codes? Why should non-purposive behavior move toward greater fitness rather than along any other line of development? And why does Mayr exemplify the view of so many biologists who persistently use purpose laden terms?

Mayr expressed great indignation toward Roman Catholic Church practices based on their convictions regarding the role of sexual intercourse, family size maintenance, and similar canons of behavior.

> Many of the evils of modern society are...the result of overpopulation...[and] the adoption of a healthier way of thinking about the perils of overpopulation is impeded by medieval, and in their effects extremely vicious, church dogmas.[23]

Evils? Perils? Vicious? Why, without purpose? Consider Mayr's description of the role of a species. He suggested that if there were only one interbreeding community of individuals in the world, there would be no mechanism to avoid the development of destructive gene combinations:

> The reproductive isolation of a species is a protective device that guards against the breaking up of its well-integrated, co-adapted gene system. Organizing organic diversity into species creates a system that permits...the accumulation of favorable genes...without the danger of destruction of the basic gene complex.... Organizing into...species, guarantees that these limits are not overstepped.[24]

These sentiments from a man who castigates church dogma. He argues that the organization that guarantees the avoidance of danger to species welfare is an accident of natural selection. But why is it *dangerous* if there is no purpose, plan, or direction? Mayr's "church" may be more scientific, but his principles are equally dogmatic, and his trinity as mysterious.

Philosophic and Scientific Positions

The interpretation of purpose, as describing interactions that transcend the physical entity, is found in the writings of many contemporary philosophers and psychologists. Adler wrote that it is useful "to regard human behavior and understand it as though a final constellation of relationships were produced under the influence of the striving for a definite goal upon the basic inherited potentialities of the organism."[25] Note the emphasis he placed on the phrase "striving for a goal." Further, the "final constellation of relationships" may itself include self-sacrifice when it is species preserving.

Adler was, of course, philosophizing; but Mayr presented a biologist's view. While proposing that preferential selection or adaptation accounts for evolution, Mayr stated that "there is no excuse...for considering adaptation as evidence of purpose."[26] But he then wrote, "a steady selection pressure...can push an evolutionary line closer to an ultimate *goal* without...showing any purposive behavior whatsoever."[26] He suggests ultimate goals without purpose. In this text, we will propose *purpose without ultimate goals.* Chardin stated that "the objective reality of psychical effort and work is so well established that the whole of ethics rests on it,"[27] adding that "objects...are only made manifest by their outward determinisms."[27] The expression "outward determinisms" represents motion toward a goal beyond the individual.

Support for the legitimacy of purpose is also found in the writings of many existentialists in spite of their focus on the individual. Wild, in his attack on the essentialism of Hegel, stated, "This over-simplified ontological prejudice has resulted in the fantastic attempt to understand human action without reference to that factor of purpose which everywhere pervades it."[28]

An attack on this type of obviously teleological interpretation was provided by Nagel in his text *The Structure of Science.*[29] His general conclusion was that "organismic biologists have not established the absolute autonomy of biology or the inherent impossibility of physicochemical explanations of vital phenomena."[30] He did concede that "purposes and deliberate goals admittedly play important roles in human activities." However, he said, "there is no basis whatever for assuming them in the study of...most [sic] biological phenomena."[31] The obvious question is: Why should purpose occur at *any* level of organic existence?

In his challenge to the use of teleological explanations, Nagel suggested that a statement such as "The function of the leucocytes in human blood is to defend the body against foreign micro-organisms" can be restated as, "Unless human blood contains a sufficient number of leucocytes, certain normal activities of the body are impaired." He also argued that any evidence warranting the teleological form would also confirm his proposed alternative, and thus that they "cannot be distinguished with respect to what they *assert.*"[32]

Ignoring the temptation to develop the thesis that "impaired" is a purposive, directional term, consider what this altered form represents. The definition of purpose we will propose is one of a *relationship* between elements of a hierarchy that culminates at some level of organic existence. Nagel's formulation merely focuses at the step-level of the recipient of the action. This is tantamount to restating "The purpose of going to the post office is to purchase stamps" as "Unless one visits the post office, stamps cannot be purchased." Surely a game of hide-the-purpose.

Nagel further contended that it is equally possible to make directionally organized statements about vital and non-vital systems. "The human body, with respect to homeostasis of its internal temperature, is an example from biology; a building equipped with a furnace and a thermostat is an example from physicochemistry."[33] Could it have escaped his attention that thermostats (as was mentioned earlier) are constructed to function in the interest of those people who construct them—to serve a purpose?

Nagel's analysis leaves open to question whether purpose may ultimately be shown to differentiate the living from the inert, although he insisted that it has not yet been accomplished. He believed, however, that the infinite regress of such conundrums as "who made the watchmaker?" destroy finalist arguments, and that the assumption of control at the level of species or life in general is absurd. The most reasonable alternative, he suggested, is that of reductionist philosophy.

Among many of those who deny purpose one finds implicit an ultimate desired state which provides a background against which beliefs are projected. It is this background that is invoked as a necessary condition and thus, in one immediate sense at least, an indication of purpose. Nietzsche, for example, made a plea for a superman, who certainly represented his idea of a desirable goal. Like Kant, he saw direction in the destiny of man which is representative of a final (or purposive) cause although he denied the possibility of recognizing causality.

Sartre provided a more contorted explanation. In his intemperate rush to deny God, morality, and law, he insisted that freedom is the universal norm and that purpose in the moral sense is meaningless.[34] However, his insistence on the individual's obligation to live freely at the risk of being "unauthentic" demonstrates an acceptance of purpose in humans, which, he contended, is to live consistently with the truth of their freedom.

Orthogenesists suggest that purpose exists on the evidence that species development is directional and that this directionality is not alterable by the accident of environmental opportunity. Its proponents point to the limited number of life forms which exist. They would question, for example, why some groups of people do not have twelve fingers or three ears, since many diverse characteristics may have similar survival value.

In studying similar types of animal species from different parts of the world, many homologous characteristics are noted. "Why," asked Koestler, "if evolution were a free-for-all, restrained only by selection for fitness, why did Australia not produce some of the bug-eyed monsters of science fiction?"[35] These interpretations may suggest some ultimate state, which is not the argument presented here. However, they do challenge the contention of those who deny directionality in the development of species.

The attack on the concept of purpose is not confined to those whose principal interest is in the phenomenon of life. It finds support among thinkers who have found an alternate explanation for purpose through the introduction of the concept of *feedback* as a characteristic of open systems. This was alluded to under the discussion of general systems theory. More specifically, cybernetics focuses on the capacity of effective entities to receive and translate information from the environment, which makes possible continual course correction, as was discussed in Chapters 2 and 3. This ability, they contend, is peculiar to certain types of systems—those with built-in sensors or components which are sensitive to specific signals.

Cybernetics deals with the communications process, taking much of its impetus from the development of complex machines. Wiener stated that "the newer study of automata, whether in the metal or in the flesh, is a branch of communication engineering, and its cardinal notions are those of message…quantity of information, coding technique, and so on."[36] His comment reflects a fascination with the idea and technique of sharing information, of language interpretation, and of data storage.

Cyberneticists have modernized teleology by demonstrating that, in principle, a machine can behave as if it has a purpose. It can be programmed to correct its errors and to maintain any path that is predetermined. Since the adaptive behavior in machines is always produced by humans, however, to what extent has purpose been removed? To whose end does a machine function? The aim of cyberneticists is to render human behavior subject to mathematical-physical analysis, and to this end they have achieved considerable success. This does not, however, legitimize their view that purpose does not necessarily involve any external causal agent.

They insist that purpose must be explained in terms of a relationship between entities or occurrences with a "concurrent" focus. Thus, the purpose of an automobile carburetor is to allow for a gasoline-air mixture, but this, they argue, does not require any reference to an ultimate or final goal which influences why or how the carburetor works. Does this reduce the causality involved to the accident of the way in which the carburetor is built, or can it be assumed that it was to meet some external objective?

Cyberneticists agree that some behavior can be called purposeful, but this does not mean it is caused by a future goal. Rather, they refer, for example, "to a final condition in which the behaving object reaches a definite correlation in time or in space with respect to another object or event,"[37] suggesting, therefore, that "some machines…are intrinsically purposeful. A torpedo with a target-seeking mechanism is an example."[37] The problem is that the target-seeking mechanism which will correct the torpedo's travel must be placed there by some individual with a purpose not intrinsic to the torpedo.

There is the further contention by some cyberneticists that a purposive object must exhibit *choice*. Purposive action must be voluntary. It cannot be fixed by anyone or anything external to the behaver. Although this may seem reasonable in the sense that an organism's activity, if not voluntary, seems difficult to relate to purpose in the behaving agent, it suffers from the same fallacy as do other arguments in positing purpose in the particular. The argument ignores the subordinate role of the behaver in its relationship to some superordinate entity. If the individual behaved with no direction (i.e., if the choice had no referent), the activity could only be capricious.

The purpose of the behavior of individuals is, in many instances, to enhance a life form which the individual manifests. This, of course, need be no more than a convenient expression for describing an observed event with the feedback mechanism (genetic code) merely representing the efficient cause. It does not, however, eliminate purpose—which is defined in this text as the behavior of individuals as influenced by the (non-immediate) form of life they represent through genetic inheritance.

In some instances cyberneticists use the term purpose in a way that *is* consistent with individual/species activities. Rosenblueth and Wiener, for example, stated that "purposeful behavior is to be attributed only to an object which forms part of a larger system...[and which is] guided by a goal."[38] This view is, however, difficult to reconcile with that of a voluntary, choice-making individual. In the case of living individuals the "goal" that guides resides in the individual/gene pool relationship, and the choice the individual makes is to some extent mediated by signals emanating from the genotype.

Taylor, like many who have opposed the cybernetic practice of allowing for purpose in machines, has taken the position that purposeful behavior *must* be desired by the behaver. "There must be, on the part of the behaving entity...a desire, whether actually felt or not, for some object, event, or state of affairs as yet future."[39]

This allows for a considerable range of error, both in determining who or what directs such action, and what is meant by desire (i.e., "felt or not"). In living forms, the *genotype* controls the activity of the biologic individual as well as the individual itself; and desire may refer in many instances to that which would be profitable to either the individual, the gene pool, or both. Taylor's insistence on desire in the behaver allows for purpose *only* where a choice of actions is possible, thus eliminating the activity of pre-aware forms of life as subject to purposive explanation. Although in higher organisms desire is an essential element in the behavior sequence, purpose is a factor at all of life's levels.

Evidence in Plant and Animal Behavior

As the phenotype moves through physical/temporal space it pursues a path that has been set at a higher level through genetic predisposition. That path is not designed only to assure the survival of the individual. If survival alone were the case, formal, material, and efficient causes might provide sufficient explanation. Rather, each organism acts and reacts in its dance with the environment, sometimes overcoming interference with its growth needs, at other times sacrificing itself to the survival of the family, group, or species, all on the basis of a signal system which is transported genetically. Built into each individual are means by which to make contact with certain environmental stimuli and a way of knowing when to struggle; when to die.[40]

The action of the flower as it bends and works around an object that stands between itself and the sun may be explainable on the grounds that it responds only to immediate causes, in that organic matter includes a vital driving force because of its survival value. At this non-decision-making level, however, much can be observed to occur which has no survival value for the individual. The practice of producing seeds, in which there is no profit to the plant, is an obvious example. Here, of course, there is clearly profit to the germ cells that are transported by the somatic entity. Beyond this, in many decision-making animals, considerable activity occurs which apparently is taken in spite of the potential for self-immolation, as in the case of the killdeer, the nighthawk, or the prairie warbler, all of whom risk death to protect their young. It is in the fact of the survival of a species, which is a non-palpable existent, that an explanation can be found.

In most forms of life the individual appears to be influenced by inputs which must be interpreted as inherent in the individual/species relationship. Thus, when it is stated that animals act in a particular way because of a species demand (or purpose), the inference is that some "law" can be identified which describes the action involved. Obviously, formal, material, and efficient causes are involved as well, but there can be little doubt that in no instance are these factors creations of the individual that expresses them. The presence of a poison-carrying stinger in some insects is one cause of the wound an enemy receives. But when that weapon is employed in such a fashion that the insect who uses it dies in the process, some assumption of service beyond the welfare of the individual must be made.

In making the statement that individuals act in a certain fashion because of a purposive outcome, a final cause or at least a predetermined direction is presumed. If it is argued that they do so because of a (formal and material) blueprint that resides in the genes, an efficient cause has been substituted which seems to play the same word game decried in others. But neither of these causal elements provides a complete account. Both statements are necessary, but they are not sufficient to a comprehensive explanation of the activity of organisms. The *goal* of activity in living beings must be included if the explanation is to be exhaustive.

Purpose is limited to the organic hierarchy and, when related to behavior, involves both an individual (instance) and some superordinate existent. (This does not, incidentally, preclude behavior which is directed toward individual well-being, since the survival of any holon includes the concept of health in its parts or instances. I *do* want to be healthy, and will accept pain—as through exercise—to become so.)

There is, apparently, some reason for the way in which life manifests itself, and that reason cannot be explained as based on the desire of the biological individual but with some more general conceptualization. Von Nageli suggested that evolution occurs in a series of leaps, explaining that some drive within each species keeps it leaping in the same direction.[41] The inference is that the species provides the drive, while the individuals carry it out. Mendel seemed to overcome the problem of species leaps (with its hint of purpose) by showing that inheritance is not determined by the blending or averaging of genetic components but the chance selection of certain pairs from within many possible combinations, with only a fixed number being possible.

But what is the nature of each genetic contributor? What information does it provide? Finalists have insisted that the explanation can only be found in a grand design by which each characteristic is expressed in terms of its faithfulness as a manifestation of some pre-existing universal. In an attempt to demonstrate this, Driesch showed that although split in half, a sea urchin embryo develops into two complete animals.[42] He concluded from this that the ultimate form of the individual is governed by what the organism is supposed to become rather than because of any efficient cause which may be operating. Causalist biologists refuse to accept his interpretation, arguing that feedback mechanisms inform each half of the embryo that it is but half an embryo, which results in corrective action.

Other researchers have reported similar phenomena. "When the gullet end of a single celled protozoon is cut off with a tiny needle, a complete new one grows back in the course of several hours."[43] Assuming the cell contains a blueprint that covers the entire organism, why is the gullet rather than some other organ regenerated? The question of the source of the feedback must be raised. On instruction from what source are the halved embryo and the injured gullet informed that their developmental courses should be altered? To what end does the development change?

Purpose Defined

When protoplasmic beings are studied, dynamic, hierarchical relationships are observed. What occurs at one level of existence does so on the basis of directions initiated at other levels, and much activity occurs which results in the preferential preservation and growth of the superordinate levels. It is here that the term purpose is applicable. Purpose, as it was born in the universe and as it continues to characterize a basic parameter of existence, refers to:

> *the relationship between living parts and instances, and the superordinate entities that their activities serve, in which the function of individuals meets dynamic survival and growth needs of the existent for which they provide an agential function.*

Thus, we offer a resolution to the problem of teleology—of the assumption that the future may cause the present. Since purpose emerged at the first reproductive moment, and since instructions then provided to the descendents predated all subsequent directives, it may be argued that "final" causes are, in a sense, "first" causes. Perhaps this relationship could be somehow embraced under "formal" cause since the holonic nature of existence demands that reality and meaning are an essential aspect of any being—organic or not. Nevertheless, this often subservient, agential relationship is peculiar to organic life in that some living form, gene pool, phenotype, population or species must always stand at the "end" of any sequence of acts appropriately defined as purposive.

Purpose deals with the contemporaneity of part/whole and instance/whole relationships, whether or not future states are involved. No intentionality, consciousness, or deliberation is required. Formal, efficient, and material causes suffice to explain action only to the extent that subservience of parts to whole is appreciated.

Purpose, as proposed here, is a characteristic peculiar to organic relationships. In one of its parameters, however, it parallels that of all existents—though its special relevance to the living must be taken into account. The common aspect is the time dimension which affects every interaction. It is in the nature of accepted causal factors that their influence is on current or future events. Events are preceded by, or are contemporaneous with, their causes. And, to the extent that future values in organic hierarchies are triggered by space events that qualify as "efficient," they follow the same sequence. The phenotype, however, is invested with features that meet two demands unique to the living.

First, activities are *directional*. Either they serve suprasystems directly (as through reproduction), or mediately through self-care (growth and safety activities). At the plant level, needs of the individual are rarely, if ever, attended to prior to those of the species. However, from simple to more sophisticated animal forms, the individual gradually increases the proportion of activity that serves the immediate biological self first. The second unique feature is that functions are all *potentially* enhancing to the individual and/or the totality. The potential nature of such functions is based on environmental unpredictability as well as, at the most advanced levels of mind, the distorted or perverse application of the individual's potential.

The impact of the future individual or species benefit, for which a purposive act is performed, is only a "potential" based on some previously useful action. In another sense, the "now" of the family, population, or species is much broader than that of the individual. Existential writers have made much of this time spread—the amount of clock time that is appropriately identified as "now." Beyond this, the entire conception of a species or class of life assumes a relatively broad time span, with "yesterday's" experiences modifying "today's" actions only in a figurative sense. In the case of *intentionally* purposive acts, the only modification is that the agent has the capacity for recognizing (experientially or instinctively) situations as they relate to a particular value.

Purpose may be assumed when a contemporary action cannot be explained in terms of profit to the actor (agent) at this time. One who engages in exercise at cost in terms of time and pain, may do so for some noncurrent "purpose." By contrast, an individual may swim, for example, simply because of the enjoyment of the immediate experience. If the skill acquired is such that at some later time a competitive event is entered, the term purpose would not appropriately relate the earlier swimming activity to the competitive performance.

As with meaning, the relational nature of purpose must be kept in focus. *Nothing has purpose in itself.* Neither the recipient nor the donor possesses such a characteristic. The term has the same limited status as the expression "taller" which is meaningless except as a comparator which demands two or more contributors, and which characterizes existence but not substance.

The term purpose often refers to relationships in which the subordinate element may be an inorganic existent. However, the interest served in such relationships is always that of some organic holon. Since this is a directional interpretation, it is in disagreement with Kant's contention that the purpose of the survival of the totality may equally well be considered to provide the individual with its survival needs. In primitive life forms it is clear that the survival of a protected gene pool is never subverted to the needs of any of its parts or instances. Only in the most highly developed forms of life, and especially in humans, does the individual sometimes strive to protect itself at risk to the totality. Such behavior is, however, considered perverse even by writers who reject the concept of purpose. It is perhaps such behavior that prompted Kant's interpretation.

The Immediate Target

The term *species* should be understood to represent a homeorhetic influence with its breadth varying greatly among forms of life. Furthermore, the focus of activity in any form of life may well be directed most immediately to other superordinate entities. The species or gene pool has been selected for discussion because it is most common, particularly in lower animals, to observe instances in which others of the same type are protected.

In describing the tendency to respond to clues external to the individual, an analogy may be useful. Physical objects are known to have a "center of gravity" (sometimes referred to as the center of mass), which roughly means that the weight of an object is concentrated at one point. If an object is cut into separate entities, each has its own center of gravity but each contributes to an "influence point" that may lie outside either of them. If, for example, a block of steel is cut in half and the halves are placed on the opposite sides of a balance, when they are positioned properly they will exert a maximum force over the center (where neither of the entities is physically located). The center of gravity of the duo is outside either item.

In the case of life, the influence point is in the direction of the involved gene pool. Again, a second characteristic is involved. In addition to the genetic "center" of gravity, the living entity possesses a psychological center or *self*, just as each half of the steel bar standing alone had its own internal influence point. At that stage where the elements of the organic being were themselves inorganic, (i.e., the simplest cells) the only psychological center was that of the total of all individuals. However, as division occurred and each instance was itself organic, the influence point or self of the totality represented one pole on a continuum, with the self of the biological part or instance at the other. The holarchy was born.

The "influence point" is apt to be quite broad. Although in very simple forms of life the gene pool may provide a highly specific influence, more complex creatures are attracted to an increasingly blunted apex. Thus, the problem of mixed allegiance as between races, families, and nations; and, the fact that obligation is neither extended to all members of an interbreeding group nor limited only to such members.

But to what existential level is purposeful action appropriately directed? If the traditional evolutionist argument is followed, allegiance would be (after self interest) first to the closest level of classification (e.g., to race or subspecies, rather than to species) on the ground that they are chronologically prior. Although such preferential obligation is widely observed, and is a predictable occurrence, the chronology described is misleading.

Dobzhansky proposed that "species evolve from races by the accumulation of genetic changes."[44] This statement suggests that races come first. But they do not. Rather, races are a refinement of a species that, over time, and with such factors as geographic isolation, come to be reproductively unique, in the sense that members share well-defined biological characteristics, since gene pools are sexually "protected." If races preceded species, they would "grow" from originally different ancestors. African Americans, for example, would be the descendants of separate genetic lines. The similarities between races is so extensive as to belie such an interpretation.[45]

This holonic interpretation of purpose mandates rejection of the assumption that the application of Occam's Razor can eventually reveal all of the essential elements of nature. Parsimony is desirable where extraneous data mask a valid interpretation, but the assumption that analysis is the royal road to understanding is not only presumptuous, it is illogical. In spite of this, efforts to explain existence through the dissecting of elements persists beyond the point at which their organizational form determines their contribution. The principle involved is that an existent is elemental to a relationship when its status as a *whole* determines its contribution. Emergence is once again a factor.

Although this seems obvious enough, students of human behavior have consistently sought explanations for deliberate activity through the analysis of its components. Nagel, in fact, insisted that statements which represent a clinging to the indivisibility of living forms "exhibit an intellectual temper that is as much an obstacle to the advancement of biological inquiry as is the dogmatism of intransigent mechanists."[46] What he failed to recognize was that analyses, while perhaps wholly appropriate to the discovery of *how* organic entities work, is incompetent to provide answers to the question *"Why?"* Such questions require relational, as well as proximate, responses.

The behaviorist contention that activity is fully fixed by reinforcement contingencies is recognized as a glaring example of the nothing-but fallacy in psychology. However, personality theorists from Freudian mystics to cognitive psychologists are equally guilty, as we shall demonstrate.

Purpose is found both in activity which conserves the useful (preservative), and investigates the potentially useful (creative). As a result of the investigatory aspect, many species modifications result in complex and delicate organic mechanisms such as are associated with aesthetic development. But this is not at all an obvious step. Grobstein asked: "What has driven life to higher levels of organization? Since bacteria are successful in adapting to a changing environment, why has the biomass produced such complex organisms as mice and men?"[47] Why then, should life attempt to express itself in ways which increase its complexity and, in consequence, subject it to additional types of survival threat?

The answer seems to lie in the notion discussed above, that whether individuals survive is secondary to the optimizing of the probability that the whole will survive environmental irregularity over time. This occurs despite the mechanism by which it happens. It is the species that endures; the genotype that persists; the biomass that evolves. In the process, the increased viability of life as a whole determines the extent to which new techniques are adopted. Individuals attempt many activities which are personally destructive. Such activity represents the investigation of possible alternatives, the outcome of which is often species preservative. The fact that many individuals succumb along the way is in one sense little more than a statistic. If the survival of the fittest *individual* were the goal, no such self-risking, and often self-destroying, characteristics could ever emerge.

The focus here is on the relationship between living organisms and species through the influence of genetics. A similar holarchic arrangement may be discerned at all levels of organic existence. Species risk and die to the enhancement of the ecologic community (though here the relationship is of a different nature). The wonderful symbiotic existence of many animals and the predatory interaction of others are evidence of the relative immortality of the community. Similarly, the organism as a system has existential priority over its components. The various elements of the body live and die, often in service to the individual. This ubiquitous directionality is damning evidence against the sociobiological claim for the ultimacy of specific genotypes.

Purpose does not require that any of the arguments offered by vitalists (or even the contention of this text) be correct. It is sufficient that the capacity of self-replication that is unique to the living be understood. A powerful case for purpose can be made on that fact alone. Consider the following: It is generally agreed by reductionists that phenotypes best equipped to survive will reproduce themselves most prolifically, and that the result will be a continually more adaptive genotype. Add to this the cybernetic view that purpose, like action, can be seen in the performance of machines controlled by servomechanisms, and there appears an airtight case for explanations that eliminate the need for purpose.

But such an interpretation is not exhaustive. There is the entailment that the preferential survival of organic individuals, as well as the perhaps contingently occurring altruistic behavior of some, results in the enhancement of the totality, albeit unintentionally. Such performance does not characterize the inorganic on the sheer basis of the lack of self-perpetuating potential—the "accumulation" of crystals, notwithstanding. If purpose cannot be ascribed on the basis of direction it has ample reason for acceptance on this account alone. Wiener's torpedoes are directed by human beings. Organic existence operates on the basis of internal or self-directed control.[48] Nor is deliberation or intention an essential prerequisite. The fact that only mentally endowed creatures deliberate does not alter the relationship between holarchic existential levels. The reformulation of concepts to avoid the suggestion of a mysterious force by those who accept the incredible mystery of self-replication is of less, not greater, heuristic value.

It should be a useful exercise, once again, to carefully consider the meaning of typical enigma-avoiding statements. "Evolution is due neither to chance nor to design; it is due to a *natural* [italics added] creative process."[49] By creating a third alternative ("natural"), Dobzhansky skirted the problem of finalism, and thus of purpose. What, pray tell, did he mean by *natural*?

The analogy between genetic information and goal-directed machinery mentioned above was said to be limited by the distinction that life processes are based on internal controls, while machines must be programmed externally. It is, of course, true that the machine's organization contributes to its interaction with the environment; but such organization is comparable to that of a phenotype, being not of its own design. The machine is always subject to the interest of its creator.

Deliberate Systems

A unique class of systemic interaction is represented by all of the structures and institutions that are employed by living creatures to the enhancement of their existence. The hunter's axe, the beaver's dam, and even the most sophisticated computer share the common characteristic of existing in a dynamic relationship with living beings. Laszlo suggested that the term *artificial* system be used to describe this type of interaction.[50] However, the term *deliberate* system seems more accurate, since it focuses on the fact that such systems are employed in the interest of *living creatures*, and often with the intention of the user.

Most difficult to understand are deliberate systems such as social and political organizations. Labor unions, bowling teams, religious orders, and nations are obvious examples. While no direction is discernible in inorganic part/whole relationships, and parts are subordinate to wholes in natural organic systems, here the whole seems to serve the interest of its parts. But such an interpretation is demonstrably erroneous.

The union organization is more accurately viewed as a *part* of the individuals who create it, although it stands in a mediate position relative to its membership. That is, although one may be said to "belong" to an organization, the association is only a convenience which is incompletely defined. The full meaning requires that the organization be related to the individual(s) whose collective purpose it serves. People create unions; they do not create species.

The problem arises because of the tendency of the holonic nature of entities to slip out of the perceptual field. The term "individual," for example, is used synonymously with human being, and it is thus difficult to recognize as a whole except in terms of its immediate parts. The scheme was exemplified in Table 3.1, to which we can add that trade unions more accurately represent parts of humans (collectively), procedural agreements are parts of trade unions, etc.

In each case, the definition (meaning) comes from above, the manifestation (reality) from below. In the case of instances, a system may be fully defined with any number of individuals or instances. In the case of parts, however, no one is sufficient since the systemic function requires the existence of other (unlike) parts. A small number of people, in fact as few as one, exhausts the requirements of a population. But the system whose whole aspect is a human, requires that many subsystems be included in order to complete the definition.

Considerable controversy has been generated over the issue of the status of the family as a natural or deliberate system. The term family itself has many connotations. The interpretation here shall be based on its usage in the nuclear sense. Does the family exist for the individual or is the reverse true?

Since the relationship between parents and children is "instinctively" known, the appropriate location for the family as an entity would seem to be somewhere between the individual and species. This would make it a natural system. The problem arises when a decision is to be made as to which has priority when one must be sacrificed. Since the welfare of humankind precedes the interest of the family unit, the order appears to be reversed—with the family representing a part of the individual, and thus deliberate.

The issue is further confounded by such arrangements as extended families, and the affinity between non-biologically related parents and children. Each of these, however, represents a learned technique for establishing a community which simulates the parent-child grouping that occurs naturally through the union of specific individuals. The extended family is considered natural—to the extent that kinships of receding intimacy are involved. However, multiple marriage, and sibling and in-law contributions nullify any effort to demonstrate a difference between such families and adoptive relationships. The allegiance, whether between children and their natural or adoptive parents, is not biological but psychological. Consequently the focus may be directed toward individuals or groups that stand *in loco parentis*.

Where a choice must be made, the evidence suggests that the welfare of natural children will take precedence. Although this may be based on genetic influence (and perhaps is), it does not make the case that the preservation and enhancement of genetic lines supersedes that of species development. It is far more likely that the psychological as well as perceptual factors or relative distance from the gene pool causes this preference for one's "own."

The Ultimate Goal

Since purpose has been defined as directional, the problem of identifying the goal or end-state remains. We suggested earlier, that the focus of the obligation of the individual as a biological unit is a gene pool, species, subspecies, or other mediate existent. But that represents only the narrow band of attention that results from the formation of increasingly isolated gene pools. Where is the totality of life *going*? What is its *mission*? The question arises naturally whether it is assumed that life emerged from pre-life as an accident, or that divine interests are involved. The latter interpretation includes a final state which is unacceptable to the scientist. It is, in fact, a keystone of the rejection of vitalist claims.

Dobzhansky typifies the scientist's view. "Theories that ascribe evolution to 'urges' and 'telefinalisms' imply that there is some kind of predestination about the whole business."[51] But such an implication is not necessary. Even if the reductionist claim that there is no ultimate state can be shown to be true, the legitimacy of purpose is not revoked.

It is perfectly reasonable to assume that the procession of life follows a path that is finite at one limit, infinite at the other. There is simply no *logical* necessity that a final goal be defined in terms of some fixed condition. As defined here, purpose requires the specification or assumption of no such ultimate state. The simplicity of this argument may suggest a gross naïveté, but its justification can be found in its analogous use both in mathematic manipulation and respected scientific formulation. Although divisibility as a matter of measurement is infinite, a mathematical distinction is drawn between *being* and *not being*. In the computation of potential (real) instances, it is appropriate to begin with zero (or one) and to proceed *infinitely*. The number system represents an obvious example of a situation fixed at only one end.

In the case of a vector (e.g., a force having direction and magnitude) some fixed length as well as direction is involved since a point is determined in terms of its relationship to another point. A beginning and end are posited. However, a point in space may simply be a convenient benchmark for the establishment of direction. Point A may be situated at some distance from point B and that distance may be increasing. No terminal point is essential to an understanding of the relationship. This is the situation with life, where the two points involved are emergence B and any contemporary moment A.

Cosmologists accept the possibility of an expanding universe which began at some finite point of maximum density. Although Eddington[52] and others have suggested the possibility of a limit, the *principle* of limitless expansion is respectable. In the case of cosmogenic theory, the logic of the position rests on the observation that remote galactic systems appear to retreat with velocities proportionate to their distances.

The interpretation of purpose as the subservience of parts to wholes that results in movement along a vector of distance from the first reproductive occurrence, can be found in the work of biologists, zoologists, and anthropologists, many of whom deny the unique significance of the observed relationships. This leads to an explanation of the ostensive paradox of "contingent" progress. When purpose and direction emerge, even as a contingency, it is neither proper nor necessary to insist that their existence as unique to life be denied. Having evolved, the manifestations of life are non-contingent. Although environmental happenstance is a limiting factor, the drive toward survival and growth provides a constant, purpose-laden element.

Purpose emerged at the moment that some organic compound *used* another entity to its own survival/growth ends. Its significance was enhanced when the first *division*, or *duplication* occurred, which would be similar to the "birth" of gravitation only when a second entity existed. If life were related in a purposeful (i.e., subordinate) way to the inorganic world, it could be said to be purposeful at the outset, but no such relationship can be discerned. The interaction and competition between various forms of life presents its own problem, if one insists that life in general, or at least at species levels, is the principal focus of activity. If life is a unity, why do some of its instances destroy others? Once again, the human analogy may be useful. In the performance of an activity such as exercising, many cells are destroyed. In some instances, they are replaced by superior entities, as when scar tissue becomes muscle. In others, they are simply consumed in the interest of achieving a "goal."

Environmental accident mandates the achievement of goals in unpredictable ways. Goals include optimal survival and growth, which vary over time and place. The way in which growth and competitive survival are accomplished is not, and could not be, determined by a static gene pool. All systems are in a state of equilibrium which is determined by the totality of existent systems (the suprasystem), and the vector of any one (such as the human species) is a property of their interaction as subsystems. "The simplest set of equations for a system of this kind simply states that each population has an equilibrium value which is a function of the existing values of all other populations."[53]

Since the value of any other population or species may vary from zero to some immense term, the behavior of each individual in any population also varies. People who live in areas where meat is plentiful develop different characteristics over time than those who have an essentially grain diet. In this way, the environment has an inevitable effect on the species and is a determinant of how the goal will be achieved. Although the goal remains a constant (i.e., optimal survival/growth), its expression varies according to opportunity.

Homo sapiens is, then, no more than an "accidental" species insofar as the particular manifestation is concerned. However, purpose is expressed by movement along the survival parameter through both conservative and exploratory behavior. Environmental factors effect the manner in which the goal is pursued, but to the extent that life is a fact in the universe they do not determine what the nature of the goal shall be.

The inference of this definition of purpose is that the goals of an organic system are inherently "good" and that the activity of the individual in meeting such goals has a moral quality. The concept "good," as a moral term, has no more appropriate definition. Clearly, however, purpose and morality are not human exclusives. They represent characteristics of living existents which predate and supersede human presence.

Purpose emerged with the presence of organic forms of existence. Concepts such as reality and meaning are also dependent on interpretation by the living. To speak of meaning as independent of description by a living being is incomprehensible. The concepts of meaning, reality, and purpose are all dependent on such interpretations, with purpose referring to the peculiar directional relationship which obtains where a living holon is served by a subordinate existent, whether living or not.

Purpose burgeons as life develops from the simplest organic entity to a complex whole. It appears to reach an apex at the species level because protected gene pools provide messages that guide action toward species enhancement. However, the principle is more general. At every organic level, the holon expresses purpose in its relationship to its *immediate* superordinate. Just as the individual monkey or man does not deliberately act to serve life in general at cost to his own species, the liver cell and the epithelial cell function to protect a specific organ, or body element in ordinary circumstances.[54] Since a superordinate holon may have a variety of parts, it may at times be difficult to identify the appropriate focus. The blood stream, for example, which serves many organs, also functions mediately in service of the individual and ultimately optimizes survival and procreative potential for resident germ cells.

We have pointed out that the term "purpose" is employed in a wide variety of contexts. It may be said that the purpose of a book is to communicate, of a nail to attach a board, of a car to provide transportation. However, the *notion* of such relationships grows out of the part/whole relationship where subservience can be identified. Furthermore, to reiterate, the *ultimate* referent is *always* some living holon.

The Mechanics of Purpose

In Chapter 3, we proposed a model that could account for the emergence of purpose. We argued that the perceptual and ultimately the cognitive/affective systems in organisms are so designed that the perceiver/thinker recognizes as worthy of care other superordinate beings as well as the physical self. In fact, *self* care is as purposeful as that of caring for others—in that the body operates in the immediate interest of its resident germ cells. However, of equal interest and persistent confusion is the fact that the welfare of others takes priority over care for the self in many instances.

We do not propose that deliberation be assigned to gene pools, subspecies, populations, etc. However, this does not minimize the impact of these entities on the individual. To the extent that the interest of other living creatures is believed to be of significance, that conviction will influence emotional attitude as well as behavior. It is in this sense that species "control" has been proposed. Where the individual responds to extra-personal life, a higher order of organic existence is served. Germ cells have—perhaps inadvertently—created somatic extensions that react to "types" as well as to the individual that transports the system.

As to those forms of life that show no interest beyond the individual, there is no reason to assume that purpose includes a protective attitude toward others—even to one's own offspring. Purpose, however, is still a factor. It resides in the drives for food that maintains the individual and sex that enhances endurance beyond the life of the individual. The capacity to perceive (recognize) certain qualities in others is seen in the imprinting of geese, where any object will be accepted as a "mother" at certain developmental stages,[55] but not in ducks who recognize only duck mothers. In the first instance, the code is more general and probably keys on something as vague as "moving object."

Sociobiologists contend that individuals "recognize" kin, or those that share genes. Our position is that the capacity to "recognize" is based on a peculiarity of the perceptual system which simply does not discriminate completely between biological self and others. The sociobiological proposal requires some "mystical" recognition which is not born out by the evidence. While the highest degree of cooperation is observed between those most closely related, altruistic behavior extends beyond such restricted relationships in humans, as is well documented.

An example of the fact that preference is based on such factors as visual similarity, physical proximity, and experience was seen in the behavior of hundreds of Polish children raised in Germany during World War II who refused repatriation when the conflict ended. Their preference was for those to whom they had become accustomed. Lest it be argued that improved life styles was a significant intervening variable, there are countless instances of children adopted into less economically comfortable homes who have refused to return when natural parents of considerably greater means attempted reconciliation.

Other forms of evidence for purposive behavior—as purpose is defined as action directed *away* from the agent—can be found in the developmental stages of human (as well as animal) life. Freudian analysts, however, as well as many others, have supposed that because children are apparently born only with self-interest (and thus must be taught to curb negative or destructive attitudes toward others in order to survive in civilized societies); such "instincts" must pervade all human motivation.

Interpretations of infant and child attitudes are based on observations of the behavior of many children. They surely provide one logical conclusion. Once again, however, the obvious has been stated and restated with scant regard to its inconsistency with conflicting data, or to the possibility of simpler, nondemonic explanations. It is certainly commonly observed that children show evidence of distress when other children or animals are injured. This has been explained away as little more than the ability to reflect the behavior on themselves. (Note, however, that it is only behavior that is not self-centered that needs such dismissal. Behaviors that suggest greed, destruction, or insensitivity are accepted as valid.)

Considering the helpless state of infants, what could be anticipated if the urge to defend others at risk to the self were active at birth? Any behavior attendant upon such an emotional state could be destructive. During the prepubertal stages it is critical that the individual develop the strength and skills to function effectively. Just as reproductive capacity is delayed in humans for ten or more years, so too, is subjugation of the self delayed until some parallel level of maturity is reached. The capacity to recognize others as appropriate objects of protective/supportive activity is not appropriate to optimal development of the gene pool until the individual can defend itself.

The strongest bonds, those between mothers and their children, are undoubtedly one-sided in the early years, and usually go through painful reorganization as the adolescent attempts to find ways to adapt to social demands. However, such developmental periods are consistent with survival advantage to the targeted gene pool. The willingness to sacrifice does not become a potent force until *after* the individual goes through those hormonal changes that make child-bearing possible––and, in most instances, until after children are conceived.

This widely observed phenomenon accounts for the confusion regarding how a sacrificing individual could pass along its germ plasm. In human societies, the artificial extension of adolescence has certainly altered the calendar. Fourteen year olds often do show altruistic tendencies—well before they are considered ready for parenthood. However, their reproductive capacity has matured many years earlier and the activities of youth groups of all types attests to the development of "sharing" emotions.

Thus, purpose, as it refers to the priority of transcendent wholes, is manifested at all levels of life. In the highest forms, affective and cognitive sophistication results in feeling states that replace taxic responses as individuals begin to weigh self and other interests in the choice of behaviors.

Summary

Purpose is a class of force which binds parts to wholes in a unique way. It is this characteristic of existence which allows living wholes to persist across time as disposable parts combine and recombine. It is not necessarily dependent on desire in the whole, but on a directionality that, prior to mind, results in mandatory activity.

The relationship between a phenotype and its same species neighbors, and that between a genotype and the gene pool from which it is drawn, represent different aspects of the altruistic portion of purposive behavior. In the first instance the individual recognizes as a perceptual matter similarity in others, and the system is geared to serve types rather than specific individuals. In the case of the genotype and its parent pool, the "other" that sister genotypes represent are in the larger context the same, since the emergence of each phenotype is nothing more than an expansion of the expression of the original totality.

Three parameters of existents have been developed in Chapters 2, 3, and 4. An entity is *real* in the sense that it is analyzable; *meaningful* in-so-far as it is related to some whole (whether or not dynamic); and *purposeful* to the extent that it functions in the interest of some organic whole in a systemic relationship. Reality and meaning are mutually entailing for all existents because of their holonic nature. Purpose, however, is relevant only where life is involved. It may be useful to point out here that the purposeful relationship that pervades each element of the biomass in no way suggests that the totality of life itself is purposeful. It cannot be shown to serve any superordinate existence and, as we stated earlier, it is quite likely that purpose is purely contingent on the nature of organic development.

This text is designed to provide a basis for the understanding of emotional health. That understanding must include the nature of such concepts as meaning and purpose. The chain of relationships is inevitable. Meaning is the existential characteristic of existence that makes purpose possible. Purpose begets morality. Morality begets such emotions as pride, guilt, and anger. Emotions beget behavior, and convictions about one's capacity and opportunity to behave are the aspects of mental life that relate to emotional health.

The next step will be to analyze the process by which individuals become aware of the world in which they live.
- How do we "know?"
- What can we learn?
- What is the nature of knowledge?

Chapter Notes

1. Schlick (1953), p. 528
2. Elliot (1972), p. 309
3. Waddington (1968b), p. 56. To the extent that natural selection refers to the contingency of environmental opportunity, he was correct. However, he was focusing on only one aspect of the process.
4. Waddington (1967c), preface
5. Koestler (1959), pp. 536-537
6. Dobzhansky (1970b), pp. 4-5
7. Runes (1962), p. 259
8. Wiener (1948), pp. 236-237
9. Kant, cited in Runes (1962)
10. *Ibid.*
11. Hatt (1968), p. 331
12. MacArthur & Connell (1966), p. 135
13. Christian (1958)
14. Wynne-Edwards (1962)
15. Grobstein (1964), p. 33
16. *Ibid.*, p. 110
17. Dobzhansky (1950), p. 36
18. Huxley (1942), p. 577
19. Wilson, E. O. (1975), p. 575
20. Mayr (1968), p. 48
21. *Ibid.*, pp. 48-49
22. *Ibid.*, p. 49
23. Mayr (1970), p. 409
24. *Ibid.*, p. 20
25. Adler (1927), p. 73
26. Mayr (1976), p. 62
27. Chardin (1965), p. 62
28. Wild (1966), p. 236
29. Nagel (1961)
30. *Ibid.*, p. 444
31. *Ibid.*, p. 402
32. *Ibid.*, pp. 405-406
33. *Ibid.*, p. 418
34. Sartre (1947)
35. Koestler (1967), p. 145
36. Wiener (1948), p. 54
37. Rosenblueth, Wiener, & Bigelow (1943), pp. 18-19
38. Rosenblueth & Wiener (1950), p. 324
39. Taylor, R. (1950), p. 331
40. The "feedback" mechanism described by cyberneticists represents only the *mechanics*—not the *purpose* of the sequence.
41. Nageli von (1884)
42. Driesch (1908)
43. Beck (1961), p. 277
44. Dobzhansky (1970b), p. 367
45. Though differences between races seem minimal, there is considerable argument that different species may well have totally independent ancestors. Ouspensky criticized Buckes' acceptance of evolution as involving only one form, "not at all admitting the possibility of other points of view: for example, the fact that each of the existing forms is a link of *separate* evolutionary chains, i.e., that the evolution of animal-vegetables, of animals and men are different, go by different routes, and do not impinge on one another. And this standpoint is entirely justifiable when we take into account the fact that we *never know* transitional forms." (1970, p. 293).
46. Nagel (1961), p. 445

47. Grobstein (1964), p. 93
48. Augros and Stanciu pointed out that "nonliving things do not have control over their activities; they are either always in action or are put into action from outside" (1986, p. 43).
49. Dobzhansky (1950), p. 40
50. Laszlo (1973)
51. Dobzhansky (1950), p. 40
52. Eddington (1933)
53. Boulding (1972), p. 80
54. However, their potential service is not limited to the body of that individual into which they were born.
55. Lorenz (1965)

Chapter 5
Epistemology

Knowledge represents the capacity to intercept and experience data (*information*) transmitted by all types of existent. It is not solely a mental phenomenon, but is a characteristic of both organic and inorganic entities.

Learning refers to change in response potential resulting from maturation and/or exposure to relevant information. It is an automatic process, that may or may not follow a behavioral sequence. *Intelligence* is a function of the degree of malleability of the learner.

At the level of life, knowledge, learning and intelligence, are employed in goal oriented pursuits. When a message is involved, the term *communication* is employed, with *drives* and *perception* representing the techniques involved in the process.

Before describing the functional relationships among elements of the phenosystem, it is necessary to define several processes involved in the transmission of data from one entity to another. In most instances, the definition employed represents an attempt to focus on an interpretation of the concept that is commonly intended. In some cases, however, definitions vary so widely that no reconciliation is possible; in others, the prevailing interpretation seems untenable.

Entities were defined in Chapter 2 as corporeal existents. They differ from other forms of existence in the ways in which they are manifested. Qualification as an entity requires the capacity to broadcast data that may reveal its presence. This represents the transmission of whatever makes possible the translation of *substance* into *existence*—*noumena* into *phenomena*. Such data shall be defined as *information*. The stipulation is merely a convention. Non-informational substances, should there be such, are not excluded from classification as entities simply because of the presumption of positing them (which is itself a powerful cause), but because this classification provides a specification that identifies useful parameters. Examples of types of information include immediate physical contact (touch), disturbance of neighboring media (electromagnetic vibration), and chemical activity.

Information is not peculiar to life but characterizes interactional activity between all existents. It is, thus, without truth value. It is not possible for information to be correct or incorrect since it represents no more than the passage of data in whatever way is possible. An optical illusion, for example, is misleading only when its interpretation is taken into account. The passage of a vagabond celestial body sufficiently close to a solar system may cause a gravitational disturbance (information) that alters orbits and ultimately destroys the system. This would not, however, represent an "error" or an inappropriate action since there is no criterion for judging the propriety of an event..

Information may be generated by an entity (e.g., illumination by a light bulb) or be reflected, as is an image created by illumination from the sun. Information may itself be comprised of entities (e.g., chemical molecules) and an informational chain may pass through a series of entities providing both direct and indirect clues to the presence of related entities. In the case of information broadcast by the sun, entities are bombarded by the light quanta, (photons), absorbing some and reflecting others in patterns which create shape, color, and other qualities, when intercepted. Interpretation of waves as color is, of course, dependent on the perceptual organization of the receiver. More critical is the fact that the entity revealed by information generated by the light from a lamp, for example, is only the fixture, not the electrical power which creates the illumination.

The reductionist interpretation, which contends that the ultimate source (e.g., the electricity generator) defines the quality of the information involved, misses the point. It is obviously possible to demonstrate that the source of the lamp's light is some agent which delivers electrical energy. However, the agitation of the glowing filament provides a form of information which need not be reduced to its elements. In fact a regression of entities may be being revealed. Light quanta reveal the presence of a bulb; the bulb of its elements (filament and glass), the filament of electrically charged wire. But the charge may be generated by 240/110 volt house current, a dry cell battery, or other source. To make an appropriate determination requires additional data, and here new information/knowledge chains are involved.

Information is of many kinds and can attest to the presence of existentials other than entities. Melting ice, for example, is being informed of the presence of heat.

EPISTEMOLOGY 131

Heat, of course, is a condition rather than an entity. There are many examples of such a confusion of concepts. Consider a magnetic force field. Such an existent is often misconstrued as an entity. Hawking, for example, proposed that a field is "something that exists throughout space and time."[1] This type of definition is common to most encyclopedias. Tryon called a field a "type of variable representing *quantities* (italics added) that may, in principle, be measured...at any point of space-time."[2] Certainly, force fields exist. However, they are better understood as types of *information* that reveal the presence of a condition, situation, or relationship which characterizes an entity or a condition which obtains between entities.

Entities vary widely in their capacity to experience, interpret, and respond to information. This capacity is the appropriate referent for the concept commonly referred to as *knowledge*. This definition of knowledge, which identifies it as a characteristic of the knower, runs immediately afoul of the platonic proposition that humans can only know (i.e., have knowledge of) that which is eternal. The idealistic philosophy sees the perpetuity of an existent as essential to its being known, which would make true knowledge an invariant state. Plato's "forms" represented these eternal realities. The degradation of perception as a source of knowledge based in part on the awareness of the limitation of perceptual accuracy springs from the same conviction. But the fact of learning and the capacity of an entity to alter its response potential provide incontrovertible evidence that knowledge states are transient, and that the permanence of the "sacred" geometric figures is itself limited by the condition of the observer (i.e., knower) as Berkeley eloquently demonstrated.[3]

The terms *information* and *knowledge* are often interchanged. However, it is essential to discriminate between characteristics of a transmitter and those of a receiver. To inform is to dispatch, broadcast, attract, emit, reflect, etc. To intercept such transmissions requires a sensitive receiver—an entity with knowledge. It is, of course, necessary for an information transmitter to have knowledge if information is to be transmitted. However, the converse is not true. The reception and absorption of information by a knowledgeable individual, such as a human, does not entail any emission.

Two classes of knowledge can be identified. *Innate* knowledge is that capacity which is inherent in an entity, prior to experience (i.e., knowledge that characterizes the entity in its primitive state). *Learned* knowledge is that capacity which an entity possesses after having been modified by experience and/or maturation. In many situations entities are observed to act without apparent stimulation as if they were excited from within. Such activity may be said to be based on internally generated information. An example from inorganic matter would be star sourced radiation. Among organic beings, growth urgency seems similarly independent of environmental influence. In each case, internally generated knowledge is involved.

Reaction to external stimulation is far more commonly observed. Light striking a photoelectric cell, a phototropic plant, or a human eye, causes reactions that are based on knowledge in the recipient. When a knowledge state is activated the response may involve only an experience, or it may include some form of action as well. The distinction between these several elements is critical. To possess knowledge is to be so organized that a response may occur under appropriate circumstances. In the case of inorganic matter and mindless life, responses are mandatory. To have an experience (i.e., be "knowing") is to sense the presence of information. To act is to respond as a result of the experience.

On the basis of the definition introduced here, inorganic substances must be considered to possess knowledge whenever they have the capacity to be altered by specific stimuli and, the capacity to experience (or know) when such an alteration is occurring. This attribute is, therefore, little more than a common feature of all existents. Knowledge is always located in some specific place, at some defined time. This feature circumscribes the identity of the knower. If a stone has knowledge its existence as part of a collection of stones may suggest that in some sense the collection has knowledge. More accurately, however, the collection simply includes knowledgeable elements within which many of its instances are apt not to possess that knowledge. This distinction, too, will be shown to be critical.

The immediate reaction to the definitions of knowledge and experience stated here will be understandably discomfiting—especially as the terms are used to describe interactive moments between inorganic entities. The cause of the problem, however, arises from the prejudice of epistemologists who associate knowledge with learning, and who assume that the possession of knowledge is unique to the living; in many ways even peculiar to humans.

This distortion is not only the responsibility of the Quines, Russells, Ayers, and Moores of recent vintage but occurred frequently in the works of the earliest thinkers. It was, unfortunately, logical to follow the ontological question: "Does X exist?" (does it, for example, meet the Kantian condition of having space/time referents) with the question "How does one *know* that X exists?" Responses were couched in terms that defined knowledge as a human characteristic. Perception seemed a necessary aspect. Democritus[4] and Anaxagoras[5] saw reason (knowledge in action) as the capacity to recognize perceptual flaws in the search for truth. Thus, truth became involved. This connection survives today. Locke echoed Plato with his suggestion that knowledge is the perception of agreement and/or disagreement between ideas.[6] More recently, Ayer (who also equated knowledge with truth) stated that "Nothing is known unless somebody knows it."[7] Again the reference was to the mental aspect.

Early behaviorists supposed that anything that might be accepted as knowledge does not come into being until the human level, when language becomes available to subserve that knowledge.[8] There is scant evidence that today's behavioral scientists have renounced that view. Such terms as mind, knowledge and truth are, thus, analyzed under a presumption that is totally untenable. It is a devastating misconception to attempt an understanding of a concept of such significance as knowledge by ignoring its basis in levels of nature more general than that of life. There is, in fact, a delicious irony in the paradoxical effort of modern thinkers to reduce life to its physicochemical elements, while simultaneously developing arguments such as that regarding knowledge which presume its uniqueness. Life does differ from non-life in critical ways. However, the possession of knowledge is not one of the differences.

The conflict between rationalists and empiricists concerning the essentiality of experience is based on an assumption of the ability to remember and profit from such experience, which would seem to be peculiar to life. But is it? The certainty of knowledge where evidence is "complete" is contested by the fallibilist claim (to be defined in Chapter 6), that empirical statements are limited to probability. But probability does not exist in the mindless world. Modern physicists have been captivated by the assumption of probability as causal, with "strict" causality being denied at the subatomic level. However, the proof of this assumption, compelling as recent evidence has been, awaits.

Discordant views of the nature of knowledge, being based on the predilection that knowledge is peculiar to mind, result in a far-too-narrow interpretation. Consider the following: When each evening at sundown the photo-sensitive electric light on a patio begins to glow, and when at dawn it expires, it seems contentious to interpret that activity as a result of knowledge possessed by the mechanism. It may appear absurd to state that the light *knows* when to go on and off, and it may be argued that the act represents no more than a mechanical necessity which should not be dignified as knowledge. But such a distinction is not supportable.

Knowledge, or knowing, is described in many ways. It includes such varied functions as cognizing, remembering, being acquainted with, intuiting, perceiving, appreciating, and understanding. Furthermore, it is seen as derived from the senses, cognitive potentiality, categories of thought, and even revelation. Thus, any attempt to define the term is limited operationally to specifying that aspect which is being addressed. If one says that to know means "to be aware of" or "to understand" the concept is ordinarily being limited to its mental manifestation. If what is meant is to know right from wrong, to be acquainted with, or to recognize, different parameters are involved. To know "right from wrong," for example, means either to have a moral "faculty" that provides an intrinsic sense of propriety, or to be familiar with particular social customs.

Any definition of knowledge is subject to the same restrictions. However, when a common denominator is extracted, *knowing* (as it is used to describe being aware or cognizant of) is based on a prior ability to realize an experience or to respond to information—which is to possess knowledge. An investigation of what is normally intended when knowledge in a human is described reveals that the same principle is involved. "I know (have knowledge of) the name of the city which is the capital of France" means that I have the capacity to recall or state the name "Paris" upon receipt of appropriate information. If I am thinking of it now, I am *knowing* or *experiencing* it. This is an example of learned knowledge. However, such knowledge could not have been acquired unless the individual possessed some innate capacity which made the learning possible.

As it relates to inorganic entities this principle is relatively simple. A stone, a lake, or a light beam possesses knowledge to whatever extent it can respond to information. Where the processing agent is more complex, as in the human brain, the term knowledge must be defined more cautiously. However, knowledge as experienced by a vibrating ear drum in a narcotized individual is no different, in principle, than that of a light sensor, except that it does not provide its intended communication. The information received by the operable light sensor would, by contrast, be sufficient to action.

Information and knowledge form a tandem. When information is being received (i.e., when knowing or experiencing is occurring), any reaction or response is itself informational. Rain (information) falling on a roof (which is then knowing or experiencing it) causes reverberations (informational action) which may result in the vibration of nearby windows (which are then knowing). The term *stimulus* is commonly used to represent not only information as it refers to the transmitter, but also knowledge in the receiver to the extent that it can respond, and knowing when it is being received and processed. It is assumed that if a stimulus has an impact the receiver possesses the requisite knowledge. When *stimulus* is used in this text, however, it shall refer only to the informational aspect of an event.

The Cybernetic Process in Living Beings

The phenotype represents an interface between the principle of life and the environment it challenges. It is subject to thermodynamic law but resists decay through the incorporation and metabolism of certain types of matter. The selection process is based on genetic information and on the accident of opportunity to express knowledge so acquired. This principle of life is a characteristic recognized by many sciences. Homeorhesis in biology, negentropy in physics, drive in psychology, and instinct in ethology all deal with this potent, persistent force.

Each living entity represents an instance of the species principle with systemic survival and growth being the ultimate goal. Because of the holarchic nature of life, conflict potential is a natural outcome of the drive toward continued existence. Each phenotype is in competition with similar individuals and divers species for the wherewithal to survive and grow. This causes little distress at those levels where decision-making is not an issue, but it becomes potentially debilitating as the individual recognizes any form of selfhood, which provides it with a conviction of independence or separate significance.

Reference was made earlier to the several terms employed to identify the unique characteristic of living entities which distinguishes them from inert matter. Whether a hackneyed expression like *elan vital* is resurrected, a scientifically respectable concept such as the open system is adopted, or a term such as holonic intumescence is coined, the principle-of-life reveals itself to the most casual observer. Its parameters are identical at all levels of existence. They include an urge toward activities which ensure continued existence, the capacity to intercept and interpret critical aspects of the environment, the ability to act when the situation is appropriate, and a satiation signal system which prohibits unnecessary or harmful perseveration. And each step in the process represents an expression of the information/knowledge chain.

Urges initiate activities which are essentially of value both to the individual, such as hunger and thirst, and other activities which are oriented more directly toward the welfare of the gene pool—ranging from that of reproductive behavior, which is relatively neutral to the individual; through exploration, which profits some while destroying others; to self-sacrifice, which is clearly inimical with the interests of the individual. Such performances are based on the possession of innate and/or learned knowledge.

To the interceptor lacking a mental capacity only the most immediate information can have an impact. By contrast, however, living entities can intercept and interpret such information through a sensorium that provides an inestimable advantage in the process of coping with and overcoming the environment. In some cases, information has a purposive characteristic in that it functions to relay a message. However, the communicative aspect may be limited to the intention of only one element in the process. The beaver, for example, observes and evaluates weather changes. In such instances, the message is not "intended" by the transmitter. On the other hand, the singer who shatters a glass by singing a particular pure tone provides information that is not desired by the receiver.

The term *communication* distinguishes this functional aspect of the process when the sender, receiver, or both have a stake in the transaction. It is exemplified by commands such as "stop" and "go"—communications which are received and interpreted by receptors and other complex elements. Such a data chain characterizes phenotypic-genotypic communion. However, the fact that either sender or receiver profits from the experience does not entail the notion that either of the two acts deliberately.

At the level of communication, potential for error is introduced. Information may be transmitted and/or received and interpreted by faulty operators, resulting in serious damage. In this text, communication between the human gene pool and the individuals (phenotypes) created by the union of genotypic plan and environmental accident are of central concern. Messages which direct growth and behavior patterns through the genetic process will be analyzed.

The position that evolving forms of life interact in a manner defined as purposeful was developed in Chapter 4. The technique by which this is accomplished represents an example of the communication process. The issue, then, is in the identification of various levels of the continuum. Where, for example, does information originate?

Certain characteristics of individuals make possible adaptation to and control over the environment in the interest of survival and growth of the individual, the germ plasm, and ultimately each gene pool or species. The transmission of valuable specific physical attributes and skills across generation can be explained mechanistically through the application of Mendelian principles. However, there is palpable evidence that information/knowledge systems are involved which result in activity that is *not* profitable to the individual and, in fact, is in many instances fatal.

This phenomenon does not require the assumption of a unique potential at the level of life. It represents only the capacity of information and knowledge to be passed up and down holonic levels, as well as between holons. A canyon created by rushing water develops, at some point, the capacity (knowledge) which makes possible the transmission of information (an echo) based on various forms of intercepted information. The peculiarity at the level of life forms is that information and knowledge pass between gene pool and individual in such a way that the species, as well as the individual, is enhanced. Purpose as demonstrably directional activity is involved since the information transmitted from gene pool to individual includes some which results in the individual's destruction.

The term *individual* continues to be awkward, in that it refers in some instances both to the germ cells and their vehicle (the body), and in some cases only to the somatic aspect. When a phenotype is destroyed, the term "individual" obviously includes both. When, however, it is argued that information is directed at the "individual," the intention is to focus on some aspect of the body as, for example, when the individual is vested with intelligence. The appropriate referent, though sometimes subtle, should be discernible from the text.

The distinction between information and knowledge becomes somewhat blurred at this point. Since what is transmitted is information, the receiver must have prior knowledge if it is to be processed. If the gene carries information, from whence does the material upon which it acts receive its knowledge? A perhaps oversimplified explanation is that the material so impressed, being organic, has a "natural" capacity to know and to gain new knowledge. By natural is meant some physicochemical quality such as cohesion, magnetism, or similar characteristic. Genetically transported information results in the organization of this material in such a way that knowledge arises as a natural characteristic of the resulting configuration. The gene, of course, is not the genesis of information but is a carrier (i.e., has knowledge) of information (here a form of communication) supplied by the germ cells of earlier generations of living individuals.

Knowledge in the living takes many forms. A wide variety of coping techniques are employed which enhance survival at the level both of the individual and of the species. Proliferation of offspring, speed in pursuit and escape, aggressive capacity, armour plate, and camouflage, are commonly observed phenomena. Each method has certain advantages and limitations in its capacity to preserve and enhance life. The photosynthetic ability of the daisy provides a method for forming carbohydrates from H_2O and CO_2—a process which animals cannot duplicate. However, mobility separates animals from plants along the parameter of attack and escape potential.

These characteristics represent varied approaches to durability and viability in life's struggle against the environment. Furthermore, some of the methods are highly efficient. Bacteria are extremely effective in their struggle for existence, as are mollusks, the lowly cockroach, and many other life forms. In spite of this, species have evolved, and from the recombinations of genetic potentiality more complex life has emerged.

Evolutionary explanations for such development are not thoroughly convincing when viewed from a particular point in time rather than retrospectively. The presence of surplus organs (as well as genes) in many animals, and the fact that few vital organs, including the brain, are ever used to capacity are embarrassments to the notion of parsimony, and to the relationship between immediate survival and selective heredity. For whatever reason, a hierarchy of techniques can be discerned in the patterns of development, among which, one shall be discussed in considerable detail in Chapter 6, since it represents a critical aspect of human behavior. The method referred to is the transference of some decision-making capacity from genotype to phenotype through the development of a variety of information/knowledge systems in the individual.

It is extremely difficult to separate experiencing from acting in the inorganic world, and even in simple plants. An example might be seen in the passage of liquid from branches into the trunk of a tree after it experiences a temperature drop. It may be that the tree "experiences" alterations in temperature prior to the point at which it is sufficiently low to cause the flow of liquid. This would, perhaps, exemplify knowing without responding. However, it is not until the emergence of mind and the potential for experiencing without responding that the distinction becomes significant, and at that level it is a vital factor.

Because of a peculiar capacity to intercept and interpret sound waves (knowledge), bats can perform unique activities. Wave data provide information that excites knowledge in the bat, thus causing an experience, which may be followed by some form of action. If the bat, for whatever reason, lacks the capacity (knowledge), no corresponding experience can occur. In humans, knowledge of sound is limited to a specific wave length range (approximately 15-20 to 20,000 hz). Although it is known that higher and lower frequencies exist, such knowledge is not *auditorially* acquired.[9]

In entities not possessing a mental capacity, there may be a form of knowledge which makes possible, for example, a reaction to electromagnetic vibration that has not as yet been deciphered. Inorganic substances are, perhaps, capable of intercepting most such oscillations. However, a substance such as glass, through which certain quanta apparently pass without measurable impact may represent an example of lack of knowledge of those light waves in that entity.

The interception of environmental data should not be presumed to represent a purely passive acceptance of such intercourse as is the case with a servomechanism. The life process includes dynamic, seeking, probing activities. Although in the highest forms of life concepts such as conation or willing are posited, the seeking of potential stimuli is evidenced in the simplest organisms, and the search for contact for its own sake represents a motivating force in many species. While the drive toward food appears to represent the genesis of activity, it should be recognized as a reaction to genetically determined knowledge. Such knowledge results from the transmission of information by which the gene pool communicates with individuals.

Principal differences in the expression of the homeorhetic process at various levels are found in the complexity and the mechanics employed. In the simplest life forms it may be only the contractibility and irritability referred to in biology, while at the higher stages reorganization of cell complexes, body temperature fluctuation, and even blood sugar and hypothalamic modification are involved. The principle remains precisely the same.

A signal which guides or controls response patterns is present in each phenotype. Recoil from noxious stimuli, elimination of body waste, the exercising of musculature, and similar essential activities occur at the beckoning of a device by which individuals are sensitized to the need for such activity. In each instance, knowledge is activated in a particular way and is classified according to some taxonomy. Unfortunately, although there is general agreement regarding the existence of such processes, many of the categories employed are ambiguous, and others are thoroughly inaccurate.

Epistemics of Life

With the advent of life, and the emergence of purpose, characteristics of entities such as information and knowledge provide techniques that are invaluable in the pursuit of survival and growth objectives. Factors that were incidental in pre-life become vehicles for the propulsion of living forms into the dominant role that they play today. Below the level of mental processing, however, information and knowledge relate only to genotypal existence. No deliberation is involved.

Inorganic existents disseminate information in the form of physicochemical or other force, generated or reflected. They are also capable of differentially responding to such information, which represents a primitive form of knowledge (sensation/ primitive perception). Interaction is contingent upon location, relative motion, shape, density, and other features which limit access to information by the nature of the interface.

Living organisms, by contrast, are equipped with specific cell assemblies that are sensitive to certain types of stimulation (perceptual knowledge) by which they respond to environmental information. They are also endowed with energy mobilization potential that directs action and reaction (drive knowledge), which translates genetically communicated information. At this level, knowledge is also constrained by the many inherent limitations of the informational systems.

Action on, as well as reaction to, the environment represent forms of information exchange. At the simplest level, responses to stimuli are of the binary (yes/no, go/

EPISTEMOLOGY

no-go) type. Such information-processing provides for survival and growth under conditions established and maintained at various holonic levels. The concept of communication is appropriate in that drive and perceptual capacities represent an effort by the genetic material to provide directives to the individual. Since the non-affective phenotype (e.g., a plant) is unaware of its existence, a concept such as anteconsciousness would seem applicable, for at this level of life consciousness has no meaning.

It is extremely difficult to find an appropriate term to describe the communication chain that characterizes those forms of life that are not believed to possess a mental or psychological dimension. Most plants and some types of animal are assumed to function without benefit of a state approximating consciousness. They are not believed to possess a will, to have ideas, to think, or to conceptualize. The "psychic process" which Wundt proposed as a most accurate description of mental activity is considered to exist in only a small proportion of all that lives.[10]

This characterization of mind led to a predisposition to focus on the cognitive aspect of mental activity, with cognition being defined as "both thoughts and visual images in the stream of consciousness."[11] Since a precognitive state is described in this text as representing a level of mind, that term cannot be employed, and with biologists offering no appropriate word, the ungainly term *pre-mind* will be introduced to describe the communication chain that characterizes all living forms without a mental aspect.

Figure 5.1 presents a comparison of the function of several characteristics of entities as they are pertinent to various existential levels. In the interest of providing an efficacious composite, several elements, to be described below, as well as their role at the level of mind (Chapter 6), have been included.

Figure 5.1

Pre-mind Information Processing System

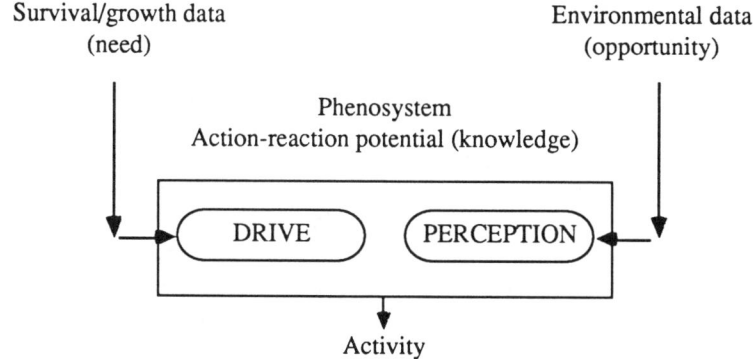

The goal oriented employment of data processing systems is unique to biological individuals. Such systems represent communication chains that have made possible negentropic action across eons. In the case of pre-mind life forms, gametes endowed with knowledge derived from a gene pool are comprised of natural, docile material which carries the message that transports the genetic idea. In turn, they impart information (based on this knowledge) to the soma cells which develop into the phenotype. The techniques employed have been defined as *drive* and *perception*.

Drive

The term *drive* is commonly used to describe biologic alterations representing the energizing aspect of organic activity. Since the organism inherits potential for interaction with the environment in ways that are valuable to survival and growth, drives (internal information) represent a form of communication. They include urges toward energy replacement, metabolic processing, growth, procreation, and the conservation of the individual and the species. As *knowledge*, they represent the organizational state which prepares the individual for action through differential energy distribution. As *knowing*, they refer to the experiencing of any such state when it exceeds some genetically established limen. When a drive energizes, it is informing or communicating information from whatever organs are activated, to whatever organs are capable of responding. It is a purely biological phenomenon, with no psychological characteristics.

Many of these propensities, each of which has the effect of providing for individual and species enhancement, are characterized by encroachment or invasion of the environment. The organism is, however, incapable of continuous action because of physical as well as energy limitations. Thus, there are information inputs or signals which cause activity to cease. In addition to fatigue factors, there are many homeostatic devices which limit activity to tolerable limits in the form of *appestats* and other regulatory mechanisms. Furthermore, there is a drive toward stabilization which is activated whenever course correction is required, as when perceptual processes are disturbed.

When Woodworth introduced the term drive, he was borrowing it from mechanics and he meant the energy supply that causes motion.[12] *Drive* was generalized to explain animal behavior where it became associated with such factors as hunger, sexual activity, and maternal behavior. It became associated with instincts and other propensities since at that time there was little distinction made between *why* a behavior occurred, and *how* it was accomplished.

An attempt was made to avoid subjective explanation by limiting the meaning of drive to activity that resulted from stimulation. Pfaff referred to drive as a theoretical concept, employed to explain the internal forces that influence the motivational process.[13] To say that a drive results from internal arousal suggests a forced response unless some mediating influence is introduced. In plants, the term drive seems appropriately related to, for example, sun-seeking; but the action must be differentiated from its source. Drives seem better restricted to the "internal arousal" or internal information/knowledge aspect.

Hull, in formalizing Thorndike's theory, postulated *needs* as conditions such that some action on the part of the individual (or species) is essential to optimal survival. Since these needs precede and apparently "drive" responses, they were assumed to produce the primary animals drives, which he described as intervening variables.[14] Miller, however, considered "any strong stimulus [to be] a drive,"[15] thus expanding the concept to include those behavioral components which Hull had termed incentives. As a result, many drives were assumed to be learned.

The confusion has not been resolved. Bergquist asked, "First, what is motivation (drive)?"[16] Having inappropriately equated drive with motivation, he stated that it is "a label referring to the activity of certain neural mechanisms, where any alteration in this activity (i.e., a change in motivation) will be reflected behaviorally."[16] He thus added the contribution of the nervous system and pinned it down with altered behavioral likelihoods and changed reward values. These neural mechanisms represent the location of the knowledge which determines whether or not a behavior will occur. Summarizing the many definitions of the term, Young concluded that the term *drive* has many meanings—energy, stimulus, internal tissue condition, general activity, behavior tendency, goal-directed activity, and motivation. He opted for *energy* as the most meaningful definition, allowing, however, that those studying behavior would equate drive with behavior, while for those studying personality it would be associated with motivation.[17]

Young's advice, which was "to recognize that differences of interpretation exist, and then to be clear about one's own position,"[18] will be followed here. However, the arbitrariness of usage results not from disagreement about what the term drive *is*, but what process is being investigated. In this text, a drive shall be reserved only to that aspect of behavior potential arising *within* the individual. The process we refer to here is the energizing of the organism in such a way as to provide an essential contribution to an action sequence. The knowledge possessed is the capacity to initiate such energy when appropriate conditions exist. The term "appropriate" is an example of purpose, in that it explains in terms of potentially salubrious action.

Knowledge possessed in the form of a drive represents an organizational framework with which the phenotype is invested. It is part of the genetic inheritance, and is an essential element in shaping the action and reaction of living individuals. Knowledge of drives in plant life is manifested as knowing when the individual seeks water or reacts to sunlight. A drive is a form of knowledge that is activated (releases information) on the basis of internal change. It is analogous to radioactive alteration, resonance, or pulsation, which are characteristics of inorganic entities, where information is passed between elements of a single existent. Internal change may arise spontaneously, or on the basis of external stimulation. The distinction will be detailed in the section on "desire" in Chapter 7.

Insofar as drives are designed to cause action in the interest of survival and growth, they can be identified as *primitive* needs. Primitive needs in biological individuals are always related to species, as well as to individual survival and growth. Their existence is a logical consequence. That is, if one is to live, one must eat. This relationship is fixed by the nature of biological existence which is itself dependent on the metabolic process. Species survival over time is, in like fashion, dependent on some form of reproductive activity. In each instance, the question of why a drive exists may be answered by some necessary connection with survival and growth.

Perception

The form of experience through which an individual becomes aware of what the environment provides at any moment represents an improvement in its ability to cope with environmental variability. The type of knowledge that makes an appreciation of such information possible is often included under the term *perception*, in the broad sense that includes sensations as well as their organization and interpretation. Perception will refer here to the knowledge residing in receptor chains which are sensitive to external stimulation. To perceive is to respond to the excitation of such receptors by some environmental information source. The information involved includes electromagnetic vibration, pressure, and similar stimuli that impinge on sense receptors. The filtering process includes the ordering of such information according to the structure of the receptor.

In defining perception as a capacity for intercepting that information which is critical to the survival and growth of the individual, an essentialist view of the perceptual process is adopted. The pre-existence of being (substance) beyond the limitation imposed by the perceptual train has been asserted, with perception representing a capacity to experience and interpret such elementary elements. Thus, it represents that form of knowledge which relates the biological individual to external events. This is not to deny the role that the observer plays in such situations. Modern physics has re-discovered the notion that, in the act of perception, the perceiving individual makes a significant contribution.[19] Experimental studies have confirmed the principle that how one establishes the rules of observation contributes to what is discovered. In the case of deciding whether light is formed of particles or waves, it has been shown that "the 'we' that does the experimenting is the common (essential) link."[20]

Once again, however, there is a flaw associated with attempts to extrapolate. There are limits to the number of possible realities that can be discovered. One assumption of this text is that in recognizing the inherent limitation in precisely defining entities, especially those that are microscopic, perceptual skill plays a critical role in *estimating* the nature of the external world. Perceptual organization is a technique, a form which knowledge takes. It is not a capricious occurrence but serves a function in the perceiving organism—that of adding a sensory parameter to substantial being.

This theoretical position is consistent with organismic development. Perception, as a capacity, represents the ability to respond to certain stimuli. It is, thus, a form of knowledge. At the point of data reception (perceiving, knowing, experiencing), it is manifested in a temporary modification of sensitive cell assemblies. It is sufficient to provide for reaction to the environment at a taxic level where the organism need not interpret or generalize about the interfering agent. It is the basis for a form of knowledge that is empirically verifiable, generally with sufficient accuracy to meet the needs of the perceiving organism.

This position parallels that of Whitehead, who suggested that all entities cognize each other—with sentient beings differing only in their awareness of the experience. A stone "sees" the rose on the basis of its capacity to interfere with reflected rays.[21] Alexander, who coined this concept, made an earlier, similar, suggestion in his contention that one principle of the universe is the mutual perceptual relationship between all things, with the sensorium simply sharpening the experience.[22]

The proposition also finds support in the Chardinian argument that the potential for life must reside in pre-life forms.[23] From a philosophic standpoint, if a visually sensitive cell is at all possible, the possibility must *precede* the appearance of such a cell. In fact, such potentiality must be present in all inorganic matter. In this sense, emergence, as defined in Chapter 3 need not be involved.

The perceptual system can provide an individual with information about *what*, *when*, and *where*. No evaluative terms (e.g., good, evil, valuable, dangerous) are involved because the system possesses no such knowledge. The system is limited to providing primitively organized sense data (information) to a more sophisticated network, which integrates that information.

Vibrations in the atmosphere encounter many entities which are in some way affected by them. The term *sensation* shall be used to identify this level of knowledge. This faculty is the precursor of perception, which itself represents an increased or specialized ability to organize such vibrations. It is a physicochemical characteristic and is equally appropriate to the description of inorganic reception, having both informational and knowledge aspects.

Knowledge, as it pertains to perception, has a slightly different connotation than with drive, in that it involves informational data that cannot be predicted accurately since the environmental location of the individual is beyond gene pool control. Such knowledge is, prior to experience, a capacity to respond to a range of possible stimuli. After experience it is in some instances altered by the learning process. It seems most reasonable to define perceptual knowledge in terms of its relationship to the development of living organisms and its usefulness in solving the demand for improved survival and growth potential. One of the results of applying definitions which do not meet these criteria is confusion about the nature of human knowledge, as in philosophies that limit knowledge to that which is derived through the senses.

When the concept of usefulness is employed, the term that was applied earlier to the patio light describes the same process in simple forms of life—especially as observed in plants. In this case, knowledge makes possible the processing of information which may provide an efficient reaction to the environment. There is no inference of awareness or feeling in either instance. At the level of the patio light (an agent which performs to meet someone's purpose) and the simple plant (performing its function as a germ cell carrier), the options are extremely limited and the presumption of knowledge is inferential. It is assumed that the light sensor and the plant *know* because they function in a certain manner. But this is simply an extrapolation, just as it is assumed that a boy knows how to ride a bicycle because, in an appropriate situation, he does so.

The fact that the only assurance that knowledge exists is provided when action occurs does not rule out its potentially independent existence. It is presumptuous, and we believe demonstrably absurd, to claim that knowledge does not exist except when it is manifested, while holding to the claim that the observer contributes to the creation of external existents. It is this point that challenges the argument of the radical empiricists who propose that knowledge is based solely on experience. The proper interpretation is that experience (knowing) can occur only when information and knowledge are joined. Experience is—*in fact must be*—based on knowledge. During an experience knowledge may be altered (i.e., learning may occur), in which case subsequent knowledge will be of a different character. But, the genesis must always be an innate or previously altered knowledge base. Piaget gave tacit agreement to this interpretation in his suggestion that the biological concepts of assimilation and accommodation may be employed to describe new learning. "No new stimulus or behavior is taken in *as is*; some aspects are always transformed by the existing cognitive organization."[24]

Consciousness is not a requirement but an evolutionarily recent improvement in the form that knowledge may be experienced. To infer that a plant is *aware* that it is a plant is unnecessary. There is no empirical evidence for such an event nor can it be shown to provide any useful function. In order to determine how the plant knows, its components can be analyzed and the processes by which information is handled may be identified.

One of these processes represents the reception and interpretation of information about what exists in the environment. Where the individual must respond in a specific way, as with the photolight, there is no justification for inferring anything beyond reaction as prescribed by the blueprint. At higher levels, conceptualization and other intellectual activities are involved. The common feature is that the perceptual system provides a technique for gathering information about the existence of environmental objects and events, and for the manipulation of such data.

It is critical to an understanding of perception that a distinction be drawn between the data which are intercepted, and the interpretation of these data. At the pre-mind level, interpretation may be limited to an awareness of the presence of some information. The difference between the signal as received, and the way in which it is organized (which itself is accomplished at another level in another system) must not be overlooked, however. As with all information systems, the focus of attention determines whether knowledge, knowing, or informing (communicating in living systems) is involved. The term perception is employed in all cases. To be capable of perceiving is to possess knowledge, to experience a percept (to perceive) is to be knowing (experiencing), to perceptually organize is an informative and communicative action.

Perceptual recognition requires a ground. Such knowledge cannot be activated unless the information is projected against some contrasting medium. If all is blue, blueness cannot be seen. Movement is similarly dependent on a field. What is perceived is that which is different. As Merleau-Ponty stated in discussing the notion that figure-ground is the simplest sense datum, "it is the *very definition* of the phenomenon in perception."[25]

The developmental level and integrity of the nervous system control what is received and how it is interpreted. Thus, sensitivity to stimuli and distortion in sense organs, limit the form in which the environment is known. The simplest phenotype is capable of responding to limited environmental stimuli with very few options. The plant cell, for example, capable of reacting in the presence of a light source, is clearly superior to the crystal which remains inert, if the survival and growth of the individual are to be considered. There are, however, much more interesting potentialities and, in fact, superior adaptive techniques. The plant cell, in spite of its cleverness, will "drink" anything placed before it so long as it is in a particular physical form. Ink, milk, and water are equally accepted, and destruction, as blatantly evidenced by the effectiveness of weed killers, is attendant on such lack of discriminatory ability.

In the attempt to clarify various perceptual terms, functions which characterize certain organisms will be defined and a term which is closely related in usage will be employed. If the plant cell cannot distinguish between alternative liquid offerings it is considered capable of responding to information only at the level of *simple primitive* perception. The stimulus impinges and, given the appropriate conditions of energy, the response is (at the macrolevel) invariant. To the extent that the response is mandated by the presence of a stimulus such knowledge does not differ in principle from that of an inanimate object. Since all existents are complex, the "simple" stimulus is, in fact, a complicated pattern. Furthermore, receptors are often tuned to a range of stimulation. This suggests that to some extent the message is always subject to some monitoring. In the case of water-seeking, for example, liquidity is itself a discriminator. However, it is important to emphasize the kind of restriction that is placed on some forms of energy reception in simple forms of life.

An improvement on this response pattern is an arrangement by which the individual can selectively respond to similar stimuli. The garage door opener is sensitive to only a narrow band of stimuli, which is accomplished by filtering out inappropriate signals. Such a filtering system in the operator protects it from stray signals from other garage door operators. The process by which this selectivity occurs may be identified as *complex primitive* perception, which itself represents the expression of a more sophisticated form of knowledge.

This subject has been extensively researched, especially by Gestalt psychologists who developed principles to explain many of the forms in which data are interpreted. As in the case of simpler organisms, which react predictably to certain patterns of stimulation, there may be some genetic advantage to certain organizational forms. For example, the law of *Prägnanz*, or the tendency of perceptions to move toward simplicity and completeness, may have positive survival value.

There is an obvious advantage to the individual (and thus to the species) that can selectively organize the data encountered. With such skills, an organism can, to some extent, avoid danger. In primitive forms of life, such as the paramecium, it is possible to ingest selectively, rejecting inappropriate food, which increases the potential for overcoming short term survival threats. Here again, however, there are severe limitations. As the environment changes, perceptual patterns may become inefficacious. Modifications may be such that perceptual organization is inadequate to provide essential cues. A more competent organism would be one capable of modifying its response repertoire as a result of experience—that is, an individual that could *learn*.

Learning

Because confounding a change in organization with deliberate activity has resulted in such a broad range of potential meanings, it is essential that a rigorous interpretation of *learning* be employed. We shall define learning as an enduring change in response potential through which an individual's knowledge is *necessarily* different (usually greater) after an experience, or following a maturational event. Excepting for the inclusion of maturation, this is a definition of fairly wide acceptance, insofar as it deals with obtaining or acquiring knowledge or skill.

Bugelski suggested that learning be thought of "as an unconscious neural process (a physiological change) such that an organism, once having undergone such a process, is now able to (but need not) respond to a stimulus in a way not previously possible."[26] However, this definition, like most others, restricts learning to that which humans or animals do, failing to appreciate that changes in response potential characterize all existents.

Any entity which is alterable by experience is capable of learning. An iron bar which can stand greater stress when bent into a 90^0 angle, or a board weakened by continued exposure to humidity has learned. The nature of the learning process in inorganic entities differs from the human in that the response to a stimulus must occur as is the case with many types of plant, whereas in the human it may not, as Bugelski suggested. Furthermore, such learning does not necessarily represent the addition of knowledge, but merely an alteration in what is known. At its minimum, learning requires only that the individual be present at the time that the stimulus impinges, and that it be docile to change. However, at the level of life, a unique characteristic is observed. The change which learning represents may be profitable or deleterious; desirable or destructive.

The acquisition of knowledge in the living individual represents an opportunity for improvement in survival and growth potential. In the simplest forms, response patterns are relatively immutable. At the level of learning, the first basic change occurs in the degree to which the individual is controlled by genetic inheritance. Here, the phenotype is produced according to a pattern which allows for response strategies to be determined after delivery into the world. The exigencies of environment are dealt with by a phenotype capable of alteration based on experience. The blueprint is flexible and responses possess greater potential effectiveness. More importantly, since specific environmental experiences cannot be predicted, the learning that takes place is to some extent free of the agency which produced it. Although such viability represents a tremendous stride toward improved potential for survival, it is not based on any deliberation by the individual. The capacity for modification is fixed by genetic inheritance and prior learning. Learning only represents a change that occurs as a result of experience or maturation.

The inclusion of maturation as a cause of learning is mandated by the definition employed here. The distinction between the two resides in the source of the information rather than in the knowledge change that occurs. Maturational changes are based on characteristics of the individual that are determined by growth-and-decay processes relatively independently of environmental contingency. Experiential changes are subject to the vagaries of chance—in spite of the fact that in many instances deliberation is involved in the choice of an activity. In living forms, learning occurs only within limitations prescribed genetically. Only certain patterns are subject to such changes but their characteristics are identical at all levels of life. Learning is entirely separate from consciousness, awareness, emotion, or any other system, although it may well be influenced by them. Learning is a process *genetically* introduced and *mechanically* accomplished.

Learning represents a relatively permanent change, ordinarily persisting until further learning causes a further change. It refers equally to motor, cognitive, affective, attitudinal, and all other determinants. We must draw attention to the fact that the word learning is not used here as a gerund. It is not an action term being used as a noun. To learn is not to *do* something, but to be *changed* by some form of action. Thus, learning is not to be understood as the activity preceding or following the changed state as some behavioral scientists use the term. Learning refers only to the altered knowledge state. To say that one is learning is to infer that their knowledge state is being altered by some activity or other influence.

At this point, the empiricist problem arises again. The contention that one comes to know only through experience, equates knowing with learning as well as with perception. The distinction made here is that an individual with innate knowledge, on the occurrence of a perceptual experience (knowing), is altered in the sense that the knowledge is *verified*. On perceiving an object with certain electromagnetic characteristics, an experience occurs which is determined by a capacity-to-know. If one learns to call that experience "green," the individual now has knowledge of a taxonomic symbol—of a term to apply. No change in the knowledge of the experience takes place. A cat who never learns the word may have the same experience and the same or similar knowledge, except for the arbitrarily assigned label. When experience alters knowledge, learning may be said to occur. A different capacity exists. A plant is born with knowledge of liquidity, but this is never altered. By contrast, a mouse may learn to "recognize" its home following a series of experiences.

In inorganic entities, learning is not functional, but refers to many types of alteration, the capacity for which is differentially held. Although little attention will be paid to such primitive forms of learning, the concept, as with knowledge, must be appreciated in a sense that may help to clarify its expression in living beings. In the simplest forms of life, where the deliberative process plays no role, the efficacy of learning is manifested in the improved viability of species. Learning is a matter of alteration in genotypes as the varied potential expressions of the genetic plan are filtered through the unpredictable environment. As the best adapted, as well as those that survive creative exploration, are represented in evolving populations, the gene pool may be said to have learned to function in increasingly efficient ways, though often at cost to the welfare of its individual "agents."

Intelligence

The term *intelligence*, like knowledge and learning, is described by most psychologists as a characteristic of mind, specifically of the cognitive process. Keenness of perception, reaction time, ability to abstract, and learning potential, all have been seen as evidence of some underlying capacity. It is usually associated with intellect, and is often defined as the ability to reason or understand.

Benner said that "the conceptualization of intelligence as a generalized problem solving/reasoning ability continues to permeate research on intelligence."[27] Psychological dictionaries are primarily—if not exclusively—concerned with that aspect of intelligence bearing on the performance of living creatures. However, the characteristic being described here must be understood in its most inclusive, and elementary, sense. Inanimate objects vary in the facility with which they respond to changes in response potential, as do the simplest organic entities.

Intelligence at every level of existence, refers to *the potential for change that is expressible through learning*. Goldman suggested that, "Intuitively, intelligence consists in a 'raw' ability to learn or perform other cognitive feats."[28] His limiting of the concept to cognition is far more restrictive than is proposed here, but the notion of docility to learning is precisely the same. Intelligence, whether it describes a human capacity or a more general flexibility is comprised of innate or previously acquired knowledge, and malleability.

Examples of such potential can be taken from any level of existence. A one quart metal container may have the potential to be extended so that it will hold two quarts. A simple alteration. For an acorn to produce a maple tree would require a change of monumental difficulty since molecular structures must be altered. Nevertheless, the difference is simply one of degree.

Along with the capacity to change, living individuals, as well as species of life, differ in the degree to which alteration is beneficial. Ability to learn is subject to such factors as the extent to which new knowledge is maintained, and the degree to which change affects the integrity of the entity. The iron bar, which is capable of supporting itself on end when bent into a "U" shape, may become weakened by the process. Of little significance in the inorganic world, this aspect of docility becomes a matter of concern in the living. Alterations resulting from high levels of malleability may result in the creation of individuals that cannot survive under changes in the environment with which they must contend.

Summary

The interpretation of knowledge, learning, and intelligence presented in this chapter reflects what is known currently as dispositional philosophy, a point of view which suggests that living entities are so constructed that they are *disposed* to respond in particular ways under the influence of internal or external stimulation. It follows also the event-event causation of the physical sciences—in that a "reaction" such as photosynthesis follows upon the receipt of photic stimulation.

These positions, taken together, represent no more than a modernization of three of the Aristotelian causes (formal, material, and efficient—today recognized as highly ambiguous) which many believe are sufficient to explain all behavior. Radical behaviorism, which attempts to reduce behavior to its stimulus-response properties, follows such an explanatory thesis and is, in fact, quite adequate to explain pre-cognitive activity. Its failure at the level of decision-making individuals will be elucidated in later sections.

By way of recapitulation: *Drive* refers to the energizing of an organism through genetically fixed mechanisms. *Perception* represents a technique for receiving and interpreting information. *Communication* refers to message bearing information. All provide knowledge potential. *Knowledge* refers to the capacity to respond, *learning* to a change in response potential, and *intelligence* to the docility of the learner.

Living beings make use of these characteristics of all entities by applying them to the issues of problem solving as it relates to survival and growth. Below the level of mind, however, all such factors must be understood as they refer to genotypic existence, which is influenced by the effect of such existential characteristics in the struggle for survival and growth.

Chapter Notes

1. Hawking (1988), p. 184. This is a common practice. Harré, and Lamb, for example, proposed that "fields are real, part of the furniture of the world.... Perhaps it is only the limitation of our senses that prevents us from experiencing [them] in as direct a way as we are aware of earth and water" (1983, p. 56).
2. Tryon (1989), p. 123
3. Berkeley (1938)
4. Democritus in Russell (1945). Democritus proposed that atomic existence is impenetrable, contending that "when you use a knife to cut an apple, the knife has to find empty places where it can penetrate" (p. 71). Reasoning, thus, he presumed could lead to truth.
5. Anaxagoras in Russell (1945). Anaxagoras argued that reason leads to such conclusions as the denial of a void in nature. "The clepsydra or an inflated skin shows that there is air where there seems to be nothing" (p. 62).
6. Locke (1959)
7. Ayer (1956), p. 70
8. Attneave (1974)
9. The specification of the source of knowledge should help to clarify this issue. To "know" of the existence of longer wavelengths results from a learning experience to be defined. However, some knowledge must reside in the learner that makes such information intelligible.
10. Wundt (1874)
11. Benner (1985), p. 178
12. Woodworth (1918)
13. Pfaff (1982)
14. Hull (1943)
15. Miller (1941), pp. 534-535
16. Bergquist (1972), p. 544
17. Young, P. T. (1936)
18. *Ibid.*, p. 79
19. Holton & Roller pointed out that "it is impossible to make a *raw* observation...without at the same time having some interpretation, some hypothesis enter the mind" (1958, p. 239).
20. Zukav (1979), p. 95
21. Whitehead (1929)
22. Alexander (1914)
23. Chardin (1965)
24. Piaget cited in Cowan (1978), p. 22
25. Merleau-Ponty (1966), p. 4
26. Bugelski (1973), p. 517
27. Benner (1985), p. 591
28. Goldman (1986), p. 283

─────────── *Chapter 6* ───────────
Mind

Mind is best understood as the focal point of a process that involves the cognitive manipulation of perceptual and drive initiated data, and the (affective) convictions so induced. The products of the cognitive process are *concepts*, which are held to be true or false as a matter of *belief*, which represent the limit of knowledge at the mental level.

Conceptualization, or the ordering of concepts into classes, which is essential to deliberative and decision-making functions, is unique to the mental process only at a conscious level. The value inherent in the mental process relates essentially to the capacity of the individual to delay, or avoid, behavior mandated by the presence of a stimulus in the pre-mind individual.

Behavior is based on *beliefs*, which represent a state with well defined boundaries. Facts, judgments and evaluations, all are known only in the sense that they are convincing to at least some individuals. Efforts to improve emotional health must operate within that framework, destined to help or hinder only to the extent that the limitations as well as the advantages of mental knowledge are recognized.

When the individual functions at the level of primitive sensation (as does inorganic substance) and compelling drive, (as occurs in most plants), action occurs as a direct response to the forces of internal and external pressure. Although the sophistication of reaction potential is increased through learning, responses tend to remain relatively rigid. Activities which maximize individual survival and growth result in species preservation through the reproductive process, and the sacrifice of the individual when such destruction enhances the survival potential of the species or supraspecies. Thus, simple organisms and all living forms in *their* service (e.g., living animal cells) serve more complex existents, surviving or perishing as the greater need demands. Under such an arrangement an individual never can act counter to the pattern genetically prescribed, although it may strive to meet requirements of the plan in a variety of ways.

If life forms are to evolve, the type of knowledge that is made available through sheer drive and perceptual organization has many limitations. Where the mere attractiveness of a stimulus or the strength of an urge is the controlling factor, pursuit may be lethal. Sun-seeking in leafy plants, an activity which ordinarily results in the performance of essentially preservative functions, is potentially deadly should the sun become excessively strong. Improvements provided by learning capacity and perceptual sophistication, while valuable, do not begin to exhaust the potential methods for overcoming environmental hazard.

The fact that the individual with greater learning capacity is more apt to live, and thus reproduce, can be a factor only through the reproductive years, since knowledge which is utilized in later life provides no Mendelian advantage. In addition, change resulting from minute learning superiority may need to survive generations of regression before it persists. Thus, a significant improvement may not be incorporated in the gene pool for aeons.

Many of these limitations could be overcome if the individual were not bound to a reaction by the sheer presence of a drive whenever an opportunity to act arose. Undesirable situations might be avoided if action could be delayed, and planning could be accomplished if the emergence of a drive or the occurrence of a specific perceptual experience did not represent a demand for an immediate response. This type of signal reception (i.e., knowledge) would resemble a rheostat rather than an on-off light switch in that the degree of urgency of a drive and the quality of the stimulus could qualitatively interact. Activities could be carried out in terms of estimates of environmental opportunity as related to level of deprivation and the urgency of competing drives.

The structures which make possible such discrimination are a nervous system and, ultimately, a brain. A variety of invaluable functions are carried out by elements of the nervous system that are found in organisms far below the level of humans, and some of these perform indispensable maintenance services. However, at the highest levels of life, the evolution of the brain has made possible several unique processes; thinking (cognition), feeling (affect), and deliberating.

These functions are collectively identified as aspects of mind, which suggests the existence of a noncorporeal entity. They are, however, more accurately understood as mental *processes* or activities performed by the brain. When mind is involved, a unique set of relationships obtains, although even in an organism with such a capacity only a fixed group of activities is subject to local mediation.

The problem of understanding and explaining what is intended by the concept of *mind* has attracted more attention from philosophers than perhaps any other issue. For centuries, succeeding generations have proposed new interpretations of the human mind, and each ensuing generation has claimed to discover fallacies in prior explanations. Ryle, speaking of Cartesian dualism, said, "I hope to prove it is entirely false."[1] Penelhum, challenging Hume's conclusion, said that the Humean interpretation "gives us, I think, an excellent example of how complex and far reaching the consequences of a mistake in linguistic or conceptual investigation can be."[2]

Many interpretations of mind have been shown to contain serious flaws and have come to be generally rejected. However, the persistence of ostensibly mutually exclusive views (e.g., monism and dualism) suggests that both may be correct in that they may be focusing on different aspects, or that both may be wrong because of an error in principle which causes the wrong questions to be asked. Ryle, for example, claimed that Descartes' theory "is not merely an assemblage of mistakes. It is one big mistake and a mistake of a special kind. It is, namely, a category mistake."[3]

The game of outintellectualizing one's predecessors is of ancient lineage. Aristotle's "correction" of Plato's idealism was an early example, and Protagoras, impressed by this practice of continually revising interpretations of reality, suggested, perhaps cynically, that "what appears to each man to be is true for each man."[4]

Ayer complained that Descartes' proof of his own existence (*cogito ergo sum*) was fallacious because the addition of an existential term to a sentence is redundant.[5] To say, for example, while pointing to a tree: "That tree which exists is green" is a degenerate statement since it is a condition of the demonstrative that what one refers to exists. Ayers concluded that Descartes' proposition "I think," presupposes his existence and trivializes his dictum.

Such vehement reactions to philosophers as respected as Descartes, Hume, and others is cause for considerable caution, and the interpretation to be suggested here represents only a possible—but hopefully reasonable—way to interpret the phenomenon of mind. It is undoubtedly worth repeating that this text is not intended as a philosophic treatise. However, an understanding of the nature of mental processing requires the recognition of various well-developed viewpoints and some reaction to their assumptions.

To understand mental function it is necessary to consider the development of stimulus response styles from the patterned responses of the simplest life form to the complex brain processes in humans. Absurd as it may seem, the nervous apparatus of a simple spider is appropriately placed in the same category as that of the most highly developed living species, when one significant aspect of response type is under consideration.

This interpretation is inconsistent with the Cartesian notion that only humans have a mind, or mental process capacity. It is, however, supported by many modern thinkers whose definition of mind includes the phenomenal experiences of simple organisms. Brain, for example, said, "The behavior of bees and birds...exhibits features which, if they occurred in human beings, we should describe as mental, and I know of no reason for denying consciousness in some elementary form to comparatively simple organisms."[6] The principle on which such a determination is made is based on the distinction between organisms with sensors that mandate responses (e.g., plants) and those whose signals are only "suggestive." The point at which such a discrimination can be made is undoubtedly indistinct, but the significance lies in a recognition of that characteristic in organisms well below the human level of the life holarchy.

Several discrete steps may be identified in the evolution of the mental process, although some are exemplified in response styles at many developmental levels. At the simplest cell level, although there are many clearly distinguishable substructures, activity is determined by interaction which focuses on the totality. Nucleic and cytoplasmic components jointly operate to carry on cellular functions based on native irritability. In many instances action and reaction are limited to direct response to internal organizational states (active drives) and/or external stimulation (perception). Thus, a phototropic cell may flourish in limited exposure to light, while significantly more or less radiation will destroy it. Here no adaptive response is available and in cell groups with interdependent properties, the destruction of some number or percentage of cells will destroy the totality.

At a more efficacious level are cells and cell groups that are capable of responses that attract positive and/or avoid negative stimuli. A plant that closes its petals against destructive illumination is an example. In some cases, as in the translocation of photoperiodicity from one leaf of a plant to another, cellular response may be transmitted—perhaps hormonally—from cell to cell.[7] However, responses are rigidly patterned and are made by the same cell or those contiguous cells that are stimulated.

A greater degree of intricacy is found in organisms and organs where cell specialization results in the development of separate receptor and effector nervous tissue. Here receptors or sense organs, in some instances comprising only a single neuron, on being stimulated transmit a nervous impulse that impacts an effector system at some central location, such as the ventral nervecord in a planaria or the spinal column in humans. Through such a network taxis in simple organisms as well as reflexes and homeostatic functions in higher animals may occur. Still, all response patterns are fixed by the reception of a nervous impulse, and the energic condition of effector systems. There are neither options nor diversity in the manner in which responses occur, and it would be specious to apply the term *mind* to such functions, though the activity of a central nervous system is involved.

It was only when the nervous system added a distinct element to its information/knowledge system that the mental function evolved. The essence of this emergent process lies in the interruption of nervous discharges by mechanisms in the brain that interface and interpret neural messages.

Four unique characteristics have arisen from this vital modification. First, information is evaluated on a continuous or analogic scale, and comparative terms are born.[8] Today, some scientific writers believe that nature is quantized; that such things as electric charges exist in indivisible "units," which rules out the notion of magnitude as a continuous function. Pap claimed that, "we know nowadays that it [the continuity of physical existence] is false."[9] This inconsistency between the scientific "fact" of discontinuity and the perceptual conviction of continuous experience (as in observing a color pattern) has created one of the many problems faced by physical identity adherents. However, beyond the problem of assuming that the discrete nature of microscopic existence requires the abdication of principles of continuity, the critical issue is that at the macroscopic level, where decisions are made, discrete separation points cannot be discerned by mind.

Second, while rigid stimulus/response bonds allow only for action deemed valuable by genetic influence, this more sophisticated type of interpretative technique allows for reactions focused on the interest of the individual. The self comes into being. Now, personal preference and egocentric interests, sometimes of a positive nature but often injurious to self or fellow beings, enter into behavioral equations. Many such concepts as "this," "that," "here," and "there" acquire meaning only as related to some observing "I."

Third, the focus of attention on the individual is based on the fact that awareness, and thus consciousness, arises. This characteristic of mind, serving to make possible reactions to internal and external stimuli as signals become subject to local mediation, will represent one of the key elements in challenging the psychoanalytic positing of a dynamic unconscious. This use of the term conscious is, of course, subject to criticism from the scientifically oriented. Ashby, for example, proposed that consciousness, "vivid though [it] may be to its possessor," cannot be demonstrated by one individual to another. "And until such a method, or its equivalent, is found, the facts of consciousness cannot be used in scientific method."[10] However, on the assumption that awareness (mental or not) of a stimulus is essential to its processing, and since no communicable action need be involved, it is necessary at this level of understanding to presume consciousness as obligatory.

Finally, the proliferation of neuron interactions has led to a capacity to transcend immediate sensory experience, to hypothesize or imagine, to cognize and perform other complex mental processes. Each of these features will be developed in detail. It is necessary first, however, to stipulate as precisely as possible the meaning of mind or mental process to be conveyed in this text. In the most inclusive sense, it may be appropriate to include as part of mind all of the neurological paraphernalia associated with thought process. But although brain and mind are certainly closely associated, the distinction between an entity and an emanation or parameter must be recognized.

At the other extreme, it may be most accurate to limit mind to thought and ideas.

However, it is common practice to include elements such as perception, desire, emotion, and other experiential states as well. This would require that mind be considered to have two aspects, one of mere sensitivity, and one of the interpretation of such experiences. Although one may be aware of a negative sensation, it may require some degree of conceptualization to determine what type of discomfort is involved. The critical problem lies in the categorization being analyzed. Strictly speaking, there is no such *entity* as mind, as there is no such *thing* as an ego. When the term mind is employed, it references a phantasmagoric construct, a convenient— –though mythical—existent.

The practice of positing entities to describe functions is common. A flower is said to *have* a scent. In fact, it *does* something. The odor results from an emanation or emission arising from the flower under particular conditions. The fact that the scent characterizes certain chemical substances does not make it a thing. The term rather describes a sensory experience based both on the chemical properties of the emission and the perceptive capacity of a recipient. This distinction must be kept in mind [*sic*] as in the following discussion reference to mind may appear to represent it as an entity. This is unavoidable since in the literature such a categorization is invariably employed.

In the homeliest sense, mind (mental processing) represents a parameter of a knowledge state. It is activated when an individual is experiencing or knowing. The requirement for such activation is the possession of a mental capacity, and the attention value of a stimulus. In action, mind involves: The *cognitive* manipulation of drive, instinctively known or perceptually received data, the *conceptualization* that results and the *affective* conviction of the legitimacy of the concepts produced, as well as the *deliberations* that follow. Just as a scent may be added to a previously odorless exudation (by the admixture of specific chemicals), so mind represents an aspect or dimension of the form in which knowing occurs.

At the lowest level of mental activity, desires and perceptions may only be sufficiently acute to create an unidentifiable disturbance or balance reorganization. At this level, they shall be identified as *preconscious*, which approaches one pole of the mental continuum with acute (conscious) attention at the other. This is not to imply that there are discrete mental compartments. The range of mental activity runs from the sharp focus of immediate awareness, through a very dim level of attention, to a stage at which sensed material is volatile but below the level of attention essential to deliberation, and ultimately to the state of inactive memory. The lower levels may be described as subliminal in that they are out of conscious focus.[11]

The term preconscious, as it is employed here, is consistent with psychoanalytic usage in the sense that material involved is capable of becoming conscious under conditions of increased attention. In another sense, however, a critical distinction must be made. The psychoanalytic interpretation posits two types of nonconscious state. One, the preconscious (*Pcs*) is assumed to represent a "screen" between that aspect which is incapable of consciousness (the unconscious or *Ucs*) and the conscious mind. Freud proposed that, "The system Pcs not only bars access to consciousness, but also controls the access to voluntary motility."[12] Here no such role is assigned to preconscious processing. It is rather an extremely low level of mental experience, having no function as a steward of unconscious wishes, though much of its content may be withheld from conscious attention.[13]

Critical to this text is the contention that conceptualization and the problem solving process are unique to the conscious state. It is, in fact, only at the conscious level, where the various intellectual functions are involved, that deliberation and decision-making, and hence the potential for deliberate action, can take place. This interpretation requires the rejection of both dualist philosophies and the materialistic viewpoint of the identity and central-state theorists.

Dualists, Cartesian or not, assume the existence of an independent entity (mind) which interacts with the physical world. Among the many arguments for such a position is the claim that the mental or conscious process always includes an object, while physical entities do not. There are further claims that mind may exist in a unique space and that it may have temporal and causal characteristics. (At the opposite extreme are those that claim that the assignment of spatial dimension to physical objects is itself a presumption.)

Many of those who support the dualist position subscribe to the legitimacy of parapsychological phenomena, contending that it is impossible to establish a correspondence between brain function and, for example, telepathic communication. They contend that there must exist some extra-biological agent to account for such occult experiences. Others, (interactionists), suggest that voluntary behavior must be explained as caused by "a transcendental mind or 'self' acting upon the automatisms of the body."[14]

Such explanations, though offered by respected philosophers, are considered by the scientifically minded to be as obsolete as vitalism itself. Ryle argued that there is no warrant for presuming a "ghostly other world" in which mental occurrences take place. Emotions, desires, reason, and other feelings, he said, are incompetent to cause behavior. Such (mental) concepts represent only inculcations or tendencies that are attached to behavior or behavior potential. Ryle proposed that one who "expects" rain is, from the time of the origin of the expectancy, in an "expectant" condition, which is a persistent brain state. To attempt to characterize it objectively at any instant is impossible. Introspection, he said, is at best retrospection, which is a description of how one felt at some previous time.[15]

Rose proposed that "mind is the description of brain activity at a particular hierarchical level,"[16] which is consistent with the view presented here. It is, in fact, as real as love, justice, or hunger, for they too represent characteristics of entities. Coulter presented a similar argument. "Any theory of mind—when we are in a position to construct one, which at present is not the case—is going to form a part of a theory of social conduct and social conceptualization."[17] He thus dealt with mind as it represents interaction with the physical world, saying that we should *"treat the mental properties of persons as generated from situated, constitutive practices.*"[18] Such a view clearly denies mind's status as an entity *in* which things are kept. Mind is not a corporeal existent. Rather it describes an active/interactive *experience*.

Identity hypothesists have tended to dispose of mind as having *any* legitimate existence. An obvious example of this "nothing but" philosophy is provided by Beloff:

> The world consists exclusively of physical entities and physical space-time events. What, all this while, we have been calling the phenomenal facts are, it transpires, merely particular physical facts, i.e., brain states and brain processes, that happen to become known to us in a very special way, namely by direct acquaintance.[19]

Fodor added, "Mental events, states and processes are identical with neurophysiological events in the brain, and the property of being in a certain mental state [such as having a headache or believing it will rain]...is identical with being in a certain neurophysiological state."[20] Phenomenal or mental events are presumed to include ideas, volitions, sense-data, and other sensory experiences. They are the stuff that comprise the world of mental events as they are interpreted by dualist and idealist philosophies.

The identity hypothesis proposes empirical equivalence between phenomena and brain states in the sense that there is a common referent—the brain. The central-state materialist philosophers (e.g., Smart[21]) go further. Attributes such as color and taste are assumed to be mere characteristics of physical objects that cause particular responses in sentient beings. "Thus, perception is simply an acquiring of beliefs about the external physical environment *as a result of* sensory stimulation [while] introspection is an acquiring of beliefs about the internal physical environment."[22]

Feigl proposed a solution to the mind-body problem by defining phenomenal or personal-private experience as *acquaintance* knowledge, and third person or scientific knowledge as *descriptive*. This brand of critical realism (and, he says, "tentative reductionism") allows for the acceptance of mental knowing as unique. "The phenomenal event and the physical event are identical and yet known in different ways."[23] This interpretation is known as the qualitative-identity theory, as opposed to the physical identity theory which maintains that phenomenal experiences are merely disguised brain processes.

These views of mind reflect the general reductionist posture recognizable in the writings of thinkers who desire to synchronize philosophic speculation with the scientific zeitgeist. But criticism is widespread. Such problems as the lack of correspondence between phenomenal experience and brain topology, failure to account for mind as an evolutionary phenomenon, and the evidence of parapsychological occurrences have all been mentioned.

There is, however, a more serious issue; that of the status of an inactive mind.

Existentialist psychologists deny the possibility of imageless or empty thought. Brentano and others have pointed out that mental states have the peculiar quality of intentionality. They always take objects or are directed toward something. One thinks *about* something or wants some *thing*. Thinking and wanting do not exist in the abstract.

Brentano denied that the content of mental activity is a special class of existents.

> What we think about is the *object* or *thing* and not the "object of thought". If, in our thought, we contemplate a horse, our thought has as its imminent object—not a "contemplated horse" but a horse. [And, this is the case] whether or not there is anything outside the mind that corresponds to the thought.[24]

This poses a problem regarding the status of mental processing as a reflection or revelation of what exists prior to its interpretation. When Brentano dealt with universals he insisted that they are immediately or imminently contemplated. Although this makes no case for their existential verity it does presume that the action is that of an aware thinker.

Does this view equate mind with consciousness? Ducasse suggested that, "a mind *exists* in so far and only in so far as one or more of its capacities are *being exercised.*"[25] But he believed that it may be "exercised" unconsciously, as Feigl suggested in his contention that philosophers who deny the legitimacy of unconscious mental processes "stick to an (unfruitful) terminological decision according to which 'mental' is defined as 'phenomenal' or 'conscious.'"[26]

Other identity theorists seem to be more obviously referring to conscious states in their arguments. Quinton, for example, said, "the mental...consists of those states of affairs of which we can have direct awareness in the psychological sense, if we reflect or direct our attention appropriately."[27] Here, again, the suggestion that some *thing*—other than the brain—is involved. The holarchic interpretation sees mind as a dimension, and, (here, consistent with materialist philosophy), contends that it would make no sense to assume an independent reality.

An object is, in the final analysis, no more or less than the synergistic sum of its parameters. Thus, mentation is an indispensable property of the brain *in one of its active states*. Just as the attractive power of a magnet is an essential characteristic of that entity, the self-replicating capacity of certain carbon bearing molecules must be recognized as an influencing element. The awareness that accompanies certain brain states is just as much a part of the totality as the touch, the color, or the weight of the physical object.

Today many physicists assume that "matter" and "energy" are unreal, with only action and interaction having any true existence. Nevertheless, it is improper to state that mind is a separate entity. Mind, or mental processing, is rather a characteristic of a knowledge state. To assume otherwise would be equivalent to stating that one had a board *and* its dimensions, its color, and other attributes. Materialist theories propose that mental events are identical with brain or other neurophysiological events. Such interpretations are inadequate since they fail to separate the fact of being in a particular mental state from the physical elements which make such a state possible. This is similar to equating the experiencing of color with the electromagnetic vibrations that produce it.

Rejection of the identity hypothesis is based further on an acceptance of the notion of intentionality and its implication. If the mind were identical with the brain it would, in principle, be possible to be conscious of nothing. There could be states of awareness without content. Living beings who possess a mental capacity possess that attribute at all times. There is, however, a *latent* aspect in that not all mental processes are continually functioning. Some are merely potential. The statement, "John has a terrible temper," describes a predisposition. At some, but not all, times John may be said to be "displaying his temper," which is the equivalent of the exercise of mental activity as one wills, wishes, or deliberates.

Unconscious states, were they to exist, would represent mental processing in one of its functional aspects. What is claimed as being included in the unconscious ranges from the simplest mechanical processes described by researchers such as Shevrin and Dickman,[28] to the dynamic turbulence "revealed" through psychoanalysis. The critical factor is whether the point at which mental processes are assumed to occur is purely an arbitrary matter.

If conscious mental processing is the last in a series of steps—with the unconscious evolutionarily bisecting taxic response and deliberate action—there would seem no defense for setting a particular limit. However, our contention is that the emergence of the deliberative process split the world of the living into two *distinct* categories. If an unconscious mentality exists it represents not a forerunner but a residual aspect of conscious mental processing.

Mental processing occurs at many levels of awareness. The minimal arousal of desire and perceptual states represents mental activity in the sense that objects are taken and are being processed. However, this may occur at a preconscious level, where the content is as yet unidentified. Since awareness is awareness-of-something, mentality is a parameter of the *experience*. Consider several analogies.

- A bit of coal has physical dimensions at all times. When the coal is burning, it may exude an odor. The odor, however, is *not* a parameter of the coal but of the experience of (the coal) burning.
- A group of individuals may or may not be a team. If a team exists, it does so on the basis of a relationship or collective function. This cannot be determined by any physical aspect of any or all of them.

This is the level at which mentality must be involved. It is a collective term for the various mental processes and their (affective) impact. It is not identical with brain process as a physiological matter, but with the psychological elements involved.

The problem created by this view, which would perhaps be acceptable to interactionists, is that it proposes that an idea may cause a physical response. If I *see* a red object and *enjoy* the experience, I may buy a red shirt. The sensation, the phenomenal experience, can be credited as causal. Yet a parenthetical caveat must be considered. Monists (identity theorists) have so many "representations" that they can no doubt find a way to accommodate any rejection of their position.

Such proposals as the qualitative identity theory mentioned above as well as the double-language theory (i.e., the contention that physicalist language and introspective language describe the same event) demonstrate a practice similar to that followed by neo-Darwinists in their effort to prove evolution. Adherents are firmly convinced of the correctness of their view and expend immense energy in attempting to wrap an all-encompassing mantle over every possible aspect of the position. And it is our contention that monism *is* more accurate a representation than parallelism or other epiphenomenological interpretation, just as evolution is superior to creationist views of the origin of life. Both, however, are dependent on the *convictions* of introspective, personal-private, phenomenal individuals, whose zeal is a product of mental processing.

The question of the function associated with the evolution of mental process must also be considered. What is it that emerges in the individual that is possessed of consciousness? In pre-mind forms of life experience may result in alteration of the composition of the gene pool which is the only terminal for such information. Individuals possessing a mental capacity possess auxiliary terminals at which points information may be acted upon far more immediately. While, for example, the focus of injury to an individual in a pre-mind species is limited to possible alteration in the characteristics of ensuing generations, mentally endowed individuals can feel (localized) pain, and take remedial action relatively quickly. The same is true for all signals that are monitored by the individual with a mental faculty. It is this aspect of the process that represents its purpose.

In order to clarify the characteristics of mental processing that are essential to an understanding of the nature of mental knowledge, its various constituents will be analyzed, with the knowledge states involved being related to both internal and external information.

Cognition

Cognition is another of the many elusive psychological terms. It is employed sometimes as a verb, sometimes as a noun, and often carries adjectival inference. Cognition is separated from affect by some scholars, while others use it to embrace all mentality. Corsini, for example, said, "The most common separation [of the mind] is in two parts: Cognition and affection."[29] However, Lachman and Lachman included understanding and storage along with the active aspects of cognition: "[The] collection, storage, interpretation, understanding and use of environmental or internal information *is* cognition."[30] This confuses the processing of conceptual data with its impact on the individual, as well as with the memory (i.e., storage) of such information. Flexner defined cognition as "the act or process of knowing; perception."[31] This is misleading for several reasons. First, it considers knowing (a state of being—cognizance) to be a process (the act of cognizing). Then it equates cognition with perception, terms of clearly different implication.

If the separate contributions of the various mental elements are to be appreciated a distinction must be drawn. Thus, in this text, cognition shall be restricted to the representation of the *thinking* process or the use of the intellectual faculty. It is not, in itself, the awareness of information that has been organized by the primitive perceptual process. Rather, it relates such information to the many affective scales to be presently described. Cognition was characterized in this sense by Restak, who proposed that it represents "a process that refers to a broad range of mental 'behaviors,' including awareness, thinking, reasoning, and judgment."[32] Thus, cognition represents a characteristic of mind that is distinct from the experiencing of "raw feels," from introspective sensation, from phenomenological awareness. (We depart from Restak in excluding "awareness" from his set of "processes.")

Cognition embraces all of the *actions* of mind including, in addition to conceptualization, such processes as abstraction, generalization, recall, and memorization (but not abstractions, memories, etc., as such). It also includes the analytic and synthetic functions which Silvern suggested be referred to as *anasynthesis* since the two ordinarily occur serially.[33] Beyond this, the cognitive process deals with the interrelating of information from all data inputs (i.e., comparing percepts with each other and to desire, as well as to the various judgmental scales). However, it does *not* represent the experience described as awareness. It refers rather to the manipulation of the material *about* which one is aware. In the case of desire and emotion, for example, it is limited to the labelling of an affective experience.

Cognition occurs at levels of awareness ranging from the highest intensity of attention to the lowest degree of consciousness. It makes possible the interpretation of things and events on first acquaintance because of their similarity to previously encountered stimuli. Further, it provides the opportunity to recognize in novel situations potential usefulness, danger, and/or other relevant characteristics. To cognize, however, is not to *believe*, but to present or order data which may or may not be affectively accepted. It is dependent on native capacity, previous experience and learning, and on the nature of stimulus patterns. In the simplest forms of mental life it functions in a relatively primitive manner. Animals that instinctively know the value of perceived situations may be unable to alter such knowledge through cognitive processing. At the highest levels it is possible to apply the process to hypothetical situations, as in conjecturing whether any form of prevention would eliminate a particular disease.

Our analysis of behavior focuses on activity which involves environmental interaction. Such activity requires opportunity if it is to be expressed. However, the cognitive process itself qualifies as behavior in that one may decide whether or not to perform a particular function, such as computation. This form of behavior also requires external opportunity (freedom from distraction), as well as internal opportunity (freedom from alternative demand for cognitive processing), if a behavior is to ensue.

To the extent that cognition is considered an action, it is not in conflict with the neo-behaviorist contention that thinking is, in fact, implicit or unobservable behavior. However, the behavior involved may or may not be the subliminal physiological response that is claimed. To think, to consider, or to measure, all represent processes that describe actions rather than actors, and their operation as neural firings or molecular reorganizations represent only their mode of operation. Two sticks may be rubbed together to start a fire, beaten together to provide a rhythm, nailed together to form a cross, or painted white to make a fence. Finding in them the commonality "two sticks" reveals nothing of their function. In summary, cognition describes the *action* involved in mental processing. It refers to what one *does* by way of manipulating data and deriving increasingly sophisticated concepts.

Conception

All types of information produce mental images. Such images, thoughts, or ideas may be defined as *concepts*. Klausmeier suggested that, "a concept is the meaning or meanings that the individual associates with words, other signs, and direct sensory experiences."[34] Deese spoke of "concept attainment" and "concept formation,"[35] while Hergenbahn spoke of "cognitive structures"[36] as representing the products of the cognitive process. These general definitions describe what we intend to be the images formed by thought processes.

Concepts are developed through the process of *conception* or *conceptualization*, which is a subset of cognition. For many psychologists, such constructs are dependent on language and are expressed only as words or expressions. The holonic interpretation of information systems, however, requires the acceptance of the notion that many animals are capable of cognitive activity and of producing symbolic images which provide for the ordering of subsequent information, albeit in a less sophisticated manner.

Conceptualization is a superior process to the perceptual ordering that characterizes the preconscious aspect of mental experience. It refers to the process of generalizing from a particular to a class or many classes, and the reverse. The concept as a product is meaningful as related to larger classes, and provides meaning to its elements. When such information as desire is involved, the problem is more complex. To know (i.e., to have knowledge of) a desire such as hunger is to have the capacity to identify the state when it occurs; but to be *knowing* it requires that it be experienced *as a desire*. In this sense, at the level of mind concepts must be consciously known at the time they are being experienced. They do not, however, require language in order to qualify as knowledge.

Affect

Although cognition is a highly sophisticated function, it does not represent the possession of knowledge but only the method by which information is processed. Concepts, similarly, are not in themselves knowledge, but rather represent that which is *known*. Affect references the many feeling states that represent evidence of the activity of internal and external information vehicles. Feelings of desire, attitudinal and sentimental reactions, temperamental and mood states, emotional experience, and the awareness of the perceptual senses all impinge on the individual as forms of mental knowledge. Each must be dealt with separately.

In this section, one of the less commonly recognized types of affect, the feeling state associated with convictions concerning the nature of conceptualization, must be considered. A distinction must be drawn between a cognitive action, a concept, which is an idea, and the appreciation or understanding of that concept, which is a form of affect. "Treeness" and "sweetness" are generalizations from experiences as identified by separate senses. As concepts, they embrace examples and are projected against the affective system for understanding. To say that a tree is a form of plant life is to move from one conceptual level to another, which is a cognitive process. However, to believe that the concept is appropriate is an affective experience.

This provides a point of view on the argument concerning which conceptualization is "correct." Is the color-blind individual perhaps as correct as others? To the extent that the information gained or the behavior of the individual is homeorhetic, it is possible to draw the meaningful conclusion that there is a *most accurate* concept. The quality of a conceptual experience has a referent which removes it from the speculative. There must be, in fact, a most accurate concept regardless of whether the individual is competent to recognize it. The expression "most accurate" deals with the knowledge in a living being which makes possible an experience that triggers those mechanisms designed to encourage an effective response.

Consider the capacity of a chicken to recognize the hawk because of its instinctively known color and shape. Genetic history has provided that species with the capacity to relate a particular form to an emotional or behavioral reaction and a conceptual error may be fatal.

But the senses are often in conflict. In a figure such as ⊥ the illusion is created that the vertical line is longer. When they are measured, it is discovered that the perception was inaccurate. When an auditory experience is in conflict with a visual one (as in studies with reversed earphones), either a priority is posited or an appeal is made to another sense—perhaps tactual. This apparently results from a flexibility at higher levels of conceptualization which makes possible superior adaptation. However, it does represent a limitation on the dependability of any specific conceptualization and indicates the subjective nature of the system.

The significance of this distinction seems to escape many of those who describe the cognitive process. In discussing the problem of how concepts are attained, such notions as "the *acceptance* [italics added] of facts" have been employed which are clearly affective.[37] Bruner, in asking how one knows when a concept has been learned, said that a "naïve" interpretation would be:

> when he *feels* [italics added] he is able to predict the status of new instances with a high degree of certainty [and that] for simplicity's sake, it is often better to bypass the question and to ask instead whether the attributes that are critical for the subject in his categorizing judgment are also the attributes that are defining of the concept.[38]

Having disposed of the problem in this manner, Bruner concluded, "Let it be clear, however, that some people require many more encounters beyond this point before they *feel* [italics added] any degree of certainty," and that it is really all a matter of judgment, which is based on "what consequences *seem* [italics added] reasonable."[39] It *seems* incredible that such an explanation could be accepted, when *affect* is so obviously the key element! The distinction among conceptualization, which is the act of classifying; cognition, which is a process of thinking or doing; concepts which are the product of such activity, and affect, which is an experience regarding the conviction of the legitimacy of these performances, must be understood.

Consider the two statements: $2+2=4$ and $2+2=5$. Each is a cognitive production (concept), but one is believed (felt) to be correct. In such simple instances, the distinction is obvious. However, a statement such as "Intelligence is an acquired characteristic," is felt to be true by some and false by others. The argument that in this case "all of the data is not in" fails, since all of the data can never be "in," except (perhaps) in the case of tautological statements.

Some psychologists have pointed out the need for an organizational system to which cognition must relate. Norman, for example, said, "it may well be that it is the cognitive component that is subservient, evolved primarily for the benefit of the regulatory system, working through the emotions, through affect."[40] But few theorists have followed his suggestion. Higher levels of cognition, in the form of more subtle manipulative techniques, represent only an increase in the ways in which data may be treated. Superior intellectual (cognitive) skill does not represent the possession of greater knowledge, but only the capacity to generate it.

Cognition relates to knowledge as the musician to music, being only an instrument of the process; or as eating relates to tasting, the latter being essential to a knowledge of what is eaten. To perform the inductive operation is a cognitive act, but the conviction that the sun will rise tomorrow because it always has, resides in an experience that transcends the intellectual exercise. The *ability* to perform a cognitive act is, of course, a form of knowledge. It represents, however, knowledge only of its *function*, not of the quality or *veracity*, of its products.

The limbic system is believed to represent the principal structural seat of affect. It includes homeostatic elements, which automatically correct deviant action, as well as providing "a neural substrate for motivational and affective (including emotional) processes,"[41] which must be separately identified. Although the limbic system becomes less rigidly regulative in higher forms of life, this is not because of its replacement by the cognitive function, but because a more sophisticated form of affect (i.e., reason) becomes increasingly operative.[42]

In simple forms of life, the chain from perception to response is tied directly to the activation of a drive. With the evolution of the cognitive process, increasingly finer distinctions can be made between concepts. The evolution of that improved facility has resulted in the erroneous conviction that a new capacity (cognition) operates to replace (emotional) affects. However, what the cognitive process replaces is instinctive knowledge. It functions in a mechanical, computer-like way. In lower organisms, the individual "knows" what to do, which fixes responses within a narrow band. In higher forms, learning occurs partly due to the cognitive process. The result is an improved potential for presenting data for affective consideration.

Many types of affect can be identified. *Desire* as a feeling state related to primitively needed experiences, (to be described in Chapter 7), includes several discrete classes. *Emotion*, a complex interaction of desire and conceptual belief, is the principal component of the motivational process.

Belief

When knowledge is activated as a mental phenomenon, knowing occurs in the form of *belief*, which is an affective experience, based on innate knowledge, or cognitively processed information. This is the epistemological limit of mental experience, regardless of whether the data are drawn from internal or external sources.

Insofar as perceptual information is concerned, the mere manipulation of data would be meaningless without resonators against which it could be tested. It is, in fact, argued by some epistemologists that no perceptual experience is "value free," or without a conceptual referent. The conceptual process is verified by the conviction that particular percepts are related to specific categories. Furthermore, even the highest level of intellectual performance would represent only mechanical cognitive computation resulting in automatic responses without the function of affective reaction, and the belief states that conceptualization generates. A paralyzing confusion in the development of theories of knowledge has resulted from an unwillingness to accept this premise.

Mental knowing is an affective experience. To know (i.e., be knowing) is to have a feeling about the legitimacy of contentions regarding processed information. This expression of knowledge is unique in the universe. Although it is based on the organizational state of the individual as tempered by learning and experience, as well as by some forms of instinctive patterning, it is held as a matter of degree. Contrasted with learning, which is a dichotomous state, mental knowing is limited to levels of strength or degree of assurance, and *no such expression of knowledge transcends this limitation*. Affect, thus, is the precursor and foundation of belief.

Because the term belief is used to describe varying degrees of conviction (e.g., I believe in God; I believe that it will rain tomorrow; I believe I have a chance to win the race), it has been widely argued that a difference should be drawn between belief and knowledge. The issue has been treated by hundreds of philosophers, for thousands of years.

Hume, highly respected for his conceptualization of belief, as well as other mental constructs, challenged the empiricist philosophy that had dominated British thinking during the previous century, proposing that the "ideas" that Locke had assumed to come only from experience were in actuality of two kinds. Substituting the term *perception* for Locke's "ideas," he suggested that those involved with experiencing or sensing and which represent "our more lively perceptions" be defined as *impressions*.[43] By contrast, *ideas* were to refer to "the less lively perceptions."[43]

The data (conceptions) of ideas, in combination with the "force and vivacity" of impressions were assumed to create beliefs, which are "nothing but a firmer and stronger conception of an object."[44] His thesis was that an idea is no different because it is believed to be true, except that it is held more forcefully. We take issue with his assumption that beliefs are no more than intense ideas. Rather, they represent entirely separate aspects of an experience.

Consider the idea of a five legged horse. As an idea (using Hume's contention), it is merely a faint image of impressions based on previous experience with "legs" and "horses." Belief about the existence of a five legged horse is a conviction based on any or all of the data available that bears on the existential verity of the idea. An idea is a mental image, a conceptualization. A belief is a degree of conviction (in this case, that such a horse actually exists). It is a matter of sense or feeling, rather than of mental manipulation. In point of fact, Hume, at another time made the point—with which we concur—that "belief consists not in the particular nature or order of ideas, but in the *manner* of their conception, and in their *feeling* to the mind."[45] Such terms are obviously affective.

Those who attempt to distinguish belief from knowledge would not disagree with Hume's description. However, they would contend that somehow, out of this affective experience, true knowledge may develop. Russell, for example, said: "Every case of knowledge is a case of true belief, but not vice versa."[46] And further, "What an asserted sentence expresses is a *belief*; what makes it true or false is a *fact* which is in general distinct from a belief."[47] His "facts" were "everything that there is in the world....The sun is a fact; Caesar crossing the Rubicon was a fact."[48]

But Ayer insisted that to know something is to *believe* it to be true, that it be true, and that there are good reasons to believe it.[49] He distinguished belief from knowledge by saying that one may be completely sure of a belief that does not meet the condition of being knowledge (being in fact false, for example). "But whereas it is possible to believe what one is not completely sure of...this does not apply to knowledge."[50] Ryle made things no simpler in his statement that although both terms refer to dispositions, "knowing refers to a capacity and believing to a tendency,"[51] adding that knowing is "to be equipped to get something right."[51] This suggests a correspondence between the knower and the "truth out there."

The confusion generated by these shifting interpretations led Stroud, a critic of Hume's philosophy, to conclude: "No adequate theory of the nature of belief has been given to this day, and that is probably because it has been investigated in virtually complete independence from the notions of passion, desire, will and action."[52]

But some current thinkers have taken "passion" into account. They have assigned the passions to belief, and set out to show that such affective states are not a characteristic of knowledge. Roth and Galis summed their approach to the belief/knowledge distinction in the statement:

> Any attempt to provide a thorough assessment of the traditional analysis must ultimately consider the objection...that knowledge is not a kind of belief at all.... Knowing something to be true and believing something to be true are *entirely* separate and distinct and neither can legitimately occur in the analysis of the other.[53]

Such interpretations suffer from a common misconception. At the level epistemologists define knowledge, its separation from belief is impossible. The process can be compared to attempting to distinguish *lunch* from *meal*, or *man* from *person*. One is a subset of the other. They can be distinguished only as to level, not as mutually exclusive experiences. Hospers claimed that they differ in that:

> In believing that *p* is true we are *merely* having a certain state of mind or attitude toward the statement we are believing; but when we *know* that *p* is true, a *further condition* must be fulfilled: *p* must really be *true*.[54]

This was augmented by the requirement that there be "complete evidence that *p* is true,"[54] which is only the case when no further evidence would make *p* more probable. Ayer, in a similar vein, argued that:

> The necessary and sufficient conditions for knowing that something is the case are first that what one is said to know be true, secondly that one be sure of it, and thirdly that one should have the right to be sure.[55]

Malcolm distinguished between *strong* and *weak* uses of the term knowledge:

> When I say that I know something to be so using "know" in the strong sense, it is unintelligible to me (although perhaps not to others) to suppose that anything could prove that it is not so and, therefore, that I do not know it.[56]

The refutation of these arguments can be made on empirical as well as rational grounds. Both the limitation of the inductive process to the prediction of probability according to Humean philosophy and the historical evidence of changes in what are accepted as truths demonstrate the inadequacy of the proposals as an empirical matter. Russell's homely example of the expectant chicken, whose inductive process led him to believe he would be fed forever, corroborates our contention that *all* mental knowledge is limited to *belief*. "The man who has fed the chicken every day throughout its life at last wrings its neck instead, showing that more refined views as to the uniformity of nature would have been useful to the chicken."[57]

But there is also a logical conundrum. An example may be taken from Chisolm's set of conditions for knowledge.[58] Along the same lines as Ayer and Malcolm, he contended that the necessary and sufficient conditions for knowledge are that the desideratum be true, that it be accepted, and that the acceptance be based on adequate (justifiable) evidence.

Gettier disagreed. He believed that he could provide "proof" that "it is possible for a person to be justified in believing a proposition that is in fact false."[59] Following Gettier's analysis, a variety of philosophers joined in the search for the proper definition of truth (i.e., true knowledge). Skyrms claimed that "all the revised definitions that have appeared are inadequate,"[60] after which he offered his own explanation.

Goldman provided a variety of interpretations. "A belief qualifies as truth [i.e., knowledge]...when its content is a true proposition."[61] And "in a loose sense, a person knows something (a proposition) if he believes it and it is true."[62] Unger offered a most strident dissent. Pointing out along the way that "as my analysis dictates, we must give up the idea that factual knowledge is any sort of justified true belief, or anything of the like,"[63] he offered his own interpretation, concluding that, "apparent problems now appear to be resolved entirely, this resolution affording further support for my analysis of human factual knowledge."[64]

The blatant immodesty of Unger's claim points up the question to be dealt with. Once again the practice of destroying a predecessor's argument is considered part of the game. But this time it raises a specter that stands outside the analysis of any of the viewpoints represented.

Take the general proposition "p is a case of true knowledge if...." Considering that each of those authorities that claim to know how to separate belief from knowledge provide different conditions, would each:

- Claim that only his was a case of true knowledge?
- Contend that a proper set of conditions exists but that to date they may not have been discovered?
- Allow that each was only one person's *belief*?

The first claim, beyond being presumptuous, makes every other position an example of "justified" true belief, which each author denies is knowledge. Of course, each claimant would argue that for others' contentions, at least one condition was lacking—the factual truth of the proposition. But, how would each "know" that his was the factually true proposition? The best that can be said about the second alternative, in the face of the evidence of so many "erroneous" efforts, is that it is a strongly held belief. But is it as convincing as the (questionable) proposition that all black cats are black? Choosing the final alternative, which is the argument of this text, would be to accept the limitation of belief. But that would be considered preposterous, since epistemologists claim that belief and knowledge are entirely separate concepts.

All such contentions fall on one simple issue: What compels acceptance of the claims? Are they known in some way separate from belief? A common answer is that to refuse to accept certain forms of knowledge as true beyond the limitation of belief (e.g., deductive relationships or analytic statements) would be self-stultifying in that it would make communication impossible. Furthermore, it is argued, if one denies that $p \supset p$ represents an example of true knowledge, and the denial is asserted as true knowledge, the very law of identity which has been denied is ostensibly validated. But this too is an unwarranted assertion. The denial represents no more than a refusal to accept the claim that the proposition is true beyond belief, not a claim that its rejection is an ultimate truth (i.e., simply do not believe that I must accept its special knowledge status).

In all cases, belief (not that which is believed) represents an affective condition. It is the nature of this form of knowledge that it can never reach an absolute state, being always limited to a matter of degree—even where mathematical propositions are involved. To claim knowledge of the process of deduction is to profess an ability to perform an operation (to know how). But, a problem would arise, if one claimed that the application of the deductive process mandated acceptance of its conclusions without the mediation of some feeling state. Why should such an argument be accepted? How much data is sufficient to warrant unequivocal conviction? Such questions require a capacity that exceeds that of the belief system.

Belief, with all of its limitations, represents the most sophisticated expression of knowledge, being a flexible, resilient, and docile medium for the interpretation of information. The deductive argument is convincing because it creates a positive affective situation. It seems correct; it makes sense; it persuades.

Much of the problem with distinguishing between elements of the mental process is based on confusion among actions, reactions, and consequences; among process, products, and interpretations. The distinction between verb forms as they describe actions and states of affairs, is not, in all instances, clearly drawn. To distinguish between these varied usages, consider the data in Table 6.1.

To cognize represents the performance of an action. The result or product of such action is a concept. Convictions regarding qualities such as the veracity of the concept are beliefs. Thus, knowing (i.e., believing) is not an action but a reaction or consequence, and what is believed (i.e., the conceptualization) is that aspect of the process that is subject to error.

Table 6.1

Action/Reaction/Consequence/Interpretation

1. Action
   (process)
   Focuses on the initiation or continuation of an event sequence; action aspect of a verb.

   behavior
   a. One *leaps* from a window
   One *studies* French
   One *thinks* (cognizes)

   nonbehavior* b. Lightning *strikes* a house

2. Reaction
   (product)
   Focuses on direct outcome; occurrence aspect of a verb.

   a. One *falls*
   One *learns* French
   One *has* a thought (concept)

   b. The building *burns*

3. Consequence
   (significance)
   Focuses on indirect outcome or contingency

   a. One *hits* the ground
   One *has knowledge* of French

   b. The building is *destroyed*

4. Interpretation
   (understanding)
   The concept is believed to be valid (affect)

* action without deliberation

Applying this model, presume that I *feel* a condition of malaise. I think about it. What do I want? I draw the conclusion that I am hungry. This concept or *belief* cannot be precisely known. It may be erroneous. However, the condition of malaise (the experiencing of discomfort) is exact. It is not subject to "truth" analysis. It is, in fact, not mental. The distinction here is between a physical or psychological feeling and its interpretation. The former is an experience, the latter an explication.

It was pointed out in Chapter 5 that epistemologists begin with the assumption that knowledge is an intellectual matter. By so doing, they confine epistemology to mind, and especially to human deliberation. Such a position is destructively parochial since it hinders the development of a thesis which can reveal the developmental characteristics of the cognitive/affective process. Furthermore, these philosophies fail to make a case even for human knowledge, since they also dichotomize knowledge and belief.

The rationalist contention that truth can be arrived at through the application of deductive, *a priori*, principles is itself only a belief regardless of its compelling nature. Modern symbolic logic with its truth tables reveals no ineluctable relationships but avoids the ambiguities of ordinary language through the application of symbolic conventions. Powerful as they are, they do not surpass belief. By reducing propositions to their formal characteristic, logicians presume to provide criteria of meaning. But this is no more valid than the pragmatist proposition that meaning is limited to the consequence of actions.

The Empiricist reaction, although it denies innate knowledge and insists on the pre-eminence of experience as the epistemic vehicle, also considers knowledge as an intellective or cognitive affair (and thus purely mental). Affective or emotive statements are reduced to attempts to communicate feelings. Along with many forms of judgment, they are considered unrelated to truth on the basis that they are noncognitive. The radical empiricist rejects even the capacity of mind to impose relationships onto the data of experience, contending that such processes themselves are experientially derived and of a cognitive nature.

The cause of the rationalist/empiricist disagreement is the erroneous assumption of each school regarding the relationship between cognition and knowledge. Such an interpretation follows naturally from the misunderstanding of such concepts as perception and learning discussed earlier.

Part of the reason for this confusion may lie in the difference between *knowing* as a conscious experience, and *having knowledge of* as a state of being. "Conscious" knowing represents simply the affective instance of an *experience* which is available in a different form at pre-mind levels. To "have knowledge of," where what is known are symbolic relationships, language, etc., may represent a result of learning based, in part, on cognitive skill. But, this is not mental; it is neuromuscular reorganization. To have knowledge of (i.e., to have learned) algebra changes the potential for action, but the conscious experience of knowing that one possesses algebraic knowledge is some degree of belief. Unfortunately, the expression *to know* is used to describe both aspects. It is essential to distinguish which usage is intended if the process is to be properly interpreted. At the level of mind, to "know" is to believe.

A similar problem arises from the use of the term *understanding*. Here the issues of how well, in how many ways, and in what relationships, a concept is known are raised. Degrees are appropriately involved. One may understand how to avoid being beaten at tic-tac-toe quite completely with minimal intellectual skill. By contrast, the game of chess may be understood at many levels of sophistication. The principle is that regardless of the degree of understanding, the limit, at that level, is the conviction or belief that one knows.

In order to deal with the problem of associating knowledge with truth, it is essential first to determine what is meant by the condition that for something to be known it must be "true." Presumably, to be *true* means to possess existential status; to be the case in the perceptual world. Knowledge by this definition is the correspondence between a knower, and something which is external to the one who knows. But the knowledge state is a contingency of the structure of the knower, which alone is sufficient to limit what is known to the peculiar organizational state of the individual. And, this is no different in the individual possessed of a mind than for inorganic entities.

To caricature the distinction between knowing at a pre-mind level (where it is precise) and belief as a characteristic of mental knowledge (which is by its nature imprecise), we offer the following example. Consider a bit of iron which has knowledge such that it responds to the presence of oxygen by combining and creating a residue called rust. Every such inorganic entity responds on the basis of a discrete knowledge system. A specific amount of oxygen results in a specific amount of rust. No oxygen, no rust. X amount of oxygen, X amount of rust. (Other factors are, of course, involved, but they follow the same principle.)

In spite of the fact that the amount of oxygen present may be measurable by some agent with such a capacity, that fact cannot be discerned by the iron. This is not due to a characteristic of the oxygen, but to a limitation of the form that knowledge takes in the iron. The iron cannot deal with such concepts as "about" or "approximately." It is competent to handle only yes/no issues. The concept of *measurement* has no meaning. It does not exist for iron. Iron can make no distinction between degrees of heat (molecular action) and the presence of one or two "units" of oxygen.

Pre-mind organic entities possess quite the same kind of knowledge, with the critical distinction that communication is involved. When a chlorophyll containing plant responds to the presence of sunlight by photosynthesizing, it is communicating on the basis of a capacity provided by the genetic plan. Except for the communication aspect, the discrete nature of responses remains the same as for that of the inorganic.

In such instances, knowledge is limited both by the peculiarities of the knowing individual (i.e., the perceptual train) and by its discrete form. Future, past, and other nonpresent elements, play no part. As a result, there is no way in which such knowledge could be a true—or false—representation of what exists-in-the-world.

With the emergence of mind, a system of knowledge appears which is unique in the universe. At the conscious level, mind is based on a continuous knowledge scale. It is a system of measurement; analogic rather than digital, progressive rather than binary. "More" and "less," "much" and "little," "almost" and "practically" come into being where the knowledge resides in the belief system, which in the living individual is a product of the cognitive/conceptual/affective system. The affective aspect is the element which prohibits precise knowledge, and which mandates the skeptical or fallibilist interpretation presented here.

Skepticism is itself widely criticized. Smythies was annoyed by "the sea-green incorruptible logical Skeptics who demand rigorous proof for every statement, especially for those asserting the existence of anything."[65] But in the case of knowledge, the "skeptical" view proposed here is only an alternative to the "sea green" presumption that some propositions are irrevocably true.

Ayer supported Smythies' view. He insisted that "there are a great many statements the truth of which we rightly do not doubt."[66] (Note that he is referring here to propositions.) In fact, he warned that "we should not be bullied by the skeptic into renouncing an expression for which we have a legitimate use."[66] His "legitimate use," of course is to equate the *almost* exact with the exact—an astounding presumption.

This rejection of the fallibilist view pervades modern philosophy. We are accused of using terms like "certain" in a far too extreme sense. "But since [the fallibilist] assigns a new, unusually strong meaning to this word [certain] his disagreement with the common sense view is merely *verbal*."[67] We would protest that such an interpretation (which infers that the common sense use of "certain" means "not quite certain," or "almost certain") is absurd. Further, it misses the significance of the distinction as it bears on human behavior. (They could, of course, discard Hume's limitation of the inductive process on the same grounds—that in assuming natures regularity, they do not mean "certain" predictability!)

Once again, an analogy may assist understanding. I believe (a) Sally is 21 years old (discrete data), and that (b) she is an attractive woman (continuous data). It would appear that the difference resides in the kind of statement being dealt with. However, it is rather a characteristic of the affective system. Compare this with the knowledge possessed by the bit of iron mentioned earlier, as shown in Figure 6.1.

In each case, characteristics of the *receiver* determine the form in which knowledge is held. In the case of the iron, the fact that the data may be considered continuous as a mental conviction makes no impression. Regarding knowledge about Sally, my conviction about her age, though based on the most sound evidence, remains no more than a belief. To expect mental knowledge ever to be sufficient to deal with the distinction between the belief that "She is pretty" and the knowledge of her prettiness where the latter represents an exactitude is patently absurd.

Although it may seem obvious that prettiness is a judgment which cannot be precise, it does appear that the statement "She is 21" is of a different nature. They are, however, both matters of belief. The problem lies in failing to recognize that in each case the conviction of legitimacy is limited by the statement, "I believe (am convinced) that she is 21," and it is *here* that the mental measurement function operates.

When the experience that knowledge makes possible is considered, four kinds of condition are involved: (a) pre-mind experience, (b) pre-mind knowing, (c) mental

Figure 6.1

Pre-mind/Mental Knowledge

TRANSMITTER CHARACTERISTICS

Pre-mind Knowledge		Mental Knowledge	
Discrete Data	Continuous Data	Discrete Data	Continuous Data
There is oxygen	There is some some amount of oxygen	Sally is 21 yrs. old	Sally is pretty

RECEIVER CHARACTERISTICS

Discrete - Digital	Continuous - Analogic
binary - yes/no functions	progressive - measurement
precise knowledge	affect - belief

experience, and (d) mental knowing. The first three of these are internally valid. As Ayer asserted, "Our experiences themselves are neither certain nor uncertain; they simply occur."[68] This, of course, is equally so for the knowledge and experiences of nonliving entities. It is only in the fourth case (d) that a difference may be noted, and here Ayer made a statement that is accurate for the conscious aspect of knowing:

> It is only with the use of language that truth and error, certainty and uncertainty come fully upon the scene. It is only such things as statements or propositions, or beliefs or opinions, which are expressible in language, that are capable of being true or false, certain or doubtful.[68]

Ayer's definition reveals the problem with attempting to distinguish knowledge from belief since the term "certain," which he employed as an antonym for "doubtful," differs only in degree. He made the statement that it is only at the level of propositions that truth is at issue, employing a simile of Ryle's (There can be false coins only where there are coins made of the proper materials by the proper authorities) to make the point that some propositions must be "true." "It is true," Ayer stated, "that no judgments of perception would be specially open to distrust unless some were trustworthy."[69]

But the statement, "There could be no blue unless other colors existed," is entirely different (though still only a belief) than "There could be no white cats unless there were non-white cats." In the second instance, the dimension of color is not exhausted by cats, for the existence of anything of another color would allow for the possibility that all cats be white.

In the case of belief, where the comparable statement would be, "There can be no imperfect knowledge (i.e., belief) unless there is perfect knowledge," the situation parallels that of the white cats. There *is* a form of knowledge which differs from mental knowledge; and there are mental and nonmental experiences, all of which are parts of the knowledge domain. It is these aspects of knowledge which represent the referents against which to project the status of mental knowledge.[70]

Returning to the concepts of subliminal desire and conception, when the only impact of the situation is a heightened, undefined tension state, the experience is described as preconscious. However, prior to the conscious conceptualization of the appropriate desire, there may be a belief state. (I believe that I am disturbed.) Knowledge is not of the same form that it takes in pre-mind and nonliving entities.

The distinction between conscious and preconscious aspects of an experience resides in the individual's determination regarding the nature of their discomfort. If people "realize" that they are hungry, a conscious conceptualization is being made. However, the mere recognition of a stimulus without specific assignment can, at most, involve only belief. In neither case is there a condition of mental knowledge that exceeds belief. Only prior to the recognition and assignment of a stimulus is belief transcended, but in this case no conceptualization and thus no potential error is involved.

This provides an explanation for the contention of Husserl,[71] Ayer,[72] and others that experiences may represent true knowledge (knowledge that exceeds belief) because there is no external criterion against which to evaluate them. While unconceptualized experiences require no external referent, neither do such experiences have a belief aspect. To assume that one is experiencing "thirst," for example, *is* a belief because the interpretation of the feeling as having a specific character represents the *labeling* of an affective state. The feeling that exists prior to the labeling does not meet the conditions that are included in Ayer's arguments. His analyses always dealt with propositional (and thus conceptualized) situations.

The reason that a belief is only held as a conviction is not necessarily because there is reason to doubt it, but because that is the form in which it is known. To insist that "I know unequivocally that I am hungry" is always constrained by the limitation of the nature of the belief process which operates on a measurement scale. To have unconceptualized experience is a form of knowing that transcends belief. To *believe* that one is "having an experience" is a different matter entirely. Phenomenologists insist that the perceptual experience defines truth. Such views make possible multiple truths—in fact quite as many as there are experiences—which itself robs truth of the very meaning they propose, unless truth (and thus "true knowledge") need not parallel external world events.

Under such interpretations, experiences may represent "true" knowledge. They may not be limited to the belief state described here. However, this is only the case as long as they are unconceptualized. *Seeing* a "green" object and *labeling it such* are different experiences; for the question arises as to whether others would undergo the same experience when perceiving the same entity. This is not to engage in solipsism. An individual with a different nervous system may, of course, have a different internal state. Proof of this is impossible, but it is unnecessary so long as there is consistency in communicating the experience. (In Feigl's terms, while the *acquaintances* may differ in their nature, common *descriptions* may satisfy the equation of similarity.)[73]

But this approach to truth avoids any mental manipulation. The Cartesian principle that the experiencing of ideas precede any investigation of truth was based on the notion that matter is known through mind. "Before examining whether any such objects as I conceive exist outside of me, I must consider the ideas of them in so far as they are in my thoughts."[74] However, by *thoughts*, or *mind* Descartes meant the *convictions* that one holds. Zen practice also separates interpretation from sensation. Truth in each instance is reduced to the primitive experience. Unfortunately, such truths are unavoidably modified by the idiosyncratic characteristics of the perceiver, when they reach the level of interpretation and communication. The critical factor is that truth, *as a mental phenomenon*, can never exceed the limitation imposed by the nature of belief.

Mental Learning

The peculiarity of mind, in that it limits knowledge as a mental experience to estimates or beliefs, must be further analyzed. To understand why belief about the world varies so greatly among individuals, the learned aspect of the mental process must be considered. Why does one learn to believe that specific concepts are valid? Learning is limited not only by the capacity of the individual, but by that which is presented; that is, by the opportunity to learn. In the absence of conflicting information one may, for example, learn that whales fly—to the extent that the source is believed dependable. Thus, the environment limits. For the same reasons, individuals may believe that they are hungry or sexually aroused, because they are told that such is the case. Therapists often "explain" to their clients which desires are responsible for their aberrant behaviors and/or distressing emotions.

When a change in knowledge occurs, what or who has learned? By this definition, the learner is the modified entity. This, too, has been a source of confusion. When a child is said to have learned, one usually means that there has been some change in the child's *total* being which is manifested in altered behavior. This is an accurate representation only in a limited sense. It is more precise to consider learning in another manner.

Learning to read refers to a change only in part of the individual child. Nothing is necessarily altered, for example, in the capacity of leg muscles when the child masters the reading process. On the other hand, when one says that the child has learned for example, to play soccer, much more total potentiality is included. Knowledge of the rules, as well as the ability to manipulate the ball, are involved. However, the child may have learned only the rules, not how to kick or pass the ball, or vice versa. In neither case could it be accurately inferred that the child had learned to play soccer. A more accurate statement might be that the rules of soccer had been learned.

Consider a more complex existent. When it is stated that a *team* has learned how to lose, or that an *institution* has learned how to handle student relations, the reference is to an entity more inclusive than any of its individual members. If the university president's newly acquired human relations skills are negated by a stubborn faculty senate, then learning is appropriate only to the president's altered knowledge state, and not to any change in relations. Only where some totality meets the criterion of change is the word learning appropriately applied.

These examples indicate that learning must be defined at the highest existential level at which knowledge alteration is complete. Learning the alphabet is less inclusive than learning to read. If a child has learned only 25 letters of the English alphabet, only in a loose sense of the word would one say that the alphabet had been learned. The child has, of course, learned a set of 25 letters, which is, of course, not the same as 25 separate and unrelated facts. However, the relationship between the letters does not justify the implication that the *alphabet* has been learned. In all cases, the learner is that entity which has necessarily been modified in the capacity under consideration.

The key term in this definition is *necessary*. When one says an individual has learned to read, it may appear that such learning is not a necessary change because the individual can choose to read, or not, in any situation. However, here is precisely where the distinction between learning and behavior becomes critical. It is appropriate to ask what has changed as a result of experience that cannot be controlled *deliberately*. The answer in this case is the individual's *ability* to read. Although he or she can choose to read or not, the individual cannot choose to *not know* how to read. This provides a clue to the answer to the general question: What is it that is being referred to when one states that learning has occurred?

If the answer is "yes" to the question "Do they know (have knowledge of) how to read?" they must have that knowledge. If the question relates to their knowing how to respond, although the answer is again "yes," the response is not mandatory in mentally endowed individuals.

Figure 6.2 shows the distinction between kinds of response patterns as they relate to experience and action at the levels of mind and pre-mind. The optional nature of action monitored at the mental level is the basis for the *decision-making* and *behavior* sections of this text.

Figure 6.2

Response Patterns

	Experience Option	Response Option
Pre-mind	Mandatory	Mandatory
Mind	Mandatory	Discretionary

Many puzzling situations may appear to be involved in the definition of learning as a change in capacity or knowledge. How may we explain, for example, learning not to respond? What has been altered? Either no response is possible or knowledge of each alternative is possessed. Since new learning does not necessitate forgetting of previous knowledge, the latter interpretation is most reasonable. A child may learn to make a request, rather than to take an item without asking. After the learning experience, both options are known (i.e., have been learned). However the child may not have learned the nature of the consequences attendant on each alternate behavior. Here we have another example of the potential for difficulty. An assumption is often made that, at some maturational level, an individual will "know better" than to act or fail to act appropriately in a given situation. Though maturation is a cause of certain types of learning, it is not competent to teach socially prescribed behaviors.

Forgetting represents the loss of knowledge. It, too, is applicable whenever any informational term is appropriate, although, once again, it is ordinarily restricted to human and other animal forms of life. Perhaps the application of such concepts as memory banks in computer language will make possible the appreciation of the situation when such a bank is cleared. If data are stored in a computer, that information represents knowledge only at some specific location in that computer. Similarly, if data are stored at some ordinarily inaccessible region of the brain, it is knowledge only in that region.

Knowledge has spatial and temporal referents. Thus, the individual who forgets, and then who under new circumstances recalls is, in fact, relearning.[75] At the time that the material was forgotten, it was erased from that part of the nervous system which was accessible to the individual who sought it. Knowledge of the forgotten material was certainly retained *somewhere*, but at a particular time, at a particular level of mental processing, information that can no longer be recalled cannot have the status of knowledge *at that level*.[76]

The biological person is a collection of "parts" analogous to a social group. If at any time a particular individual does not possess knowledge, the fact that others do would not warrant the contention that the target individual knows simply because the group does. Although hypnosis or other experience may cause the recall of previously known data, (i.e., the restoration of knowledge), it would be inappropriate to say that the individual really "knew it all the time."[77] Although, admittedly it was known by some portion of the person's nervous system, it was not knowing as a mental experience. The difference between recalling and learning for the first time lies only in the information source. The recaller is learning from information provided by some other part of his or her own biological being. A similar explanation can be provided for the ostensible exception of adventitiously blinded individuals who claim not to have lost knowledge, since they can still, for example, detect the presence of others through hearing, touching, or other sensorial experience. However, losing the sense of sight is parallel to forgetting.

To understand this, the definitions of information and knowledge must be kept in mind. The blind person no longer has knowledge that makes possible the interception of visually presented information emanating from external sources. Even if the sound of a voice calls up a visual image, the knowledge is different. Here, it represents the capacity to respond to information projected by some part of the nervous system which, itself knowledgeable, passes that knowledge on in the form of information which causes a *knowing experience* based on that information.[78]

When learning refers to modified conceptualizations, several factors are involved. Beliefs change. Learning to ride a bicycle probably changes one's belief regarding the premise that he or she knows how to do so. (Behavior is based exclusively on such beliefs. Some individuals may not believe that they are capable of riding a bicycle in spite of the "objective" evidence.) Beliefs are often accompanied by emotional reactions. The belief that one knows how to ride a bicycle may cause happiness, while knowledge of a murder may cause grief. Thus, learning at the level of mind represents a change in affective states as conceptualizations are processed.

Consider a complex series of events which represents a holon chain of learning. The selection of items at each level is, of course, arbitrary. A series of learnings has been sketched as they may be applied to knowledge concerning the sport of soccer. Each factor represents one of many that could have been included, and in each instance the terms employed refer to complex activities. For example, "knowing how to kick" refers to a great variety of activities including punting, place kicking, etc. The assumption embedded within Figure 6.3 is that the learning is complete—although such a situation would, strictly speaking, be an impossibility. There must, inevitably, remain some aspect incompletely learned.

- If learning occurs at level A, it changes A completely, E less completely, and C and D, not at all.
- If it occurs at level B, it changes B completely, E less completely, and D indeterminately. (No matter how completely B is learned, D is not necessarily approached.)
- If learning occurs at level D, then A, B, and C are learned more or less completely, E less and F also somewhat less.

Once again, in the strict sense, by this definition it would be impossible for anyone to meet all of the conditions essential to "know how to play soccer." Thus, beyond the simplest example, such as having knowledge of the alphabet, which can be more accurately specified, learning is difficult to pinpoint as to exactly what is included.

If one wishes to determine the appropriate level at which to describe the process, the holon chain to be pursued must first be determined. The level at which learning should be identified is that at which continued learning would not affect the next highest level. In our example, learning the rules is fixed below the level of learning how to play. In regard to learning what to look for when watching a soccer game, the learner can be identified at a higher level.

Conceptual learning refers to the content that has been added, while cognitive learning refers to new mental tasks that can be performed. Motor learning follows the same pattern. One can speak of the total person, a leg muscle, or the parts of a muscle, with the criterion simply being that entity which has the capacity to respond in a particular way following an experience. It was pointed out earlier that in the case of a person, or parts controlled by that person, a response may or may not occur, while knowledge at the experiential level must take place. This definition of learning is designed to clearly distinguish it from behavior, and to avoid the confusion which occurs because of the tendency to speak so loosely of what happens when learning occurs.

Since much learning in living beings results from experience, it is obvious that sensation and perception are integrally involved. To learn, the individual must receive a signal, process it, and change as a result. If the individual, for any reason, cannot process the signal, no learning can result. If it can be processed, it must be. The individual may react to the stimulus at the level of sensation or even of primitive perception, but without the capacity for change, the organizational state will remain unaltered. Thus, the potential for learning may be diminished either by a weak or ambiguous signal, or by any other cause of impotence in the learner.

Figure 6.3

Learning Holon Chain: A Soccer Example

Level	Learning Concept
1 A	Knowledge of one rule of soccer
2 B	Knowledge of all soccer rules
2 C	Knowledge of how to kick, pass, etc.
3 D	Knowledge of how to play soccer
4 E	Knowledge of what to look for in a soccer game
5 F	Knowledge of all that is required to become an expert soccer player

Ascending Knowledge Sequence

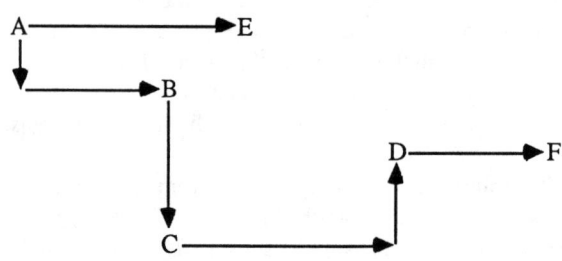

*Note that knowledge of C, D, and F includes the learning of many skills.

Mental Intelligence

Learning and intelligence are at their zenith in humans. At this level, intelligence includes both the ability to learn to perform functions (cognize) and to appreciate relationships (to believe appropriately). It is not considered a sign of intelligence to recognize that one is hungry, or to realize that murder should not be committed, except as such issues bear on the individual's well-being. If one knows that to kill another human is *illegal* as an intellectual fact, it is because it has been learned, and this requires some level of intelligence. Since knowledge represents the capacity to experience, intelligence refers to the malleability of pre-experiential knowledge, which embraces both learning potential and innate or instinctive capacities.

Such genetically prescribed docility represents the potential for action in the interest of survival and growth. Because of this, controversies are generated in relation to racial and ethnic differences. The definition of intelligence as the capacity to be altered by new information bears on the issue of whether intelligence varies between groups. If intelligence is the interaction of innate knowledge and docility, it would appear that it is fixed at conception—or perhaps at birth. Deutsch, Katz, and Jenson,[79] as well as many others subscribe to this interpretation.

But the difference may be one of degree of difficulty in arriving at the same learning level, rather than an eternally unalterable situation. A dissenting school of thought considers intelligence to rest not only on innate knowledge but also on what the individual has learned. The more one learns, the more one is capable of learning. Environmentalists, such as Staats,[80] have argued that, excepting those with central nervous system damage, the only difference between the learning potential of individuals is their exposure to opportunity under appropriate conditions. Thorndike,[81] and many of his followers, believed that the evolution of intelligence was essentially a straight line of increasing intricacy. However, recent research has revealed that "brain structures evolved by higher animals do not serve merely to replicate old functions and modes of intellectual adjustment but to mediate new ones."[82]

A common interpretation of mental intelligence was offered by Perkins who suggested that "intelligence means intellectual competence."[83] He broadened the term to include such diverse aspects as "power models, tactical models and knowledge models,"[84] which he suggested be employed in various situations in terms of which theory best fit the data. Whichever model is employed, however, our contention is that the function of intelligence in living beings (i.e., the way in which docility is genetically employed) is to improve adaptability. Since it deals principally with perceptually derived data, it relates to efficiency in dealing with the environment, which in this sense refers to all that is known separately from drives. Ostensibly, such a characteristic has the potential for producing individuals who are able to provide maximum development for the species. If this is so, it would be difficult to consider a definition of intelligence which restricts it to abstract thinking except to the extent that such thinking is useful in providing the individual with a more efficient life or, in terms of its original purpose, with a more species profitable existence.

The concept of *creativity* is assumed to describe a facet of intelligence—a capacity which has been shown to be distributed fairly evenly across the sexes among bright children.[85] However, there remains a wide difference of opinion as to what should be included under that rubric. The holarchic model posits creativity as a capacity for exploratory and risk taking behaviors that provide valuable growth opportunities for individuals as well as species.

Intelligence is often used (and measured) in ways that describe the possession of information. In this sense, it is equivalent to knowledge. Such usage leads to many strange and misleading consequences. It is sometimes assumed, for example, that the intellectual scale leads from a lack of ability to comprehend at the lowest levels, to an appreciation of the truth, as the highest degree of mental sophistication is reached. It is erroneous, however, to suppose that overcoming intellectual immaturity means to arrive at the truth.

Such elitism is insupportable from either a logical or evidentiary standpoint. Individuals, at every level of intelligence, have a capacity for understanding the world. They cannot go beyond this understanding, and their beliefs are limited at some point along a scale of potential truth which is never completely fathomed. To assume that at some level "right" responses can be identified is absurd, if only because of perceptual/cognitive limitation, and the analogic nature of belief.

Stages of moral development have been proposed by Piaget[86] and Kohlberg.[87] Kohlberg proposed that moral choices are made on the basis of intellectual maturity in the same way as are rational decisions, with intelligence making a significant contribution. He contended that at the highest levels of maturity a "proper" solution to moral dilemmas may be reached. The reliability of such schemata has been challenged, however, in a number of studies by Wonderly and Kupfersmid.[88,89,90]

In simple forms of life, the intellectual span is not extensive and it is appropriate to distinguish intellectually immature from mature thinking. It should be obvious, however, that the most mature thought process in the highest ape falls far short of that of humans, and that the adult animal of such a species would not be considered to possess "truths" except of a very limited kind. What is not so obvious is that the human intellect represents only another level of ability along the same scale. Conceptual knowledge varies from person to person. At levels of increasing education and research, different interpretations of data are made. However, all such interpretations are only relatively locatable on the scale of adequacy.

If the relationship between intellectual skill and metaphysical commitment is considered, again no clear pattern emerges. Faith in the occult is not peculiar to the unintelligent, but can be found at all levels of intelligence, with varying interpretations designed to make it conform to conceptualized information. Belief in God, finalism, and teleology in general cannot be dichotomized as to those who accept articles of faith and those who "know better." Rather, such devotion can be found manifest in different forms at all levels of understanding. It is critical, therefore, that intelligence not be assumed to imply access to knowledge of truth as opposed to belief about the speculative. Although some ultimate external truth may be postulated, intellectual facility represents only the extent or degree to which the data that is intercepted can be rationally interpreted.

If intelligence is defined simply as the level of complexity of the cognitive process, machines may be assumed to possess such a characteristic. However, mental intelligence represents a capacity for learning, which provides the potential for superior adaptation and control in the interest of living creatures, and ultimately their parent systems. Since machines cannot function deliberately—on the basis of their own interest or that of "machinehood,"—they do not qualify. Thus, although it is certainly possible to create an instrument capable of duplicating the efficient aspects of the central nervous system, especially as it performs logically or intellectually, "artificial intelligence" cannot be construed as a meaningful concept.

The intelligence of a machine parallels that of pre-life existents, in that it refers to mere docility. However, it is specious to assume that a machine can learn to "win" a game or correct an "error." Such concepts have no pre-life significance, and the construction of a machine capable of relating a function to a *goal*, presumes a purpose that is not inherent in that entity. The goal is defined by the operator.

Dreyfus[91] pointed out that the reason machines can not duplicate the brain is because they cannot determine what the problem *is*. He was, of course, referring to the total mental process. What the machine can duplicate is the cognitive aspect of the brain or the manipulation of perceptual data. MacKay, however, suggested that machines can duplicate most of the functions of mind:

> What then of consciousness and mind? I should be prepared to defend the thesis that *as far as we can find words for tests for these attributes*, it is possible for an artifact (i.e., a machine) to meet those tests.[92]

MacKay's thesis deals essentially with cognitive and conceptual functions. He did make comments, in passing, about the ability to include emotion as well but failed to develop this most critical aspect.

The ability to deal with symbols; to remember; to recall; to interrelate concepts; to produce artistic, aesthetic, or other works are all differentially subject to learning. Thus, individuals may, at any point in time, be characterized in terms of the ease with which they may be altered in any such area. The quotient derived in a test of such ability would represent their docility along some normative scale—their intelligence.

Higher Mental Processes

The ability to perform the process of abstraction is peculiar to the highest forms of life. The spider makes an estimate of the distance to a fly, and a cat estimates his degree of hunger when food is proffered. However, neither ponders the probability of rain during the ensuing week or the relative nutritive merit of various foods. This capacity represents the manipulation of perceptual data at the hypothetical level. Information which is neither present nor even necessarily real can be dealt with. Its verification is considered by many philosophers to depend on experience, but some extrapolation is approved. Logical implication, for example, is accepted regardless of the factuality of the premises.

Just as cognitive skill at higher levels makes possible the rational analysis of conceptual data, the moral sense can be recognized as applicable to such information in the abstract. The moral censure that accompanies the observation of a particular act, such as deliberate injury of a child, is also applied to a generalization such as "children should not be abused."

When one argues that if $A \supset B$, and A is true, B must follow, a correctness is sensed which need not be verified empirically. As in the case of the Law of Identity discussed earlier, the validity of the claim is *convincing*. Similarly, the conviction that life should be preserved is compelling, in spite of the fact that no experience could prove it to be correct. Aesthetics are also generalized. The contention that "blondes are beautiful" is an example of such a judgment, and principles of artistic excellence are taught as faithfully as those of mathematics.

In the realm of the abstract, reasoning can be applied even to desire. For example, it would be considered rationally sound to conclude that a seven course meal should destroy the desire to eat. It may be because of this that the nonrational nature of desire has been obscured. However, if one stated in honesty on completion of such a meal that they wanted more food, the incompetence of reason to explain desire at the practical level would become clear.

Assessments may be made about emotional states as well as other forms of information, and in such cases it is proper to consider the emotion as occurring prior to the assessment. However, it is common to erroneously assume that this is the case with all judgments. The reason for the confusion comes from several sources. When such evaluative scales as reason and morality are involved, disinterested responses are relatively rare. In considering whether it is reasonable to jump from a building from a height of 50 feet, the one who judges, in imagining the situation, is apt to relate it to desire and thus to emotion. Asked to judge whether vanilla or chocolate ice cream tastes better, desire and an imagined (or perhaps real or recalled) experience are involved. Hence, once again, emotion is involved. However, it is quite possible to make judgments about generalities (i.e., how many peas would it take to fill a quart jar?) where the correctness of the estimate is ostensibly of little consequence to the estimator, though some level of tension could probably be discerned.

The critical nature of this distinction lies in the practice of making what are assumed to be impartial assessments of reasonableness or morality when emotion is inappropriately involved. If a candidate for public office is judged to be honest because he or she is attractive and personable, a judgment based on emotion rather than purely on situations, events, or behaviors is being made. This form of self-deception, a casualty of complex mental processing, leads to conflicting beliefs which are related to many emotional health problems.

Summary

Any interpretation of *mind*, or the mental *process*, is of necessity subject to criticism. Putnam pointed out that "each previous period in the history of Western thought had a quite different idea of what such a term as *mind* or *soul* might stand for."[93] However, some effort must be made to describe that nebulous concept in a manner that makes possible an approach to emotional health. Our definition has been based on no more than that concern.

Mental *processing* results in the creation of many classes of data. Mental *knowing* refers to, and is limited by, belief regarding the propositions so developed. Ayer and other empiricists have made a persistent attempt to identify some knowledge beyond belief. The search is made in terms of the distinction between *cognition* and *affect* which associates knowledge with cognitive processing. Unfortunately, the pursuit is destined to fail on the basis of the affective limitation on the knowledge they seek. The sequence involved may be displayed as follows.
- Processes:
    Conceptualization - the anasynthetic process by which sensations are translated into concepts.
    Cognition - the manipulation of conceptualized data.
- Products:
    Concepts - knowledge that is created by cognitive and conceptual processes.
    Beliefs (affects) - feeling states which represent the form in which mental knowledge is manifested; convictions regarding the validity of cognitively derived concepts.

For all philosophies of mind, the realization that knowing is neither peculiar to perception nor to mental manipulation of any kind should provide the sobering conclusion that their prey is chimerical. Human knowledge simply cannot stand the test of priority to which philosophers subject it. But the appreciation of such a constraint need not be pessimistic. Rather, it provides a basis for the development of a program that may be more effective in the search for improved human adjustment.

One of the disturbing issues concerning the concept of mind is the status of purpose as defined earlier. Does it have ontological verity beyond the realm of consciousness, or is it a contingency of the structure of mental processing? There is little doubt that a concept such as purpose, as well as the paradoxes of infinity, time, and extension, can be resolved by taking the position that they are mind dependent. However, activities cannot be planned and executed without taking such "fantasies" into account. In either case, it is the *psychological* impact manifested in the search for meaning that has a bearing on emotional health. The paranoid conviction that one is under surveillance is no more or less affected by Essentialist "truth" than are the beliefs of commuters that they must hurry through time to catch their trains.

Chapter Notes

1. Ryle (1949), p. 16
2. Penelhum (1955), p. 571
3. Ryle (1949), p. 16
4. Protagoras cited in Gomperz (1901), p. 456
5. Ayer (1956)
6. Brain (1965), p. 55
7. Flowering, for example, may occur if only part of the plant receives an appropriate amount of sunlight.
8. "Fuzzy mathematics" in computer development follows a somewhat analogous plan.
9. Pap (1953), p. 23
10. Ashby (1960), p. 12
11. At subliminal levels, considerable reaction to external and internal stimuli is involved, with subtle motor responses occurring that cannot be considered purely reflexive.
12. Freud, S. in Brill (1938), p. 544
13. There is extensive evidence that such mental processing includes the operation of the cognitive function below the level of awareness. However, the impetus for such control does not arise in the unconscious but as a protective mechanism based on signals emanating from a conscious source, or where the process is of a mechanical (non-mental) nature. Although the impact of such subliminal signals has been clearly demonstrated, their influence is only indirectly on the decision-making process. A useful comparison may be made with the influence of one's age when deciding whether to take a course of action (e.g., to run in a foot race). While the determination may hinge on one's ability to run at a certain speed, for example, and where that facility has diminished with advancing years, age per se would not ordinarily be considered the reason for a decision *not* to participate. The ability to run would be the critical factor regardless of the underlying cause. Another older individual, in better physical condition, may not respond in the same way.
14. Beloff (1965), p. 54
15. Ryle (1949)
16. Rose (1973), p. 21
17. Coulter (1983), p. 145
18. *Ibid.*, p. 128
19. Beloff (1965), p. 37
20. Fodor (1981), p. 116
21. Smart (1959)
22. Beloff (1965), pp. 38-39
23. Feigl (1975), p. 8
24. Brentano (1966), p. 77
25. Ducasse (1965), p. 81
26. Feigl (1975), p. 30
27. Quinton (1965), p. 233
28. Shevrin & Dickman (1980)
29. Corsini (1977), p. 5
30. Lachman & Lachman, (1979), p. 7
31. Flexner (1987), p. 399
32. Restak (1988), p. 318
33. Silvern (1971)

34. Klausmeier (1961), p. 155
35. Deese (1958)
36. Hergenbahn (1976)
37. Klausmeier (1961), p. 157
38. Bruner (1973), p. 134
39. *Ibid.*, pp. 134-135
40. Norman (1980), p. 1
41. Young, P. T. (1936), p. 764
42. We are describing here, not the reasoning process, but the conviction of the reasonableness of a proposition.
43. Hume (1938), p. 300
44. *Ibid.*, p. 301
45. *Ibid.*, (1952), p. 467
46. Russell (1948), p. 154
47. *Ibid.*, p. 111
48. *Ibid.*, p. 143
49. Ayer (1946)
50. *Ibid.*, (1956), p. 16
51. Ryle (1949), p. 134
52. Stroud (1977), p. 74
53. Roth & Galis (1970), p. 7
54. Hospers (1953), p. 148
55. Ayer (1956), p. 35
56. Malcolm, N. (1963), p. 72
57. Russell (1965), p. 144
58. Chisholm (1957)
59. Gettier (1963), p. 121
60. Skyrms (1967), p. 373
61. Goldman (1986), p. 17
62. *Ibid.*, p. 19
63. Unger (1968), p. 165
64. *Ibid.*, p. 170
65. Smythies (1965), p. 248
66. Ayer (1956), p. 68
67. Edwards and Pap (1965), p. 116
68. Ayer (1956), p. 52
69. *Ibid.*, p. 38
70. In fact, our claim regarding the nature of knowledge should be preceded by "I believe that..."
71. Husserl (1931)
72. Ayer (1956)
73. Feigl (1975)
74. Descartes (1972), p. 179
75. A stroke patient whose illness makes inaccessible bits of coded data may have such knowledge elicited under excitation by clinical electrodes. At the conscious level, relearning is occurring.
76. Obviously, such a distinction is a *reductio ad absurdum*. It is employed here only for emphasis.
77. The *mental* experience is not spatially located, although the *source* of the experience is.
78. In the (obvious) case of an individual unable to communicate because of mutism or other debilitating condition, knowledge may not be demonstrable. The constraint on such expression requires that the definition of knowledge include the restriction, "where response capacity is not impeded."
79. Deutsch, Katz & Jensen, (1968)
80. Staats (1968)
81. Thorndike (1911)
82. Bitterman (1965), p. 100
83. Perkins (1986), p. 102
84. *Ibid.*, p. 104
85. Wonderly (1964)
86. Piaget (1954)
87. Kohlberg (1958)
88. Wonderly & Kupfersmid (1980)
89. *Ibid.*, (1981)
90. *Ibid.*, (1982)
91. Dreyfus (1965)
92. MacKay (1965), p. 185
93. Putnam (1986), p. 48

Chapter 7
Mind: Information Channels

Desires, the mental representations of drives, may be classified as *assertive*, *protective*, and *transcendent*, all of which are experienced as negative affects. Only assertive drives arise spontaneously. Of these, only *hunger*, *thirst*, *stimulation*, and *sex* are controlled by appestatic devices. The behaviors, situations, and events that are presumed to satisfy desires are defined as *needs*, the vast majority of which are learned.

Mental perception functions to reflect external existence in order to provide the information necessary to act and react to the environment efficaciously. Perception is, however, constrained by limitations inherent in its structure. The observed (existential) world is, to a considerable degree, a creature of each individual's perceptual acuity and the modifications that have been wrought by experience.

Desire

At the level of mind, drive knowledge is expressed as information which communicates with the affective system in the same way as do percepts. Instead of being driven to a response in the presence of an urge, the individual is aroused by signals of varying degrees of force; by feelings of *desire*. Desire, the psychological manifestation of drive, is an affective state having both conscious and preconscious aspects. Signals take the form of recommendation rather than commands, and intensity is a factor in the deliberative process.

To the extent that a desire is expressed as an alteration in the nervous system—as a modification of elements of the limbic system—it is infallible. It cannot err. By contrast, *belief* about desires, or the attaching of a label to the affective state, is not unfailing. Individuals may make incorrect assumptions about why they are experiencing a particular feeling. They may *believe* that their distress is caused by hunger, for example, when the reason for their restlessness is mere boredom.

Most psychologists use the terms drive and desire interchangeably. This effort to avoid mentalistic terms has resulted in serious misinterpretation of many behaviors. The substitution of terms like "deprivation" for hunger, though blessed with the potential for reducing introspective terms to measurable increments (e.g., time) has had a proclivity to breed unwarranted assumptions about much of human behavior.

In pre-mind individuals, urges related to assimilation, reproduction, growth, probing or searching, and self-preservation can be clearly identified. These signals, which mandate action when triggered, were classified in Chapter 5 as *drives*. Assimilative and reproductive drives are essential to the maintenance of life. Thus, they are mirrored in hunger and sexual desires. The signal that triggers automatic recoil in the pre-mind individual is analogous to the desire to escape from pain, while the exploratory effort of pre-mind forms is paralleled by the desire for stimulation. The urge to belong, to be a part of, arises when it is possible for an individual to feel a sense of separation or the lack of significance that isolation creates. It is a mental manifestation of the drive in pre-mind life toward species enhancing actions.

The quality of an experienced desire is a function of maturation, affective integrity, and deprivation level. Thus, the nature of a child's "hunger" may vary considerably from that of a mature person. Similarly, what is described as hunger may be a totally different experience at the level of mild interest in eating as opposed to being at the point of near starvation.

Since desires, as the mental representation of drives, function to enhance survival and growth, and since the survival of life is commonly considered to be desirable they represent a *positive* force. Such ostensibly abhorrent activities as pillage, looting, and rape, as well as expressions of hate and disgust, are all based on motivational sequences that include positively directed desires. They are considered deplorable because they represent socially unacceptable manifestations. "Sins are not sins at all but [propensities]...that lead us to sinful behavior."[1] This is a clearly misunderstood relationship. Programs for improving emotional health cannot be developed around the notion of "good" and "bad" motives but rather on the acceptance of the role of desires and the opportunity for their expression in the most effective ways.

The Negative Aspect

Desires, in spite of their positive value for the development of life, are experienced as negative affects. The awareness of an urge is a signal to rid oneself of that feeling. At this level the Freudian homeostatic interpretation is applicable in the sense that homeostasis refers to the dissipation of uncomfortable feelings. Stimulation seeking, the widely observed phenomenon which has been used to challenge the psychoanalytic principle, is no different than that of food seeking. Lack of stimulation causes a feeling of distress, differing only in quality from a feeling of hunger.

The notion that desires are negative experiences is well-recognized by motivational theorists. In discussing the orthodox conception of drives (referred to here as desires), White said, "the tension of an aroused drive is interpreted as unpleasant, at least in the sense that [one] acts in such a way as to lower the drive."[2] Some philosophers have proposed that from a species standpoint the pain caused by desires is of little consequence since it is through the suffering of individuals that their progeny are made superior over time. This accident of evolutionary development, good for the gene pool or species, is in many ways bad for the individual. There is even a theological notion that the pain produced by desire is an outcome of human wickedness.

Moral philosophers have considered desires not only as negative but sources of evil as well. Kant proposed that:

> [Desires] are impediments to the development of humanness.... There is no denying the preponderance of evil in idealized and extreme refinements of taste, in the scientific luxuries that feed men's vanity, begetting and diffusing endless insatiable desires.[3]

He believed that such negative behavior is part of the human legacy. "It is not [man's] nature to rest and be contented with the possession and enjoyment of anything whatever.... The inconsistency of his own *natural dispositions* drives him into self devised torments."[4]

Biblical references to the negative aspect of desire are extensive. The Book of James, in the New Testament of the Christian Bible provides several examples of the negative impact of allowing desire to run free. "Each person is tempted when he is lured and enticed by his own desire. Then, desire when it has been conceived gives birth to sin."[5]

The reason that desires are not always recognized as negative is, first, because (especially in wealthy societies) they are ordinarily satisfied long before they are experienced in an extreme state, and secondly because the gratification of some desires is a highly pleasurable experience.

The positive feeling is that associated with the awareness (either through current perception, imagination, or recall) of an experience which has the capacity to gratify the desire. It is not the experience of the desire but the conceptualized resolution or the experiencing of that resolution which carries the positive valence. It is therefore most accurate to think of a "desire sequence" which includes both a negative and positive aspect. In this way a number of apparent paradoxes may be explained. Such riddles as the agony of unrequited love and the "desirability" of frightening experiences are based on the same postulate.

The person who skips lunch to increase the enjoyment of dinner creates a mental scenario which focuses on the feast which will remove the hunger. The attractiveness of a dangerous experience is quite similar. The ecstasy of the threatening situation is coupled with the conviction that it can be resolved. In much the same manner, the rapturous experience of the pining lover is positive to the extent that the wooer believes that the suit may be won. The acid test of the accuracy of this interpretation of desire would be to eliminate the possibility of gratification and then to examine the affective state.

Positive food tastes—the sought after experiences—are positive only as they relate to the appeasement of a desire to enjoy them, or to the extent that one has learned of the excitement of the senses associated with such appeasement. Thus, condiments come to be sought because their flavors "thrill" the sensorium. The source of their attractiveness lies in the fact that they represent powerful stimuli. It is here that the term *appetite* is often employed. It refers to the affective state arising from the contemplation of the positive experience associated with the gratification of desire.

In the information/knowledge chain, desires represent knowledge in respect to internal and external signals—information in respect to deliberation. For example, the capacity to know sexual arousal as a psychological experience (i.e., desire) contributes to the individual's reaction to sex-related situations.

A critical issue is the point at which an urge is recognized as hunger, thirst, or some other form of desire. At the level of minimal excitation the individual is aware only of some distress or discomfort not associated with a specific signal. Evidence of agitation at this level of awareness is plentiful. The infant displays restlessness which may be due to hunger, constipation, need for stimulation, or other disquieting feeling. Humans, as well as many animals, display uneasiness when in a state of sexual arousal or when danger is imminent. Dieters find themselves irritable after fasting; a woman may be fretful due to the phase of her menstrual cycle. Therapeutic examples are found in certain anxiety experiences, where, for instance, one mistrusts a particular individual solely on the similarity of their facial characteristics to those of another person that they believe to be dishonest.

It is often possible to pinpoint the cause of malaise. However, it is a common experience to realize that one has been "on edge" without relating it to any recognizable issue. At this level, it is appropriate to speak of the situation as mental, but to the extent that the reaction is fixed by the situation it is an aspect of the preconscious mental state. It may, thus, be defined as "subliminal" since it is related to no identifiable desire.

It is quite probable that when in the course of evolutionary development a species comes to possess a nervous system that is excited by a deficit of any kind, the nature of the distress is not appreciated at minimum excitation levels. Thus, infants know only that they are uncomfortable. They must learn to associate ingesting food with

MIND: INFORMATION CHANNELS

both a positive affective experience and relief from a state of annoyance. Such learning may occur quite rapidly.

Desires, however, are not learned. Rather, one learns the kind of situations and events which reduce discomfort, or are experienced as enjoyable. Ultimately, a conceptual state is arrived at in which a belief is held regarding the type of deficiency that is causing the uneasiness. At this point consciousness is involved. Not all conceptualizations are learned. For many animals the significance of a perceptual experience in conjunction with a state of hunger is appreciated on first exposure. This is an example of instinctive need.

Types of Desire

Desires may be grouped in three categories. Deficit desires include those that arise spontaneously as drives in pre-mind forms of life and are based on tissue change which occurs as a function of time. Deficit desires shall be described as *assertive*, in that their gratification is related to aggression or acquisition—a propulsion of the individual into the world.

The second class of desire includes those related to threat. Such desires will be defined as *protective*. They are aroused when the integrity of the individual is at risk. The signal is one of pain or discomfort, and relief rather than pleasure is sought. In addition to cues that arise when one is physically or mentally injured or diseased, are the signals associated with elimination needs, the urge to relax after expending energy, and the desire for safety that attends the awareness of a perilous situation.

The third category, *transcendent* desires, deals with the threat of isolation or the desire to identify with other individuals, or with various forms of institution. Transcendent desires include the desire for intimacy and meaning, which is critical to emotional adjustment. They arise only when individuals are capable of action which separates them from some group or institution. As with the protective desires, these urges are contingent on the awareness of situations which have the capacity to threaten one's opportunity to belong—to be a recognized part of.

Each form of desire has features which must be appreciated if it is to be dealt with effectively. Table 7.1 lists examples of the varied types and some of their characteristics. Such categorizing of desires into several subcategories has been widely criticized. Psychologists have been accused of positing an endless array of mysterious forces whenever a new behavior required interpretation. From McDougall's "propensities,"[6] to Madsen's "primary motives,"[7] many respected theorists have provided lists of such forces, defining them as drives, needs, motives, "Ergs," etc.

While such a proliferation of desires may seem unnecessarily confounding, appropriate responses to human behavior require that some discriminatory process be followed. It is often the case that identification of the appropriate desire is crucial to the effectiveness of programs designed to deal with ineffectual or unacceptable behavior.

Table 7.1

Desire Types

Desire Type	Spontaneous	Cyclic	Contingent	Pleasure	Relief	Appestatic
Assertive						
hunger	X	X		X		X
thirst	X	X		X		X
sex	X	X		X		X
stimulation	X	X		X		X
potency	X			X		
power			X	X		
Protective						
order			X		X	
integrity			X		X	
safety			X		X	
Transcendent						
meaning			X	X		
intimacy			X	X		
belonging			X	X		

* Some desires have an orientation beyond those listed. Assuaging desperate hunger will have a relief aspect, while the establishment of order can be a pleasing experience.

Assertive Desires

The functions included in this class are often referred to as basic or "primary," appearing to represent the most primitive urges. Rapaport suggested that they be called "instinctive drives."[8] He was, once again, using the term as synonymous with desire. However, *any* form of desire may take priority in the course of overcoming environmental interference. Maslow's hierarchy of preference[9] cannot be shown to be thoroughly dependable.

Assertive desires are, in most cases, associated with obvious and specific gratifiers. Assimilative and sexual urges call for fairly specific experiences. Furthermore, many emerge either cyclically or as a result of deprivation, and their satiation is usually predictable (although activity at a conscious level does not necessarily obey "appestatic" commands).

Despite the fact that assertive desires may be aroused prior to awareness of the opportunity for expression, the behavioral response potential is not equally arbitrary in each instance. The emergence of sexual interest directs behavior toward a variety of techniques from masturbation to intercourse. It cannot be satiated by eating or drinking although its urgency may be temporarily reduced by the introduction of attractive food, just as a sexual opportunity may distract a hungry individual. In many cases, where sexual gratification is unavailable, eating is substituted over extended periods. It is clear, however, that eating does not fully resolve the problem of sexual arousal.

Hunger. Most easily identified as an assertive urge is the desire to eat and, for most individuals, for specific foods. That certain foods taste good is based on the associated affect. The food's potential value as a metabolizing agent is not the reason it is eaten. Either the individual desires some experience or outcome (to live, to gain or lose weight, to be loved, to enjoy the taste, etc.), or the act is not expressed behaviorally. Thus, drives, at the level of desires, are expressed less dependably than if they were forced. The specification of the driving force as directed toward self-preservation and growth identify it as assertive.

When people eat because they choose to, one motivational element is the wanting of food, but since the desire is based on taste which is affectively positive there is no assurance that the proper amount or type of food will be eaten. Thus, desire as a substitute for compulsive drive includes a great deal of potential for undesirable outcome. Consider medicine taken because it cures. When a pill is swallowed because of a desire to get well, the drive purpose is met rather directly. But when the tablet is coated to appeal to taste, as in children's aspirin, the increased likelihood that it will be taken (which is a positive factor) is accompanied by the possibility that it will be taken for its flavor; because it is seen as a form of confection. This is when desire may create a problem.

The desire for food, drink, sex, and other assertive urges often leads to behaviors which exceed, distort, or prevent their appropriate function. Eating, liberated from genetic control in order that account can be taken of the occasional need to eat excessively, develops to the point where one eats only because of taste, and the individual responds to gratification far beyond what is desirable from a health standpoint. Sexual behavior follows a similar pattern. Such excesses are based on motivational sequences in which behaviors have been developed to excess because of the sophistication of the cognitive/affective system.

Differing from hunger and thirst in the degree to which they can be avoided, delayed, or subverted are such desires as sex and potency. Sex has been questioned as belonging in the same category as hunger and thirst, and potency could be similarly questioned on the grounds that, appearing to be non-essential to survival, such desires may better be recognized as learned. However, their expression is essential to the health and welfare of the gene pool, directly and indirectly, in the sense that they must occur in some individuals. The necessity for sex is obvious. The inclusion of potency comes from the observation of a striving toward freedom and independence observed at all levels of life, the presence of a recognizable affective state in those enjoying such a condition, the logic of locating an informational system for indicating an optimal state, and the extensive evidence of behavior associated with the opportunity to express such a desire.

Sex. The aspects of sex which are of primary interest are the nature of its expression, the results of deprivation, and the import of satiation. Although social control makes a contribution to the ultimate expression of sex in all cultures, the contention that sexual desire is learned must be rejected, where the implication is that it does not qualify as a primitive motivating force. Beach's contention that it is inappropriate to assume the existence of a sex drive (desire) in a non-stimulated animal is puzzling.[10]

It is true that in the case of hunger, deprivation causes increased body movement which itself provides a clue to the presence of some need state, and in many cases such behavior is not observed in the case of sexual deprivation. But what is it that becomes excited when sexual arousal occurs? The females of many species alter their behavior patterns during a certain portion of estrus and males in many cases actively seek females only at specific times. Must the conclusion be drawn that the desire for sex is born anew in each situation, or does such use of the terms simply cause confusion? It seems more reasonable to assume a latent desire in each case which is aroused by either some perceptual experience or cyclical glandular alteration. This suggests an inactive—not an unconscious—urge. Knowledge may have dissolved; knowing is certainly absent.

Of all forms of drive, and thus desire, only sex appears to present itself in distinct forms for each gender. Female excitation levels fluctuate cyclically while in (human) males no comparable pattern has been identified. In human males, short term lack of opportunity for sexual gratification leads to frustration as tension mounts. But abstinence over a protracted period is believed by some sexologists to be a cause of impotence and reduced urge while frequent sexual activity is said to increase interest.

Since in lower animals of many species only certain males ever indulge in sexual activity with no apparent ill-effect on the non-participants one might conclude that deprivation does not increase desire. This explanation is, however, not sufficient to deny the primitive status of sex as a desire for two reasons. First, in those instances where a limited number of a group practice sex, the death or loss of a sexually active member will bring about the activation of sexual behavior in another. If, on the other hand, the lost individual had learned other activities, his replacement would not necessarily imitate him in those behaviors. Second, in humans, the fact of extensive inactivity does not necessarily make the appropriate affective state unattainable. As to the fact that extended abstinence does not cause an ever increasing desire for sexual contact we should point out that similar reactions may be observed where any desire is subverted over time. Hunger, for example, diminishes after a short period of fasting. The reason for such a reduction in desire is that the genetic plan, being incompetent to foresee the many causes for a failure to eat, is designed to provide a warning signal only for a limited time.

This is analogous to the alarm clock that rings for only two minutes, or the buzzer on the oven that sounds only briefly. In constructing the equipment, an assumption is made that after a certain period it is no longer reasonable to assume that an appropriate response is available. The distinction between the loss of signal in the cases of food and sex is that only in the former is the result inevitably death. Thus, the reduced desire for food that dieters observe after a few days without sustenance cannot be expected to continue unabated indefinitely. Liquid deprivation, which is more immediately life threatening, does not in fact result in loss of interest at all until mental activity level (i.e., degree of consciousness) is itself significantly diminished.

Satiation presents another interesting inconsistency. While the assuaging of hunger or thirst produces a stronger, more capable individual, sexual activity is believed to deplete the body. This has been noted by a variety of authorities and is difficult to contradict. However, there seems an obvious explanation for such a difference. The purpose of many assertive desires is to produce a healthy organism, while the purpose of sexual intercourse is to create new individuals. The sacrifice of parts to whole is manifested not only in the trivial exhaustion in higher animals, but in the actual destruction of the reproducing animal in many forms of life, including the threat to existence that leaf or fruit bearing poses to plants that require such energy for survival.

Why is sexual gratification so highly stimulating? Some writers have suggested that the purpose of high sexual interest in humans is to provide a family tie, implying that the enjoyment of the experience will cause families to remain together. A more reasonable explanation is the need to ensure that at least some members of a species pursue sexual behavior at any risk. However, speculation by those who see in sexual activity other purposes, on the basis of the evidence in its many forms of practice, are not without value. They point to the aspect of sex that causes its great potential for damage to self and others.

The twin issues of the importance of sex to the preservation of the species, and the fact that its expression is not essential, anticipate that it should be a powerful motive. If the individual can live without it, and species survival demands that it be expressed in spite of its disadvantage potential, its urgency level once aroused can be expected to be high. Its importance is obvious; its non-essentiality in each individual requires a more detailed explanation.

When the assertive desires that are not essential to sheer physical survival (sex, potency, and stimulation) are considered, we discover a phenomenon that seems to violate the principle of the individual/system relationship in which needs of the gene pool are defined as having first priority. Reproduction and growth seem not to have priority over sheer metabolic need. Individual sustenance appears to take precedence, and indeed the individual suffering from both severe hunger and coital deprivation prefers food to sex in most instances.

There are, however, many obvious reasons for such a priority. The nature of the metabolic limitation is such that unless nourishment is taken the individual would not survive and be able to reproduce. On the other hand, in most individuals reproductive capacity is not irrevocably lost despite extensive deprivation. The same is true, to a great extent, of growth potential.

In many forms of life it appears that differential sexual expression is most advantageous. The restriction of sex practice to certain members of a community provides the optimal reproductive plan. This requires that lack of opportunity to experience sex be a non-debilitating factor. Thus, sexual desire is a highly important spur to behavior—which is most efficient if it is not essential to existence in each individual. Each of these considerations provides support for the unique characteristics of sexuality.

The force of this desire, when it is operative, is awesome. Murder and other forms of destruction are practiced in the pursuit of sexual gratification. When sexual desire is accompanied by the emotional state known as romantic love it inspires incredible acts. The victims of such a relationship will often violate almost any tradition, rule, or law. That love laughs at locksmiths is a terrible truth.

Potency. Less dramatic than sex, but of critical concern, is the positive affect associated with the sheer sense of being independent, capable, and free. The motivational input referred to in this case is potency or the assertive urge that was referred to earlier, as observed in the flower that "tries" to find the sun. It is true that the feeling associated with control of one's destiny mingles with and even perhaps triggers a sense of safety or mastery. However, the two experiences have separate referents; one to the desire to *grow* in all dimensions (potency) and the other to the feeling associated with *control* (power).

We will employ the term potency to describe the growth urge that is manifested in living things, since the term growth is both awkward and non-dynamic. This desire to grow is in many ways similar to that for sex. Unessential to fundamental existence, its taste is attractive to most normal beings and its pursuit is observed in every form of life. Philosophers have dealt with this characteristic under such concepts as *will*, while psychologists in the existentialist and humanistic fields have encompassed it under the rubric of *self-assertiveness*.

Psychoanalytic writers often represent it as a reaction to the need to compensate. For the Freudian, potency is an adjusting mechanism; for others, it is the source of one's identity as a unique, dynamic individual. The notion that emotional health is a function of one's autonomy, and that societies which demand strict conformity are brutalizing, are based on a recognition of the desire for potency.

Adler saw the desire to overcome inferiority as resulting in a striving for superiority.[11] (Beyond this, he relegated sex to the role of providing such superiority.) Rank insisted that neurosis represents the blunting of the expression of potency (will),[12] while Fromm,[13] and Sartre,[14] saw humans as obligated to be strong and free.

For the extremists of this school of thought, such a process represents the only true behavioral urge. Moustakas stated that "all life is one, a constant urge to become."[15] Goldstein was similarly adamant taking the position that "we have to assume only one drive, *the drive of self-actualization* and...the goal of the drive is not a discharge of tension."[16] Maslow followed this line of thinking in his definition of self actualization. He assumed that mature individuals seek "to be unmotivated and non-striving, i.e., to behave purely expressively."[16]

Although analytic thinkers, with their emphasis on conflict and tension reduction, differ from humanists who stress the creative potential of the urge to humanness, each sees within the organism a contributing dynamism. Behaviorists, on the other hand, not only emphasize dependence for stimulation on the environment, but see people as docile victims of chance encounter—desire, purpose, and emotion having long ago been discarded as nonheuristic concepts.[18]

It may appear that the proper heading under which to discuss this concept would be that of *self* or *personality* and, indeed, many writers (e.g., Maslow and Allport) have denied the validity of an animal-like drive as a basis for the creative and individuality need. However, such behavior is simply evidence for an affective component which has been identified as the growth or potency desire, while self is a construct related to its locus.

A strong contribution to the idea of potency comes from the vitalistic writers who repeatedly refer to some force or energizing factor which characterizes living beings. This view is not universally accepted because of its varied interpretations in the writings of psychologists, possibly due to its mystical nature (as discussed earlier), and to the observation that it is not essential to survival. As with sex, however, the potency urge must be reckoned with whenever it becomes active. When the condition for the expression of such desires as sex and potency arise the individual can be expected to weigh them heavily in decision-making, often to the exclusion of other factors.

Stimulation. The desire for stimulation or adient activity represents the conscious experience of the drive which leads to the seeking of energy replacement. In higher forms of life the desires for sensual gratification, thrilling physical and psychological experiences, and for risk taking and exploratory behavior all stem from the desire to probe the environment and exercise the body, as well as the mind. Certain behaviors are appropriate to specific needs in the case of many assertive desires, while they are far more arbitrary in the case of stimulative and potency desires. This is central to the interpretation of the motivational process. The opportunity for stimulation and growth experiences is essential to optimal adjustment, but they may be experienced in many ways.

The recognition of a stimulative urge is found in the works of many motivation theorists. It occurs under such labels as "curiosity," "activity," "exploratory," and other terms denoting an urge to interact with the environment. Butler and Rice contended that:

Stimulation is so pervasive for every organism that the very concept of a completely unstimulated organism is meaningless...[proposing that]...there is a drive—we shall call it *stimulus hunger* or *adient motivation*—which is a primary drive, perhaps even the most pervasive primary drive.[19]

Researchers point to the evidence of developmental arrest attendant on restriction of opportunity for interaction with the environment. Solitary confinement and limited intellectual stimulation lead to personality alteration that exemplifies the stultifying effect of such experiences. The taste of sugar is, for most people, appetitively attractive. The positive experience associated with smoking and back scratching may be based on the fact that they provide evidence of the vitality of the individual through contact with the sensorium. On the other hand, such behaviors as reading a novel, playing chess, or riding horseback are apt to be primarily associated with a desire for stimulation. This urge is the basis for many of the behaviors of humans and lower animals, especially when there is a low level of interest in other experiences, or where other desires are incapable of expression.

Pre-affective percepts impinge on the individual despite personal desire and force responses to the limit of drive potential. When the affective system becomes a factor, individuals are aroused by the positive or negative feeling associated with experienced stimuli as they identify the world and thus in one sense *verify the sensorial capacities*. Experiences associated with the seeking, probing activity of the simplest forms of life have led over evolutionary time to the development of a desire for the heightened tension states that accompany such interaction—often for sheer stimulation.

Behaviors associated with such desire are a casualty of affect. When the exploratory drive becomes internalized as affect, it creates behavior potentiality that is not directly related to the well-being of the individual or species as a conservative force but rather arouses activities of a purely sensual nature because of their capacity for immediate gratification. Although the urge to search—to investigate—arose from the drive associated with stimulus seeking, it has evolved into a force of its own. There may be survival advantages associated with the stimulative urge, but many of its expressions seem purely sensuous.

Many aspects of the stimulative desire are conservative at the level of minimal indulgence, and to the extent that they have a homeostatic effect (as in listening to a gentle musical sound) they may well represent an aid to optimal survival. Behaviors which can be subsumed under this category range from the cognitively oriented (where an individual studies for the joy of learning) to those such as drinking alcoholic beverages where one indulges in order to become intoxicated. Less obvious are those behaviors that are credited to the desire for aesthetic gratification. The enjoyment of art for its own sake in any form represents the recognition of a pleasurable affect which arises when a particular sensual experience is encountered.

This interpretation would seem to equate drug and alcohol consumption with attendance at the opera or an afternoon in the Louvre. This precise equation underlies the theoretical position on which this text is based. Stated in the briefest terms; given the opportunity and the capacity to recognize the experience, most individuals will find receptor stimulation a rewarding experience, to a certain level of excitement. This represents a desire for stimulation that grows out of a need for contact which has a creative component. McClelland and his colleagues have taken a similar position.[20]

The urge for stimulation may, *but need not*, be related to other forms of desire. Its appreciation will be based most significantly on the sheer fact of its presence. Although the many barriers to expression that are visited on sensually or cognitively stimulating experiences shall be considered, the fact of their existence must first be accepted. Prurience and patronage may be examples of the same basic urge—the desire to experience a specific stimulating sensation.

Power. The concept of power has been developed by so many philosophic and psychological writers, with such a wide variety of interpretations that it may seem necessary to provide a unique definition. In fact, it is a relatively simple matter to show that the many uses of the term can be reduced to a common notion. Whether an author refers to political, economic, physical, mental, or other kind of power, the feeling state experienced by individuals believing that they possess such power is based on their possession of "needs" essential to the meeting of desires or access to such needs at manageable costs.

It is, thus, misleading or inappropriate to speak of a "will to power" where will is equated with desire, or of an urge to control or dominate. More accurately, such behaviors are based on the belief that particular statuses or situations (e.g., being a dominant male) are most apt to provide access to the expression of desires. Such behaviors can, and often do, become separated from their exercise as need-fulfilling, becoming "needs" in themselves. This occurs because they create an aura of desire fulfilling potential that is itself satisfying.

The idea of a power motive has been expressed in many ways. Nietzsche saw power as the appropriate goal for exalted persons. "The noble man is essentially the incarnate will to power."[21] Russell, however, interpreted Nietzsche's concept of power to more accurately represent a sense of apprehension: "It never occurred to Nietzsche that the lust for power, with which he endows his superman, is itself an outcome of fear."[22] Dewey believed that power should reside not in individuals but in communities—that social power is the appropriate human goal.[23] Locke, in his criticism of inherited political power,[24] and Machiavelli, in his proposal to princes of techniques for gaining and retaining power,[25] thought of power as essentially a political concept.

Concern here is with the psychological connotation of the term and its role in human adjustment—the generalized motivational element that guides acquisitive or aggressive behavior. White suggested that a separate motive be recognized. He proposed that "activity, manipulation, and exploration...be considered together as aspects of competence, and that for the present we assume that one general principle lies behind them. I propose that this name be *effectance*."[26]

White considered this an aspect of competence, by which he meant the fitness of an organism to achieve, "to interact effectively with its environment."[27] The holarchic view differs from McClelland's notion of achievement in that effectance or competence—and thus need access—may be accomplished in a variety of ways, with achievement representing only one.[28]

The term power is preferred because it identifies both an urge and the many objects of competent behavior. One wishes to act competently in order to gain power to access needs, and here the term seems to stand midway between desire and need. A motivational sequence may begin at the level of fear or frustration related to a sense of danger and proceed to a condition of control. The resolution of the problem may also be accompanied by a feeling of *pleasure*. A martini, taken to reduce tension, often becomes, over time, the two martinis that heighten pleasure.

Power represents only one aspect of pleasure. Another meaning of pleasure is sheer joy; titillation—which may be unrelated to control. The pleasure in an alcoholic drink need be associated with nothing but the thrill of the taste and the resulting euphoric state. This distinction is also significant. The feeling associated with need access is quite different from the urge to pleasure, which is represented both in the pursuit of appetites because of the associated excitement and in the desire for stimulation of a general nature. Pleasure is, in fact, a term that describes the feeling associated most commonly with the gratification of the assertive desires.

Power must also be distinguished from potency, which we described earlier as the urge to grow. Power, by contrast, involves control or dominion. In the sense that it is employed here it is a positive term and may thus be most accurately seen as a need. It refers to the feeling that one has the capacity and opportunity to live a satisfying life. Furthermore, unlike the more specific desires, the urge to power does not arise spontaneously, but is triggered during the contemplation of methods for gaining control.

Although its "positiveness" is valuable to both individual and gene pool, the motivational sequence associated with it, especially in humans, is often a threat to the welfare of the species. Holarchic inversion is again in evidence. Power, sought by individuals whose sole motive is to gain political, military, financial or other type of control, without regard for the impact on others, has often resulted in widespread destruction.

Protective Desires

In contrast to the urge to satiate assertive desires is the desire for safety, control, organization, tension stability, and the ability to cope with the environment. The desire for an intact sensorium and for maintaining contact with the environment is part of the general homeostatic urge, which includes optimal states of physical and psychological equilibrium based on temperature, humidity, etc.

This form of desire is activated in situations that threaten survival or growth. It represents a *reaction* to information from the environment as well as from internal mechanisms. Confused perceptual states, distortion of images, and any inability to interpret needed information causes an alarm system to function which is experienced as an urge to alter the situation.

Unlike most assertive desires, protective urges are not periodic, or based on privation. They arise only when situations result in threat or interference with stability. Assertive desire may thus be considered *spontaneous*, while the protective desires are *contingent*, being aroused in states of confusion or conflict.

Integrity. Each of the information sources has an input which is received along a continuum of clarity and integrity. When information systems are out of control, ambiguous, or conflicting, and as a result do not produce a faithful or consistent message, an alarm is provided. The individual becomes "disturbed." This is not a characteristic of pre-affective systems since at that level perception provides only raw data. Clarity is at issue only where it can produce a negative emotion. An individual experiencing weightlessness for the first time is quite apt to feel severe anxiety.

This desire must not be confused with the affect which identifies an experience as it may be enjoyed (or avoided). Integrity desire identifies the extent to which the sensorium is, or is not, functioning properly. Proper functioning here refers to reliability, consistency, and lack of ambiguity. Stimulation was identified as a spontaneous desire for the exercise of the sensorium and a feeling of elation when it occurred. Integrity refers to the contingent desire to restore stability when a threat is experienced.

Safety. The tendency to seek safety (to be safe) is considered by many psychologists to be a primary urge. However, it does not meet the condition of spontaneous arousal. Individuals who are capable of feeling discomfort in situations of intense cold, heat, and danger, learn to find or to create protection against the vagaries of weather as well as the threat of predators. The practice in human societies of providing shelter long before the infant is aware of any such need is simply evidence that at the highest cognitive levels individuals are capable of preventive action—a capacity to be dealt with in detail in the section on emotional health.

The fact that one experiences a desire to seek safety does not mean that the behavior which follows the reception of such a signal will necessarily be directed away from the danger. Homeostasis represents a state of the organism which describes a comparatively low energy level. The behaving individual may or may not prefer such a state. The net motivational urge may be to allow the condition to continue. For example, in a state of anxiety, one may decide to live with the tension rather than risk potential destruction.

Brown[29] and others have concluded that because a behavior tends to lessen when an individual is negatively reinforced it can be assumed that the movement is toward a negative tension state. It is more appropriate to describe motivation as impelling the individual toward a preferred positive end state. Although the behavior reduces tension, (or the individual avoids any activity), the behavior is directed *toward* some desired state. Just as one cannot technically correctly state that coldness is added when the temperature is lowered, one cannot be said to move in a negative (psychological) direction.

The wish to avoid or escape from situations which cause physical or psychological damage is appropriate to all desires. The desire for safety, however, always requires reference to some specific urge. To be safe is meaningless in isolation. It requires the qualifier *from* (i.e., safe from what?), which identifies the desire that is specifically threatened.

The distinction between power and safety is subtle. Obviously, to feel safe provides a sense of control, and to be possessed of power causes a feeling of safety. But the safety feeling is one of calm, a homeostatic condition, while the sense of power is one of agitation or stimulation. More importantly, the lack of power is experienced as a negative feeling associated with a sense of impotence, while the need for safety is associated with an awareness of danger.

Appestats. The desire for relaxation following a stimulating or appetite-gratifying experience represents a signal of a strange nature. The word "enough," ostensibly of obvious connotation, is difficult to relate to its physical concomitant. There is clear evidence of an affective experience associated with the sense of sufficiency. This desire to cease behaving, or to terminate a situation, is an aspect of the protective urge. The term *appestat* has been used by many psychologists to describe this type of signal.

Appestatic function represents a form of (contingent) desire, and not simply a cessation of interest in continuing a behavior. When individuals have had "enough" to eat, it means not merely that they do not want more, but that they *want* to have *no more*. The peculiarity of the appestatic urge is that it is appeased by what individuals avoid doing, rather than by what they do. Thus, the appestatic desire to relax represents a wish to cease some—or all—activity.

Appestats function automatically at some levels where they terminate an activity when some predetermined level of sufficiency is reached and are appropriate to activities which are potentially harmful if some limit is exceeded. For this reason not all desires have appestatic controls. Metabolic needs have points of optimal intake while the urge to grow has no limitation. Although the physical limit to which an individual grows is approximately preset, the desire to *pursue* a growth course is unrestrained. Healthy individuals exert a continual effort toward challenging the environment.

Transcendent Desires

The transcendent urge is one of the signals that appears in some life forms as they reach the level of mind. It is at this stage that such a signal relates the individual to the species and other transcendent entities. With pleasure and pain a localized matter, it would be reasonable to expect individuals to lose interest in their relationship to a more inclusive existence without some form of knowledge of their partness.

In the pre-affective state transcendence is represented by total control through the fixing of responses that direct activity toward system preservation. The sexual activity of plants occurs automatically. The urge to relate or contribute to a significant institution is an example of the same type of response at a higher level of life. Where the drive toward belonging or membership is recognized as a desire, the source of motivation lies in the relating of the biological self to a more general existence.

Behavior motivated by a transcendent desire is either carried out or avoided on the basis of the positive or negative feeling that the pursuit manifests in the individual. People who share or give because it "feels good" are enhancing their meaning as they identify with a larger system. (The urge to give in order to belong must be distinguished from that desire as it refers to the welfare of others.)

The transcendent desire arises in the same fashion as do protective and assertive desires. "Go" signals are provided by perceptual experiences that encourage activity which relates the individual to a system. They inform the individual of the isolation inherent in self-oriented behavior. This desire encourages activity which in many instances appears to violate intellectual soundness, as shall be demonstrated. The affective state that accompanies behavior which meets the urge toward belonging is as positive as that related to any other desire. However, the activity that results in such a feeling is directed away from the immediate survival and growth needs of the individual. It focuses on some system to which the individual relates as a part or instance.

The focus of obligation, or belonging, is not static in view of the homeorhetic nature of species existence. This to some extent explains why obligations are not clear in highly complex individuals. Simple organisms deal relatively directly with a particular goal, the priority of which is instinctively known. Higher animals must sort out a preferred target in situations where learning and experience tend to obscure the "proper" goal. The critical distinction between transcendent and other desires lies in the fact that the former is gratified by the experience of *giving*. By contrast, all other desires are satisfied through experiences related to what one *obtains*. The focus in the former is on the relationship with some superordinate existence while in the latter it is on the enhancement of the biological or extended self. The transcendent urge represents the basis for the process of identification to be detailed in Chapter 10.

The emergence of mind, desire, and cognition has resulted in the appearance of many forms of life that are simultaneously capable of the most rapid and efficient self enhancement and the proclivity for species destruction. Humans are, until now, the ultimate example. The holarchic principle seems clearly involved. There is a tendency for parts of the living chain to possess varying degrees of autonomy. This characteristic of life is of inestimable value until the decision-making elements evolve. At this level action occurs on the basis of deliberation. The desire for power and safety interfaces with the desire for meaning and purpose. Choices pit personal gain against profit to others. Appetite is set against considerations of health and safety. "Getting" conflicts with "giving." The challenge is to find a solution to this inevitable dilemma.

Needs

Although pure desire lies at the root of behavioral impetus, desires ordinarily become identified with some form of gratification. To satisfy the desire to eat, some form of food is *needed*. The sex urge calls for action in some form. At the simplest levels needs such as the appropriate sex object or potential food are instinctively known. Since interest here is in human behavior, our analysis will be restricted to those experiences which individuals learn to pursue because of the belief that they have desire-satisfying properties. Such entities, experiences, and events shall be identified as *learned needs* and bear the same relationship to individual desires as primitive needs do to species survival and growth.

An example of the sequence as it relates to food/hunger follows:

Primitive need - food is needed to sustain life

Desire - food is pursued because of the desire for life, taste, etc.

Instinctive needs - comestibles innately known to satisfy hunger

Learned needs - comestibles that one learns to be satisfying

As needs are learned, they are also invested with value. At the same time that adolescents discover that pornography excites, they may also be taught that it is considered immoral. Giving to others, by contrast, is apt to be experienced as gratifying while it is concomitantly learned as a morally desirable action. Desires, then, are usually manifested through associated learned needs and their related (learned) values. Needs are, of course, not only for objects. They may be (and often are) for experiences, events, and behaviors. Whenever the term is employed, therefore, the appropriate referent must be taken into account.

There is a temptation to reverse this usage of need and desire so that hunger, for example, is considered a need, with a particular food said to be what is "desired." There are several reasons for preferring the definitions we employ here, and it is important to clarify the distinction since it is used extensively in the diagnostic section of this text.

It is clearly inappropriate (though often observed) to claim a need for an experience which is in no way as urgent as is argued. Need is erroneously treated as if it had drive status. To say "I need a cigarette" means that my desire for a particular experience can be met with a cigarette—and that the desire is particularly strong. While the cigarette represents an item that can satisfy the craving, unless the individual is beyond the capacity to make a decision, the relevant element is the *desire* to smoke. The most important reason for the choice of terms is that if one continues to ask the question, "Why do you need this experience?" the ultimate response must be "I don't know, I simply desire it." Desires, as such, are inexplicable An example may help.

Asked why one purchases a particular food, the reply may be, "Because I want (desire) it." As to why, the response may be, "Because I *need* to eat." When again asked why, the respondent may say, "Because I must eat, if I am to live." The answer to whether one desires to live is obvious except in a situation in which one desires to die but has some competing desire (e.g., care for his or her children) that requires one to live.

Unless such a further reason is given, it would not be appropriate to close the issue with the insistence that one "needs to." It is obviously a matter of desire. Only if one further analyzes the question would "need" be appropriate. But even to say, "I need to live—in order to care for may family" would only delay the ultimate. (Why do you need to care for them?)

The principle involved is that all needs must yield to the issue of what is *desired*, while desires require—and can provide—no such justification. Where a fearful or dangerous situation is involved, one may be said to desire to escape. Here the *incentive* that arouses the desire is the threatening situation, while the associated needs include the potential activities or routes to safety.

Desire/Need Interaction

Consider first an illustration of the interaction between a desire (a negative feeling) and a perceived need (which causes a positive anticipatory feeling) in the case of an assertive desire. The experiencing of hunger provides a good example.

From any point in time at which complete satiation is achieved a desire for food gradually but consistently develops, depending on energy expenditure and metabolic rate. At first this urge is so minimal that it makes no impression, especially if attention is focused on other matters. When the desire reaches some degree of urgency it is manifested in a general (preconscious) uneasiness or discomfort, still subject to the competition of other interests. At some point a conceptualization of the situation is made based on discomfort, awareness of the amount of time that has passed, and similar factors. All of this is manifested in an increasingly negative comfort state approaching some maximum level of intensity.

When, during this increasing distress, an edible substance is introduced (actual or imagined), an arousal state is triggered based on the gratification or need value of the food and the degree of hunger experienced. The amplitude of the arousal state is a function of this interaction. (Many other factors, such as energy level and previous experience are involved. We wish, however, to focus on the interplay of desire and perceived gratification potential.) Stated as a formula, *Arousal level* (A) is a function of the interaction of the need value of a perceived food (nv) and the degree of deprivation (dd) involved.

In Figure 7.1a, x is obviously of greater appeasement value than y, since the same degree of deprivation causes a higher arousal level. The x may represent a bar of chocolate while y is a carrot stick. If one is sufficiently hungry, the carrot may be as exciting as the chocolate bar would be under a lesser degree of deprivation.

In the case of threat-oriented desires the situation is quite different. Dangerous situations are first recognized at the level of some unspecified (preconscious) malaise. As the degree of threat increases a corresponding negative alarm is sounded.

212   MOTIVATION, BEHAVIOR, AND EMOTIONAL HEALTH

Figure 7.1

Arousal Levels for Classes of Desire

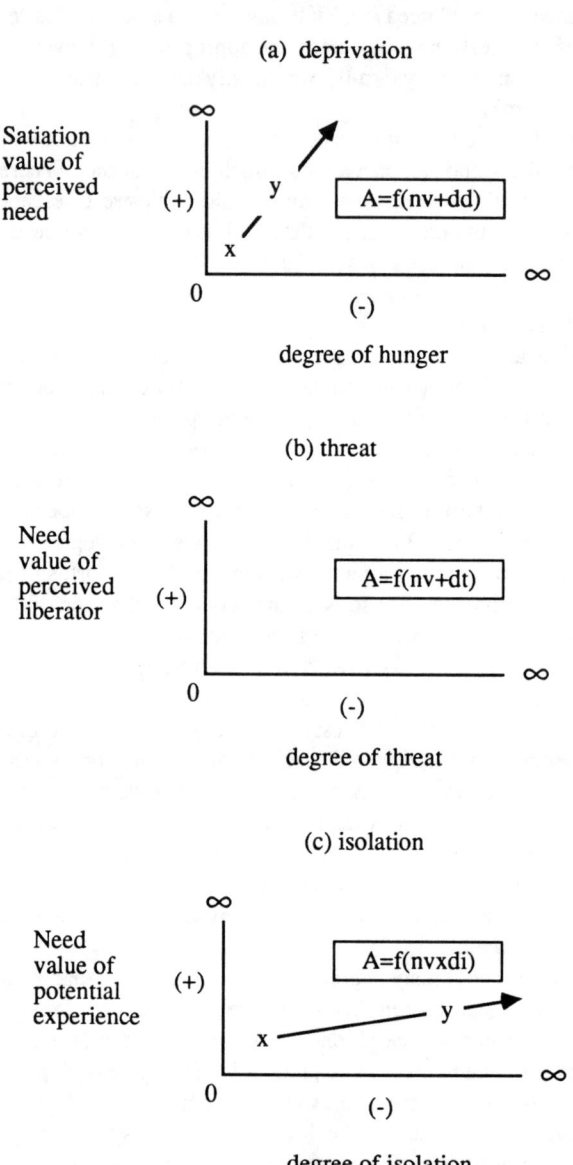

The term threat refers to potential damage to, or the destruction of, the individual. The signal that is experienced is one of fear, pain, or discomfort. When an entity, experience, or event (need) with the potential for reducing the threat is perceived, a positive signal is experienced. The arousal state is a function of the degree of perceived threat and the succorance value of the perceived liberator. The formula in this case (Figure 7.1b) is: *Arousal level* (A) is a function of the interaction of the (need) value of the liberator (nv), and the degree of perceived threat (dt).

The term incentive may be applied both to the initiating perception (the awareness of a dangerous situation) and the desired escape (the needed experience or situation). The incentive for running may be considered either (or both) an attacking lion or a perceived door that leads to escape. The distinction is important. Consider the case of dental hygiene. Teeth that are not cared for will ultimately decay. While the appropriate measures (e.g., brushing, flossing) require relatively little effort, the perceived threat is at such a low level of awareness that many people do not experience an arousal level of sufficient strength to bring about the necessary action. The incentive provided by pleasant tasting toothpaste is often similarly ineffective. Sound educational programming may encourage individuals to routinize positive dental hygiene practices. (The addition of fluorides to drinking water may, in fact, solve the problem in another way.)

The desire to escape isolation, being also contingent upon a perceived situation (i.e., the possibility of being alone), follows the pattern of the threat-oriented desires, differing essentially in the fact that the positive value of belonging is often one of pleasure (gratification) rather than relief. The formula (Figure 7.1c) is: *Arousal level* (A) is a function of the product of the gratification (need) value of a related experience (nv) and the degree of isolation being encountered (di). The individual with few friends is apt to be attracted to undesirable individuals and situations in the search for a meaningful relationship. By contrast, the well adjusted person is apt to find such experiences distasteful.

Although the appeasement of deprivation and transcendent desires is essentially pleasant, there is, foremost, a relief aspect involved. This is also true for assertive urges as when hunger, sexual, or other desire is at an extreme level. Thus, the sexually "starved" person may seek a sexual experience for the sake of eliminating tension. There is also apt to be some degree of pleasure experienced as one is freed from a threatening situation. The excitement associated with the feeling of liberation is a well-known phenomenon. Thus, gratification and appeasement refer only to the principal aspect of the resolution of desire.

The addictive power of television as an incentive is based on the fact that its stimulation value is extremely high, while demand on its audience is minimal. The appestat functions much more slowly than it would under more demanding conditions. Reading, for example, typically tires a reader in a much shorter time.

Arousal levels are determined not only by the awareness of presently existing appeasers, but may be caused by imagined or recalled experiences relative to the desire involved. An example of this may be observed in the case of experiencing an itch in the center of one's back. The onset of that feeling is negative and an effort is made to reduce the annoyance. The scratching experience is extremely pleasant and one is apt to seek such experience in the future. What happens is that when individuals consider the possibility of having their back scratched the arousal level is not tantamount to an increase in desire but is based on the pleasure associated with its gratification.

This is the situation as it relates to the abuse of gratifiers in any of the desires where the positive state is one of pleasure rather than relief. Having learned the voluptuousness of particular experiences their contemplation can lead to a high arousal level in spite of a very low degree of desire. Sugar and salt are examples of tastes of such high appeasement value that they are apt to be consumed even when the degree of desire is relatively low.

The model depicted here reveals that as one behaves in the interest of satisfying any desire that is appestatically controlled, each succeeding step in the experience is less satisfying than was its predecessor. The first taste of a strawberry sundae is more delicious than any that follows at that sitting. This is not true for desires that are not appestatic. Thus, behaviors associated with the desires for potency, power, and identification do not lead to a diminution of arousal but, on the contrary, often result in an increase of interest following relevant experiences. Thus, the corruption associated with power can be explained by the lack of appestatic signal and the pleasure associated with gratification. (The first time than one ever tastes a strawberry sundae, their desire for a second taste at that sitting will be increased, but the increase will not persist.)

Perception and Mind

The term perception has been used to describe every class of information reception from the experiencing of a simple sensation to the complex organization of data. This practice has resulted in a literature which includes apperception and conceptualization as aspects of perception, along with many other features of the process.

In the following discussion, the general term perception will be employed since it is under that name that philosophers as well as psychologists have presented their theses. However, when the individual becomes sensitized to an environmental experience, considers the information, and categorizes it according to some class (conception), discrete mental functions are being performed.

Conception or conceptualization has been defined as including such processes as abstraction and generalization. It is also sometimes referred to as *apperception*. This is a more puzzling term. It has been defined by philosophers as the perception of the mind's own state; perceptions made clear through interpretation or recognition of their appropriate classification. Herbart provided a psychological interpretation,

MIND: INFORMATION CHANNELS 215

suggesting that apperception refers to the absorption or accommodation of new percepts or ideas into the totality of understanding, thus expanding the nature of the knowledge system.[30]

At this level, conceptualization is occurring. However, there is a preconscious process that parallels that of "subliminal desire." This is the process of *recognition*. The distinction to be made, is that to recognize is to perform an act which requires no *interpretation* by the cognitive system. Knowledge, it will be recalled, is no more than a characteristic of an entity that makes possible a reaction. No consciousness or intention need be involved. Thus, the ability to recognize and to respond is not necessarily associated with the conscious reception of a signal any more than the heart requires *conscious* awareness in order to alter its pace when a stimulant is introduced into the body.

The "blooming, buzzing confusion" that James believed to represent the mental experience of an infant[31] is experienced by everyone when the signal strength of a stimulus from the environment is insufficient to allow for deliberation to occur. What occurs is not the conceptualization or deliberative assignment of a signal to a particular class, but the recall or activation of that assignment after learning has occurred or on the basis of instinctively related stimuli and responses.

This interpretation of subliminal conceptualization and desire suggests that a demarcation be made between the two types of signal systems and several levels of signal where mind is involved. Table 7.2 describes the relationships, as well as other elements, to be defined.

Gestalt organizational principles, such as that of closure, are involved at all experiential levels. The completion of a whole occurs at the simplest perceptual level. To the extent that it is outside the ability of the individual to deliberately modify it, it is nonmental. The sensitization that the individual experiences at exposure is preconscious recognition, while the assignment of the closed figure as a particular geometric form is a conscious conceptualization.

During the twentieth century, philosophic views of perception have dealt almost exclusively with vision, and reflect efforts to explain the phenomenon without reference to the desire or need of the perceiving agent in the true scientific spirit. The science of perception should certainly be developed independently of the will of the observer. However, such a separation does not *ipso facto* rule out the purpose of perceptual experience.

Explanations are offered along what might be called the sense datum line. Broad[32] and Russell[33] were proponents of the position that the perceptual experience includes a perceiver, *sensa*, and external objects. Sensa are entities with an existence of their own. They are logically deduced from experiences and propositions such as "the penny appears round" which infers that there is *something* which is in fact round at this perceptual moment. There remains the question of how the sensa are seen. Having gotten rid of the object as the source of sensation, these theorists replace it with another ghoul which must somehow be apprehended. Their explanation is that

Table 7.2

Pre-mind/Mind Signal Systems

Pre-mind Level	Mental Level	
Pre-affect	Preconscious	Conscious
Drive	Subliminal agitation	Conceptualization of desires
Perception	Subliminal recognition	Conceptualization of perceived data

sense data are the objects of immediate or "direct" perception. An opposing view—the multiple relation theory—as expressed by Moore,[34] Hicks,[35] and Barnes,[36] is that the perception of ellipsisity in the penny merely expresses a particular relationship between the perceiver, the concept of an ellipse, and the object. This theory posits no sensa between perceiver and perceived. The relationship fully accounts for the experience. Intervening entities are unnecessary. Observed or perceived sensations are a product of both object and perceiver. Here, the conceptual aspect is in focus.

A third view is that every existent presents many faces, each equally legitimate. One sees the penny as round, another sees it as elliptical. Each has an accurate perceptual experience. This view in a way parallels the wave-quantum theory of electromagnetic impulse in that it reconciles apparent difficulties in the perceptual presentation of matter. It also presumes an infinite number of perceptions for each object, since any number and type of distortion are possible. As a result, all entities would seem to have the same perceptual potentiality. To deny this would be to infer some ultimate difference, which is precisely what the theory seeks to avoid.

Another thesis, introduced by James,[37] was that perceptions are not comprised of sensations. His argument was based on the observation that many qualities besides color and shape seem to be perceived. Such characteristics as "gracefulness," he said, are perceived immediately and without sensation. This places beauty as well as redness in the object. What is perceived is not the sense datum but the sensually clothed object. The sensory aspect is not separable from the total object.

The interpretation of perception proposed in this text would nullify the possibility of "perceiving" tragedy or beauty. Such descriptors are based on interpretations or conceptualizations that are affectively mediated and, in most instances, learned. This makes possible a reasonable explanation of alternate interpretations of the same information as "comic" or "ugly."

Theories of perception seem to have been developed as logical exercises with no necessary relationship to the precursors of such an information flow in the inorganic world. But internal consistency alone is a poor argument for legitimizing an explanation. In drawing a conclusion, one must either assume that living beings—because of the accident of the characteristics of organized sensation—create the world they live in or that perceptual skill represents the imperfect reflection of external essence.

Kant's "thing in itself," and Hegel's essentialism have been challenged on logical as well as psychological grounds. The essential contribution of the perceiver and the difficulty of proving the existence of matter free of the influence of the nervous system led many thinkers to an abandonment of the view that humans have their world imposed on them.

This is a most unfortunate interpretation. First, it ignores the problem of whether the "redness" that one sees reflects *anything* external. Unless the answer is no, it must be assumed that an object is dependent on perception only for the *way* in which it is perceived. (The distinction between substance and existence was developed in Chapter 2.) Second, there is the issue of the role of perception as evidenced by evolutionary progress. Increasingly sophisticated perceptual skill, the superiority of vision over more primitive senses, and the survival advantage of the perceptually superior individual are obvious examples. Third, if internal states (e.g., desires) are accepted as representing knowledge with a function (i.e., communication with genetic information), it would be consistent to recognize the parallel with external knowledge that perception represents (communication which elucidates environmental information).

The holarchic interpretation is that, through genetic inheritance, apperceptive sensitization and conceptual skill enhance individual (and thus species) survival and growth potential. Individuals are freed from the tyranny of environment by a technique which in its narrower sense refers to the interaction between organized sensations (which present a shared experience of external existence) and the process of conceptualization. They are, however, not free in an absolute sense, remaining subject to the limitations imposed by the belief system.

This view, which separates perception from sensation, and which represents a phenomenological approach, argues that one "sees" (perceives) all of an object, not just the surface. There may be a series of physical steps that can be identified, but when it is reduced to human awareness (a psychological experience), the perceiver is aware of the whole object. Perception involves entering into a relationship with the totality.

Obviously, such an interpretation of perception deals only with the phenomenon as it bears on the interpretation of the world which each individual must make. Technical aspects have not been discussed. Structuralists suggest simply that "perception...implies the grouping of sensations under the law of attention."[38] The most complex interpretations propose that perception is a part of the transactional process that implies an awareness of environmental impingements that may be relevant for behavior.[39]

Gestaltists have insisted on the ultimacy of wholes as the elements of a perceptual experience.[40] Bruner and Goodman believed that perception is a function of the individual's directive state, and is thus without meaning when studied in isolation.[41] Hebb believed that perception should be understood in terms of the cell assemblies and phase sequences that determined its expression.[42] More recently, Gibson and others have offered the proposal that perception is purposive—in that energy that exists at the receptive surfaces (i.e., sense organs) includes potential information about the environment, and that perceptual experiences represent an effort to interpret the information correctly.[43]

Most theories of perception describe only the *mechanics*, not the *role* of the perceptual process. Gestalt principles assume that perception is always of wholes. The "New Look" of Krech,[44] and Bruner and Postman,[45] proposes that individual *needs* or *motives* color perception, which is hardly a novel interpretation. Others, such as Werner and Wapner insist on the influence of body tone and the interaction of perceptual systems.[46] None, however, deals with what perception provides to the perceiving individual.

The most extreme interpretation of the nature of perception is found in the writing of those who have been instrumental in the development of quantum mechanics as an approach to an understanding of the universe. Here we find the persistent contention that the infinitesimally small cannot be perceived because of the uncertainty principle which says that "particles no longer [have] separate, well defined positions and velocities.... They [have] a quantum state, which [is] a combination of position and velocity."[47] Since primitive particles cannot be perceived in any state, it is presumed that *such a state does not exist*. Perception, under this interpretation clearly does define existence. But what has happened to *substance*?

All such analyses are of value in the attempt to understand perceptual dynamics. However, it is the role of the process as it contributes to behavior and behavior potential that is the concern of this text, and here perception as a mental experience provides for the recognition of one of the critical elements in the determination of deliberate action.

This mirroring process suggests acceptance of the Representative Theory of Perception which is in some disrepute today for a variety of reasons. A principal concern is that if the agents of communication are the sense data described earlier, there is no possibility of ever proving that an external world "really" exists. But defenders of the theory argue that "physical events bear causal relations to sense data

MIND: INFORMATION CHANNELS 219

(or to our sensations) on the grounds that we observe the physical events *by means of* a representative mechanism."[48] It is this relatively brute interpretation that is proposed here. The function of the perceptual system is to reflect the environment in the manner that the limits of electromagnetic and other impulses make possible.

Summary

Desires may be classified in three categories (assertive, protective, and transcendent)[49] and recognized as arising spontaneously in some cases, contingently in others. The subcategorizations employed, a technique abjured as nonparsimonious by many, is based on the conviction that its heuristic value can (and shall) be demonstrated when programs designed to appeal to different types of desire are evaluated. *Needs* have been defined as those entities, behaviors, situations and events that represent the satisfaction of desires. They are to a great extent learned, and play a critical role in human adjustment.

Perception theory must align itself with either the notion that a real external world is intercepted, or that externality is a creature of the perceptual system. While no disagreement with the notion that the perceiver contributes to the experience is offered—such an assumption would be ludicrous—it is proposed here that as an evolutionary matter, the capacity to recognize and respond to, rather than to create, represents the most reasonable interpretation of the perceptual process.

In analyzing information systems, an attempt has been made to explain both the reasons for identifying various factors and their interaction effect. All information sources are, of course, subject to error in the sense that they may not accurately reflect to the individual what they purport to measure. There is a systematic variation from objectivity which is based on the structural limitation of the systems.

Perception, designed to measure the world, falls short in its construction. Knowledge of external events is always subjective and personal despite the ostensible similarity of observed phenomena. Conceptualized desires provide a rough guide to the degree of negative affect that is being experienced as well as the source of the malaise. Nevertheless, as with perception, innate idiosyncrasies and learned interpretations result in many misunderstandings.

The question of whether the affect related to a desired item is "correct" must also be answered in terms of its relationship to a perception. To say "I should have enjoyed an experience but did not," would be nonsense. I mean that, as the total situation was perceived by *me*, it was not likeable. Failure to remember or recognize what made the experience unpleasant, represents perceptual/cognitive error. Thus, belief about the nature of a conceptualized desire represents a limitation no less significant than that associated with a perception. Together these systems provide the basic information essential to the deliberative process. The manner in which such information is organized as knowledge, and those faculties which are essential to an appreciation of the status and the value of such data will be considered in Chapter 8.

Chapter Notes

1. Greeley (1981), p. 1
2. White (1959), p. 315
3. Kant in Blakney (1960), p. 271
4. Kant in Green (1957), p. 442
5. James, Saint, (1952), p. 218
6. McDougal (1908)
7. Madsen (1959)
8. Rapaport (1960)
9. Maslow (1970)
10. Beach (1956)
11. Adler (1927)
12. Rank (1936)
13. Fromm (1947)
14. Sartre (1956)
15. Moustakas (1956), p. 273
16. Goldstein (1956), p. 17
17. Maslow (1970), p. 135
18. Watson (1930)
19. Butler & Rice (1963), p. 82
20. McClelland, et al. (1953)
21. Nietzsche in Russell (1945), p. 766
22. Russell (1945), p. 767
23. Dewey (1900)
24. Locke (1969)
25. Machiavelli (1952)
26. White (1959), p. 321
27. *Ibid.*, p. 2
28. Political manipulation, brute force, and sexual enticement, would not be considered examples of "achievement" in the sense that McClelland proposed.
29. Brown (1961)
30. Herbart (1896)
31. James (1891)
32. Broad (1914)
33. Russell (1926)
34. Moore (1918-19)
35. Hicks (1938)
36. Barnes (1944-45)
37. James (1891)
38. Titchener (1905), p. 214
39. Kilpatrick (1952)
40. Heider (1958)
41. Bruner & Goodman (1947)
42. Hebb (1949)
43. Gibson (1966)
44. Krech (1949)
45. Bruner & Postman (1949)
46. Werner & Wapner (1952)
47. Hawking (1988), p. 55
48. Smythies (1965)
49. Koestler used the term *integrative*, rather than *transcendent*. "[One] aspect of the holon is its *integrative tendency* to function as an integral part of an existing or evolving larger whole" (1969, p. 208).

Chapter 8
Mental Components

Mental processing makes possible the distinction between many forms of knowledge. *Facts* are distinguished from *judgments* in that the former represent data about which total agreement is a possibility. *Truth,* which is peculiar to the mental process, refers to the relationship between belief about facts, and their *existential* actuality, while *proof* is limited to claims that are subject to public verification.

Reason, aesthetics, and *morality* represent classes of assessment that are not subject to standards of truth or proof. While reason is a form of judgment, morality is an evaluative scale. The conflict between these forms of assessment represent critical elements in the deliberative process, and thus in the extent to which behaviors influence human adjustment.

Each level of existence (identified as *pre-life, pre-mind,* and *mind* in earlier chapters) is characterized by a particular expression of the information/knowledge/communication system. Although at the highest level epistemological elements are processed cognitively and appreciated affectively, it is presumptuous to assume that they are mere Kantian figments since pre-mind knowledge has been shown to be a legitimate (if unexciting) trait. Berkeleyan idealists may have been saved the problem of proposing a universal mind had they realized that consciousness is not essential to, but is merely a unique element in, the process of information exchange.

The discriminant features of each stage of existence although apparently not intelligibly communicated below the conscious level, are not created by mind but must be recognized as ineluctable. As more complex forms of existent evolve, informational characteristics are not superseded but are appended by more sophisticated techniques. Thus, any characteristic of pre-life epistemology obtains also at the level of life, though the reverse is not always true.

Pre-life existents are real and have meaningful relationships. They act and react, transmit and receive information, possess knowledge, experience knowing at times, learn without purpose, and interact on the basis of chemical/physical, energy/mass interchange. Within narrow limits, this interchange causes a continual reorganization of existential elements according to thermodynamic and similar material laws. Terms such as *accident* and *caprice* are meaningless since all action is fixed by the physicochemical condition of the holonic elements involved

With life comes purpose, and an array of terms that grow out of the fact that goals are involved which may or may not be realized. While disinterested action and reaction characterize pre-life, internal striving and external impact make a difference where an effort is made to overcome annihilation. An intrinsic action may result in a successful or positive outcome or in an error that requires correction. Where environmental elements cause a course change, accident is involved. The term "accident" takes on meaning because of the fact that progress, a goal-related term, is impeded or facilitated. Mutations, for example, result in species alterations on the contingency of their occurrence.[1]

The cybernetic process, discussed in Chapter 4, can be re-evaluated at this point in terms of its applicability at the various levels of existence. It was pointed out that inorganic systems cannot possess feedback characteristics as that concept is ordinarily defined since a course cannot be "corrected," there being no meaning to the term. Further, if pre-mind organic systems, and machines, had feedback elements they could be only of a purely negative type since there is no profit in informing system elements of the propriety of an action.[2]

At the level of mind, positive feedback as a corrective device becomes meaningful. The individual operates on a decision-making, payoff-expectancy basis. While negative feedback remains a valuable technique the signal that a right action is being taken is also useful in its potential for assuring its continuation. Where no choice is involved, encouragement is useless. However, where the awareness of a desired outcome is involved, action may be accelerated or otherwise positively altered in the presence of knowledge of its relevance.

Because of the limitation imposed by belief, many concepts are defined in ways that cause confusion as to their legitimacy as forms of knowledge. As discussed earlier, pre-mind entities are controlled by drive and perceptual/conceptual interaction which, under appropriate conditions, results in automatic activity. At the level of mind, cognitive function, the development of concepts on that basis, and conviction or belief regarding their legitimacy is added. The category into which conceptualized data falls plays a significant role in the effect it has on behavior, and ultimately on emotional health. Here, the characteristics of "factual" and "judgmental" conceptions, and the distinction between them, will be described. Figure 8.1 describes the relationship between mental concepts, both conscious and preconscious, and the parallel elements in pre-mind life.

Fact

The information that is broadcast by an existent provides a clue to its existence at any level. The psychological phenomenon involved in its mental interpretation is defined as the knowledge of a *fact*, which is a "value free" parameter of a total experience.[3] The process involved is that of identifying an existent (It is the case that ...). The experiential or affective state is based on the conviction of the legitimacy of the factual conception that is involved. When the term fact is employed hereafter it will refer to this conceptual experience. This condition is imposed on all mental experiences. What one recognizes as a particular desire, as a specific need, or as any other aspect of mind, is always known (as described in Chapter 6) as a form of *belief*.

The interpretation of fact as value-free proposes a fact/value dichotomy which has been challenged as artificial by those who take the position that facts are only a class of value. Such argument is based on the contention that for a percept to have meaning, it must be interpreted by an individual in terms of previous experience, learning, maturation, or desire.[4] The term *interpretation* hints at some latitude on the part of the person receiving the data, which involves some choice in the application of value. But, such freedom cannot be universally inferred. The argument that raw data must be interpreted, and thus evaluated, is understandable. However, "evaluate" as used in this sense may represent no more than the assignment of an object to a class. To make the further claim that it must be related to desire or personal interest cannot be supported.

Psychologists, biologists, and physicists have developed many theories based on observations of special conditions. Freud made assumptions about normal personalities from studying the abnormal. Indeterminists in physics presume randomness because measurement distorts either location or velocity. Perception theorists, noting that a hungry individual "sees" an amorphous object as a form of food, presume that all percepts are colored by individual interests. There is, however, a stratum of experience at which certain entities, situations, etc., are reducible to factual status.

Whether or not one approves of Hitler's action in declaring war on Russia in 1940, it is an accepted *fact* that such a step was taken. The distinction to be developed here is between Hitler's attack on Russia and any interpretation of it as a "wise" or "foolish" decision.

To understand the nature of a fact, it must first be recalled that insofar as a fact is a *mental* representation of an existent it can never be precisely pinpointed. It is, at its limit, subject to acceptance as a form of belief. At the simplest levels of mind, data

Figure 8.1

Experience/Activity Sequence

Pre-mind	Mind Continuum		
	Pcs ──────────► Cs		
Drive/Perception	Desire/Perception		
Activation of drive in presence of perceived experience. This may be totally internal (e.g., arousal of urge in seed pod may cause eruption).	*Process*	*Product*	*Experience*
	cognition	concept	**affect**
	identify	factual conception	
	measure	measurement	
	judge	judgment	
	estimate	estimation	
	compare	comparison	**belief**
	evaluate	evaluation	
		moral	
		aesthetic	
	reason	rational appraisal	
	relate desire to situation	joint conceptivity	
	consider capacity & opportunity	conception of capacity & opportunity	**emotion**
Taxis/reflex/automatic activity	Behavior/emotional health		

is presented as essentially "factual" (yes/no, go/no-go), and an object of perception is "known" as being or not being some innately determined item. At the highest levels, assumptions are made about the "exactness" of certain information. However, such discrimination represents only the limiting case of belief about the data. Factual information may closely approach an abscissa of precision, but it can never quite arrive. The limitation of the inductive process exemplifies this perennial disappointment to those who seek the factual truth as a mental absolute.

The relationship between facts and existents is highly significant. An existent is the focal point along a hierarchy of perceptual being. The underlying substantial basis is independent of its conscious revelation and is not subject to analysis along a truth continuum. Not to exist is not a falsehood any more than to exist means to be true. The dichotomy does not have any meaning except where mind is involved. Facts are mental representatives of the presence, *not the truth*, of existents.

Facts include not only those experiences which are presumed to identify existents but also the relationships that obtain between them. Twoness, for example, is a mental concept employed to signify a condition that is nowhere to be discovered—inside or outside—the observer. Neither of the (two) objects possesses the quality and when taken together another holonic level of existential unity is represented. Furthermore, the awareness of a specific experienced entity in terms of a quality such as color is subject to the phenomenological peculiarity of the observer who is incompetent to precisely describe an existent since such knowledge is limited at least by the perceptual acuity of the perceiver.

To assume the (factual) being of substance which cannot even be potentially perceived is considered presumptuous in that it deals with the proposition: "I know *(believe)* there exists that which I do not *know*." However, there are several compelling reasons for accepting the assertion in spite of its ostensible audacity. First, there is the obvious fact that individuals have different perceptual experiences. Furthermore, people continually add to their store of knowledge by new learning. To assume that at any time what is being perceived by any individual is in precise factual correspondence with all that exists would be more difficult to accept than the alternative hypothesis.

Second, when an attempt is made to distinguish between what is being experienced perceptually (It is raining here now) and what is assumed to be the case where information is less precise (It is raining a mile away now), the error resides in a misunderstanding of the meaning of the proposition. The intention of the statement, "I know that there exists that which I do not know" is "I believe there exist things which I cannot at present prove to exist." The knowledge that it is raining here now is itself simply a belief which has greater potential for verification. Its factual status never exceeds the limit of belief but is simply more compelling.

Several classes of factual knowledge may be identified. The first deals with facts about the environment. Perceptual information is processed mentally by an act of ratiocination or rationality. Awareness of particular stimulus patterns results in a conviction that some external existent is present. To "see" or "hear" an object means to intercept a perceptual signal and to interpret the stimulus according to its persuasiveness as concepts are generated.

Facts based on percepts may be considered public in the sense that they are believed to be shared or are subject to sharing. They represent *descriptive* knowledge. They include knowledge of such things as existence (There is a tree), quantity (There are three people), relationships (John is taller than Harry), meaning (That is a river), purpose (That is a clock), activity (It is raining), and behavior (He is running). For each such fact, the data are required to meet specific conditions.

Other factual conceptualizations include implication (A ⊃ B), generalization (Trees are green) and abstraction (2 + 2 = 4). Such facts are generated out of a capacity of mind which is more sophisticated than that which deals with existents as "simple" wholes. In recognizing an existent as being red, the percept is related to a scale and requires no intervening percept (although the scale may represent a learned concept). On the other hand, a concept like "brother" requires another existent in order to be reduced to a scale. That is, asked if John is six feet tall, only John and the scale of height are considered (there need be no other person of that (or any) height). To determine whether he is a brother, another existent (a sibling) must be taken into account. This is, of course, no more than the analysis of the elements of a more inclusive holon.

If a fact deals with meaning, "This is a mountain," and if the term "mountain" is defined by physical characteristics such as "at least 2,000 feet above sea level," then any existent which does not meet that condition is not in *fact* a mountain. If a fact deals with function, "It is a clock" and if the term "clock" is defined by a function such as "capable of telling time," then any existent which does not meet that definition (a broken clock, a crushed clock, a clock that does not tell time) is not in *fact* a clock.

Another class of facts represents the knowledge of internal states which may be considered private because they cannot be shared. They represent knowledge defined in Chapter 7 as *acquaintance* rather than *descriptive* knowledge. Belief about desires is an example of such facts. Facts about desires do not meet the condition of reasonableness. For example, it is not "reasonable" to be hungry. However, desires can be conceptualized in the sense that hungriness, for example, is generalized from knowledge gained from many experiences of hunger. By contrast, drives are descriptive facts. They are not known or experienced as such but are assumed to exist on the basis of reason, just as knowledge of other desires is known.

In addition to the belief that specific desires are factual, it is possible to compare the strength of different desires which represents the same type of relational knowledge that is possible with perceptually derived facts. Desire facts as related to wholes cannot be known *exactly* for the same reason that perceptual facts cannot. (Conceptualizations are limited to approximation as characteristic of mental processing.) However, when compared, the reduction to exactitude is approximated once again by the apparent exclusion of certain alternatives, as "more hungry than thirsty". Desire facts cause negative affects which call for resolution while need facts cause positive affects which call for continuation. The satiation of desires results in positive affective states which are also factual in nature.

When percepts and desires are defined as factual, it is their conceptualization and not the experience that is being described. To experience a feeling that one may come to describe as hunger is not, in its preconceptual state, a fact since the cognitive system is not involved. Existents are without truth value because they cannot be false, while facts appear to be excluded from truth since, being inexact and limited estimates of existence, they cannot be true! Where, then, does truth become meaningful?

Truth

In addition to beliefs about concepts and inferences, individuals possess the ability to communicate—to make verbal and nonverbal statements about existential verity. It is here that the appropriate definition of *truth* shall be discovered. It lies in the correspondence between *beliefs*, *inferences*, and/or *statements* and the *existence* of the entities, situations, or events, that they purport to describe. As with meaning and purpose the term *truth* is relational, being a property of neither entity but of their interaction. Truth is created by, and is peculiar to, the mental process.

Ayer suggested a similar interpretation. "Truth is a property of beliefs, and derivatively of sentences which express beliefs."[5] Unfortunately, he added that it "consists in a certain relationship between a belief and one or more facts *other than beliefs* [italics added]."[5] In our text, the relationship is described as between a statement or conviction about a fact and the general acceptance of that conceptualization as being factually accurate (i.e., between a belief and the existential accuracy of that belief). Since the nature of substance is beyond certain knowledge, truth in that relationship is trivial. The more important correspondence is that which relates belief about facts to their acceptance as such because of the limitation that facts are themselves restricted by belief. Thus, truth is doomed to the status of approximation. There is, however, a far greater irony.

In the development of theories of knowledge based on the contention that cognitive processing produces the highest form of knowledge, it is assumed that the evolution of mind is from belief or feeling to intellect and truth. The situation is, in fact, quite the opposite. Conviction regarding the legitimacy of a conceptualization is an affective state. As knowledge is more refined, in that the cognitive/affective system becomes more sophisticated, truth as it relates belief to actuality becomes increasingly less stable. The more that is known about a concept, the less possible it is to consider the data "true" or "false." The reason for this is that what is being added is a series of measurements each of which adds a limitation to the final determination. Clearly, the relationship between an experience, which is in its nature neither true nor false, and the labelling of that experience (e.g., I see a tree) represent an attempt to achieve correspondence. However, the constraint of approximation must again be appreciated.

Proof

Although truth is applied to statements or beliefs about all facts, proof is differentially applicable to those involving public (descriptive) concepts and those related to privately held experiences. Empirical verification is limited to data which can be supported by evidence which, in the strict sense, refers to the presentation of signs that are publicly or outwardly visible. For practical reasons, it is often appropriate to make assumptions about private facts such as hunger or anger, and even to accept certain behaviors as evidence of the existence of factual states. However, the act of stealing bread after a month of starvation is not proof of the existence of a state of hunger (in the same sense that proof of the act of stealing was observed) in spite of the reasonableness of the presumption.

The freedom of the experiencing individual to interpret factual data is extremely limited. To the extent that a fact is either publicly or privately known it is fixed by that datum regardless of any feeling that may accompany the experience. Three eggs are appropriately considered to be three eggs regardless of one's hunger, their cost, or their size as long as they meet the demands of their definition. If they are defined as "things laid by a chicken," they qualify in almost any condition. On the other hand, if they are defined as "food," they are only eggs if they are edible. The agreement of the belief with the named fact fixes its interpretation until and unless new data are introduced.

Proof is reduced to the common acceptance of interpretations that are subject to experimentation, to replication, to continual verification. This, however, is no more than a convention, since no degree of proof can ever exceed the limitation of mutual agreement. The ultimate difference, then, between proof regarding public and private facts is to be found in the nature of inferences based on observation and those dependent on reason.

Measurement

The evolution of measurement skill represents a refinement of the knowledge system. In Chapter 2 the point was made that knowledge as a mental experience is analogic. In simple forms of mental organization stimuli are experienced as discrete. The phototropic cell responds at some exact level of light, and degrees above or below are meaningless. It is at this level that knowledge is essentially of a "factual" nature. In higher organisms, it is possible to make finer interpretations of the data. Shades of light are discernible and, in addition to the ability to apply numbers and physical measures, individuals can recognize such variations as bright, dim, very bright, almost dark, etc.. This is not true of all information at all levels, and measurements are not always appropriate. One would not claim to have *almost* or *about* two brothers, but they might be said to be *rather* tall or *very* bright.

This restriction does not rest on the fact that computation produces exactitude but on the lack of refinement which would be essential to a distinction. Are one full brother and one half brother closer to two brothers than one brother alone? Would the miscarriage of a male fetus represent "almost" a second brother? The problem lies in the practice or constraint of defining certain "facts" at some less than ultimate level of refinement. Asked to determine whether the distance from New York to Chicago is 800 or 1,000 miles, the former response may be considered correct although a finer response is available. However, if no measurement skill had been learned, the limit of ability to discriminate may be that Chicago is "close to" or "far from" New York. The distinction in this instance is between computation, which appears to have an exact locus, and measurement, which clearly does not. However, computation owes its sense of finality only to the inability of mind to make finer discriminations.[6]

There is a further limitation on the use of computational terms. Since the purpose of measurement and evaluation is to arrive at decisions, in many cases rough approximations are sufficient. In order to purchase Christmas cards, the number of individuals to whom they are to be sent (e.g., two) would be sufficiently refined. However, if each person is to receive a gift of a pair of skis, much more information about them would be needed—data regarding their height and weight, for example.

All data that describe *attributes* of wholes are measures and, thus, irreducible to exact status on the ground that measurement is always approximate. By contrast, many types of relationship can be stated with more precision. The number of states in the Union (whole to part) has an answer which seems to clearly exclude certain responses. Similarly, "taller than" or "older than" are dealt with as non-approximate, although their ultimacy remains non-demonstrable.

Judgment

Beyond the ability to conceptualize data in order to identify facts, higher levels of mental activity include the capacity to relate information to many more subtle scales and to appreciate additional characteristics of the data. This process is known as the making of a *judgment*. Here again, the cognitive aspect represents the performance of a function (i.e., a behavior), while the affective component refers to the conviction of the accuracy of the derived concept.

In practice, there are two quite distinct uses of the term. To *judge* is, in one sense, to take an action. One may, for example, consider (judge) the probable length of a room by taking into account various cues. But arriving at a *judgment* (to judge it to be 30 feet long) is affective. It is a belief state, a conviction, an opinion, a matter of faith regarding the presumed 30 foot length. Thus, a judgment, as an experience, is not something that one does, but what one feels. It is a *consequence* of an action.

Two uses of the term judgment as an *action* can be distinguished—estimates of factual data and relational judgments. Estimates of factual data deal with classes of data that are considered to be subject to verification as ultimately correct or incorrect. One might, for example, estimate the number of people sitting in a room. The limit of such an estimate would be the *factually* correct number. However, to the extent that the estimator does not have information regarding the correct response (the number of people in the room), the response can never be more than an estimate.

A slightly different form of estimate would be that related to measurement. One may estimate a room to be 42 feet long. In this instance, the limit is the actual length of the room, but the inability to derive a precise answer is a function of the nature of the information as well as the limitation imposed by belief. The process is analogous to approaching the number one (1) by way of the infinite series $1/2 + 1/4 + 1/8 \ldots$.

A graphic representation of the focus is shown in Figure 8.2a.

Judgments regarding desires are essentially limited to estimates of the strength of an urge (how hungry) or of a comparison between wants (more hungry or more thirsty). Such judgments are far less complex than those related to perception, which is the area in which the greatest evolutionary development has occurred. To the extent that judgments represent measures of desire or concepts exclusively, they are, like facts, value free. To judge one building to be taller than another, a shade of red to be nearer to crimson than scarlet, or that one is more hungry than thirsty, are theoretically "objective" estimates.

The distinction between knowledge defined as factual and that considered judgmental is critical. A fact is a *situation*, a *condition*, an *event*, etc., about which rational individuals would agree.[7] There is, of course, a suspicion of circularity in that by considering doubters irrational, any datum may be accepted as a fact. In spite of the limitation of mental knowledge that makes it impossible for any belief to be exactly correct, this interpretation is sound. The discrimination to be made is that facts are beliefs which rational individuals consider to be related to inferences or statements in such a way that the assumption of truth (and in some cases the possibility of proof) is applicable.

Judgments are beliefs that such individuals would consider incompetent to meet either condition. The proposition that a particular entity is a tree is accepted as being subject to some form of ultimate verification, while the judgment that an individual is "obese" is often limited to opinion. (It matters not that such verification represents only the collection of beliefs that strengthen the status of another belief.)

This interpretation is equally valid when the judgment deals with an issue that as a statement of fact is subject to proof—as in estimating the number of people in a room. In spite of the happenstance of an exact correspondence between estimate and fact, the judgment is not "true," since a non-corresponding estimate would not be considered a *false* estimate. The term commonly used to describe this relationship is "correctness," which, to make a confusing issue more so, also is used to describe correspondence of varying degrees of precision. However, having been operationalized, it is the appropriate term. Asked when Napoleon Bonaparte died, an *estimate* of the year 1820 would be considered incorrect if the specific year (1821) were required and correct if the decade were sufficient. In no instance could the response be considered a "true" estimate.

Judgments may be made about any form of knowledge. As with facts, judgments about characteristics of wholes are always a form of measurement ("He is 6 feet tall" or "He is old"), while those dealing with relations between existents may be considered to at least exclude certain possible responses. When quantitative estimates of the former are made, they are always estimates of approximations. In the case of relationships, a more precise interpretation may be provided.

The second class of judgment is one which compares an existent to itself in other circumstances or to other existents. I may believe that I am shorter than Harry, but taller than I once was. These are *relational* judgments. Qualificatory terms such as "rather," "very," "somewhat," "decidedly," "and extremely" are appropriate. Terms such as "tall," "short," "young," "fat," "happy," and "silly" are also descriptors of this type. As with estimates, because of the fact that objective states are approached, confusion is often created.

Figure 8.2

Estimation and Evaluation Standards

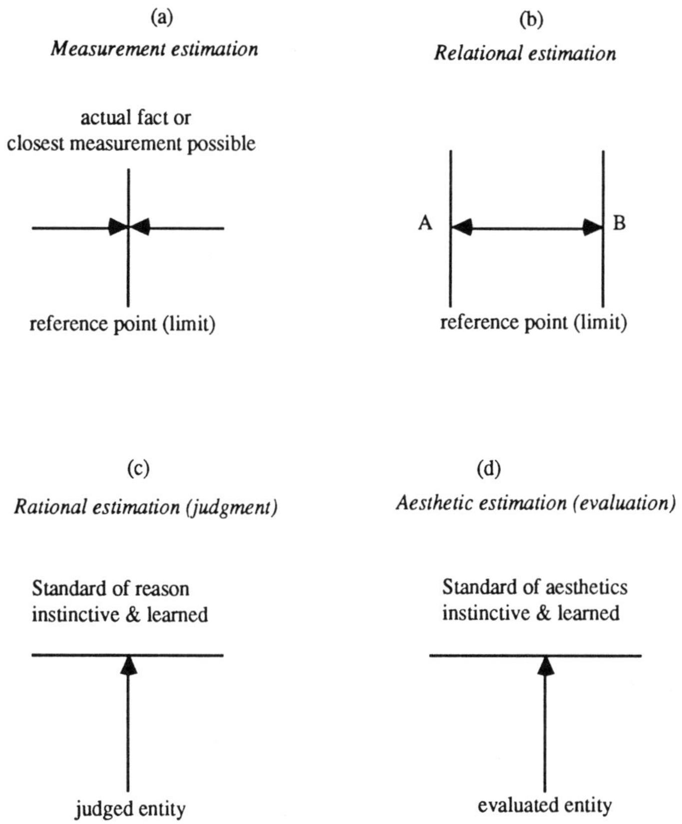

(a)
Measurement estimation

actual fact or
closest measurement possible

reference point (limit)

(b)
Relational estimation

A ↔ B

reference point (limit)

(c)
Rational estimation (judgment)

Standard of reason
instinctive & learned

judged entity

(d)
Aesthetic estimation (evaluation)

Standard of aesthetics
instinctive & learned

evaluated entity

The critical issue is that each relational judgment has as an appropriate criterion depending on the reference group one wishes to consider. She is a "tall" woman (5 ft. 10 in.) is quite appropriate although such a height would not be considered tall for a man. It is even proper to speak of a tall pygmy (5 ft.), a young vice-president (age 41), or an old high school student (age 20). A graphic representation of this focus is shown in Figure 8.2b.

Here the descriptor applied to B is meaningful only in relation to A, where A is B in another circumstance or another existent. A in this case may be "average height of women" while B is the woman in question. Given a different reference point (e.g., the height of all people), the distance between A and B would vary.

The distinction between estimates and relational judgments is obvious. The criterion of the accuracy of estimates is some parameter of the estimated entity. Of course, the parameter is itself a relative concept. The notion of length, for example, identifies entities only on a scale which projects them against an arbitrary relational referent. Relative location, rather than mere accuracy of estimate, is involved in relational judgments. Accuracy in this instance refers to the extent to which the location of both the referent and the referred datum are properly identified.

Reason

The process of ratiocination and the conviction of the veracity of facts and judgments refer to an ability to manipulate data on a scale which involves intelligence, experience, and other intellectual attributes and to draw a particular type of conclusion. This capacity is defined as *reason*, and it deals with the appraisal of probabilities where behavior is involved, and of the validity of belief where facts and judgments are in question. The adjective *rational* will be employed as synonymous with *reasonable* (rather than with *sane*) in order to avoid awkward sentence structure and to be consistent with accepted use.

Terms such as those employed in relational judgments are appropriate, but the limit (again beyond reach) is at one extreme—an "upper" limit. It would be erroneous to argue that one could be *too* reasonable. (It may be that one's reason caused difficulty, but that would not mean that on that *scale* the limit was exceeded, but that other considerations made being reasonable counterproductive.) A graphic representation is shown in Figure 8.2c.

Reasonableness as it describes behavior relates only to the behaving individual and not to interpretation by others. I may believe that you are not being reasonable. You may or may not agree. Only *your* experience is involved in this determination. Because behavior is based on a summation of all mental functions, any deliberate action will be discovered to have some underlying rationale (i.e., reason) that contributes to the decision making procedure.

In simple forms of life, the "fact to act" sequence occurs almost immediately on presentation of a stimulus in the presence of a drive. Higher forms of life are capable of an intervening process which deals with such issues as success, failure, the cost of failure versus the profit in success, or the relative merit of alternative behaviors.

To consider whether a belief about a situation or a contemplated or practiced behavior is reasonable, it is necessary to ask: Compared to what? Since an endless and diverse set of conditions may be considered, a judgment (or a behavior) can never be shown ultimately to be right or wrong, correct or incorrect, reasonable or unreasonable. However, judgments do seem subject to being scaled as "better" or "worse" as a proposition, situation, behavior, or event is considered.

Unlike factual data and related estimates, rational appraisal is not fixed by perceptual information but involves intellectual skill in an experiential context. If reason is applied to the estimation of a situation that is reducible to a factual state, new information may cause the judgment to be altered. Asked how many people are in a stadium, one may respond "20,000." Informed that such a number would collapse the edifice and that the response is thus untenable, the estimate is likely to be reduced. This, however, represents no more than the adding of knowledge to a data bank or previous experience and the new estimate, though considered more "reasonable," is neither right nor wrong, though it is probably closer to the factually accurate response.

Although judgments are qualitatively different from facts, the limitation that a fact cannot be exactly true at one extreme also causes confusion where it collides with judgment. The term "tall" is judgmental, but to say that a 7' man is not a tall man would cause some suspicion of mental incompetence. Thus, at the limit, judgments are practically indiscriminable from facts, which provides still another cause of confusion. (Judgments may, of course, be "rendered" factual by consensus. People may agree to call all 7' men "tall." Such a labelling process does not, however, alter the limit imposed by non-discrete data.)

The role of the reasoning process is to recognize situations of this type. To claim that there are eight days in a week is irrational; it violates a well accepted (factual) datum. To claim that there is sufficient time to cross a railroad track when a train 20 yards away is approaching at 60 mph is a matter of reasonableness. Close to impossible, it may be accomplished by some, not by others; it is not inherently reasonable or unreasonable.

The application of reason to the relationship between situations and events, as in calculating the success probability of a wager, may represent the pitting of desire against cost. Here is an example of the projection of manipulated data against the rational scale where personal interests are involved. The summative feeling that is produced still represents a form of knowing only as an affective state. To reason is to perform an action, to believe that the response is reasonable is an affective experience, just as to "hit" is a behavior while to "hurt" is a feeling state.

Evaluation

Judgment, in the sense that it refers to the ability to make increasingly refined computational and dimensional estimates or to compare entities, represents a *measurement* function. The focus is limited to particular mathematical physical scales. Beyond the capacity for assessing "how much," and "how many," mental constructs are subject to *evaluation*, which represents the projection of measurement data against scales of a different type. Here the question is one of *value* which requires a referent of a higher order and represents a unique type of assessment. Where judgments are considered on the scale of reason, for example, an evaluation is made, not of their accuracy as a physical matter, but on their propriety as a rational issue.[8]

The concept of *value* is particularly difficult to explicate. It came into existence when purpose emerged, and originally had a moral connotation. An action, a situation, or an event had value as it enhanced life. Over time, as the sense of self developed, the term has become far more general. It is now employed to describe everything from the relationship between a datum and a desiring individual to the seemingly disinterested association between elements of a mathematical equation. Exhaustive analysis would demonstrate that all such usage can be reduced to the initial moral intention.

The rational scale (described as an instrument of appraisal) represents an evaluative instrument in that estimates of the validity of beliefs and/or the relationship between a behavior and the probability of the associated outcome deal with the notion of *worth*. Thus, an issue such as the probability that one may commit a crime undetected may be evaluated in terms of the degree of risk, the penalty if discovered, etc. The process of projecting a datum against a standard such as reason is a cognitive performance. The standard may be learned or innately known. The sensory distinction between salt and sour is recognized because of an inborn capacity, while the desirability of a taste (e.g., the enjoyment of bitter foods) may be acquired.

The class of assessments in the value category also includes morality and aesthetics. Each represents a form of assessment which is independent of both the estimated entity and its comparison with other entities. Since the distinction is critical to the behavioral model to be developed in this text, each type of value judgment will be discussed more fully.

Aesthetics. The aesthetic sense has been a puzzle to philosophers since the positing of its status as parallel to reason and morality. Emerson, for example, believed that beauty represented one of the faces or modes of all existents.[9] But the role of beauty has had widely varying explanations.

Plato believed that beauty revealed God's essence to humans and suggested that the impulse toward goodness is revealed through the artistic quality of each individual's work, which may be that of artist, carpenter, or bricklayer.[10] Kant, Hegel, and many others, saw in beauty a window to ultimate truth. Kant believed that the appreciation of beauty represents a sympathetic bond between the viewer and the reality behind perceptual experience.[11] Hegel, who saw poetry as the highest form of art, believed that phenomena are captured in art forms in a sense which reveals that reality which is mind determined.[12] This relationship between beauty and God (Schelling also suggested that God is manifest through the artist's creative work) is obviously related to morality.[13] Shaftsbury and Hutcheson contended that evil behavior is based on a deficiency of aesthetic taste, while good conduct results from the ability to appreciate the beautiful.[14] Schiller felt that the beautiful helps humans to avoid many of the attractions of evil, "thus the will and desire are brought into harmony."[15]

The holarchic interpretation, while not wholly consistent with any suggested above, is to some extent similar in its essence, being based on the contention that aesthetics are functional. That which is perceived as beautiful, although culturally influenced, has value as an instinctive or learned *need*. Aesthetic evaluation represents the projection of percepts on a scale that, in instinctive forms of life, relates to their ostensible need value. For example, at the lowest levels of life an individual is recognized as a sex object because of a certain combination of characteristics such as shape and color. However, as generalization becomes possible (at higher levels of life), certain features of the sex object become stimulating in themselves.

Such stimulation relates most noticeably to the assertive and transcendent urges and is experienced through all perceptual modes. The sexually attractive individual may excite visually or through any of the other senses. Hunger is affected in the same way, with a highly desired food being sometimes described as "beautiful." The beauty residing in objects with no discernible relation to specific desires, as in the sound of poetry or the sight of a landscape, may well be related to the desire for stimulation, relaxation (serenity), or other less obvious urges.

Since this scale relates to so many types of desire—because the desire for stimulation, for example, leads to a seeking for diversity, and because learning is ubiquitous (repeated discords may become attractive)—many unusual forms of aesthete have developed. In order to provide evidence for this interpretation of the development of an aesthetic sense, it would be necessary to show that each percept with aesthetic characteristics could be traced to some instinctive behavior. Some simple organism would need to respond to that feature by behaving in some way related to a specific drive. This would be a particularly difficult, but nonetheless theoretically possible, task.

It is an assumption of this text that feeling states are inevitably related to percepts in some way that potentially leads to profitable activity, and aesthetics must meet that condition. Although this is an evolutionary argument, it falls short of the Darwinian notion that aesthetics helped civilized people to prevail. Rather it assumes only that since aesthetic situations or objects are desired, there must be some historic purpose for such feelings. As with reason, aesthetic evaluation is geared to a scale outside the limits of comparison with others, (Figure 8.2d).

It is quite appropriate in the ordinary course of consideration to make the statement that "Alice is prettier than Gladys," just as one might say that "Alice is taller than Gladys," and even that "Alice is tall for a woman." But it would seem absurd to compare (or even perhaps to discuss) the beauty of two warthogs since no matter the relative appearance of the two, the best falls far short of any conception of attractiveness. (According to humans, of course! For warthogs, the standard is the same; what differs are the physical characteristics that are projected against it.) Here is a further example of the distinction between innate and learned standards. One culture may teach that obese females are most beautiful while another may find slimness more desirable. They would, however, agree that the characteristic they were describing is *beauty*, and that the capacity to recognize such a characteristic precedes its manifestation.

Morality. A most critical evaluative scale, for which the term *morality* is commonly used, is represented by a sense which communicates at the conscious level the propriety of situations and events as to their self and general life enhancing characteristics. The expression *moral intuition* used by scholastic philosophers to identify the source of knowledge about God, survives as a branch of moral philosophy which takes the position that objects and events have certain "non-natural" characteristics which are recognized only introspectively. The terms *morality* and *ethics* are often used interchangeably, and shall be so employed here. (In Chapter 16 a distinction shall be drawn.)

The mandatory activity and end-states that characterize preaffective life provide for a survival and growth parameter. The evaluative scale defined as morality at the level of mind performs the same function. It invests actions and outcomes that are fixed at the taxic level with a sense of propriety. It sanctifies drives and their associated desires, as well as perception and the intellectual process, coloring all such experiences with feelings that are the basis for such concepts as "should" and "ought." The model for moral evaluation parallels that of the aesthetic scale which was depicted in Figure 8.2d.

This capacity to recognize the value of human feelings as well as the relative correctness of situations and events, binds the individual to the species, to other individuals, and to life in general. The moral faculty, in making possible the evaluation of propriety along the scale of self care and species enhancement, is as determinate as any other affect. The sense of the value of life is not situational, in spite of the fact that decisions which must be made about who should live and who should die in a particular situation often make it seem so. The concepts of ethics and morality that have developed out of this sense and its relationship to emotion and behavior will be considered in detail in later sections.

Although moral evaluations are imposed on factual and judgmental estimates they are themselves measurements along more subtle scales. Moral control resembles that of the appestats in some respects. Despite the fact that signals related to sufficiency remain in force in affective beings, they are in many instances overwhelmed by compelling data, as, for example by the powerful attraction of a particular experience. In such cases, the moral sense provides an additional braking mechanism. However, its range includes both positive and negative input, and the "go" aspect is equally significant. The interchange of active and feeling states, as cognition and affect are involved, is once again a source of confusion. To study relevant elements in the attempt to determine whether a condition is moral is a matter of cognitive manipulation—a behavior. But to conclude (i.e., believe) that it is or is not moral is an affective experience—a consequence.

A significant aspect of moral and aesthetic evaluations is that they are not subject to rational appraisal. The statement "abortion is immoral" is not subject to rational inquiry. However, it would be considered unreasonable for one who professed to believe that abortion was immoral to take the position that "Mary, in having an abortion, acted morally." Although reference to a supreme being is not involved in this text, there is clearly present in much of life some *a priori* conviction regarding the value of life. Morality seems an appropriate descriptive term in spite of the fact that the faculty is derogated as, "a term in popular rather than scientific usage."[16] But it seemed something more than a "popular" term to men like Einstein, who stated: "The moral imperative is the most precious traditional possession of all mankind."[17]

The moral sense must be understood to be distinct from the transcendent urge. When individuals perform in the interest of others because they believe it to be *right*, what is meant is that in addition to the desire to belong or to share, there is a recognition that such behavior is morally correct. (The same analysis may be applied to the contention that one wants to act rationally or intelligently. If, for example, money is saved, it will be because of what desires the money may cause to be satisfied and not because of a simple desire to act wisely.)

In the case of the transcendent desire, moral judgment is especially potent because it must deal with the paradox that self-sacrifice and self-care introduce. All desires as they are expressed in behaviors, relate to morally and rationally positive outcomes. Transcendence is, thus, no different than other urges in its moral aspect. A Kantian interpretation may help to clarify the distinction. If the reason one performs a socially approved behavior is to attain approval from the group, the action is not moral, but merely instrumental. If in considering possible alternative behaviors, an individual selects one considered to be moral, regardless of any resulting sanction, that person may be said to be influenced by a moral sense. The two concepts may be difficult to distinguish in a particular instance, but they are quite different in their nature.

The role of both the moral and rational systems is judgmental. In the motivational sequence, they are involved as estimators of the quality of potential activity along each scale and have a significant impact in many cases. Nonetheless, *neither is a form of desire*. They follow and judge potential or actual situations and events which are believed to have moral and/or rational components.

The concept of a moral sense that transcends the urge for personal profit is of ancient lineage. From Aristotle's notion that the highest good is the contemplation of truth, through the modern thesis of "enlightened reason," morality has been seen as a branch of intellect. The commonest view has been that reasonable behavior is moral behavior, since the purpose of such faculties is to guide the individual along appropriate paths. Others, however, such as Hutcheson,[18] have proposed that the ability to appreciate moral virtue is not a matter of reason but of a unique capacity which is related to the contemplation of ethical issues. Reid took a similar position, saying that "some philosophers, with whom I agree, ascribe this to an original power or faculty in man, which they call the *Moral Sense*, the *Moral Faculty, Conscience*."[19]

The view proposed by Kant two hundred years ago is reflected in the works of many contemporary thinkers. Ellington suggested that "Kant's greatness as a moral philosopher is rarely disputed...even among those who think his teachings grandly misconceived."[20] Few would take issue with that statement. The essential aspect of Kant's moral philosophy, as it relates to the definition employed here, revolves around the concept of a *categorical imperative*. This, he suggested, is the basis for moral law. It is peculiar to reasoning free willed beings (i.e., humans) and is a type of "golden rule." In simplest terms, it represents the assertion that individuals should act in such a way that their behavior would be appropriate to anyone, at any time.[21]

Kant's argument is complex and grows out of the contention that, unless pure reason could control one's action and unless the will were free, morality would be impossible. "An 'ought' can arise only when man has a choice between doing what his inclinations, if unchecked by reason, would inevitably lead him to do, and doing what reason tells him is in accordance with moral law."[22] This interpretation reveals the problem of relating reason to morality. Although one may well assert (reason) that a particular act, such as aiding an ailing person, probably is moral, it is beyond one's *reasoning* capacity to demonstrate that such behavior *should* be carried out.[23]

Kant believed that acting according to moral law represents a form of freedom or autonomy. "In obeying the moral law for the sake of the law alone, the will is autonomous because it is obeying a law which it imposes on itself."[24] If people are to be free (of "inclinations," baser motives, or physical causes), they must accept the categorical nature of lawfulness. By categorical, Kant meant a rule of action unrelated to its goal. Thus, while the knowledge of swimming is only hypothetically imperative to the avoidance of drowning (there are other methods), a maxim such as "thou shalt not kill" is a moral (categorical) truth independent of any end.

There is little question that Kant's analysis is "reasonable." For example, if one obeys a self-imposed constraint on one's own behavior, it may be argued, with reason, that this is a form of freedom (i.e., freedom from control by God or physical cause). And to be free one must accept the categorical nature of moral law. But the conviction that one *should* be free (*ought* to accept lawfulness as a rule of action) cannot be arrived at as a matter of reason, but on the basis of a separate and distinct faculty. Kant's reasonableness would describe mechanical people, automatons– a form of life more like the pre-mind species that function in strict response to preordained signals.

It may seem that conflict could be avoided if a term like "logical" rather than "reasonable" had been employed in this text to describe intellectually correct thinking. Unfortunately, that would have created worse confusion, for the term "reason" is most commonly employed in precisely the sense suggested here. Dictionaries, thesauruses—even Harriman's *Handbook of Psychological Terms*,[25] and Rune's *Dictionary of Philosophy*,[26]—make absolutely no reference to morality in their definitions of reason, reasoned, reasonable, etc. But, it is not simply a semantic issue.

The ability to reason, to think, to consider, is applicable to situations as they relate to the cost/gain balance of potential behavior. The capacity to appreciate the propriety of self-care and other directed activity, including the value of life in general, is based on a different evaluative capacity. Although some behaviors may be both morally and reasonably sound, in the vast majority of instances it is the *conflict* between these faculties that causes emotional problems.

Morality represents an evaluation of all other judgments (including reason). In principle, the function of reason in the evolutionary scheme is to make possible optimal experiences which "should" (i.e., ought to), ultimately profit the gene pool. Since reason provides the individual with the potential for mastering the environment, the outcome should be a healthier developing species, a continually improving gene pool. The dilemma that has resulted is an unforeseeable contingency in the evolutionary process. Possessed of awareness and the ability to recognize a biological self, individuals have increasingly turned their attention first to personal interests. As a result, their relationship to a more comprehensive existence has suffered. The denial of the past and cynicism about the future that mark so many in an opulent society, as described by Lasch,[27] are evidence of the ascendancy of reason.

Once again, culture and other sources of information have led to the creation of many arbitrary "rules" regarding moral conduct. Kohlberg's moral dilemmas provide examples of the conflict.[28] In the situation that requires a man to decide whether he should steal medicine needed by his wife from a pharmacist whose fee is beyond the individual's ability to pay, it is pointed out that the level of moral development shall determine the outcome. While this is a "reasonable" assumption, there may be a difference of opinion as to whether stealing is morally appropriate here. There is no confusion as to what is meant by moral propriety. The maxim, for all evaluations, follows that of morality in that *one learns what is "good" but has innate knowledge of what "good" is*. Where aesthetic and moral evaluation and reason are involved, confirmation is limited. An evaluation of "pretty" may be corroborated only by general agreement of one's placement on the aesthetic scale, while the contention that one is honest could be substantiated by instances of behavior which themselves were judged to be honest. The "truth" of such statements, however, can not be determined since beauty is not a matter of fact, nor is honesty independent of the moral scale.

In earlier sections we pointed out that many biologists explain moral behavior as activity which is designed to profit either the self, one's closest kin and most broadly the genetic line of the individual involved. A similar interpretation is offered by behaviorists, whose principles mandate such an explanation. Although psychological behaviorism was described by Wilson as offering a definition of the human mind "as a virtually equipotent response machine [which is] neither correct nor heuristic,"[29] reductionism is not denied. He did, however, say that Skinner's dream "will surely have to wait for the new neurobiology. A genetically accurate and hence completely *fair* [italics added] code of ethics must also wait."[30] Saints preserve us! It is strange that so many thinkers that find it easy to accept the notion that individuals are equipped with a signal system that underlies the desire to protect themselves, have such great difficulty in agreeing that the source of that desire (i.e., the species) may be transmitting signals that relate individuals to existence beyond themselves, and thus to feelings of responsibility and obligation.[31]

Obligation is, in the case of many individuals, to a form of life as it is represented in those with particular *perceived* characteristics. As members of a species strive to do that which is profitable to their own genotype, they also feel a responsibility to those who are perceived as alike. Serving the germ plasm of the individual becomes serving those with similar characteristics. Although this obligation fades as likenesses recede, it is recognizable across the species for many forms of animal life. In the case of humans, a generalized sense of the value of life extends to members of other species as well.

Superspecies,[32] semispecies,[33] and sibling species,[34] as well as such labels as "transitional populations" created by biologists to classify individuals, exemplify the confusion that lies in attempts to specify the precise target of moral responsibility. They do not, however, explain it away. A living existent, be it a class of individuals or a biological entity, has the propensity to survive and grow as a whole. But its organic parts have the same holarchic self-directedness. When the parts are physically separate (e.g., as instances), they are often invested with urges that conflict with their obligation to the totality as they struggle with their personal environment.

This concept of self-interest seems quite acceptable to biologists. As we mentioned earlier, selfishness of one kind or another is posited to explain away altruism. Why this is not as mysterious as selflessness is its own riddle. There seems no difficulty at all with accepting the notion that individuals are genetically endowed with the desire to protect themselves. *This* mystery apparently poses no problem! But if selfishness in the individual is understandable, why not some parallel characteristic in a superexistent (species or other level of influence) as it interacts with its parts or instances—even though such control is contingent on perceptual skill or instinctive knowledge? Does it matter which whole is targeted? Or what label is applied?

The parts of an individual biological entity are accepted as serving that total individual. Why should not the same relationship *for whatever reason*, be accepted between individual and species since such activity is continuously observed? Our contention is that individuals experience the same relationship with their species (recognizing the slipperiness of that concept) in the sense that it is synonymous with "protected gene pool." From a psychological standpoint, the critical factor is that individuals sense an affiliation with something outside their biological selves *and even outside their kin*, and that the opportunity to express that relationship is experienced by a moral sense, and is related to levels of emotional health.

When no choice between self and species is involved an individual's survival seems the only concern as we see in every instance of competition for food and shelter. Such viability represents a legitimate goal of the living individual. Self-care serves a purpose at both levels. However, in the highest forms of life, groups of individuals are sometimes sacrificed to the protection of one. An appreciation of the reason for such paradoxical activity is essential to an understanding of moral principles.

Efforts to explain generous and altruistic behavior in neat reductionist terms are observed at every hand. Darwin explained such behavior by claiming that "each man [learned that] if he aided his fellow men, he would commonly receive aid in return."[35] As to the sacrifice of individuals which results in the enhancement of the whole, we pointed out earlier that Neo-Darwinists argue that if in any organic collection some individuals possess the proclivity for self-destruction when necessary to the group's defense or growth, that group will have a survival advantage. Furthermore, such a predisposition will be transmitted. We do not dispute the logic of the argument. But somehow the reality, and more significantly the priority, of the group as a moral target goes unnoticed.

The sociobiologist's solution is properly directional, although the target is inappropriate. Wilson suggested that the many levels of kinship create an ambivalence in the individual as to which of conflicting moral behaviors is correct. He optimistically predicted that when sociobiology and neuropsychology combine, they may "transform the insights of ancient religions into a precise account of the evolutionary origin of ethics."[36] Under such interpretations the apparent morality of individuals would be reducible to activity found in the inorganic world. Systems outlast nonsystems. However, it is quite impossible to describe a relationship between inanimate objects which includes occurrences determined by change which is more than transitorily directional. For some period of time, and under certain well-understood principles of mechanics, matter may flow in a specific and predictable direction. But, as numerous physicists have observed, there is a great deal in the physical world that could be equally well understood if time were reversed.

> There is no difference save of initial positions and directions between the motions of an orrery turned forwards and one run in reverse.... If we were to take a motion picture of the planets...and were to run the film backward, it would still be a possible picture of planets conforming to the Newtonian mechanics.[37]

Thus, in physical affairs, directionality is in many cases arbitrary. It would be meaningless to relate the activity of iron particles around a magnet to any purpose, or moral attractiveness, in either component. By contrast, the activity of organic individuals is often directional and is geared to the homeorhetic survival of some living form which is the ideational parent of the behaving entity.

Elliot suggested that purpose, (and thus morality) is no more than a matter of "interest," and that "if planetary action were of intense interest, gravitational action, which affects the motion of planets, would be believed to be purposive."[38] How they do reach! If fantasies were horses, such philosophers would surely ride. The point is that— interesting or not— in living beings much altruistic behavior is observed.

There are several serious problems with current biological interpretations of moral behavior. First, as the focus of moral responsibility descends from species to tribe to kin to self, there is a tacit acceptance of ultimacy at subordinate levels of life. This violates principles of the concept of purpose and meaning developed in Chapters 2 and 4. If each individual's gene line were the ultimate focus of moral affect, genetic predecession could be shown to be independent of species influence. Gene "lines" would of course, be "meaningless" since meaning requires a referent. More importantly, feelings associated with propositions regarding the propriety of preserving human life in general would be impossible to interpret.

Second, as the object of benefit comes closer in kinship to the biological individual, the moral aspect of a situation takes on the characteristics of reasonableness. Helping my child is likely to profit me and helping another who is in a position to reciprocate is certainly rational. But the rational character of the action negates its moral status. We have pointed out that reason is a separate, distinct, and often conflicting evaluative standard.

The sociobiologist's philosophy has been shown to be racist. Barash claimed that races were an evolutionary possibility on the basis of sheer distance and naturally isolated gene pools.[39] This was offered as an explanation for racial, ethnic, and other types of hatred, based on long-standing locational or social separation. Race preference is a step in the direction of kin preference. Wilson plunged all the way. He contended that human beings, rather than having overcome selfishness, have "acquire[d] the intelligence to consult the past and plan the future...the primary 'goal' of a social vertebrate is the best arrangement it can make for itself and its closest kin, within the society."[40] Once again, the equation of reason with morality. Selflessness is said to be a game people play to provide the "best arrangement" for themselves and their families. The moral act is the one most apt to provide an advantage to individuals and those related to them, in order of receding kinship. The prescription is for *deceit, trickery, misrepresentation*, and other forms of activity that appear altruistic while being, in actuality, self serving. Evil? Immoral? Not in terms of sociobiological theory which would describe such action as appropriate to all forms of life. The moral aspect represents no more than a delusion.

In spite of the fact that some of the principles of sociobiological thought are worth serious consideration, their pronouncements (especially those of Wilson) on moral behavior are not. Kitcher, in a penetrating analysis of the shortcomings of this approach to an understanding of human behavior contended that the very writings of its proponents "make startlingly clear the shallow absurdity of pop sociobiology's repeated claim to provide a scientific foundation for ethics."[41]

The genesis of self-sacrifice in early human behavior is explained by anthropologists, many of whom subscribe to sociobiological principles. "A crucial aspect of operating [the economy]...was enhanced social interaction, particularly the psychological and emotional complexities of reciprocal altruism."[42] Hamilton argued that Darwinian fitness (i.e., preservation of the genetic line) is increased if a parent risks its life for its child because of genetic material they share.[43] Further, he showed that a gradually diminishing altruism is found as the relationship between the sacrificing individual and the recipient is lessened (with which we have no disagreement).

Trivers developed this line of research. He hypothesized even more specifically that the individual who acts altruistically with limited risk is apt to be helped in return and thus has greater survival potential.[44] Wilson accepted this interpretation adding that the gene line rather than the individual is the focus of altruism.[45] These two notions were the foundation on which sociobiology, for a period, a highly respected biological school was erected. The mystery of the "gene line," as suggested earlier, posed little problem.

Wilson and other sociobiologists found the gene, which they apparently interpreted as a physical blueprint, the most suitable focus of the activity of living creatures. The species and the individual are each assumed to serve this master. This "modern" synthesis in biology offers the explanation that since self-sacrifice is most apt to be performed in the interest of those of near relationship, and since the altruistic individual is most apt to share genes with those saved, the altruistic characteristic will be preserved in that genetic line. In the attempt to explain why others of the same species, who do not share common genes, are protected, Wilson suggested (using the case of protective calls in birds) that it is "owing to the probability that close kin are [physically] near enough to be helped."[46]

A prodigious effort to avoid the idea that other-directed or purposeful behavior may cause individuals to sacrifice themselves to the living principle as manifested in species, can be found in Wilson's hypothesis that:

> Warning calls...actually help the bird giving the call.... Feasting on a neighbor can sustain the predator long enough for him to continue hunting, encouraging him to remain in the neighborhood. It can teach him how to catch members of the species, and give him a preference for the species.[46]

Leakey and Lewin suggested that the achievement of common goals requires much sublimation of personal interest, concluding that "beyond this [is] the desire—conscious and unconscious—to ensure that the system of reciprocal altruism operates as it should, with no one gaining unfair advantage."[47] What do they mean by unfair? From what source does the concept arise? If one individual violated the rule, they continued, "[it] could be biologically beneficial [to him] in the short run."[48] His genetic line would profit. Since this is precisely how they presume evolution to operate, it may seem an embarrassment to their argument. But they were prepared. "Natural selection," they pointed out, "inevitably gave rise to individuals capable of detecting cheating."[48] If neatness counts, the problem is solved.

But what of self-serving behavior? Since that type of activity is believed to be the root of all other-directed action, is it not appropriate that we all act for ourselves? And, why not do it openly? The proposals of sociobiologists are indeed strange. The dilemma they have created is as unnecessary as it is absurd. Consider the reasoning involved:

- Sociobiologists are evolutionists. Thus, they accept the principle of the survival of the fittest, which is a basic evolutionist postulate.
- This requires the belief that individuals, as carriers of genetic material, must serve themselves first.
- Much human and animal behavior is directed toward the self.
- Self sacrifice and other ostensibly altruistic behavior which are an embarrassment to the position must be explained as being ultimately self-serving.
- Yet the selfishness they see as the underlying motive is also discomfiting.
- Thus, they conclude, *we must rise above it*!

Dawkins' proposal was a classic example of this incredible recommendation: "[We] have the power to rebel against the dictates of the genes, for instance in refusing to have as many children as [we] are able to."[49] If my genetic inheritance proclaims, "be selfish—enhance yourself," from whence arises Dawkins' feeling that we *should* overcome it? Or was he saying do it though we *should* not? Or do our genes say, "preserve yourself—though you should not?" But that would represent a feeling that we should sacrifice in the interest of others.

This schizophrenic position is reflected in the writings of social learning theorists who, although they agree in denying an inherent (genetic) urge to altruism, propose that such behavior be taught to children! Examples may be seen in a report by Yarrow, which provides guidelines for parents: "Generalized altruism would appear to be best learned from parents who not only try to inculcate the principles of altruism, but who also manifest altruism in every day actions."[50] And in a review by Grusec, who contended that, "The more examples of altruism provided the easier it should be for children to abstract a general rule about the importance of showing concern for others."[51]

But why teach children altruistic behaviors? Either they would be violating the basic principle of selfishness, or they could use such behavior to achieve their own ends. In fact, what "general rule" could be abstracted from examples except that by appearing generous one would gain applause—ultimately an advantage over one's neighbors? Hoffman, in a rare dissent, (with which we are in total agreement), made the point that:

> The doctrinaire view in psychology has long been that altruism can ultimately be explained in terms of egoistic, self-serving motives.... It is always possible, when viewing an example of human action that appears to be motivated by an interest in the welfare of others to induce a hidden, unconscious or tacit self-regarding motive (e.g., social approval, self-esteem) as constituting the real source of such behavior.[52]

More recent interpretations of ostensibly sacrificial activity include the hypothesis of "selfish DNA." Since each genome contains far more DNA than it can ever use, it is speculated that "sequences whose only function is self-preservation can arise and be maintained simply because they are successful in that endeavor."[53] Sequences which provide the protein necessary to the fitness of the organism are most apt to survive. But so are "non-coding sequences that are simply effective in spreading themselves through the genome...'selfish DNA'."[53]

There was also a proposal by Thomas, mentioned earlier, that we are no more than the unwitting environments for "selfish" organelles. Thomas proposed that our notion that organelles are "enslaved creatures captured to supply ATP for cells unable to respire on their own"[54] may be quite wrong. "From their own standpoint," he suggested, "the organelles might be viewed as having learned early how to have the best of possible worlds, with least effort and risk to themselves and their progeny."[54] This, he supposed, they accomplish by avoiding the manufacture of increasingly more elaborate DNA strands and "electing" to remain small. To make this possible "they got themselves inside all the rest of us."[54] Every action of organic individuals is reduced to self-centered motives. But why should they serve their progeny? Is this not *unquestionable* evidence of altruism? Does the one or group that profits from such activity matter? Why is helping my own child not conclusive evidence of the existence of an altruistic motive?

Each of these sociobiologic interpretations represents an attempt to provide for a part/whole explanation that avoids the human/species conjunction, and specifically refutes the sense of allegiance to humanity that guides behavior in a morally positive direction. Moral behavior is rejected as evidence of a purposeful relationship between the behavior of the individual and the enhancement of the species. This dismissal of a paradigm that was accepted for many years is based on what some believe to represent a break-through in genetic understanding.

The principle involved was that the mystery of purpose is not essential to an understanding of the worker bee's behavior, which is simply a characteristic of genetic function. Purveyors of the no-purpose, no-altruism, look-out-for-number-one position in biology are sometimes quite vehement. Ghiselin, for example, in presenting their position stated that, "given a full chance to act in his own interest, nothing but expediency will restrain [man] from brutalizing, from maiming, from murdering his brother, his mate, his parent, or his child. Scratch an 'altruist' and watch a 'hypocrite' bleed."[55]

Adherents to the modern synthesis, in statements of this kind, demonstrate an arrogance which can be found in the works of many who herald new discoveries. As often as not, however, rejection of conventional wisdom does not stand the test of careful scrutiny.

Evidence is sometimes provided that a ravenous mother may take food from her child—perhaps even kill it for the food its body will provide. The conclusion drawn is that at the level of starvation her true nature is exposed. This fatuous interpretation is assumed analogous to that of the contention that the authentic personality is revealed when an individual is under the influence of alcohol. The greedy mother is perchance believed to mask her selfishness for social reasons—another example of a *"discontent"* of civilization.

It may be that such theorists would suggest that to understand how an automobile *really* functions, we should foul the carburetor, or to test their ability to swim, we tie people's arms behind their backs. The starving mother is functioning with a crippled cognitive/affective apparatus. *Her behavior under such conditions is no testament to her intrinsic urges.*

Consider, further, some of the technical aspects of sociobiologist's claims. They contend that since each person has two sets of genes (one from the fathers two sets, and one from the mothers) there is a 50% probability that any particular gene in a given individual will appear in a full sibling. Washburn, however, challenged that notion. "This whole calculus upon which sociobiology is based is grossly misleading. A parent does not share one half of the genes with its offspring; the offspring shares one half of the genes in which the parents differ."[56]

Geneticists estimate that humans share 99% of their genetic material with chimpanzees. Since the best estimate is "that the races of man are 50 times closer [to each other than to chimpanzees] individuals whom sociobiologists consider unrelated share, in fact, more than 99% of their genes."[56] Washburn, in this analysis, was not denying the fact of difference as genetic lines separate, but his data pose a problem that is of considerable interest. With perhaps .01% of the genetic material variant, the genetic capacity to discriminate must be awesome; even occult!

Sociobiologists contend that when species live in family groups, genes for altruism will increase whether or not family members can be recognized by those carrying the genes. What then should be expected about the concern of a parent for a child *not their own*, who through a hospital error was given to them without their knowledge? Though the sociobiologist may claim that the genetic potential to know was overpowered by, perhaps, a maternal instinct, the issue is not resolved.

What the sociobiologist has done is to attempt to rid biology of the "mystery" of self-sacrificing behavior and the notion of purpose; to get at what *really* causes behavior. Not some nebulous species centered genetic idea, but a real, finite little mechanism; a clever little entity that directs individuals, without their knowing why, to prefer their own kind; a molecular collection that reads self enhancing potential in the future behavior of a recipient of self-sacrifice. What they have done is to sacrifice one mystery for another, and in the process they have created a less adequate—in fact highly misleading—explanation. Washburn suggested that:

> The power of the genetic theory of natural selection gives sociobiologists the confidence to provide genetic explanations for social customs without producing careful analysis or supporting facts.... They are not worried by their repetition of the errors of the eugenicists, social Darwinists, or racists.[57]

The idea of the selfish gene provides comfort to those who object to the notion of species or gene pool priority. An appeal is made to a characteristic of living things that is more acceptable, more easily observed; the notion of selfishness. But even here, the action of the gene is in the interest of its successors. There remains the disconcerting problem of allegiance to an existence beyond the individual.

This insistence on minimizing of the role of selfless behavior is based on the assumption that such action would not only challenge evolutionist principles (by moving the focus from individual to species) but would require the acceptance of the notion of purpose, and this is to be avoided at all cost. To the extent that the difference between species membership and a more immediate relationship (i.e., close kin) is one of degree rather than kind, it may seem of relatively little significance to determine which view is the more accurate. From an emotional health standpoint, if there is agreement that the individual has an evaluative component that directs behavior and emotion away from self, what matter the ultimate focus? But the focus is critical if educational programs designed to provide guidance are to be based on a coherent philosophical model.

If the underlying motive in altruistic behavior is to improve one's probability of being helped in return, surely children should be taught to consider the future return potential when performing a generous action—even one of oblation. It is quite likely that sociobiologists, like other scientists desperate for concrete, visible explanations, have been deluded. The individual inherits its genetic direction *through* the family, but unless families have a source separate from the species, the message conveyed is more general than that of kin supremacy.

When sociobiologists trace the lineage of an individual, they are surely aware that in little more than thirty generations, the number of unions involved would equal the world's total population. This is, of course, an absurdity since many of the same people are involved, and in a period of a mere 500 or 600 years the degree of common ancestry is staggering. Gene line, or kin purity is a myth to the extent that as an evolutionary phenomenon it could represent the *ultimate* focus of purposeful behavior. Stent referred to such efforts as "the corrupted use of the antonymous concepts of altruism and selfishness,"[58] adding, "It would be marvelous if those two movements [sociobiology and creation science] that threaten to pollute the intellectual environment...were to consume each other and let the rest of us get along with our task."[58]

Summary

The cognitive/affective function of the mental process has created a unique class of concepts, which must be understood in their separate significance. *Factual* and *judgmental* data describe distinct types of categorization. Facts represent a class of data that are believed competent to be evaluated as true or false. Judgments are not subject to tests of truth or proof, there being no standard of accuracy against which to test their validity.

Facts, judgments, evaluations, and other concepts come into being with mental processing, with truth representing the relationship between beliefs about such things as propositions and situations, and the existential verity of the concepts involved. In the case of facts, the relationship to belief is subject to analysis on a truth continuum, and, where the facts are public, to proof. As to judgments, no such claim may be made since the scales against which they are projected remain private. Proof, which can be ascertained only for factual data, is shown to be subjective and limited. The fact that some forms of knowledge are subject to proof means only that convictions about such knowledge can be shared. *Reason* and *morality* represent assessment scales against which behavior is measured. Being judgments, they too are beyond verification by any more ultimate criterion.

The most controversial aspect of the material that we have presented here is the contention that humans have a moral sense which identifies right and wrong as species preservative characteristics and the assumption that as a "scale" it is infallible. Appreciating this makes possible the fullest development of the self. It is within this system that meaning becomes significant. For the moral sense to be in error, it would be necessary to call on an evaluation from outside the gene pool—since the genetic code does no more than define a relationship that is observed throughout organic nature, both in the conscious and preconscious activities of life. Error can occur, of course. However, the error source is at the individual perceptual/cognitive level. The correctness of the moral faculty is as arbitrary as the weight of a kilogram, but the arbitrariness is visited on the individual genetically. It is the associated (learned) behaviors that are subject to distortion.

We stated earlier that reason and morality often induce conflict. The immediacy of the biological self, and the role of reason in acquiring what is desired, often swamp urges that are evaluated as morally proper. Since morality in the individual represents the reason of higher levels of life, and since such levels tend to be much less in perceptual focus, activities that are self enhancing often take center stage. The guilt associated with such behavior, can be extremely debilitating, no matter that the "proper" focus of behavior in such instances has been learned. Thus, murder and mutilation carried out for personal gain, for revenge, or for the interest of some subgroup of human beings, may well bear on the conscience of those taught that all life is precious. We shall deal with the defense mechanisms that alleviate such negative feelings in Chapter 14.

In this chapter attention was paid to the prevailing view of biologists who see moral behavior as reducible to self serving activity, in that those who perform generous acts expect recipients of their largesse to reciprocate. This interpretation, which grows out of the Darwinian philosophy of the survival of the fittest is without merit. The view of positivists such as Ayer, who argue that moral statements are no more than emotional expressions[59] have not been presented since so many philosophers have denied their validity. Milne, for example, said "the emotive theory of values...is philosophically unacceptable,"[60] adding that "[Ayer] did not notice that intelligibility is logically distinct from and logically prior to verifiability"[61]

Chapter Notes

1. The contingency is, of course, only such as it relates to the species, not as independent of those specific factors that cause it to occur.
2. The fact that an "effect" such as the travel of siphoned water may contiguously "cause" water to flow has a feedback characteristic only in the peculiar sense that an action may cause a reaction in a geographically prior entity. The chronological flow is only in a forward direction. "Positive" feedback may, in this sense, be used to describe any effect that triggers further action.
3. The term *value*, as it is used here, refers to the interest or concern of one who assumes the factual status of any datum.
4. Proponents of the so called "New Look" interpretation of perceptual experience argue that biological and psychological needs as well as levels of stress and particularly the "set" or stimulus expectancy all determine the interpretation of a perceptual experience. Thus, they would challenge the contention that any proposition can be said to represent a "fact," if such status requires universal accord.
5. Ayer (1956), p. 148. The definition proposed here is recognized as an arbitrary stipulation. It does, however, meet Ayer's concern that any theoretical position be "intelligible and coherent." (Ayer, 1979).
6. Probability theorists, and perhaps molecular biologists, shall ultimately demonstrate that a datum presently considered to be an entity represents only the apex or gross interpretation of an approximation. The "twoness" that describes a pair of entities will be seen as the mean or locus of a collective existence. There is already serious consideration of the possibility that existents are simply extreme expressions of what in minute entities would be wave forms. The notion that an individual may be "reducible" to representing the locus, the peak or trough of a wave is not particularly bizarre.
7. On the principle that facts have a truth dimension, and since truth is often considered a characteristic only of propositions, it may seem that facts themselves must be limited to propositional existence. However, to have factual status, a situation need not be communicated (even internally). Only the truth regarding a claim about it is subject to that limitation. For example, Chicago *is* in Illinois prior to any claim as to its whereabouts. A statement about its location is made on the basis of one's belief about what is the *pre-interpreted* case.
8. To judge the size of the earth as

one-tenth that of the sun would be inaccurate but not wholly unreasonable. To assume that a 10 pound test line could withstand the pull of a 100 pound fish would be considered both inaccurate and unreasonable, regardless of whether in some situation it did.
9. Emerson (1841)
10. Plato in Bacca (1945)
11. Kant cited in Kemp (1968)
12. Hegel (1975)
13. Schelling (1845)
14. Shaftsbury & Hutcheson, in Fowler (1883)
15. Schiller cited in Hibben (1911), p. 191
16. Drever (1952), p. 177
17. Einstein cited in Bohr (1949). Einstein did not accept the personal God of western religion but the God of Spinoza "who reveals himself in the orderly harmony of what exists, not in a God who concerns himself with fates and action of human beings" (p. 18). It is to the invariable and magnificently orderly laws to nature that obeisance is due, yet Einstein said that science provides no insight into morality, which is rather, revealed by men of religious genius. He believed moral codes are revealed "through the medium of powerful personalities." (Ethics comes from all religions.) "Cosmic religion," Einstein said, is the "noblest motive for scientific research" (1985, p. C4). However, he could make no case for his position except his feeling. His science helped him only to a belief based on the *order* he saw in the world.
18. Hutcheson (1971)
19. Reid (1965a), p. 291
20. Ellington (1983), p. xi
21. Friedrich (1949), said that Kant believed that man's "good will" would lead to acceptance of the rule.
22. Kant cited in Kemp (1968), p. 57. Kant contended that behavior is based on "inclinations," to which reason goes counter.
23. "Hume's Law," or the concept of the naturalistic fallacy, dealt with the problem of drawing moral conclusions from rational premises. However, philosophers such as Reid, believed that by *moral reasoning*, individuals can determine the value of particular behaviors, "as all human actions, considered in a moral view, are either good, bad, or indifferent." (1965a), p. 291.
24. Kant cited in Kemp (1968), p. 60
25. Harriman (1974)
26. Runes (1962)
27. Lasch (1979)
28. Kohlberg (1958)
29. Wilson (1975), p. 551
30. *Ibid.*, p. 575
31. A fascinating study has been made of the behavior of dolphins where every individual, "mothers, babies, old, powerful, weak, renegade," has the power to kill others whenever it so chooses. Instead, they elect to live in so-

cial harmony, providing no evidence of conspecific struggle. "They may live in a balance of personal and social constraint, analogous perhaps to the gentleness of a giant aware of its capacity for power." Morality is nowhere more clearly manifested. It is suggested that this "provides hope that we, too, [in spite of our destructive capability] will gain control of ourselves" [Calypso, 1982, p. 4).

32. Amadon (1966)
33. Mayr (1959)
34. Dobzhansky (1970b)
35. Darwin in Montagu (1952), p. 85
36. Wilson, E. O. (1975), p. 129
37. Wiener (1948), p. 42. Strictly speaking, there is reason to doubt the reversibility of time. Cronin and Fitch have discovered a flaw in one of the assumed physical symmetries. "The laws of physics...must change if one reverses the direction of time—they do not obey the symmetry T" (cited in Hawking 1988, p. 79).
38. Elliot (1972), p. 318
39. Barash (1977)
40. Wilson, E. O. (1975), pp. 380-381
41. Kitcher cited in Kamin (1985), p. 78
42. Leakey & Lewin (1977), p. 61
43. Hamilton (1964)
44. Trivers (1971)
45. Wilson, E. O. (1975)
46. *Ibid.*, p. 123
47. Leakey & Lewin (1978), p. 61
48. *Ibid.*, p. 62
49. Dawkins (1976), p. 141
50. Yarrow, Scott & Waxler (1973), p. 226
51. Grusec (1981), p. 74
52. Hoffman (1981), p. 41
53. Science and the Citizen (1980), p. 92
54. Thomas (1974), p. 71
55. Ghiselin (1974), p. 274
56. Washburn (1976), p. 415
57. *Ibid.*, p. 416
58. Stent (1984), p. 141
59. Ayer (1946)
60. Milne (1987), p. 89
61. *Ibid.*, p. 107

Chapter 9
Emotion

Emotions are a form of affective knowledge which is activated by an awareness of the interaction between desires, associated needs, and the conceptualized environment. They are an essential aspect of the deliberative process. Although all desires are experienced as negative affective states, some emotions are positive, since they include the belief that desires may be assuaged. *Attitudes* represent emotions that persist over time, and are aroused in situations where characteristics are recognized as similar to those of earlier experiences.

Hope is an emotional parameter that comprises both desire, and the conviction that the desire may be gratified. A *wish*, by contrast, describes a situation in which there is no reason to expect the associated desire to be relieved. *Excitation* levels relate only to hope and are based on the interaction of desire and expectation.

The conceptual system includes a technique for identifying, categorizing, and evaluating desires, their related needs, and the nature of the environment, whether real or imagined, contemporaneous, anticipated, or recalled. The experience that results from this complex process, and which evolved simultaneously with desire and the conceptual system, is commonly referred to as *emotion*. It represents a mediational component of the affective system at the conscious level. It is, thus, a form of knowledge and, like desire, is a type of *private* fact.

As with so many terms employed in the description of introspective experience, emotion has been defined in many ways. In general, psychologists have avoided subjective accounts of the phenomenon. A psychological dictionary, in defining the term emotion and describing the behavior associated with its intense manifestation, states that "emotion refers primarily to perceived feelings, while affect includes the drives that are presumed to generate both conscious and unconscious feelings."[1] Again, the notion of unconscious affects.

While many theorists attempt to ignore or avoid the introspective aspect, some writers like Chein have castigated those behaviorally oriented who "avoid the phenomena of inner feeling and emotion as mentalistic poisoning.... The price they pay is that they lose much of the human being and what makes him do what he does."[2] Those who appreciate the vital contribution of emotional experience offer a wide variety of interpretations. Hilgard pointed out that rather than to develop theories of emotion based on recognized mood states "the specializations within psychology assigned such matters to personality or to abnormal and clinical psychology."[3]

Among psychologists who have dealt with the concept, some have considered emotion and affect to be synonymous. Harriman defined affect as "the totality of feeling—emotion."[4] But as belief is a subset of knowledge, so emotion is one of many types of affect. Harriman, in fact, referred to desire as "longing;"[5] and Funk called desire an "impulsive motive tendency."[6] These are clearly affective states, as is *belief*, which both writers referred to as dealing with convictions regarding the validity of propositions.

Philosophers are no less vague. Emotion was defined by Runes as "the inner motive as distinguished from the intention...of action."[7] But intention is another affect laden term. Fernald & Fernald suggested that emotion is "a complex feeling state accompanied by physiological arousal and overt behaviors."[8] However, desires are no less accurately described as "feeling states," though they are perhaps somewhat less complex. Although Young seemed about to break through the fog of contradictions with his inclusion of desire, moods, and temperament along with emotions as types of affect, he failed to recognize the normalcy of emotion in his proposal that it be defined as "an acutely disturbed affective process...a departure from the normal state of composure."[9] He argued, unfortunately quite correctly, that "nearly everyone, in describing emotion, uses such terms as *stirred-up state, disturbance, disruption, upset, turbulence, perturbation*, and similar words that imply disorganization."[10] Such definitions, however, are not appropriate descriptions of emotion, but only of tumultuous emotional states which occur in those conditions in which the system is out of control.

The result of these imprecise interpretations is manifested in a number of positions taken in the field of cognitive psychology. In the early 1980's, a running feud regarding the order in which mental events occur was waged by Lazarus and Zajonc. Lazarus referred to Zajonc's position as an effort to "prove the primacy of emotion, *or affect*," [italics added].[11] Nor did Zajonc draw any distinction, claiming that *emotion* may precede cognition in some "mental" sequences.[12] Lazarus responded, however, that "cognitive activity is a necessary precondition of emotion."[13]

They were simply not addressing the same issue. The problem of such ripostes is that in confusing the terms they preclude possible resolution. Emotion is one *class* of affect. It may be that cognitive activity must necessarily precede emotion (itself a debatable postulate since instinctively recognized percepts may call for no intellectual processing). However, it is quite likely that such activity must be preceded by some *belief* about the presence of pertinent information, and its conceptualization; a different class of affect.

Feelings are sometimes described as mild affects, while emotions are said to represent extreme affects. Theories have been developed which purport to explain emotion without any reference to its evaluative aspect. The definition of emotion as a disorganizing factor by some psychologists has been mentioned. Others credit emotion with providing for the efficient organization of protective behavior.

The view of emotion as facilitative has been expressed most adequately by Leeper,[14] and the interpretation of emotion employed in this text is consistent with his position. It represents a rejection of the assumptions of the James-Lange theory that behavior causes emotion rather than the reverse. James[15] contended that when a perceptual experience affects the central nervous system, impulses are distributed to glands which, in returning the signals to the brain, create a state of emotional awareness. His interpretation was that this characteristic of an event does not cause behavior but results from it. The view of emotion as no more than the conscious aspect of an experience fascinates behavioral psychologists—who enjoy demonstrating that it is difficult to frown and experience joy, or to smile and sense sadness.

That such a viewpoint demands the acceptance of emotion as an unnecessary component of behavior seems to concern very few of those experimentalists who see such feeling states as no more than an interesting spin-off of consciousness, and apparently interpret behavior as a necessary outcome of certain perceptual, and perhaps drive level, interaction. As in the efforts to verify Cannon's Emergency Theory of Emotion,[16] concentration has been focused on attempting to support or refute the idea by frightening college sophomores instead of considering the strange implications of the argument.

In Cannon's case, only those emotions which have physiological components and which prepare the organism for fight or flight were dealt with. As for the James-Lange position, it is true that in higher organisms emotions often do not occur prior to the initial experience with a situation. But this is because the individual does not yet recognize the implications of the experience. In such a circumstance, the emotional system would be incompetent to make an evaluation. However, after a behavior is attempted or a situation is experienced, subsequent events arouse emotional states on the basis of recall, generalization, and other factors, and may even be generated by vicarious experience. It is critical to an understanding of this vital signal system that it be recognized as only one of the many types of affect and one with a unique function—that of providing the impetus to potential behavior on the basis of a special type of feeling.

Entities, situations, and events are often recognizable as want-related by simple animals (i.e., as instinctive needs) prior to experience. The spider recognizes the fly as gustable before one has been tasted. In higher life forms, the cognitive/affective process makes possible the association of past experience with future satisfaction. As a result, emotions become attached to learned experiences, situations, and events. An experience which results in a negative feeling, for example, will tend to carry that connotation when perceptually similar occasions arise. Although desire is often related to innately known or learned need, an emotion may occur upon the awareness of sheer desire and the contemplation of *any* satiating experience—as when one feels hungry and considers the availability of any comestible. It is essential, however, that a distinction be made between sheer desire as an affect, and the emotion which requires the inclusion of some situation, however imprecise.

While an affective arousal state may involve only the awareness of desire and/or perhaps a potential source of gratification, emotion is based on a complex interaction of conceptualized elements, including all of the judgments that may be involved. This does not require that a desired resolution be specified where a negative emotion is experienced, but it does demand that some situation be discernible through analysis of the contributory elements. Although needs are often the focus of emotional reactions, underlying desires must be considered if feelings are to be understood. For this reason, and because the term *need* has many levels of interpretation, emotion shall be described as *want* related in this and future chapters, with want referring to either or both aspects of a situation.

It may seem presumptuous to state that such feelings as *relief, satisfaction*, and *guilt* are appropriate to the evaluative process in simple organisms, but the anthropomorphism is intended. To presume the presence of a signal system in lower animals, similar to that observed in humans, is far less arrogant and much more consistent with the evidence than to suggest that humans are unique in this respect. The similarity can be appreciated if the language terms that are ordinarily employed are ignored, and an attempt is made to determine whether separate and distinct feelings accompany specific acts or events.

Instead of saying "I feel guilty," "I am frustrated," or "I believe that I should act in some manner," consider only the uncommunicated and unlabeled affective experience. It is this signal, that must be present in some form at all levels of life where local mediation precedes an action, that qualifies as emotion. Wherever a response is not fixed by a perceptual experience, some interaction between desire and the stimulus must occur. Although the mechanism may be extremely simple in lower animals, the principle is the same.

Emotions represent feelings about situations which, under appropriate conditions, may lead to behavior. They are *always* and *only* the result of the interaction between desire and associated needs, and the conceptualized environment. Judgments about situations or events in the abstract are without emotional quality. A judgment that leaping across a six foot gorge would be dangerous has no emotional aspect until it is related to an attempt, observed or contemplated, real or imagined, where desires are brought into play.[17] Although emotions may be aroused by conditions under which no action is viable (one may feel sad or angry to hear that children are being massacred in a distant country), our focus shall be on those associated with the contemplation of some possible behavior.

Among the elements involved in some emotional states are beliefs regarding one's capacity and/or opportunity to act. However, these factors arouse emotions only on the condition that desire and assessment of the total situation are involved. There must first be both some level of desire and some belief about a real or imagined situation that is related to that desire. The combinations are endless and a wide variety of emotions may be experienced in the consideration of a simple act. If, for example, one is hungry, an emotion is possible if that feeling is associated with the opportunity to eat. The presence or lack of such opportunity and the capacity to take advantage of it, as well as any judgments about the quality of food available, the propriety of accepting it, the probability that it is safe, each and all contribute to the prevailing emotional state.

Since emotions include estimates of the price to be paid for a potential behavior, it is obvious that costs as well as desires have emotional characteristics. A precise definition is, again, essential. Costs, as they relate to behavior, represent *actual* or *potential* interference with the expression of competing desires or of the relinquishing of alternative needs relevant to the same desires. Thus, the cost of eating may include energy consumption vs. a desire to relax, or the probability of gaining weight vs. the desire to be slim etc.. Additionally, the item eaten may be taken in the place of some alternate possibility. At least some such situation must be identified when cost is assayed. If the cost of a meal has an emotional impact, there must be both a known pecuniary consideration, and the judgment that this is either exorbitant or inexpensive. The same is true for each input. Judgments, for example, include both the factual data ("it is about three hours until sundown") and the feeling that this is a "short" or "long" time, depending on the relationship to other factors.

Emotion, like desire and conceptualization, is an emergent form of knowledge. The simplest forms of life operate only on the basis of drive and perceptual information which results in forced responses and where no local mediation occurs. The "partness" of any living form at this level is clear. It belongs to a more persistent form of life and performs to the limit of its ability in meeting genetically determined needs. At the highest evolutionary level, the phenotype is invested with a technique for evaluating potential and actual experiences as they relate to future behavior through the introduction of desire and emotion. Emotional affects are associated with many desires, all of which represent information that suggests activity. However, the deliberative process must take into account capacity and opportunity which are probabilistic. Inputs are weighed in terms of deprivation degree, opportunity, and energy level. The resulting behavior is fixed by a *dominant* emotion which is determined by the prevailing need or desire in terms of the cost that activity entails. As the evolutionary scale is ascended, the capacity to make long range cost estimates and to apply cognitive skill and rational and moral judgments, which are potentially valuable techniques, often result in emotional maladjustment.

Only *some* activities become associated with affect; others continue to operate automatically. Even at the highest levels, the decision to metabolize or to pump blood through the body is not left to the discretion of the individual. Such activities continue to be mediated genetically. The knee jerk and the sucking reflex are instances of genetically mediated responses to stimulation at the level of the human. Furthermore, the nature or state of desire is not subject to moral evaluation (e.g., "Should I be hungry?") Such urges represent *desire facts* in the same sense that daylight is a *perceptual fact*. Each has a claim to existence and each is potentially value laden, but it is only when a situation arises that relates them to the individual or the gene pool that the emotional aspect is involved.

Emotion provides a communication form which makes possible the identification of experiences in terms of their satisfaction potential. The woman who accepts the loss of a lover because she has learned an obligation to care for her invalid mother may well be grief-stricken and depressed before, during, and after her decision. However, if she persists in her behavior it will be because of the urgency of the identification and the associated emotional state which is based in part on the sense of moral propriety.

The introduction of emotion broadens opportunity to take into account many of the accidents of existence. All of the idiosyncrasies of the individual can come into play. The larger organism can judge as unworthy of its time and effort a food particle that a smaller neighbor may find attractive. Such a system can accommodate much of the diversity of environmental opportunity which plays a significant role in determining behavior. With the advent of emotion, a new set of relationships and existents enters the world of reality. Motivation, self, behavior, and many other terms become appropriate only at this level of organic existence. The capacity for emotional evaluation sets the stage for the developmental pattern that has led, for better or worse, to the appearance of humans as an example of animal life in which cognitive sophistication has resulted in bizarre forms of behavior, conflict, and defense.

The contribution of emotion to deliberate activity is one of relating the contemplative or mental to the physiological. Through alteration in the cognitive/affective system, glandular components are modified. This activation of the mental parameter of the knowledge system represents the mechanism that separates the mentally endowed from the tropistic individual, and the complex and often mysterious results of the process are recognizable in the ills as well as the achievements of humans. The process is an evolving one, with lower forms of life manifesting a similar, if simpler, communication system.

Most simple animals are limited to judgments of present situations and neither learn to generalize from experience nor to take into account more than a few variables. Whether in such cases it is proper to refer to this process as emotion is moot. The principle involved is that a capacity to interrelate desires with existing situations is often present, and when it does not function effectively, distress may follow. It is of little consequence that a spider may be unable to "imagine" a meal or to recall a previous experience—the evidence suggests that such activities are unique to higher animals. The critical issue is that whenever an emotional mediating capacity exists, some form of decision can be made. Such decisions are always made through deliberation that involves cost and such costs may be so exorbitant that maladjustment results.

The Emotional Experience

Since emotions function to recommend behavior, they relate only to potential experiences as they are contemplated, imagined, or recalled. Judgmental estimates as well as abstract interpretations are involved, but must be recognized as representing a fundamentally different process; that of classifying and interpreting information along such scales as morality and reason with no necessary behavioral implication. Whether killing is immoral is an issue which can evoke a judgment just as would the question of whether the purchase of a lottery ticket is a good risk. No emotion is required so long as no action is contemplated (even as minimal as responding to the question). Abstractions are peculiar to higher life forms, but the estimates which are also judgmental are found at all levels at which emotions occur.

The fact that emotions serve the purpose of initiating behavior does not suggest that they cannot occur where no experience is possible. We pointed out earlier that one may become quite angry about a situation that is beyond alteration. However, although emotion may occur without a behavioral reaction, unless an emotion is experienced no deliberate response is possible in any situation.

The work of recent motivation theorists has been somewhat helpful in that a continuum of arousal states is posited, with the occurrence of behavior dependent on some level of energy which has an optimal point. Despite this, there remains the implicit (and sometimes explicit) inclusion of desire and emotion under the same rubric, even though the terms refer to essentially different affects.

The level of desire represents only one element of an emotion. It may arise spontaneously (assertive urge) or be aroused by the situation (a protective or transcendent desire). The other contributor includes the *conceptualized data* relevant to the satisfaction of the desire. The data which is conceptualized includes:

1. *Needs* - Any and all possible ways in which desires may be satisfied including learned and instinctive behaviors, situations, and events
2. *Abetting and hindering environmental elements*
    • events - It is raining, vs. It is a clear day

- circumstances - I do not have enough money to buy a meal (i.e., capacity), vs. funds are no problem
- behaviors - I am not permitted to take a particular trip, vs. someone has invited me to go (i. e., opportunity)
- all other costs - Risk of danger, etc.

All elements are included in the general term referred to here as the *situation*, which is that state of affairs which the individual perceives (believes) to be the case. Emotions, then, may unequivocally be defined as *affective signals arising from the interaction between desire and relevant, judged, and evaluated, conceptualized situations*.

Since emotions represent the evaluation of conceptualized situations they cannot be spontaneously generated. True emotions represent an evaluation of some considered event. Emotions are a significant clue to one's identification level since many such feelings are based on the extent to which individuals empathize with or include others as part of themselves. Emotion is not merely a feeling associated with experiences which the individual has learned in terms of what the environment offers. Rather, it is a specific, though often poorly translated, information/knowledge center which is built into the individual's central cortex, autonomic nervous system, and hypothalamus. It provides messages that suggest "go" or "don't go," "do" or "don't do," as each situation is assessed in terms of want and moral/ethical, rational, legal, and other issues.

This ineluctable component of non-taxic response in all forms of life is badly misconstrued or overlooked in many theories of emotion. Arnold and Gasson stated that "it is possible to go counter to emotion...when the goal we want to achieve is so important that we are willing to suffer to achieve it."[18] But the willingness to suffer, and the evaluation of the importance of the goal, represent evidence of the presence of conflicting emotions associated with the anticipated behavior. If I lunch on watercress despite craving a pastrami sandwich it is because I feel more strongly about controlling my weight than about immediate appetitive gratification. In the course of judging the situation, the value of lowered weight becomes a factor that contributes to the emotional reaction and the decision to diet.

The inability to appreciate this facet of behavior is puzzling, although it is probably related to an unwillingness to accept the notion that mental events can influence physical entities. The obvious reliance on emotion for decisions, and the ultimacy of such evaluation, have been discussed by many writers in many ways. Ouspensky, who called *will* the resultant-of-desires, stated, "As to the men with a so-called 'strong will,' these are usually men of one dominating desire, in which all other desires vanish."[19] His meaning is clear. Individuals of strong "will" have a powerful emotional reaction to the desire under consideration, and they act to satisfy that urge in terms of whatever opportunity is available. When deliberation determines action, it does so because of the nature of the want/cost ratio, with emotion being an essential element.

If a positive emotion is experienced on seeing a type of food, the positive connotation is probably related to a desire for food. By the same token, in the case of identification, a positive feeling must relate to a desire for other-directed or meaningful activity. Rational and moral judgments, when they represent evaluation of a desire/perception related event, cannot produce an emotional state independently of either. If upon hearing of a potential killing, one has a morally related emotion, some want must be included ("I want it to happen and it should," or "I don't want it to happen and it should not"). If guilt is felt because one has sinned, that individual must include their having wanted to act in such a manner in spite of believing that they should not have done so.

When any activity has individual or species value characteristics (although the specifics may have been learned), there is also a moral aspect. This is a principal reason for our contention that humans do not (*cannot*) learn what morality *is*, but only the moral characteristics of a situation or event. Although one may learn that infanticide is morally sound and even experience a positive emotion on contemplating such behavior, its propriety cannot be explained except by appeal to an *innate* capacity to hierarchize events on the moral scale. Rational appraisal is equally dependent. Chagrin, based on some past behavior judged foolish, must include the wish that one had acted differently. It is only when the action resulted in an unwanted situation that the emotion could be evoked.

The fact that "emotional" states can be induced by artificial methods does not alter the contention that their function is to relate experiential with desire components. In some instances, a clear distinction can be made between a true emotional state and one that is created by nerve manipulation. It is, of course, possible to identify the instrumentality by which emotions are expressed and then by stimulating that element, to duplicate the feeling. This means at best, however, only that the mechanism is being manipulated by an artificial technique.[20]

Free floating anxiety is, almost certainly, an example of a distorted nervous system. The sense of dread, of anticipated disaster, of unexplainable distress, can be logically predicted from a disturbance in the limbic system resulting from adventitious insult or genetic flaw. Similarly, severe psychotic states are now recognized as perverse outcomes of what are normally essential human mental operations.

Emotion terms are, unfortunately, used to define both behaviors and feelings. Since the word *emotional* is used as an adjective, there is the erroneous implication that there exists non-emotion based behavior. Other practices, such as the tendency to employ such broad categories as *love* and *hate* and to identify some emotions in terms of their levels of excitement make it difficult to recognize the appropriate referent. This has undoubtedly contributed to the practice of equating *drive* with *motivation*.[21] At the opposite extreme, the very richness of language and the proliferation and varied use of words has produced a formidable array of terms to describe subtle nuances.

Most confusing is the practice of using the same term to describe quite unrelated feelings. Apathy, for example, refers to a condition in which one experiences minimum levels of emotion over an extended period of time. However, it is used both as a synonym for a mere lack of interest (indifference or minimal affect), and is sometimes equated with depression or despair (a pathologic condition). Apathy shall be used here only to describe a measure of emotional intensity level.

Pleasure and pain are equally awkward terms and cause confusion for a similar reason. They are ordinarily employed to describe states of gratification (pleasure) or physical injury (pain). However, some usage produces the paradox of pain that is "pleasant" and pleasure that is "painful" (as in sexual frenzy). The terms shall be used here only as they identify positive and negative emotional states. Pleasure shall be restricted to affects that are desirable, while pain shall refer to negative emotional experiences. As with taste, pleasure and pain are end-states. In the case of pain, the emotion that precipitates action is *fear*. When the feeling of pleasure or pain leads to behavior, the emotion is one of expectancy of a future, similar experience. Pleasure is assigned anticipatory as well as consummatory status, since no term that may be compared to fear is available.[22]

Eating or sexual activity may be enjoyed in process as exhilarating, and in the outcome by the sense of well-being which is experienced. However, there is a critical difference in why the activity is indulged which can help to explain many maladaptive behaviors. Some behaviors are enjoyed purely because of their stimulative value, and a drive based desire for such stimulation has been posited. Watching a baseball game, listening to a radio, or even recalling an exciting experience are all related to the stimulation-seeking aspect where the desired state is the emotion that accompanies the process rather than the outcome it produces.

In describing the feeling associated with the achievement of power or the control of one's destiny, the term *exhilaration* still seems appropriate although the emotion includes the anticipation of a desirable outcome. The sense of well-being (even at the level of the thrill that may be reported on the consideration of one's state of freedom) refers to a sense of the capacity to behave in desired ways which can be identified as a feeling of power. To move from an impotent state to one which allows access to many experiences is attractive because positive behaviors can be anticipated.

Tension reduction theory failed as a complete explanation of behavior because it assumed that the basic urge was toward the reduction of excitation which would ascribe only negative characteristics to emotional states.[23] This interpretation adequately accounts for such uncomfortable feelings as guilt, anger, and frustration from which refuge in the form of diminished tension or relief is sought. However, the anticipation of exhilarating experiences—where a heightened stimulative level is sought—is as legitimate a signal to behave, although the action results in the accretion of tension.

When such positive high level states are sustained over a period of time, a desire for relaxation arises. This represents movement from a positive state of high tension to a positive state of lowered or balanced tension. In some instances, persistent stimulation may become exhausting or otherwise painful to the point that relief is sought, just as with situations that are inherently undesirable.

It is unfortunate that the term *tension* has come to denote a negative condition. Muscle flexing and sensual stimulation certainly represent non-slack states insofar as oxidation, synergistic interchange, and glandular secretion, are involved. However, the exercise or exertion involved in physical or mental "stretching" is often a highly positive experience, and, as tension accretion is used here, the positive aspect is often intended.

Although deliberate action may be taken in order to achieve any of the emotional states described, in emotionally healthy individuals negative emotions are never sought as ends in themselves. They are either aroused by unavoidable situations (where they are designed to prepare for corrective action) or are tolerated as part of the cost associated with some competing present or anticipated future positive feeling. The contention that fear, for example, is apparently sought in high risk entertainment can be shown to be erroneous by considering whether dangerous behavior would be indulged if the stimulative aspect were removed. If no concomitant exhilaration is involved, personality disturbance may be confidently predicated.[24]

In the evolution of species, the bonding of an emotion and an experience represents an example of genetic learning. Since certain interactions between phenotype and environment result in outcomes that have preservative and growth aspects, some of the characteristics of the environmental contribution are invested with affective qualities. However, if the only occasion on which an individual could experience an emotion came after an activity, it would be of little value to the gene pool. Although the consummatory emotion (CE) would appear to represent positive or negative "reinforcement," it could not lead to a repetition or avoidance of the act. It is essential that the individual be capable of anticipating the reinforcing state, and of experiencing an anticipatory emotion (AE) that encourages action. This interpretation bears on the concept of purpose that was described earlier and has the same significance for positive and negative emotions.[25]

If the feeling of guilt that attends an action that one believes to be immoral, or the feeling of excitement that accompanies a particular sexual experience caused no change in future action, they would, respectively, represent punishment and reward of the type described in the Old Testament of the Christian Bible. They would function as capital punishment sometimes does when the notion of retribution is involved. "An eye for an eye" assumes that the treatment of the guilty need not be related to a change in behavior but is just in its own right. The significance of both anticipatory and consummatory emotions as they relate to a behavioral sequence must be taken into account.

The introduction of the anticipatory phase of the emotional experience is based both on the capacity to predict future events on the basis of sense receptors and the sophistication of the cognitive process. An olfactory or visual experience, the recall of a previous event, or the imagination of a generalized activity may arouse an affect which anticipates a desired emotional experience.

In the simplest forms of life, this arousal is attached both to a sense experience and the emanating source. Taste that accompanies a specific food is related to the food's smell, and one may respond to the smell by eating the appropriate food. Sexual activity is accompanied by characteristics of the sexual partner which become associated with the anticipated act. The sight, smell, sound, or other signal from the "proper" target arouses an anticipatory emotion which leads to appropriate activity. In the case of activity which leads to the potential debilitation or destruction of the individual in the interest of others, and ultimately the gene pool, the same paradigm may be employed. As the appropriate behavior becomes necessary, an anticipatory positive emotional state is aroused. The feeling that accompanies the consideration of self destruction in the greater interest is at a high positive level and must be assumed to represent the dominant emotional state in humans, as well as in simpler animals.

Positive Emotions

Some of the terms used in describing emotional states that accompany the anticipation and/or outcome of a desired event are listed in Table 9.1. Though they are scaled according to degree of excitement, they do not necessarily merge into each other as the Table may appear to suggest. Positive emotions include both those which anticipate high levels of stimulation and those that relate to relaxation or rest. In a general sense, positive emotions are feelings which project a desired state, and the anticipatory emotion is essentially the same as the consummatory. In all instances, the desired behavior is related to balanced or increased tension—activity which maintains the experienced emotional state.

Included among the positive emotions are those associated both with the behavior of the individual experiencing the feeling, and situations and behaviors of others which bear on the well-being of the individual. When one is protected or otherwise abetted by another, there is a sense of belonging or intimacy that enlarges the sense of self and is a signal regarding the desirability of such interaction. When emotion is related to the potential for fulfillment, either of any specific desire, or desires, or the general urge to power, the anticipatory emotional state (AE) may be described as an *aggressive* feeling. Consummatory emotions (CE) are variously labeled and Table 9.1 includes many terms applied in both senses.

Positive emotions, whether anticipatory or consummatory, have the commonality of being enjoyable in spite of the fact that they differ in subtle ways. The anticipation of eating a meal, or attending a sporting event, cannot be described with the same term as the emotion which accompanies the expectancy of a state of relaxation. In one instance an increase in the level of excitation is desired, in the other not. However, no attempt shall be made to discriminate between these forms. The terms in Table 9.1 are meant to include feelings associated with each type of desire satisfaction. Anticipatory emotions recommend action which (at least in higher organisms and in those cases where behavior is profitable to the individual) is likely to result in an associated consummatory emotion. Such emotions may be activated at any point in an experience and, although they are essential to all decisions, need not lead to action where it is not appropriate.

Table 9.1

Positive Emotional Terms

calm	happiness	friendliness	merriment	delight	ecstasy
relaxation	cheerfulness	pride	mirth	ebullience	rapture
comfort	pleasure	warmth	gaiety	elation	affection
contentment	gratitude	joy	buoyancy	glee	

Relaxation ◄——————   ——————► Tension accretion

Excitation Level

When one perceives a generous action or is the recipient of such action, the emotion is at its consummatory point. Similarly, observing a beautiful painting or hearing a brilliant musical performance may create a totally satisfying experience. The act of observing or listening is at the positive end of the scale of affective desirability. In these cases, the desire for stimulation is also at the consummatory level. By contrast, the smell of food when in a state of hunger may lead to behavior intended to achieve the more desired emotional level.

Before dealing with those signals which recommend escape from unpleasantness, an emotion must be identified which has consistently resulted in a misinterpretation of behavior. The boy who studies, although he prefers to play, the man who works at a distasteful task, and the woman who foregoes pleasurable experiences to care for a sick child, each provide evidence for the existence of an emotional state which appears to violate the principle. If the function of emotion is to recommend behavior, it would appear that such ostensibly negative activities must be, in fact, desirable.

The error lies in the assumption that the defined activity always represents an intrinsic behavior—an activity that is desired for itself. In many instances this is not the case. If a behavior which would not otherwise be indulged is believed to lead toward a desired state, or if the culmination of the act does in fact lead in such a direction, the anticipatory emotion cannot adequately be explained in terms of any of the types described above. Individuals who are required to work on a holiday may experience anger before, during, and after the task. However, if they go to work, the dominant emotion is determined by the consideration that they are meeting the conditions of approaching longer range goals. This feeling shall be identified as one of *satisfaction*, a concept that shall later be associated with *will*.[26]

Satisfaction represents an example of an emotion peculiar to the highest levels of life, since it is dependent on the ability to delay gratification. Any element of a behavioral sequence in which the dominant emotion is one of satisfaction shall be defined as *instrumental* behavior. As such, it represents a cost to the total sequence. There are other senses in which the term satisfaction is commonly used. It is sometimes synonymous with "pleased"—where desire is thoroughly gratified. Another use refers to situations in which the fulfilled desire exceeds the cost by very little. In such instances, the behavior is *intrinsic*, or complete in itself. No further need is involved. For diagnostic purposes, only the sense of instrumentality shall be intended when the term satisfaction is employed, since its function is to discriminate between completed and continuing behaviors. Instrumental and intrinsic behaviors shall be further defined in Chapter 13.

Negative Emotions

It is a fact of life that not all desired emotional states can be achieved. In addition to the conflict between competing desires, limitations on behavior are imposed by the many types of cost related to each potential act, and by the interfering or supportive behavior of others. In every instance an emotional state is associated with such interference, and for every type of frustration an appropriate emotion can be identified. Unlike the positive emotions, which recommend behavior that will excite or relax, these feelings are uncomfortable and call for a change in the situation. The anticipatory emotional state, being unpleasant, is unlike the consummatory state which, if achieved, is one of relief or tension reduction.

Desires have been described as negative in the sense that they represent signals which call for action that will change the situation. In some instances, that change will be toward relief from the feeling, while in others it will call for some activity that is desirable. Emotions, on the other hand, may be either positive or negative, since needs and other aspects of a situation are involved.

Negative emotions may be categorized in terms of: (a) Interference with the expression of a need or desire; (b) an attitude toward the source of such interference; and (c) the impact of reason, morality, and other judgments. In the following classificatory scheme, the appropriate focus for a variety of emotions is indicated.

Some terms are included in several classes because of the varied ways in which they are commonly used. Charts indicate intensity levels with extreme feelings at the left.

Type I. Emotions focusing on the affected individual

Class A - *Inability to Recognize or Properly Assign Stimuli; Confusion or Ambiguity of Signal (integrity loss)*

Anxiety Group

dread	anxiety	worry	confusion
panic	apprehension	distress	fretfulness

Behaviors that clarify perception and reduce confusion represent *needs* and are felt as positive. These behaviors may be carried out by the individual involved or any other person which improves the situation. Perceptual integrity refers to the capacity of the informational system to provide dependable data. The individual who avoids a dark place does so because of the absence of the figure-ground relationship that makes vision functional, thus allowing for the presence of imaginary—perhaps threatening—apparitions.[27]

Individuals who cannot estimate the relative morality of their acts, or even which of several motivators is ascendant, face the same dilemma. Kierkegaard suggested that anxiety, (which he expressed as dread that is closely related to sin) represents a moment of awareness of what one *could* be, since reality relates to our imperfect selves. It "enters into the world quantitatively every time an individual posits sin."[28] Thus, anxiety may be a spur to freedom and creativity. Since anxious times are often accompanied by bizarre ideas, and creative individuals are assumed to be comfortable in ambiguous situations, there may be reason to accept this explanation. However, the feeling seems designed to encourage behavior that will abort such situations regardless of their creative potential.

Class B - *Interference with Desire in the Biological Self, Where the Focus is on the Desired Experiences*

Frustration Group

agony	anguish	depression	discouragement
gloom	despair	anomie	vexation
melancholy	impotence	frustration	alienation

Any behavior that moves toward overcoming the feeling of inability to achieve a desired state will produce a positive feeling. Each of these negative feelings represents a sense of helplessness or a separation from what must be overcome. The search for tickets to a sold-out ball game, or the attempt to operate a jammed vending machine, are examples of such situations. No danger is necessarily involved.

Since one of the significant desires is for identification, the inability to achieve meaning results in a feeling of impotence. No threat need be perceived and where no "other" is seen as interfering, the prevailing emotion is apt to be one of helplessness. Anger in such situations would be inappropriate if it persisted. The cause of distress should be pursued in a clinical situation, to ascertain whether any morally responsible agent is believed to be involved.

Class C - *Interference with Projected Desires in the Identified or Extended Self*

Empathy Group

grief	sadness	empathy
pity	sorrow	sympathy
frustration		compassion

The emotions depicted in Class C extend the feeling of frustration to the distress of others who are seen as part of the self, although physically separate. There is an appreciation of their unmet desires. These feelings are experienced on seeing or hearing that others are without the minimal necessities of life, or when life itself is lost. Behavior is sometimes possible, as in providing financial assistance to those in need, but in some instances the focus of the emotion is on individuals beyond help, as for those destroyed in a fire—although, in such cases, it would be more efficacious to tender the feeling toward those left behind by providing consolation. A critical issue here is the appreciation of the fact that, in the case of a lost life, the emotion represents an awareness that there is no behavior that could possibly recall the deceased person.

Class D - *Encountering Unanticipated Experiences*

Surprise Group

shock	startle	wonder
bewilderment		surprise
awe	astonishment	amazement

This group is difficult to categorize since the feeling is in some instances believed to be positive. It is closely associated with anxiety in that there is at least a momentary loss of perceptual balance and, to this extent, it is a feeling-to-be-dispatched.

As to the contention that there are positive surprises, consider the impact on the nervous system of a continued series of such experiences. What one desires is an *occasional* surprise, similar to the desire to experience controlled danger. There is a titillation that is attractive, but, as with hunger, the signal system is a form of alarm— —it seeks to be turned off, although at manageable levels, it may be experienced as a positive stimulus. Startle is included as a level of surprise rather than as a reflexive response.[29]

Type II. Emotions which include the frustrating agent

Class E - *Situations, Events, or Behaviors Which Cause One to Recoil, Where the Cause is Obscure*

Aversion Group

loathing	odium	annoyance
disgust	repugnance	dislike
	revulsion	

In this group are included feelings attendant on experiences which, although they often cannot be explained, cause a desire to recoil. The sight of vermin, as well as many smells and sounds, are as frightening as more understandable dangers. Similarly, many tactile experiences, such as touching slime, cause such negative emotions and induce a desire to escape. These feelings probably represent instinctive knowledge which has not been genetically extinguished. Such feelings are, however, often felt toward the behavior of humans.

Class F - *Threat of Harm to the Biological or Extended Self*

Fear Group

horror	fear (AE)	trepidation
alarm	pain (CA)	worry
panic	fright	

This class of emotions focuses on the possibility of seriously damaging experiences. There is present or impending danger which is recognized as such (as contrasted with unfocused anxiety). When the feeling of fear includes a responsible causal agent, anger and other emotions may be aroused. A threat from a non-moral source—such as in being attacked by an animal or buried in an avalanche—would also cause fear. Any behavior which reduces the threat to the expression of desires will cause the emotion to be relieved. Such behavior qualifies as a *need*, as was indicated earlier.

Fear is related to frustration in the sense that there is interference with some desire. It differs in that it includes the belief that harm may be involved. Pain is included because, although it seems a different experience than that ordinarily considered an emotion, it does include (at the psychological level) both a desire (to avoid the aversive stimulus) and a conceptualized situation. In Chapter 11 we shall deal with the notion of unconscious pain, which shall be shown to be an unsupportable fiction.

Class G - *Frustration Caused by the Possession of Desired Individuals or Objects by Others. Morality is not necessarily involved.*

Jealousy/Envy Group

jealousy yearning
envy pining

The evolution of the sense of identity includes a reaction to the lack or loss of desired persons or things. As the concept of self becomes more pronounced, the awareness that desired individuals or objects are not owned or controlled may lead to a feeling of distress. When the feeling relates directly to the involved object, yearning or pining occurs. When a third party interferes, jealousy and/or envy may be experienced. Envy, which relates to another's possession of a desired object, calls for some alleviating experience. There is little doubt that envy relates to the desire for power. Since the presence of this emotion represents a recognition of relative security, it is obvious that few humans can ever attain sufficient power to relieve it completely.

Jealousy, which deals with another's possession of a love object, is also directed at some interfering individual. To remove the threat results in a positive feeling. The disappearance of a love rival is an example. As with envy, because of the impossibility of achieving sufficient mastery over other individuals through any of the techniques ordinarily available, this emotion leads to behaviors which are often in precise opposition to those that can provide relief.

Type III - **Emotions which include moral and rational judgments**

Class H - *Behavior of the Biological or Extended Self Which is Believed to be Morally Wrong.*

Guilt Group

guilt regret embarrassment
shame remorse

Feelings of guilt arise whenever a behavior is related to an outcome that is believed to be morally wrong. In such cases, in addition to the conviction that what one is doing as damaging to self or others, there is a belief (often learned) that the behavior is inappropriate. Killing an animal for food causes little or no guilt, and overeating because of an anticipated famine may also be accepted as proper. However, wanton destruction of life, as in murder for pleasure, or excess of stimulative experience is ordinarily accompanied by a negative evaluation on the moral scale.

An appropriate behavior would be any which moved toward goals believed to be positive (which include the well-being of the individual and other forms of life), and which may be accompanied by a feeling of pride. An example of a situation which could create such an emotion is that of a youth who steals from his parents. The awareness of the impropriety of such an act may lead to an alteration in behavior or some defense against this awareness (e.g., they have plenty of money...they can afford it).

This process represents the development of (rational) principles—those guides to action that grow out of the conflict between reason and morality. The instance mentioned demonstrates a common belief that those with more *should* share, and is in conflict with the thesis that one *should not* appropriate the goods of another. Both positions can be defended logically, and the selection of the former by individuals who want what they do not have is not difficult to understand. The practice is indulged by many of those with limited assets, and perhaps accounts for a majority of the negative feelings that obtain between socio-economic groups.

Shame must be distinguished from *guilt*. The former is a feeling of moral inadequacy where the individual is incapable of behaving in a way that will alter the situation. A man may feel ashamed of his parentage, his size or skin color, etc. The feeling is akin to, but is not identical with, guilt because it places the responsibility for unworthiness in the self as part of a family, race, or other group identity where it is believed that no behavior can erase the stigma.

The term *embarrassment* is included in Class H, since situations that cause such a feeling are often those in which individuals believe that they are acting in some way that they should not. The ten-year-old boy whose mother praises him profusely in front of others may be embarrassed by being made obvious, very much as does the adolescent who comes face to face with an attractive member of the opposite sex. In such instances, there is likely to be a desire for immediate extinction in that one's self worth approximates zero. Somehow, exposure causes a feeling that one should be able to do something to alter the situation. The term embarrassment, like many others, is often used to convey other sentiments.

Class I - *Behavior by a Responsible "Other" which is Believed to be Morally Improper, in Addition to Frustrating the Self or Those With Whom One is Identified.*

Anger Group

fury	anger	scorn	odium
rage	animosity	contempt	indignance
abhorrence	antagonism	disgust	ire
revulsion	repugnance		resentment

This category is highly significant since it includes a type of emotion which is instructive in the analysis of personality integration. The continuum runs from rage to relief with the positive affect being difficult to adequately characterize. The emotion occurs in situations in which individuals feel that someone's behavior or situation is interfering with their ability to get what they believe they should have. It extends to all things that are desired, with the emotion relating to others' right to interfere. Unlike fear and frustration, it includes the belief that some morally responsible agent (some human being or institution) is behaving in a way that illegitimately frustrates a desire. Hebb stated that:

> Anger is characteristically aroused *by the behavior of others*...when the behavior is not consistent with what one is proposing to do, when one expects resistance in having the behavior changed, and finally, when one thinks one may be able to change it.[30]

In Hebb's interpretation, "others" represent morally responsible others. Regarding his last phrase, the idea of capacity for change is the factor that separates rage from despair as experiences are considered. When the feeling includes change potential, energy is at a higher level—but on the same continuum. However, though despair decreases as hope increases, rage is not necessarily reduced. In many instances, the conviction that some retributory action is immanent may actually *increase* the intensity of the anger being experienced.

The identification of rage as an emotion represents a denial of its conceptualization as a drive or desire. As a desire, it would represent a compulsion to anger or an urge-to-hate which is suggested in psychoanalytic literature. This is another example of the attempt at elegance which characterizes parsimonious approaches. In reducing behavior to its elements feelings are simplified beyond their appropriate level. Rage is an emotion. It is comprised of the frustration of desires plus a conviction of the moral reprehensibility of the one who frustrates.

The moral value of an activity is, of course, subjective. A behavior that angers one person may please another. This may occur because of a differential evaluation of the behavior or because of different degrees of identification with the individual whose behavior is in question. In this list of feelings that relate to the moral blameworthiness of another many terms have been included that describe pervasive emotions or attitudes. They also identify feelings toward individuals as they relate to specific situations and are thus applicable as defining immediate emotions. For clinical applications the distinctions become important in that different attitudes call for diverse therapeutic approaches.

Class J - *Behavior by the Biological or Extended Self which is Believed to be Rationally Inadequate*

Chagrin Group

humiliation   embarrassment
remorse   chagrin

The capacity to process information cognitively is, theoretically, a positive characteristic. In spite of the fact that intelligent activity is often inimical with the needs of others, the failure to perform optimally causes a negative emotion which relates to *should* in its logical or rational sense. If a man does not take full advantage of an opportunity to profit himself, he may feel bad although the act from which he would have profited may be seen—even by himself—to be morally reprehensible. ("I know I shouldn't cheat my client, but he would have paid me more had I asked.") In its anticipatory phase, it is a recommendation to act more intelligently in future transactions. It is unrelated to the moral evaluation of any proposed behavior.

Remorse is included in this group as well as in the guilt category. It covers those situations in which one feels sorry for an action that injures another without intention. It is the feeling associated with causing accidental harm. The driver of a car that strikes a child darting into the road experiences a self-punitive emotion which includes both sorrow and a sense of at least some responsibility. This occurs even where no negligence seems assignable, and varies significantly among individuals, as well as between cultures.

Class K - *Behavior by Others Which is Believed to be Rationally Inadequate*

Contempt Group

contempt   scorn   impatience
disgust   irritation   vexation

This emotional state presents evidence of the moral value that we have indicated as residing in rationality. The feeling associated with irrational or unintelligent behavior includes the judgment that one *should* act in an intellectually sound way. No matter that behavior cannot be shown ultimately to have an intellectual basis, there is a firm conviction that people should use their intellectual powers at every opportunity. Contempt may also be experienced as one recognizes weakness, disorganization, or any characteristic deemed immoral, but which does not interfere with one's desires. Law violators who are excused by tolerant judges learn both scorn for the judicial system and a sense of meaninglessness in themselves.

This categorization of emotions is designed to serve two purposes. First, it represents an attempt to identify the function of emotion as an essential aspect of the deliberative process. The thesis developed here is that, at many levels of life, signal systems that function as emotions must be understood to operate as guides to behaviors. Second, it may serve to disclose sources of discomfort in those suffering from inadequate adjustment, as beliefs are revealed in counseling situations. The distinction between anger and frustration, for example, may well be critical to the amelioration of emotional distress. More importantly, information about how individuals interpret the actions of those under whose direction or control they must operate, should provide valuable information in the planning of preventive emotional health programs.

Parameters of Emotion

Attitudes

Attitudes are enduring emotional predispositions. They represent affects which are attached to situations, behaviors, individuals and events, and which are aroused on the perception of relevant situations. Emotional states that arise because of the peculiarities of a particular situation, such as on the observance of inappropriate behavior, are rarely evidence of an adjustment problem. By contrast, when such arousal represents a persistent personality trait, in that the level of intensity and the methods employed in responding to emotional demands are significantly unusual, some degree of abnormality may be predicated.

Love. Terms like *love* and *hate* represent emotions that persist as personality correlates. Each relates to a disposition based on the experiencing of a certain emotional state over time. Hate refers to an attitude toward a person or situation where rage or disgust is involved. There is a moral connotation in each instance. It is inappropriate to hate the weather, a recalcitrant auto, or taxes, although all three receive their share of abuse. To say that one hates a tax, or to be confined because of rain, represents a reification that is as common as it is absurd.

By far the most troublesome term used to describe an attitudinal state is *love*. It is used to identify every feeling from the agony and ecstasy of sexual involvement, or *amour*, to a respect for family ancestors, unselfish love for others, or a love of God, known as *agape*. This tendency to use the same term in many ways is understandable, when the purpose of a self-transcending drive in the service of species development is considered.

First, in the most general sense, the experience of love has an identification connotation which refers to movement of the self along the scale in the direction of more inclusive selfhood. This scale, which defines purpose, morality, identity, self, and system, is represented affectively by a feeling which can be referred to as love. In this sense, it is not an emotion but a desire. Although any such movement along this scale qualifies as a love experience, the system referent need not be the species since deliberate systems, such as labor unions have the capacity for attracting the same response, as was developed in Chapter 4.

A common interpretation of love is the one sometimes defined as *platonic*—with the implication that it is qualitatively different from amorous love. Such love refers to a spiritual or idealistic relationship and includes such subsets as friendship, camaraderie, and fellowship. This experience represents information about the desirability of self-denial, and self-subservience. At this juncture friendship and amour melt into one another. To love another by giving to the relationship is, in fact, to grow in selfhood in the sense that growth involves movement toward totality. Although such a process of identification has tremendous implications for potency, it is, in its desire aspect, essentially a recognition of the relationship of the individual with a more inclusive existence and ultimately with the totality of humanity.

As with all drives which are mediated affectively, love, as a desire for union, represents information which replaces *must* signals with *want* signals as the individual recognizes a feeling which can be analyzed as representing obligation beyond the biological self. This feeling makes possible the sacrifice of the individual when a situation so demands. When it is attached to another individual or an institution, it results in an emotion which, over time, becomes instilled as an attitude.

With the development of the cognitive process, the relative strength of the urge toward selflessness is diminished. Self-awareness, the cult of here-and-now, and the focus on personal biological aggrandizement result in the devaluation of this desire. Self love, in the sense of respect for one's humanness, however, implicitly requires that others may take priority. Moser, who believes that respect for others grows from freedom to respect one's self, proposed that the truly free person is responsible to others because although he is "free from the pressure of forces and value outside himself...he accepts others, and affirms in them *their own* valuing process."[31]

Lasch, by contrast, suggested that we live in an age of progressive narcissism: "The narcissist has no interest in the future because, in part, he has so little interest in the past. He finds it difficult to internalize happy associations or to create a store of loving memories."[32] A critical contention of this text is that the self-centeredness that Lasch deplored is not a Twentieth Century phenomenon. It is rather an expression of the interaction between evolving intellectual capacity and social systems that encourage it.[33] The awareness of one's biological self and its locus of pleasure and pain, in fact, predate the human species. The genesis of such an alteration of focus came with the advent of mind, an evolutionary step some millions of years removed.

At the human level, love is often unable to compete with other desires. It conflicts with assertive and defensive interests in many cases, and it is ritualized so extensively that the essential intimacy is destroyed and the attitude becomes flaccid. The relation of man to God, as regimented by many religious denominations, suffers from the insinuation of so many levels of priesthood, and so much catechismal rigidity, that the love relationship often becomes hopelessly obscured. The connotation of love that describes the relationship between a man and a woman in the sense of physical desire, represents a somewhat different function which is expressed through the same general desire. The "love" in sexual love has the same self-transcendence as it does in any other form, but it is combined with a possessiveness that is essential to its ultimate purpose. In order to clarify this, the evolution of sexual individuation must be considered.[34]

In the simplest organic forms, budding, fission, and similar techniques provide for reproduction. When the sexual aspect is included, for the many obvious biological reasons, its first manifestation includes no desire or selection other than that introduced by environmental contingency. Pollination occurs if the proper winds or insects provide for communion between stamen and pistil. In lower animals, sexual contact occurs whenever desire and opportunity coincide. Following the union, the interest subsides and the maximum interaction is coital. While such an arrangement can produce sufficient progeny to provide for the maintenance of the species, it provides less viability than can be generated by individuals who care for their young, which occurs in some of the more complex forms of life.

Under the most primitive method, each new organism has only drive and perceptual systems operating at the reproductive level. The advantage of selectively avoiding sex requires that its practice be associated with affect. Thus, levels of desire provide a more sensitive manipulator of the reproductive process. At a still more sophisticated level, the profit that accrues when offspring are cared for not only increases potential for sheer survival but also for qualitative improvements such as schooling.

For these reasons, love—valuable in the general platonic sense—is also useful in the upgrading of the reproductive process. If the seducer is also seduced, the ingredients of a family are present. When the bestower of sexual joy finds in the total relationship an identification with the individuals involved (i.e., mate and offspring), the probability of providing for the care and feeding essential to more effective learning is enhanced. Here, emotion becomes a factor. The individual who has a desire to love can evaluate situations in which such (implicit) possibilities obtain.

With sex in higher organisms comes a sense of identification which is precisely the same as other forms of love, except that it is associated with the sexual urge which is possessive or individuated. The path from plant to human is, of course, not a straight one. A perfect correlation between evolutionary level and affective relationship cannot be shown. Although this must be accounted for, many explanations are available. Nature experiments with many methods, and the socialization or ritualization at many levels of life over aeons may have significantly altered natural patterns. Obviously, sex and love are not simply joined. Safety, hunger, and power needs, as well as the desire for sheer pleasure, have all perverted the relationship so that the practice of sex may represent a response to any of a wide variety of desires. Such deviations and their consequences will be considered in Chapter 10, in the section on conflict.

Hope. Since emotion is a signal which encourages action, all emotions must exist as continua along which the affect ranges as behavior occurs and/or situations change. Furthermore, it must be possible to anticipate such a change if these signals are to be efficiently employed. In the case of organisms whose activities or behaviors are instinctive, however, the consummatory characteristic (CE) need not be involved. The spider, on feeling some emotion, may "decide" to spin a web, but since the activity is unlearned there is no reason to assume any positive feeling associated with the outcome.

In organisms capable of learning, the situation is of a different nature. Not only is there some ability to anticipate an emotional state (AE), there is also a capacity to recall the emotion which accompanied previous events. Such recollections are also experienced in the form of emotions—which is perhaps one of the reasons why emotions have sometimes been considered irrelevant to behavior, as was discussed earlier. However, some recall is essential to the capability of anticipating future emotional states, and it is here that the term *hope* takes on meaning. Since the level of hope is related to the probability of the occurrence of an event, intellectual capacity and learning are also involved.

To hope is to anticipate. A deliberate act is carried out because some emotional outcome is expected. The suicidal individual hopes for relief; the hoarder for security. The continuum of hope ranges from despair, where there is little faith in the possibility of success, to the elation associated with a high probability of achieving a desired outcome. Because hope involves both anticipation of what is to come, and recollection of what has occurred previously, it represents a link between past and future which is peculiar to the highest forms of life and is particularly extensive in humans. It relates desires to situations in terms of the probability of achievement. To feel "hopeful" is to believe that something desirable has a satisfactory prospect.

One may hope for an outcome that is not anticipated. For example, the imminent end of a war may be much desired, although it seems quite impossible. This represents the use of the term hope as a synonym for desire, and anticipation as it means belief. As employed in this text, the terms refer to emotional states—where hope refers to desire plus expectancy along the continuum of probability. It is only when behavior is involved that the terms are used in this sense. Thus, to hope for the end of a particular war demands some measure of belief in its possibility.

Hope provides another example of the fact that all emotional states involve some desire. To state that one hopes that the war ends, but does not want it to, would obviously be absurd, but it would be equally nonsensical to express the hope while claiming disinterest. In the latter instance, it might be argued that the hope is based purely on a moral evaluation of the situation. However, moral judgment can only enter into an emotional state after desire is involved. And to state that one believes a war should end and therefore hopes so *but does not want it to* is equally untenable. (One can obviously also hope against an event. The essential elements remain the same—some level of desire and expectancy).

This does not imply that hope is always in the direction of moral propriety. An individual may hope to find a cigar in the humidor because of a craving, despite an acknowledgment that smoking is an undesirable behavior. Similarly, individuals who state that they hope no dessert is served because they believe they should not eat any, are expressing their awareness of a conflict between wants. In such cases, there is also a desire to avoid an anxiety-provoking situation based on moral judgment and a recognition of their limited resistance.

Wish. The term *wish* is sometimes employed as synonymous with hope—as when a child says, "I wish I were grown up," or when one says, "I wish the driver of the car ahead of me would hurry." But wishing, strictly speaking, represents an emotional state quite the opposite of hope. It refers to *impossible* situations in which desire is involved. In the case of the child, the wish is to be an adult *now*, which cannot be, just as one may wish that they were wealthy now while hoping for financial success in the future.

One cannot wish and hope for the same situation or event. More specifically, one cannot hope for any past or present event, and one cannot wish for any future event. One can only hope for future events and can only wish that past or present events were, or are, true or untrue. Past, present, and future are all related only to the observer's knowledge or belief. If a boy states that he hopes his sister won yesterday's race, he means that he has not yet learned the results.

To wish you success in a coming venture can be translated as a hope for your success. However, to say I wish I could lend you $10.00 (which I have irrevocably decided to use otherwise) cannot be similarly transposed, although it appears to be a possible event. In this latter instance, the belief is that, given all present data, it cannot occur although being a future event it is subject to alteration, and I want it to happen if circumstances permit. This is an example of the wish/hope interface. The term wish is appropriate because of my conviction that, with all available information, I see no possibility of altering the decision. The ambiguity is similar to that involved in saying I wish that Mr. X, who I believe to have died, were alive. To the extent that my knowledge of his death is indirect, I may learn one day that he is, in fact, alive. Nevertheless, the statement of wish would have been appropriate—lest all things were subjected to the same analysis.

A simple example describes the range of hope, the location of wish, and the gray area in which the two often become confused. Assume that we desire rain, with the limitation that at the time under consideration, we believe it to be true that:
- It is not raining here.
- Rain is not imminent here.
- It has sometimes rained here.
- It has sometimes not rained here.

EMOTION

Given this state of affairs, the following must be the case:
- We cannot hope that any of the above data are true or false.
- We cannot wish that they are (or were) true (since they *are* true).
- We can (*only*) wish that they were false.
- We can (*only*) hope for rain to fall in the future.

Each of the emotional characteristics exemplified in Figure 9.1 represents higher level affective states. They are probably not appropriate to the simplest organisms. However, it is difficult to avoid the implication that the cat who sits patiently at a rat hole is experiencing some emotion which combines want with probability of occurrence. If the same animal is placed in a situation in which it is separated from a mouse by a sheet of glass, it will certainly continue to desire the object although it may believe that it is unattainable. In this case, *hoping* would be replaced by *wishing* (that the mouse was obtainable).

Figure 9.1

Wish/Hope and Rain Potential

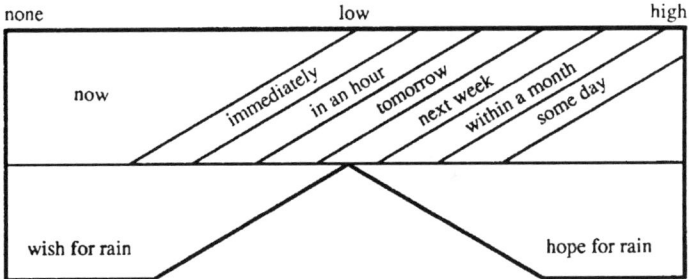

The contention that emotions are purposeful seems clear enough in explaining hope, but it appears at best useless and even somewhat cruel that people are invested with the capacity to wish for impossible situations, since such wishes are sometimes accompanied by painfully distressing emotions. Several explanations are available.

First, at the lowest level of hope, the wishing sentiment may be a spur to action (since some tiny shred of hope may exist), which is why the distinction has been drawn. In the absolutely hopeless situation, the residual feeling that exists probably represents the fact that desire cannot be shut off simply because opportunity fails. The tiger that stalks a zebra is experiencing hope. If the prey escapes, the tiger is left with the same want, mixed with the intellectual awareness that it is not to be met at this time. In the simplest animals, "out of sight" may be "out of mind," but as the evolutionary ladder is ascended, wishing becomes increasingly involved as the cognitive apparatus begins to operate.

In the case of humans, wishing performs another function since the imagination is sufficiently powerful to provide for vicarious experience. Thus, children who wish they were (now) astronauts can play "as if" in their personal mental spheres. This continual wishing that one were an astronaut can be translated into hope as the potential for such a career is recognized. The result may be the development of a discipline and the aggregation of skills which culminates in opportunity to enjoy the desired experiences.

The hope paradigm is complicated by many factors such as previous experience, desire deprivation level, and intellectual capacity, and Figure 9.2 represents only a rough attempt to describe it. The fact that estimates are involved further indicates the need for some local decision-making ability for efficient reaction to occur. At zero probability, it is not possible to hope for an outcome, and wishing against can only occur when the probability of occurrence is at the 100% level.

The level of hope is represented by the intersection of a line drawn between the level of desire (line A-B) and probability (line C-D), on the "hope range" line. Each must be above zero and below 100% if hope is appropriate. If they are at zero or 100% only wishing is appropriate. An example may be useful. A line drawn between Q, the current desire level and R, the conceptualized situation, would cross the hope

Figure 9.2

Wish/Hope Paradigm

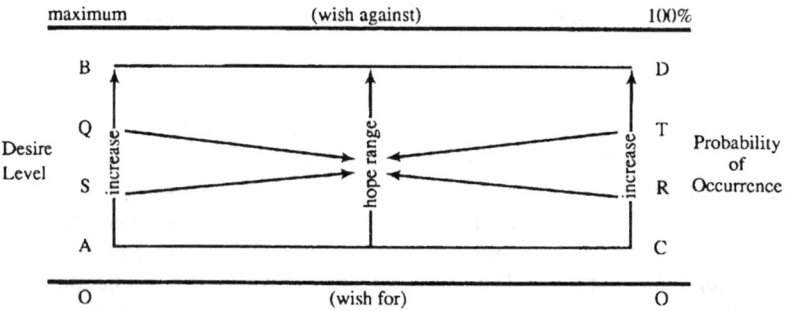

range line somewhere near the average point. But a line connecting S and T would cross at approximately the same point. Thus, as desire increases, lower probabilities will suffice to cause a feeling of hope while, when desire is low, very little hope is apt to be entertained unless the probability of occurrence is comparatively high. The critical distinction to be drawn is that in no situation may one experience both feelings, though they may be difficult to distinguish.

Excitation. The term *excitation* may be applied to the *level* of desire as it is related to or accompanies the anticipation, recollection, or practice of any behavior, situation, or event—whether associated with positive or negative emotions. It is not an emotion related to any specific drive but a description of a state of heightened tension. Its purpose as a stimulant to behavior is related rather to the physiology of energy mobilization than to any particular outcome. It is appropriate to situations involving fear and guilt and other negative emotions as well as to pleasurable experiences.

Excitation runs parallel to probability in many cases but is essentially an independent process, and the total pattern of hope has been shown to be dependent on a complex interaction between estimate of desire and estimates of the probability of the occurrence of an event. The individual who has not eaten in several days will become highly excited on smelling a broiling steak, even if the probability of eating it is low. The same person, after eating steak for several days, will be at a low excitement level even where the prospect of having it is great.

Summary

The contention that emotion is purposive is based on the conviction that no desire or conceptual experience (regardless of whether it is accompanied by any form of evaluation) could in itself cause an emotion, and that an emotional experience requires the presence of both forms of information. The positive emotion associated with a sexual encounter, eating a meal, or enjoying a book is evidence of a desire for some such activity. Although one may not actively seek safety except when existence is threatened, the arousal of fear indicates that some desire must also be involved.

An emotional response cannot be evaluated as to its propriety against some constant referent. If one is said to overreact to a situation, the inference is that one's perception of the situation is faulty (e.g., the situation is less threatening than that individual believed it to be) and/or the affect is counterproductive. Such interpretations are, however, presumptuous. Although one may argue that in previous similar situations nothing untoward happened, it is beyond the capacity of mind to determine the *point* at which a situation should be considered dangerous.

In the case of guilt, shame, and related emotions, desires and perceptual information are fed into the emotional system, where they are also judged on the moral scale. In addition to the desire for an experience or a state of affairs, there is sometimes a problem of moral appropriateness. The behavior is learned, but the moral aspect is innate. Although emotions with a moral component, such as guilt, shame, and anger, relate almost exclusively to actual rather than to theoretical considerations, their occurrence provides impressive evidence of the presence of an affective capacity that is invoked when a situation calls for such a measurement.

This does not fully account for every emotional state in humans, nor does it explain the majority of feelings that guide simpler organisms toward their goals. In the same manner, and for the same reason that other characteristics of life have been genetically modified, the role of emotion has been transformed as cognitive capacity and the ability to learn has increased. The result of this evolutionary development has been to obscure the relationship between the individual and other humans. The function of emotion has become difficult to understand and much human behavior has been interpreted in strange ways.

The role of emotion cannot be over-estimated. It is essential to any and all forms of deliberate activity. It is, thus, responsible for the superior adaptability of higher life forms. The price of such progress has, however, been immense. The capacity to express preferences has resulted in many decisions which are in conflict with goals established at the level of the gene pool. In primitive life forms, little deviation from the needs of the species occurs since the relative strength of assertive, protective, and transcendent desires is comparable. Furthermore, the simple organism, having little cognitive skill, is incapable of making (biological) self-serving decisions. In higher forms the situation is altered as the individual begins to conceptualize, predict, and recall. Here the potential for significant deviation arises.

Koestler's notion of self-transcendent or integrative and self assertive emotions must be considered in this light. Beyond his concern regarding the "poisonous aspect of the self-assertive emotions,"[35] Koestler expressed great concern about self-transcendence.

> The glory and the tragedy of the human condition *both derive from our powers of self-transcendence.* It is a power which can be harnessed to creative or destructive purposes; it is equally capable of turning us into artists or killers, but more likely into killers.[36]

Koestler, following MacLean,[37] employed the terms *emotion* and *desire* interchangeably as others have been shown to do. The term *self-transcendence* seems to more accurately describe *desire* than *emotion*, and we have so used the term in this text.

Assertive and protective desires are related to personal profit, while the urge to identify as well as the moral sense are transcendent in that they relate the individual to some superordinate existence. *Reason* is an assertive element since it represents the capacity to appreciate the probability of achieving positive emotional states by meeting desires of either type. An appreciation of the role of reason is critical. Koestler argued that *emotions* are too much involved in decision-making, while *reason* should be ascendant. However, it is reason, or the perceptual cognitive system, which allows for learning how to meet desires that is at fault. Humans learn to satisfy desires in ways that are self and species destructive, such as in believing that other races or people are inferior. Here is the cause of the problem. Fortunately it may yield to an aggressive educational program.

Our interpretation is based on the thesis that as emotion becomes involved and as the biological self assumes primacy, the holarchy of life suffers its principal perversion. The self—a creature of emotion—comes increasingly to be considered the apex of life. This involvement of emotions is the focal point of much of the psychological distress and mental aberration to be detailed in the section on emotional health.

Chapter Notes

1. Benner (1985), p. 353
2. Chein (1972), p. 277
3. Hilgard (1987), p. 348
4. Harriman (1974), p. 6
5. *Ibid.*, p. 48
6. Funk (1963), p. 689
7. Runes (1962), p. 89
8. Fernald & Fernald (1985), p. 329
9. Young, P. T. (1973), p. 750
10. *Ibid.*, p. 757
11. Lazarus (1984), p. 126
12. Zajonc (1984)
13. Lazarus (1984), p. 124
14. Leeper (1963)
15. James (1892)
16. Cannon (1927)
17. Certainly an affect, in the sense of a conviction regarding the probability of falling, is essential to the determination.
18. Arnold & Gasson (1968), p. 218
19. Ouspensky (1971), p. 118
20. Appetite suppressors and a host of drugs that have been developed to control the desire for food, alcohol and cigarettes, do not provide evidence that the desires involved are not essential to normal behavior. Nor would an intelligent Martian who dismantled a typewriter and discovered alternate ways to manipulate the mechanisms fail to recognize that those parts in the intact machine performed an essential word processing function.
21. This practice may have been, in part, because of the similarity of the terms *motive* (which does refer to drives), and *motivation* which references a more complex process.
22. The paradigm *fear* —> *pain* is probably quite similar to *pleasure anticipation* —> *pleasure experience*, and fear may be equated with pain anticipation. But since the term fear is in common usage it will be so employed here.
23. Both psychoanalytic and behavioral interpretations have focused on the urgency of the desire to reduce tension. Sublimation, rationalization and other defense mechanisms are presumed to operate in order to keep tension at manageable level.
24. The assumption that those seeking negative emotional states are mentally unhealthy, arbitrary as it may seem, is quite consistent with both lay interpretation of guilt- or anger-seeking individuals and professionals who find self-deprecating and pervasively hate oriented individuals to be suffering from various forms of maladjustment. As to those who pursue dangerous entertainment, the appropriate model sees the stimulating value of the experience as worthy of the risk. Every attempt is made to minimize the risk factor, but there remains the fact that stimulation is heightened when risk is

present. The fear element is accepted on the assumption that the danger will be overcome.
25. The consummatory emotion (CE) is that affective state that is experienced during, and/or after, the occurrence of a behavior or event that identifies it as positive or negative. In addition to those anticipatory emotions that are awakened instinctively, the recollection of earlier experiences arouses an anticipatory emotion (AE) when a similar experience is considered.
26. Freudian psychology errs in its assumption that individuals who behave in ways that are self-punitive must enjoy the attendant negative emotions. That interpretation is, among other, things contradictory, as will be developed in Chapter 11.
27. An individual falling through space, and who cannot make contact with any substance will feel states of anxiety and even panic unless the experience is believed to be under some form of control.
28. Kierkegaard (1944), p. 49
29. There is, of course, an automatic triggering of elements of the nervous system. However, it is the *experiential* aspect that we wish to emphasize.
30. Hebb (1949), p. 257
31. Moser (1973), p. 234
32. Lasch (1979), p. 23
33. One group of "pop" psychologists has proposed that love of self should come first and a "look out for Number 1" philosophy has been preached by a radical few. Such self-serving behavior is a recipe for the attraction of negative emotions ranging from sympathy to disgust.
34. The analysis that follows relegates homosexual love relationships to a form of perversion of the purpose underlying male/female intimacy. Homosexuality represents a combining of platonic caring with the physical gratification accompanying coital activity.
35. Koestler (1967), p. 231
36. *Ibid.*, p. 245
37. MacLean (1971)

Chapter 10
Conflict, Control, and the Emergent Self

The *self* is the focal point along a continuum of awareness—with the corporeal individual at one extreme and the totality of living existence at the other. It is a meaningful concept only at the level of life at which it is possible for the individual to act counter to the survival and growth interests of the parent gene pool. As cognitive skill develops, the sense of self becomes increasingly responsive to the demands of the palpable and immediate individual.

Identification and *identity* are interdependent process, with the desire for an identity being rooted in one's relationship with some identificatory system—with some whole from which the individual elicits significance. It is only through such an affiliation that an efficacious and enduring identity can be developed.

Parameters of the Self

In the simplest organisms, drive information is spread evenly across the range of possible responses. Urges toward eating, sexual activity, and stimulation all bear on the individual as impulses to action, and arouse similarly powerful emotions when appropriate situations arise. The individual has a relatively limited cognitive capacity and does not differentiate significantly between itself as an independent organism and as a part of the species. As a species matures, this situation is modified by an increasing capacity to manipulate the environment, to profit from experience, and to associate activities with the capacity to satisfy desires.

To describe techniques for solving adjustment problems it becomes necessary to refer to the individual in terms which suggest the presence of a separate, and in many ways independent, entity. This existent is known as the *self*. It is *as if* there were a conscious, internally sufficient force which causes action and determines the mental state at any point in time.

Under the principles of holarchic existence, the individual is recognized as having some identity separate from the gene pool from which it is generated. However, the self in the conscious individual represents not the *cause*, but the *result* of the interplay of genetically fixed dynamisms and environmental opportunity. It exists along the individual/species continuum and has developed on the basis of its potential for species survival and growth. It emerges only at the level of potential for separation of personal interest from that of the gene pool.

The causes for the conflict between biological self and species membership are manifold. At the most sophisticated level of phenotypal existence, the sensations of *pain* and *pleasure* are experienced only by individuals. The organism recognizes a relationship between its experiences and their impact on its physical and psychological well-being. As intellectual capacity increases, more techniques for finding and sustaining pleasure, and for avoiding pain, are learned.

Such intellectual development in many instances moves away from the needs of the species. While "intelligent" behavior is equitable with species preservative activity in primitive life, it begins to separate at higher levels. Not only is sensation localized, but the partness aspect of individual existence is not so clearly manifested. Individuals can be perceived acutely, but the generality of the form of life represented is apt to be conceptually blurred.

The shift of focus in the mediating of environmental data from the higher life echelons to a wide variety of instances or individuals results in the emergence of an entity which is often considered to be the embodiment of "appropriate" significance. It is a spin-off of local decision-making capacity and is expressed through the cognitive/affective system. The fact that many decisions are made by the individual results in a conviction of autonomy, and in some cases even a reverent attitude toward the psychobiological center of such activity.

As cognitive skill becomes more sophisticated, the sense of individual self becomes more pronounced. The potential advantage of such a construct to species enhancement is obvious. Individuals who are sensitive to their own significance and are capable of experiencing the positive and negative affects associated with many behaviors as well as possessing the skills essential to their consummation are equipped more effectively than those forms of life not possessing such sensitivity. This capacity, however, includes the potential for maladjustment. In the process of directing behaviors toward personal goals, a separation from identification with the species often leads to conflict, particularly of a moral nature.

Many profound thinkers have concluded that selfhood demands a relationship between the individual and some external, more inclusive existence. Some writers, demonstrating a keen sense of this union, recognize not only the validity of the premise, but problems associated with attempting to avoid it. Lawrence said, "Individualism is really an illusion. I am part of the great whole and I can never escape. But I *can* deny my convictions, break them, and become a fragment. Then I am wretched."[1]

Royce contended that in the process of learning one realizes that the self which thinks "is identical with the deeper self which possesses and truly knows the object."[2] All thoughts are part of larger thoughts and they must be somehow nested in some all comprehensive self. "There is, then, at last, but one Self, organically, reflectively, consciously inclusive of all the selves, and so of all truth."[3]

This synthetic idealism is a form of Berkeleyism, but James offered a similar interpretation from a pragmatic position. *"In its widest possible sense, [a man's] self is the sum total of all that he can call his."*[4] This represents another example of the notion of biological transcendence, since the self is said to include that which is "owned." Although James posited several types of self (material, social, spiritual, and pure ego), he concluded that all are known or centered in the physical being, which the knower assumes to be "me" or "I."

The individual/species relationship is not universally accepted. The notion of an individual soul for each human being and the many philosophical arguments on the value of individual life imply that something exists within each living being which is independent of any more comprehensive existent. Portman, in his concept of *interiority* suggested that living organisms "overcome their corruptibility through reproduction and hereditary transmission...[and] are capable of relatively autonomous activity."[5] Such interpretations exemplify the tendency to point toward the biological individual as the proper focus of selfhood.

The organism is said to overcome extinction by reproducing itself. This view represents yet another example of the presumptuous and wholly inaccurate suggestion that the individual is anything more than an agent of a process with which it is invested by its genotypic ancestors. It does *not* reproduce itself, but is an element of the reproductive process. The holarchic position, which assumes the existence and superordinacy of life at the species level, mandates the conclusion that behaviors define the self *on the individual/species continuum.*

The psychoanalytic interpretation of self is another example of the persistent view of life as emerging from part to whole, with individuals having some evolutionary, as well as developmental, priority. Weiss, in describing the phenomenon of belonging, said "the 'ego feeling' *extends* [italics added] to a 'we feeling'.... It *grows* [italics added] to include a drive for preservation of the group, society, and mankind.... The 'we' may be felt as the ego continuation."[6]

This view reduces the external world, and all that is not ego, to secondary status. The ego is first purely narcissistic (an accurate interpretation) and later takes into itself the identified world. But the "world" it embraces includes the life form of which the individual is inherently a part. The relationship between the individual and the group may be said to "grow" only in the sense that the maturational process leads to a *recognition* of one's partness not the creation of an external world.

Another example of this focus comes from a philosophic camp quite differently oriented. Sartre suggested that "man is nothing else but that which he makes of himself."[7] That self includes a *mitwelt*,[8] which suggests a degree of responsibility for all individuals. But, said Sartre, the responsibility is personal. "If...I decide to marry...I am thereby committing not only myself, but humanity as a whole, to the practice of monogamy."[9]

This view is an unavoidable consequence of the premise that essence is only a contingent reality. We must begin from the "subjective," insisted Sartre. "There is at least one being whose existence comes before its essence. That being is a man."[7] Such an interpretation is based on the priority of experienced phenomena which, of course, are creatures of an experiencing individual.

With such an orientation, models of human nature as diverse as those of Freud and Heidegger must be stretched to painful limits in order to accommodate the phenomenon of self-subordination. The holarchic interpretation sees the experienced self as a focal point of the interface of the genetic totality and the biological self. The only aspect of selfhood that is unique to the biologic entity is the location of the organs of awareness—the implanted signal system. And here is the battleground; the arena for the struggle between opposing pressures. The conflict between the urge to control and the urge to belong represents the principal issue in the holarchic emotional health model.

Self is said to be the object of awareness. But awareness of what? Following earlier arguments concerning the evolution of information systems, the limit of awareness is the perceived world, the urge toward activity (power) and safety, and the recognition of the individual as part of a life system (purpose). The emotional system, in that it refers to the interpretation of interacting signals, represents the hub of selfhood.

It has been pointed out that the term self becomes meaningful only at the point where an individual is capable of activity which is in conflict with the purpose of the species that it manifests. The individual is part of *all* life. However, since signal systems emanate directly from the protected gene pool through the genetic process, the critical relationship occurs between these two existents. Although this may seem a negative description, it follows both logically from the emergence of awareness of localized affect and (especially) from the observation of behavior. There is, however, a more positive interpretation and one which should help to clarify the relationship between the individual as a whole and as a part.

The human self represents the convergence of the relationship between the individual and some superordinate existence. It is judged by the quality of behavior in a succession of reference points which associate it with that higher order of being.

CONFLICT, CONTROL, AND THE EMERGENT SELF

The most insignificant limit of the relationship is that at which the totality of selfhood is the fleeting physical being, and it is this trivial entity that is acclaimed as the pinnacle by many existentialists.

This interpretation does not, of course, limit selfhood to humans. In simpler organisms, individuals are often described in terms of behaviors which (as with humans) represent what they characteristically do. The personality of an animal is ordinarily limited to this type of description, since it seems presumptuous to ascribe motives that have a moral aspect. However, if an animal is called "sly" or "clever," the anthropomorphic equivalent is recognized and there is a sense of self of the human type implied. In fact, when any animal decides to act consistently with, or in opposition to, species needs, selfhood is meaningful. The problem is to recognize when such assumptions of motive are accurate.

The dimensions of a self are extremely difficult to identify, in part because of the flexibility of the experience. Clearly, the self is not diminished because a part of the body is lost or nonfunctional. The self of a one-armed person is quite complete. When one speaks of a self that includes more than the physical body, however, the concept is more difficult to accept. If John is known as a "family man," or, in political parlance, that Henry is a "party man," the reference is to an individual who gives priorities to some person or organization outside of his body, and this is an appropriate interpretation. The man who gives his life for his child can be said to recognize a self which transcends his physical being. Although the locus may be biologically determinate, the extension is not limited to the physical body.

It is proper to say that the individual who gives, or shares, is identifying with a larger system, but it is equally meaningful to say that the self includes more than the physical person. The self expands as the locus of behavior shifts from personal desire to the welfare of the larger existence. Although awareness of the self is located within the biological entity, the object of such awareness can range from the body itself to the totality of life. "Who am I?" becomes "What is the self of which I am aware?" The answer defines the self as that with which one identifies.

The "I" that identifies represents another point along the continuum, somewhere between biological individuality and species totality. The self-transcendent desires can, thus, best be interpreted as referring the biological or physical being to the more comprehensive existence—species or gene pool. This incorporation of others into the self as an act of identification represents a recognition of species superordinacy rather than a creative enlargement of the self. For this reason, the "expanding self" of the existentialist, which never moves its existential center from the biological being, cannot be accepted.

Since the focal point of the self is in the individual, existence is viewed in two directions. Looking outward one finds meaning; inward, the object of praise and blame. In addition to seeing myself in terms of all those with whom I identify, I see the elements of my physical body as other objects to be evaluated. When I state that "I do not know why I eat so much," the focusing agent (or self at some level) is criticizing another level of self because of its incontinence. I become angry or pleased with myself because of a capacity to hierarchically recognize the propriety of my behavior. If the focus of the question of selfhood is located, the issue of *who* in the sense of "To what totality do I belong?" is species directed. The issue of *what* I am represents an analysis or an identity question. It may be more fully stated as "What is that of which the individual is composed?" Figure 10.1a describes the relationship involved.

Figure 10.1

Identification and Behavior Continua

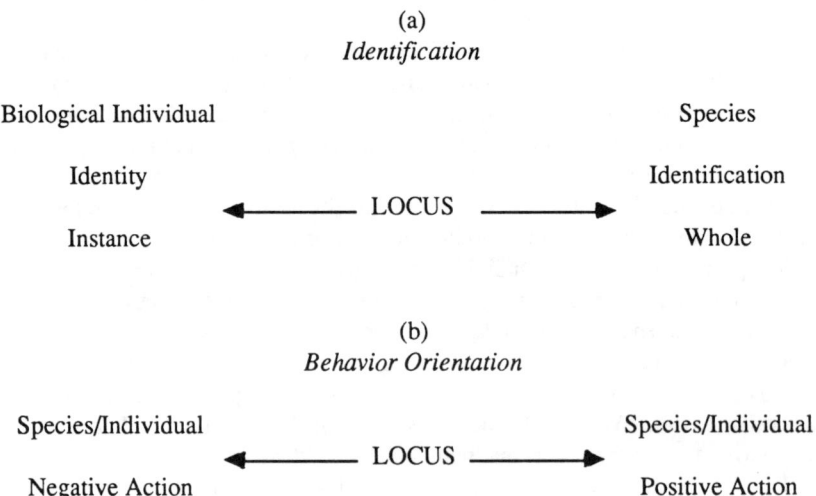

In this analysis, the direction is from "evil" to "good," and the self stands in judgment of experiences as exalting or debasing. The point on the "locus" line at which individuals see themselves identifies their degree of meaningfulness as human beings. The continuum can be described in another way (Figure 10.1b) because of the potential in the decision-making individual to violate propriety. Here the *behavior* of the individual is considered, with that which is self serving being contrasted with that which recognizes the priority of the whole. It points up the holarchic basis for conflict. In this usage, "self" serving refer to those actions which are carried out despite the fact that they may injure the individual who performs them, or the species, or other transcendent existent that they represent. Thus, activities that may result in a disease such as AIDS[10] and the transmission of that disease to unborn children would be an example of self serving behavior.[11]

The self is roughly analogous to the ego in that it is the "me-ness" aspect of the mental structure. Although it cannot be isolated, it must be inferred. This is not as presumptuous as it may seem. Living protoplasm can be observed to move toward food. *Drive* is a construct that is inferred from such behavior. The environment, however, is also a construct which is generalized from observation of specific instances of impeding or encouraging situations, events, or experiences. A wall that may stop movement is an example of what qualifies as "environment."

The self has the same limitations, and the task is to infer its nature from behavior. The first inference is that the self is an aspect of the physical body since the individual seems to focus considerable attention on its corporeal being. Western culture has in fact reached the point where individuals are so highly prized that a *cult of self* has developed. Part of the contemporary tragic incapacity for improving conditions of emotional health is the insistence with which many educators and educational philosophers hold to this view. Social scientists have continually expressed concern about the denial of an innate urge toward belonging which could put the biological being into proper perspective. Montague proposed that "the infant has no ego. The evidence, on the other hand, suggests that it is conditioned to become egocentric by processes of culturalization which emphasize egocentricity."[12]

This emphasis on independence and the priority of the individual with the minimizing of the relationship to all human life leads to a loss of identification and to interpretations of convictions of *obligation* and *duty* as undesirable feelings. Deprivation in the area of assertive desires gives rise to negative affective states. Signals associated with such other-directed demands as *responsibility* often appear as barriers to action. It is only when the individual is interested in some form of activity which is not species positive that such morally charged affects are experienced. They function in much the same capacity as the appestats, which indicate when a behavior exceeds some optimum.

The moral sense, however, also provides "go" signals, and in some situations, the positive nature is obvious. Individuals who serve their family because of a positive sense of obligation may be "tempted" by some opportunity to profit themselves at cost to the larger group. Here the message may be interpreted in the same "stop" sense as moral obligations usually are. A more accurate interpretation would be that a conflict exists between "go" signals with the assertive often more potent than the transcendent, and, with increasing intellectual skill, more apt to be heeded. What could be termed wisdom in the primitive organism—which acts on the basis of a powerful (moral) input—becomes replaced by *expedience*, with the physical individual often viewed as entitled to first consideration.

It is obvious that selfhood and identification are closely associated and that knowledge of the relationship is, in part, a form of moral awareness. The scale of morality and the desire for identification proceed from a level at which parts and whole are indiscriminable. In the simplest life forms, no behavior is possible, and total identification obtains. In humans, the existence of much competing data make identification a sometimes serious problem. The evolution of identification is charted in Table 10.1.

Evolving individuation is a valuable process in that the sense of identity increases concern for self-care, and thus, potentially the well-being of the species. It is, however, characterized by a concomitant increase in the ability to identify with exclusive subsystems. In humans, the creation of deliberate systems has resulted in inter-human competition and intra-human conflict.

Emotion and the Self

The method by which individuals interpret both the nature of the world they inhabit, and their own needs and obligations, provides the potential for homeorhetic survival. It represents a sensitivity to existence which, optimally, makes the living organism a model of efficiency in dealing with its environment; one that is without parallel in the universe of the inorganic. However, even at its maximal adjustment level, the mere fact of choice in a garden of alternatives presents considerable unavoidable difficulty. Information systems are attuned to a wide spectrum of stimuli and provide an impetus to many potential behaviors. With each decision, some alternative activity is denied, some behavior eschewed, some outcome precluded. The personality, or self, that ensues is a kaleidoscope of emotional experiences. Emotions, in fact, *define* the individual. The self is no more or less than the feeling states that are experienced and displayed.

The emotion generated by conflict is *anxiety*—to fight, to run, to risk a fortune on the turn of a wheel. Each such decision carries with it some negative emotional component, and each can immobilize. Where the competition is between different types of desire, the emotion is the same whenever the issue is one of uncertainty. The hungry animal that risks its life in the pursuit of a meal, is operating in a tension-laden situation.

Similarly, if the problem is whether to save one's life or to protect another, and the inability to decide is based on a lack of sufficient information about the outcome, anxiety can be anticipated. When sexual behavior is hindered by uncertainty about the receptivity of a potential mate, the same is true. When a driver who exceeds a speed limit (even where deemed essential) is unsure whether their explanation will be accepted, anxiety is again a consequent.

Another source of conflict arises when a need is inconsistent with some form of evaluation. If a decision includes both the desire to perform a particular act, and the coexistent feeling is that it should not be done, the consequent guilt may interfere with the expression of the act. Deliberating about whether to smoke a cigarette, when the cognitive data as well as the moral sense provide negative signals, may arouse anxiety.

Table 10.1

The Emergent Self

Level	Individuation	Behavior	Example
Pre-affective	none	All species demands met	simple cell plant form
Affective			
A	slight	Some decisions but species needs take priority	simple animals (ants, bees)
B	moderate	Appestat control and strong sense of responsibility to species	higher animals (cats, apes)
C	extreme	Appestats weaker and sense of responsibility to species low	humans

A similar problem arises when a choice must be made between behaviors that relate the individual to one system while at the same time alienating them from another. The young person who must decide whether the responsibilities of military duty takes priority over the call of conscience faces such a dilemma. The same emotion occurs when perceptual information is unclear. When the meaning of signs is ambiguous, or when the same stimuli change meaning without warning, a state of anxiety develops which can be reduced only with the return of order and the integrity of the perceptual/cognitive system.

Researchers have demonstrated that neuroses can be created in relatively simple animals by placing them in an undependable environment. In humans, the same type of reaction is observed when behaviors or language that have had a particular meaning are altered rapidly and without a decodeable pattern. Culture shock represents evidence of this type of conflict. More dramatic is the panic of animals who sense that a predator is near but cannot locate it, or the reaction of the infant whose mother has disappeared from sight.

The great majority of such decisions are made at a level at which the systems can handle the shock. Temporary surges of hydrochloric acid released in anxious situations are neutralized by chemical action in the digestive tract. Furthermore, in lower organisms, where the interpretation of signals is limited, few natural occurrences result in significant physiological damage. Even here, however, continued uncertainty and the need to make decisions without reliable information can be fatal. Classical studies, in which monkeys were placed in uncomfortable situations, revealed that those with the opportunity to improve the situation through attempting to outguess the experimenters developed ulcers, while their counterparts forced to suffer the same discomfort without options did not.

In humans, a variety of physical disorders are associated with the inability to make decisions. The most significant contributor is ambiguity which prohibits decisions from being made. Individuals who say they do not know what to do often mean they cannot understand the situation. The outcome of a behavior is uncertain. The demands being made are unclear. In each of these situations, the emotion that is experienced is *anxiety*, a potentially painful and often destructive affect.

The conflict state characterized by anxiety demands attention—ideally, some behavior that alleviates it. The type of activity observed in animals placed in anxiety-provoking situations often fails to meet this criterion. Uncontrolled defecation and severely diminished activity are observed in such conflicts. This does not refute the argument that the purpose of anxiety is to encourage a change in the situation. Ineffective activity merely manifests the fact that the genetic plan has not produced a phenotype capable of coping with the specific threat. Ostensibly random movements or elaborate activity may also reflect imperfection at the genotypic level—the behavior in each instance representing an attempt to alleviate discomfort.

The importance of recognizing the presence of anxiety is that the behavior associated with its relief is different than that, for example, associated with guilt. Anxiety is, in fact, an extreme state. The anxious individual often cannot even assign guilt, the acceptance of which may be the first step toward recovery, although the feeling of guilt is neither a happy nor desirable experience. In many instances, guilt may be a step toward conflict resolution in that through recognition of responsibility a more viable situation may be created. Persons who believe they are contributing to an untenable condition are in a position to modify their behavior. Guilt, however, is an extremely destructive emotion when it is strong enough to cause preoccupation and where resolution is difficult. As with anxiety, an effort is made to dispose of the emotion by conceptual modification or whatever action is available.

Guilt may be relieved to some extent by blaming others or denying responsibility. Such methods, which have been defined psychoanalytically, have the facility for relieving distress and, in fact, of leading to equilibrium. By translating feelings from guilt to anger, conflict may be significantly lessened. Individuals may blame their fellow workers for their own inadequacies, resorting perhaps to the "incompetency of institutions" or whatever agency is sufficiently impersonal that the emotion may be successfully attenuated. Such an approach may excuse ineptness, disloyalty, or other peccadillo.

Another signal of distress—the anger associated with inability to reach a desired goal—does not yield as readily. If someone is believed to be deliberately interfering with one's opportunity to gratify desires, the conflict has a different character. Here, merely blaming another does not solve the problem, and, except at the level of extreme apathy, there remains the desire to alter the situation.

The reason for conflict in such cases is the awareness that the situation *could* be altered. An obnoxious fellow worker could be fired, transferred, or even have his career destroyed. Each potentiality may be flirted with, depending on the extent to which the need has been suppressed. Such feelings are often observed in teenagers whose sense of justice is insulted by a world that limits their freedom to indulge their desires while they observe adults practicing all the forms of hypocrisy that are decried in adolescents. Even more devastating is the impact on fully mature individuals who are prohibited because of race, ethnicity, gender, or other characteristic from sharing in what they believe is legitimately theirs. Conflict is inevitable in such situations, and the behaviors that result represent the type of decision that each individual makes as situations are weighed in affective terms. Is destruction worse than slavery? Is immolation preferable to humiliation? Such questions demand—and usually get—answers, in one form or another.

Fear-provoking situations are not included here since fear is not based on conflict. It is only when confusion about how to get out of the situation is added that conflict is involved. Furthermore, there is often an element of *value* in a conflict situation. The question of whether a behavior or event *should* occur, whether such a response is intellectually sound, or both, may be under consideration.

In dealing with conflict, two types of resolution are possible. For many conflict combinations, there is the possibility of resolution by taking action which removes the conflict. This is the function of negative emotions. Anxiety may be relieved by learning the nature of the problem. Guilt can be assuaged by behaving in such a manner as to be subject to self-approval. Anger can be reduced by removing the interfering agent. If a man *wants* to attend a baseball game but an employer will not allow the time, he can busy himself with activity until such time as the game is over, at which point his level of interest will be greatly diminished.

Unfortunately, the nature of situations, the interaction between them, and social and other devices do not allow for such a direct assault on the problem in many instances. The solution may be so complex that it cannot be learned. Guilt may be so heavy as to defy expiation. The forces that inhibit growth may be of such magnitude as to seem insurmountable. Furthermore, in some instances every conceivable resolution seems to include some extremely negative element. But the world cannot always be changed. Desires cannot always be denied. Values cannot always be altered. However, the information that is transmitted by the various systems may be interpreted in such a way as to minimize distress. The technique has been identified by psychoanalysts as the employment of *defenses*, which shall be dealt with in Chapter 14.

The Problem of Identity

In earlier sections, we presented a classificatory scheme which included the basic drives as well as their mental manifestations as desires. Obviously absent were the concepts of an urge-to-life and a desire for an individual identity. Each of these constructs has been offered as an essential human desire by a variety of philosophic and psychological theorists. However, they are deliberately excluded from the holarchic paradigm.

Consider first the so-called will-to-live or the desire for continued existence. An assumption is often made that such an urge has a separate, independent, legitimacy. However, no such unique desire can be identified. The test of this interpretation would rest on the response of those offered a continued existence in which they were convinced that no desire of any type could be met. Evidence is available from studies of elderly and incurably ill people who reflect no hope of ever again enjoying any form of gratification of their desires. Shorn of such potential, death seems preferable. In many parts of the world, euthanasia is becoming a legitimate and respected technique for terminating the existence of those whose lives are without satisfying experiences. Such experiences represent the gratification of desires. (Ostensive exceptions would be those where hope for such experiences remains.) It seems more reasonable to consider the urge to live as a general term which, like power, embraces, and consists only of the specific desires.

As regards identity, the very nature of holarchic existence is inconsistent with the notion of an *independent* desire of this nature. Here, too, the concept can be both logically evaluated and empirically tested. From an ontological standpoint, one begins with the question of the level at which one's identity is established. In dealing with identification, we suggested that individuals seek meaning through belonging to more inclusive entities. Identity represents no more than one pole of the same principle. "I am a teacher" not only posits some relationship to a group, but at the same time makes assumptions about the group's significance. Identification must itself be recognized as a form of identity when it is related to some still larger entity, and this is a necessary requirement of its definition. Thus, one's teacherhood is a self, with an identity as well as a projection of biological or physical existence. A series of identities descending from the species (itself related to life in general) to the smallest element in the living chain can be demonstrated.

And what of the desire for an identity? Why does one say, "Look at me," "Notice me," "Attend to me?" One explanation is that it represents a way to gain potency and power, since power represents a general term for access to all desires. But, consider the evidence. If I wanted you to notice me when I was evil, weak, or incompetent, I would be considered emotionally unhealthy—seeking demeaning sympathy and physical or psychological support. Only well-adjusted people—those that are successful, competent, and capable—seek to express their identity in ways that are considered healthy and desirable.

What then of the identification aspect? If I have a desire to belong, why should I not desire to be recognized as separately significant? Again, the test would be to offer an identity where no identification was involved. Presume that an individual were to be provided with the power and potency that would make all desires available except identification. The arrangement may be: *You are to have at your disposal anything that you may desire except that you shall never be "allowed" to be obligated, expected to give, or indebted in any way. You shall not be responsible to any one nor to any thing.* How many people, on consideration of the implications of such an offer, would accept? And, what often happens to those who achieve such a status—deliberately or not?

Another test would be to ask what price a person would pay to be "me." Obviously, many die for others, but how many would give up all identification in exchange for a totally free self? When artists defied their patrons, the argument they offered was that their work was more important than the individual who interfered. Identification with *a particular* individual was merely avoided. Identification with their art was more important. In point of fact, identity could never be established without identification. They are, rather, two ends of a continuum. Individuals identify, and seek recognition of their contribution.

This is a species-positive assertion. It provides legitimacy to the aggressing individual. Of course, the term individual is, once again, appropriate at many levels. Teachers represent an identity as they perform collectively. They, for example, teach. Such a statement is reasonable in spite of the fact that some of them may *not* do so. The development of an identity represents a technique for establishing some form of identification. The awareness of one's relationship to a targeted transcendence, provides a potential deterrent to the socially inappropriate expression of naked urges.

Perhaps most unfortunate among the consequences of selfhood and identity is the distortion of the sense of purpose. As the biological self assumes increasing importance, the feeling of purposefulness decreases and the search for meaning (identification) becomes greater.

We stated earlier that the sense of selfhood becomes more pronounced and increasingly focused on the individual as species become more highly developed, with the direction being away from the system. As the growth of an individual from the time of birth is studied, the opposite phenomenon is observed, with maturation and experience causing a progression from absolute narcissism in the infant to the humanitarian philosophies that typify many of the aged. Not all individuals pass through all stages, nor do they achieve them at highly predictable ages. However, as with cognitive development, there are recognizable interactions which imply that identification develops through experiences that are appropriate to various culturally determined statuses.

The first individuals with whom the infant comes into contact are the objects of the initial attempts at projecting a self. Imitation and other activities not only provide the child with techniques for handling the environment, but also allow for the cathexis which enlarges the personality and increases the scope of the self. As rules of conduct are incorporated, the self is elevated to include the rule-maker, and children can evaluate their own behavior from a higher level.

As growing children encounter and interact with siblings and other peers, identification potential is increased. Although successful identification with a parent is not essential to success at this level, it can facilitate the experience. As children expose themselves to parents and risk their sense of power, the extent to which the investment is successful will have an impact on their willingness to risk with others. And the urge to identify is so great that attempts of all sorts are made at every critical point. The boy or girl who wants to belong because of a sense of the value of relating to a larger system may perform in undesirable ways in order to be accepted. In young adulthood, communal cults and religious fanaticism are as much associated with the identification problem as their alienated opposites who resist immersion in any type of organization.

Concepts such as friendship and intimacy refer to the need for identification and the rewards associated with the establishment of affective bonds that represent the expansion of the self. However, when friendship is expressed by fawning, and intimacy by submission, the growth potential is lost and the behavior of those who search desperately becomes an impediment in its excess of zeal.

The concept of selfhood is dependent on the recognition of one's physical body, and one's behavior potential, in relationships with others. This awareness has a valuable characteristic. The world is perceived in terms of its potential to aid or hinder power expression, with the identification process referring to perception of environmental sources as supportive or not. This is how the self expands at each developmental stage. If an environmental agent is seen as assisting deliberately, it is embraced as *self*. If it is seen as hindering, it is rejected as *other*. Continued growth demands that one believe in the most facilitative perceptions. For this reason, perceptions are structured to meet power/potency needs, and the result of all such modifications of existence produces the only self that qualifies as real.

Since the "self" comes into existence only where species interests can be subverted, and thus as an outcome of the capacity for deliberation, the only reasonable interpretation would be that the self is a characteristic of a *conscious* being. It would be specious to argue that unconscious reactions represented any form of selfhood. Responsibility is a function of an aware and capable individual. The cognitive/affective interaction which characterizes decision-making occurs only at this level, and it is only here that the term self is appropriately applied. Although selfhood is distributed along the individual/system continuum, the contribution of the biological component cannot be avoided. To deny this, as in claiming that "this is not really *me*," or that "*I* am really not that kind of person," is tantamount to saying, "under all of this fat, *I* am really quite thin!" Similarly, to argue that submerged forces have taken control is to assume the unconscious motivation of Freudian psychology, which clearly removes all behavior from praise or blame.

Hospers pointed out that the psychoanalytic position has been elucidated by many philosophers. *"It is the unconscious that determines what the conscious impulse and the conscious action shall be."*[13] Nowell-Smith added that "[the] conscious mind and will are puppets activated by wires pulled by the unconscious."[14] Skinner's denial of responsibility in *Beyond Freedom and Dignity* provides a refutation from another viewpoint.[15] Not surprisingly, such interpretations are rejected by the holarchic approach. Certainly each conscious moment is impacted by information that arises from nonconscious sources, as well as environmental contingency. However, the operation on these diverse sources of information is carried out by the *conscious* individual at the only level that the deliberative process occurs.

Analytic Dynamisms and the Self

The ego may be compared with the conscious self as it is characterized here, rather than as a creature of the preconscious. Although the notion of the ego as an independent agent is rejected, it must be recognized as more than a mere result of the interaction between desire and perception because of the dynamic nature of the affective reaction to information inputs. Ego function must include a coordinating or synergistic activity. It cannot be understood solely as a passive reflection of species-directed needs manifested in biological impulse. To the extent that one identifies with a larger self, the ego functions in the interest of more than the biological being. By contrast, the so called "id" processes relate only to the physical "me." In spite of the fact that the behavior generated by "id" impulses has potential self and species positive outcomes, the urges that are psychologically experienced are based on satisfactions of a physical nature. They are based on feelings of pleasure and pain that are experienced by the individual. Quite often, what the physical self wants is inimical with what the larger self can tolerate. Here arises an appestatic barrier that is psychoanalytically identified as the *superego*.

The superego is posited as the censor of human behavior. It rewards, punishes, recommends, and prohibits. But thoughts are not suppressed because they are identified as evil by a strict superego, rather they are suppressed because of a conflict in which individual gratification is prohibited because of its inconsistency with larger self integrity.[16] The individual does not insist on carrying out every wish. Some are restrained as unacceptable. If individuals observe "evil" behavior on the part of their physical being, they are apt to ascribe it (as some psychotics overtly do) to a part of their being which is rejected—in the sense that its influence is alien, is visited upon them from an external source, and is inimical with their relationship to a more encompassing self.

Determining which of competing behaviors shall be expressed involves, then, two facets of the self. The "id" component may be described as comprising all of the self-assertive drive systems. The larger constituent, or superego, includes the awareness of a systemic relationship expressed through the desire for identification and the moral faculty.

One may have an impulse to commit a sexual assault, based on what has been described as a libidinal urge. "Freud called libido only the cathexis pertaining to the sexual drives."[17] If that sexual act is not committed, it may be because of an identification with a larger self than that which the physical gratification encompasses. It is for this reason that the behavior may be suppressed. It is a matter of survival threat (sanity or equilibrium of self), and the vacillation that is sometimes observed provides additional evidence of the presence of several "levels" of selfhood.

Cheating is seen as immoral because it gives an unfair advantage. Ultimately, it may represent a threat to one's potency. If I believe an act that I commit is immoral, I am in a position to discern the limits of my self since the species aspect of my self is inherently good. If I condemn behavior in another that you condone, that person is part of your self but not of mine. If I know with whom you identify, I can predict what you will see as moral, and what you shall decry as immoral.

This position differs from the psychoanalytic interpretation in that the defenses, which involve moral choices, are not seen as beliefs designed to resolve conflict between ego and superego structure as it represents parental or other social forces. Morally relevant defenses are related to the conflict between biological and species wide aspects of the self. When morality is attached to belief, it refers to deliberate behavior in "others" that affect one's power or equilibrium.

To understand this, the terms "me" and "others," which refer to the identification process, must be clear. Identification refers to a dividing of the world into abetting and impeding factions, and the healthy person identifies with that which is species positive. Identification has been described as dynamic, unstable, responsive to learning, and as a definer of the self. I am that with which I identify. This, as has been stated, may or may not include all of my own physical being or behavior. Recalling that the spatial and temporal parameters of the identified self are capable of a tremendous range (from less than the physical body to all of humanity), it can be said that one's level of comfort, adjustment, or sense of adequacy will depend on the extent to which one believes that the potency to express a "self" is present.

Belief and the Self

Perception, as cognitively processed, affectively interpreted, and modified by defenses, may be viewed as an interpretation of the world as self or other. The self is, thus, perceived to be an existent, with the perception being limited to belief. Beliefs, however, are learned and the perceived self is therefore a transient being. The extent of the transience is determined by genetic potential for change, the opportunity to change, and the risk to self in accepting belief modifications. The rigid personality is, in many instances, a product of experience which has represented actual or potential threat to self stability.

Infants have relatively undistorted perceptions because they are limited in terms of available concepts within which to assemble experiences, or of immaturity of intellectual and physical endowment. Thus, beliefs about the self are fairly stable. As children develop, new experiences are assimilated into the network of beliefs in terms of previous patterns. Dissonance begins to disrupt equilibrium, and they learn to distort perception to suit their power and safety needs. By this process, the self begins to feel more complete.

The conditions of learning or belief modification are functions of the power level of the individual, the dissension level of the introduced material, and the identification level. The description of self portrayed here is one of an agent *organizing*, rather than *causing*. Identification, which is related to the self/system hierarchy, is a defense mechanism in the sense that it is a belief regarding one's meaning, and thus provides a source of potency and power.

White, Anglo-Saxon, Protestants (WASPS) in modern times may perceive themselves, because of their reference group, as very powerful. This strength is seen as comfortably extensive so long as nothing happens to alter that view. As long as WASPS control of the world's goods remains constant, this persistence is probable. Such individuals have the potential for a very broad identification front. For specific individuals, the extent of identification may be far less in other areas, such as in their relationship with employers or colleagues where the sense of relative incompetence may be extremely threatening.

Members of minority groups, by contrast, have "selves" which are apt to be reduced almost to sheer physical existence; and their impotence is such that subservience may be essential to survival. Their defense may be to believe that their status represents "God's will" which is a technique employed to retain a form of power. They may feel that they are not important physically, but God (and through God they...) shall prevail in the struggle. "The meek shall inherit the earth."

Today, the larger identification potential within minority groups allows for behaviors which conflict with the "establishment's" desire. Assertive behavior by this newly emancipated population is viewed by many as a sign of maladjustment and "treatment" for offenders is recommended. Such a point of view presumes that, properly handled, these "deviants" will learn to revert to an attitude toward identification which does not disturb the status quo. It is a futile appeal to the miracle that the defense systems of these people will revert to an earlier level; to a time when they were without hope and *needed* to believe differently. At its worst, such "maladjusted" individuals are considered to have "emotional problems" which are peculiar to their inner inadequacies. They are seen as sick and the focus of treatment is on restoring *correct* interpretations! (In the middle of the 19th century, slaves who ran away from their owners were identified *by physicians* as having a disease called drapetomania—which they described as a 'runaway' disorder.[18])

An example of belief breakdown or confusion at an identification front occurs when, for example, a son performs an act which his parents would find evil in others.

Either they see the act as evil and hate *that* in him (which is not *really* him), they do not believe he is at fault (they excuse him), or they reject him and he becomes other, like the "otherness" in themselves. What they do is a clue to what they believe. If they defend him without reservation, they probably do not accept the truth of the charge. It is *beyond* belief. If they separate the act from the child, they reject that part of his being. If they totally reject him, their identification is diminished. They lose part of themselves.

Because the self is so equivocal, one can appear to love and hate at the same time. But this is a misinterpretation. If I love, that with which I identify is the totality of the entity involved. That is, the extent of my love is determined by all that is identified. If I love someone with a defect that I recognize, that particular part of their being is excluded from my love (which is not to say that I would, or should not accept that person as a friend or colleague).

This characteristic of the self, and its relationship to others, is also appropriate to the evaluation of the physical individual by the fluctuating self. The concept of Thanatos which Freud described as a death wish is better understood as a rejection of the biological self as dangerous to, or unworthy of, humanity. Many suicidal individuals are engulfed by this deprecation of physical self, especially as they deem themselves unworthy of belonging. This view of identification, which leads to power as well as meaning, suggests that it would be desirable to provide individuals and groups with maximal opportunity for widening their identification front. Efforts in this direction have been largely fruitless, but in this text we shall introduce a program which is designed to increase the probability of such an occurrence.

The Continuity of the Self

A much discussed issue concerning the nature of the self involves the question of the extent to which selfhood retains its identity across time. Are middle aged conservatives the "same" persons as the radical teenagers they were, and whose counterparts' behavior they now deplore? Recognizing that all of the body parts with the exception of the germ cells have been replaced many times, how can it be assumed that the self remains the same throughout life?

To deal with this issue we shall first consider the point at which the "self" is assumed to come into being. Kagan suggested that the sense of self emerges only at some time during the middle of the second year of life. "All the interactions in the world won't lead to the sense of self until you're in the middle of the second year because the brain is not yet mature."[19] While the ability to recognize one's being as separate from others may well arise as early as Kagan proposed, few people recall events that occurred at such an early age, and it may be better for the purpose of characterizing continuity, to consider selfhood as appearing at approximately the age of three, or perhaps slightly later.

From the time that the memory becomes active, there is a continuity of identity which makes the self appear to remain the same. Locke assumed that sameness of self is based on the individuals ability to be conscious of both present and past actions as parts of an unbroken chain.[20] Hume, in a similar manner proposed that the self is a matter of one's recollections. "The thought alone feels personal identity, when reflecting on the train of past perceptions that compose a mind."[21] Many philosophers have argued that such interpretations are invalid, since at varying times in life, different events can be recalled.[22] Furthermore, a number of cases of amnesia and other disorders of mind that result in the loss of all but a sense of the present have been documented. The character "Clive" in Restak's book *The Mind,*[23] lives exclusively in the immediate present, yet those that know him would insist that his memory-less "self" is intact.

Since over time, every entity changes in some respect, if only in terms of its temporal location, the relevant question would seem to be to determine which criteria should be considered to bear on the issue. Factors that are undoubtedly different in an individual at different ages include needs, interests, capacities, knowledge, size, shape, attitudes, and social and legal status, to name a few. On the other hand, a significant number of factors remain constant. Recollection of a past that is uniquely one's own, relationships with certain others (e. g., a son to his mother), possession of a name (and in many countries a number) that indelibly labels, and even the role that one plays both as a member of a society and a culture, and as a member of the human race.

Clearly, the question of the continuity of self must be reduced to an arbitrary determination. Just as the problem of when life begins cannot be settled beyond some legal designation, so must the decision as to whether one's self survives each developmental stage be determined on the basis of the purpose to be served by the stipulation. In Chapter 12, we shall, for example, consider the identity of the self as it bears on personal responsibility.

The Self as Independent

The sense of self as an independent entity, is believed to transcend sheer desire. But the term *self* is, once again, misleading in many ways. It hints at a form of existence free from constraint. To be "me," "my own person," "self made," is the goal of adolescents of every era, legitimized in the philosophy of existentialism, the politics of anarchy, and the ethics of situational morality. Before dealing with the impact of such guides to human behavior, it should be useful to consider what processes and products the term *self* identifies.

What is the nature of the "I" to which the self refers? Ryle suggested that it is improper to posit an "I" somewhere inside the individual which would theoretically make it subject to discovery some*where.*[24] He contended that the term is used differently at various explanatory levels. When I say that "I like myself," Ryle suggested that the subject of the sentence is of a higher order, ad infinitum. For Ryle, there appeared to be no end to the continuum. This is a result of his general objection to any concept of mind as an entity. (Ryle believed that the mind, which houses the self, is a term which collectively describes "the person's abilities, liabilities, and inclinations to do and undergo certain sorts of thing and of the doing and undergoing of these things in the ordinary world."[25])

Ryle's thesis is similar to that put forward by Hume, who denied the possibility of the existence of a self independent of its experience:

> When I enter most intimately into what I call *myself*, I always stumble on some particular perception.... I never can catch *myself* at any time without a perception.... When my perceptions are removed for any time [I] may truly be said not to exist.... If anyone, upon serious and unprejudiced reflection, thinks he has a different notion of *himself*, I must confess I can reason no longer with him.[26]

This argument parallels that of the denial of mind when it is inactive, but with a serious difference. Who is it that Hume referred to as the "I" who "stumble[s] on some particular perception?" Hume seemed to make a case for the very entity he denied.

The positions taken by Hume and Ryle are sound in terms of the denial of self as having a specific tangible locus. This makes the concept relational which is precisely the holarchic interpretation. However, when Ryle described the mind, he suggested that the "person" can be completely described in terms of abilities and inclinations which are located within the individual—specifically in the information/knowledge systems. But selfhood as a dynamism must be appreciated as relating the individual both to the environment and to a life system.

We stated earlier that "a self must be inferred," and that "I see my physical body as another object to evaluate." The reference in each instance is to the fact that selfhood may be located at any point along the part/whole continuum, as observed from some other point. The inference was *not* that the self is free of its constituency, or that an "I," *separate from its elements* can be identified. The assumption of an orchestrating entity has, in fact, been denied by many philosophers who find the positing of such a being gratuitous. Consider first the argument of those who support the "bundle" or "nothing-but" theory of selfhood.

Hume exemplified that position in his proposal that the self is no more than the body it represents. He believed (as in dealing with the continuity of self) that if a separate self existed, it should persist over time and in every circumstance. "But," he said, "there is no impression constant and invariable.... It cannot therefore be from any of these impressions, or from any other, that the idea of self is derived; and consequently there is no such idea."[27] Hume, who had made a strong case against the possibility of deriving "ought" from "is," was making a similar attack on the attempt to derive "is" from "has." On what grounds, he would ask, may we assume an existent when we use the possessive form to express a relationship? Perhaps, simply because the assumption is never challenged.

To say "*I* have a mind, or a body" is to assume that there is *something* that possesses a mind or body. For those like Russell, who followed Hume's argument, the notion of an independent self is insupportable. "There is not, in addition to thoughts and feelings, and actions, a bare entity...which does or suffers these occurrences."[28] The statement "I have a body" means only that I *am* a body.

Interactionists, (those who assume that the mind and the body act on each other), find the denial of a separate self absurd. Reid argued that every thought requires a thinker. "The thoughts and feelings of which we are conscious are continually changing...but something which I call *myself* remains under this change of thought."[29] Reid's contention was that there is some*thing* which remembers the past and considers the future and "judges, reasons, affirms, denies...eats and drinks, and is sometimes merry and sometimes sad."[30]

The interactionist position is popular with many modern philosophers, who have offered an extensive collection of arguments in its support. In general they have complained that materialists have made unreasonable demands on the concept of self. The argument that a mental image such as the self is fictitious, they say, grows out of an expectation that such an entity must meet the requirements of physical bodies. But, they claim, the self is not a spatio-temporal entity at all. Like such things as love and honor, however, it is a legitimate existent, and one that can, and does, exert an ineluctable force.

Several factors have been proposed as offering support for the assumption of an independent self. First, regardless of the coercive nature of the emotions, it seems possible to continually add new data to a deliberative equation. The cost of a meal may be "ignored" or overridden, if we are sufficiently hungry. We may, or may not, decide to pay what, under other conditions, we would consider an exorbitant price. Secondly, there is an incredible *range* of choices. The immensity of options leads to the conclusion that there must be a directing or controlling entity. Free of so many constraints, it seems that "I" may be capable of controlling "my" behavior. It may be that "I" can make decisions that exceed the information provided by the emotions. And here is where the interpretation is vulnerable. Neither the ability to consider additional data, nor the seemingly infinite number of choices is sufficient to warrant the denial of the compulsion of desire based motives. To develop the thesis further, we would contend that the issue is not one that is peculiar to the phenomenon of mind, but is rather a general semantic issue.

To say that an automobile "has" a carburetor is to presume some entity that possesses that part. However, *no such entity can be discovered.* It would be as impossible to identify the automobile separate from its parts, as to locate the "I" that has a body. The automobile *is* the parts of which it is comprised. (In Chapter 2 we developed the position that reality is manifested in the parts which comprise a whole at any level.) The problem is encountered equally often in describing mathematical, geometric or other theoretical entities. The rectangle, which is said to *have* four sides with 90° angles at its corners, *is*, in fact, such a collection of factors.

The practice of assuming entities that have an existence above and beyond their constituency is based on a misconstruing of the nature of wholes as holonic entities. Certainly, as a whole an entity has synergistic characteristics. The interaction of parts and instances results in configurations that are unique to the relationship. However, the wholes that emerge do not take on a reality that makes it possible for them to function as agents, independently of their elements. The human self, with all of its significance remains only the interactive sum of its many contributing factors—including both the corporeal and the extended existence it manifests.

Summary

The self may be identified as a vacillating point on the individual/species continuum. It is a product of the capacity to employ the many information/knowledge factors that are peculiar to life, and to experience the emotions that result. Whether it survives the flow of time is best resolved in terms of one's interpretation of the needs of a situation (as in a therapeutic setting). The notion of a meaningful, independent self is, by contrast, insupportable.

To understand the nature of the self, and the motivational process, makes possible an approach to altering unsatisfactory behaviors. However, such knowledge is probably far more useful in developing educational programs and practices which will minimize the inculcation of beliefs that are so difficult to alter. It seems more reasonable to attempt to provide a milieu in which an effective personality can develop, than to attempt to reshape it after fifteen or twenty years of debilitating experience.

Recognizing that identity and identification are equally essential to the development of an adequate personality provides a basis for building effective child development programs. The child who develops a personality in which identity occurs at a high level of identification is most apt to possess the requisites for an effective and satisfying life. That is the goal toward which our energy as educators and political leaders must be directed.

Chapter Notes

1. Lawrence (1932), p. 200
2. Royce (1892), p. 371
3. *Ibid.*, p. 379
4. James (1890), p. 291
5. Portman (1949), p. 16
6. Weiss, E. (1960), p. 29
7. Sartre (1955), p. 124
8. Hergenbahn (1984). Existentialists consider three categories of human existence, within which the person exists simultaneously. The mitwelt refers to "the realm of interpersonal relationships" (p. 341), and as such identifies that area in which the needs of others is considered.
9. Sartre (1955), p. 125
10. AIDS is the acronym for the disease "acquired immune deficiency syndrome."
11. This interpretation of selfhood places the target of evaluation at the behavioral level. Thus "goodness" includes biological self care as well as altruistic behavior. "Evil" resides in behavior that is injurious to any aspect of the life continuum.
12. Montagu (1976), p. 83
13. Hospers (1965), p. 77
14. Nowell-Smith (1965), p. 88
15. Skinner (1971)
16. This repeated rejection of psychoanalytic dynamisms is not based on a denial of their value as describing processes, but because of the persistent reification that has led, in many instances, to misinterpretation. The term "superego," for example, understood as no more than a descriptor for clarifying a tendency to sense a superordinate relationship, is a valuable concept.
17. Weiss (1960), p. 164
18. The term survives in such places as The American Pocket Medical Dictionary as "an insane desire to wander away from home." (Dorland, 1946, p. 318)
19. Kagan cited in Restak (1988), p. 61
20. Locke (1969)
21. Hume (1965), p. 195
22. Reid (1965b) provided an example of a situation in which an individual would have to be considered at the same time to be—and not be—the same 'self,' because of different stages of memory.
23. Restak (1988)
24. Ryle (1949)
25. *Ibid.*, p. 199
26. Hume (1965), p. 187
27. *Ibid.*, p. 186
28. Russell cited in Edwards & Pap (1965), p. 176
29. Reid (1965b), p. 200
30. *Ibid.*, p. 253

Chapter 11
Motivation 1: Theoretical Concepts

The holarchic motivation model is based on the contention that behavior occurs as a result of a conscious deliberative process in which desires, needs, and environmental factors are weighed cognitively and evaluated affectively.

Behavior is controlled by a continuous affective stream that is fed by a consideration of some future (consummatory) emotion. Neither motivation models which ignore the contribution of internal states, nor the psychoanalytic view which relegates desires to an unconscious realm, can adequately characterize the behavioral process.

Psychological literature groans under the weight of an endless array of motivational theories purporting to provide a meaningful approach to an understanding of human behavior. Centuries of research and analysis have, however, produced few definitive concepts. Brown summarized the dilemma, pointing out that: "Although a concept of motivation...is to be found in nearly every theoretical account of behavior, an amazing divergence of opinion exists as to the nature and function of motivation."[1]

Among the many theories regarding the wellsprings of behavior are interpretations that are optimistic (individuals are motivated to act morally), pessimistic (people are basically evil), and indifferent (human actions are fully determined responses to prevailing stimuli). The intention of such paradigms is to discover that focus which will reveal the most useful elements in the effort to predict and control human activity.

The extreme interpretations posed by the founders of the various theoretical models has led to a continual attack from those less radically oriented. Positions have been modified both by their originators and by the lieutenants that such viewpoints have attracted. The seminal contributions of such creative thinkers as Watson, Skinner, and Freud have been so diluted that their theses can often be reconciled with less revolutionary positions. Most psychoanalysts today reject the notion of a death instinct and the pervasiveness of sexual desire, while many applied behavioral analysts accept inner (mental) states as legitimate—if noncontributory—concepts.[2]

Unfortunately, such modifications do little to solve the problem created by the acceptance of the basic tenets. Psychoanalysts cling to the essential contribution of a dynamic unconscious, and behavioral scientists restrict their research to the analysis of behavior and its components. Introspective accounts are denied by one group, while they are the critical factors for another. Humanist phenomenologists appeal to the inherent goodness in humans in restive fellowship with religious existentialists and theological clergymen.

Certain common features may be discerned among all psychologies. While only the psychoanalyst claims an esoteric foundation, all views are mired in complexity. Each seeks to understand the human personality by renouncing the layperson's claim regarding the impetus of observed behavior. The persona is assumed either to be masked by defenses designed to mislead or protect, warped by environmental contingencies, or of marginal value as an aid to understanding behavior.

The Holarchic Model

It is such interpretations as these that have led to the development of the holarchic model, which holds to the naïve or brute contention that behavior is motivated by the arousal of desires in conjunction with beliefs regarding the capacity and opportunity to satisfy them. Such a model suffers, of course, from its lack of sophistication and its use of prosaic language. However, slippery as introspection may be, mentalistic as desire may seem, and as subject to nonaware stimuli as split-brain research has shown the mind to be, human behavior can best be understood by focusing on the elements of conscious experience.

In pre-affective life forms, the organism is forced to respond even where it is accurate to describe the activity as aggressive. The flower that seeks the sun is acting under the pressure of a compulsive drive which it cannot choose to ignore. The leukocyte which sacrifices itself to the welfare of its host because of genetically fixed knowledge performs appropriately in spite of itself. In each instance, the genetically prescribed organizational state of the individual determines the occurrence of an activity in the presence of particular stimuli. The emotional system in higher forms of life provides a technique for improving the efficacy of such activity.

MOTIVATION 1: THEORETICAL CONCEPTS

In defining motivation as the introduction of an affective element which transfers the impulse to action from maturational/environmental demand to desire in the individual, it must be understood that such a change did not occur suddenly, or without problems, in the evolutionary sequence. The fact that humans have the capacity to find certain experiences pleasant does not guarantee that they will recognize the specific source of the affect or know how to increase it. If a motivational sequence is to be initiated, many of the contributory components identified earlier must be present. However, the arousal of an emotion, the wedding of conceptualized desire, need, and environmental factors, is only one step in the process. It is necessary but not sufficient to trigger the motivational sequence.

None of the many interpretations of motivation—though each describes some of the contributions to the motivational process—provides the elements essential to fully determine a deliberate action sequence. The problem is not to discover what motivation is, but on what process attention is to be focused. Sex and hunger represent only the urgency of desires of a physiological nature, while integrity demands deal with the desire for stability. The desire for identification, as modified by the moral sense, is also insufficient to exhaust the motivational scheme.

The difficulty with most approaches to the problem lies in attempting to locate motivation at some point. But no constellation of inputs can do more than describe a moment in the succession of experiences that contributes to a motivational pattern. Motivation may best be understood as *a process that flows continually from any emotional state through deliberate activity, which is directed toward the maintaining or improving (optimizing) of the affective state, (Figure 11.1)*.

In addition to emotional experiences, a motivational sequence includes belief about *capacity* and *opportunity to act*. It is a ubiquitous condition which is characterized by the inception and culmination of behavioral sequences, including many actions that are impossible to define in isolation. Motivation is *always* and *only* related to behavior. This definition distinguishes motivation from desire, drive, and any of the judgmental scales that are sometimes considered to be independently causal. It also discriminates between feeling states that recommend action, and the techniques involved in the satisfaction of such urges. Unless such an interpretation is employed, desire and motivation, behavior and forced reaction shall continue to be confused.

The holarchic view of motivation finds sympathetic roots in the hedonic purposivism which McDougall[3] found so distressing. It is unfortunate that many of those who reject such a position do so because of a narrow interpretation of pleasure-seeking or "happiness," which has resulted from a social convention that mandates disapproval for the terms because they suggest irresponsibility. What would be the correct emotional term to apply to McDougall or Skinner as each prepared tests of behavioral sources? Hopefully, each had a goal in mind and found his work enjoyable—perhaps even thrilling! The contention that "other things are more important than happiness," is an apparently not-so-obvious contradiction in terms.

316   MOTIVATION, BEHAVIOR, AND EMOTIONAL HEALTH

Figure 11.1

The Holarchic Motivation Model

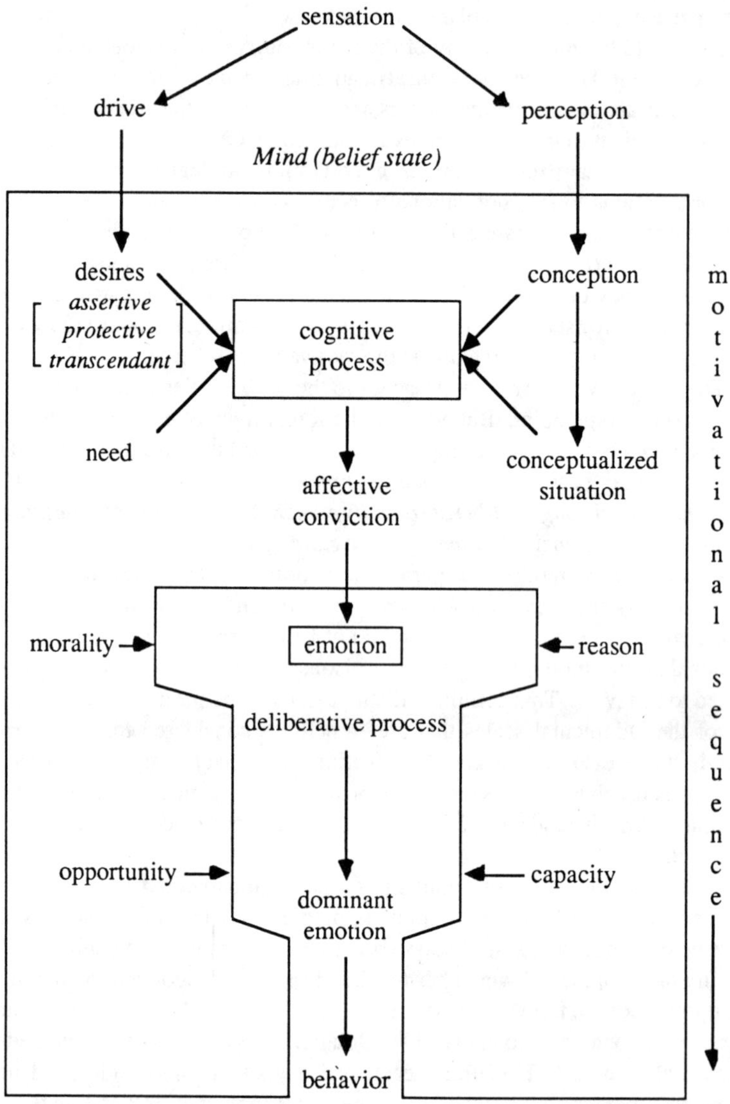

The nature of holarchic organization represents the increasing freedom of individuals from the rigid demands of species enhancement. Thus, desires have been defined as self-assertive (power), self-protective (safety), and self-transcendent (identification). Drives, and thus desires for survival and growth, are based on species needs as represented in the phenotype. Both survival and growth are, within limits, more adequately attended to where the focus of activity moves from the totality to the individual.

Motivation includes the total process that is rooted in desire and opportunity and proceeds to ultimate, although transient, decisions. Hunger is manifested as a desire which may initiate behavior. Individuals may learn to feel "hungry" in the presence of a certain food or to feel nauseous in the presence of another, but they begin with the capacity for (knowledge of) such a reaction.

The presence of food, a sex object, or a threat to survival may contribute to the ultimate response. However, only in an organism with a specific capacity can a particular response be anticipated. That response is subject to degree of deprivation, learning, and competing response potential which spreads its manifestation across a broad range. It is this essential attribute of behavior that caused Hebb to separate the environmental aspect of an event from its impact on the individual.[4] Hebb saw desire as a source of energy which is essential to behavior—although not a specific determinant. To this extent there is no problem. Unfortunately, Hebb's explanation of deliberate activity as the association of energizers with habits lacks the vitality that characterizes human behavior. This tendency to minimize the role of deliberation, while focusing on essential but incomplete elements, is found in the work of many motivation theorists. The effort to reduce the number of factors involved, results in the loss of some that are critical.

The holarchic analysis of motivation makes possible the embracing of aspects of each of the varied interpretations. Drive states and perceptual information have an impact on the individual prior to their being mentally experienced. When such forces become sufficiently strong, they enter the realm of awareness as *sensations*, which identify them as conceptualized percepts and classes of desire.

These preliminary sensations are processed cognitively, culminating in a conviction or belief regarding their nature. Conceptualized situations are labelled both as to their existence and their meaning, while desires are classified as to type and level of intensity. Concomitantly, the moral and rational aspects of the situation are evaluated. This interactive process results in the creation of an emotional state, which is a composite of positive and negative factors.

The deliberative process, or the consideration of potential behaviors, includes an assaying of the need value of action alternatives in terms of the potential costs associated with such behavior, as well as the contemplation of one's capacity and opportunity to act. The consummatory phase includes the emergence of a dominant emotion, and the resulting behavior which the dominant emotion mandates. As each behavior occurs, the motivational process continues, with new data continually introduced and with new deliberations constantly restructuring the mental configuration. This suggests that *conscious inner states*, those ephemeral elements of introspective psychologies, must be reckoned with. Such view is at variance with most of the interpretations offered by the leading psychological theorists. There are, however, serious problems associated with the acceptance of any of the major alternatives.

Problems of Interpretation

Among the many factors that cloud attempts to explain the motivational process is the practice of employing a wide variety of expressions to reference the same concept, while subsuming many concepts under a single term. We see here the same consistent interchange of terms that has led to the misunderstanding of purpose, knowledge, and emotion. Madsen, for example, in his analysis of theories of motivation, stated that he "selected from among all discourses those which contain explanatory terms like *motivation, motive, drive, need, instinct, force, incentive, valence, etc.*"[5] The confusion is understandable.

There is no question that human behavior is complex, nor that much valuable research, as well as successful therapy, have been carried out by individuals employing a wide variety of theoretical models. However, in the case of research findings, it can be shown that practically identical results may be obtained on the basis of quite disparate assumptions. As for therapeutic effectiveness, the unique skill of practitioners plays more of a role than the hypotheses under which they proceed.[6] It would seem that a less intricate representation of the motivational process may prove at least as effective, and with far fewer extreme assumptions. The holarchic model, based on premises that were described earlier in this text, is designed to address that issue.

The term *motive* is often applied to identify the genesis of a behavior sequence, where it purports to answer the question of why such action occurs. Because of its common usage, it will be employed here as a synonym for desire. It will not, however, refer to a drive state. Although drives, as peremptory, have been shown to be essential to the action of mentally endowed as well as pre-mind forms of life, we must recall that desires differ in the degree of coerciveness of their contribution. This formulation excludes such external factors as environmental conditions such as opportunity, as representing motives, though they play a vital role in the initiation of many behavioral sequences.

Psychologists do not necessarily assume any critical "starting" point in a motivational sequence. Drives or impulses generated from within the individual are usually accepted as essential elements, with many of the self-assertive urges believed to be mere biological phenomena. Hilgard said that "if drives vary in strength according to the degree of deprivation...differences in drive strength should be measurable according to the amount of arousal that the deprivation generates."[7] This

MOTIVATION 1: THEORETICAL CONCEPTS

type of analysis, risks overlooking the affective component which represents the translation of drive into desire.

Janis et al attempted to distinguish motive from drive, stating that "in simplest form, a motive is a wish."[8] This usage would seem to equate motive with desire as is proposed here. By *wish*, however, they included not only the naked urge, but also some desired object or experience with which to assuage the desire, which we refer to as a *need*, and which psychologists often define as an *incentive*. Finally, they took the position that "motives, then, are cognitive processes and have no necessary relation to overt behavior."[8] They were dealing essentially, with the hope, or wish, that some procedure may prove efficacious. The process, they argued, is that of considering or contemplating courses of action that are believed apt to solve a problem. Behavior seems only tangentially related.

Hebb suggested that the nervous system is always active in the waking state, and that the purpose of motivation is to organize and direct (rather than to arouse) behavior. He viewed motivation as a constant function, which he, too, described as a cognitive process. He also asserted that motives are learned, representing a cognitive reorganization of activity.[9] Under such an interpretation, they would certainly differ from drives or desires.

Hebb's thesis was that any organic deficit leads to disruptive, restless, disorganized activity. The central nervous system organizes and directs activity toward a "solution" which is a state of less disruption. This is, at least implicitly, a tension-reducing activity.[9] It defines motivated behavior as an organized, learned response which follows a state of disequilibrium. Although he did not deny that drives are related to the organic deficit, he considered the motivating force to reside in the central nervous system.

Since this postulate places the principal cause of behavior within the perceptual/cognitive system, it risks the consideration of behavior as automatic—a simple reaction to external stimulation. This was quite specifically proposed by Hull, who stated: "The organism is...a completely automatic entity...[without] entelechy, no disembodied mind, soul, or spirit which in some way tells the various parts of the body how to cooperate behaviorally."[10]

This statement should make Hull's outlook obvious. He argued that behavior is fully explainable on the basis of its probability of occurrence in terms of drive, stimulus trace, incentive reinforcement, and habit strength. If this suggests hope, in that drives may at least represent a dynamic element, consider this statement regarding the role of drives in his definition of motivation:

> Primary motivation (D), at least that resulting from food privation, consists of two multiplicative components: (1) the drive proper (D') which is an increasing monotonic sigmoid function of h, the number of hours of food privation; and (2) a negative or inanition component (Σ) which is a positively accelerated monotonic function of h decreasing from 1 to zero.[11]

This is an example of the type of description that Eysenck criticized as pseudo-intellectual. While such a model may be useful for specifying elements of the process, the synergism of interactions is essentially ignored.

McClelland and his colleagues disagreed with Hebb's suggestion that behavior occurs simply because of a discrepancy between expectation and perception, substituting the notion that moderate increases in stimulation are always pleasant, while beyond some optimal point they become unpleasant. Their position was that *"a motive is the redintegration by a cue of a change in an affective situation."*[12] That is, stimuli which result from discrepancies between what is expected and what is perceived result in, what McClelland referred to as "primitive affects."[12] Cues or signals which occur in contiguity with these affective states are capable of modifying the state. This is a learning process. For McClelland, motivation is dependent on such affective states. To the extent that affect itself is the result of minimal stimulation without necessary reference to the motivational modes, this is consistent with the holarchic position.[13]

McClelland's thesis, like that of many others, was that all behavior is directed toward pleasure and away from pain. He assumes that motives are universal if the same environmental conditions result in the same human expectations. Since achievement is observed to produce a positive affective state in many humans, he assumed it to be universal, contending that it is as basic as hunger or sex.

McClelland proposed that the reason that some individuals develop higher level motives (e.g., achievement) is because during their developmental stage they are encouraged to act independently and rewarded when they do so. Since this is the case, McClelland considered achievement motivation to be inherent in all humans. However, the term achievement represents an evaluation or description of behavior, which, to use McClelland's words, is dependent on the cultural arrangement. It does not represent a basic urge, but rather a technique (need) for gaining power and is expressed through accomplishments of many types by the male in most societies, and it is often masked or sublimated in females so that it appears in other forms. Furthermore, a vicarious form of power is widely observed in the "pride of the matriarch" and in some cultures, including that of mainstream North America, many women are overtly achievement oriented.

McClelland failed to explain the selectivity and uniqueness of a form of disturbance in the organism that makes an essential contribution to the motivational process. As with models such as Hebb's, the first step was to minimize or "explain away" the contribution of desire, which is unique to certain forms of life. After that, it was a simple matter to show that the facets of the process are mechanical. McClelland stated that "certain stimuli...are sources of primary, unlearned affect."[14] He compared this affect with instinct in animals. At another point, he stated that "certain types of situations innately release reactions."[15] It is these *certain* stimuli and *certain* types of situations that must be involved in determining behavior. Obviously, the individual learns how to gratify many desires, but the unlearned affect cannot be ignored. Since McClelland used the term motive to describe learned behaviors, sex, duty, and even hunger could be disposed of in favor of achievement which, apparently, may become as compelling (and is certainly more socially acceptable).

Efforts to provide research evidence for achievement motivation have not been particularly satisfactory. DeCharms contended that "the measure of achievement motivation, despite several attempts to refine it, remains...the same crude instrument with a discouraging penchant for quixotic fluctuations in any single experiment."[16] Beyond the difficulty of providing sufficiently sensitive instrumentation, there is the more serious problem of construct validity. What McClelland considered the uniquely human motivating force can better be considered as the more highly organized cognitive system which makes possible the ability to recognize the utility of achievement as a technique for improving the probability of satisfying desires.

Applied Behavioral Interpretations

Stimulus-response theory, which is the basis for behavioral psychology, and which Hall and Lindzey called the "most elegant [and] most economical" view of human behavior, with "tough-minded, empirical strengths,"[17] is essentially a theory of learning. Kalish argued that "most psychologists today are behaviorists [because they believe that] psychology is the objective study of behavior."[18] He did claim that "no one asserts that people do not have inner lives, or private experiences."[18] Unfortunately, in the attempt to understand this aspect of the human personality, many essential contributors to behavior that leads to learning have been ignored because of their introspective nature.

This has not been true in all instances. Miller and Dollard stated that "in order to learn, one must want something, notice something, do something, and get something."[19] They reduced this formulation to "drive, cue, response, and reward."[20] Since the term want was equated with drive, it was possible to ignore the conscious aspect. Miller, in fact, postulated that any stimulus (incentive or need) with sufficient intensity will arouse a drive (i.e. desire) that will force a response.[21] This view took him well on the way to the development of a mechanical model of personality. Unless stimuli are defined as only those provocations that arouse a desire, his argument is logically absurd. If he does define it in this way, it is banal.

Perhaps the most bizarre conceptualization that has grown out of the S—>R model is that of learned drives. Psychologists from Watson to Hull had dealt with drives (i.e., desires) and responses as interactive elements. However, Brown noted that "when they began to speak of *acquired* drives, which embody the characteristics of both a learned reaction and a motive, precision of expression faded and the concepts of drives and habits lost their individualities."[22]

Brown's comment points up the insistence by experimental psychologists that only *reactions* are to be considered scientifically respectable. Reactions are, of course, what one measures in a laboratory, and it seems an obvious preference to the use of "outmoded" introspective techniques. One of the serious problems with such an interpretation is that it eliminates from consideration any condition in which the situation does not have sufficient impact to result in behavior. How, they would ask, could one be said to have a desire for an item of food if nothing were done to obtain it?

Brown said that "to have an acquired drive is to learn a response possessing the characteristics of other responses and, in addition, the capacity to act as a drive."[23] But no response *ever* acts as a drive. It represents only a learned sequence that will, as a potential form of action, *interact* with a desire (as a need or incentive) if that desire is sufficiently strong on future presentation of an incentive.

A glaring example of the result of assuming that responses become drives appears in research studies that purport to show that fear is learned. In principle, it is argued (appropriately) that many habit patterns are established in response to aversive experiences. Over time, (conditioned) stimuli not originally associated with the habit come to evoke the same behavior. This occurs because the awareness of the stimulus arouses an internal pattern of stimulation similar to that of the primary drive—in this case, the desire to avoid pain. The conclusion is drawn that because the conditioned stimulus is learned, a *secondary* drive is created. In the case of the primary drive of pain avoidance, the secondary drive is said to be fear.

By way of distinguishing between primary and secondary drives, "the latter have been given the distinctive label of anxiety or fear.... Thus fear is both a learned *response*...and a learned or secondary *drive*."[24] Apparently, it was assumed that fear is not only learned, it is also a behavioral sequence. The genesis of this incredible confusion of concepts can be traced to the work of psychologists like Neil Miller, whose experimental data was of such psychological respectability that many palpably erroneous pronouncements are reproduced intact half a century later.

It was pointed out in Chapter 10 that Miller, among others, employed the term drive to identify *any* action-provoking stimulus. This may seem to justify his contention that fear is just another drive. However, after introducing the topic in an article entitled, "Studies of Fear as an Acquirable Drive," he wrote in the first paragraph: "An important role in human behavior is played by drives, such as fears, or desires for money, approval or status, which appear to be learned during the socialization of the individual."[25] His experiments, he said, had "demonstrated the drive function of fear as a response which presumably produces a strong stimulus."[26]

What Miller had shown, in fact, was that some situations or events can elicit fear. Such feelings as fear are, however, *neither drives, primary or secondary, nor behavior of any kind*. Rather, they are *emotions* which represent the reaction to experience in the presence of desire, or the awareness of a situation that has relevance to the expression of a desire. The desire is not learned, the meaning of a situation is. Fear is an innately known capacity, an emotion potential actualized in a situation perceived as threatening.[27]

Pain represents an affective reaction to an undesirable physical or psychological experience. Although pain may occur as the culmination of some experience or event—a consummatory emotion (CE)—it arouses an anticipatory emotion (AE) in succeeding motivational sequences in that the recollection of the painful experience suggests action in the direction of relief. Fear is an anticipatory emotion (AE) which relates desires to *potential* pain, or the awareness that something may occur which will cause the individual to feel pain. Like pain, it cannot be learned. However, an individual who experiences pain in a particular situation may ultimately learn to associate new exposures to the situation with a previous negative experience. What is learned is the relationship. What is felt is the signal which recommends action.

If the individual had no innate capacity to feel physical or psychological pain, no fear would come to be associated with a "painful" experience. If there were no innate capacity to feel fear, whether or not the capacity for pain existed, fear could not be associated with the response. Furthermore, if the pain was equivocal, some would learn to experience fear while others would not. By calling fear a response, a drive, or a learned feeling, and by equating it with pain or pain avoidance, a semantic curtain is drawn over the experience making an understanding of much behavior impossible. However, if S—>R theorists were to alter their language to allow that what is meant is that one learns to believe that certain situations are fear provoking, their theory would lose its elegance. Maze running cannot provide the data necessary to account for such interpretations.

Similar formulations have been developed for guilt, anxiety, and other emotional elements. In this respect, the behavioral formulation is in agreement with the psychoanalytic interpretation. Little wonder that motivation has been such a slippery concept. The only point at which these polar positions coincide is when both propose ambiguous (and stultifying) interpretations.

The most extreme view of the argument that motives are learned has been provided by Skinner, who stated that "the exploration of the emotional and motivational life of the mind has been described as one of the great achievements in the history of human thought...but it is possible that it has been one of the great disasters."[28] Skinner began with the postulate that behavior is a continuous activity and that interaction with the environment simply causes a change in direction whenever reinforcement occurs. He contended that reinforcement is rewarding because it reduces a deprivation state.

Skinner's position is similar to that of Kelly,[29] who claimed that a living organism is inherently active and that this condition is an essential aspect of being alive. It is, in fact, what Kelly believed being alive means. An example of the wondrous conclusions drawn from this type of argument is a statement by Ebel:

> Human beings will continue to make choices among the alternatives they see as being open to them, but these choices are more likely to be made on the basis of anticipated consequences than on the basis of built in motives.[30]

The practice of replacing motives with anticipated consequences is a hallmark of behavioral writing; but they fail to recognize that their "consequences" (i.e., needs) are only consequential because of the "built-in" motives (i.e., desires).

Skinner's compulsion to rid the science of psychology of terms that denote inner states is evident in his definition of drive. Although he apparently felt that he must use the term in order to communicate with those who had become accustomed to it, he said "the term (drive) is simply a convenient way of referring to the effects of deprivation and satiation and of other operations which alter the probability of behavior."[31] It is not a cause, he said, but an effect. By eliminating this "phantom" element, it was possible for him to proceed directly from deprivation to activity. There seemed no need to introduce a troublesome—and for Skinner unnecessary—term.

In relation to the problem of behavior and motive, Skinner denied the essential role of motivation and enabling inputs. "The emotions," he said, "are excellent examples of the fictional causes to which we commonly attribute behavior."[32] He assumed that appropriate reinforcement would automatically cause learning and thus behavior. Skinner's work with pigeons is illuminating. He showed that if the proper reinforcement schedule is maintained, what the animal will do can be predicted to a high degree of probability.

There is certainly no question about the veracity of the research. Furthermore, much of the behavior of humans is amenable to a similar approach. In view of the interpretation of the responses pigeons manifest, the prospect is, however, not particularly exciting. The reasons for concern are by no means subtle. First, the high level of success with pigeons is related to the relatively few behavioral alternatives with which the experimenter has to contend. Pigeons do not diet, play chess, or feel chagrined if they make an error. They either eat or do not eat for the most part, especially when other sexually attractive pigeons are absent. Over their entire life span, pigeons expend perhaps 90% of their energy looking for food. Skinner owned the refrigerator.

In itself, this may not seem fatal to the argument, since Skinner suggested that people are different from simpler animals—if only slightly. "Man is much more than a dog, but like a dog he is within range of psychological analysis."[33] Thus, he proposed that the difference in shaping the behavior of a human is essentially one of degree. If food is proffered when one dances, dancing will be learned.

Such an interpretation ignores the vital contribution of the living being. Organisms not only react to stimulation, but actively contribute to it. Even the pigeon seeks food, *pursues* stimulation, *desires* contact. The fact that the experimenter intervenes by placing the sought after items in the path of such activity does not explain anything, except that a response can be shaped. The response will, however, be based on an urge that the experimenter chooses to ignore as being critical.

A second problem is posed by the characteristics of a response. Even at the reflex level, it has been demonstrated that only the totality of a response is fixed. In the case of deliberate behavior, only the goal is determined. The pigeon's eating is a process

MOTIVATION 1: THEORETICAL CONCEPTS

that can be accomplished in many ways, with many styles, and at any pace. To this extent, it is not a sheer mechanical process but is based on an organized *decision.* In spite of the similarities observed, it is a unique process in each individual.

This is not an appeal to complexity. Weiss[34] and others have shown that organisms follow a structural pattern that although macroscopically determined, is microscopically free. Ethologists see instinctive behavior as fixed at some levels, free at others. If behavioral scientists accept such premises, they must recognize that the inflexibility of the responses they observe are determined only in *some* characteristic at *some* level. Indeterminacy, both in physics and biology, suggests that an event cannot be specified exactly. Although the environment provides a necessary component, it can fix responses only at some holonic level.

Desire without environmental opportunity cannot cause behavior. Environmental opportunity without desire is equally incompetent to initiate action. The only type of situation in which the environment provides a sufficient condition is one in which the individual is forced to respond in some precise manner, which disqualifies the resulting activity as motivated.

The ability to communicate verbally is considered a cause for many of the motives that characterize humans. Washburn reflected the view of most anthropologists in his contention that "language (speech and cognition) separates human behavior from that of any other animals."[35] However, the language aspect may be the least unique part of the motivational sequence. Language, which theoretically increases freedom and individuality, is so highly structured and stylized that it is probably very low on the scale of differentiators. The ways in which a human can behave far exceed the ways in which it can be described.

Those who contend that motives are learned, and that language has its own causal function, ignore the difference between stimulative and other assertive desires. Their position is based on the observation that many behaviors are not directly related to drive reduction, and that all kinds of bizarre responses can be habituated. They seem to conclude from such evidence that anything can be learned as long as it is reinforced, without attending to the innate factors that determine what is reinforcing.

The behavioral position is that individual variation is a result of early reinforcement and that had reinforcement been begun early enough, more similar individuals would be produced. As a generalization, there can be no disagreement. The problem is that so many factors enter into behavior which are not identical, that the process makes extremely ambitious demands. Individuals differ in height, weight, gender, energy, intelligence, sensitivity, appearance, strength—in fact, in an endless array of characteristics. They do not vary in possessing desires that contribute to motivational potential. The result is the wide variety of personalities that develop and the impossibility of positing any response set or reinforcement schedule as ultimately explanatory.

The failure of behavioral interpretations lies in the refusal to appreciate the fact that one behaves in order to arrive at some emotional state. From the time that reflexive, pre-mind responses were superseded by the evolution of an affective system, behavior has had a goal determined by affective demands. Skinner seemed unaware that he was admitting this when he referred, for example, to "the naturally reinforcing consequences of making things."[36] Why did he suppose making things (craftsmanship) is a "natural" reinforcer?

Behavioral views have, of course, been challenged by many theorists. Hayes contended that the attempt to account for thought exclusively in S—>R terms is "a task which has distant similarities to building a skyscraper from damp kleenex."[37] Others have been less kind. Restak, a prominent psychobiologist, warned: "Behavioral psychology as a legitimate explanation of human behavior is a failure and should be quietly buried at a small private funeral [with mourners] limited to B. F. Skinner and other members of the immediate family."[38]

A number of psychologists have taken the position that some behavior is not motivated at all. McFarland said "it is [today] generally recognized that it is not necessary to account for behavior in terms of motive forces, rather a particular activity is a result of an animal being in a particular motivational state."[39] Other similarly strange interpretations have been offered. Taylor, for example, proposed that "some behavior qualifies as motivated, but some does not...someone might be so euphoric, or overwhelmed by an urge to shout, that he does so."[40] Is an urge to shout not a motive? Peters was perhaps most extreme in his effort to demonstrate alternatives to motivated behavior. He proposed substituting a non causal "means to ends" framework for motivation in some instances.[41] Most critics found this too extreme. However, Taylor, in support of Peters, said that "opponents naturally grumble that the relationship of motives to deeds is then too mysterious, and that compliance accounts [such as Peter's formula] are nothing but a species of causal explanation."[40]

Kagan offered a specific example of what he considered unmotivated behavior. He held that when a child takes a seat in a chair on being called to dinner, the behavior is fully determined by the appropriateness of that action.[42] Belief regarding the suitability of a response may contribute to a motivational sequence to the extent that it includes an idea of a desired experience. However, the act of sitting in a chair requires far more data consideration than that of its social propriety. In many instances, individuals perform behaviors which, considered in isolation, they do *not* want. An obvious example is the deliberate taking of painful treatment in the hope of curing a disease. It may seem that this represents a violation of the principle that all behavior, and thus its motivational source, includes desire. It may appear to be an example of "unmotivated behavior." But this is not the case. To understand why any behavior is undertaken, the ultimate goal or the total behavioral sequence must be taken into account. Willingness to take the treatment (one interpretation of the concept of "will" was defined in Chapter 9 as *satisfaction*) is, incidentally, further evidence of the purposiveness of behavior.

One method for distinguishing between the deliberate and the involuntary is to determine whether a sequence can be avoided. If, and when, it can, it is deliberate, otherwise not. In the case of a child seating himself in a chair, the interpretation varies according to his awareness of what is occurring. Being called to dinner may set in motion a behavior pattern to which he does not attend (and which is mediated at a very low level of the nervous system). However, if such acts are called to his attention, it is quite likely that he can explain whether or not he wanted to sit in the chair. He would, of course, still have to explain why in more specific terms for his motive to be understood, since it is the *net* effect of many movements, which may include some rigidly performed and others of a negative quality, that determines the total behavioral sequence.

The behavioral interpretation of the human personality is pessimistic as to the hope, as well as the responsibility, of humans. Behavioral scientists may insist that the application of appropriate reinforcement contingencies will lead to a better society, but that would belie their denial of the significance of internal states. *Better* is a value term rooted in an affective system that can only be experienced introspectively. But perhaps proponents of the behavioral approach would deny that their approach has any value at all.

Consciousness

The holarchic model is based on the primacy of affect. *All behavior is driven by a contemporaneous anticipatory affect.* Beyond that, affect is assumed in the holarchic model to be a characteristic that is unique to the conscious state, with nonconscious disturbance representing a closely related, but separate experience.

The concept of consciousness as a characteristic of some life forms received little attention in philosophic thought prior to the past few centuries. It has become a matter of interest largely as a reaction to the development of the notion of an *unconscious*. Descartes, in his epistemological argument, embraced conscious mind as a given, believing that it included both active and passive aspects.[43] Sartre, following this thesis, remarked that "all knowing is conscious knowing."[44] Such explanations were based on efforts to understand human knowledge, with consciousness accepted as an essential vehicle.

Many other interpretations of this unique phenomenon have been suggested, including the view of consciousness as indefinable because of its apparent tendency to infinitely regress. Fichte stated that, "each definite act of consciousness may be made the subject of reflection, and a new consciousness of the first consciousness may thus be created."[45] Chein attempted to interpret this regression by relating consciousness to aspects of behavior, "a behavior that takes the primary behavior as its object."[46] He concluded that there are degrees of consciousness, with awareness and attention differing from one another. "We must admit the possibility of highly conscious bare awareness; thus in the dark, we may be acutely conscious of seeing movement of which we are hardly aware."[47] This poses a semantic enigma: Chein apparently believed that "acutely conscious" and "hardly aware" are not contradictory terms.

Others have categorized consciousness in nonhierarchical terms. Eccles proposed that "it is convenient to think of...consciousness as being of two kinds. There are firstly, perceptual experiences. Secondly we have the self-consciousness of inner experiences."[48] He suggested that these experiences, in combination, provide information about the external world, the memory of past experiences, and the "deliverance of imagination, emotional feelings, wishes, and planned actions."[48]

Beyond these descriptive accounts have been the many theories about why consciousness came into existence. Nietzsche considered it a necessary outcome of the human need to communicate. *"Consciousness generally has only developed under the pressure of the necessity for communication.... From the first it has been necessary and useful only between man and man."*[49] He argued that this is a matter of "species genius," which makes it possible for humans to compare themselves to others, as well as to communicate. By contrast, behaviorists have ignored the contribution of the conscious mind. "An epiphenomenal view would imply that consciousness had no causal efficacy and therefore little interest for science."[50] Such an interpretation manifests the consistent failure to recognize the essential nature of consciousness as the arena for emotional experience. Without consciousness, such concepts as desire, perceived situations, and their interaction would be meaningless. While there is no doubt that one of the many valuable aspects of consciousness is that communication is enhanced, to assume that interaction with others is its principal role is to lose sight of the far more general contribution of the phenomenon.

The Psychoanalytic View

For psychoanalysts, consciousness is no more than a sense organ by which one may observe what is taking place at more primitive levels. Kohut and Seitz contended that "consciousness is not, at any time, an essential quality of mental activities."[51] This parallels the Freudian view that "[consciousness] is a special psychic act, different from and independent of the process of becoming fixed or represented.... Consciousness appears to us as a sensory organ which perceives a content proceeding from another source."[52] The basis for the claim that desires are active, prior to emergence into the conscious/preconscious realm, is the assumption of a dynamic, autonomous unconscious, which represents a reservoir of desires that are unavailable to the individual's immediate thought processes.

The Unconscious. While behavioral scientists deny the relevance of inner states, whether conscious or unconscious, the psychoanalytic motivational scheme includes the acceptance of mental determinants, relegating them essentially to the unconscious and preconscious facets of mind. Since they cannot be experienced directly, they must be inferred from behavior. The unconscious is said to house instinctive needs (id processes) and personalities that vie for expression with their conscious counterparts. Repressed desires are considered to be associated with id demands that have not managed cathexis with the ego. Brill equated the unconscious, or "primitive self," with the *id*.[53] Other interpretations have separated the two. Kohut and Seitz suggested

MOTIVATION 1: THEORETICAL CONCEPTS

that "the term id is not synonymous with the term unconscious: The unconscious is composed of the id and the unconscious layer of the ego."[54]

In describing the id, Freud painted a picture of irrational, illogical desire which operates on the basis of a balance between desire for pleasure and desire for minimal stimulation (which we have defined as the self-assertive and self-protective desires). Freud viewed the primitive personality as a boiling kettle with steam attempting to escape at every joint. Life, he believed, begins with unbridled lust, immediate demand, and insane desire. The urges toward sexual expression and belligerent behavior seem to dominate the themes of analytic writers, drawing from the works of Freud. When Freud settled on sex and aggression as the principal sources of anxiety, he was aware that other desires exist. However, he pointed to "the remarkable fact that want of satisfaction of hunger or thirst...never results in conversion of them into anxiety."[55]

Remarkable? Fact? It is neither. There is nothing remarkable about the fact that most societies lay few sanctions on the opportunity to eat and drink. Offspring, wanted or unwanted, are not apt to be generated by such behavior. By contrast, many cultures place strict taboos on sexual expression but where they do not, sexual anxiety is often "remarkably" absent. As to the "fact" that hunger is never associated with anxiety, psychotherapists regularly observe phobias and compulsive actions in their bulimic and anorexic clients.

The production of memory images by the id for the purpose of cathecting energy (primary process) is a logical interpretation of how, in a pre-perceptive individual, (i. e., an infant child) it may be possible to dispose of tension. However, since the id is not in contact with the external world, these images must be also innate, which would require instinctive knowledge of relevant objects. The individual must instinctively know some of the appropriate techniques for meeting desires.

The elements of the unconscious system are defined in so many ways that a nightmare of confusion results. Such terms as instinct, longing, liking, drive, wish, need, desire, urge, motivation, emotion, impulse, and intention are interchangeably employed throughout the literature with little attention to their essential differences. Weiss, a prominent analyst, used the first ten of the above terms on one page to describe the same concept as well as (on the same page) such combinations as "instinctive drives" and "emotional motivation."[56] Mechanisms and processes which have the responsibility for accomplishing certain tasks are posited. These entities sometimes become reified not only unnecessarily but, more seriously, to the point where their explanatory value is lost. When, for example, the id is referred to as an "agent," it seems to take on existential status.

Some have argued that analytic thinkers do not intend such interpretations. Hall and Lindzey stated, "It should be pointed out that the id, ego, and superego are not to be thought of as manikins which operate the personality."[57] But, Hall's own description of id processes suggests the presence of a homunculus. Such statements as: "The tendency of the id to treat objects as though they were the same,"[58] certainly imply a directing agent. Benner even defined the id as "a *container* [italics added] of instinctual drives."[59]

A patent example of the practice is seen in Freud's description of the conscience:

> It would not surprise us if we were to find a special institution in the mind which performs the task of seeing that narcissistic gratification is secured from the ego-ideal and that, with this end in view, it constantly watches the real ego and measures it by that ideal.[60]

Freud thus posited an "institution" that watches which would require another accounting agent to see that it performs adequately. There seems a risk of the infinite regress that disturbs so many theorists.

The acceptance of a dynamic unconscious did not come quickly or easily. However, its capacity for providing explanations for puzzling behavior resulted in the development of a cult of believers whose faith has been bolstered by the detailed interpretation of chance behavior, parapraxis, and taboos; the analysis of multiple personalities; and by the revelations produced through hypnosis, narcosis, and free-association techniques. The literature provides analogies in the writings of poets and story tellers from Ovid to Shelley. Dreams reveal feelings and dispositions that seem undeniable. Thus, the many interpretations of psychoanalytic theory, including several of Freud's own "periods," as well as the wide range of latter day analytic interpretations, have made the concept of unconscious motivation practically impervious to attack.

The contention that preconscious and unconscious processes account for most psychic activity was, at one time, basic psychoanalytic dogma. Freud referred to an absolute psychic determinism which is exemplified in such statements as: "It is impossible to think of a number, or even a name, of one's own free will."[61] But, more recently, analysts have allowed that the control of thought by unconscious determinants is only partial. Kohut and Seitz, for example, said that "mental processes *may* (italics added) occur outside of consciousness."[62]

Such terms as "psychic determinism" and "endopsychic continuity" refer to an ongoing, struggling, decision-making process that requires no awareness. Endopsychic activities are said to "take their course...whether observed by the 'eye of consciousness' or not."[62] Freud contended that "'unconscious' is no longer a term for what is temporarily latent: The unconscious is a special realm, with its own desires and modes of expression and peculiar mental mechanisms not operative elsewhere."[63] Kohut and Seitz supported the Freudian contention that "the clinical evidence for the relevance and validity of these concepts is overwhelming."[64]

A spate of studies, such as that of Shevrin and Dickman[65] have been offered as evidence in support of the notion of a dynamic unconscious. Such research is presumed to have demonstrated that cognitive functioning can occur unconsciously, that such cognition has a different organizational form than that of its conscious

MOTIVATION 1: THEORETICAL CONCEPTS   331

counterpart, and that defense mechanisms deliberately interfere with the emergence of threatening material. There is little doubt that one possible explanation for the experimental findings would be the presence of an active, subterranean personality with desires that mandate the repression of certain data.

Psychobiologists have taken a parallel, though not identical, view of the unconscious. They challenge the notion that mentality is a unitary concept. Restak said, "we now have good reason to believe that the experience of mental unity is an illusion."[66] His viewpoint was based on studies which show that the separate hemispheres of the brain perform different functions. Sperry asserted, "There is no indication that the dominant mental system...is concerned about, or even aware of, the presence of the minor system under most ordinary conditions."[67] To which Restak added, "[This] sounds strikingly similar to the Freudian concept of the unconscious."[68]

As powerful as the evidence is, each example of independent processing by the separate hemispheres appears to represent a *reaction* to environmentally introduced data where the material is processed by a nonconscious system. This is radically different from the psychoanalytic unconscious which is said to house its own desires that attempt to force themselves into consciousness through the medium of the preconscious.

The Preconscious. The psychoanalytic interpretation posits all of the rational or reality-oriented functions in this nonconscious arena. Without any concern for consciousness, the preconscious is said to go about the task of struggling with id impulses. The dynamism that is assumed to function at the preconscious level is the *ego*, which is designed to operate on the external world in such a way as to make available avenues to drive satisfaction. This is necessary because "our civilization is, generally speaking, founded on the suppression of instincts."[69] The self (or ego) observes and judges. To judge requires a separate energy source which is assumed to be diverted from the id and attached to the ego in order to provide psychic energy.

The ego, "a system composed predominantly of mature, preconscious functions,"[70] is presumed to participate in the nonaware decision-making process that results from the conflict between unconscious libidinal forces and preconscious reality orientation. It is seen as an arbiter, choosing between behavior alternatives and limiting the expression of the desires which comprise the id. Intelligence and other endowments are seen as part of the executive aspect of the ego rather than of the biological portion of the self. The ego is presumed to possess its own intelligence––to have a capacity beyond such primitive sources of data as instinct and desire.[71]

An example of the dynamic nature of the ego is seen in its effort to control the id. The defenses are believed to be barriers created by the ego to protect its integrity. "Pressure from repressed instincts...is felt by the ego as a danger."[72] "To ward off dangers the ego must resort to...defense mechanisms."[73] Such interpretations suggest that "immoral" or socially unacceptable libidinal urges are controlled by the ego for its own sake.

Anna Freud[74] stated that the ego senses an enemy in every instinct. But an enemy against what? Apparently, against the superego with which the ego is armed. Broadly interpreted, this would mean that the ego knows what is good and what is bad, what is harmful and what is safe, that it is embarrassed by bad behavior, afraid of dangerous behavior, and that it puts up defenses against such activity. It would seem to Freudian analysts far too simplistic to state that individuals, possessed of rational skill and social awareness, appreciate that some potential behaviors, based on (amoral) desire violate moral or ethical codes.

This rational characteristic of the ego is supplemented by a cleverness in controlling the id. In order to defend itself against what may be disintegrating or disturbing influences arising from the id, the ego can shift cathexis in order to prevent the id content from being egotized. Ego defenses are seen, then, as constantly moving; weakening, or strengthening the flexible ego boundaries.

A variety of interpretations of the role of the ego have been proposed. For Erikson,[75] ego identity is paramount. This identity depends on successfully integrating libidinal urges, native ability, and environmental limitation. The balance provides a sense of continuity in one's self as well as in others. Erikson spoke of identifiable crisis points in life which are culturally determined in terms both of when they should occur and how they should be handled. Lewin's topology[76] accommodated Erikson's position by describing the ego as a point in a force field (life space) which is comprised of differentiated areas that become increasingly numerous with maturity. The identity to which Erikson referred is accomplished through the integration of these many regions.

Federn described an affect which he called ego *feeling*, which is associated with the experience of mediating between the id and the environment. "It is an entity which stands in relation to the continuity of the person in respect to time, space, and causality."[77] More than knowledge of the self, it refers to an awareness or affective reaction to self. Federn argued that "the familiar phenomenon of ego feeling...proves the existence of the ego."[77] This is a Cartesian explanation, but one that must not be underestimated. In all such interpretations, the ego is seen as a dynamic energy system capable of decision-making outside of and beyond the insistence of drives and frustration. It is, however, subject to attack through various subtle techniques.

The Superego. That part of the mental apparatus which is said to represent an internalized and "egotized" authority, and which directs and judges behavior, is identified as the *superego*. It is said to arise from the incorporation of the parent or parent surrogate during that stage of ego development when the world around the individual is taking shape through introjection (i.e., the oral stage). While the ego is learning about the qualities of objects through the digestive tract, id impulses are monitored by the superego which provides a moral evaluation of its activity.

The development of the superego is believed to be caused by the survival need of the weak and helpless child. A boy must identify with more powerful figures. As he gives up his wishes toward his parents, he incorporates their value system. This results in an ego state which cannot be fused with the "authentic" ego which, for an analyst, is the "real" self. This ego state is autonomous, developing its own boundaries separately but as part of the true ego. Morality is seen as a feeling growing out of restrictions in behavior assigned by the superego. One avoids acting in a certain way because the superego says not to (conscience), or because one wishes to be like a parent (ego ideal). Having posited a structure and observing behavior, the force of law is ascribed.

The specific development of morality is seen by many analysts as resulting from the experience of acting in a self-controlled manner. Weiss offered an explanation:

> For it is not (as we ordinarily think) that we desist from aggression because we have a very rigorous moral ideal but, rather, we have a rigorous moral ideal just because, or to the degree to which, we have renounced aggression.[78]

This interpretation is akin to the behavioral view. It assumes that the logical sequence is from the experiencing of a particular form of behavior (e. g., aggression) to the emergence or creation of a moral sense. It assumes that the moral sense grows from the reward/punishment paradigm. The superego, which is called the moral arm of the personality, is believed to develop as a reaction to what it receives from the environment, and especially from parents. "To obtain the rewards and avoid the punishments, the child learns to guide his behavior along the lines laid down by the parents."[79] In spite of the fact that rewards are recognized in the form of emotional reactions (e.g., guilt and pride), it is ostensibly what children get for themselves that determines activity with moral characteristics. The holarchic interpretation is that when one acts in a particular manner, a sense of morality, which existed *prior to* and *separate from* the act or event, contributes to the attendant emotional state.

The psychoanalytic view is not only inaccurate, it is *a violation of the very function of the moral evaluative system.* Moral feelings are associated with behaviors, situations, and events that are perceived to be related to the enhancement of human life, not to personal profit or loss. (This, of course, does not obviate the fact that many perverse interpretations are offered regarding *whose* life is to be valued and *what* techniques are to be employed.)

Freud argued that the moral sense is developed on the basis of imitation of parents and reaction to their admonitions. There is no way in which the experiences that a child may have with parents, peers, or any cultural group could result in guilt by their sheer occurrence, or in behavior that can be described as moral. The only kind of data the perceptual/cognitive information system can provide is an awareness of acts, events, or experiences.

Why should the boy, punished by his father, learn anything except that he will suffer if he persists in such behavior? How can such an experience lead to a sense of value or of moral propriety? Although the child can learn that his father associates "goodness" with an act, from where did the father learn this affective state, and why should the child incorporate the selflessness it implies? Unless there were some information system to provide a sense of moral value, the only result of such experience would be fear or personal satisfaction. Anger, guilt, and similar affects require a relationship which cannot be created environmentally. The analytic interpretation is that morality is "introjected from parents or parent surrogates,"[80] and is thus learned. However, what the child, in fact, learns are the socially evolved rules and behaviors to which that form of evaluation may be applied.

The Holarchic View of Nonconscious States

The existence of mental states to which one is not attending cannot be questioned. There are clearly processes occurring which do not meet the condition of awareness. This aspect of mind, however, is not an agent of a subconscious ego which employs its wit to provide opportunity for primitive desires to be expressed. At the active or dynamic stage, the preconscious is comprised of material that has been conceptualized but not yet resolved for whatever reason. Issues which represent problems to be solved or understandings to be reached, as well as those that arouse emotions which are not dissipated through behavior or other methods, are the material of the active preconscious. At this level of mind, habituated behaviors are mediated and incoming stimuli are often monitored. The "decision-making" that characterizes this level of mental process, however, resembles that of a sophisticated computer which is equipped with an extensive ROM[81] and is capable of "learning" to shut out urges or perceptions that if experienced consciously, would be undesirable.

In spite of enthusiastic claims, no evidence has been provided that would authenticate the claim that a *continuity* of subconscious activity obtains. There is no evidence that the state with which the aroused individual is dealing, has *progressed* from its previously conscious condition. There is, however, a significant characteristic of the preconscious state which must be considered. As the conscious state descends from the point of acute attention in the direction of the preconscious condition, the effectiveness of the various evaluative scales is diminished. Reason and moral judgment become progressively less operative. Desires of all types, including the transcendent, operate on an instinctual or primitive basis. This represents no more than the inability of evaluative systems, which operate at the conscious level, to operate profoundly without maximum energy. It is *not* a weakness that allows an evil personality or immoral wishes to be expressed. The inactive extreme of the preconscious function is better understood as *memory*, which is comprised only of congealed concepts. Desire and emotion as such are not part of this aspect of mind which provides no more than a storage function.

The preconscious state represents an aspect of mind that includes data not available for deliberation. Material that is emotionally charged, or where resolutions are incomplete, remains in an active state, while that which is of no immediate concern passes into memory. The so-called "decisions" that are made resemble those

MOTIVATION 1: THEORETICAL CONCEPTS   335

of complex machines. The distinction between the psychoanalytic and holarchic positions is not a mere semantic. It may seem that what is being suggested is no more than the substituting of the term "preconscious" for "unconscious." However, the reason for disposing of the unconscious completely is because of the nature of its operation.

This is not to deny that desires arise from sensations operating below the conscious level. Such sensations are, however, elements of the drive system, which when active emerges as desire at the conscious level. There is also no doubt that perceptual signals are, in many instances, monitored preconsciously. However, behaviors are mediated by a conscious affective system that is influenced by rational and moral judgment. This may be clarified through the use of diagrams that represent the alternative views. It is necessary, first, to point out that the types of illustration typically provided in psychoanalytic writings do not accurately reflect the process to which the psychoanalytic literature refers. The Kohut and Seitz diagram, Figure 11.2 exemplifies the problem, in that it does not provide any evidence of the persistence of unconscious dynamic processes.[82]

Figure 11.2

The Eye of Consciousness

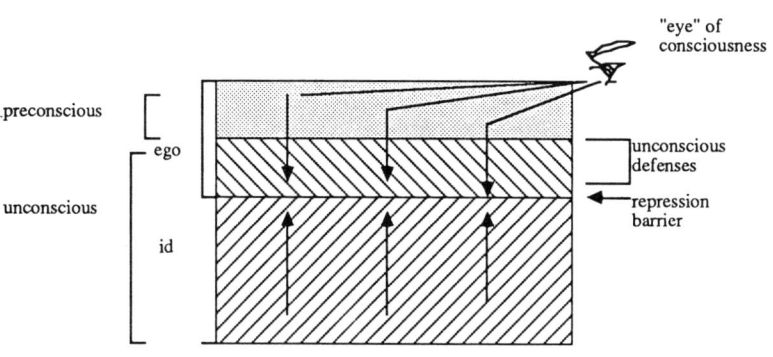

Adapted from Kohut and Seitz (1963)

The Kohut and Seitz model does not adequately account for the temporal aspect of the "psychic continuity" to which psychoanalytic writers consistently refer. A more accurate interpretation of the analytic model is depicted in Figure 11.3.

Figure 11.3 represents the psychoanalytic notion that the unconscious, in a state of permanent agitation, forces itself against the ego-managed preconscious which

336   MOTIVATION, BEHAVIOR, AND EMOTIONAL HEALTH

Figure 11.3
Psychoanalytic Mental Model

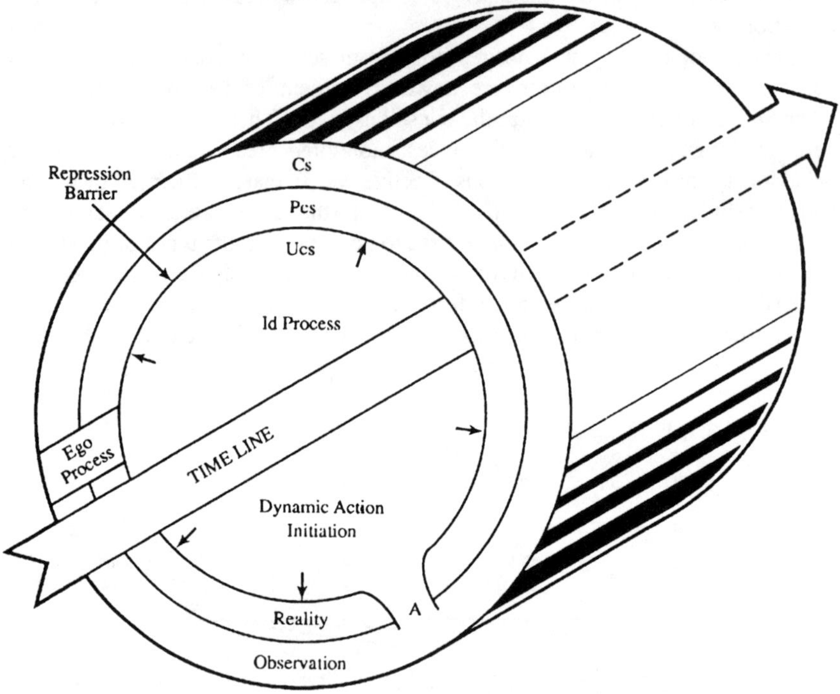

Labels on figure: Repression Barrier; Cs; Pcs; Ucs; Id Process; Ego Process; TIME LINE; Dynamic Action Initiation; Reality Observation; A

attempts to control its expression. Occasionally, it breaks through and reaches the conscious level A. The arrow represents a timeline. The model suggests that the individual's personality manifestation is the result of this continuity of mental action. It also presumes that all action is initiated at the unconscious level, with the preconscious operating to control or direct such action. The holarchic model, Figure 11.4, indicates that the conscious person is continually bombarded with environmental stimuli and by desires that arise both spontaneously and in response to stimulation.

Much of this interaction is mediated at the preconscious level, especially where the individual has learned to avoid distasteful, confusing, or threatening signals. It will be recalled that learning is an automatic result of experience in any entity (here the Pcs) capable of modification. It does not require conscious attention. The "struggle" that characterizes the interaction of mental elements is carried on between

Figure 11.4
Holarchic Mental Model

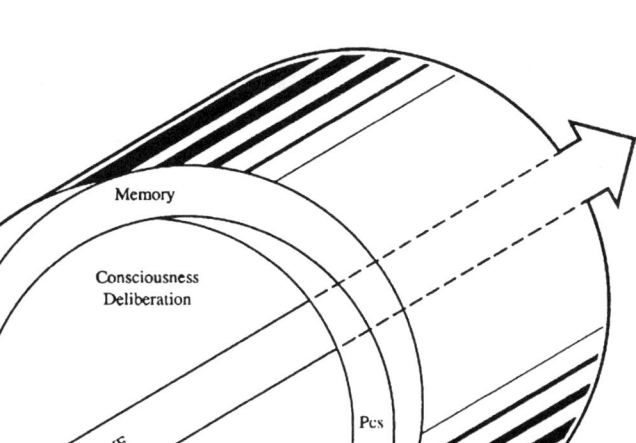

the Cs and the Pcs. Attempts to avoid confrontation with undesirable material is accomplished at the level of dim awareness which makes it difficult to deal with. Once again, however, this does not represent the desire of the material to become conscious but the difficulty with continually denying its presence. The only dynamism involved in preconscious material is its volatility. It does not posses a continuity of its own except as remaining in a state of agitation, and of persevering in its dealing with data that has not achieved resolution.

The memory state represents the storehouse of available (learned) material. Its availability to consciousness is determined by many factors including time delay, the organization of material, and the emotional quality of what has been stored. Where the information is distressing, its emergence may well be inhibited by preconscious processes. However, unless the individual disposes of an issue by dealing with it, traces of the stimulus will remain in the preconscious until they are either dealt with or, over extended time, dissipated.

Psychological occurrences are, by their nature, the products of mind in its conscious or immediately aware sense, or in its preconscious or nonattentive aspect. Desire, pain and pleasure, emotion, and all such experiences are based on the function of a part of the nervous system which contributes to the deliberative process. The preconscious screening of material that is offensive to attention is not a device for avoiding the expression of desires or emotions that are struggling to emerge. It is, rather, a mechanism for restraining the egress of thoughts that, when meditated upon, may cause negative feeling states. The affective condition only follows on the presentation of data, which carries with it all of the judgments that are likely to cause distress.

When an individual is continually depressed or anxious, it is because the information, being volatile or unresolved, continues to rise to attention. This action, however, is no more than an unfortunate by-product of the capacity of conscious mind to fasten itself on significant issues and the imperfection of the psychological screen that the preconscious represents. The same principle accounts for the arousal of pleasant or thrilling thoughts when desire becomes active. The attractive person and the savory meal are images that in the conscious mind of an interested individual result in positive feeling states.

If the dream is considered a conscious experience, it is reasonable to argue that desires are present which may be attached to a great variety of expressive forms, since the cognitive process functions without many of the restrictions that waking states impose. The fact that bizarre and sometimes hideous connections are made represents no more than the immediacy of recall of recent events and the arousal of sexual animals and/or very young children. It seems equally accurate, if less romantic, to consider that dreams allow, not for the cathexis of id impulses, but for the expression of persistent desires, often in unexpected ways. Certainly there are many cases in which dream states are recalled as having been "frightening" or "pleasing," and if dreams are assumed to be unconscious, such experiences would seem to provide interest in proximity with such a thought. The dream may, for example, include homosexual contact believed by the dreamer, in a waking state, to be of a revolting nature. However, this need not lead to any conclusion regarding "latent homosexual wishes." It is far more sensible to treat the dream state as a process by which drives are dissipated through any form of expression that becomes available.

There is, in fact, no excuse for positing dream states in the individual prior to experience unless some instinctive concepts may be associated with the desire in evidence that one can experience emotion unconsciously. However, the contention that dreams are vehicles for the release of latent desires and are to be included as part of the unconscious state, is expressly denied here.[83]

There is a further logical argument against the hypothesizing of a dynamic unconscious and the emotional states presumed to invest it. In the pre-mind world,

MOTIVATION 1: THEORETICAL CONCEPTS

as we discussed in Chapter 2, interaction between entities is a matter determined by immediately present factors. The development of a conscious state makes possible the weighing of immediate factors with desire levels, evaluative capacity, and estimates of the efficacy of potential behavior based on the recognition of many contributory elements. Consciousness makes possible an incalculably greater potential for control of the environment. Deliberations are the unique functions of a mental state that requires awareness. To respond to pain or hunger, one must be aware of it. One must feel pain, not merely *experience* injury. To assume unconscious pain, desire, or other mental experience is not only unnecessary, it disregards the role that consciousness plays as a forum for the unique experiences that contribute to potentially superior lives.

The oft-jilted person recalls some past experience and now feels a negative emotion. The assumption of unconscious feeling would include the experiencing of pain and other sensations without awareness. It is a common occurrence to discover that one has been injured without realizing it. But to assume that it hurt, "but I didn't know it," is as nonsensical as to claim that "I enjoyed myself" when my back was scratched as I slept.[84]

In discussing the positions of behavioral scientists and psychoanalysts, and the works of Skinner and Freud in particular, it may seem that relatively minor aspects of their arguments have been stressed. Unfortunately, it is the inferences of such points that cause the difficulty. The acceptance of the ego as an independent director, the environment as principal determiner, and motives as learned represent principles which have led to inadequate interpretations of human behavior.

Many significant and valuable aspects of human sexuality as well as other personality characteristics have been identified and developed by the psychoanalytic school. The recognition of the tendency to deny or ignore many feelings, and to pay a high price in terms of personal adjustment for doing, so must be credited to Freud and other psychoanalytic thinkers. Nevertheless, many of the conclusions and associated implications for treatment cannot be accepted on the basis of their scholarly presentation where the nexus is so tenuous.

Issue is taken, especially, with the notion of a dynamic unconscious, suggesting that the entire process represents a basic misunderstanding of the mind's role. It is only by stretching the concept to include nonmental determinants such as recallable events, or by positing a dynamic unconscious, that mind can be considered to include the nonactive present. And the latter practice is common. There is no question that a reservoir of nonconscious material exists. Memory and other aspects of the preconscious represent a legitimate domain, although they do not comprise mentality in the sense that the conscious state does. The problem-solving aspect of mind is peculiar to the conscious state, and it is in assuming that one lives a private subconscious life that the unconscious motives of Freudian psychology are necessitated. Such failure to distinguish between processes is at the root of the development of the fantasy of an unconscious mind.

The behaviorist denial of desire as essential to the motivational sequence provides an equally mysterious explanation. The nauseous reaction by those who believe only what they can see and what can be measured should be tempered by the knowledge that their mechanical model describes everything but human life. When Skinner conceded that there may be something occurring within the organism, but that there is no necessity for dealing with it, he put himself in an awkward position. By what evolutionary error did he assume that these feelings, sentiments, and emotions came to be part of the human experience? If they play no role in the deliberative process, how—or why—did they evolve?

Most incredibly, the reputation of radical behaviorism seems to have blinded many otherwise competent thinkers. Hall and Lindzey described a situation in which a wounded soldier developed a paralyzed arm, where no physiological cause could be discerned. They stated that Skinner would explain the reaction by saying that the soldier elected this condition because he wished to avoid punishment, which is an aversive stimulus. Following this, they stated, "Notice...that there is no reference to what the soldier is thinking, feeling, or trying to do."[85] This is gross intellectual naivete. If it is assumed that the soldier's feeling is unessential to an understanding, why not argue that a rock would respond in the same manner?

Aversive? Deprivation? Satiation? Can anyone believe that these terms are not all based on affective, emotional, motivational, internal events?

Summary

Individuals are motivated by perceptions in the presence of desires which are common to all. That they learn, persevere, order their universe, and respond predictably are peculiarities of their being. Self-sacrifice and obligatory behaviors, as well as those based on the assertive urges, integrity, and even thrill-seeking, must be dealt with in terms of the nature of the information systems which contribute to their occurrence.

To assume desire to be unconscious because it appears to explain the otherwise unexplainable, or to deny conscious contributions to behavioral sequences because they cannot be measured, is no excuse for positing ghosts or denying the obvious. Each view avoids the "pitfalls" of introspectionism by ignoring vital determinants. The "myths and superstitions" of psychoanalysis have been countered by an approach to an understanding of behavior which has replaced "soft headed" feeling with "hard-headed," objective research. Unfortunately, the application of scientific rigor does not excuse the ignoring of informational inputs into the motivational sequence because of their messiness. While such an approach may provide an antiseptic laboratory, it will not lead to understanding.

Furthermore, current research into brain physiology does not support the S—>R paradigm. Sperry, a professor of psychobiology, commenting on recent developments in brain research, stated that after over 50 years of strict avoidance by behaviorists, terms like "mental imagery" are now employed in the literature on cognition and perception:

> The revised interpretation brings the conscious mind into the causal sequence in human decision making—and therefore into behavior generally.... This swing in psychology and neuroscience away from hard-core materialism and reductionism...tends now to restore to the scientific image of human nature some of the dignity, freedom, and other humanistic attributes of which it had been deprived by the behavioristic approach.[86]

The problem faced by many psychological theories is that they require the acceptance of premises that violate reason. Accept the notion that fear is a learned response, suggest the behaviorists. Allow that the id is a reservoir of destructive desire, propose the psychoanalysts. It seems so little to ask.

Critics of a model which bases human motivation on conscious desire, may object to the dynamisms which have been described here. But there is nothing fantastic about a feeling commonly experienced, although it cannot be seen. Hunger and love, sexual arousal and hate, are as real as the distress experienced by Harlow's monkeys. The ulcers in their primate stomachs were simply palpable evidence that there is something intangible which plays a significant role in the impetus to behave.

The desperate foraging after mysterious or mechanical explanations has resulted in a ruck of viewpoints, with each position being denied by its opponents as having any validity. However, the relative simplicity of the holarchic approach makes its acceptance highly improbable. For the behaviorist, it is too cabalistic. For the psychoanalyst, insufficiently obscure.

Chapter Notes

1. Brown (1961), p. 27
2. Even in Freud's lifetime, many members of the "Vienna Circle" challenged his most extreme pronouncements. Similarly, only the *radical behaviorists* have insisted on excluding the contribution of affective states. Skinner, however, contended that radical behaviorism does not deny consciousness. "It does not sweep the problem of subjectivity under the rug" (Skinner, 1974, p. 219).
3. McDougall (1930)
4. Hebb (1955)
5. Madsen (1973), p. 673
6. Congressional hearings were held in Washington, D.C. in 1986 to determine which therapeutic approach is most effective. Every psychologist who testified agreed that *all* therapies are effective depending on the skill of the therapist. But imagine Rogers employing rational-emotive techniques, or Albert Ellis using a client centered approach!
7. Hilgard (1987), p. 356
8. Janis et al (1969), p. 424
9. Hebb (1949)
10. Hull (1952), p. 347
11. *Ibid.*, p. 6
12. McClelland et al. (1953), p. 28
13. These "primitive" affects are apparently feeling states not identical with, but similar to, emotions. It is the contention of this text that when such affects represent an interaction between a conceptualized need, a related desire, and an awareness of (belief about) a relevant situation, emotion is the appropriate affect involved.
14. McClelland et al. (1953), p. 28
15. *Ibid.*, p. 32
16. DeCharms (1968), p. 190
17. Hall & Lindzey (1970), p. 417
18. Kalish (1981), p. 6
19. Miller & Dollard (1941), p. 1
20. *Ibid.*, p. 2
21. Miller, N. E. (1948)
22. Brown (1975), p. 37
23. *Ibid.*, p. 38
24. Hall & Lindzey (1970), p. 426
25. Miller, N. E. (1948), p. 89
26. *Ibid.*, p. 99
27. A "latent" or "potential" emotion, like a potential desire, is a genetically prescribed affective state that is activated under appropriate conditions. The notion of "potential" is no doubt distressing to many psychologists. However, the practice of referring to concepts (i.e., emotions) such as fear as "drives," "behaviors," or whatever seems to fit the occasion is sheer mumbo jumbo!
28. Skinner (1974), p. 165
29. Kelly (1958)
30. Ebel (1974), p. 488
31. Skinner (1953), p. 144
32. *Ibid.*, p. 160
33. Skinner (1971), p. 291
34. Weiss, P. (1969)

35. Washburn (1978), p. 405
36. Skinner (1974), p. 163
37. Hayes (1978), p. 41
38. Restak (1979), p. 418
39. McFarland (1983), p. 401
40. Taylor, I. (1983), p. 403
41. Peters (1958), p. 7
42. Kagan (1971)
43. Descartes (1972)
44. Sartre (1956), p. 53
45. Fichte (1848), p. 471
46. Chein (1972), p. 108
47. *Ibid.*, p. 112
48. Eccles (1967), p. 8
49. Nietzsche (1960), p. 298
50. Marx & Hillix (1973), p. 177
51. Kohut & Seitz (1963), p. 117
52. Freud, S. in Brill (1938), p. 224
53. Brill (1938), p. 12
54. Kohut & Seitz (1963), p. 121
55. Freud, S. (1943), p. 357
56. Weiss, E. (1960), p. 44
57. Hall & Lindzey (1970), p. 35
58. Hall (1954), p. 40
59. Benner (1985), p. 558
60. Freud, S. in Riviere (1959), p. 52
61. Freud, S. in Brill (1938), p. 151
62. Kohut & Seitz (1963), p. 117
63. Freud, S. (1943), p. 188. Nagele, in fact, proposes that "the most important dynamic in the analytic process takes place between the analysts unconscious and that of the analysand." (1987), p. 180. He seemed to assume that a conscious state is quite unnecessary.
64. Kohut & Seitz (1963), p. 117
65. Shevrin & Dickman (1980)
66. Restak (1979), p. 202
67. Sperry, quoted in Restak (1979), p. 202
68. Restak (1979), p. 199.
69. Freud, S. in Riviere (1959), p. 82
70. Kohut & Seitz (1963), p. 133
71. A careful study of the nature of ego processing shows that it is believed to be competent to organize behavior without recourse to the basic urges—it is an independent force.
72. Weiss, E. (1960), p. 339
73. *Ibid.*, p. 327
74. Freud, A., (1946)
75. Erikson (1963)
76. Lewin (1936)
77. Federn (1952), p. 212
78. Weiss, E. (1960), p. 45
79. Hall & Lindzey (1970), p. 35
80. Harriman (1974), p. 193
81. ROM references the "read only memory," or permanent program items on computer storage media.
82. Kohut & Seitz (1963), p. 134: "Eye of consciousness."
83. There persists among most psychotherapists the conviction that dreams represent the manifestation of hidden, guilt-laden desires, and that they must be deciphered by one who understands their meaning. This legacy of Freud's occult philosophy has withstood every effort to provide alternative interpretations. Most recently, Hobson, in his text *The Dreaming Brain*, (1988), suggests that dreams are improvisations on normal brain functions, and that, as Jung proposed long ago, they have no deceptive function at all. It is highly unlikely, however that such non-titillating explanations will be accepted until studies of

sleep rhythms, and the mechanisms of rapid eye movement (REM) sleep sequences can be proven to describe normal, perhaps creative, moments in our resting phase.
84. Back scratching may cause a relaxation of tense muscles or the physiological arousal of quiescent nerves. While such an experience may cause pleasure in the conscious individual, the appellation is no more appropriate to the sleeping individual than to a robe as it is caressed by a luxuriating person.
85. Hall & Lindzey (1970), p. 510
86. Sperry (1975), p. 30

Chapter 12
Motivation 2: Cognate Factors

Beyond the problems associated with the major theoretical positions, as described in Chapter 11, lie a series of implications based on such theories as well as a number of beliefs held by those who reject both behavioral and psychoanalytic polemics. In many instances these diverse views are also inimical with holarchic principles. A series of premises based on material introduced in earlier chapters will be developed here. The principles involved bear heavily on the preventive and intervention strategies to be described in Chapters 14, 15, and 16.

The role played by desires in the motivational sequence is often misconstrued. Beliefs about non-existent moral and rational urges, the ability to "rise above" the basic desires, the possibility of free or undetermined behavior and its attendant responsibility, and the negative interpretation of aggression, all interfere with attempts to understand and ameliorate emotional problems. Here we shall offer brief analyses of the holarchic interpretation of some of the parameters of desire and its impact on behavior.

Desires as Limited

Premise 1: **All behavior is based on a fixed set of innate desires.** The principle applies at every level of animal life. Although desires vary in intensity between individuals and from time to time, they cannot be superseded or overcome.

The classification of desires as *assertive*, *protective*, and *transcendent* in Chapter 7 was intended to identify urges to action, on the basis of their relationship to survival and growth. The subtlety of their expression is not sufficient reason to assume the emergence of "higher order" motives, unless such motives can be shown to provide survival and growth advantage unattainable through the gratification of the three classes of desire that we have identified. Despite the claims of evolutionists, there is no evidence that interest in the arts or allocentric perception provides such leverage. This limiting of motives to the basic urges is denied by many psychologists, especially those identified with the "third force," an approach to motivation which rejects many of the rigid determinants of behavior proposed by behavioral and psychoanalytic principles.

Although humans spend considerable time and energy attending to primitive needs, phenomenologists claim that there is a persistent desire to be free from the press of such noncreative experience. The truly whole person, they say, is one who breaks the shackles of such oppression. Schachtel suggested that maturity represents a capacity to view the world for itself, free of the neurosis of dependent perception.[1] Maslow was quite specific. He did allow that basic needs provide the motivation for *some* behavior.[2] He contended, however, that their frustration results in the inability of many individuals to rise to higher, more "humanizing" motivational levels. For Maslow, the basic needs represent only a small proportion of the total range of motivators.

The Maslovian hierarchy represents a view of motivation in which desires emerge in some approximate order. In the Maslovian interpretation, reference is often made to those objects, situations, or events that meet the demands of desire, and which we have defined as needs. Thus, food is a need related to the hunger desire. For those deprived, the meeting of such needs, according to Maslow, will take priority over all others. In people with adequate emotional health, basic needs (i. e., desires) are met with little effort, and attention is turned to the higher level motives.

The assumption that individuals will attempt to meet needs in a fairly fixed order is, however, inconsistent with much observed behavior. Self-sacrifice as practiced by mothers for their children and artists for their art are commonplace. The reason for such deviation from Maslow's proposed pattern lies in cultural arrangements as well as in the cognitive/affective sophistication of humans. Maslow's hierarchy is accurate only at a low level of life. The scheme increasingly breaks down, as parenting and social recognition become influential factors. "Higher order" needs often become as compulsive as their basic counterparts.

There is, in fact, a more serious problem. For Maslow and those who follow his argument, self-actualization is considered to be separate from growth. It is described as an openness to creative experience; an approach to full potentiality. It represents a stage of existence where ordinary motivational factors are said to be inadequate to describe what Maslow termed "character growth, character expression, maturation and development."[3] This is a recognizable, understandable condition and one which describes many individuals. But why is it necessary to assume that it *transcends* the basic desires? Why deny that this is an aspect of the growth urge that is applauded in the bursting rose bud, and admired in the fawn as it struggles to gain its feet in its initial attempt at independence? Why propose a mystical component when there is a reasonable alternative which does not violate what is known of living beings? Clearly, the self-fulfilled person is one whose desires are essentially expressible, and this includes the desires for potency and power.

The assumption of a class of desires that transcends drives is not peculiar to phenomenologists. The urge to potency was described by White as a non-drive based desire. He defined it as a desire for *competence* which "cannot be wholly derived from sources of energy currently conceptualized as drives or instincts."[4] White felt that a complete understanding of human motivation must include this factor which, he said, "represents what the neuromuscular system wants to do when it is otherwise unoccupied or is gently stimulated by the environment."[5] This strange statement implies that the musculature has a desire to act in certain situations. Furthermore, in such circumstances, individuals may have to do what they do not wish to do. We have included the competence motive under the desires for *stimulation*, *power*, and *potency*, all of which are based on drives, and all of which occur in many forms of animal life.

Hunt, while not denying the legitimacy of drive-based motivation, argued that "there is a highly important system of motivation...that has a developmental basis...quite different from that of the now traditional acquired [*sic*] drives."[6] He labelled this system "intrinsic motivation," by which he meant behavior which occurs when no desire can be identified. In fact, we have included such desires in the "exploratory" category. (They have also been studied under the labels "exploratory" or "curiosity" by many researchers.)

The psychoanalytic school also assumes a number of non-drive based motives. Freud's ego, though arising out of the id, was said by Hall to be capable of using id energy "for other purposes than that of satisfying the instincts."[7] The inference is that reason can take humans beyond their drives. Hass made much the same statement, asking, "How free is our ego in its emergence?"[8] referring to its ability to "prevail against individual members of the parliament of instincts given that 'differences of opinion' arise."[8] Hass was not dealing with how the ego decides *which* instinct (i.e., desire), to support, but proposed that the ego can "prevail" against all of them. This image of the rational being as one who can rise above desire is eminently appealing. It seems a route to the freeing of the individual from base motives. Morris, for example, decried the reducing of human behavior to a series of responses to primitive urges as legitimizing such behaviors as rape, promiscuity, and other abominations.[9] However, rape, and other widely detested behaviors are *not* desires, but nonessential *needs*. Kitcher's response was of little help. In agreement with Morris, he denied that people "ought [necessarily] to do what comes naturally."[10] Like so many theorists, he proposed that humans should overcome many of what he assumed to be undesirable innate desires. Such views are, of course, consistent with those preached by every form of religious injunction.

Ethologists, on the other hand, have taken a strong stand against the notion that individuals may rise above their instinctive nature. Morris stated that "optimism is expressed by some who feel that since we have evolved a high level of intelligence and a strong inventive urge, we shall...dominate all our basic biological urges. I submit that this is rubbish. Our raw animal nature will never permit it."[11]

Ardrey was equally convinced of the ubiquity of the animal residing in humans. "The individual may and must grapple with the animal within him."[12] He quoted Anthony Storr as saying "we know in our hearts that each one of us harbors within him those same savage impulses which lead to murder, to torture and war."[13] Ardrey further disagreed with Koestler for assuming that most of the horrors of human interaction come from the self transcending tendencies. He accused Koestler of "denying ultimate evil as rising from the greed and selfishness of the individual."[14] For Ardrey self serving behavior is the norm.

To the extent that animal instinct is similar in its nature to learned human behavior, holarchic theory parallels that of ethological conviction. Human activity is no more than a sophisticated expression of the instinctive behavior of simpler organisms. Furthermore, each level of the chain of life, while independent in much of its performance, functions in the interest of higher levels of "authority." Through the genetic process, individuals are bound to the species in many subtle ways. Principal among these is the technique by which actions are encouraged. Motivation represents an ongoing process with the potential for maximizing species—as well as individual—enhancement.

Morality and Behavior

Premise 2: **Behavior is not motivated by a desire to act either morally or immorally.** There is no inherent urge to be "good" or "evil," kind or cruel, honest or dishonest.

The basic urges were shown in Chapter 7 to be *negative* as they are experienced and *positive* in that they provide the impetus for individual and/or species enhancement. The capacity to learn and to define the world in terms of the biological self, however, has resulted in the identification of many behaviors, objects, and situations as *needs*. It is in the *behavior* directed toward the expression of such needs that moral evaluation resides.

Hudson asked whether people desire to be moral and concluded that "the question is, of course, ambiguous."[15] In one sense, he said, "it seems clearly to be that all men some of the time, and some men all of the time, do *not* want to be moral."[15] His assumption was that morality is a form of desire that is not always operable. The holarchic interpretation is that behavior (not desire) may be evaluated as good or evil as it meets survival and growth demands. Kitcher denied the contention that species profit defines moral behavior. He would not accept the argument that "a property or form of behavior is good if it provides survival (regardless of other features)."[16] He was apparently reacting to situations in which one individual injured others for personal gain, with which we would agree. But Kitcher went further. He questioned the very claim that life is inherently valuable, concluding that you can only believe in the value of the preservation of life, if you have "antecedently held beliefs about the value of survival."[16] Whether he assumed that such precedents for belief are taught or innately known is not clear. The holarchic view is that the sanctity of life is an inherently held conviction, and that "good" behavior relates to its preservation.

Philosophers have, of course, found it extremely difficult to determine precisely what "good" behavior would be. Moore, for example, claimed that, "'Good'...if we mean by it that quality which we assert to belong to a thing, when we say that thing [behavior] is good, is incapable of any definition."[17] Others have attempted an explanation. Fichte proposed that good behavior is that which is spiritually elevating. He spoke of a moral impulse, which represents a higher spiritual striving, contending that "we raise ourselves from this abyss [of annihilation] and maintain ourselves above it, solely by our moral activity."[18] Schopenhauer, although he believed that "deeds and ways of acting...can be very much modified by dogmas, example, and custom,"[19] proposed that when an individual acts morally "he performs such a deed because he is *good*."[20] All such views assume behavior to spring from positive or negative moral motives. Not, however, because certain behaviors are good or evil, but because people *desire* to be good or evil. (The holarchic position—that morality is *not* a desire, but rather an evaluative mechanism—was developed in Chapter 8.)

Phenomenologists have taken the position that humans are inherently moral, but that retardation of emotional maturity and lack of recognition as having worth, cause many people to fail to realize their potential in that dimension. Rogers, in many works,[21] and Maslow, especially in *Motivation and Personality*,[22] argued that people should be encouraged develop their sense of self as fully as possible. Roger's thesis was that if people are appreciated without reservation or correction, they will be free to achieve the highest level of humanness. To the extent that love and trust can be freely given, the individual can become fully actualized. This view is based on the assumption that motivation includes a desire to become fully functional and that fully functioning individuals will act in morally positive ways. A diametrically opposed position is taken by psychoanalysts, who assume that immoral activity is an innate human characteristic which must be controlled either by the superego or by social sanction. The quintessential example of this urge to indulge in immoral behavior is expressed in the positing of an infantile incestuous urge.

The Oedipus Complex

The earliest sex object of a boy, according to psychoanalytic theory, is said to be his mother; "an *incestuous love choice* is in fact the first and the regular one,"[23] and that he desires to destroy his father whom he sees as a rival. Freud suggested that this perverse aim is "a natural result of the immature constitution of the child."[24] Whether the mother is instinctively preferred is vital to the theory, but Freud was inconsistent in his explanations. At one point he said "he directs his earliest sexual desire...to those nearest him...his parents, brothers and sisters or nurses."[25] This would suggest a learned attachment to those nearby. In still other of Freud's writing, there is an inference that the mother-as-object is part of the instinctive package. He wrote, for example, that unless there was such a natural attachment to the mother, the negative aspect is such that: "The avoidance of incest would have been automatically secured, and we would have been at a loss to understand the necessity for stern prohibitions which would seem rather to point to a strong desire."[23]

Further evidence for the incestuous urge was provided in the work on repression where it was suggested that "the sexual instincts are (then) apparently brought into submission and required to procure their satisfaction by circuitous regressive paths, where in their impregnability, they obtain compensation for their defeat."[26] Causing an instinct to *submit* and considering that submission a *defeat* would imply that the instinct included its object as an integral part, and that such activity is inherently immoral. Freud was adamant in this, complaining that his critics provided absurd explanations for this obnoxious, but inescapable, concept. "The most preposterous attempts have been made to account for this horror of incest,"[27] and (derisively), "What has not been invented for this purpose!"[28]

The distinction to be drawn, is between sexual desire as it is directed toward a member of the opposite sex, and an instinctive desire for the mother. Although most interpretations lean toward the former, the travails of the individual are assumed to be based on the latter. What would the ego be struggling *against* if it were no more than a desire for sex? There is nothing immoral or undesirable about such an urge in a normal individual. The ego need only struggle if the desire is attached to an *inappropriate* object. Ego forces would represent only guides or prompts designed to aid in the selection of appropriate objects, and infantile striving should respond without inordinate difficulty to whatever object is selected. The problem is, more likely, related to the conceptual naïveté of the infant, than to an instinctive preference for the mother or any other person.

This is not the interpretation, however, that can be taken from psychoanalytic literature where a constant struggle goes on to overcome incestuous interests. How must such a potentiality be understood? Perhaps such a relationship is simply not socially desirable. This, however, would ignore both biologically recognized disadvantages and the universality of the objection. The social argument cannot be accepted. A second possibility would be that while children *instinctively* desire sexual congress with their mother, older individuals *instinctively* abhor it. This explanation, though equally untenable, would set the stage for the ego/id struggle which analysts claim goes on. In order to believe it, however, one must accept an evolutionary hypothesis that is both absurd and unnecessary. Absurd, because it requires that an advantage be attached to investing various developmental stages with antagonistic characteristics. Unnecessary, because a far more parsimonious explanation is available.

The sexual urge, like the desire for nourishment, is an active aspect of the mental process from the earliest stages of life. In simpler animals, the individual has instinctive knowledge of the needs relevant to all forms of desire, including the recognition of appropriate sex objects. In humans, most desires must be related to needs through the learning process. Maturation alone does not necessarily result in an awareness of the proper targets of any urge. The fact that desires are active before learning takes place provides a tremendous advantage for creative adaptation. However, it is inevitably accompanied by a number of ostensibly negative characteristics, such as the indiscriminate sexual experimentation of the infant.

Freud's notions of Oedipal sexuality have been attacked as fraudulent and self-serving.[29] Masson provided an extensive analysis of Freud's vacillation and ultimate discarding of the seduction theory of neurosis in favor of the assumption of an "oedipus complex." In view of the wide acceptance of the later interpretation of childhood sexuality, Freud's motives in making the substitution deserves careful attention.[30] (It should be pointed out that Malcolm offered an extensive rebuttal of Masson's work, accusing him of deliberate distortions in the interest of promoting his publication.[31])

In addition to the compulsion for incestuous relationships, other forms of immorality as exhibited in sexual deviance are presumed to pervade the unconscious mind. In the analysis of a young man (Ray) concerned about a possible homosexual encounter if he were to take a hike with a man to whom he felt attracted, Janis stated that interaction with this male "stimulated Ray's unconscious homosexual wishes, fantasies, and memories...[his] unconscious homosexual conflict was so intensified that it could have become conscious.... By hiking alone, Ray avoided further stimulation of his unconscious conflict."[32]

An interpretation not relying on such mysterious postulates would be that Ray had associated his desire for sex with males, and had learned that it was unacceptable. In a compromising situation, his feeling about sex with a male being positive *and conscious* created a conflict between a desired sexual experience and moral judgment which would cause distress if it persisted. The holarchic interpretation is that one *learns* that the desire for an incestuous relationship with one's mother, for a homosexual experience, or for any other type of sexual expression is considered immoral or is expressly socially or legally forbidden. It is after this is learned that an attempt may be made to avoid dealing with the desire for that particular form of behavior.

As to the desire itself (e.g., sheer heightened sexual interest), in some cultures it is considered immoral for certain individuals—especially adolescents, and females—even to feel the urge. In such cases, the individual may attempt to suppress specific *thoughts* related to the sanctioned behavior, to ignore the feeling, or to engage in some activity which interferes with the arousal of the desire.

The occurrence of thought relative to desires is based on the capacity to explore, experience, and imagine many forms of gratification. In some instances, a form which is highly attractive may be culturally unacceptable. It may, in fact, be stimulating or attractive to a degree beyond that ordinarily associated with the desire.

Thus drug use, sexual perversions, compulsive eating, and high speed driving, though learned to be exciting and desirable, are not acceptable in many communities. In all such instances, the specific behavior carries the moral connotation. The desires on which such actions are based are, however, positive in their genesis.

Reason and Behavior

Premise 3: Reason, like morality, is not a desire but represents an evaluative capacity. The role of reason as it relates to behavioral consideration is in the evaluation of the relative efficacy of potential alternatives.

The appeal to reason as motivating has fascinated thinkers from the time that philosophers proposed that human behavior must be based on motives of a higher order than those of animals. When Aquinas, following Greek thought, proposed that humans are possessed of a rational soul, and that, unlike animals, their behavior is rationally determined, he was expressing a sentiment that has found wide acceptance in the scientific community. His interpretation followed the millennium old Aristotelian view that saw the good in humans being realized in the actualization of their intellective rather than their vegetative faculties. Thus, humans were considered capable of action based on the rational, as well as the moral sense.

Kant posited a will that controls passion, implying that the will includes reason. Believing that human action is based on a free will, he contended that "pure reason by itself can determine the will,"[33] and that "the necessity of acting from *pure* respect for the practical law is what constitutes duty, to which every other motive must give place."[34] Kant proposed that acting out of respect for law is a necessity, concluding that individuals are motivated to act lawfully because it is reasonable to do so. He did not view rational activity as necessarily different from behavior based on a moral sense, and "prudence" was (and is) said to represent behavior which is both intelligent and moral. Many schools of thought continue to identify rationality as a force associated with *goodness*, a motivator that, in the absence of conflict, is believed to cause individuals to live moral lives. "Right reason" is considered to be an essential tool of thinking people in their search for appropriate action.

Most phenomenologists represent humans as reasonable beings, including an oft-quoted assumption that their most compelling desire is to be rational, excellent, and free. However, in existential circles, where rationality is ostensibly demeaned, the appropriate goal of humans is believed to be authenticity. Ellenberger argued that humans are free to choose whether they shall submit to the indignity of collective existence or accept responsibility for themselves.[35] Cofer and Appley advised people to "experience the world and themselves as they *are* [italics added] rather than as some theory, belief, or convention would make them appear."[36] Such arguments spring from the conviction that individuals sometimes behave solely on the basis of a desire to be reasonable. The rational aspect has not been associated with behavioral psychology since that interpretation of behavior calls for the downplaying of desires of any type as useful in understanding behavior. However, psychoanalysis includes a clear rational component. Freud's ego is "wise," thus it must act on the basis of reason. "The ego becomes 'reasonable,' is no longer controlled by the pleasure-principle, but follows the Reality-principle."[37] Since the ego is not considered a desire, it apparently seeks to act reasonably for its own sake.

The holarchic interpretation of motivation identifies behavior as resulting from an emotional state which represents the relationship between desire and belief about an existing situation, expectancy about a future situation, and belief regarding the capacity and opportunity to take action. The actual situation is somewhat more complex. Desire is ordinarily experienced in association with a learned need, with reason (and morality) applied to each step of the deliberative process. However, such evaluations *follow,* rather than precede, the contemplation of a behavior. The conviction that the odds are 1,000 to 1 against being killed when crossing a highway at a certain time calls for a judgment regarding the reasonableness of making the attempt. Whether one crosses, however, is determined not only by the odds against injury, but by the *desire* for the attraction (need or incentive) on the other side, and the willingness to take the risk. The reasoning process represents the manipulation of, and conviction about, data on which decisions are made since cost factors are considered in relation to desire.

It is true that humans (as well as many animals) make use of knowledge and intellectual skill and take into account probabilities and potentialities beyond the data of the immediate present. However, all that such calculations provide are the techniques for getting to those points in space and time that are desired. Since reasoning, or the cognitive process, is employed to achieve what is desired and since desire is not rational, the intellect is no more than a useful tool.

This limitation on the role of reason has been recognized by many philosophers, especially where reasoning is related to the search for truth. Moore, in explaining pragmatism, asked, "If truth be the satisfaction of a special instinct...what is this instinct's peculiar satisfying material or object...? The content of any thought always turns out to be the material of some other instinct."[38] This is not to deny that one form of stimulating activity is the search for solutions to problems—even where the problems may be created merely to entertain. However, it is the excitement, or stimulation of seeking that is involved, and the closure provided by an explanation (integrity or order) or the attractive giddiness of ambiguity are more accurate explanations.

The holarchic model allows that a behavior may be both moral and reasonable, but not in the same aspects. It is *neither moral to be reasonable nor the reverse.* Exercising and eating wholesome foods may well provide for both personal health, which is a reasonable course of action, and for the well being of the species which we have defined as moral. The motivating factor, however, is not the reasonableness of the activity but its efficacy in meeting a desire. Joggers do not desire to be reasonable, but to improve their health. The fact that such behavior may be evaluated as reasonable is only a spin-off—desirable as it may be. Similarly, when individuals make generous, anonymous, charitable contributions, the appropriate interpretation would be that they *desire* to help others, though such behavior is usually evaluated as moral.

The role of reason in such transactions has to do with the identification of behaviors which may be evaluated as to their rectitude. The question to which reason applies would be: "To what extent is a behavior morally sound?" Is it, for example, *reasonable* to assume that stealing from a church poor-box is *morally* appropriate? In such instances, the potential behavior is weighed against previously established convictions regarding a set of moral principles.

Freedom and the Dominant Emotion

Premise 4: **Behavior is fully determined by a "dominant emotion."** Decisions are as causally fixed as are other events, varying only in the nature of the determinants. They are not free of the emotions that are involved in the deliberative process. This contention poses a dilemma in that behavior appears to include an element of choice, being neither genetically rigid, as is a reflex, nor totally subject to environmental happenstance. Many philosophers object to the thesis that behavior is fully determined. Edwards summarized the view of those who deny strict determinism. "Our experience of freedom is a datum of immediate experience, while determinism is at best a complicated theory. If the two conflict, this indicates that there must be something wrong with determinism."[39]

James was concerned with the essentiality of freedom as a criterion for the evaluation of interhuman behavior. "The only consistent way of representing a pluralism and a world whose parts may effect one another through their conduct being either good or bad is the indeterministic way."[40] Like many philosophers, James appealed to the *need* to accept an indeterministic world. Hume had made a case against strict determinism on the grounds that it represented a semantic error. He said that when we say "free" in ordinary life, we do not mean without cause, but rather that the behavior is based only on the *will*, or *desires* of the individual. "By liberty [freedom] then we can only mean *a power of acting or not acting, according to the determinations of the will*; this is, if we choose to remain at rest, we may; if we choose to move, we also may."[41] He concluded that "an action is free...if it comes from an unimpeded *rational* desire on the part of the agent."[42]

Schlick offered a similar explanation. "A man is free if he does not act under compulsion, and he is compelled or unfree when he is hindered from without in the realization of his natural desires."[43] Such a philosophy is defined as "soft" determinism, which represents a heroic effort to provide for some measure of freedom of the will. The holarchic view finds Hume's use of the expression "rational desire" to be wholly inappropriate. Desire, alone, is quite incompetent to mandate behavior.

Mill proposed another argument for accepting the freedom of behavior, contending that although behavior may be *predictable*, it is not therefore *predetermined*. With perfect fore-knowledge, he allowed that behavior could be predicted, but only if the predictor knew *every* factor that contributed to the occurrence of the behavior under consideration. He held, further, that "human actions...are never...ruled by any one motive with such absolute sway that there is no room for the influence of any other."[44] Thus, the influence of a multitude of causes was offered as evidence of freedom. Furthermore, Mill argued, "to call this [multiplicity of causes] by the name necessity is to use the term in a sense so different from its primitive and familiar meaning...as to amount to almost a play upon words."[44] The issue, of course, is to determine which interpretation represents the "play on words." The holarchic position is that behavior is fully determined by desire as modified by those factors that bear on its expression. How can the influence of many determinants be construed as representing freedom?

If behavior is fixed, and if the limit of potential is genotypal capacity as well as temporal/spatial opportunity, how should the term *deliberate* be interpreted? Deliberation is a uniquely conscious mental function. Its peculiarity in its relationship to behavior is that the element of desire is included as a determinant. The decisions that result fully determine the action that follows. If this were not the case, it would be inappropriate to assume that a decision had been made. The determinism that is involved refers, however, only to the *focus* of the decision, its fixed aspect being in relation to the totality of the activity involved. If one decides to buy two pounds of candy, the specific way it is accomplished and the sizes and flavors selected are not determined unless they represent an integral part of the decision.

The fact that behavior is based on emotional evaluation which results in resolutions that mandate activity challenges the claim that human behavior is free. Do humans have the capacity to decide their own fate? Or are they merely pawns that play out a predetermined game in which, as Descartes suggested, all the moves have been preordained? This issue cannot be ignored, since the approach to behavior recommended here, hinges on how the behavioral act is interpreted. We indicated earlier that in the effort to understand human behavior, many thinkers have attempted to develop descriptive laws in a scientific manner. But science of any kind develops principles which are assumed to have universal application. Because this reduces the subjects of science to mechanistic status, there is an understandable resistance to any attempt to understand human behavior under laws of the type that apply to physical matter.

In spite of this reticence, there is a rhythm in the behavior of living beings which can be teased out and identified if one is sufficiently diligent. Moreover, if a characterization of behavior is to be offered, the axioms that are discovered must be applicable generally. For this reason, the acceptance of some form of determinism seems essential, although it poses considerable psychological repugnance.

Perhaps the contention that behavior is not free can be better understood through an analysis of the connotation of the term *free*. The most general sense in which the term could be used would be that related to sheer caprice. In speaking of such an act by any agent, it would mean uncaused, without referent, going nowhere, and arising from nothing. Of course, this entails the assumption that the free agent referred to has no structure since this would determine some aspect of its movement. It could also have no history, no experience, be frictionless, timeless, beyond entropy or catabolism, irresistible, immutable; in fact, indefinable.

But this is a fruitless endeavor. If anything recognizable has been described, it would be the notion of God as some interpret this form of perfection. Certainly, nothing short of divinity could qualify on the basis, ultimately, of the sheer impossibility of identifying the entity, since the act of describing puts a limit on the freedom to vary that this meaning of free entails. (It should be unnecessary to point out that even a deity, once specified, falls short of freedom on the same grounds.)

What, then, might the term free mean? Apparently, as with so many labels, it represents a continuum which at one extreme means fixed by a simple causal agent (which would represent the only—though impossible—instance in which no freedom existed) and, at the other, the caprice referred to above. In this sense, reference to the freedom of an agent must not only specify, at least implicitly, those agents which are causally related, but also those which are not. The term free indicates that there are some potential causes *to which the individual is not subject*. It means free *of* something—*not* fixed by some specific factor that might have exerted control.

Consider several uses of the concept of freedom and their common interpretations.

- "The wheel revolves *freely*." There is relatively little friction, drag, or control by the axle.
- "Americans are *free*." We elect officials as opposed to their choosing themselves.
- "I am *free* to accompany you." My work, or other factors, do not stop me.
- "I attended the concert *free*." There was no fee involved.

In each instance, although one or more restrictions is removed, at least one remains. If a man states that he is free to breathe or not, consider the problem with the alternatives. He *is free to avoid breathing*. If asked why, then, he fails to decide not to breathe, at least occasionally, any reason that he offers can be shown to be a limitation. For example, if he says that he "wants to live," his freedom to choose has that restriction. Freedom from breathing, means to be required (i.e., determined) to die. One is unable to behave *free of cause*.

There seems no way to resolve the problem of apparent choice without relegating it to the status of a mental construct. This, however, need not minimize its legitimacy, since determinism has been accused of being no less a phenomenological figment. In Chapter 6, the concept of belief as a limiting form of mental knowledge was introduced. The problem of absolute knowledge at the level of mind was demonstrated to be insupportable. Thus, the issues of cause, implication, and necessity, versus chance, freedom, caprice, *causa sui*, etc., all must be settled in terms of the pervasiveness of the argument presented.

Among those who have adopted or concur with the notion of holonic existence, disparate views of freedom have been offered. Weiss contended that determinism is most appropriately applied to holons as wholes (macrodeterminism), with freedom characterizing the parts. He described this phenomenon of indeterminacy of parts in living organisms. In studying a spermium, he demonstrated that while its totality is genetically fixed, its constituency is unpredictable. "The individual mitochondria, for instance, are capriciously different from one another, and yet, the composite structure as a whole is of impressive regularity of over-all design."[45] The principle of organismic theory described in Chapter 1 is, thus, supported in Weiss' concept of stratified determinism. He, in fact, challenged the capacity of science to discover causality at the microlevel. "I submit...that modern science cannot deliver such a picture in good faith, least of all life science."[45]

This view, an impressive and well documented argument, was challenged by Koestler, who took precisely the opposite position.[46] In both *The Ghost in the Machine*[47] and *Janus*[48] Koestler developed the argument that living holonic elements are relatively fixed (determined) at some levels and become increasingly free as a species develops. As new "wholes" emerge, they provide new freedom to solve nature's problems.

> The evolution of life is a splendid game played according to fixed rules which limit its possibilities but leave sufficient scope for virtually limitless variations. The rules are inherent in the basic structure of living matter, the variations are derived from flexible strategies which take advantage of opportunities offered by the forms.[49]

Koestler's rules and strategies are best understood through his analogy with the game of chess, where the rule of movement of the Queen, for example, is: Any number of squares diagonally, vertically, or horizontally. However, these few options provide for a vast range of strategic uses of the potential. Thus, the individual who plays as a beginner is much less "free" than the expert, although both abide by the same code of play. Koestler's argument looks as convincing as Weiss', and the problem would appear to be one of determining which is most persuasive. But strategies need not be seen as free in the sense that rules are parts of them. They may be described as subsets or elements of the rules, which are the wholes in this case. In this sense, creativity in the organic world represents the employment of new (free) materials in new ways to approach a solution that is fixed by the needs of an evolving form of existence.

Since this text is based on the contention that life expanded "downward" into parts, with the first division of a living cell, there are two elements which together describe the one existent which is life—the abiding form—and the transient parts or instances. As a result, the freedom may appear to be in the parts as they combine genetic potential with environmental opportunity. (The original cell or "whole," in the sense that it represents life, does not change in the transition.) Koestler did not agree with this directionality, contending that such alterations are not "down" to parts but "up" to new forms. But the disagreement is unnecessary. A closer look at these positions suggests a third interpretation which both enhances and denies each of them. It is our contention that *freedom and determinism are mutually entailing*, just as are such concepts as tall and short, light and dark. Koestler's freedom is Weiss' determinism.

Confusion about the terms may well be the result of a failure to recognize that they describe situations and events according to arbitrary referents which signify both causality and freedom at the same time, depending on the focus. This, of course, represents a subtle acceptance of determinism since the contention is that all events are (must be) both free (of) and caused (by) which is entailing within the limit of belief. It is, however, no Orwellian interpretation. Freedom and determinism are not equivalent. Rather, any description of an event which includes an element of freedom is, by definition, identifying a determinant.

Consider again the diagrams in Chapter 2 (p. 52). A square made with four coins spaced equally is fixed as a square, whether the coins are pennies or dimes. The parts are free. But the four pennies may be aligned to form a square, a diamond, or a rectangle. In this case, the parts are fixed (as pennies) but the forms they create (new wholes) are free of determination as to shape.

In essence: To be "free of" implies a constraint. All of which individuals are free of is separated from them and locked out of their options. The falling parachutist who is free to continue to fall is, at the same time, constrained from remaining aloft. As freedom (or determinism) "increases," a set of determinants (or freedoms) increases simultaneously. Specific constraints may provide access to desired freedom by increasing options. The rules of play (constraints) of a ball game provide opportunity for optimizing—"freeing up"—playing time, since it is unnecessary after each play to debate the number of players on each side or the number of points needed for a victory. Constraints, in general, represent the organization of elements which, in many cases, allows for a greater number of potential behaviors.

Consider the nature of freedom in pre-life existents. Gravitational constraint represents freedom from centrifugal force. The vaporizing of water represents freedom from the bonding of the hydrogen and oxygen involved. To be determined (forced) by A means to be free of A'. Since a condition of reaction potential is a knowledge state, differing degrees and types of knowledge alter the freedoms of each existent. Conditional terms such as *may*, *might*, and *could* refer only to ignorance of the factors to which a reactor is subject and those of which it is free. Chance, in the sense that an event has no cause or is spontaneous, has no useful application. Caprice may be the ultimate explanation for the occurrence of an event, but if so it has no predictive value. Concepts such as *accident* and *error* are also meaningless at this level, being, in fact, creatures of the mental process.

Living existents possess forms of knowledge (e.g., drive and perception) which change the equation. To be subject to drive states is to be free of entropy. The plant is forced to respond to light signals which free it from decay. It is forced to produce a seed which frees the species from extinction. In Chapter 4, the qualitative difference from pre-life forms was shown to be the emergence of *purpose*. Terms such as *right*, *better*, and *useful* are involved in spite of the fact that each agent of life responds to stimuli within sharply defined limits. The term "may" refers to lack of knowledge of the presence of an active drive or of perceptual integrity in the conscious observer.

Of critical interest is the ostensible freedom that mind brings to the situation. That freedom includes several elements. The first and most significant is the emergence of desire. Organisms that weigh desires in deliberating are free of the mandates of drives. They are not bound by compulsive urges. Beyond this, the very richness of intellectual skill frees the individual from the limitations of simpler neurological systems. But the difference is only one of the degree, quantity, and characteristics of knowledge. The highest forms of life are invested with the ability to respond to a wide variety of signals. Furthermore, there is the qualitative distinction that learning is possible. Docility to potentially purposeful alteration in a short length of time makes it possible to express desires with an almost infinite number of techniques. This does not, however, justify the assumption of complete freedom. At best it represents relative freedom; a greater number of factors of which individuals are free, and which identifies, as a corollary, a greater number of causes to which they are subject.

The notion of choice comes from the fact that wants and costs are weighed as a decision is made on each course of action. But the balance scales are no different in principle than those at the post office. Experience and the contributions of judgment and evaluation have an impact, but these, too, are fixed determinants. The dominant emotion—that emotional state which is most influential—is an inevitable result of the process.

Most important to this text is the classification of behaviors according to their desirability in spite of the constraints involved. Children who have learned to swim have freedom in the water that their nonswimming neighbors have not. This is true of any discipline at any level, and it does not deny causality. Freedom, in neither pigeons nor humans, represents the ability to avoid a response to new data. Rather, it means that such data must be included in the balance sheet. Individuals who are "free" from responsibility to some standard setting entity are vulnerable to (driven by) the demands of intemperate desire. Such freedom is better recognized as licence.

Returning to the classification of decisions, the point was made that the fixed aspect is in relation to the totality of the activity involved. Buying a specified amount of candy is not only free of its parts or instances (individual pieces), but as a whole it is free of all other possible purchases. That is, the decision frees the decider from all possibilities that are excluded in making the choice.

Many other freedom-related concepts take on meaning at the level of mind. *Accident, error, mistake,* and other terms of that nature were said to represent occurrences which violate intention or deliberation. But accident is not an antonym for *cause* or *contingency*, but for *intended*, or *planned*. Within the sphere of cognitive/

affective processing, facts, judgments, emotions, and the decisions based on them can be distinguished in terms of their invariance. At each level cause/effect relationships hold, as do their attendant freedoms.

It is a characteristic of the mental process that deliberations, and thus behaviors, are based not merely on factual data (which is sufficient to action at the pre-mind level) but on judgments regarding the relative merit of such facts. However, at each step, an additional (and independent) set of freedoms (and thus determinants) operates. Facts about the environment are constrained by the perceptual and conceptual systems, in that knowledge of what is externally the case is determined in part by the integrity of these systems. Perceptual judgments are free of facts only to the extent that they may be erroneous, as in estimating distance, while judgments are free of factual data in that they are based on scales which are themselves independent of the facts. Similarly, emotion and desire as facts represent no more than an acceptance of signals as interpreted.

A bowling score of 175 may be considered "good" by one individual and "poor" by another. The fact (175) represents only one determinant. But, no collection of facts fixes the judgment. It is free of any such mandate. Tastes differ, experience intervenes, biological variability plays a role, and the face that is considered beautiful by one observer, may be deemed plain by another.

A degree of indeterminacy is involved although the perceptual facts remain constant. A common example of the freedom of judgments from facts may be observed in the change that takes place in what might be thought of as a "reasonable" expenditure for an item as one's income fluctuates. However, the apparent freedom of judgments is also illusory. An individual can no more "decide" that a bowling score of 175 is "good" than that it is "176." If it is believed to be good, one may say that it is not, but the belief remains. The difference is only one of degree.

Judgments are fixed by the interaction of the facts and the scales against which they are evaluated, remaining constant until new information is added. Emotions, which represent the consideration of specific desires as they relate to perceptual events, are also fixed by the data. The distinction, made earlier, is that an emotion cannot be caused solely by either desire or perceptual information, being thus free of either alone. The observation of two children fighting may cause anguish in one breast while it leads to exultation in another. However, neither observer is free to alter the emotion without additional information.

At the highest level is the capacity to relate situational data to desires in such a way as to optimize their realization. The resulting action is defined as behavior, with the determining factor being the establishment of a netwant/netcost ratio or decision,[50] which results from the consideration of all innate or learned needs, judgments about them, comparisons between them, and the opportunity and capacity to express them. The resulting (dominant) emotion is the outcome of the deliberative process, which is fully fixed by the interacting information.

When all data are considered, behavior is mandatory and occurs according to the formula described above unless new information intervenes, but after which the same determinism applies. However, another restriction has been lifted, since no single input into the process is sufficient to compel action. No fact, no judgment, no emotion can, by itself, force a decision. It is only the comparison between emotional states, which is not a characteristic of any one taken separately, that determines action. The relative freedom of the various levels of mental function is such that each is free of the others but is fixed at its own level. Decisions cannot alter facts, judgments, or emotions; and no single emotion nor its components can fix a decision. Such factors as capacity and opportunity must play their role. It must be clear that decisions are not behaviors *per se*. They are affective experiences that precede and determine behaviors, just as desires are prerequisites to emotion.

Determinism and Responsibility

Premise 5: **Responsibility is an arbitrary, legal concept.** The question of human responsibility is obscured by the fact that determinism represents the obverse of freedom. Since behavior is at once free of certain constraints, and fixed in other dimensions by the same constraining conditions, how shall the actions of each individual be evaluated? To what extent is behavior based on "free will" and, thus, possibly subject to sanction. And should *any* individuals be absolved of responsibility for their actions?

The reason that seems to underlie arguments regarding responsibility is that, in the case of humans, morality is involved. While it is not considered offensive to accept determinism as it describes inorganic action, it becomes distasteful when applied to humans. The moral sense alone should "free" the individual from the blind force of indiscriminate urge. However, given a situation in which one may be tempted to commit an immoral act, the moral sense is apparently not, in many instances, powerful enough to resist the force of the passion. The individual seems to be a victim of uncontrollable coercion. The self, as subject, observes but, apparently, cannot overcome, the self as object.

The fact that emotions control behavior means that they are, at least, an essential element in the process. Whether they are sufficient, though a matter of controversy, does not effect the responsibility of the behaver. Neither caprice, nor the existence of some "transcendent self," that stands between thought and action alters the equation. Responsibility must rest on some mutually acceptable set of rules—on some type of implied "social contract," as has been described by Rousseau,[51] Rawls,[52] Milne,[53] and many others. These philosophers are interested in the moral basis of human action. However, our concern is with the pragmatic aspect of such an arrangement, since ethical propositions are considered by many to be vacuous.[54] Consider several relevant arguments.

- *I am no other than the body I inhabit.* This position (with which we are in agreement), may seem sufficient warrant to place responsibility. We pointed out earlier that morality is an evaluative—not a driving—mechanism. If the self is considered to be no other than its collective parts, responsibility must reside in the totality. Even in a case where moral considerations mandate a particular response, the self is not free of ordinary causal factors. However, if the interactionist view that the self stands outside the mental process is accepted the situation is no different. The monitor of behavioral acts cannot evade responsibility.

Assume that the cause of my failure to arrive at a meeting I was expected to attend was some sort of problem with my car. It would be equally accurate to say "my car wouldn't start," "the carburetor on my car wasn't functioning," or even "the flutter valve on my carburetor was broken." Although the first response is most likely to be employed, all would be accepted as meaningful explanations. What would not be appropriate, would be to excuse the automobile, by assigning the cause to its parts. In so doing we would be denying responsibility in an entity whose *existence we cannot demonstrate*. We would be reifying—then excusing—a mental figment. We could not exempt the (total) car from responsibility, in-so-far as the term responsible means "to be the cause of."[55]

The response to the claim that the compulsion of emotions is no excuse for behavior would be that humans are subject to such contingencies as environmental happenstance, genetic error, circumscribed learning and other factors for which they should not be held accountable. Behavior is regulated by as many external, as internal factors. Placing responsibility is a precipitate undertaking.

- *The function of the moral sense is to identify behavioral propriety.* Like all of the senses, morality is purposive. In Chapter 9 we pointed out that emotions may be classified in terms of whether they include a moral component. Anger for example, represents frustration plus moral evaluation, which places responsibility on some individual or group of individuals believed to be morally accountable. It is, furthermore, deemed inappropriate to apply sanctions to the performance of machines or subhuman forms of life. Thus, we possess an innate instrument which invariably posits responsibility in humans. The only task, it would seem, is to determine *which* human or humans are to be held liable. The determinism inherent in behavior would appear thus to provide no excuse.

The transparency of the fallacy in this argument would seem obvious. However, it has in many forms been an underlying factor in various branches of philosophy. Such issues as the search for synthetic a priori statements, the positivist denial of the meaningfulness of metaphysical statements, and dispute concerning the validity of theological claims for the literal translation of hallowed behavioral commands all fall on the fact that they pursue a chimera.

Two factors introduced earlier in this text provide an explanation for the confusion. The first of these, the limitation of belief, is sufficient in itself to render the pursuit of absolutes futile. The human mind is, by its nature, incompetent to provide answers to any question that calls for absolute or incontrovertible truths. The second problem is based on the fact that while humans possess a moral sense, they are not instinctively aware of where and how it is to be applied. Simpler animals seem, in many instances, to be cognizant of appropriate moral activity, similar to that of a mother who risks her life for her child. However, when an issue such as the morality involved in lying, or otherwise violating a community standard is involved, cognitive skill and depth of understanding make possible many disparate—and often equally reasonable—exceptions. Thus, determinations of responsibility are limited to judgments, with the innate sense of the preciousness of life providing only an imprecise guide to appropriate action. A third argument revolves around the social need for responsible behavior.

- *"Without morality there could be no social life...because morality makes trust possible, and trust is essential for social life."*[56] This, of course, sounds like a pragmatic or utilitarian statement. However, it is based on the same moral presumptions. Not only is there no way to *prove* that social life is superior, but the unfortunate fact is that an individual may be far better off being irresponsible in an otherwise responsible community. The argument, however, does lend itself to application on the grounds that it appeals to many people—including a number of moral philosophers. Bridgman denied that determinism provides an excuse for behavior, contending that "we disregard determinism when dealing with ourselves—we have to disregard it, within reason, in our everyday contact with others.... The insistence that punishment is unjustified can lead only to social catastrophe."[57] Lerner challenged Bridgman's argument. "The suffering of the punished criminal is not balanced by a benefit to the rest of society.... On the contrary, the rest of society suffers further losses from the costs involved in providing justice and keeping the man in prison."[58]

Each argument assumes a monolithic approach. However, despite the fact that accountability resides in the individual—wherever the self is presumed to be located—moral responsibility need not be assigned. To punish an individual who had no legs for not saving someone from a fire would be nonsensical. At the other extreme, to absolve a person whose excuse for stealing from a wealthy person was that "they can afford it" would be equally absurd. However, between these extremes are many acts that are assumed to occur under varying degrees of compulsion. The manic depressive, or the abused person, may or may not be considered subject to sanction. In dealing with such ambiguous situations, an approach may be taken based on the interpretation of freedom as a *relative* concept that was described earlier. Individuals may be deemed subject to sanction to the extent or *degree* that their behavior is believed to be free from internal or external compulsion. To allow that emotions may be warped by illness or contingency, and that actions are based on many—often undiscoverable—causes, would seem a sensible guide to judicial action.

The Role of Aggression

Premise 6: Aggression is a positive feeling and the precursor of potentially positive types of behavior. Aggression is often used as an expression of the desire for control, but it has become synonymous with negative behavior in many instances because of the association of certain acts with the abrogation of the rights and freedom of others. Harriman, defined aggression as "hostility resulting from underlying frustration."[59] Dictionaries and thesauruses have, in general, provided similar definitions.

The psychoanalytic school has used the term with both positive and negative connotations. Erikson's "effective aggression"[60] referred to actions that lead to the overcoming of developmental problems. Fromm suggested that "to be aggressive in its original meaning of 'aggressing' can be defined as moving forward toward a goal without undue hesitation, doubt or fear."[61] These views, though offered by respected analysts, see in the aggressive urge a positive valuable human characteristic. But they are out of step with the mainstream of psychoanalytic thought.

In order to appreciate the nature of aggression, it is first necessary to discriminate between the terms as it describes an affective state and as it characterizes a behavior. As an affect, it may relate either to particular desires or to the general urge to power, safety, and/or belonging. It is a *positive* feeling caused by the anticipation of experiencing a desired outcome.

Some examples are obvious, such as the feeling associated with anticipation of eating a fine meal or of earning money. Others are not, as is the feeling associated with planning to return home after attending a sporting event. Although in the latter instance, there may well be no immediately discernible reason for going home, it is obviously the place that one prefers to be as compared to any other, when all positive and negative aspects are considered. The aggressive feeling is an *anticipatory* emotion, while the feeling that one is satisfying a desire is *consummatory*. Individuals desire to *feel* powerful, safe, and meaningful. To do so, they engage in aggressive behavior.

As a behavioral descriptor, aggression describes deliberate action taken in the interest of meeting any or all desires. Thus, to feel aggressive means to have a positive feeling regarding an action to be taken. To *behave* aggressively (i.e., to aggress) means to act in such a way as to optimize the achievement of a particular state which includes both a positive valence as the environment is controlled, and a negative aspect where others are hindered by such action.

The term we have employed to describe deficit desires is *assertive*. But that term is inappropriate to describe the general feeling as well as the behavior associated with the achievement of needs. Here the term *aggression* is more appropriate, since assertiveness has a connotation among personality theorists that differs significantly from that of aggression.

Assertiveness is, itself, often considered negative. Bosley, for example, defined asserting one's self as "to *compel* [italics added] recognition esp. of one's rights."[62] Its meaning includes the thrusting of the self into situations as a significant person. Assertiveness training, in fact, deals with overcoming one's fears in dealing with others. However, many individual actions are not necessarily directed toward the display of the self. The general desire to control the environment is in no way restricted to, or dependent on, the insinuation of the self into human situations. Building a home, creating a work of art, or even carrying out the trash are aggressive behaviors. Some theorists have argued that characterizing an act as positive or negative can be done by the one toward whom the action is directed. This is tantamount to saying that whether an action is negative is determinable by the opinion of an observer. Such an approach is incompetent to reveal the nature of aggression, hostility, or any other motivational determinant.

The potential for abuse that is inherent in the holarchic structure of life is manifest in much aggressive action. In the process of seeking gratification, aggressive feelings, though positive, often lead to the injury or destruction of others possessed of the same urge. Evolutionists contend that this struggle tends to "balance" a species. And, indeed it may. Survival of the strongest, the most clever, as well as the most prolific, should result in the enhancement of the species. But there is little reason to anticipate such an attractive outcome when the most self- or clique-oriented individuals can gain access to control in a world where power can be carried in a tiny flask of deadly radiation.

In much psychoanalytic literature, reference is made to the cruel and punishing (aggressive) behavior of children. In the famous "Wolf Man" case, the subject was said to be forced by his sister to look at a picture of a wolf and that she was "delighted at his terror."[63] The interpretation offered is that she enjoyed his suffering. This gleeful reaction to sheer destruction is considered part of the human legacy, being related to a hostile urge which must be kept under control. Freud specifically equated aggression with destruction. "Man's natural aggressive instinct, the hostility of each against all and of all against each, opposes [the] programme of civilization. This aggressive instinct is the derivative and the main representation of the death instinct."[64]

Freud contended that unless humans had a destructive (i.e., aggressive) instinct, frustration would lead only to sadness and uneasiness. White, in agreement, stated that: "There is an unacknowledged pleasure in having the power to hurt others and also in using it for that purpose. This is the essential evil in human nature that some optimistic liberals have fought hard not to see."[65]

Many psychoanalysts deny the legitimacy of a desire for destruction and death. However, they do so for a variety of reasons. "Some opponents of Freud's death instinct aim to deny what seems to them a pessimistic outlook on life. Other psychoanalysts do not find that Freud's death instinct leads necessarily to such pessimism. Still others remain noncommittal."[66]

It should be clear that in revoking the principle, they retain no basis for accepting the notion of spontaneous hostility—of hostile feelings that arise without provocation. The concepts of hostility and destructive impulses directed toward conspecifics at an *unconscious* level have no rationale from an evolutionary standpoint, and would certainly provide no useful addition to the human personality from the point of view of a Creator. What service is performed by the incorporation into the information system of a set of forces whose total impact is negative?

Although it is true that the id is often seen as being amoral and of representing drives in the biological sense, the thrust of psychoanalytic literature is in the direction of the destructive characteristics of unexpressed and innate, as well as suppressed, deleterious desires. Munroe, for example, stated:

> All psychoanalytic schools are fully cognizant of hostility as an extremely potent factor in human psychology. No one can look honestly at the delightful baby who bites, hits, and scratches, and smirks as he deliberately "hurts," or at a human race whose record of cruelty appalls us even in our "civilized" times, without drawing the conclusion that sadism, aggression, hostility, whatever *you want to call it*, [italics added] is a prominent feature of the human psyche.[67]

Klein was more specific. She contended that from the middle of the first year "the increase in oral sadism çauses the release of oedipal impulses.... The impulse is then aroused to destroy in various primitive ways the mother's body and its contents."[68] Other analytic writers have been similarly vitriolic. Anna Freud claimed that "infantile sexuality is...not only shown to exist, but to be of a purely *perverse* nature."[69] Menninger added: "The destructive instinct that slumbers within the heart of even the tiny child begins to be apparent as externally directed aggressiveness accompanied by rage almost from the moment of birth."[70] Beyond being destructive, aggression is considered by some to be an unnecessary instinct. Hass suggested:

> Indeed, it has become a disadvantage to us because in a well-ordered society, we lack the opportunity to *work it off* [italics added]. This manifests itself in sporadic moods of aggression or irritability which originate within us and are not occasioned by our environment.[71]

Regarding the analytic contention that the thrust of individual behavior and feeling is toward using the world only for self, the implication that the biological being is prior in significance parallels the view of some existential philosophers. The fact that humans struggle to survive, and in so doing sometimes destroy others, is evidence only of a capacity which represents one facet of existence. The individual who can be characterized as being "against the world," humanity, or life itself, is considered perverted.

The argument that people watch auto races in the hope that a serious accident will occur, or who attend boxing matches because they enjoy the sight of blood, seems to offer incontrovertible evidence that humans are bloodthirsty, cruel, and sadistic animals. This explanation suggests that aggression is evil and occurs either because of genetic error or because cruelty is considered desirable from a species standpoint. Such negative interpretations are unnecessary and inconsistent with a total accounting of the emotions that accompany destruction. In spite of the apparent evidence for an innate urge to carnage, arguments to the contrary which are equally convincing must be considered.

Consistent with the assumption that all desires are positive, aggression must be recognized as a desirable characteristic from the viewpoint of species survival and growth. Much aggressive action is nonthreatening, as when one creates a work of art or tills the soil in order to plant a garden. However, in order to effectively cope with interference with the acquisition of desired commodities, an individual must have the will to destroy that which frustrates, and even to kill when food and other survival needs are hopelessly thwarted.

Although carnivorous animals are described as "predatory" forms of life, there is no difference in principle between the slashing jaws of the shark that rips its victim and the gentle hands of the farmer working a scythe through a field of wheat. Life is taken so that life can go on. Fromm, in fact, suggested that predation, rather than hostile behavior, is perhaps the basis for aggressive feelings.[72] The focus of the individual's attention, however, is on the affective state which accompanies the experience, whereas the focus of genetic attention is on a potential outcome.

Hunting for sport represents one possible perversion, in that although the desire to kill in the interest of acquiring food is positive, the feeling associated with the act often results in killing for its own sake. Wars of aggression as well as individual and group conflict are more accurately understood as unfortunate consequences of the abuse of this necessary and highly desirable capacity.

The destruction of lawn weeds and the neutering of house pets represent examples of killing or crippling that which interferes with the desires of an individual, even where it is not essential to the life of the destroyer. Arguments that plants are without feeling, or of less value than animals, or that cats do not care if they cannot procreate, do not alter the principle that to improve living conditions, killing and other forms of destruction are often practiced and that in each instance the ability to aggress is involved. The question that must be dealt with is whether aggression is normal in all its manifestations.

If a lioness is observed stalking and slaying a zebra, the carnage may be sickening, but the fact does not offend. When a hunter brings home a rabbit or a deer when food is needed, the act is considered positive on the basis of survival needs—although this is often unsupportable in developed societies. When one person destroys another in self-defense, or for the safety or honor of others, or even in certain forms of mercy killing, the behavior is often accepted and on some occasions even lauded. Each of these acts, from the lion's attack to the destruction of an enemy in war, requires the capacity to aggress effectively to the point of annihilating whomever or whatever must be destroyed. The problem that causes concern grows out of the arbitrariness of the decision regarding the point at which violence is necessary. When must killing be done? How shall we determine how much blood should be shed? And whose?

There are any number of people who profess to know the answers to such questions but, above the level of the organism that knows instinctively, proof cannot be provided. It seems, at first glance, that certain guidelines could be established. Self-defense is one example. Others include reaction against tyranny (the French, American, and Russian revolutions were bathed in the "red blood of freedom"), and the defense of one's principles (e.g., religious wars are notoriously brutal). If these forms of aggression are accepted by many as necessary and positive, consider the "evil" forms.

Gangster slayings, rape, murder, and similar behaviors are usually believed to represent violations of propriety which deserve punishment. But putting down tyranny with great force and its attendant cruelty is claimed as appropriate by the tyrant in quelling rebellion. King George was enraged at the American upstarts, just as Ku Klux Klan members resent the "aggressive" Black. What one group considers unacceptable, another finds admirable. Pascal suggested, centuries ago, that "larceny, incest, murder of children and of parents, all have had their place among virtuous actions."[73] Thus, it is inappropriate to draw the conclusion that aggression is a purely negative concept.

There are, in fact, few people who do not desire that aggressive feelings be preserved. What reaction would come from parents if an educational program were proposed that would eliminate all aggression in their children? It is only when aggressive behavior is practiced by someone else, in an unacceptable form, that it is viewed as negative. How then do we explain the ostensive general desire to see violence and death?

As one observes bombs being dropped from an airplane, the fact that people are being killed may be ignored. Victims cannot be seen; the explosion creates a highly stimulating experience. The ten-year-old who is thrilled by atomic explosions does not need death to accompany the mushroom cloud. At the bull ring, people may well desire to see the animal destroyed since they identify with the matador, who becomes fantasized as overcoming a monster. However, most observers experience a concomitant catch in the throat as the slaughter is observed. The emotion associated with success in battle is tempered by an instinctive sense of the value of life. When a battle ends, whether at war or in a prize ring, observers often applaud and experience a compassionate feeling toward the victor who assists a fallen foe to regain his feet.

If a race-car driver is violently injured in a high speed crash, there are feelings of several types involved including the stimulative, which is related to the majestic power of the crashing vehicle, and perhaps a sense of elation which is associated with the desire for power because of the potential elimination of a rival. In addition, however, there is a surge of grief that is based on the moral sense. As the injured driver

MOTIVATION 2: COGNATE FACTORS

is lying in a hospital bed, what percentage of those who attended the show would hope for his death on the operating table? To assume that people attend auto races in the hope that a tragedy may occur is to ignore much relevant data.

Although it is a well-documented fact that animals rarely destroy others except for food, a controversy exists as to whether humans are similarly nondestructive in their natural state. Leakey and Lewin stated that "anyone who argues for inbuilt aggression in Homo Sapiens must see aggression as a universal instinct in the animal kingdom. It is no such thing."[74] Rochlin also denied the animal referent stating that "many have been led to think that the wish to be destructive is a primary condition of existence."[75] On the other hand, Lorenz[76] and other ethologists have contended that the destruction of conspecifics is a natural occurring desire because it is ultimately species profitable. Neither position provides a satisfactory explanation for the conservative use of aggressive capacity in lower forms of life, but Rochlin denied that it should be compared to humans "since [in humans] it satisfies no animal need or craving."[77] Furthermore, he argued, "there is no reservoir of 'aggression' awaiting its inevitable 'discharge'."[77]

Is it reasonable to conclude that humans are possessed of contradictory desires? Given the apparent sense of life's preciousness, why, from an evolutionary standpoint, should individuals so desire to wreak destruction? People are capable of learning that activity of many kinds may become paired with unexpected affective states, as when one learns to enjoy discordant tones or hot peppers. Why, then, is it not more reasonable to assume that the act of destroying, being associated both with power potential and with stimulation at a high level of excitement, becomes, in some instances, a perverted form of pleasure as well as essential to the learning of a technique for gaining control of one's enemies?

Whatever explanation is offered, humans do, at times, kill for pleasure, and often when it is unnecessary. Fromm pointed out that "only man seems to take pleasure in destroying life without any reason or purpose other than that of destroying it."[78] In less intelligent forms of life, aggression, as expressed when competing for a mate, ordinarily terminates short of killing an opponent. One explanation for this may be found in the relatively strong sense of the priority of the group in more primitive species. Humans, in spite of their feeling that life is precious, have a far greater capacity to appreciate the efficacy of totally destroying an enemy as well as an ability to employ much more subtle techniques for accomplishing their end. The development of the intellect and the separation of self from species, as manifested in philosophies that idealize freedom, make possible the greatest deviation from appropriate expression of the aggressive urge.

The fact that desired goods are unavailable in great enough quantity to meet everyone's needs is not sufficient explanation for all destructive behavior, since many activities are related to desires that are relatively easily expressed, or where needs are abundant. Wealthy individuals, in many instances, aggress against those of limited means, which springs from the fact that power is a nonappestatic urge. Aggression, as a feeling associated with power acquisition, may also lead to undesirable behavior when it is paired with potency and stimulation. In the excitement that accompanies growth and self-expression, there is a euphoria which resists interference, and any attempt to frustrate the enjoyment of such experiences is apt to culminate in violence.

The fact that negatively expressed aggression is unavoidable does not pose an insurmountable problem. Death, too, is inevitable, but its arrival can be delayed with considerable success. This is accomplished because of the belief that life is a positive experience. Many are willing to sacrifice some practices (e.g., smoking) in the interest of preserving their existence.

One additional explanation for the destructive urge in humans was offered by Koestler, who argued that those who kill for selfish motives are insignificant as compared to those who destroy for "love of one's tribe, nation, dynasty, church or ideology."[79] He contended that the desire for identification with a group is so powerful that it supersedes reason, self-interest, and even self-preservation. "The trouble with our species is not an overdose of self-asserting *aggression*, but an excess of self-transcending *devotion*."[79] Koestler's thesis was that the cause of much destructive behavior is the desire to belong and to identify with some powerful institution. But the evidence, impressive as it is, does not prove that the desire to identify is destructive. Rather, the self-transcendent urge is often directed inappropriately or is coupled with the experiencing of assertive desires. Devastation can become an admirable practice when it is condoned or encouraged by one's fellows:

> Destruction and cruelty can cause [humans] to feel intense satisfaction; masses of men can suddenly be seized by lust for blood. Individuals and groups may have a character structure that makes them eagerly wait for—or create—situations that permit the expression of destructiveness.[80]

Is this, however, because of love and obligation, or because of the unleashing of the predatory instinct that may no longer be essential to human life? Does the desire for power, unshackled by the moral and rational senses, overtake such individuals? It seems improvident to suggest that self-transcendent interest be eliminated. It would seem far more useful to consider alterations in the world which would result in some different distribution of commodities and values, as well as in the education of people regarding their beliefs about what is and what is not appropriate. Because of the many negative outcomes of aggressive activity, there is much interest in controlling or even eliminating it in specific individuals at particular times. To the contrary, an effective emotional health program would call for the acceptance and *nurturance* of this capacity, with attention being paid to the direction in which it is expressed. Aggression is not a necessary evil, nor synonymous with a desire to destroy, but is a desirable and valuable capacity which, under appropriate conditions, contributes to positive emotional health.

The explanation for human violence and intra-species destruction is that the positive affect associated with overcoming obstacles and the anticipation of desired behaviors becomes generalized across many types of activity, and, at its extreme, with explosive and violent destruction. There is, however, another interpretation of so-called aggression that may provide a clue to its misunderstanding.

Hostility

When the various terms interchangeably used to describe feelings and behaviors that pit the individual against others are considered, it is obvious that several distinct affective states are involved. Munroe's "sadism, aggression, hostility, whatever you want to call it" is an unfortunate example of the tendency of so many authoritative sources to mistakenly equate diverse motivational forms. Since the success which attends effective aggression is likely to represent a threat to others desirous of attaining the same goals, *reactive* emotional states are commonly aroused.

This reactive feeling, which represents a form of anger at the level of preparation for response may be defined as *hostility*, which includes a sense of moral indignation. Although it is a normal emotional state, it is not inevitable and does not arise spontaneously. It functions as a spur to counterattack in the defense of the self against destruction. In spite of the fact that it is classified as an emotion, it is most important to attend to its behavioral manifestation. To act in a hostile or violent manner represents a form of behavior that is clearly different in its motivational components than that based on aggressive interests.

Toch suggested that hostile reactions are the result of a buildup of frustration. "Ultimately, violence arises because some person feels he must resort to a physical act, that a problem he faces calls for a destructive solution."[81] Toch may have added that the committing of a violent act is often accompanied by the experience of added status among peers and in many cases by gaining power and control very quickly. Observing the fear and submissiveness that armed violence creates is apt to be an incentive—for some—to continuing that type of behavior. Especially where frustrating conditions are pervasive. It is important to realize, however, that violence is not the only form that hostility takes. Any action designed to overcome interference by others may be an expression of hostility. A negative comment designed to injure another, even excessive "praise" for a fellow worker may represent behavior of a hostile nature.

Sadism

Sadism is different in its nature from either aggression or hostility. It refers to behavior designed to hurt or destroy because of the positive affect associated with the destructive act or outcome itself. No further goal is involved as is the case with aggression or hostility, and such a desire may be properly considered perverse, since is related to no species essential outcome. The distinction between aggression, hostility, and sadism is shown in Figure 12.1.

Figure 12.1

Characteristics of Aggression, Hostility and Sadism

	Normal	Necessary	Emotion
Aggression	yes	yes	positive
Hostility	yes	no	negative
Sadism	no	no	positive

Because of the psychoanalytic emphasis on sex, sadism has been commonly associated with the desire to mistreat or abuse a sex partner, but this represents no more than one of the many forms in which this misdirected application of a desire is manifested. The genesis of the sadistic impulse is not clearly understood. It may represent an innate desire to inflict injury which is caused by genetic error, or it may result from a learning experience in which some damaging action that occurred without intent to punish caused an intensely stimulating reaction. There is, of course, the possibility that in any instance ostensibly aimless destructive behavior is a primitive response to frustration which persists because it represents the only type of satisfaction (i.e., revenge) that seems available. In such cases, the distinction from hostility lies in the goal, with a hostile action focusing on relief and a recovery of power, while sadistic behaviors are directed toward no such solution.

Since completely different, and even conflicting, desires may be involved, no behavior can, of itself, reveal the underlying motivational force. Aggression, hostility, or sadism may be intended. The identical act may be caused by any of the three anticipatory affective states. The individual who strikes out may be testing the environment (aggression), reacting to a threatening situation (hostility), or anticipating enjoyment when another suffers (sadism). This distinction represents one of the problems with behavioral therapy which abjures historical diagnostic analysis. But, it is just as great a challenge to the theoretical contentions of psychoanalytic writers, whose interpretations are difficult to reconcile with biological evolutionary principles.

Summary

Several issues that grow from the holarchic model must be considered whenever planning intervention strategies. The role of morality and reason, and the limitation of motives to the classes of desire identified earlier, are central. Further, the holarchic motivational model represents an approach to the interpretation of human behavior that accepts its deterministic nature while recognizing its freedom from drive and perceptual compulsion. Whether the "self" is believed to be nothing more than its constituency, or whether it is considered to stand outside and judge the "parliament of emotions," responsibility is a matter of judicial or social judgment.

Aggressive, hostile, and sadistic behavior are defined in terms of their different motivational bases with the positive nature of aggression being emphasized. A further discussion of this interpretation, may be found in a text on the control of assaultive youth, where recommendations are made for the redirection of excessively aggressive behaviors.[82]

The capacity to distinguish between these varied motivational sequences, along with an appreciation of the commonality of human desires and the diversity of their needs, provides a framework for the treatment of behavioral anomaly with attention to the emotional consequences.

Chapter Notes

1. Schachtel (1959)
2. Maslow (1970)
3. *Ibid.*, p. 211
4. White (1959), p. 1
5. *Ibid.*, p. 3
6. Hunt (1977), p. 221
7. Hall (1954), p. 44
8. Hass (1970), p. 69
9. Morris (1974)
10. Kitcher (1982), p. 190
11. Morris (1967), p. 197
12. Ardrey (1970), p. 359
13. *Ibid.*, p. 360
14. *Ibid.*, p. 358
15. Hudson (1970), p. 277
16. Kitcher (1982), p. 200
17. Moore G. E. (1967), p. 323
18. Fichte (1848), p. 488
19. Schopenhauer (1966), p. 368
20. *Ibid.*, p. 369
21. Rogers (1951, 1961)
22. Maslow (1970)
23. Freud (1943), p. 187
24. *Ibid.*, p. 286
25. *Ibid.*, p. 185
26. *Ibid.*, p. 357
27. *Ibid.*, p. 186
28. *Ibid.*, p. 293
29. Masson (1984)
30. While no further discussion of that period in Freud's life will be developed, interested persons should follow both Masson's argument, and the rebuttal offered by Malcolm (1984), who accuses Masson of deliberate distortions.
31. Malcolm (1984)
32. Janis et al. (1969), p. 317
33. Kant quoted in Kemp (1968), p. 57
34. *Ibid.*, p. 315
35. Ellenberger (1958)
36. Cofer & Appley (1967), p. 633
37. Freud (1933), p. 312
38. Moore (1903), p. 115
39. Edwards (1965), p. 6
40. James (1965), p. 35
41. Hume (1938), p. 363
42. *Ibid.*, (1965), p. 7
43. Schlick (1962), p. 150
44. Mill (1865), p. 419
45. Weiss, P. (1969), p. 28
46. Koestler (1978), Personal Communication. In an informal discussion in 1978, Koestler made the point that creativity is a function of the freedom that arises out of the potential inherent in the multitude of ways in which holonic elements may be combined at higher levels of integration.
47. Koestler (1967)
48. Koestler (1978)
49. *Ibid.*, p. 211
50. *Netwant* and *netcost* represent the balance of positive and negative factors that is established during the deliberative process.
51. Rousseau in Grimsley (1972)
52. Rawls (1971)
53. Milne (1987)
54. Ayer and many logical positivists provide powerful arguments that ethical and all other metaphysical propositions are not legitimate, in that they do not meet any test

of verifiability.
55. Flexner (1987, p. 1641), includes among the definitions of responsibility, "chargeable with being the author, cause, or occasion of something." Of course, the "mental figment" that is an automobile does have a synergistic influence.
56. Milne (1987), p. 103
57. Bridgman (1961), p. 156
58. Lerner (1961), p. 194
59. Harriman (1974), p. 7
60. Erikson (1963)
61. Fromm (1973), p. 189
62. Bosley (1979), p. 67
63. Freud, S. (1955), p. 16
64. Freud, S. (1961), p. 122
65. White (1968), p. 208
66. Weiss, E. (1960), p. 248
67. Munroe (1955), p. 623
68. Klein cited in Blum (1953), p. 39
69. Freud, A. (1949), p. 39
70. Menninger (1938), p. 24
71. Hass (1970), p. 76
72. Fromm (1973)
73. Pascal cited in Copleston (1963), p. 170
74. Leakey & Lewin (1977), p. 58
75. Rochlin (1973), p. 342
76. Lorenz (1963)
77. Rochlin (1973), p. 81
78. Fromm (1973), p. 186
79. Koestler (1972a), p. 13
80. *Ibid.*, (1972b), p. 18
81. Toch (1969), p. 5
82. Wonderly & Rosenberg (1987)

Chapter 13
Behavior

The deliberative process represents the weighing of all factors that bear on potential action. It is always and only associated with behavior. However, behavior is not peculiar to the highest forms of life. Though instinctive knowledge may cause unlearned response patterns to occur in the simplest animals, such responses qualify as behavior, to the extent that they are based on even the most primitive choice of options.

Two classes of behavior may be identified. *Instrumental* behavior refers to activity carried out in the interest of achieving a goal for which the behavior represents a cost. *Intrinsic* behavior is activity which is valued for itself. In all instances, deliberate activity is based on a balancing of costs against gains, and the capacity and opportunity to act.

Unique and essential to the motivational sequence is the deliberative process, which represents the balancing of desire, need, and associated costs in order to arrive at a behavioral decision. Once again, it is essential to distinguish between an action and an outcome. The scheme to be employed was introduced in Chapter 6.

A *decision* is a consequence—an affective condition which results from considering or weighing the relative merit of competing behavioral possibilities. But to *decide* is, in one sense, to arrive at a resolution, or conclusion. Here, it also represents a passive state. Unfortunately, each of these terms (decide and decision) is used as an active verb as well.

The term decide is defined by Bosley as, "to arrive at a solution that ends uncertainty."[1] Now, to *arrive* somewhere is not a deliberate behavior but the result of an action—a consequence or state of being. Flexner, however, defined the term *decide* as "to bring...to a decision."[2] Here it appears that an action is being described, which would identify it as some type of performance. But what is intended by a statement such as "I decided to leave the country"? Here the term includes both the action of deliberating or considering the potential options and the arrival at a state of mind that stipulated leaving as the preferred behavior.[3]

The term *decision* is similarly ambiguous. Bosley defined it as "the act or process of deciding."[1] In this usage, it is a noun which describes an action. As with thinking and believing, cognition and affect, and studying and learning, confusion may result from the failure to accurately define the concept. In this section, the term decision and the nonactive sense of the verb "to decide" shall be used to reference the state at which one has arrived rather than to the deliberative process. A proper understanding of the nature of a decision is essential to the appreciation of the degree to which it is appropriate to consider it "free."

Decisions relate only to behaviors. One cannot decide, for example, what to believe, what is preferred, or what is the case. In such instances, a *determination* may be made, which refers to the judgment or analysis of the data under consideration. Similarly, behaviors occur only on the basis of deliberation. Actions that occur spontaneously, or are brought about by irresistible force, do not qualify as behavior under this definition. Behaviors are of many types. Whether one decides to accept the terms of an agreement, to conform to a rule, to respond with the truth or a lie, or not to react at all, a decision is being made about what to *do*. In some instances, of course, stimuli are judged irrelevant or noncompelling. Here the data lead to an interpretation that does not call for any behavior.

Decisions are based on the interplay of emotions which are influenced by such factors as attitude, experience, deprivation level, and perceptual set. This anasynthetic process produces a constantly fluctuating decision state which is the climax of the deliberative process. It compels behavior at some appropriate time. This follows from the fact that a decision is not free of the impact of deliberation, just as one is not free from "hurting" after being struck or of believing (or not) that something is the case, after having thought through an issue.

All decisions result from a comparison of the price that is involved with the satisfaction value of the contemplated behavior. Whether the choice is between positive options (attending the theater or a ball game), negative options (cleaning the basement or mowing the lawn), or some combination, the situation is the same.

Netwant/Netcost

Because many desires are operative and many potential needs are involved in the deliberative process, the expressions *netwant* and *netcost*, introduced in Chapter 12 are used to describe the sequence. The term *want* is employed to reference either an identified need and/or the desire that it is presumed to meet. For the purpose of analysis, the needed experience, situation, or event is often that on which analysis is focused. However, what is considered (needed) in any situation will invariably represent some experience that is believed will meet some *desire*, and that desire can be identified by analysis.

In the deliberative process, an anticipatory emotion (AE) is attached to each potential behavior. Thus, the netwant/netcost formula actually deals with behavior alternatives, and might be expressed as potential behavior A versus potential behaviors B, C, and D. The netwant refers to the sum of the judgments of all positive characteristics of behavior A, while the netcost represents all of the positive aspects of alternate behaviors. The cost, in most instances, is the potential loss associated with rejecting behaviors B, C, and D. In each instance, deliberations involve *beliefs* about the probabilities of various outcomes.

There are several reasons for employing the term net in each instance. First, judgmental and evaluative elements are involved in both the need and cost assessment. Secondly, behavioral considerations cannot be made in isolation. Deliberation *always* involves alternatives. But even here, it is not a simple matter of weighing the positive valence of each. The very notion of cost as the rejection of alternatives means that as any behavior (A) is considered, other behaviors as well as other needs or desires represent counterbalances. When another behavior (B) comes into focus, (A) contributes to the decision as a negative, or cost, element.

This is true of any deliberation, including, for example, the consideration of a palpably negative act. If one is considering whether to rob a bank, the behavior must provide some positive anticipatory emotion. In considering not to do so, the potential gain from the act is experienced as a negative factor weighing against that decision. Obviously, the strength of the negative valence is determined by attitude, opportunity, and a host of factors about which judgments must be made. (Individuals who claim they would never rob a bank must mean either that they could not or have not considered all of the possible circumstances which may encourage such a venture.)

The Deliberative Sequence

The deliberative process, which is a characteristic of all affectively endowed forms of life, represents the interaction of the several forms of judgment where potential action is considered. The factual data are not at issue, since the process only arises in the presence of (factual) desire and (factual) situations or events. One does not *deliberate* about whether X is the case (a judgment or determination may be made), but only about the value of X in terms of Y, where X is a need or desire, Y a potential behavior or outcome, and the relative values are judgments.

The difficulty with accepting the notion that very simple organisms make decisions is based in part on the extent to which human decisions so often lead to maladaptive outcomes, whereas lower animals function more conservatively and under more efficient appestats. Not all living individuals are capable of making decisions that are potentially destructive. In the most primitive deliberative systems, individual and species related experiences are both endowed with powerful affective components. Such individuals, in many instances, find activity in the interest of others as compelling as that which is directed toward personal gain. They are often also effectively monitored appestatically. These limitations on behavior are due to the relatively small step from total external control toward the individual decision making that their genetic equipment provides.

When mediated by emotion, drive becomes a valance (desire) associated with many activities which were automatic in pre-affective life. At the lowest level at which deliberation is a factor, the individual, controlled by appestatic devices and sensing a powerful intuitive guide toward species appropriate acts, performs optimally. The catfish father resists devouring his own fry; the mantis copulates though death attends the slightest error.

In each of these instances, the individual is aware of some form of information which identifies a situation as it relates to desire and, in some cases, of the fact that there is a conflict between competing desires. The mantis, which avoids danger in other situations, risks its life in pursuit of a mate. A decision, however primitive, is made. It is accomplished, in this case, on the basis of data inputs which include competing urges toward copulation and safety. (This is an example of altered desire priority in lower animals, where there is less flexibility in decision-making capacity.)

The result of the deliberative process which weighs emotion against emotion is a class of action which in this text is defined as *behavior*. Motion of a reflexive or taxic nature, where the individual makes no decision, is referred to simply as *activity*. Many writers have used the term *conduct* where deliberation is involved, which restricts its application to human action. Animals are assumed to act on the basis of "instinct" and the term is not considered appropriate to their behavior. Since no such distinction is made in this text, the term conduct shall not be used.

To behave is to act on the basis of deliberation. However, this does not require that such deliberation include the highest cognitive processes, or that responses be learned. It demands only that emotional evaluation be involved. Each decision relates to a behavior in spite of the fact that the behavior may be one as simple as sitting still, or as passive as not speaking. Behavior is based on an expectancy and no analysis of its efficacy can be made in terms of the outcome except as it bears on future behavior. In any instance where an ostensive goal is not achieved, it must be assumed either that the individual expected to succeed, that the "failure" was a satisfactory expectancy, or that for the behaver the result does not represent a failure. The distinction between these three alternatives is critical to the development of effective therapeutic intervention.

Each behavioral element is comprised of factual data about which the individual has varying degrees of information. Odds against success, for example, are factual although they may not be known precisely. Whether a fact relates to need or cost, judgments are made. Beyond those judgments related to measurement (e.g., estimates), are those that relate facts to values. Reason and morality, for example, have been shown to represent judgmental scales against which each fact is evaluated. How dangerous a behavior may be is one aspect of a behavior, while the seriousness of the social or legal consequences of failure assay the action on other continua.

Behavior Classes

It is essential that a determination be made of the level at which a behavior is to be identified. Teaching is a behavior whether it refers to what one does occasionally or habitually, or whether it is what one is at any moment actively doing. It may be analyzed into its components (lecturing, examining) or synthesized into a general lifestyle. There is no "correct" point at which to specify what is intended. There is, however, a difference to the clinician in terms of diagnostic efficiency, and for this reason several levels of behavior must be distinguished.

- *Behavioral incident*: A single behavioral action with its motivational genesis and its resolution (e.g., throwing a ball).
- *Behavior sequence:* A series of behavioral incidents which includes all related elements as they focus on some desired action or outcome, as well as instrumental behavior where relevant. The dominant emotion is one of anticipated stimulus accretion, relaxation, or relief (e.g., playing a ball game).
- *Behavior pattern:* Typical, but not continuous, actions performed to meet various desires. It represents a mode of operating on the environment. One gambles, teaches, golfs, pursues power. The individual may employ distinct styles in different situations, and a life is comprised of many patterns. The term also describes styles or "habits" (e.g., John is typically late for appointments; Harry is trustworthy).
- *Intrinsic behavior*: Action which is valued for itself. The behavior is satisfying in the performance, and no specific outcome is essential to its execution. Playing tennis, making love, or reading a novel may be examples. When in focus, each may represent a complete behavior sequence.
- *Instrumental behavior*: Deliberate action performed in order to facilitate another action or outcome. Taking medicine or washing dishes may qualify. The concept of *satisfaction* was introduced in Chapter 9 to define this type of behavior. It refers to the willingness of an individual to perform actions that, in themselves, are not desired. Such actions may consume a great proportion of available energy, in which case general depression is apt to be involved. To detest one's job or any activity that must be accomplished regularly creates a pernicious situation. The fact that so many people live in a state of perpetual discomfort is testimony to the strength of their will. The critical issue is that to behave in a way that is not in itself desirable represents a willingness to

perform that must presage a situation which is in itself desirable. The value associated with an instrumental action is some intrinsic need, while the behavior itself is reckoned as a cost in that sequence.

If an outcome is desired but the behavior is not, it cannot qualify as intrinsic. However, intrinsic behavior may include many actions that would be instrumental under other circumstances, and this peculiarity must be understood. The bride who resented cooking in her mother's home may be thrilled with every step in the preparation of a honeymoon breakfast. A golfer may enjoy each aspect of the process, from climbing demanding hills to searching for balls that have strayed from the fairway. Such elements form unanalyzable components of the sequence which carries the emotional flavor. The desirability of the total experience swallows up trivial negative feelings.

In determining whether a behavior is intrinsic, it is insufficient to consider simply whether it would otherwise be indulged, since in other settings the behavior (e.g., cooking) may be negative. The appropriate procedure is to determine whether it is negative or positive in the situation under analysis. The fact that one is delighted to pay a small price for a sweater does not legitimize that behavior (paying) as intrinsic unless the sheer enjoyment of spending is the motivating factor.

In many instances, it is desirable to transform an instrumental behavior (cost) into an intrinsic one (need). This is the only type of cost that can be so altered. Other beliefs may add to needs by being so high that a particular need becomes appropriate. A very tall man, for example, may consider professional basketball as a career. For shorter men, costs are supplemented until they reach a point beyond which the need value of such an enterprise is not sufficient to action. Height, per se, however, does not create a desire, nor does it represent a need. It merely represents a characteristic (capacity) that allows differentially for the emergence of a behavior as a need.

Since all behavior involves some cost, the distinction between an intrinsic behavior and a total sequence may seem to be simply a matter of degree. However, the distinction is vital. In many cases it would be contentious to consider parts of an action as behaviors in themselves, as in the movement of one's hand toward the pocket to grasp a package of cigarettes in order to select one. It is sufficient in such instances to focus on the behavior of "smoking a cigarette." However, if the person desired a cigarette so badly that he or she asked a stranger for one, considerable embarrassment may be experienced. Such action should be dealt with as an instrumental aspect of the total sequence.

Organisms capable of learning but not capable of evaluating stimuli, as well as organisms with only perceptual information (i.e., without any desire referent), cannot behave. They may respond to a stimulus, but if they do so, the action must be described as taxic or reflexive. If the response pattern is complex, it may be called instinctive. However, the appropriate use of that term is its application to a situation where no learning is involved, or to that aspect of the response that is genetically rigid.

Instinctive Knowledge and Instinctive Behavior

Unlearned behavior which represents a transitional state between tropisms and learned responses is sometimes referred to as *instinctive*. Complex, unlearned response patterns qualify as instinctive under this definition, but a clear understanding of the limitation of the concept is essential.

As species develop from plant to animal forms and decision-making begins its descent into the phenotype, the physiological link between stimulus and response is gradually altered. The simplest interaction is based on a system which binds affective reaction directly to specific stimuli and requires a minimum of judgment. At this level, motor patterns are often completely specified on the basis of genetic rather than phenotypic learning. The term instinct has been applied to this transition in each of its manifestations.

In the 19th century instincts were considered to be closely related to reflexes. "To compare instincts with reflexive action...had become a commonplace."[4] Early American psychologists such as McDougall[5] took the position that instinct is that which *causes* individuals to attend to certain objects or events, representing a psychophysical disposition toward perceiving. In this sense, the relationship to the reflex was preserved. Since the disposition is innate, however, it must be related to information that has value to the species. When birds perceive a change in weather, they sense that they "should" fly in some direction. Whether the information is provided through a force which makes them fly or a suggestion which advises them to go was not made clear.

This was a rather loose use of the term and criticism came from those who saw in instinct a "mysterious agent" explanation. By the simple application of a label to a puzzling concept, the process was offered as scientifically respectable. Those who were concerned with clarifying the issue intended that the identification of the process lead to further study. However, the stimulus-affect association and the unlearned motor pattern were soon confused. Activity was said to be instinctive where it did not involve learning either of any quality of a stimulus (e.g., as dangerous) or of the method by which the desired affective state could be achieved.

Not all psychologists believe that the concept of instinct is any longer of scientific value. Scott argued that "while the concept of instinct was a very useful one in an earlier period of scientific thought, it was in fact a collective name for a whole array of unknown evolutionary, developmental, physiological and behavioral mechanisms."[6] We believe, however, that an understanding of behaviors described as instinctive, as well as the notion of instinctive *knowledge* are essential to any type of behavioral analysis.

Current views of instinct stress the behavioral aspect with the most critical feature being that the activity is not based on reason. To qualify as instinctive, an action must be unlearned, adaptive, and common to most members of a species. An instinct is, quite specifically, "a set of behavior patterns which contribute to a common function (reproduction, feeding) which are shared by all members of a species and which develop in the absence of conventional learning or practice."[7] Under this interpretation, the behavior or reaction is emphasized and the cause is unspecified.

Hebb[8] contended that instinctive behavior is that in which innate factors are dominant. He did not separate it from learning because he sought a common neural principle for both. Instinctive behavior, he said, is that "in which the motor pattern is variable, but with an end result that is predictable from a knowledge of the species."[9] However, even the predictability of results was denied special significance because such behavior, varying with environmental opportunity for expression, "is still continually under sensory influence."[10] Nest building in rats was explained as "the simple result of a disturbed temperature control,"[11] which implied that some signal in the individual leads to a complex act resulting in a broadly predictable outcome.

Morgan argued that the instinct concept confuses "behavior that is impulsive or automatic with behavior that is inherited or unlearned."[12] Part of the problem stems from the fact that many complex unlearned responses do not occur until some level of maturation is reached, since they depend on the development of certain anatomical and/or neurological mechanisms. For this reason, it is difficult to separate learned behavior from that which occurs spontaneously or instinctively at the presentation of a stimulus. The critical distinction is not between behaviors, but between the causes of a behavior and the resulting activity.

A second source of confusion comes from the various uses of the term *learning*. Learning that an experience results in an affect (eating cake causes a pleasurable feeling), and learning to play golf result in different kinds of knowledge. In the latter, response plasticity is required which involves both neural and muscular potential, while the former requires only the ability to recognize a relationship. When theorists discuss the learning/instinct issue, both types of learning are involved and the distinction is not always made clear.

Ethologists have used the term instinct both as a stereotyped response pattern of the reflex type and as a broader concept embracing the stimulus seeking as well as the consummatory aspects of behavior. Stimulus-seeking is ostensibly a different activity than experiencing an emotion when a stimulus is encountered. Instincts, such as that for reproductive activity, are shown to be hierarchical with each level having greater variability, although the outcome of the behavior is fixed.

Tinbergen[13] suggested that each major instinct is expressed through subinstincts and what ethologists refer to as "appetitive" behaviors. The function of such appetitive activity, they say, is to "bridge the gap between the energized organism and the particular environment."[14] Since environments vary while instinct is constant, it is argued that behavioral variation can provide for essential adjustments.

The fact that ethologists describe instinctive activity in terms of a neural hierarchy, whereas instinct was seen earlier as being associated with a single neural center, seems to meet the requirement of objectivity that science demands. This explanation, however, still includes both the causal and the consummatory aspects.

On the one hand, the presence of certain environmental and/or drive determinants are assumed to be sufficient to cause the organism to respond. In this sense, the term relates to the stimulus or informational aspect of the activity.

But the response aspect is also included. The individual may be so programmed that certain visual stimuli (e.g., shapes) will trigger or release specific types of response. If the response is stereotyped, it, too, is described as instinctive. This capacity seems to be minimal in humans and is one of the reasons for separating human from animal behavior. However, the distinction is spurious. If an individual automatically responds to some pattern of stimulation, the action is no different than that of plants when water is encountered, except that the receptors in the latter case are not visual or olfactory.

The migrating bird is said to respond to glandular alteration which is a pattern in still another form. In all cases, some form of external stimulation in the presence of a specific desire (where the individual seeks the stimulus) or desire in the presence of external stimulation (where the organism responds when a pattern is presented) represents the initiation of a behavioral sequence.

But this is also true in reflexive or taxic activity, where the reaction occurs as a direct result of stimulation without intervention by an evaluative system. The reacting plant, for example, possesses only those systems which say "respond" or "don't respond" and terms such as reflex are used to describe such activity. Holarchic theory allows that such a situation can be envisioned so long as one does not infer with the term reflex a microdeterminacy which cannot be justified by the evidence. Reflexes, such as sneezing, in higher organisms, may appear to represent a simple response. However, even the sneezing apparatus may employ any of several strategies in reacting to initiating stimuli.

Although an individual may be programmed to react to certain stimuli, the way in which the activity is carried out may vary widely, through the complex machinations of the neural hierarchy. This does not, however, justify elimination of the role of emotion. The inadequacy of the explanation is demonstrated every time an individual does not respond as anticipated. The chick that usually pecks at kernels of corn may not do so as competing stimuli (e.g., threat) are introduced.

We shall relate instinct to emotion and activity on an anticipatory-consummatory continuum. First, it is essential that we reconsider the process that we referred to earlier in the case of the patio light that automatically illuminates at dusk. The ability to respond to photoelectric stimulation in a specific way resides only in certain entities. When we suggested that the light knows when to go on, we meant that, given the proper stimulation, it must respond. Only this light (and no other) goes on in response to this particular signal, and we must accept the implication that the capacity to respond is a characteristic which is unique to that type of fixture. By analogy, only plants and not animals are capable of photosynthesis and only certain organisms have the ability to regulate body temperature.

The living organism, like the patio light, is so constructed as to be capable of certain responses. Something beyond the organism, whether it is explained as the result of random mutation or species purpose, endows the individual with that capacity. The observation that many organisms appear to act according to some predetermined plan—even when responses are not reflexive—led to the adoption of the term instinct. To the extent that it refers to super-individual control, it is indeed a useful concept. However, as has been indicated, it includes acts forced by the genetic pattern, in the presence of a specific environmental opportunity.

If instinct is defined as an inborn tendency to act in the same way that other members of the species ordinarily do, the action of a plant in turning toward the sun would qualify as an instinct. But the term is also used to describe the rushing of salmon up river, the care of the young by a mother and even "a natural or *acquired* [italics added] tendency...as an instinct for doing the right thing."[15] In the last instance, the term is often applied to what has been learned. Small wonder the distaste for the term and its low status among scientists.

In order to identify activity as it relates to these several processes, we shall once again employ the information system model. When a stimulus encounters a body that lacks any form of knowledge that would call for a response, it is simply interrupted or passes through the entity. When it meets a receptor in a living organism that is attuned to react immediately, the resulting activity is considered reflexive, or taxic. At the level of plants and simple animals, an energized drive in the presence of an appropriate stimulus, demands such a reaction. No decision is made regarding whether or not to respond to such stimulation, which may come in such forms as electromagnetic vibration or pressure.

Since the reaction is related to stimulus intensity, the only function involved would be that of measurement. The requirement for a response, insofar as the environmental aspect is concerned, involves only the presence of some amount or degree of stimulation. The nature of measurement is not as objective as positivists might insist, however, since size and other stimulus characteristics are relative both to other entities and to the perceiving organism.

The confusion caused by the failure to recognize the limitation of activity based only on perceptual and drive information systems is observed in all types of literature. In his text *The Mind*,[16] Wilson defined taxis as an activity that must occur in the presence of external stimulation. Then he stated that paramecia move "to the more *comfortable* [italics added] end of a tank of cold water."[17] The implication of a desired state and thus decision-making in the organism belies the taxic label. Either the paramecium *must* move toward a specific temperature, in which case its comfort is not a factor, or the activity is not taxic.

We are more interested in this tendency to explain behaviors with only perceptual and drive referents in the activity of higher animals. The practice of caring for the newborn, which occurs in so many forms of life, is called instinctive, but the impression given is that some form of activity must follow specific stimuli. The sheer presence of a perceived threat, for example, must result in some automatic response.

This is a more flagrant overestimation of the contribution of the perceptual and drive systems which leads to a predetermined response only at the taxic level.

When an organism judges a situation and makes a decision as to whether or not it will respond, any activity which results from a drive belongs to another class. Because learning, maturation, and other factors complicate its manifestations, it seems appropriate to refer to such activity as being on a continuum which includes reactions not involved in reflexes and which may be thought of as instinctive. Insofar as the reference here is to the interpretation of a signal, the focus is on the affective reaction to the stimulus, rather than on the motor response. This represents the first phase of the sequence and it cannot be derived from the most complex reflex chain.

If the mother peahen believes that an intruder is dangerous, either such knowledge has come from an emotionally judged earlier experience, or the intrusion of some stimulus on the sensory field has become a genetically developed signal which triggers an emotion that recommends action. In either instance, the presentation of sensory data represents only information regarding the existence of some external event. Its judgment (e.g., as dangerous) is a mental interpretation. The interpretive mechanism is a characteristic of the affective system whether the specific response is genetically fixed or not.

At the most primitive levels, desires are relatively strong as compared to the perceptual information system. The individual feels an urge to indulge certain activities and is often unaware of alternatives. The pigeon in the Skinner box is aware of a positive feeling when eating is anticipated or accomplished. Furthermore, it cannot read the evening paper or play billiards. Activity is limited essentially to food acquisition, sexual activity, and escape from threatening situations. Even at this level, considerable conflict can be generated, but there is little doubt that the bird is functioning at a simple level of behavioral response. Few competing desires interfere with movement toward satiation of hunger, thirst, or sex drives, and the method by which the pigeon can be reinforced is limited. The fact that pigeons may learn to use their talons to take food and are thus trainable does not alter the fact that their typical response method is highly predictable.

When attention is turned to activity resulting from an evaluation of a stimulus, the problem involves determining which behaviors to identify as instinctive. The distinction on which most of the literature on instinctive behavior rests is on the complexity of certain unlearned activity which removes it from the reflex category. The spider, under optimal conditions, spins a very elaborate and predictable web, and the building of this food catcher is called *instinctive*.

The failure of humans to exhibit such a variety of complex unlearned responses has resulted in the erroneous notion of their rationality. A more accurate interpretation would be that more sophisticated organisms are gradually freed from stereotyped reactions as the genetic pattern allows for learning and experience to play a role. The fact that humans are the most capable of such learning to date, does not legitimize the argument that their responses are based essentially on reason, since the emotional system plays the same part in humans as in the house cat, and human behavior is subject to the same interpretation. Lower animals seem more closely tied to the stimulus-response pattern, in that predetermined cues direct them to much invariant and unlearned activity. This, however, represents only the limited plasticity of the various information processing systems.

The hierarchy of emotional potential begins with the introduction into the individual of a signal system that identifies an external situation or event as related to some desire. Since the simplest forms of life respond only to stimuli which are immediately present, the most rudimentary relationship between a stimulus and an affect would probably be a tactile experience. The performance of a behavior would result in a positive or negative feeling which has been identified as a consummatory emotion (CE).

Because the occurrence of such affects is dependent on the accident of opportunity, their value is limited and it is difficult to isolate dependable examples of action patterns that include only a consummatory emotion. We can, of course, find many instances of individuals at all evolutionary levels who, on encountering some experience, seek its repetition, as when a cat encourages having its head scratched, after realizing how positive it feels. In such cases, however, it is more likely that the scratching experience is simply one of many ways in which the desire for stimulation might be satisfied.

For such an affect to be of value, the individual must be capable of learning, at least to the extent that the experience and the affect can be intellectually related. Although physical pain requires that it be experienced if its impact is to be known, it would be of no value unless, in future, similar experiences might be avoided. In the same way, the positive affects associated with the taste of food and the ecstasy of sexual behavior must be guides to future action, and thus subject to learning if they are to be useful.

There is, however, an alternative technique which could provide solutions to the same problems with relatively little learning involved. It would require that an affective state be associated with an experience before it occurred. If an organism could experience a feeling upon becoming aware of a future event, it would be possible to approach or avoid the stimulus as desired without experience. Reflexes may operate in an anticipatory manner, but without the benefit of internal affective mediation. The stimulus in this case is sufficient to a response. However, at a higher level the stimulus triggers only an appropriate feeling, which is designed to recommend a salutary response. Since it occurs in the form of an affect, this feeling has been identified as an anticipatory emotion (AE).

Whenever the presentation of a stimulus not previously experienced, or cognitively unrelated to other previous experience, causes an anticipatory emotion, the individual may be considered to have *instinctive knowledge*. This refers to knowledge which associates a stimulus with an emotion for the purpose of encouraging a response, where the stimulus has been learned (in the gene pool) to have certain characteristics.

BEHAVIOR

The predator may be avoided because individuals capable of the appropriate emotional reaction have attempted to escape and the species has learned the value of escape behavior. In the same way, the association of positive emotions with specific characteristics of appropriate objects leads to the ability to recognize nutritious food and fecund sex partners. Just as with the CE the method represents only a suggestion or guide to action as opposed to a taxic response, and the activity which results is based on a decision made by the individual.

Instinctive knowledge, as well as instinctive behavior is essentially unalterable in the simplest organisms. Learning does not occur. At higher levels, there is some ability to modify beliefs as when animals come to accept natural enemies with a minimum of fear.

The increasing complexity of response patterns is exemplified in the following (highly oversimplified) illustration:

1. **Taxis (pre-affective activity)**

    A stimulus in the presence of a drive will cause a response.
    $$S \longrightarrow (d^n) \longrightarrow R$$
    Example: The touch of a finger will cause many members of the mimosa plant family to close their leaves.

2. **Affective continuum (mind)**

    a. A previously unexperienced stimulus in the presence of a desire will cause an anticipatory affect (emotion) which, depending on judgmental consideration, may cause an unlearned response, and perhaps a consummatory emotion.

    $$US \longrightarrow (d^n) \longrightarrow mind\ (AE) \longrightarrow UR \longrightarrow CE\ (?)$$

    Example: the *musca domestica*, or house fly, and sex consideration.
    $$Female \longrightarrow sex \longrightarrow positive\ affect \longrightarrow sexual\ activity \longrightarrow CE\ (?)$$

    The male fly, on seeing (and perhaps recognizing the sex pheromone of) a female, receives a signal which is dependent on the sex drive that suggests the desirability of sexual activity, which is present in the motor pattern as an unlearned response. The male considers such factors as hunger and danger which represents competing urges. If the sex urge is sufficiently powerful to outweigh other desires, instinctive behavior occurs. The CE need not play any role since the AE may be sufficient to trigger repetition of the act. This insect knows the appropriate target of his ardor. The affect is associated directly with the type of individual with whom mating will result in the species desired outcome. If no competing desire is perceived, the cognitive aspect is limited to cost (e.g., energy output) consideration.

b. A previously unexperienced stimulus, in the presence of a desire (dn), will cause an anticipatory emotion which, depending on judgmental consideration, will result in a choice between unlearned behaviors and, in some instances, a consummatory emotion (CE) will be experienced.

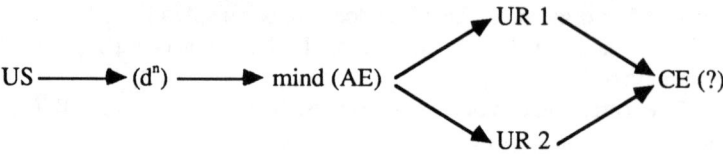

Example: the killdeer and self-sacrifice.

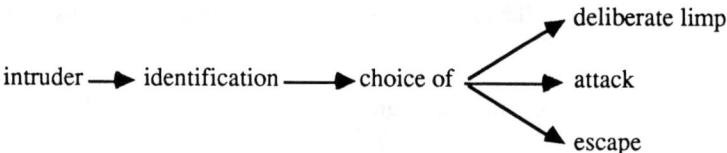

The appearance of an intruder, in the presence of a desire (and perhaps a sense of obligation) to protect the young, causes an emotional evaluation which, in conjunction with cognitive consideration of the implicatory type, results in one of several responses, of which none requires learning. The CE may operate to suggest similar future activity. The killdeer experiences a positive feeling regarding the saving of its young on the basis of an emotion that precedes or accompanies the behavior. (There is no reason to assume that the bird understands why it acts as it does.) At this level, the moral quality of an act is ascertainable. The fly knows which *specific* behavior is appropriate. (Both the activity and the target are specified.) The killdeer, by comparison, knows only what *types* of behavior are appropriate.

c. A previously experienced stimulus, in the presence of a desire (dn), will cause an anticipatory emotion, which, depending on judgmental consideration, may result in the selection of an appropriate unlearned behavior in order to experience some consummatory emotion.

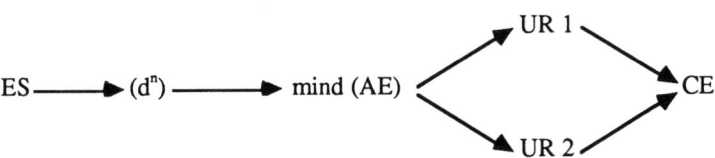

Example: scratching a cat's head.

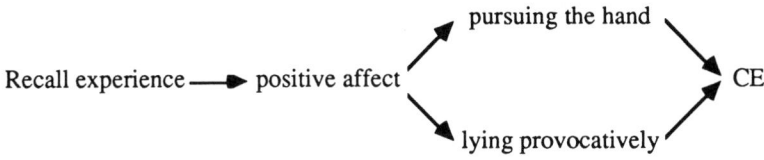

If a cat's head is scratched, it experiences a positive affect which leads to the seeking of similar experiences in the future. The method of attempting to repeat the experience may include activities that are relatively rigid, such as rubbing the head against someone's hand, or lying in a provocative position.

Learned Behavior

Next, we approach the level of behavior that is not instinctive and which characterizes much human activity. It provides an insight into the problem of why higher animals must learn what simple organisms know on the basis of instinctive knowledge. The progression that begins with instinctive knowledge, where emotional reactions are associated with a highly specific stimulus, develops to a stage where cognitive sophistication and other factors make the connection difficult, if not impossible.

d. A previously experienced stimulus, in the presence of a desire, will cause an anticipatory emotion which, depending on judgmental consideration, may result in the selection of some appropriate learned behavior in the hope of experiencing some consummatory emotion.

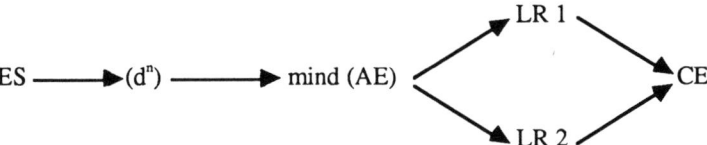

Some theorists argue that sophisticated organisms are qualitatively different because they must learn many behaviors. Responses that appear to be instinctive have been shown to be dependent on experience. The work of Reiss[18] which showed that rats deprived of certain experiences did not build nests at the appropriate time, seems to support this viewpoint. However, because it can be caused to malfunction, the essentiality of an evaluative mechanism that is designed to ensure efficient behavior must not be overlooked. The deprived rats missed the appropriate cues, but this does not prove that instinctive patterns did not exist, only that they could be distorted, or even fail to be manifested.

Simple forms of animal life operate relatively directly in terms of what the environment offers at face value. As we move up the perceptual scale, where cognition becomes increasingly involved, competition for satiation between drives becomes a factor. The chimpanzee who works for chips that can be inserted in a food vending machine also learns to use them for alternative rewards such as cigarettes or even more subtle payoffs. Motives related to sheer physical contact become significant competitors as the individual develops the capacity to recognize how to attend to them. Behavior moves away from immediate attention to survival and growth motivators and complex patterns of response are developed. In ethological terms, the levels of the subinstinct hierarchy become increasingly complex. In highly evolved organisms, this procedure results in many puzzling situations. Monkeys have to learn copulation techniques, and humans have to be taught to care for their young.

These occurrences are the result of cognitive sophistication combined with delayed maturation which allows for the development of such complex learning repertoires that by the time the individual reaches the age at which the appropriate desire matures, its expression must be learned in competition with many already ingrained habit patterns. For example, by the time sex becomes relevant, individuals have already learned how to get food, to protect themselves, and to satisfy the growth urge to some degree. Higher organisms have also learned that contact motivators have potentiality for positive and immediate emotional gratification.

The sensing of this new (sexual) desire may be insufficient, in spite of its energy level, to guarantee that it will be expressed efficiently. The individual has to learn how, as well as when and where, such behavior may be indulged. A behavior which would occur as a result of mere exposure to a stimulus in simple life forms requires learning as the organism becomes more complex. The sheer docility of the individual, in that learning ability modifies reaction potential, contributes to the problem.

As the cognitive information system becomes more sophisticated, the capacity of a simple cue to evoke a response is vitiated. Although the reception of a stimulus may still trigger an affect, it is fed through such an intricate intellectual maze that associations with other stimuli are apt to distort the message. The sight of an ordinarily desirable food may recall a distasteful experience and the net affect may be so negative that it cannot be eaten.

Simple organisms cannot make such connections, and may not even associate the positive feeling that attends the presence of a stimulus with the behavioral or consummatory affect. The reason that a housefly does not masturbate or practice other perverted forms of sexual behavior is because the sex act is tied to the opposite sex member by cues that specify the appropriate object. Further, the fly does not learn to make the connection through experience.

In humans, the reaction potential is quite different. Children, who without education may feel a positive emotion on the anticipation of overcoming a rival, are taught in some societies that such behavior is undesirable. Since children also have a desire for belonging, the resulting affect may cause a diminution of interest in aggressive behavior. However, this does not provide evidence that there is no desire for power. It represents only the ability for learning to modify or suppress the expression of particular desires.

Theories that suggest that all men have latent homosexual tendencies are similarly based on a bizarre interpretation of this evolutionary phenomenon. Sexual interest is cathected onto a series of potential individuals during the development of the personality as suggested earlier. However, the selection of a like-sex mate is not dependent on an innate perversion of interest except where genetic error leads to the possession of distorted information systems. For others, the cues associated with appropriate partners are either masked by convention (sex-linked smells are passé in many cultures!), or other characteristics of a potential sex partner are of greater attraction at the time that sexual imprinting occurs. Males who admire strength and females who seek tenderness may well find those characteristics more predominant in members of their own sex. Such behavior does not destroy the argument that sexuality includes a proper partner in spite of the gay liberationist protest. (The fact that young men raised on farms sometimes copulate with animals does not legitimize the contention that there is a genetic sheep interest, nor is the glove fetishist expressing an innate attraction to particular clothing.)

The sense of malaise on impending danger, or the confidence that things will go well that have been lightly ascribed to "intuition" are, in fact, evidence for the remnants of an ability to relate a specific stimulus to an affect. When a woman says that she has an intuitive feeling about a situation, she may well be experiencing a form of instinctive knowledge that has been buried under the avalanche of experiences that have altered her interpretation of the cue. The fact that females are more often considered to have intuitive reactions may be legitimately based on a difference from males, who some researchers suggest, have lost that facility.[19]

Decision-making has, as its principal function, the initiation of behavior. Although decisions are often made which require no immediate action, or even mandate that no action be taken, they represent the drawing of conclusions which are binding on any behavioral situation that may arise. We are concerned principally with behavior which commonly follows a decision immediately, and shall describe some of the parameters of deliberate activity.

Characteristics of Behavior

In identifying the elements of a behavioral episode, we shall refer to those factors which make possible movement toward *something*. We have not as yet indicated what that something may be. Ostensibly, it refers to some physical experience such as eating or smoking. However, we cannot analyze behavior in this way without risking assumptions that will lead to misinterpretation.

An obvious example of the problem would be to confuse behavior which leads to eating in the case of: (a) a starving person; (b) a satiated person interested in an attractive dessert; (c) a frustrated person seeking security; (d) a bored person who wants to fill time; and (e) a person preparing for a normal meal. In each instance, the anticipation of the act of eating is associated with a different type of emotional experience. These acts are contemplated on the basis of such emotions as fear, anxiety, depression, boredom, or desperation. A change in emotional state or the continuation of a desired affect with a broad range of potentiality is sought. The factor which is of significance is movement along the affective scale. Behavior is based on a decision to maintain or alter an emotional state and it is this goal that must be determined if behavior is to be understood.

Since behavior represents a valance dependent on many potential inputs, it is obviously erroneous to claim that an individual's desires can be determined solely by an observed behavior. It is the very nature of decision-making that some desires must be excluded from expression. It is, furthermore, a peculiarity of behavior that it represents conflict in many instances. In such cases, it is only a resolution in the sense that some desire has been overridden. In other situations, although there may appear to be no conflict involved, the decision to act is made only in terms of the relative quiescence of alternatives.

The deliberative process peaks at the crest of dominant emotions (the sequential awareness of anticipatory emotions which fluctuate with new data). Thus, the essential contribution of a final cause represents a critical distinction between the decision-making individual and all other forms of existence, including pre-mind life forms. Reflex, taxis, and habit, insofar as the functioning organism is concerned, may be explained by formal, efficient, and material causes alone. However, in the case of decisions, the future, as represented in the anticipatory affect, plays an essential role. While it is true that the anticipatory affect is either triggered by instinctive knowledge or based on the recollection of previous experience, its role in the deliberative process is related to potential future behavior.

In order to adequately define a behavior, it is essential that the outcome that is desired be fully identified. We spoke earlier of the behavior of a child on being called to dinner and the question of why he sat down in the chair. Kagan[20] argued that the child's action in sitting was determined by its appropriateness. Since such an explanation rules out the possibility of exception (appropriateness is offered as a sufficient condition which, Kagan assumed, is not motivational), it does not adequately explain what occurs. The child may have found the experience positive, or as a price to be paid to avoid punishment. A total behavioral sequence must be distinguished from instrumental behavior as well as from techniques that may be automatic or habituated.

Behavior is based on the interaction of perceptual/cognitive data and desire/need levels. In considering the contribution of the cognitive aspect in more detail, we see that it deals only with data such as "a healthy condition will be more likely attained if this unpleasant medicine is taken." It cannot deal with "a healthy condition is desirable."

We cannot explain the taking of medicine on the basis of individuals' wanting it. However, if we try to prohibit them from using it, they may insist on the premise that they want to take it so that they will get well. In this case, the proper interpretation of what their behavior comprises must include their ultimate state of health. Medicine-taking is not the appropriate referent. If it were, it would not be taken. The total behavioral sequence is "acting to improve health." Of course, a behavior may be both satisfying in itself and facilitative. The former aspect defines it as complete. However, if it leads only to *satisfaction* or the acceptance of discomfort, it is only a part of a total sequence (i.e., it represents an instrumental behavior).

The same interpretation can be applied to sitting at the dinner table, which is only a complete behavior if as such it represents the desired outcome, in which case it would be termed a *netwant*. If the reason is that the individual wants to "feel relaxed," sitting in a chair represents an intrinsic behavior. As for the specific manner in which the act of sitting is performed, the term habit or habit pattern has been employed. *Habitual behavior* refers to a pattern of action which was, at one time, deliberate at some holonic level, and subsequently attached directly to motor controls which require little or no cortical intervention. The stimulus becomes sufficient to initiate behavior when no competitive desire or perceptual input is at the focus of attention. If a motor response which was never deliberate becomes habituated, it is not an habituated behavior, but only an habituated activity or response.

Habits can, of course, be extremely complex, including practically every step of the process as for example in preparing for work in the morning by dressing, shaving, etc. In this case, the desired outcome may be as remote as the security that the income from the job provides. The test of which behavior is being dealt with is the specification of the level at which it is wanted. The reinforcing agent must be located and related to some desire if the sequence is to be altered.

In spite of the necessity for decision-making in order for deliberate activity to occur, there are many forms of behavior which seem to occur without any such choice-making involved, or where the relationship is difficult to identify. Examples of several types of decisions may help to clarify the issue:

- A situation in which no alternative appears to be involved. "I wish to play golf and there are no apparent constraints." There are, however, many factors to be considered. The price of green fees, the time required to play, and other competing forces are involved in spite of the fact that their input may be so minimal as to appear nonexistent.

- A situation where the choice is between indiscriminable items. "Two shirts are offered for sale which are identical in every perceptual way." I must simply pick one up from the counter. The choice may be considered trivial, but it involves selecting the nearest, the one in my hand, or simply asking the clerk to give me one. The decision has not been avoided.
- A situation in which the data clearly indicates that one choice is superior. "I can purchase a particular ticket to the theater for $20.00 or $40.00." Although it may seem that I am not required to decide, I must still make a determination and the possibility that I want to spend a great deal of money, remote as that may seem, must be taken into account.
- A decision which seems to be removed from the individual. "A judge is called upon to sentences defendant who has been found guilty of a crime for which the mandatory punishment is one year in prison." In spite of the legal mandate, the judge must decide whether to pronounce the appropriate sentence.
- A decision which seems counter to netwant. The example of medicine taking has been suggested. The decision involves a much more inclusive outcome. Many decisions are of this type, and in some cases, they seem even more difficult to reconcile with netwant. If a spouse insists that the press of work demands that an individual give up the opportunity to play a round of golf, the harassed person may well experience anger. However, if they carry out the assigned tasks, the emotion associated with maintaining a positive marital relationship, as well as perhaps a feeling of obligation or responsibility are sufficient to produce a positive net affect. The dominant emotion is based on a more compelling desire.

All behaviors—following an employer's instructions, hiring a baseball player, coming to dinner when called, fleeing from obvious danger, or twirling a handlebar moustache—are based on a decision to act in some way at some level of consciousness. The requirement that one be conscious has been challenged by psychoanalytic theorists as an essential feature of the process. Jaynes said "consciousness is...not necessary for judgments, reasoning, and problem solving."[21] His contention was that although "consciousness studies a problem and prepares it for struction [his term for the nonconscious mental process] it is not essential to the reasoning that takes place."[21] Our concern is that some mode of thought other than that defined as unconscious be understood to precede and fix behavior. Many behaviors are relatively insignificant. We have little interest in whether a belt or a pair of suspenders is chosen to support one's trousers. What we wish to understand is why one adolescent decides to rob a bank, another cheats on exams, and a third does neither.

Why does Sally live on yogurt and rye crisp while Helen eats her way into a size 24 dress? Why does John, the college professor, detest his $60,000 a year job and drink excessively to forget it, while Marvin, the shoe shine boy, is delighted with his pittance and treats his customers as friends? Why are blatantly dishonest officials continually re-elected, and innocent children physically and psychologically abused? Why do embezzlers persist in committing crimes that almost guarantee detection? These questions must be dealt with in terms of the various inputs into the behavioral sequence rather than on the basis of "character traits" or other such simplistic explanation.

The Behavioral Event

The affective point at which a decision/behavior sequence is initiated may be thought of as possessing a relative zero valence. Although it is not an energy free state, it is as yet unrelated to the new stimulus pattern. Since each stimulus is imposed on an existing emotional state, only the direction of emotional responses can be estimated, which is insufficient to explain the ensuing state. If, for example, one is depressed, the perception of some positive opportunity may result in a condition that, although improved, is still extremely negative. The husband who elects to inform his wife that he has damaged the family car at a time when she is in high spirits is taking advantage of the fact that although the direction of her response is predictable, the net emotional level and behavioral response may well be tolerable. He may avoid an unpleasant episode.

In summarizing the behavioral episode, we see a pattern which makes possible an approach to educational development that can significantly improve adjustment which leads to positive emotional health. Although it is not a simple task, it lies within the capability of every public institution and every home. Many attempts are already being made in this direction and some are based on relatively sound interpretations of behavior. However, the dissemination of information and the distortions that occur at the level of implementation seriously handicap their effectiveness.

The principles that have been outlined are dependent on a view of the nature of motivation and the roles of desire, perception, cognition, and affect that must be fully understood if the proper interpretation is to be made. When we state, for example, that every behavior is based on desire, we include the desire to belong. This reveals the potential for programming that includes opportunity to give, because giving provides meaning. When we state (in Chapter 16) that there are no inalienable rights, we intend to make the point that it is fruitless and often damaging to argue on such indefensible grounds but not that the issues should not be debated. When we state that decisions cannot be evaluated on moral or intellectual grounds, we are suggesting that a freedom to decide can be generated which is not ridden with the fear that failure must be avoided nor the practice of avoiding a mistake by not behaving at all.

This section concludes with the introduction of a formula (Table 13.1) that represents the mental process which results in the initiation and maintenance of a total behavioral sequence.

Table 13.1

The Behavioral Progression

Desire/Need Elements	D •	desire of any or several of the three types existing in some degree of arousal and manifested in learned need.
Cost Factors	C •	current active desire(s) similarly identified, e.g., self-enhancing vs. self-transcending.
	•	future competing identified desire(s), (long range goals).
	•	future competing unidentified desire(s) which may be met with resources considered for use in expressing a current desire (e.g., money, energy, material).
	•	alternative behaviors which may meet the same desire (e.g., swimming vs. hiking).
Pertinent Factors	P •	judgment of behavior in terms of success probability, long range goals, capacity, opportunity.
	•	institutional constraints.
	•	legal constraints.
Evaluative Factors	E •	moral, cultural, ethical, rational aspects of behavior and/or outcome.

Netwant $\quad NW = D + P + E$

Netcost $\quad NC = C + P + E$

Since the deliberative process involves choosing between alternative behaviors, the behavior that eventuates may be described as:

$$B = \frac{NW^1}{NC^1} \wedge \frac{NW^2}{NC^2} \wedge \frac{NW^3}{NC^3} \wedge \frac{NW^n}{NC^n}$$

Each equation represents the relative value of potential alternatives. Substituting values of 1 to 100 for NW and NC potential scores range from .01 to 100. The behavior that occurs will reflect a value in excess of **1.0**.

> *Example*: The desire for stimulation may be at a level of **40**, while the cost has a value of **30**. At the same time, the desire for food may be at a level of **60** with a cost value of **40**. Assuming that a ride on a roller coaster is the form of focused available stimulation, that a hot dog and root beer comprise the competing focused desire for food, and that only one can be accomplished, the relation of the fractions (**4/3** to **3/2**) indicates that the decision will be to eat. Many other desires are simultaneously involved and are included among the costs.

The formula is based on the contention that all behaviors are functions of the relationship between desire and a perceived situation. The fact that one must want to behave does not mean only that positive emotions are involved. The desire may be simply to rid oneself of a noxious feeling, or to avoid a threatening situation. However, the netwant must exceed the related cost in each case.

The selection of the value exceeding **1.0** does not imply that others are not close to that point and the fact that the composite emotional state is positive is no assurance of positive adjustment. The relative strength of competing desires and the nearness of the fraction to **1.0** are, in fact, evidence of the emotional health of the individual as they persist over time.

Summary

This text is concerned with those factors that influence human behavior and emotional adjustment. An understanding of such factors requires a study of the evolution of response potential and the capacity to learn from experience. At all levels desire/need and cost considerations represent the most salient contributions to the deliberative process whether behavior is identified as an incident, a sequence, or a pattern. Whether the action is intrinsically valued or only instrumental to some future goal, the principles are the same.

In studying behavior, it must be recognized that perceived actions cannot, in themselves, reveal the deliberative sequence that underlies their occurrence. Actions cannot necessarily be identified as *behavior* until the motivational elements are understood. The clinician, or institution whose roles shall be discussed in Chapters 14, 15, and 16, must pursue the motives for each relevant behavior until some basic level and class of desire is discovered.

Chapter Notes

1. Bosley (1979), p. 291.
2. Flexner (1987), p. 517
3. In fact, the statement, "I decided to leave the country" *must* include reference to both the action and the consequence.
4. Murphy (1973), p. 5
5. McDougall (1908)
6. Scott (1973), p. 718
7. Harre & Lamb (1983), p. 310
8. Hebb (1949)
9. *Ibid.*, p. 166
10. *Ibid.*, p. 167
11. *Ibid.*, p. 168
12. Morgan (1961), p. 36
13. Tinbergen (1951)
14. Cofer & Appley (1967), p. 65
15. Guralnik (1966), p. 390
16. Wilson (1964)
17. *Ibid.*, p. 195
18. Riess (1950)
19. That (highly controversial) interpretation is based on the argument that mental faculties, such as *reason*, have evolved further in males.
20. Kagan (1971)
21. Jaynes (1986), p. 53

Chapter 14
Emotional Health and the Counseling Process

Mental health covers a broad spectrum of psychological functioning. The holarchic model was developed to deal with one aspect—that of *emotional* adjustment, which is a function of behavior potential. It represents a pervasive emotional state aroused and maintained by belief regarding one's capacity and opportunity to express needs related to all classes of active desire, which, with their associated needs are often in competition for expression.

A system of *defenses* operates to monitor the conflict that obtains between assertive, protective, and transcendent desires. Defenses, which are positive phenomena, are a class of *beliefs*, which oper :e at conscious and preconscious levels. Emotional maladjustment results when defenses do not operate effectively; when one believes that no behavior will provide for need expression at an acceptable cost.

Counseling, or therapy, represents a technique designed to assist in belief alteration, both in order to facilitate more efficacious behavior, and, to improve adjustment in situations where there is little reason to believe that behavior alternatives can be expected to solve an emotional problem.

Mental Health

Mental health is an omnibus concept which has been defined along such parameters as cognitive acumen, social adaptability, addictive predisposition, glandular imbalance, and emotional stability. Individuals are apt to be considered mentally unhealthy, if, for example, they are intellectually defective or morally insensitive. The DSM III-R[1] includes such "mental" disorders as pyromania, masochism, alcohol dependence, and malingering. It does state, however, that "neither deviant behavior...nor conflicts that are primarily between the individual and society are mental disorders unless the deviance or conflict is a symptom of a dysfunction in the person."[2]

Labelling of this type is perhaps valuable for the purpose of distinguishing certain psychologically tinged anomalies from frank physical defects, and, to some extent, for establishing treatment regimens. However, the practice of using such an all-embracing taxonomy has the untoward effect of resulting in misunderstanding in some instances, with inevitably ineffectual treatment.[3]

Consider the example of a rapist, a sociopath, or a schizophrenic recluse. An individual with any of these characteristics may be a quite happy person. Unlikely as that may seem, there is nothing in the nature of the behavior that such individuals evince to guarantee that they suffer from chronic despondency. Individuals may, in fact, enjoy good *emotional* health though they suffer from poor *mental* health. If more effective preventive and ameliorative programs are to be instituted, more accurate distinctions must be drawn.

The holarchic schema is not designed to deal with problems of intellectual defect, addiction, chemical imbalance, psychosis, or psychopathic deviance. Significant as such abnormalities are, there are many tens of millions of individuals whose psychological debility is a function of emotional distress—of the incapacity to envision a future in which desires may be met with tolerable cost. It is to the quality of life of this population that the holarchic model addresses itself. The issues to be dealt with are best subsumed under the label *emotional* health.

The Holarchic Model of Emotional Health

The holarchic principle provides the infrastructure on which the emotional health model introduced in this text is based. The many factors that are involved in the psychological process have been described in earlier sections of the text. A brief iteration may be of help in relating the elements to an emotional health paradigm.

All existents are holonic in nature, being at once both wholes with constituent parts and/or instances, and being parts or instances of greater wholes. Among living holons, wholes have priority over parts, but descendent levels tend to take on independent characteristics. As levels of life move from totally genetically determined activity to individuals endowed with the capacity for deliberation (i. e., where mental processing is a factor), the holarchic concept is increasingly involved. The sense of autonomy and selfhood, and the focussing of pleasure and pain in the biological individual make possible adaptive and creative actions that improve the viability of gene pools.

Individuals pursue the gratification of aggressive, protective, and transcendent urges. They do so by weighing potential gain against potential cost in each instance. The emotional system is a highly sensitive barometer of successes and failures in the continuing effort to gratify desires which represent the psychological awareness of primitive drives. At every step in the motivational sequence, the goal of behavior is the achievement of an optimal emotional state—a positive consummatory emotion. Although details of the process vary in terms of idiosyncratic characteristics of behavers and environments, the principles are invariant.

This process is an outcome of the ineluctable function of the emotional system, and its appreciation makes possible an understanding of the most bizarre behavior. It may be reduced to a quasi-mathematical equation, though the vagaries of psychological experience limit its application. In essence it says:

> *If an individual has consistent, positive, emotional experiences, (i. e., is a happy person), the conclusion may be drawn that that person is either convinced that desires can be met through available behavior at an acceptable cost, or that they are being, or have been met at a reasonable price.*

The terms of the equation may be reversed without loss of accuracy, as is described in Figure 14.1. This ostensibly simple relationship must be appreciated if behavior or belief alteration is to be successful, where the goal is the optimal adjustment of the individual or group involved.

Although this text is designed to provide a framework for the development of emotional health programs, the focus has been on the nature of behavior. This approach has been taken because emotional adjustment is a function of behavior and behavior potential. Since emotions relate needs and desires to beliefs about the perceived world, emotional health has been defined as the extent to which individuals believe they have the capacity and opportunity to satisfy active desires.[4]

The kind of personality that is considered most emotionally healthy has been characterized in many ways. A common theme is found in the programs of philosophers and psychologists, although it is expressed in different ways and supported for different reasons. The humanists call for self-actualization, the analysts for conflict-freedom, and behavioral scientists speak of a society in which individuals learn to act in a manner conducive to effective community living. The common suggestion is to behave in ways that are not significantly deviant while allowing for some degree of individuality which, in holarchic terms, means to act in ways that are profitable to the species or the total social group in ways that also provide for individual development.

Figure 14.1

Emotional Health and Behavior Potential

EMOTIONAL STATUS: HAPPINESS

Negative		Positive
are not being met because the cost of behaving is believed to be too high		are believed attainable with reasonably priced behavior
or	DESIRES	and/or
are being met though the cost of behaving is very high		are being attained with reasonably priced behavior

The theme underlying most emotional health (usually referred to as mental health), models has been some notion of happiness and the performance of moral and rational behavior. Aristotle said: "It is the life which accords with reason then that will be best and pleasantest for Man, as a man's reason is in the highest sense himself. This will therefore be also the happiest life."[5]

Forem, in describing the philosophy of Maharishi Mahesh Yogi, and the practice of meditation emphasized the pursuit of happiness: "In all ages and places men and women have sought happiness and fulfillment of their potentialities as human beings."[6] He thus added "fulfillment," by which he meant the carrying out of their role as humans. Mueller defined mental health as a function of emotional maturity. He emphasized "being able to carry on happy, helpful, successful relations with others [and] to live in harmony with accepted social, moral, and ethical standards."[7] This would represent a view of emotional health that includes a relationship with others in one's community—a response to the transcendental urge. In each instance, happiness is considered synonymous with positive emotional adjustment.

Maslow and Mittelmann listed a number of characteristics that they believed would describe the emotionally healthy person. These included:
- Adequate feelings of security
- Adequate self-evaluation
- Efficient contact with reality
- Adequate bodily desires and the ability to gratify them

- Adequate self-knowledge
- Integration and consistency of personality
- Adequate life goal
- Ability to learn from experience[8]

The assumption of Maslow and Mittelmann was, in agreement with Goldstein,[9] that those who possess these characteristics can be said to be "self actualized." But, beyond the problem of defining *adequacy* in each case, what is the meaning of *self-actualization*? Maslow stated that self-actualization is found only in older people. "It tends to be seen as an ultimate or final state of affairs, a far goal, rather than a dynamic process."[10] If this is true, it is hardly useful in describing the emotionally healthy state in a growing child.

Rogers was more inclusive. He too contended that the fully-functioning person is a self-actualizer, stating that such a person is "able to permit his total organism, his conscious thoughts participating, to consider, weigh, and balance each stimulus, need, and demand, and its relative weight and intensity."[11] This, of course, could apply to any person whose emphasis is on openness and trust. Fromm stressed the necessity for each individual to "[relate] to man lovingly...rooted in the bonds of brotherliness and solidarity...experiencing himself as the subject of his powers rather than by conformity."[12] Here the emphasis is on love, compassion, union, creativity, and respect. Further support for this relating of the self to others may be seen in the similar characteristics found by Allport in *Creative Becoming*,[13] and Riesman in *The Autonomous Person*.[14]

Since such characteristics are surely acceptable to Rogers and Maslow, it may seem that we are on the right track. In each case, the nature of positive emotional health is described in terms of tenderness and goodness with evil resulting from the brute forces of a hostile environment and/or an inflexible society.

The illusion of agreement, and thus legitimacy, is to be rudely shattered, however. The state that is described by each of these writers is one which is available to only a limited part of a community. The view, in fact, represents a form of elitism which has been under attack in one form or another since people have written of the glories of war, the challenge of conquest, and the impetus to domination, control, and destruction. From Attila to Nietzsche, a philosophy of self which calls for the domination of others and the ethical justification of naked power has existed side by side with the compassionate suggestions of the humanists.

Accounting for these diametrically opposed manifestations is not difficult. First, it will be observed that the great majority of those who decry lust and aggression hold a disproportionate share of scarce assets and many are at an age where such fires are diminished. By contrast, the advocates of struggle and blood feel the challenge of such action in their veins, being predominantly youthful and in possession of relatively little security.

Although one must respect the integrity of those who argue for nonaggression, self-acceptance, and other cooperative and self-negating behaviors, there is one characteristic that almost all such philosophers possess. When Carl Rogers (whose sincerity is above reproach) suggests that we accept each other without judgment and love each other without reservation, his vantage point is suspect. It is very much as if Helen of Troy (who is neither to be faulted for her superiorities) were to suggest to a group of females that it was unladylike to aggressively compete for a mate. Such advice suffers somehow in its limited applicability. It is the wealthy who are conservative, the have-nots who want change at any cost, and emotional health is a function of very different behaviors in each case.

This is not to say that all such arguments are, therefore, unsound. It suggests rather that each be considered in terms of its relevance to others, and that some determination be made of the relative merit of each contention. If any conclusion can be drawn, it will be based on an analysis of personalities developed in a setting where a self-serving philosophy is taught as opposed to those which include the obligation to accept fairly extensive social constraints. It must be appreciated, however, that each stance is based on the conviction by its adherents that they are describing the true nature of human propensity.

Emotional health represents a state of being in the sense that the emotional condition is in part caused by reflection on what has happened in the past or is now happening. But it is more importantly a form of *becoming* in that it includes a consideration of desires or needs recognized as relevant to future satisfaction in terms of anticipated costs associated with their achievement. Emotional health is a function of the belief that one has the capacity to satisfy desires at any time, *as compared to their previous ability to do so.* It is directed to the future. A starving child who has just received a bit of bread is likely to be happier than a wealthy child who has just learned that his new ten-speed bicycle has no horn. Of course, emotional health is a description of a pervasive state, not of any particular moment in one's life. The principle involved is that individuals who see their lot as improving across time—poor as it may be in real terms—are in better emotional health than those whose access to needs (though perhaps relatively high) is seen as diminishing. We have characterized individuals who see life as improving as *happy,* and happiness, as Aristotle and other have suggested, is the best gauge of one's emotional health status.

Reference was made in Chapter 9 (Emotion), to the fact that there is considerable resistance to the equating of happiness with emotional health. Once again, we are dealing with the contention that the positing of such an equation is no more than a mere semantic exercise. The fact is, however, that to assume that a person who is consistently, happy, could be in poor emotional health is to stretch the definition of adjustment to include wholly inappropriate concepts, as is shown in Figure 14.1.

On this basis we may explain more explicitly the suggestion made earlier regarding the possibility of their being a "happy rapist." While a society may determine that any behavior is to be stigmatized, and declared illegal, and that the taking of another for sexual purposes without their consent is to be severely punished, there is no foundation for the assertion that such persons are necessarily emotionally unhealthy. They may, in fact, be quite joyous in the performance of their actions. They may even consider their socially deviant behavior to be wholly appropriate—at worst that it be condoned.

Until almost the twentieth century, the rape of a woman was considered an offense against her husband or father—not against the woman who was the victim of an attack. In primitive societies, the forcible capture of a bride was an acceptable social custom. Armies of an earlier period, and to a lesser extent today, often considered the rape of the women of a defeated enemy a reasonable activity. To assume that all such individuals suffer from poor emotional health would be patently absurd. Today, a substantial group of individuals insist that sex with young children should be accepted as normal. It would be futile to attempt to 'prove' that such views are wrong, as was developed in Chapter 7 on the nature of judgments. This is not, of course, to argue that such behavior should be approved, but only to distinguish between social acceptability and emotional health.

This is true for any form of behavior that has moral characteristics. Homosexual behavior is considered by many to evince a severe psychological problem. Wife beaters are assumed to suffer from a psychological defect. A prime example of the tendency to label socially disapproved behavior as psychologically based was cited in Chapter 10, in the admonition by physicians that slaves who attempted to escape from their masters suffered from a disease labelled drapetomania, or the "runaway" disorder. It is such interpretations of non-conforming behavior as evidence of emotional maladjustment that lead well intentioned societies to "fix" individuals whose philosophies they decry, so that they can lead well adjusted, socially acceptable, (happy?) lives.

Since the satisfaction of desires (through the gratification of needs) is determined to a great extent by what people have learned to be truths about themselves and their world, a critical factor in the analysis of mental health is the study of what individuals *believe*. It is not factual access to gratification, but the conviction that gratification is accessible that determines one's state of emotional health.

Emotions vary in the extent to which they are modifiable through the adoption of appropriate behaviors. Grief and shame, for example, cannot be assuaged through behavior—except as diversionary—since they represent reactions to situations outside one's control. The fact of the death of a loved one or shame about one's heritage cannot be altered by behavior, and must therefore necessarily be modified by belief alteration.

Frustration, fear, guilt, and anger, are, by contrast, amenable to change through appropriate action. They are, however, often extremely resistant because of the lack of awareness of ameliorative techniques and/or the high cost believed to be associated with behaviors that may be effective. Emotions, unresolved, tend to persist and are synonymous with character, personality, and emotional health over time. All emotions are subject to modification through the application of protective or defensive techniques.

Defense Mechanisms

The purpose of defenses is to provide a state of optimal mental equilibrium, usually in a homeostatic direction. In order to deal with the many ways in which this is accomplished, it is most efficient to employ the language of Freudian psychology. It must be recognized, however, that the development of these concepts is based on an assumption of unconscious desire which is expressly denied in the holarchic interpretation of mind.

In order to demonstrate the distinction between the two points of view, several common types of defense shall be defined according to a series of somewhat loose groupings. This attempt to reconcile interpretations across many authorities will certainly cause some distortion of meaning. However, the purpose here is only to identify a classificatory scheme that is based essentially on the operation of unconscious manipulators. Following each definition, the holarchic interpretation is provided in italicized form.

Class A - **Defenses which focus on avoidance of a stimulus.**
- REPRESSION (Dissociation, Disowning): An unconscious ego function designed to prevent the emergence of id impulses This represents the nearest thing to an unconscious defense. However, it refers more accurately to an *automatic reaction similar to that of shock, where the nervous system is simply short-circuited. Threat to equilibrium results in a reflex type of action, which is designed to maintain stability.*

Interpreters of the psychoanalytic position, which sees repression as a dynamic, unconscious ego performance, are not unaware of this potentiality. Weiss said: "repression seems similar to the involuntary physiological phenomena, such as the reflexes. We do not perform them, they take place in us."[15] But, he pointed out, "although we become aware of some reflexes, we remain unaware of the phenomenon of repression.... [Such] withdrawal can be considered as an intermediate act between a physiological reflex and a voluntary act."[15]

If repression were dynamic, unconscious, and completely ignored by the ego, it should have no impact on behavior, and in some instances this surely occurs, in that an individual is not aware of any process being involved—if such be the case. The holarchic interpretation is that what impacts the emotional system is partially or incompletely erased negative content. This applies to all of the following defenses.
- DENIAL: Ego prohibition against believing some external reality. Sometimes considered a form of forgetting designed to avoid painful recollections. A *conscious cognitive function by which an effort is made to alter perceptual information to fit acceptable beliefs.* The concept of cognitive dissonance (more accurately cognitive/affective dissonance) is appropriate here.
- SUPPRESSION: Conscious interference with the emergence of id impulses. *The cognitive process of rejecting thoughts (concepts) which arouse negative affects.*

Class B - **The "general" defenses.**
- ATTENTION ALTERING: Ego activity designed to avoid id impulse expression by attending to unrelated percepts. *A conscious effort to focus attention on non-threatening stimuli in the interest of avoiding a negative affect.*
- FANTASY FORMATION: Fulfillment of id desire through imagination. *The deliberate employment of the imagination in the interest of provoking, exciting, satisfying, or relieving affect.*

Class C - **Defenses defined essentially in terms of cognitive processing.**
- RATIONALIZATION: Ego action by which repressed id impulses are explained in a way which makes thoughts acceptable; usually accomplished by substituting "reasonable" for true explanations. *The cognitive process of projecting a thought against many possible interpretations in the search for the relationship which will provide the least debilitating affect.* We will pay considerable attention to the undeniable fact that humans are capable of believing whatever fits preconceived notions and justifies existing need.
- DISPLACEMENT: Attachment of affect to objects with similar physical characteristics. *The arousal of similar affects by objects with similar perceptual characteristics in the process of generalizing.*
- PROJECTION: Ego function by which undesirable id impulses are checked through the assignment of the desire to others. *A cognitive process by which an effort is made to negatively evaluate other individual or group practices in order that one's own desire or need may be judged acceptable.*
- ISOLATION: Ego function whereby the affect associated with some recollection is separated from the recalled experience. *A cognitive process by which a recollection is severed from its negative affective reaction by relating it to neutral or positive issues.*
- INTROJECTION (Identification): Ego technique for allowing the partial expression of an id impulse through cathecting energy onto another individual or group. *Providing for the expression of desires either vicariously, by observing others, or actually, by imitation.*

Class D - **Defenses defined essentially in terms of behavior alteration.**
- REGRESSION: The fixation of libidinal impulse at some pregenital level because of traumatic experience, resulting in abnormal psychosexual development. Stress situations in later life cause libidinal energy to be discharged toward objects or behaviors that were appropriate at as yet unresolved levels. *The scanning of the memory, when one is threatened, in an effort to discover techniques that were previously effective.* In some instances, the process results in behaviors which are considered to be age-inappropriate.
- SUBLIMATION: Ego function by which libidinal expression is modified by the practice of socially acceptable, often artistic, behaviors. This form of

defense may have no basis in fact, except in the general sense that attempts are often made to express desires in acceptable ways. *The many forms of creative expression may be equally well explained as springing from aesthetic or stimulative interests as from the repression of sexual desire.*

- REACTION FORMATION: The ego function by which negative id impulses are checked by actions which indicate positive feelings. This represents perhaps the most bizarre of psychoanalytic interpretations and will be developed slightly more fully since it exemplifies a common problem with defense mechanisms. Reaction formation is considered a primitive form of sublimation, whereby an individual unconsciously rejects some impulse the ego considers unacceptable. Freud held that when infants realize the positive response that their displaced (sexual) interest-based behavior produces, they persevere in such action. "The general perverse sexual disposition of childhood can...be esteemed as a source of a number of our virtues, insofar as it incites their creation through the formation of reactions."[16] The holarchic interpretation requires no reaction to sexual excitation to account for behaviors which are considered virtuous. *The moral sense and the social sanctions which accompany particular actions serve to develop behavioral repertoires. The expression of positive feelings toward an individual whom one, in fact, dislikes represents an effort to assuage guilt based on the awareness that the individual so disliked is one that social or moral convention decrees "should" be admired, or at least accepted.*

In summary, in the holarchic view defense mechanisms are seen as cognitive/affective functions designed to provide for some optimally non-threatening emotional state. When this occurs below the level of awareness, it is more appropriate to consider it either a preconscious process or a reflexive reaction which is hard-wired into the nervous system as a "fuse" which is blown when some emotional limit is reached. This may occur prior to the individual's consciousness of the event.

The psychoanalytic contention is that as the developing child learns various defensive techniques, the stage is set for behaviors which are apt to be inappropriate at a later date. This is a valuable point and one that finds considerable evidential support. However, it is the inadequacy or *incompleteness* of the defense that causes emotional breakdown. This distinction is essential to an understanding of the positive nature of defenses, in spite of the debilitation with which they are often appropriately associated.

Defenses modify beliefs about situations, thus limiting the ability to accurately assess information. Defense mechanisms are normal, frequently adaptive, and consequently desirable. In fact, defenses are unavoidable components of mental life which, when operating appropriately, *do not represent neurosis*. On the contrary, neurosis describes the condition of an individual in whom the defenses are *not* functioning adequately. This is true whether the defense is as simple as denial or is associated with a psychotic episode.

Defense as Belief

Every conscious defense is a belief network whose function is to maintain equilibrium in the face of threat. One need only consider beliefs about "rights" and "responsibilities" to appreciate the defensive nature of such convictions. It is a characteristic of beliefs that they are not based on an objective appraisal of the perceived world, but are heavily influenced by what one needs to believe. Thus, they are not subject to alteration by the mere application of rational or moral judgment. Although they may change dramatically in response to fluctuating needs, they are singularly resistant to reason or evidence. In view of this, emotional health must be interpreted as including the effective functioning of the defense mechanisms, in spite of their incongruence with external reality.

In Chapter 5, information systems which provide access to knowledge essential to effective functioning were identified. Each of these systems is warped by its organizational limitations and altered by the learning process. However, learning is also dependent on the need to believe, which results in further modification of data. It is clear that increased capacity to profit from experience has survival value. Perceptual modification based on interaction with the environment increases the opportunity to express desires. Less clear, perhaps, is the reason why distortion of beliefs should be valuable. This capacity is due to the complexity and intellectual skill of the highest life forms.

Although organisms can manipulate the environment better as their ability to understand it increases, the potential of the most primitive animals to act is great compared to their total store of knowledge. Having a relatively uncomplicated cognitive system, simple organisms, especially where drives, appestats, and moral signals are strong, have little ability or occasion to evaluate their activity or to ponder the nature of their personality. Much of the activity they perform is accomplished at a level that exceeds their capacity to understand the motive.

As capacity increases along the evolutionary scale, the power/intellect ratio is altered until a point is reached where understanding is greater than power. This can result in disequilibrium since threats posed by the environment may be clearly recognized. When the individual appreciates that a situation is dangerous, an attempt can be made to prevent it. This is the positive aspect. However, the individual who can plan, avoid, delay, and worry is in a position to be destroyed by such competence. To know that one must eventually die represents potentially distressing knowledge. In order to maintain equilibrium, the individual has the capacity to modify beliefs (i.e., defenses) which are related to all forms of information. Some control is exercised over each form of knowledge.

Defenses are established when, for fleeting moments, the data of perception, desire, and judgment, move into the focus of mental operation. This neural activity occurs in millionths of a second and can easily escape detection. However, it represents an entirely different interpretation than that which assumes a descent into the unconscious and the manipulation of conscious mind by desires which must be warded off by an ever-vigilant ego. The function of defenses is to reassemble information in some plausible form, and this is a conscious or preconscious process.

Consider regression. If it is complete and can be maintained, it provides essential solace. It is a fragile technique and very apt to prove ineffective over a long period, but this suggests only that it is a relatively poor form of defense. Repression represents a similar technique for avoiding painful experiences. This technique is also considered the basis for neurosis because the repressed material is assumed to maintain its capacity to direct and cause distorted behaviors. However, such activity represents the failure of the repressive attempt. The compulsive, perseverative, ineffective activities of certain individuals arising out of the discomfort associated with conflicting beliefs demonstrates that they are still dealing with the data at a conscious level.

The "multiple personality" is another example of the analytic claim that there live within the psyche other selves whose emergence must be controlled. There is no question that most individuals act differently in different settings, and even that they may be said to be "quite different people." The schizophrenic represents only an extreme manifestation of the decision to respond in specific ways for particular reasons. For one "Face of Eve" to deny knowledge of another is no different *in principle* than the forgetting of a telephone number under stress. A change in the demand of a situation results in a reorganization of data which serves as a (defensive) screen for maximizing the opportunity to express power or safety needs.

The view of defenses as positive in no way minimizes the desirability of assisting those in conflict toward reducing their anxiety levels. However, in so doing, the therapist is dealing only with the alteration of beliefs in directions that are more consistent with what is commonly accepted. The reason for this is that such beliefs tend to be more resistant, not because it is desirable that the distressed individual live with the "truth." This distinction is crucial to diagnosis and treatment and is the reason for the inclusion in this text of a consideration of the nature of mind, where the limitation of belief, as a subset of knowledge was developed.

Even when one is operating from a positive emotional base, adjustment problems arise in the selection of needed actions and outcomes. Desire is not always expressed in behaviors that are consistent with long term values. Primitive needs are, in some instances, unmet or unsatisfactorily reduced because of the many possible activities which result only in satiating desire without solving the underlying need. This is a consequence of the fact that humans have the capacity to learn varied techniques for meeting desires, and often ignore those of less intensity and immediacy in favor of those that are more highly stimulating.

The relationship among the three levels of drive presentation (primitive need, desire, and learned need) becomes more tenuous as cognitive skill, experience, and opportunity increase. More subtle techniques for stimulating the senses are constantly being discovered. Those viewed as socially unacceptable are accompanied by negative social and moral judgments. Where they include physical or psychological risk, there may also be negative rational reaction. Furthermore, since not everyone is provided access to all forms of behavior, there are often predictable frustrations and feeling of envy. The result is an increase in the attractiveness of behaviors which may not effectively meet a balance of desires. The kind of signals that individuals receive will be dependent on their own previous experiences and other determinants which may distort the messages.

Because of the many forms of interference that have been discussed (conflict, cost, lack of opportunity, etc.), the ultimate reaction to any situation has been described as a function of the netwant/netcost relationship which by its nature represents a compromise. Behaviors, and thus adjustment, are based on the affective states that such reconciliation arouses. In simple organisms, an affect such as rage may not be experienced, but in humans it plays an important role. Although it is by no means a pleasant experience, it is not necessarily destructive. Such affects provide valuable indices of those factors which contribute to each decision.

Behavior that provides for an emotionally healthy personality must represent the expression of many desires in such a balanced state that serious conflict does not persist. However, not all desires are active at equal levels of intensity at all times. It is necessary that many factors such as age, sex, and experience be taken into account in determining the appropriateness of the behavior of any individual. In so doing, it must also be recognized that the opportunity to satisfy a particular desire may cause others to be ignored and that when a desire of one type cannot be satisfied, others are apt to be substituted.

The person who endures by continual sacrifice and who in so doing renounces all potency, power, and other self-assertive feelings may survive physically, but is not apt to develop a healthy personalty. In like manner, the individual whose behavior is directed toward the assertive and protective desires only, and who in no way meets the need for meaning that obligation can provide, will find that life lacks something that is essential to complete satisfaction. In each case, desires of some type are unmet, and here, the holarchic conflict becomes an issue.

While sex and hunger are aroused without external incentive, the manifestation of some desires varies on the basis of cultural practice. Desires such as belonging, as well as many specific forms of stimulation, require the opportunity for behavioral expression if their nature is to be revealed and they can become powerful enough to have a significant impact on future behavior. However, their status in terms of political and moral philosophies varies widely from one community to another, which results in examples of both the most desirable (emotionally healthy) and undesirable practices.

Some philosophies, while perhaps recognizing the need for meaning, consider the existential individual the apex of significance and thus fail to provide for the kind of belongingness which is essential to the satisfaction of this crucial urge. Others have reduced the significance of humans to the level of accidental outcome of environmental influence or to their role as witness to an omnipotent power. However, since behavior represents the vehicle by which desires are satisfied, the urge toward meaning or belonging that is sometimes overlooked or, in many instances, considered less critical than the self-assertive desires, must not be ignored. The crucial factor may well be the target toward which self-transcendent behavior is directed.

The value of other-directed behavior through the socialization process is learned and the outcome can be profitable to both individual and group. To appreciate the positive affect associated with obligation, individuals must have the opportunity to experience such a relationship. By the same process, of course, they may learn to indulge in many forms of unhealthy behavior including a variety of practices which are both physically and emotionally destructive.

In light of this, it may seem paradoxical that we take the position that emotional health is a function of the individual's belief in their capacity to meet desires. Such a view appears self-contradictory both because one may want behavioral outcomes which are manifestly unhealthy and because even if one's desires were only positive, meeting them all would appear certain to lead to a state of ennui. In order to appreciate the implication of the statement, consider each form of objection.

Regarding individuals who may, for example, abuse themselves with some form of stimulant, the question of their emotional health must be considered in terms of the extent to which such activity represents an interference with other desires. It is only if drug addicts or alcoholics are concerned about unsatisfied desires that their emotional health may be considered poor. The total destruction of their bodies and the welfare of others is only a factor to the extent that they want something different from what their behavior produces. In the case of those whose behavior has resulted in a condition of dependence (to the extent that responses are beyond their control), their actions barely qualify as behaviors. As with any situation in which forces outside the individual mandate action, emotional health may be affected because of the helplessness which is felt in attempting to overcome the obstacle.

To claim that addicts must realize that they are paying a high price in terms of their inability to meet other desires begs the question. When this is true, there is an emotional health problem. But defense mechanisms, the luxury of euphoria, and other factors may cause a condition which effectively minimizes the impact of competing urges. It was pointed out earlier that emotional health cannot be defined in terms of the social acceptance of behaviors. On the other hand, it cannot be assumed that continual abuse satisfactorily meets desires. The need to consume ever increasing quantities of alcohol, or to persist in the ingestion of narcotic substances, may be accompanied by a consistent awareness that they are, in fact, a poor substitute for some unattainable behavior.

As to the contention that individuals who have everything will not enjoy positive emotional health, the confusion is caused by the failure to clearly appreciate the word *everything*. It is a matter of simple semantics that if individuals have all that they want, it cannot be argued that such a state would provide life with no challenge. If

EMOTIONAL HEALTH AND THE COUNSELING PROCESS   419

a challenging life is desired (and lacking) then all desires are obviously not being met. This is no polemic. It is critical to the argument that *all* desires must be taken into account if an emotionally healthy condition is to be anticipated.

The desire for stimulation is as legitimate as any other, but in many situations its urgency is disregarded. It is even more common to ignore the desire for meaning because of the failure to appreciate what is required for its satisfaction. The fact that giving, sacrificing, and other self-denying behaviors are not recognized as being essential to meeting the desire for identification creates the kind of societal arrangements that attend to only a limited number of human motives. The unfortunate outcomes are the concern of this text. To meet all of one's assertive urges will not result in positive emotional health where other equally pressing desires go unattended.

In spite of the desire for meaning that is basic to adequate adjustment when it is active, many individuals (especially children and disadvantaged people) are treated as if meeting other desires could satisfactorily substitute. Unfortunately, not only does such an approach fail to satisfy, it often leads to the perversion of practices and an ultimately destructive contempt for society. Children who are free to indulge themselves because of a parental conviction that this will make them happy may ultimately become convinced of the triviality of their existence; just as the welfare recipient, unable to offer anything of value to a community, must find a path to meaning in some other way. In each case, behavioral outcomes are often socially undesirable.

Behaviors are reinforcing because of an inherent capacity for feelings of satisfaction or dissatisfaction. Such feelings occur in spite of the social, legal, or moral appropriateness of an experience. The desire for identification may be met by some individuals because of the accident of mental or physical superiority. The willingness of the football player to shed blood for his school, and the conviction that "the show must go on" attest to the potency of the urge. Philanthropic contributions by wealthy families are, undoubtedly, often equally sincere efforts to meet the desire for meaning.

Experiences of all types affect wants in a variety of ways, and unless a balance is achieved, it is quite possible that some desires will receive a degree of attention that leads to unfortunate consequences. This problem is manifested in such behavior as the use of illicit drugs and alcohol, or other abusive activity. However, it is a more subtle destroyer in many other areas. The nurturance and development of "achievement" motivation, which McClelland[17] and several others claim will lead to happy lives (and, where striving to achieve is accomplished at risk to the expression of other desires), is a glaring example. Although achievement represents a form of behavior that has positive reinforcing effects, its potential for providing for positive emotional health must be tempered by a concomitant recognition of the desire for meaning. Otherwise, it poses a no less serious threat to adjustment than excessive indulgence in any other activity that satisfies a limited number of desires.[18]

The constantly changing social scene, plus the various interpretations applied to emotional health by proponents representing different segments of the population, are evidence for our contention that mental health cannot be identified as a specific state. There is considerable additional evidence for this relativistic interpretation. The reason for this is that emotional health is a *reaction* to what individuals believe about their situations. Efforts to modify society along Maslovian principles to ensure a guaranteed universal minimum subsistence level cannot succeed. Even if it were accepted that having enough to guarantee some level of subsistence would result in positive emotional health, how much would that be? How much income would be required to provide relatively happy, satisfied people? How much power would satisfy the need for control? How much potency to satiate growth demands?

A characteristic of emotional health that is often overlooked, and which relates to its quality as a reaction, is the fact that it cannot be guaranteed to anyone. No action on the part of an individual or society can confer emotional health. Many things can be given. Money, control, even love may be offered by one person to another. Their acceptance, interpretation, and management must, however, be determined by the receiver. This suggests another highly complex set of interactions. Gifts may represent opportunity for growth, identification, and hope. They may equally be construed as demeaning, aborting, or alienating. The school boy's allowance, his freedom of action and choice, have potential for devastation that somehow has not been made as clear to parents as the equally stifling outcomes of consistent denial or distrust.

When an attempt is made to assure emotional health to others, the very factors that are essential to its development are often removed. To become powerful, one must overcome; to love, one must give. To grow in any area requires that the individual be aware of and compete successfully against some type of force. Only when it is *earned* does a commodity have value.

This interpretation of emotional health clearly assumes that the individual's personal contribution is a critical factor. It suggests that positive emotional health cannot be visited on an individual, but rather that it may only be encouraged and supported by the action of a family or a community. Governments, schools, and other institutions in a democratic society bear the responsibility for providing the opportunity for the expression of human desires. This is not proposed as a moral imperative, but only as a recognition of the operative forces.

Many individuals have professed to know what people desire and/or need, and even the behaviors that would guarantee the acquisition of such needs. Adolph Hitler and Martin Luther both took such positions. Although their approaches were not necessarily admirable, they did demonstrate that to the extent that desires are expressible through a wide variety of behaviors, the opportunity to become aware of such activities can be provided by the group that holds power. In the United States of America, at least in theory, this means the political organization that protects the interests of franchised citizens. Educational programs that identify and encourage behaviors that are most apt to produce well-adjusted individuals, and political practices that foster such programs, can be initiated. Some of the factors that may be effectively influenced will be introduced in Chapter 16 where the argument shall be made that a preventive approach offers the greatest hope for significant positive change.

Emotional Maladjustment

The affective system, while it provides the potential for a highly sensitive interpretation of all forms of information, may in the very performance of its function cause intense distress. Such experiences can be charted at various locations on the emotional scales. Accurate identification is invaluable both for the establishment of preventive emotional health programs and for the treatment of individuals afflicted with varying degrees of maladjustment.

The principle that has been stressed in this text is that whether maladjustment is labelled as neurosis or psychosis, whether distress is caused by catastrophic life experience or induced by stimulation with an electronic needle, psychological disorder is *always* and *only* based on the status of the belief system. It is influenced by reality only to the extent and in such form as such externality is conceptualized and evaluated.

While any negative experience may cause discomfort, the label "emotional maladjustment" is ordinarily reserved for distress which persists over extended periods of time. Thus, the chronically depressed, anxious, or resentful are considered to be beset by some abnormality in the way in which data are conceptualized or in the relationship between elements of the deliberative process.

The principles developed in this text apply in precisely the same way to those who are so incapacitated that they may require hospitalization, sedation, or other intense therapeutic intervention. However, our concern is with the application to the millions of people who find little satisfaction or enjoyment in their daily lives. It is not to the "blizzard" of extreme dislocation, but to the intermittent threat of unpredictable and debilitating emotional experience that attention is directed.

To appreciate the sequence of events that leads from a state of relative comfort to one of distress it is necessary to review the description of mental characteristics provided in Chapter 8 (Mental Components), and the definitions of emotional elements in Chapter 9 (Emotion). The first chronological step in the process occurs as an individual becomes aware of environmental data that presents itself as factual. What follows represents the tracing of a single thread of thought through a jumble of psychological interactions. Consider three examples of factual propositions. One may believe that:
- My father drinks whiskey every pay day.
- My husband allows me no freedom.
- No one wants anything from me.

This awareness of situations, though an essential step, is not in itself judgmental.

In many instances the knowledge of such facts precedes the capacity for judgmental reaction, as when a child, unaware of personal or social consequences, learns that "father drinks whiskey."

At some point, judgments come to be made about these facts. Thus, beliefs about facts become:

- My father drinks *a great deal*.
- My husband *punishes* me.
- I am n*ot wanted*.

Such judgments may be made on the basis of formal or informal learning experience. One may hear others make pronouncements, or react on the basis of a capacity to make comparative assessments. The critical factor is that these characterizations are not subject to proof, but represent opinions which vary between individuals facing parallel situations. Another person with a father drinking the same amount may, for example, consider such behavior the norm for men in his occupation, social class, or other defining category.

In a similar manner, judgments may come to be evaluated on moral scales, as defined by religious or other canons of propriety. Thus judgments may come to be evaluated as:

- My father drinks *too much*: His behavior is *selfish*.
- My husband has no *right* to *mistreat* me.
- I am *unworthy*.

Here the individual moves from the simple gradation of behavior on comparative scales, to those which include a measure of disapprobation. The behavior is believed to violate standards of decorum, or to provide evidence (as in the last case), of one's lack of value as a human; that one is despicable, shameful, or vile.

Each of these characterizations of existing situations is accompanied by feelings of desire. The resulting interface was defined in Chapter 9 as emotion, and in the three examples cited here, they can be recognized as guilt/anger, frustration/anger, and depression, respectively. In each situation, the emotional experience is, of course, far more complex, being influenced by many factors that are unique to the individual. However, for the purpose of analysis, the categorization employed here should be sufficient. Each individual experiences some sort of negative emotion, though it is apt to be intermingled with many other psychological occurrences.

As emotions persist over time, they come to congeal as *attitudes*, or enduring emotional states. The attitudinal aspect is that state in which particular emotions are not persistently active. The emotions are aroused only when the individual—be it the self or some other—or a relevant situation, is being considered. When this happens, the emotion is aroused as an inescapable aspect of the person or situation involved. Thus, when under consideration, "my husband" is seen as "my mean husband etc."

As these negative attitudes harden, feelings of *hope* (Chapter 9) for a desirable resolution diminish. Though desires may remain strong, convictions about the probability of their being assuaged are reduced to the level of *wishes*, at which point efforts to take ameliorative action are often abandoned.

The sequence of mental events described here is accomplished through a process that has made human mentality the most efficient among all forms of life. At each level of conviction, judgmental and evaluative assessments of factual data are sufficient to trigger behavior. It is not necessary—and often not desirable—to refer to the underlying knowledge base. Appropriate behavior may be carried out comparatively rapidly, and potentially more efficaciously.

This capacity underlies the phenomenon of generalization, which makes possible reactions to novel situations on the basis of limited contact with perceptually similar experiences or events. We have given the label *peripheral thinking* to this process. Compulsions and phobias as well as less extreme forms of what appear to be irrational behaviors result from this tendency to respond to the world in terms of convictions whose foundations are rarely examined. Such practices may, in some instances be recognized as defenses in action, in that efforts to scrutinize one's motives may be threatening. However, in the vast majority of cases, the sealing of the lid over substructures of thought is a purely mechanical process.

Three classes of maladjustment may be identified. The first of these is *anxiety*, which represents a malfunction of the mental process, either because of congenital or adventitious insult or injury, or because of situations where demands are so great, that the psychological apparatus is incompetent to handle them. This problem is manifested in a blurring of the perceptual field, or from a persistent inability to make decisions.

Anxiety associated with integrity-loss is a principal cause of psychosomatic illness, with severe tissue damage attendant on the lack of resolution. Colitis may be an outcome in children who lack the ability to predict parental reactions to their behavior. It may also occur in an individual who cannot decide which among moral options to select (e.g., the abortion dilemma), and it is probably associated with any situation in which decisions must be made on the basis of unstable data. Beliefs become so unstable that it is impossible to take action of any type.[19]

If beliefs become sufficiently amorphous or threatening, *free floating* anxiety may be experienced. This is a condition in which individuals become convinced that some indefinable tragedy lies in their future. Emotions range from confusion to panic. Although there is little question that such distress is often physiologically induced; the terror is related solely to the belief state.

The second class of disorder is *impotence*, which results from the conviction that one cannot meet desires in any of the three classes identified (i.e., *assertive, protective*, and/or *transcendent*). Unlike anxiety, which may result from factors generated solely within the individual, feelings of impotence are heavily culturally influenced. Individuals living in a society in which caste distinctions are clearly defined and instilled early in life may exhibit relatively little distress regarding their stations. They may have learned to believe that a prioritization of privilege is appropriate. By contrast, in a political system that purports to offer equal opportunity to all, those who are thwarted by subtle maneuver may experience feelings of impotence. Goals that seem reasonable are prohibited from expression. Remedies seem unavailable.[20]

The conviction that one lacks the capacity to take the action necessary to aggress effectively, to defend one's self or to develop a sense of meaning often results in the evolving of counterproductive attitudes. Whether individuals feel guilty because of past behavior, ashamed because of some characteristic for which they are not responsible, or grieve because of the loss of a loved one, the distress is caused by the belief (often well-founded) that they lack the capacity and/or the opportunity to behave in such a way as to alleviate the negative emotional state. Jealousy, envy, humiliation, frustration, and anger are similarly debilitating to the extent that one believes that no course of corrective action exists. The woman who remains married to a man she abhors may feel incapable of undergoing the horror that she associates with separation or divorce. No acceptable alternative behavior seem available.

The perception of impotence is accompanied in many cases by the conviction that the situation *should be* altered. In the United States, this state of despair is felt not only by the millions of blacks, hispanics, women, and other groups who are automatically excluded from certain privileges, but by the millions more who, though perhaps relatively powerful, have come to believe that they are entitled to more. Such impotence is sometimes accompanied by feelings of rage, which can become a pervasive, disabling experience. Although in the emotional scheme it provides the potential for initiating action designed to change the situation, it can become destructive when ameliorative action fails to eventuate.

Alienation represents a third class of maladjustment. It refers to the estrangement resulting from the belief that relationships with others cannot be developed, either on an individual basis, or because significant reference groups are not acceptant. Alienation is, in many ways, a form of impotence. In America, blacks and other minorities, in varying degrees of severity, have managed only limited entry into the predominantly white society.

Since white students represent a threat to those blacks whose academic credentials may not be as impressive, an effort is often made to avoid social confrontation. "Better to stick together, so these subtle but painful difficulties will not arise."[21] The result is, however, by no means satisfactory. While making every effort to avoid exposure, many members of minority groups continue to believe in their relative impotence. They cannot conceive of any behavior that would solve the problem. The same problem, of course, is encountered by those who, for whatever reason, are jealous or envious of those whose possessions they cannot acquire.

There are also whole classes of people who believe that they can find meaning within themselves. Ensnared by the vision of total freedom and self-importance, they are left hanging in midair when their bubble of omnipotence bursts. Such individuals fail to appreciate that freedom in an absolute sense represents a most dreadful experience.[22]

In all such cases, beliefs are established that have the potential for providing a defense against personality disintegration. We pointed out earlier that psychological distress is not caused by excessive defensive reactions, but *by their failure to function effectively*. Thus, psychological intervention must be carried out with careful attention to the client's need to retain even the most bizarre beliefs until acceptable alternatives can be substituted.

The principle that bears yet another repetition is that each class of maladjustment is tied directly to the conviction that no behavior resolution is possible. The individual can conceive of no action that will solve the problem—or is convinced that any potential action will be fraught with extreme cost. Hopes have become replaced by wishes, often of a vague and uncertain nature.

This interpretation makes possible an understanding of the emotional discomfort of many of those who commit anti-social actions, abuse their bodies with food, alcohol, or other stimulants, or otherwise act in ways which cause them extreme guilt, but from which they seem unable to extricate themselves. The distress persists because they see no affordable behavior that will relieve the situation.

In many instances pain and frustration cause an increasingly myopic view of the world, with protective behaviors dominating time and energy. While this is a doleful portrait of a large number of individuals, it is also the key to procedures most apt likely to prove ameliorative.

Counseling

The capacity to distinguish between the varied motivational sequences, along with an appreciation of the commonality of human desires and the diversity of needs, provides a framework for the treatment of all types of emotional distress and behavioral anomaly. Such treatment involves the alteration of belief patterns of individuals who are free to act as they see fit, both where alternative behaviors may be made possible through belief alteration, and where there is little prospect of achieving a positive emotional state through any form of behavior. Although behavior change is often possible—and desirable—the focus in all cases is on belief alteration. Appropriate diagnosis is an essential element of the process.

Clienthood

Perennial disagreement regarding the assignment of client status to various groups and individuals has led to a plethora of bitter, as well as expensive, legal disputes. As with so many of the concepts developed in this text, much of the confusion could be avoided by attending to a simple, direct, and defensible definition of the term.

> *A client is that individual, or group, whose interests take priority over those of all others, consistently with established legal guidelines.*

The test of an individuals status as a client can be made on the basis of the question: To whose interest, other than their own, is the individual subject in a given situation. In the vast majority of cases that question can be satisfactorily answered.

There are, of course, many situations in which legal inconsistencies—as well as outright pettifoggery—obscure the issue. However, for the purpose of determining the limit of a counselee's privilege, it is important that the counselor be aware of the legal niceties of the situation. The issue of legal rights (and thus of client status) as it bears on decisions regarding the operation of a public school shall be discussed in Chapter 16.

Diagnostic Principles

- Emotional health must be recognized as a reaction to an *assumed* state of affairs. It is not a matter of being in touch with reality, or of understanding the difference between right and wrong. Rather, it is an emotional state which is based on convictions about the self and others that over time have contributed to the formation of cognitive sets of varying degrees of resistance to modification. The types of belief that are to be addressed are almost universally learned, and are heavily influenced by a need to believe. Thus, no assumption can be made that any experience is or is not needed, or that any cost is or is not too high. The task of the therapist is to identify such beliefs and to work toward alteration of those that are deleterious where feasible.
- The emotional state is permeated by a melange of moral and rational convictions that are highly resistant to alteration. They are often, in fact, extremely difficult even to identify since the foundations on which a belief is held may be several layers removed from the stated position.
- Language represents both a vehicle for, and a barrier to, understanding. Even where a client is anxious to reveal inner feelings, a lifetime of interactional style and remnants of guilt feelings are likely to interfere with the disclosure of relevant data.
- The personality is an amorphous collection of beliefs, many of which are conflicting, and others which have achieved an incompletely resolved level of cognitive consonance. Information is continually considered and reconsidered, leaning first toward one interpretation, then another. Issues are rarely, if ever, finally settled, and where convictions approach a level of dogmatic persuasion, the very mercurial nature of existence is such that serious maladjustment may be anticipated.
- Almost all mental processing of data occurs at the fringe of attention. We have introduced the term *peripheral thinking* to describe this phenomenon. Just as tying a shoe lace calls for little or no conscious awareness, most decisions are made without intense consideration. This process is an extremely valuable asset in ordinary situations. It makes possible the ability to quickly recognize and react to threatening situations. A hand need not be burned a second time

since one immediately senses the fire's potential to harm. There is, however, an extremely negative aspect. The ability to generalize from one or very few cases makes possible efficient behavior, but it also accounts for prejudice and premature convictions. The person observed to have drunk excessively on one or two occasions may come to be considered a "drunk;" the child who takes a coin from his mother's purse may be called a "thief;" the woman who smiles provocatively on a few occasions is likely to be labelled a "flirt." The problem with such labelling is that the original epithet often becomes buried in the detritus of a multitude of negative beliefs and ultimately becomes extremely difficult to alter.

The diagnostic process involves the evaluation of reported behavior and emotion on the basis of which underlying beliefs are deduced. Such deductions must be continuously checked through proposing various alternative views and gauging emotional reactions. Behavior of the counselee and any others with whom they are involved must be stripped of evaluative terms to separate factual occurrence from moral interpretation.

Intervention caveats

- The therapeutic process represents a special application of educational principles, the chief distinction being that the focus is ordinarily on adjustment rather than learning. However, the beliefs one learns contribute significantly to adjustment, and both procedures are designed to direct learning in some desired direction.
- The terms counseling and therapy are sometimes assumed to refer to different forms of treatment, with therapy being reserved to the treating of those who are seriously maladjusted. However, once again, a common set of principles is involved. More accurately, both terms should be distinguished from guidance, which ordinarily represents the furnishing of information on procedures essential to the achievement of a goal (need) rather than to a restructuring of beliefs about the quality of the goal involved.
- Theoretical Eclecticism is a contradiction in terms. One must accept one or the other of conflicting tenets. Is one ruled by unconscious motives? Do inner (mental) states play a significant role in determining behavior and thus adjustment? Answers must reflect the denial of one of ineluctably polar positions.
- *Forgiveness* is a fatally flawed practice. It is common to hear the admonition that offenders should be forgiven. Unfortunately, such a practice both demeans those who are excused for their transgressions, and assumes an authority to forgive that humans do not possess. It creates an atmosphere in which one member is morally superior, and the other appropriately penitent. It is far more reasonable to *understand* another's behavior in such a manner as to appreciate precipitating factors, and to respect their accepting of

responsibility and their plan to behave differently in the future.
- Each type of emotional discomfort can be dealt with in a variety of ways. Not only can conditions which result in inadequate situations be altered, but treatment can be provided which may be effective if offered in conjunction with essential opportunity. In treating an individual with persistent emotional distress, the therapeutic process must involve more than advice to "change employment" or "stop worrying." Only in those instances where ambiguity is the cause will such changes help. If an employer's moods are unpredictable and threatening, a change of scenery may be appropriate. However, if the cause of the symptom is a feeling of worthlessness, incompetence, or guilt, such change will simply place the individual under a new threat. "Keeping up with the Joneses" and other such American cliches contribute regularly to the disasters documented in the Peter Principle and other commentaries on the times.

Setting the Stage

The counseling relationship represents a prototype of all human interaction. The effective counselor or counseling therapist uses the model of human organization that we have presented either deliberately or inadvertently. Whether the interaction is formal or informal, planned or haphazard, professional or not, a situation in which one individual is influenced by the personality of another must be analyzed along the self-system continuum. It must also be measured in terms of the access to power through identification that is provided to the individual who seeks assistance in altering an unsatisfactory situation.

The form that counseling takes may be frankly educational in the sense that knowledge is believed to be the critical component, or it may rest on a subtle affective interchange between the participants with the educational aspect sublimated. In all cases, if a counseling relationship exists, at least one party is desirous of self-expansion through successful identification. This experience is described in various psychologies under a variety of labels, each of which may provide a useful interpretation. The critical factor is that as the client approaches a counselor psychologically, some cathexis is attempted. In spite of the fact that cathexis represents the channeling of mobilized energy from the biological self into a more comprehensive system, the focus remains within the individual who must continue to feel the guilt and pain that experiences create.

In a valid counseling situation, one (or more) of several problems is being encountered. Conflicting perceptions may create ambiguity and thus anxiety. Frustrated desire may cause grief, agony, or other emotional reaction. Want/cost ratios may be intolerable. Impotence may be causing depression, fear, or similar feeling. In all cases, the potential value of the counseling relationship lies in the opportunity for clients to include the counselor in their sense of self. *You* must be included in *me*. *We* must become an entity that includes *you* as an element in the totality that is *me*. When this situation obtains, it becomes possible for beneficial change to take place.

The principle involved was developed in Chapter 10 where the nature of selfhood was discussed. Here, the counselor hopes that the client may be able to enter into a psychological relationship that makes possible a breaking down of defenses that ordinarily resist attack. If another person tells me that, I am "too fat," I am apt to resent the remark and set up defenses that will somehow legitimize what I believe represents a failing. (It's my glands; a family tendency to being large boned, etc.) By contrast, if I say to myself that "I am too fat," the defensive wall need not be constructed, and when the counselor shares my selfhood, that same recrimination can be a stepping stone to progress.

The way in which identification is accomplished has been variously described by authorities on counseling. Rogers suggested that "unconditional positive regard" be extended to anyone in a counseling situation.[23] This kind of advice, sound in theory, is often interpreted in ways which may increase alienation. To regard unconditionally, since it frees the client from responsibility, is of little or no value and may even make a situation worse. Glasser developed an entire counseling model based on the need for responsibility that he discovered in his clients.[24]

The opportunity for the client to grow comes, as in all of life's experiences, at the point that an expectancy is developed which provides a path toward meaning. When the counselor can instill in the client a sense of debt (which must be accomplished in steps small enough to avoid serious anxiety), and when the reaction of the client to a challenge is on the guilt rather than anger continuum, an effective relationship has begun. Positive change can be anticipated only after emotional alteration has occurred. This sense of debt represents a microcosm of the general human principle that meaning, and thus significance, is based on a part/whole relationship that the client can recognize.[25]

The process of developing a responsible relationship with a counselor is referred to in psychoanalytic literature as *transference*, which is another unfortunate term since it is sometimes construed as the passing of an attitude from one individual to another, as if it were a projection. It is also described as a form of intimacy with related sexual characteristics. The holarchic model sees it rather as an expansion of the self which makes possible the acceptance of cognitive information in such a way that affective reaction may be more positive.

Counselors must represent an avenue to safety and security. They must be worthy of trust and as consistent and demanding as they would be in their relationships with other human beings. They expect their tennis partners to arrive at the court on time. If this agreement is consistently violated, they ultimately change partners. The counselee who is excused from any expectancy is in fact reduced in stature, demeaned, and further alienated.

Over-expectancy is, of course, as destructive as total freedom, and especially at the outset. Clients' fear of risking the little power they possess must always be taken into account as counselors plan their strategy. For people who have difficulty in dealing with authority figures, care must be taken that their identity not be challenged by a counseling approach which smothers individuality.

We have, by using the terms "plan" and "strategy," perhaps offended those who do not accept the contention that an effective counselor is manipulative. They are correct in assuming that many counselors are not. We believe, however, that such counselors will fail in their task unless they possess an instinct for feelings and a rapid reaction potential that is found in very few people. For a counselor to state—as Rogers has—that he has no desire for clients to accept his ideas, is indefensible unless he is unconvinced of the value of the ideas that are to be shared.[26]

The use of the term "manipulate" here must be clearly understood. The counselor must not use clinical skill to determine which decisions a client should make, but only to direct attention to those the psychological structures that are significantly related to the distress being experienced. The procedure represents no more than assisting counselees to attend to those factors that are the basis for their unhappiness. The role is one of opening doors that may lead to the resolution of conflicts that stifle ameliorative effort.

When the counselee reaches the point at which identification has taken place, some personality modification has occurred. As the three aspects of the decision-making process are considered, it becomes clear that although the first two, (desires and needs), remain exclusively part of the counselee, the perceptive/cognitive input and thus the emotional responses are altered. The self, now including the counselor, has much more information to deal with. The new relationship provides a forum for the reconsideration of data that had previously been interpreted in ways that led to negative emotions. Since the self now includes the intellect of the counselor, data which was either ignored or misunderstood can be reexamined. *It is this restructuring of the cognitive map which comprises counseling*, and it is a *directed* process if the counselor is skilled. (Directed only, however, to the extent of revealing potentially successful paths to conflict resolution.)

The acceptance, warmth, and humanness recommended by therapists are essential to setting the stage, but counseling represents a changed interpretation of the world which is based on an alteration of beliefs about netwant relationships, cost factors, etc. If effective change takes place it will come about because of cognitive reorganization and associated belief alteration.

The term *reality* represents only some accepted interpretation of the world. Reactions to a particular "reality" may vary widely. The same situation may, for example, be viewed by one observer as morally appropriate and by another to be ethically unsound. The phobic individual may well be fully convinced that the odds against an airplane's falling from the sky to be one in a million. It is not a denial of the fact that the degree of risk is minuscule, but the focus on the potential experience––the reaction to the possibility at another level of mind—that is immobilizing.

If an individual with hysterical symptoms is counseled and the symptoms disappear, the counselor has not been dealing with reality, since the symptom termination occurs because of a changed emotional reaction to a belief, or a reaction to, an assumed reality. Such individuals deal only with an interpretation of the meaning of what they perceive, which is predominantly a learned reaction. This requires that change occur in perceived or believed reality, which is a cognitive experience. One need not search for ultimate truths but must build on the previous experiences of the counselee. The client's response to situations can also be attended to without reference to any inherent characteristics of an experience.

Since counseling involves only the *reinterpretation* of the viability of the environment in meeting desires, many of the activities in which a counselor may become involved are not counseling per se. If a woman complains of a drinking husband and the counselor encourages him to attend meetings of Alcoholics Anonymous, the action may be effective, but such action is guidance, not counseling. If, on the other hand, she learns how to live more comfortably with her husband in spite of the fact that he continues to drink, an effective counseling experience has occurred. The situation is no different than that involving a terminal illness. Although a cure would certainly be desired, a counselor's task is to assist in the acceptance of a helpless situation with minimum discomfort.

Counselor Characteristics

The image that an effective counselor presents to the client has a significant impact on the probability that successful intervention will eventuate. Some counselor characteristics such as appearance, sex, age, and speaking voice are subject to little if any modification. This may account for the notion that counselors are born rather than made. However, the most influential factors are amenable to change through a rigorous training program.

A counselor must exhibit *strength*, *competence*, and *confidence* while maintaining a warm and accepting appearance. In this respect, a counselor is no different from a physician, an attorney, or an accountant. People seek help from those they believe have the capacity as well as the willingness to provide assistance. This contention raises serious questions regarding the practice of passive responding (uh-huh) and clarification (what you're saying is...) that have been advocated by nondirective psychologists. Unless such responses are employed only in specific situations, the counselor is operating under no theoretical structure at all (except that clients will ultimately heal themselves), or the client is being misled.[27]

Many clients, particularly children, are only in a counseling situation because of someone else's desire that they be there. The gambling husband, the defiant teenager, the drug abuser, or the sex deviant who reports for treatment because it is a condition of freedom is the worst form of risk. To say that under such conditions effective counseling is apt to occur represents a form of blindness that evidence of failure does little to alter. Counseling represents an attempt to alter beliefs on the basis of *at least* the client's confidence in the skill of the therapist and the capacity to accept the counselor as an identification figure. This is rarely the case in such situations.

Even where effective rapport is possible, the counselor must recognize a number of potentially counterproductive situations. One of these grows out of the fact that the client is relatively weak and seeks an individual whose strength may be employed in coping with life's problems. However, counselees must believe that they can make a significant contribution to the relationship if identification is to take place. It is here that the value of Rogerian and other types of Gestalt therapy is manifest. Clients must believe that although the counselor is strong, the counselee can represent a valuable input into the total self. If this relationship is not developed, the client may be advised or led but the intent of a counseling experience, which is to make possible growth toward ability to handle the world, will not occur. As in encouraging a husband to join Alcoholics Anonymous, such a procedure is, no doubt, desirable in many instances but it does not represent counseling.

An equally serious matter concerns the result of assisting individuals toward freedom from unproductive defenses. There shall inevitably occur periods of time during which counselees find themselves alone, threatened by despair growing out of the emptiness of shattered belief. This experience of anxiety or consternation is for most people extremely threatening and may precipitate crises as one gropes for support. It is during these periods that efforts will be made by counselees to employ reason (rationalization) in explaining their behavior, and with the personality in such need of shoring up, logical implication of relatively low fidelity may be accepted.

People who are desperately seeking an explanation for their own behavior as well as that of others may accept an interpretation that they would ordinarily reject. In a panic state, the belief that one is being hounded by relentless forces can be supported by enough evidence to give it the credibility that is necessary to maintain some minimum of equilibrium. By acting in a particular manner because they believe that others control them, the guilt, shame, or other embarrassment may be significantly lessened. The counselor must therefore take care that conditions in which defenses have crumbled, and which cry for explanation, are kept at a minimum.

The Counseling Process

Having arrived at a level of trust which makes possible the fusion of the counselor's world with that of the counselee, the conditions for probing are set. The client's defenses are usually highly resistant to attack and their value in preserving integrity must be clearly understood. The fact that clients are relatively powerless suggests that they will not give their few weapons over easily, and it is imprudent to make advances that will cause them to recoil.

At the outset, any beliefs should be supported to whatever extent they can later be modified without risk of loss of credibility. To a man's complaint that "no woman is to be trusted," for example, the effective counselor does not begin with either a countercharge or acquiescence. It is far more effective to react in a way that will disarm without commitment.[28]

Ambiguity of perception, frustrated desire, want/cost imbalance, and/or a sense of impotence, alienation, or guilt are all possible sources of need for alteration. In every case, anxiety is generated out of belief conflict which seem unresolvable. Whatever other emotions are involved, anxiety is aroused in the event of an inability to clarify the rational and/or moral aspects of a situation. Perceptual distortion may be a result of incomplete information about an environmental situation, or faulty need/desire connection. Impotence and alienation may stem from inability to establish an effective reference group, and guilt may represent the projection of the ideal against the actual self. In each instance, the counselor functions to alter conflicting belief patterns. The task is to identify beliefs and to assist the client in modifying those that interfere with adjustment. This approach requires that at some point the counselor begin to challenge the perceptions and conceptions on which beliefs are based.

Here we arrive at a critical point. If the counselee is to emerge from the therapeutic experience with beliefs that make resolution possible, and with improved coping skills, the role of the counselor must not be one of leading, directing, or determining optimal outcomes, but of *accompanying* the client on a sometimes perilous journey. The "challenging" of perceptions must represent an invitation to review beliefs in much the same manner as would occur if they were self initiated. The counselor must not function as an external guide or mentor, but as an aspect of the totality of the client's self.

The need for identification in order to cause a change in belief is increasingly less as personality breakdown becomes greater. This is due to the need for integrity in all individuals and is manifested by the ease with which confused people tend to follow the most unlikely leaders. In contrast, when defenses are strong and the interpretation of the world is relatively clear, there is little demand for change.

A putative paradox arises here. If greater breakdown decreases the need for identification before effective change can occur, why do counselors run into so much resistance to change from "neurotics?" The reason, in this instance, is not because of a sense of confidence in their potency, as is the case with relatively well-adjusted individuals, but because of the panic that arises when they consider the potential loss of control. Individuals with one satisfying belief to which they can cling will resist change in that area, while those without any stable or anchoring conviction are apt to be amenable to almost any suggestion.

An appropriate example of the situation can be seen in the reactions of typical school students. Having relatively little information about a subject, they are very apt to believe their teacher. However, as they become more skilled in the concepts with which they are dealing, beliefs become increasingly fixed and ideas of the teacher that they view as heretical are apt to be discarded. It requires a great deal of skill to challenge beliefs that have become entrenched in strongly held belief patterns.

Certain steps must be taken at various levels of the counseling relationship that may represent a further source of discomfort to those who believe that counseling must be based on a sharing of feelings at the deepest level of intimacy. At the outset, clients are often at a point where they are immobilized since the want/cost relationship is so obscure or is in such tenuous balance that they cannot act. At this time, it is most important that the moral sentiment of the counselor be prohibited from influencing a client. This issue has widely discussed by personality theorists, with many believing that it is not only impossible, but would be highly undesirable, to avoid being personally involved with a client to an extent that demands the expression of the counselors own set of values.

Personal feelings color all of our reactions. However, where decisions of another person are involved, therapists are ethically obliged to distinguish clearly between their own probable course of action in a situation and that of their client. First, such individuals are seeking to justify behavior that they will have to live with when the counseling relationship is terminated. Secondly, the task of counselors is to make possible a reconsideration of data by adding new information and revealing previously unconsidered relationships. To allow personal reactions to affect a recommendation would result in filtering the input through another's feelings which would compromise the integrity of an emotional state which is at this point so dependent on the expanded self. Furthermore, the capacity of the counselor to present a valid approach to a more meaningful existence is apt to be vitiated by the very involvement that is experienced. Although data may be shared by counselor and client, the decision must be that of the client alone.

The Therapeutic Theater

When all of the procedural elements have been identified, whether the model is psychoanalytic, behavioral, client centered, or eclectic, the arena in which the struggle for relief from emotional distress is fought is to be found in the series of steps from fact to attitude described earlier. The presumption of therapeutic intervention is that at some level an alternative set of beliefs may provide a more optimistic prognosis. The process involved is the stripping away of layers of conviction until levels are reached at which deleterious cognitive/affective inputs into the attitudinal state are revealed, and to explore belief options.

The technique may be thought of as analogous to a situation in which a physicist realizes that an error in some previous calculation has led to an erroneous or ambiguous conclusion. The difference is that in the psychological realm, what is sought is not an error, but a belief or a series of beliefs which have led to emotional maladjustment. Uncomplicated in theory, the pursuit of motivational determinants is apt to be tortuous in practice.

Beliefs at any level may be appropriate focal points for intervention. Is it a *fact* that my father is an alcoholic? Is *extensive* drinking inherently *immoral*? Is my anger at an incident appropriate to the development of a pervasive negative attitude? The task is to determine the level at which significant beliefs are held and to expose such beliefs to reassessment. The requirement is threefold; to *listen*, to listen *further*, and to listen *still further*.

Such listening may, of course, be accomplished through conversation, but it may be abetted through the use of psychometric and other psychological tools. (One may "listen" to what an intelligence test or a projective device has to say.) However, in most instances the best source of information will be provided by what is specifically said or done by the client. Behavior is apt to be the best indication of otherwise unarticulated beliefs.

The practice described here, is in many ways, not dissimilar from that followed by psychoanalysts or therapists of other theoretical convictions. The difference lies in the abjuring of "unconscious" determinants, and a rejection of the behavioral approach that minimizes or ignores the significant contribution of emotional elements. The holarchic procedure involves the meticulous diagnosis of influential beliefs and an endeavor to assist the individual in restructuring such convictions in the hope of achieving a state of improved adjustment.

As a relationship develops, the perceptive counselor may become aware at some time that the client has settled on a probable course of action and is seeking confirmation for the aptness of the decision. This is a second crucial point. If the counselor believes that it is sufficient to simply support the action, the opportunity to provide the greatest service that the relationship affords will almost certainly be missed. In fact, such action may totally destroy the value of the experience. Consider, for example, a case of anxiety, which we have defined as a response to an ambiguous situation, and guilt, which is a conviction of one's moral reprehensibility.

A woman forced to face a pregnancy with the alternatives of aborting the fetus or bringing an unwanted child into the world is probably dealing with a difficult moral choice. Her anxiety may include the concern that she will be guilty of a moral transgression regardless of her choice. Killing a fetus may be morally wrong, but so may her lack of courage in not respecting her right—and obligation—to make a free choice. Her decision, when it comes, will not in itself relieve the guilt/anxiety state, and the verbal support of a counselor for either choice represents only one more vote for a particular behavior.

The counselor, in agreeing with the chosen behavior is, in effect, attacking another identification system which provides meaning, and thus potential emotional support to the client. A mature[29] decision can be arrived at only after each alternative is understood, and the behavior is carried out in full awareness of the arguments against it. This is essential since much of the anxiety involved is based on one's feeling that, in the absence of a clear understanding of the opposing position, either action may be morally inappropriate.

The common approach to such problems is exemplified in the shrill demands of pro-choice advocates and the bellicose responses of right-to-lifers. The virulence of the behavior of those on each side is based, in part, on the fact that they cannot unequivocally demonstrate the invalidity of the arguments of their opponents. A belligerent display of self-righteousness masks the insecurity of those involved.

Given such principles of human emotion, the counselor in dealing with an individual who is leaning toward a decision between moral alternatives can help to reduce anxiety by presenting the alternate choice in a way which retains its morality but reduces the conflict. This ostensibly complex process is, in practice, often simpler than it sounds. In the case of the child whose alcoholic father has been divorced by his mother, consider one of several ways in which the father's case may be presented.

Experience teaches us that if a woman divorces her husband because of his uncontrollable drinking or gambling, the surest way for her to destroy her relationship with her own children is to constantly criticize her ex-husband for his shortcomings. Such parents must understand that a different approach be taken because children identify with both parents and are likely to defend their helpless father when his behavior is attacked. Even for children who are beaten or abandoned, the desire for identification is so strong that they often resent any denunciation of the parent who failed. Although it is true that at some time in life such children are likely to develop a strong revulsion for such inadequate parents, it is fruitless for anyone to challenge them on the subject. The mother who complains will find that she only increases her child's distress.

Although to berate the father as an inexcusably irresponsible person will only increase anxiety, it is equally useless for the mother to argue that his behavior is defensible since his absence and lack of support are daily reminders that something is amiss. Children cannot escape from the facts of social living which will constantly provide evidence that such activity is not acceptable. There is, however, an interpretation that makes it possible for the child to appreciate the conditions that led to the father's problem, as well as the mother's reaction in divorcing him if she chooses to do so. Alcoholism can be explained as a medical disorder and one which deserves understanding, if not sympathy, at the same time, that irresponsible behavior, though it is related to excessive drinking *cannot be condoned*. The mother can share with her children an empathic reaction to their father's behavior which does not destroy his personality. An example from an actual case, with names changed, and stripped to essentials, may be useful.

The case of Madeline G

Madeline was a woman in her early thirties. Her mother had died and her father, a man in his late sixties, had been recently diagnosed as being diabetic, and in need of considerable physical, psychological, and financial assistance. Madeline reported that she had rarely seen her father since her mother's death some twelve years earlier. She stated that during her childhood and adolescent years she had been so "disgusted" with her father's wasting much of his income during "bouts of drinking," that she had come to hate him. Because her mother had defended him, and perhaps because of some instinctive sense of obligation to a parent, this negative feeling was accompanied by a sense of guilt, which had been greatly increased since she had learned of his newly diagnosed illness.

Madeline said that she was "totally confused" about what she ought to do, since ignoring her father heightened her guilt. But to excuse him for years of irresponsibility was "quite beyond" her. She felt, in fact, that forgiveness would represent a betrayal of her mother who, though she had defended him, "had suffered 35 years of neglect and abuse." (The abuse was ultimately understood to have been only psychological, and the neglect—serious as it was—related only to financial matters.)

Early in the interview stage, it became clear that the option of ignoring her father was highly unlikely to prove felicitous, since the guilt associated with such behavior could be expected to persist, with his death likely to add to its intensity. The decision was, thus, to "accompany" Madeline as she moved in the direction of reconciliation. The difficulty revolved around which belief alterations were essential, and what conditions were most apt to bring them about. What must happen if Madeline were to come to understand and respect her father without having to erect defenses against her memory of his past? How could she, for example, avoid forgiving him?

The first step involved the determination of the level at which negative beliefs might be challenged. The fact of his drinking, its *excessive* nature, and the *cost* to the family would be highly resistant to belief alteration. In point of fact, his drinking was not, in itself, the problem, but his expenditure of such a large part of his salary. Furthermore, Madeline had made it clear on many occasions that she believed he had no concern about his family's welfare. It was because of this that she had come to "hate" him. The issue then was one of her father's motivation.

Madeline's mother's approach across the years had been typical, and ineffective. Both in forgiving Mr. G. and in telling Madeline how she ought to feel, she could not bring about the desired reaction. The therapist proceeded on the principle that beliefs are most apt to change when the individual expresses them personally. (It is not what counselees are told, but what they *tell*, that is apt bring about change.[30]) Further, working in the counselor's favor was the evidence of guilt that Madeline displayed when discussing her father. The procedure involved the recreating of scenarios in which Madeline would be required to defend her father's actions against attack. Moreover, recalling that the counselor had made every effort to be accepted as part of Madeline's self, the defense could be seen as essentially personal—no outsider would be criticizing her action.

With this goal in mind, the counselor asked Madeline to recount incidents that she could recall. At first, responses were general, simply that he "usually" stopped to drink, or that he "never came home to dinner on a Friday evening." Under a continual request for examples, however, she was finally able to describe a specific Friday afternoon. Excerpts of a taped session follow:

> Madeline: Well, he walked in about midnight with a stupid grin on his face, fell asleep in a chair, and woke up around noon on Saturday. When my mother

yelled at him, he got up, didn't say anything, and went out to work in the garage.

Counselor: What do you suppose he was thinking on the way home from work?

Madeline: Well, he probably wasn't thinking anything. He didn't care what happened...

Counselor: That seems clear. He was thinking "I don't care what happens to my family"...

Madeline: I don't think it even occurred to him.

Counselor: But isn't it clear that he was saying "to hell with my family?"

Madeline: I don't believe he thought about anything except the beer that he was going to get.

Counselor: Madeline, we know he didn't care about you. He must have thought about it.

Madeline: But he...

Counselor: OK lets talk about some of the other things that were going on.

Here the counselor dropped the topic and moved on to other aspects of the family's life. The purpose was to leave the issue unsettled; to allow Madeline the opportunity to contend—at a low level of awareness—with the question of what her father was thinking about, what his motive was in spending much of his salary on alcohol. In the session that followed, after some preliminary conversation, the counselor returned to the topic:

Counselor: Madeline, last week we were discussing the fact that your father must have decided on those Friday afternoons, that he didn't care what happened to his family. Whether you had enough to eat...

Madeline: No. I don't think he thought about us at all. He probably just thought about how good a glass of beer would taste.

Counselor: But he knew he was expected home. He knew he was planning to spend his salary. He knew you would all be angry.

Madeline: (laughing) My father never planned anything. I suppose he was just an alcoholic.

Counselor: Probably so. But that wouldn't excuse his deliberate abuse of his family.

Madeline: But I don't think it was deliberate. It was—well—it just—well--happened.

Counselor: And that was his excuse, wasn't it.

Before waiting for a response, and again allowing time for the issue to be dealt with at a subliminal level, the counselor turned to another topic, this time asking Madeline to explain what she meant when she said he "never planned anything."

Counselor: Did he ever do anything for you? Make you anything? Buy you anything?
Madeline: Well, he never bought me much of anything, but he did make me a doll house, and when I was about six years old he made me some silly little dolls.
Counselor: Silly?
Madeline: Well, they were just made out of scraps of wood, and pieces of metal and rubber left over from some work he was doing at the mill.
Counselor: What happened to them?
Madeline: Most of them got broken. I saved one—but I don't know where it is anymore. And I don't care.
Counselor: I can't blame you. I'm sure they meant nothing to him.

Once again the counselor dropped the subject. Over the next five weekly sessions, the counselor continued to return to scenarios in which he berated the father as selfish, uncaring, a "worthless" alcoholic, etc. Gradually Madeline began to defend her father's action, at first as thoughtless, and increasingly more as a sickness, with the counselor criticizing her comments as "defending a guilty man."

In the final (12th) session, the counselor explained to Madeline that he had been attempting to put her in the role of defending her fathers actions. She commented that she had never before tried to see the world through her father's eyes and that she could now appreciate the pain that he must have felt as he watched his wife and children "grow away from him." In a follow up phone conversation, four months later, Madeline reported that she was visiting her father regularly and was "trying to make up" for the lost years. She had obviously come to hold a different set of beliefs about his motives, but was not required to deny that the result of his behavior had been extremely negative.

With the assistance of a counselor, she had pierced the protective layers of thought that had led to the peripheral thinking that marked her father as evil, and made possible the embracing of an alternative set of beliefs.

The contention of the holarchic model is that in the vast majority of cases, belief alteration can change an emotional state, even when conditions would appear to proscribe it. A father who believes that the behavior of an unmanageable child is essential to that child's ultimate achievement of effective maturity, will enjoy better emotional health. A woman who is without hope of ever being able to leave, will be happier if she believes that an abusive husband's behavior is excusable. Strange as such convictions may seem, they are consistent with reactions that are observed every day. Beliefs are modified to make life most bearable. The role of the counselor is to assist in the process.

In carrying on a series of counseling sessions an effort must be constantly made to assure that the shared personality that faces a problem is not threatened by cognitive input which the client cannot handle. The counselor's beliefs are based on different experiences, learning, and problem-solving style. New factors must be carefully introduced into the critical situation, and conclusions must not be drawn on the basis of data that may not be available to the client, or on logical implication which is not completely clear.

The final test of the effectiveness of a counseling experience is based on the extent to which the counselee has incorporated skills which increase the capacity to handle future crises. Apprentice bricklayers, under expert guidance, develop assurance about their ability to do the job independently as their skills approach those of a journeyman. The confidence that knowledge provides is expected to remain once they no longer have a supervisor to assist when a problem arises. To the extent that the counselee reaches such a stage, the effect of the counseling experience can be said to be positive. Although the reason for conflict may have been centered around one crisis in life, the experience should extend to a generalized increase in the capacity to handle difficult decisions.

In describing the counseling relationship, we have developed the thesis that emotional health represents a condition of the individual which is dependent on the relationship between desires and beliefs and that these beliefs are dependent on experience and opportunity. We would extend this concept to include the adjustment level of a total community or society and contend that the experiences are capable of being provided systematically . Furthermore, the relationship between a counselor and a client is no different in principle than that between any tertiary prevention agency and the people it serves. This relationship can be extended to include every situation which involves the intervention of either member of the transaction which is designed to direct behavior into more desirable channels.

Sometimes those who cannot cope with need conflicts manifest the problem in criminal behavior. In other cases, it may appear in the form of withdrawal, indecision, or other expression of unhappiness. Unless the purpose of intervention is punishment or sheer control, the desired alteration will depend on the extent to which identification with some powerful entity provides the rationale for change. Penitentiaries, schools, and homes must all provide an opportunity for living a meaningful existence. The child who steals a cookie and the adult who robs a bank, as well as the timid adolescent and the suicidal retiree each behave in part on the basis of belief about the value and meaning of their existence.

Summary

Emotional health is a function of the behavioral process, in that it is based on the conviction that one has the capacity and opportunity to satisfy desires. The manner in which individuals shape their world represents an alteration in the interpretation of data which provides a network of defenses against threat to equilibrium.

The personality that develops out of the established defenses represents the biological focus of the self which, in the healthy individual includes far more than the physical body. The initiation of behavior is dependent on the perceived needs of the self at whatever level it is experienced.

Since the motivational process is based on informational inputs which are subject to the modifications that defensive beliefs create, and since behavior is based on motivation, it should be possible to draw inferences about beliefs on the basis of performance. Furthermore, this is not as obscure a relationship as it may first seem, since desires are common to all, with variation based only on the needs selected, and with the notion of self being critical to the type of behavior that is practiced.

This is not to suggest that there is a formula which can be applied in each instance, but it does suggest that the deductive process may be employed. If, for example, children steal from their parents, some degree of guilt can be anticipated. Some aspect of the self is evaluating another. Where no guilt is present, possible explanations include a lack of identification or rejection of the relationship which may pervade all of a child's processes, or a deliberate attempt to punish parents for some alleged mistreatment. The latter interpretation is most optimistic in that the angry individual shows evidence of an active moral sense to which one may appeal.

In the case of relationships that involve identification—as with Madeline G.—a particular characteristic obtains. One always identifies with an *idealization*, never with a physical entity. Thus, the father, the child, or the friend with serious faults, may be identified with in spite of a multitude of failings. Similarly a profession, or even a country may be revered, though many of constituent individuals are abhorred. This peculiarity of mental organization may be a deterrent or an aid in the development of a counselling experience. On the negative side, persistence in clinging to destructive relationships interferes with efforts to restructure behavior patterns. The positive aspect is, however, of extreme potential value. It makes possible a renovation of attitudes toward individuals or groups which can provide for acceptance formerly denied.

Madeline's father could be seen as first as a parent; an individual to be respected, and only secondly as a human being with a weakness. One's social or professional group need not be castigated because of the irresponsible behavior of a few—even because of minor faults that are pervasive. Identification with the total group as an *idealized* entity makes possible actions designed to improve the quality of the total organization.

Emotional distress occurs as the sequence that begins with the awareness of facts, is modified by judgments and evaluation, culminating in pervasive negative attitudes accompanied by a virtually complete lack of hope for a resolution. Because defenses are a form of belief modification, they may produce a stable and resistant bulwark against attack. This positive characteristic also has a negative side, however. The very strength of the defenses makes education and therapy difficult where ineffective defense patterns result in maladjustment.

The majority of maladjustment that therapists encounter is manifested in the form of experienced anxiety, impotence and/or alienation, as desires are believed to be thwarted. Much of the distress associated with such negative emotional states may be avoided through the introduction of preventive emotional health programs which shall be described in Chapter 16.

Counseling, or therapy, is the process of reviewing the content of belief levels at which fixation has occurred, and of revealing alternative courses of action, where options are available. The purpose is to assist clients to develop independence in dealing with factors that have led to a state of emotional distress. In those instances that there is little reason to anticipate that behavioral change can improve a situation that threatens emotional adjustment, the approach involves assisting in the alteration of beliefs that will make an uncomfortable situation less so. The success of this process is contingent on the capacity of the counselor to appreciate the subjective nature, as well as the tenacity, of beliefs that would appear to defy reason. This requires that counselors be sensitive, knowledgeable, and dedicated to the growth of their clients.

Chapter Notes

1. American Psychiatric Association (1987)
2. *Ibid.*, p. xxii
3. Sattler (1988), pointed out that "although the DSM III-R is considered to be the definitive guide to psychiatric classification, its psychological and practical utility have been questioned. The reliability and validity of some DSM-III-R categories have not been substantiated in empirical studies using multivariate procedures" (p. 552).
4. *Active* desires refer to those urges that have sufficient force to impinge on the individual. Desires may be considered *inactive* either when the individual is satiated, when age or other condition renders them passive, or when defense mechanisms cause them to be sublimated.
5. Aristotle (1972), p. 423
6. Forem (1974), p. 4
7. Mueller (1963), p. 30
8. Maslow & Mittelmann (1951), pp. 14-15
9. Goldstein (1939)
10. Maslow (1970), p. 25
11. Rogers (1974), p. 18
12. Fromm (1947), p. 362
13. Allport (1955)
14. Riesman (1950)
15. Weiss (1960), p. 38
16. Freud (1949), p. 626
17. McClelland et al. (1953)
18. The term "excessive" is used here to refer to such behavior only when it interferes with the gratification of other desires. Individuals who indulge in every luxury, and at the same time believe that their lives are highly significant, need not have any emotional health problems, though such behavior may be ultimately destructive.
19. The terrible demands made on a generation that must reconcile convictions regarding equality and freedom represent an obvious example—belief in the primacy of either requiring denial or compromise of the other.
20. Efforts to limit the access of blacks to homes in desirable residential areas are well documented. However, the same type of confusion and distress can be seen in those situations where the action of any subgroup is ambiguous. Fourteen year olds, almost without exception, accept the prohibition against driving, which is relatively rigidly enforced, while the ambiguity surrounding their right to smoke often results in extensive confrontation and mutual recrimination.
21. Bloom (1987), p. 96
22. What people seek is freedom from oppression. However, this normal desire is often distorted to an interpretation that severs the tie to those individuals and/

or institutions that provide the focus of a meaningful relationship.
23. Rogers (1951)
24. Glasser (1968)
25. This sense of debt represents a microcosm of the general human principle that meaning, and thus significance, is based on a part/whole relationship that a client can recognize. Reference to the guilt continuum may seem inappropriate. However, responsibility is a product of no other emotional class. To agree that individuals should act responsibly is to recognize the roots of that concept. This is not, however, to deny that individuals desire to act responsibly, which is the avenue to self-transcendence, but only to provide a key to the identification of the appropriate emotion.
26. Rogers made the point that he had no desire to change a counselee's mind in a session videotaped by Shostrom (1965).
27. The principle underlying Rogerian therapy is that individuals have the power to heal themselves. While in many instances mere listening can be of assistance, the value of such a technique (which has become popular among many who find it a simple, and thus convenient, procedure) has been vastly overstated.
28. The counselor may state that certainly a great many women have demonstrated a degree of rascality. Such a comment does not represent a commitment to an acceptance of the client's extreme position.
29. A mature decision is one that is robust—one that is apt to survive challenges to its propriety, or veracity.
30. A poorly understood characteristic of human behavior is the fact that as a point of view is defended, it gradually begins to take on legitimacy. This phenomenon underlies the practice of getting adherents to a cause to shout and sing its praises. The mouthing of adulatory phrases "stamps in" conviction. Demagogues seem to understand the process instinctively. Effective counselors follow a similar procedure.

Chapter 15
Behavior/Belief Alteration

The focus of this chapter is on the application of holarchic principles to early intervention, or secondary prevention issues where the behavior of individuals is monitored. The purpose of such programming is to identify motivational elements at the earliest signs of behavior deviance in order that ineffective or unacceptable beliefs, attitudes, and practices may be altered in the direction of more productive and emotionally healthy behaviors.

The Behavior Adjustment Paradigm (BAP) is introduced as an aid in analyzing the motivational elements impinging on behavioral patterns. Case examples utilizing the BAP are cited in both their diagnostic and treatment aspects.

In this chapter we shall consider the application of holarchic principles to the management of the behavior of those whose activity is under some form of monitoring––and especially to populations in schools or other social institutions. Although the approach, once again, involves the modification of systems of belief, the focus is on restructuring behavior patterns in the direction of the improvement of both performance and emotional adjustment. The distinction to be recognized is that in the following analysis, behaviors of those in treatment are far less free than are those that were considered in Chapter 14. The individual in treatment is not the client.

The function of diagnosis may be viewed from the standpoint of predicting what an individual or group will *do* and/or how they will *feel* in particular situations. Treatment of a behavior or adjustment problem, therefore, requires the consideration of what they *did* and how they *felt* in previous situations, as well as an understanding of the elements of the motivational process. If the purpose is to develop a prognosis solely to control or direct behavior, the conditions under which an action or reaction will occur should provide sufficient data. However, concern about an individual's emotional state, which is the rationale for the development of the holarchic model, requires that the extent of costs involved in behaving or failing to do so also be considered. Thus, a belief analysis is an essential part of the process. Although treatment strategies vary as elements that apply essentially to behavior (e.g., contingency contracting) or those that relate to emotional adjustment (want/cost interaction) are emphasized, the same principles apply to all behavior and the related affective impact.

Emotional Elements

The chronology of diagnosis is ordinarily such that the prevailing emotional state is identified late in the process. The logical order, however, places emotion prior to behavior, and the chain of beliefs prior to emotion. The holarchic motivation model that orders data, as described in Chapter 11, and as discussed in Chapter 14, applies in all instances. There may seem to be a certain chicken/egg comparison here, and behaviors certainly alter beliefs, but the holarchic diagnostic method always returns to a belief base whether the plan is to establish preventive programs or to treat the disturbed or recalcitrant.

The analysis of response patterns is of value in this pursuit. It is useful to know what individuals typically do as evidence of what they believe. (The researchers that profess to show that behavior is not based on attitudes are victims of the absurd notion that what individuals report about their attitudes is a valid indicator of their true feelings.) Although personality theorists suggest that behavior provides information about an individual's defense mechanisms, it must not be presumed that such psychological phenomena necessarily represent distortions that should be corrected. In some instances, of course, it may be desirable and effective to alter such beliefs. However, individuals who respond to provocation by physical force need not give up their belief in the efficacy of such a practice. They may simply be aided in learning alternative techniques.[1]

Response patterns also provide valuable clues regarding those situations and events which arouse emotions. Of what are individuals afraid? Whom do they resent? What do they find desirable? Such information is useful in predicting and controlling both behavioral and emotional states. It makes possible the substitution of situations, the elimination of events, and even an alteration of personalities. In all such instances, however, the determination rests on far more data than the sheer discovery of a precipitating incident.

Information relative to these issues can be drawn from behavioral observations of the individual involved, questioning those who are in regular contact with that person, considering how he or she is seen by peers, and studying any available records. This process makes possible the ranking of desires in order of ascendance, which can be roughly approximated by the evidence of how much and how often activities of a particular type are pursued. Equally important, it provides for the establishment of the emotional state against which potential behaviors are projected, and thus to an analysis of relevant beliefs.

Behavior Elements

In order for a decision to be made and a deliberate action to occur, a variety of factors must be considered. Not all are involved in each situation because of such limitations as lack of knowledge (i.e., belief) or low level of desire. However, all play a part in some decisions and their relevance must be determined in each instance.

The initiating factor may be the arousal of a desire, the imagination of an activity, or the awareness of an existing situation. Although all three occur, modern civilized behavior is so highly ritualized that the last two probably account for the vast majority of motivational indicators. In Western societies, hunger is not ordinarily allowed to become extreme before meals are served. Potency and other urges are organized into planned activities which either encourage responses, as in physical exercise and sexual discussion, discourage them through the influence of spectator activity (e.g., television programs), or label them as unacceptable, which relegates the stimulating material to the imagination.

In seeking to understand a behavior, it is important to discover those elements of the environment which may be initiating factors. Examples of this would be any situation or event as *perceived by the individual involved.* It would include such factors as the action of parents, peers, colleagues, supervisors, and institutional rules as they bear on the potential of the individual to express desires. In each instance emotions are aroused that, on being traced to desires, needs, and costs, may be altered under appropriate conditions.[2]

It is inconceivable that an individual could pass extensive time in pursuit of a single behavioral goal. The demands of an extensive set of desires and the exigencies of opportunity cause a kaleidoscope of intermingling activities. Individual actions may lead toward several alternative goals, while a series of actions may be related to a single desire. Furthermore, many complex activities are continuous. One works for an income and interacts with others without careful deliberation in each instance and with little direct attention to the consequences. Such sequences may be thought of as maintenance activities, having many of the characteristics of habit. Beyond this, much of each person's time is devoted to self-optimization or the acquisition of power and meaning.

The unraveling of the total fabric would be an incredible task, but in most instances the individual, group, or situation in diagnosis provides a series of clues which makes possible the identification of critical aspects, much as a dye inserted into the blood stream identifies anomalies in the system. Occasional deviations are the rule in normal individuals, but patterns of highly unusual behavior stand out in bold relief when a motivational sequence is traced.

The Behavior Adjustment Paradigm

The Behavior Adjustment Paradigm (BAP) shown in Figure 15.1 represents a general model which is applicable to all behavioral modes—a behavior incident, a total behavior sequence, an instrumental or intrinsic behavior, and/or a behavior pattern.[3] On the model, letters designate scale points, while numbers denote the behavior adjustment location. The diagram refers to the focused behavior or outcome. The location of a desire or cost on the model is purely arbitrary in that there is no "proper" or "correct" location in spite of a commonality of opinion. What is considered serious by one individual may be of little consequence to another as judgments are based on experience and other factors.

The behavior threshold refers to the point at which netwant and netcost are equal. The upper left area (OAF) represents the decision to perform a specific act, while the lower right (OCF) represents the decision to reject that particular action. OeF does not describe the direction of the behavior. However, the areas OAF and OCF do represent the intensity of the emotion accompanying the relevant action.

Behavior located at 2/1 (point w) is of modest value with low associated cost, while nonbehavior 1/2 (point x) is of less need than cost value. Behavior at 4/3 (point y) represents high need and some distress, while 5/4 (point z) represents high need and more extreme distress. Position 3/5 represents distress where the need value of a potential behavior is insufficient to outweigh the associated costs, and 4/5 describes extreme distress though the pertinent behavior does not occur.

The area bedF identifies the location of behaviors or alternatives which are associated with psychological discomfort. The dividing line is obviously not distinct. The increasing width of the crosshatching signifies that the discomfort is more intense. Behaviors approach this area as costs and needs become mutually higher. If either need or cost value is very low, no distress is involved. The model applies to each behavioral type as follows:

- **Intrinsic behavioral incident**
  OA desire/need strength (netwant)
  OC cost elements (netcost)
  (+) *Area* domain of netwant/netcost where the dominant emotion results in behavior. Either positive or negative emotions may lead to a behavior as one anticipates continuing or eliminating a behavior, situation, or event. The action in such instances is itself desirable in the sense that it does not depend for its

Figure 15.1

The Behavior/Adjustment Paradigm

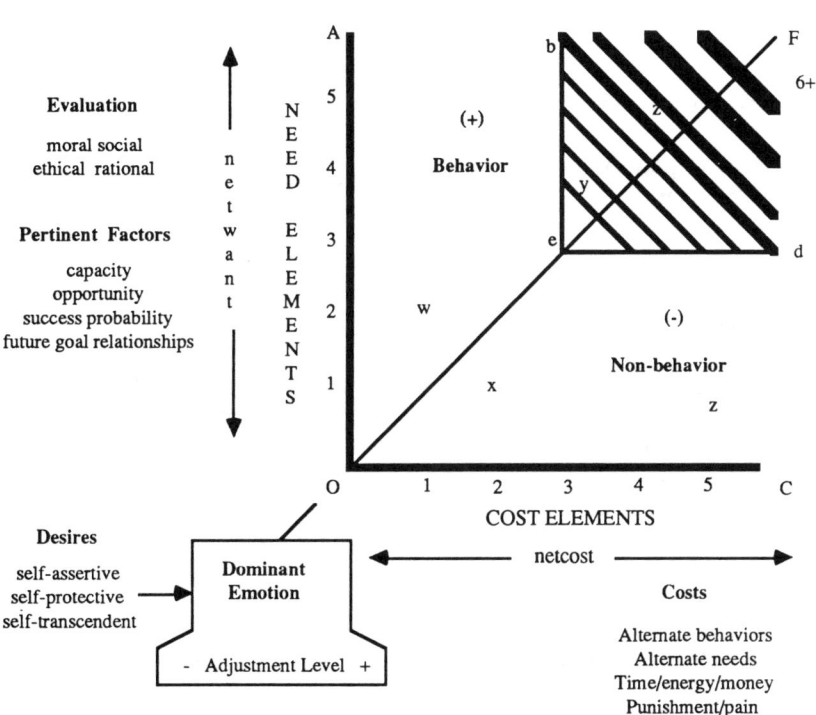

positive valence on some future or external behavior, situation, or event. (-) Area domain of netwant/netcost where the dominant emotion results in alternative action. It is identified here as nonbehavior in order to indicate that some considered behavior is not carried out.

- **Instrumental behavioral incident**
  OA instrumental value; need strength of total behavior sequence
  OC instrumental action which is added to all other costs, pertinent beliefs, and evaluations
  (+) *Area* domain of behavior; the dominant emotion is *at least in part* one of satisfaction

(-) *Area* domain in which satisfaction or willingness is insufficient to cause a particular (instrumental) behavior

- **Total behavior sequence**
  OA netwant
  OC netcost
  (+) *Area* domain of all action, including instrumental behaviors
  (-) *Area* domain of activity directed differently from the total behavior sequence under consideration

- **Behavior pattern**
  OA netwant
  OC netcost
  (+) *Area* domain of all action, including total behavior sequences
  (-) *Area* domain of activity directed differently from the behavior pattern under consideration.

For the purpose of treatment, the BAP Model is used to locate behavior on the scale, not to predict it from the scale. Although a dominant emotion in the + Area predicts behavior, the diagnostician ordinarily begins with reported behavior and from this attempts to determine the dominant emotion.

In order to demonstrate certain types and combinations of behaving as they are applied to the model, a series of examples of decisions and behaviors is provided. Each is highly oversimplified and represents only a possible set of conditions. In the first three examples, the emotional state preceding the decision is positive.

- **Intrinsic behavior**: Deliberating about whether to attend a baseball game:
  a. desire: stimulation
  b. need: attending the game
  c. focus: behavior
  d. costs: (including instrumental behaviors)
     (1) before: ticket, gasoline, parking prices, obtaining tickets (energy), driving to the stadium, family objection
     (2) during: cold weather, food costs
     (3) after: driving home
  e. pertinent factors: probability of an exciting game, previous experience as a player
  f. evaluative elements: expectancy as an alumnus

Since the focus of the experience is on stimulation during the game, the sequence ends at the conclusion of the contest. Although driving home is a cost that is considered at the time of deliberating about whether to go, it also represents part of a new behavioral sequence at the termination of the game. If the game is attended, the costs must be understood to be acceptable, (i.e., of lower strength than that of the related need).

This Sequence		Next Sequence	
instrumentality	*focus - behavior*	*instrumentality*	*focus - ?*
all costs before, during, and after game	stimulation during game	driving home	

- **Instrumental behavior:** Deliberating about whether to buy a pair of shoes while shopping:
  a. desire: attractiveness - stimulation
  b. need: shoes
  c. focus: outcome
  d. costs: usual, including other desired items
  e. pertinent factors: whether item is on sale, bank balance
  f. evaluative elements: spouse reaction, appropriateness for specific occasion

Ordinarily, the desire is not to buy, but to own and wear the shoes. Owning is an outcome; wearing is a behavior. Here the next diagnostic step can be taken. *The need may be reduced in the direction of desire by asking the question "why?" until no appropriate response can be provided.* One always *needs* something in the interest of meeting some desire, while the reason that one *desires*, as to desire food, is unexplainable, except in terms of a theory regarding human motivation. The relationship between desires and needs was developed in Chapter 7.

The shoes being purchased may have utilitarian value; they may provide attractiveness or protection. "Attractiveness" remains a (lower level) need, which could be reduced to one or more of the basic desires. It is not always essential to pursue a desire to the ultimate level. The shoes as a need are positive; their cost negative. By determining their desire-satisfying potential, alternatives at many levels are revealed. If the shoes are purchased, the cost must be understood to be acceptable.

This Sequence	Next Sequence
instrumentality	*behavior and outcome*
all costs	stimulation when wearing shoes

- **Intrinsic behavior:** Deciding whether to drink a proffered martini before dinner:
  a. desire: stimulation + relief: the drink may be exciting as well as soothing
  b. need: the martini
  c. focus: behavior + outcome: the martini may be enjoyed for its flavor, as well

as for the relaxation that follows its indulgence
   d. costs: immediate or long-term health hazard, accepting other proffered drinks
   e. evaluative elements: possible social/moral reservation or positive sanction

If the martini is taken, the cost must be understood to be acceptable.

Focus

Behavior	*Outcome*
stimulation	relief/relaxation

- **Differentially motivated behavior:** Deciding whether to attack another person:
  a. desire: (described in each example below)
  b. need: attacking behavior
  c. focus:
    1. Outcome:
       (a) the relief associated with reaction in response to an action which caused anger
       (b) stimulation associated with a sense of power on observing the recipient's response
       (c) sadistic stimulation on observing suffering
    2. Behavior:
       (a) relief during attacking as a reaction to an action which caused anger
       (b) stimulation during attacking as a feeling of power
       (c) sadistic stimulation on observing suffering
       (d) costs: usual, including instrumental actions as in outcomes (2a) and (2b)
       (e) pertinent factors: size and strength of the individual to be attacked, presence of authorities or others who may intercede
       (f) evaluative elements: antisocial interpretation by authorities, positive response from friends who encourage violent behavior

In cases of this type, excitement and relief may both be involved, and the behavior and outcome each represent a part of the total focus. It is essential to identify the emotional state of the individual prior to and during the precipitating incident in all such diagnoses.

A psychologist is usually not involved in situations of the types described above, since they represent isolated behavioral sequences. As such, they are neither particularly disturbing nor do they necessarily portend emotional health problems. However, if inefficient or unacceptable behaviors persist over time, they may become serious enough to warrant study. There is no difference in principle between a single act and a succession of actions, except that learning must be included in the equation. In the case of the individual who is destructive, the learning may have involved both the feeling associated with the behavior and the costs involved. The fact that a behavior persists in spite of what seem to be extremely high costs provides no dependable explanation in itself. Possible explanations include the high need value of the experience, failure to associate the price with the experience, and lack of awareness of alternative responses. Each possibility must be explored.

The Diagnostic Process

The first step in diagnosing a problem is to determine both the behavior to be analyzed and the alteration desired. Here, the distinction must be drawn as to whether adjustment or control is to take priority. The desired outcome must be specified with sufficient precision to elicit an appropriate prescription. Is it the quality or the quantity of the behavior that is of concern? Does it occur only at the wrong time or should it never occur at all? Most importantly, is the adjustment of individuals involved or the management of their behavior to take precedence?

It may be assumed that when individuals refer themselves for assistance, and when they are of majority status, emotional adjustment is of first concern (though they may complain of an inability to control such behavior as smoking or drinking). Where the individual is socially dependent, as is a minor at home or school, or is in some form of custodial center, the problem may well be essentially related to behavior control, with adjustment a secondary consideration.

The next task is to accurately identify the behavioral sequence and the emotional state under consideration. Simple as this sounds, the inability to correctly identify a behavior leads to misdiagnosis in many cases. Consider the complaint, "John is late for school several times a week." Dealt with at this level, such an explanation as "He is lazy" is apt to be employed, although it is obviously not of diagnostic value. It may seem that if the statement is altered to read, "John comes to school late several times each week," a behavior has been identified. But it almost certainly has not.

This description would be (diagnostically) accurate only if John were *deliberately* late, which is ordinarily not the case (if it were, another analysis would be appropriate). As it stands, lateness represents not a behavior, but only one aspect of the cost. In point of fact, it does not describe what he does but what he does not do. While it is true that John does *not* come to school on time several times each week, it would be equally valid to say that John does not milk the cows before coming to school, which would be true if John had no such responsibility. The fact that John habitually arrives late provides important diagnostic data, but to define his behavior it is essential to learn what it is that he *does*.

Since the behavioral sequence is determined by the relationship between want and cost, the error in this description of John's behavior can be revealed by asking, "What is the priority status of John's wants?" Coming to school late is obviously not the answer in most instances. By contrast, consider the report that "Henry does not speak in class although he is capable of speech." In this case, the undesirable action is far more likely to be deliberate, although his silence is very apt to be only instrumental.

Consider further, such statements as "Sally jumps up and down on her mother's furniture, although she is punished for doing so," which describes a behavioral sequence plus a cost factor; and "Alice continually fights with her sister." The latter includes some interpretive material (although fighting may not be what Sally believes she is doing). Once again, the data are useful, but the nature of the interaction must be further studied. Either child's activity may be instrumental, but the first is more apt to be intrinsic.

The task is to identify behaviors and emotions in order to discover why they occur. This requires a number of determinations. First, what is it that the individual does (instrumentally and/or intrinsically), and/or what feelings are described or manifested? Second, how regularly does the behavior occur? Daily? Weekly? Rarely? Third, does the impetus come from some apparently spontaneous interest that arises within the individual, or does it occur as a reaction to certain types of situations or the behaviors of others? To deal with the first possibility, the analysis concentrates on want/cost relationships. Where the behavior represents a reaction to others, further study must be made of such factors as the conditions under which it occurs, the extent of provocation that is necessary, the form the response takes, and the type and intensity of feeling associated with the response.

At this point it should be possible to establish a conditional hypothesis. This is accomplished by the application of principles of behavior defined earlier. Behavior provides evidence of some desire that demands resolution, of some belief regarding the efficacy of the behavior, and some evaluation of associated costs. The form in which a behavioral hypothesis is stated must include some type of desire and some culminating emotion. It presents a hierarchy of interests which makes possible an understanding of the status of the activity under consideration.

Taking the four cases cited above, a study of the situation may reveal that John wants to lie comfortably in bed (relaxation) more than to be on time for school; Henry wants the security of silence (integrity); Sally wants the thrill associated with jumping (stimulation); and Alice wants to establish control over her world (power). Such hypotheses must be understood to be tentative. The task is to determine how valid the inferences are, and, of equal importance, to learn why they persist in the face of what often seem to be extremely high costs.

The diagnostic process now moves to a study of the elements involved in the behavioral sequence. Considering first the desire related aspect, it is necessary to determine whether the behavior has intrinsic value. This is apt to be difficult because of the vagueness of the emotion, as described earlier. An individual, for example, may be seeking comfort, as in putting on a robe and slippers. This may qualify as both stimulating and relieving, but should be recognized as a different goal than that of preparing to sleep, which represents the desire to reduce activity to a level of minimal tension.

Action may also be preventive in nature. Donning clothes for warmth, threatening another person, or even injuring someone (where the action is nonpunitive) may be accomplished to avoid negative consequences. For this reason, it is important to thoroughly understand the nature of the desire(s) involved. This is done by identifying the need and reducing it step by step in the direction of a desire. The earlier example of a purchased pair of shoes demonstrated the process. In the case of a destructive child, the steps may proceed from the need to be recognized as independent of authority, to acceptance by a subgroup, to the achievement of a position of power, to access to members of the opposite sex. The hierarchy must be pursued.

A major difficulty is that most individuals perform psychologically within one or two levels of need immediacy. They are often unable to understand why they desire certain behaviors or events. However, through analysis in terms of the holarchic model, such desires can be deduced. At this step, it is ordinarily not possible to make an accurate estimate of the strength of the desire. This often requires considerable information regarding costs and other elements, especially where the behavior is difficult to understand.

Cost analysis may be accomplished in several ways. First are the obvious costs such as time and energy. These can be determined in many cases by interviewing the individual. Knowledge of legal constraints, the price of failure, alternate behavior possibilities, etc., must be ascertained. A second technique, which may be employed where a subject cannot or will not cooperate, is to consider various aspects of the behavior. If, for example, the action was obviously covert, one may assume knowledge of some institutional limitation.

The analysis of pertinent beliefs and evaluative elements is a much more familiar process and one that psychologists have developed extensively. It may involve all of the psychometric and personality assessment devices that make possible a description of the strengths and limitations of the individual. The problem here is in the tendency to use the data as fully describing an individual's motivation. Such an analysis cannot provide this information. The motive for action must be sought first in the need/desire pattern. The study of costs and pertinent beliefs and evaluative elements is useful in revealing why the particular method is employed, why alternative approaches are disregarded, and even, in some cases, why certain desires are apparently ignored. For the child who is perennially late to school, what is the need value of arriving on time––and the cost if he or she does not?

When employing the holarchic behavior model, each step must be completed in whatever detail is necessary. Behavior is constrained not by what is the case, but what the individual *believes* to be the case. Furthermore, belief is limited to that which has been learned. Thus, in estimating costs, need value, and other factors, it must be remembered that elements cannot exceed those which have been learned to be "true."

There is the further limitation of attention and relevance. If one owns only a blue car, its blueness is probably not a relevant element. (The question "Why did he drive a blue car?" would be specious.) Furthermore, if one owns cars of several colors, the selection of the blue one on any occasion may have been made with a minimum of attention. It is here that the concept of habit becomes important.

Outcomes are obviously not behaviors, although they may sound as though they were. "I burned my back" or "I failed the examination" refer, ordinarily, to unplanned experiences. But the exceptions are equally significant. Perhaps I burned my back to cure a skin disease (instrumental), or because it is considered attractive to be seen sunbathing—even getting a sunburn—in my social group (intrinsic).

It may seem that limitation of capacity in some instances represents a motive for action and thus should not be simply appended to costs. Children with severe brain damage may appear, at times, to behave because of their affliction. This is, however, not the case. Their motives are identical to those of all people, with the distinction being that their belief about their limitation adds to their estimate of the cost (e.g., risk) involved in employing a particular technique to achieve a goal. They may not even know they have a deficit, but only that the world they live in is bounded by their skill in that area. The child with dyslexia may want to learn, but the difficulty of studying or performing, which is a risk/pain cost factor, may cause him or her to seek potency and stimulation through other behaviors.

Perceptual set may also add to cost considerations. What one believes about the world provides situations with characteristics that determine how extensive a cost they represent. It also affects the establishment of needs. Prejudices, stereotypes, and labels, as they are applied to individuals, groups, behaviors, situations, or events, result in the specification of needs as deliberations are made. A teacher's need for power, combined with the conviction that students have few—if any—rights, may result in destructively oppressive action.

The diagnostician must be aware that emotional stress is often carried over and contributes to reactions where no cause is assignable. The individual who smashes a dish because of anger aroused in observing a sports telecast has no quarrel with the china. Similarly, the child who manifests rage in a situation which could be expected to elicit only frustration is very apt to be partially out of control because of nagging, unexpressed feelings. Explosions in such instances may, beyond their possible cathartic effect, provide an opportunity for probing sensitive areas.

Capacities can be measured relatively objectively in some cases, but they must still be considered in terms of the individual's beliefs. The issues of opportunity and social constraint are more obviously subjective in nature, and must be exposed through discussion and the use of objective tests and projective devices which categorize responses according to appropriate scales.

The practice of employing normative data, although invaluable for many determinations, is another potential source of serious error. First, there is the problem of the constellation in which the data occur. Achievement scores, though high, may be well below potential. Intelligence, though low, may be the highest in a particular child's family. Because of this interaction, ipsative interpretations[4] must not be ignored, and relevant reference factors must be taken into account. Second, there is an assumption of equal weight among beliefs that is apt to lead to attempts to balance strengths against weaknesses. This is a far more common error than is assumed. She is "fat but pretty" and he is "dumb but pleasant" are interpretations that suggest adjustment potential which is often not there. To be extremely overweight may be so depressing that the most beautiful face cannot attenuate it.

The problem with data interpretation must not be construed as minimizing the value of psychometric evaluation. All of the procedures for collecting and analyzing data should be followed meticulously. Beyond this, however, the information must be considered idiosyncratically as well as normatively. The rule to employ is to *measure exactly; interpret broadly.* Thus, an IQ of 95, or 108 should be painstakingly determined. However, its contribution to a behavioral sequence must be estimated in relationship to many other factors which may significantly alter its interpretation.

Instrumental behavior is often the cost which provides the most insight into the problem which has brought an individual to the attention of a mental health professional. (It is the area in which a discrimination must be made between activities which are carried out because of the positive feeling they produce in themselves, and those which are undergone as requisite to some other—often obscure—end.) Why does Johnny hit when each occasion brings punishment? What is his emotional state when he strikes his neighbor? Does he believe in advance that he will be hurt? Why does he arrive late at school when detentions are guaranteed?

Several techniques may be employed for making determinations in this area. The first involves the alteration of costs. This can be accomplished to some extent through simulation (discussion of changes), by analysis of projective data, or by actually modifying the situation. Opportunity, for example, may be altered by presenting a situation in which a restraint is removed either obviously or through misdirection. A second method is the removal of the payoff. This, too, can be accomplished in several ways. The purpose is to discover whether the actual or projected behavior persists when it is viewed as the culminating event in a behavioral sequence. Will Sally continue to jump on the furniture if her parents do not respond? How much is the behavior worth?

Employing the Behavior Adjustment Paradigm

The following figures represent locations on the Behavior Adjustment Paradigm (Figure 15.1). Consider the child whose behavior is analyzed as being focused on the outcome "possessing money" as a need related to the desire for power, and where the behavior ("stealing") is instrumental. The action may be plotted at 4/1 - a strong desire for power associated with an extremely low cost (little risk is assumed); 4/2 - strong desire for power and some concern about cost with, perhaps, few known alternatives; 3/1 - average desire, with somewhat less cost; or 3/2 - average desire with some concern about cost. Obviously, if the emotional state can be properly located, effective treatment is most apt to be applied. For example, a 3/1 location should respond more quickly and easily to increased costs than should locations 4/1 and 4/2. The possibility of applying inappropriate techniques can be reduced by the accuracy of such an assessment.

The same model can, of course, be applied to analyze a "nonbehavior." As indicated earlier, the term nonbehavior refers to a failure to carry out any specific behavior under consideration. The action of an individual who does not comply with a directive may be plotted at 1/3 - little need for anticipated reinforcement and little anticipated cost; 1/4 - higher cost and trivial payoff; 2/3 - although need is a consideration cost is higher; or 2/4 - high cost and still far from sufficient incentive.

Assessing Emotional States

The most valid indicator of the degree to which an activity is intrinsic or instrumental is to be found in a study of the emotion involved in its perpetuation. In order to make this determination, the activity must be isolated and the feeling of the individual evaluated. Sally's behavior was described as "jumping on the furniture." The question is, how does Sally feel about the act of jumping? Would a mattress or trampoline be equally satisfying? In many cases, it is not possible for the individual to specify the emotional state. However, by a process of comparisons (e.g., would you prefer to do X or Y?), it is possible to make reasonable assumptions.

When an emotional state is properly identified, it is possible to determine the source of the feeling. Anger, for example, involves desire, frustration, and some responsible agent. Thus, if anger is experienced, each of these elements must be pursued. Anxiety, which results from ambiguity, calls for a thoroughly different resolution.

The determination of an emotional state consists of several steps including theoretical, clinical, simulated, and behavioral facets. To this extent, it is similar to (and often simultaneous with) that involved in identifying a behavioral focus.

- The theoretical aspect refers to an analysis of the situation in terms of normal expectancy. If a hungry individual is placed before a meal and separated by a glass wall, frustration can be anticipated. Thus, if frustration is observed, an attempt must be made to identify the desire or need that is being thwarted.
- In the interview phase, questions should be asked which are designed to elicit feelings. This is often possible in the most direct way as, "How do you feel when he does this to you?" However, respondents may use inappropriate terms unless the meaning is explained. For example, the term "angry" may be found to be incorrect if, on further discussion, it becomes clear that the respondent does not believe that some individual or institution is culpable. It is the appropriate term only where moral turpitude is believed to be involved. The treatment would be quite different in each instance.
- Simulation refers to the use of projective devices to approximate situations in which costs are altered or needs are substituted. Here it becomes possible to test responses and reactions at low risk and to expose desires that may be

masked by the expressed need. The value of the projective response resides in its potential for revealing attitudes that are not otherwise apparent. This is not to suggest that a blind analysis is appropriate. In principle, diagnoses should be made in terms of observed behavior, with psychometric and other devices utilized for confirmation. However, wherever results are significantly different from what is anticipated, whether it be a measure of capacity, achievement, or personalty, there is reason to pursue the issue.

- The behavior of the individual insofar as emotions are expressed provides perhaps the most valuable clues. Violent reaction, physical or verbal, is obvious evidence of the presence of an agitated emotional state, although the cause of the disturbance may be difficult to pinpoint. However, passivity and more subtle affective states may be equally informative.

No one of these, nor all in concert, represents positive assurance of one's degree of emotional distress, even when supplemented by such physiological signs as flushed appearance, rapid pulse, elevated blood pressure, or excessive perspiration. However, they often provide the best information available. Although emotion is involved in all behavior, the diagnostic process should discriminate between normal reactions which involve only temporary discomfort from those which are pervasive. It is important to describe as accurately as possible the degree of distress and the prognosis for adjustment as well as for behavior.

Having completed the netwant/netcost analysis, a behavioral sketch can be drawn which both explains why individuals perform as they do, and why they do not behave in ways that others expect or desire. The diagnostic conclusion is, of course, speculative. It represents an educated guess and, in the area of psychological interpretation, this is the limit that the state of the art permits. In drawing conclusions, one must be careful to avoid as many as possible of the common pitfalls of psychological diagnosis:

- Failure to behave is not proof of a lack of desire. The fact that an individual does not perform in a certain way may rather be related to capacity, opportunity, or other pertinent motivational element.
- Such factors as capacity must take into account all possible components. Intellectual level is only one aspect. In order to perform, individuals must believe that they can exceed some minimum requirement in every area that they believe to be related.
- The fact that an individual behaves is no guarantee that he or she enjoys positive emotional health. Many competing desires may exist and costs may be very high. Nonbehavior may be similarly misleading, as when a desire to act, though strong, is inhibited because of unacceptable costs.
- Expectancies tend to color interpretations. Data should, as far as possible, be able to stand alone. The "halo" effect is an example of a situation in which one's skill or interest level in one area is assumed to predict behavior in another. Stereotyping is a similar practice. It should be remembered that

diagnosis is, at its best, based on assumptions which are deduced from speculative relationships.
- No behavior is based on one desire, one cost factor, one anticipated outcome. Treatment based on such an assumption would be irresponsible. The focus on one aspect is often desirable because of its efficiency, but even here, systems thinking would suggest that each modification that is induced alters the relationship between desires, needs, and costs. The risk of falling from a high place may be very small. However, beliefs about the seriousness of falling vary greatly among individuals. Similarly, although the odds against success in a venture may be extremely high, the value of the payoff may be so great that some will find the risk acceptable.
- Diagnosis is often based on limited contact. Individuals being studied may, because of duress, display a mood that does not typify their response style. They may attempt to impress, be willing to lie, or be anxious to escape from the diagnostic situation. They may adopt the most exaggerated characteristic of the group with which they identify (e.g., swaggering, insolence), which may signify only that they are experiencing threat.
- Knowledge is always limited. Responses are predicated on what has been learned. Terms such as "nigger" or "honky" may or may not be used pejoratively. "Bad" manners may reflect accepted family behavior patterns. Dress and cleanliness are no less apt to be affected by mores that may be unknown to the diagnostician. It is essential to recognize which factors are deviant, as well as to assume the responsibility for accepting those which vary from the preferred behavioral style of the diagnostician.
- Facts must, once again, be recognized as no more than a special class of beliefs. Although they are essential to judgment, they do not mandate specific interpretations. They do not represent "true" knowledge. Similarly, desire, emotion, and motivation must be recognized as related, but critically different, functions. To reiterate, emotion requires only desire plus a situational referent, while motivation includes both of these, plus beliefs regarding the extent to which capacity and opportunity to behave are believed to exist.

Behavior Alteration

In this section, procedures are described which facilitate redirecting behavior. This may or may not include an alteration in the behavioral sequence, since in some instances only the method, and not the goal, creates the problem. The technique involves a prognosis regarding what to expect under specified conditions. Thus, one can anticipate behaviors both in terms of what the behaver wants and as it meets the expectations of those who control such behavior, including social and legal institutions, and parents and parent surrogates.

In dealing with behavior reorganization, the same principles which apply to diagnosis pertain. The alteration of need/desire or want/cost relationships may be accomplished by increasing or decreasing need value or costs, or by any combination of these. Both what the individual is doing, as well as what he or she is *not* doing must be addressed. This provides clues to want/cost elements, which must be taken into account in determining how to encourage individuals to alter their behavior with maximum efficiency. Adjustment may or may not represent a prime consideration.

Desire is not subject to direct alteration (i.e., by manipulating that factor), but by the restructuring of needs and costs. For this reason, a desire alteration approach is not included as an option. Costs may be reassessed in terms both of any particular scale (e.g., capacity), and of the relationship between scales (achievement in terms of capacity). As to social sanctions, costs refer to the existence of rules "smoking is forbidden" or of recommendations "charitable actions are moral." Want/cost ratios refer to the application of the rules. The concept of want/cost alteration is not unique. It is, in fact, what is intended in any educational program.

The effectiveness of this method is based on the contention that beliefs about needs and costs are learned. The characteristics of this procedure which set it apart are the emphasis on behavior—as opposed, for example, to learning—and the attempt to account for all relevant inputs. Such factors as opportunity and the awareness of alternative needs receive special attention. Furthermore, the process is developed out of a consideration of what would cause behavior or adjustment change as opposed to the practice of eliminating potential solutions on the grounds of their impracticability.

Deviant Behavior Types

In order to relate diagnostic information to programming, behavior can be categorized by a labelling process which must be understood in all of its limitations. The descriptors refer to what individuals typically *do*, rather than what they *are*, and a language is employed that is commonly understood. Although this does not eliminate the possibility of misinterpretation, it may help to maintain an appropriate focus since behavior and adjustment are the business of those with social responsibility. Any individual may be so atypical that no classification is sufficiently representative to be useful, and an individual's behavior may fall into several categories. Furthermore, the types are not to be thought of as in any way causal, but merely descriptive of common sets of relationships which may provide a guide; to be altered in term of the unique characteristics of the individual. Behaviors amenable to analysis and treatment using the BAP model may be classified as *non-productive*, *disruptive*, *bizarre*, and *perverse*.

Disruptive behaviors are those which interfere with others, ranging from the annoying to the criminal. A critical diagnostic question is whether the behavior is *aggressive* (power-oriented), *hostile* (anger-oriented), *desperate* (panic or anxiety-oriented), or *transcendent* (meaning-oriented).

When individuals violate rules or laws that have been accepted by the society in which they operate, a vital diagnostic question is why they are willing to risk paying the price (e.g., incarceration) that is ostensibly associated with such activity. Examples of nonproductive and disruptive behavior, with a discussion of possible treatment and some probable consequences, follow.

Diagnosis/Treatment Examples

Nonproductive Behavior: General Deficiency

Nonproductive type behaviors are inefficient either in achieving desired outcomes (persistent failure) or in providing the sense of gratification that would be anticipated (pervasive discomfort). A critical diagnostic question is: Which factors are most amenable to alteration?

Referral data: Anna (age 13) does not complete assignments even under supervision in the classroom. She daydreams and indulges in a variety of time-consuming and apparently random behaviors (current behavior). Teachers and parents desire that her performance and attitude improve (desired behavior).

Diagnosis: The first task is to determine what Anna is *doing*, and what desires are being expressed. In this case, it may be most efficient to consider pertinent beliefs and evaluative elements since the costs (ridicule, reprimand) seem sufficiently high that the desired behavior should occur unless other factors are involved. Test results suggest a below average level of ability (IQ: 85-90) and a performance level several years below that of most of her peers. She has no special skills (athletic ability, musical talent, artistic facility), and interests are in relatively solitary recreational pursuits (riding bikes, roller skating). She is the poorest of four siblings as a student, and parents have "given up any hope" of altering her behavior. (Anna is representative of perhaps five to ten million American school students.)

Little potential for power or meaning can be found. Anna is not needed by anyone (her work is of low value), and she has few techniques available for gaining control over her world. She has learned that she can satisfy herself in a few sports activities and can tolerate fairly long periods of boredom in school and at home by daydreaming about future behaviors. Moreover, she has learned that the cost of such behaviors is relatively low (can often be ignored). Her integrity is, thus, not in immediate jeopardy. Current behavior (i.e., daydreaming), is probably located at 5/1 or 5/2 on the Behavior Adjustment Paradigm. The high need value is, in part, due to the lack of perceived alternatives.

Children exhibiting this type of behavior are commonly referred for psychological analysis. Tutoring, special class placement, or other approaches may be indicated. However, such procedures should always be based on a careful analysis of all costs. This involves a task analysis, the purpose of which is to locate the most efficient starting point for remediation. The psychologist's responsibility is to provide an accurate assessment of costs. These will vary from the type described above to resentment at being expected to perform, task-specific weakness, and non-existent discipline, with guilt feelings about failure added to the price.

Unsound Approaches: Focus on current behavior.
- Increase netcost (punish). Assign poor or failing grades. Such a method may increase the threat to integrity, in which case the child's attitude will remain negative. It is applicable only when need value is not high, and costs are close to the limen (3/2 or 2/3). Anna's need is relatively high.
- Decrease netcost. Provide no grades or ignore her performance. Accept substandard work as satisfactory. This reduces cost only where the individual is so threatened that escape is of prime concern. Since it has the potential for demeaning, it may actually increase the price being paid. It is obviously not apt to eliminate the behavior, and in Anna's case, has no value.[5]

The Holarchic Approach:[6] Focus on the desired behavior.

This procedure is based on the holarchic principles of want/cost interaction developed in Chapter 7. The goal in this case is to increase the need value of school related work such as studying, by associating such behavior with *power* and *meaning* interests. In this respect the process parallels that of a typical behavior management regimen.
- Relate tasks to immediate or near future payoff.
- Assure an opportunity to perform.
- Shape behavior through use of incremental rewards.
- Perform work against time. This associates academic performance with stimulation and identifies the time element as the cost factor.

The critical distinction in the holarchic approach lies in the last item, which deals with the nature of the reward system. While candy and similarly attractive payoffs have a function, they are ancillary to the principal focus. Such rewards are extrinsic to the process, and in fact specifically identify work as a cost factor—as an activity which is to be disposed of.

A common characteristic of poor or nonperformers is their inability to perceive any linkage between the prescribed activity and the acquisition of power or meaning. Power may be enhanced when the individual understands that skills may be employed to achieve a broad range of desires. School work, no matter how elementary, must provide access to control of this child's world. Reading and mathematics must be related *directly* to a sense of mastery. Too often, they are limited to mechanical, repetitious parroting.

Equally important, and often overlooked, is the lack of identification, of belonging, of being needed, of having an opportunity to give, that such individuals often feel. Although they may develop skills that provide for the expression of power, they will not necessarily experience a concomitant sense of worth. In fact, it is more efficient to plan first to provide opportunities for the individual to find a way to be useful and needed. It is out of such a personality that responsibility and discipline may ultimately result in an adequate power/meaning base.

Determine the locus of meaning. Who or what can appeal to the desire to belong? In most instances, especially with younger children, the most dependable sources of meaning will be found within the parent structure. The crucial step is to link academic performance to whatever behavior provides meaning. This is a most difficult procedure, since it must not represent a threat. Rather, it must enhance or complement behaviors related to identification. Examples would include the improvement of mathematical and/or reading skills essential to the performance of some specific, useful, task. The key concept here, is that the performance of the enhanced skill must be needed by other family members. It must play a significant role in the family's well being.

Recall the example of the bride who *enjoys* the task of preparing a honeymoon breakfast, (although she is ordinarily averse to such tasks) because it is part of a desired total experience. The pertinent question is: What will cause ostensibly negative behaviors (as studying may be for Anna) to be endowed with positive emotional characteristics? The answer is—when these elements are essential aspects of a desirable existence; when instrumentality has become intrinsic; when the focus is on the totality, as when a mother bakes a cake or writes a letter at a time that she is not feeling well.

In the example of Anna, the process begins with her viewing academic performance as a pure cost factor. The need aspect is extremely ambiguous. Rewarding schoolwork with sweets is useful only where it is reasonable to expect that the child will learn to enjoy such activity for its own sake. The appropriate pairing is between the product and *the desire for power and meaning*. When work is seen as functional, it may become sufficiently attractive that the want/cost ratio is altered significantly. The ultimate goal is to make academic performance an intrinsic behavior as far as possible—at least one that is more easily tolerated.

Disruptive Behavior: Aggression

Referral data: John hits other children in his classroom without provocation both during class and on the playground. His behavior is similar at home, especially with girls and smaller playmates (current behavior). His teacher and his parents wish him to interact in more socially acceptable ways—to refrain from employing physical force to intimidate his classmates (desired behavior).

Diagnosis: The psychologist determines that John hits children because it creates a sense of power and control, as evidenced by the response he gets from his classmates. He is not isolated or seriously disliked, and, in many situations, he is sought as a leader. His hitting behavior is apparently a technique (need) which is employed to express aggressive emotion. It is an intrinsic behavior pattern, since he enjoys the behavior as well as the outcome. The positive emotion is not associated with the pain that his victims endure, but with the control over them that it provides. The desired behavior is some alternative method for meeting his urge for power. Current behavior is probably located at 6/3.

Unsound Approaches: Focus on current behavior.
- Increase cost. Punish such behavior in some strict way. This may stop the behavior, but since the desire remains such action will either have a temporary or only superficial effect. Furthermore, it will probably cause anger and frustration, which may result in other undesirable action. It is an excellent example of a technique believed to be disciplinary. It is, in fact, not discipline at all, but punishment—*a diametrically opposite concept.*
- Decrease cost. Ignore the behavior. This is a common response which grows out of a sense of despair, a hope that it will stop spontaneously, or an insensitivity to the needs of both John and those whom he punishes. It is sometimes referred to as "decriminalization," a practice based on the assumption that everybody sins in one way or another. This approach will ensure that they do!

The Holarchic Approach: Focus on the desired behavior.
- Decrease need value. The value of such behavior will be diminished when it fails to produce the desired effect. This is often out of the hands of a teacher, since more rewards are distributed by peers. However, it may be possible to encourage those who provide the incentive to alter their responses. Since the cost of the current behavior is fairly low, this approach is difficult but can be dramatically effective.
- Increase the need value of alternative behaviors that satisfy the power urge. Since aggression is based on the desire for power and potency, certain principles may be taken into account.
  a. Potency or growth can be realized through skill acquisition in academic, social, physical, or other fields. Expressed talent is most apt to provide positive feelings.
  b. Power can be gained through many forms of leadership. The fact that leading through example or by successful performance encourages imitative behavior, and that a strong constituency is more satisfying than a weak one, make optimism reasonable. However, although aggressive individuals are often possessed of leadership potential, they sometimes lack the skills for employing it effectively. Here, once again, the cost aspect is involved. The procedure involves ignoring the undesired and rewarding the desired behavior. It is, in fact, such behaviors which are most amenable to a "behavior management" approach.

A subtle, but often critical aspect is that in employing an alternate approach, a high price may be paid in terms of loss of status or esteem. This must be taken into account, since the acquisition of alternative techniques will not necessarily eliminate those that have been successful in the past. It is because of such possibilities, and because of the need to discriminate the aggressive from the hostile, that indiscriminate use of Pavlovian principles is abjured.

Disruptive Behavior: Hostility

Referral data: Glenn, (like John), hits others at the slightest provocation during class and on the playground. He reacts violently to parental expectations and to any form of institutional control (current behavior). It is hoped that his attitude and behavior can be altered in the direction of social conformity (desired behavior).

Diagnosis: The psychologist learns that Glenn's behavior is a reaction to the conviction that he is being controlled, frustrated, and mistreated by people and institutions *that he believes have no right to do so*. He has no tolerance even for accidents that he may in any way construe as deliberate. His behavior represents an attempt to achieve relief from distressing situations. The tension is created because of his belief that his power potential is wrongly interfered with.

Unsound Approaches: Focus on current behavior.
- Increase cost. Assign strict punishment to such reactions. Since Glenn believes he is already being unjustly provoked, this will be seen as an additional affront. Again, there is a conviction that this is discipline, which it is not.
- Decrease cost. Ignore the behavior. In the case of a single outburst, this is perhaps the most appropriate response. However, in dealing with a habituated response, it can represent a serious error. Continual deference may lead to the adoption of such behaviors as a power gaining technique.

The Holarchic Approach: Eliminate the value of the undesirable behavior.

The holarchic interpretation is based on the contention that Glenn (as is the case with all people) does not enjoy anger.[7] Rather, he has either learned that hostile reactions often produce desirable results or his responses have become severely habituated. In this instance, there is no alternative desired behavior nor is another action appropriate for meeting the need to express anger. The appropriate procedure is to eliminate the necessity for the offensive actions. The reason is that hostile reaction is based on a normal but unnecessary emotion (Chapter 13). Unlike aggression, which is essential to positive emotional health, feelings of anger, particularly of a pervasive nature, can be avoided in many cases. The behavior may be located at any point along the limen. The cause of the location is not directly related to the cost of the behavior but to the situation that precedes it. The behavior is designed to reduce the negative emotional state. However, there may be high costs associated with the expression of anger, and this distinction must be carefully analyzed.
- Decrease the need value. Eliminate the payoff. This is extremely difficult, since those being punished are not apt to ignore their tormentor. It is, however, a possible test of the question of whether the emotion is desired for itself, and, in some well-defined situations, it may prove effective.
- Alter the elements of the situation that cause the need to arise. This is the

treatment of choice in such situations. It represents the restructuring of the belief pattern underlying the behavior. Although it is a complex process, it is by no means impossible.

It is often said that people with paranoia find many legitimate reasons for their fears, the interpretation being that they distort and magnify their interpretation of situations with the result that inappropriate emotions are experienced. In the case of the hostile individual, a parallel may be seen. Certainly, in American society, there are inequities. Status differences arbitrarily confer and withhold privilege. Beyond this, individuals may personally have undergone degrading or embarrassing experiences. The result may well be extreme sensitivity to interference, particularly when they have learned that their cause may be "just."

Treatment involves changing beliefs about those elements of situations or actions that are believed by the angry child to be offensive. When this happens, anger should be reduced, and the behavior, usually associated with high social costs, should subside. If a child learns that teachers who are viewed as arbitrary and unsympathetic are themselves carrying out instructions that emanate from a higher level, the child's emotional reaction may be dramatically changed. In this case, the change that is made in the emotional state makes it possible to alter the behavior.

Socially Unacceptable (Perverse) Behavior: Drug Abuse

The term abuse is applied where the continual exercise of a behavior is believed apt to have life or health threatening consequences, and is thus evaluated as immoral. Behaviors involving the abusive ingestion of psychedelic substances are based on the desire for pleasure (stimulation), power (impressing others), or relief (escape from an unsatisfying life). Other forms of abuse include smoking, overeating, and immoderate or perverse sexual activity. In many instances physical or psychological addiction is involved. However, the two concepts are entirely different. Abuse is the more general term for alcohol and other drug use that is potentially dangerous to the self or others. It includes addiction as a subset.

For most comestibles it is difficult to specify the point at which use becomes abuse. (How much coffee, cholesterol, sugar, butter, salt, or alcohol must be taken for the experience to qualify as abusive?) The same problem applies to high speed driving and other extreme behaviors. Addiction is also enigmatic, especially as it applies to psychological compulsion. The holarchic model does not address itself to the problem of addiction. However, we must repeat the caution that the fact that an individual is addicted is not incontrovertible evidence of poor emotional health. Unlikely as it may seem, an addict may be a quite happy person.

The urgent demand for programs that may have an impact on the use of stimulants and narcotics is based on the concern that untoward behavior may result, and that addiction may eventuate. Because of this, many programs, and especially those that receive state or federal funds, stipulate total abstinence as goals. The slogan *Say No to Drugs*, carries the message that morally sound individuals need never start to drink alcohol, or "share a joint (marijuana)," with a friend at a party.

Although guidelines for grant supported programs often speak of drug abuse prevention, they require that such programs "clearly and consistently teach that illicit drug use is wrong and harmful."[8] There is an obvious oxymoron created by pairing the message that *any* use is "wrong and harmful," with the advice that *abuse* should be avoided. The reason for this extreme position is that there has arisen a vociferous demand for drug free schools and other public institutions. A panic state has been created by the awareness that there is a significant proliferation of incidents of criminal behavior—especially among younger people—associated with an increase in the use of illicit drugs, accompanied by a loosening of regulatory controls. There is a persistent clamor for an approach that will stem the tide of behavior that violates community standards.

Public and private schools have been targeted as appropriate settings for the introduction of drug abuse prevention programs. In many instances, the principles on which a program is founded are sound (within the limitation of the state of the art in drug prevention), but the evidence suggests that they have not been particularly effective. There are several reasons for this. School curricula are designed around need priorities, and drug abuse prevention must compete with needs often considered more urgent. A three day seminar or an occasional classroom discussion in a health class are apt to be the extent of the implementation of a project. Teachers already overburdened and parents with competing demands on time and energy do not—or cannot—make the necessary commitment. Abuse prevention programs such as Quest[9] and CAP[10] require a considerable amount of concentrated effort. Beyond this, evidence of the effectiveness of any program is dubious, payoffs are obscure, and, as with all preventive programs, impatience for cures results in the implementation of projects that offer solutions that they cannot produce.

Unsound Approaches: Focus on cost factors.

As with behaviors described earlier, the commonest practice is either to punish offenders or to excuse their behavior: "Treatment" involves the manipulation of costs in the form of some type of chastisement. Although the application of punishment or control may be unavoidable in any particular instance, it is not curative where the need value of a behavior is high.

Figure 15.2, page 470, (a miniaturization of Figure 15.1, the Behavior/Adjustment Paradigm), locates a behavior described as *very heavy drinking*. The locus, (BAP 5/2), represents a situation in which need value is quite high, while the cost is low enough to be accepted with a reasonable degree of comfort. (It is important to understand that the behavior under consideration is believed to represent *abuse*, not merely the *use* of alcohol.) A narrative statement may be that "John abuses alcohol, but feels little concern about the price associated with his behavior."

A slight increase in the cost of such behavior (BAP 5/3) through reprimand or moral admonition will have little or no effect. More stringent punishment (BAP

5/4) will result in continued behavior, accompanied by resentment directed toward those who are seen as interfering. The strict application of rigorous controls (BAP 5/5) will stop the behavior, but will undoubtedly result in John's feeling—and perhaps expressing—hostility toward all forms of authority. Decreasing the cost (BAP 5/1) will do nothing to eliminate the behavior, and risks an increase in the behaviors that a society seeks to reduce. Absurd as such a procedure may seem, there is a persistent conviction that such individuals may "grow out of" such behavior. Many do not. Far too many women marry abusers, confident that they will change under the influence of a caring wife and a supportive family atmosphere.

The Holarchic Approach: Focus on need elements.

This approach is based on the conviction that the desire for stimulants, as is that for sexual behavior and exciting lifestyles is a normal human phenomenon. Thus, the program is restricted to the monitoring of such behaviors through focusing on the conditions under which they occur, as well as on the manner of their expression. The purpose is twofold. First, the maintenance of a stable society requires that some degree of control over behavior be exercised. Careless, immature and other irresponsible behaviors are not only dangerous, but represent an infringement on the "rights" of the victims of such actions, which inevitably lead to moral and legal sanctions that are inherently divisive. The second goal is the enhancement of the potential of each individual to live an emotionally healthy life. Disease, accident, and other undesirable outcomes are believed reducible through the application of constraints on excessive behavior.

Before dealing with specific steps, it should be clear that there is no easy road to a "cure" for problems of abuse. In the first place, as has been pointed out, there is little consensus on what constitutes abuse. In Chapter 14 we pointed out that emotional health is defined differently by groups with varying interests, capacities and opportunities. The "generation gap" that has been offered as an explanation for differing attitudes toward lifestyles is an indisputable factor. To this must be added a media that exploits the urge for excitement and freedom, along with the (tacit) licence to display materials that appeal to prurient interests.

While many 20 year olds do not participate in abusive practices, they do not, as a class, lead the fight against drug use; they are apt to be far more tolerant of their improvident peers. The fact that most preadolescent children share with the older generation of adults a rejection of abusive behavior provides another clue to the fact that the influence of powerful—often coercive—desires, must be appreciated. While programs geared to the interests of primary and elementary grade children appear to offer hope for forestalling or avoiding abusive behavior, they appeal to an audience not yet influenced by the types of behavior that attracts adolescents. Similarly, the entreaty of senior citizens for more 'mature' behavior on the part of adolescents speaks to an inability to recognize the fact that young and old will always have difficulty in communicating. Life is less precious at 21; risks less threatening;

Figure 15.2

The BAP and Alcohol Abuse

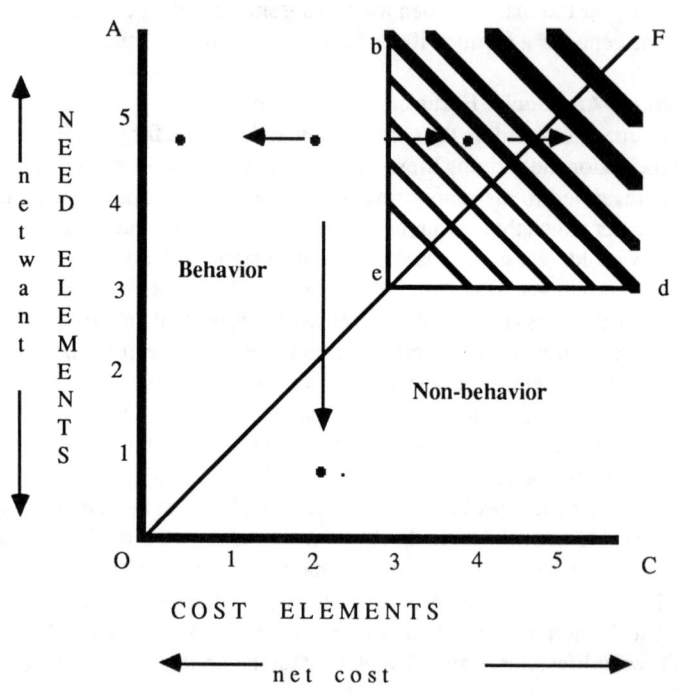

unconventional behaviors more alluring.

The most auspicious approach to the problem of controlling abuse is to reduce the need value (BAP 1/2) associated with the undesirable behavior. This procedure calls for an understanding of principles discussed in Chapter 7, where it was explained that needs are subject to manipulation. Desires are not. Furthermore, needs have relative rather than absolute value. The need value of a particular meal (e.g., a bowl of rice) as considered by a hungry person, is quite likely to be significantly reduced if a more appetizing meal (e.g., a chicken dinner) is proffered.

Several factors must be considered. Which desires are involved? Does the individual drink to escape or forget, to impress others, for its stimulative value, or–

—most likely—for some combination of all three? Given the high level of value with which the behavior is imbued, what behaviors (needs), are apt to represent attractive alternatives? For each class of desire, a menu of options must be considered. In some instances this calls for the provision of substitute behaviors; in all instances it calls for a modification in belief patterns.

Consider first the case in which individuals have occupations that they find distasteful. They dislike their jobs, their employers, and often their fellow workers. They see work as a necessary evil, as a part of life that must be endured, but is never to be enjoyed. In Chapter 16 we shall discuss the role of work as it may be dealt with in a primary preventive program. Here we must deal with individuals who have already learned to hate their work. Although many jobs are undoubtedly difficult to portray as positive, an appalling number of people develop a negative attitude toward work as part of a cultural bias. Such a stance provides a convenient excuse for antisocial or irresponsible behavior. The procedure in such cases is to reeducate; to alter beliefs about the nature of work.

For many individuals the recklessness associated with excessive drinking provides not only a high level of stimulation, but also attracts the applause of others. The man who habitually drinks so much as to reach a state of oblivion becomes a center of attention. He is noticed; talked about; holds special status in some group. A nonentity from nine 'til five, he becomes a personality at midnight. It matters little that such attention may be accompanied by ridicule. Clowns take themselves seriously—in some cases seeing themselves playing an indispensable role in their social clique.

The difference between these motives for excessive drinking lies in the fact that the behavior of the individual who drinks to escape is *instrumental*. That of the person who enjoys the experience is *intrinsic*. For the former, since the behavior (working) cannot be eliminated, it is necessary to change beliefs about the role of work. For the latter, the behavior (*excessive* drinking) can itself be altered, and the task is to change beliefs about the relative value of alternative behaviors. However, the procedure is essentially the same. It is necessary to penetrate the curtain of peripheral thinking; to carry out a meticulous study of causal factors, and to instill a different set of beliefs.

The belief pattern that emerges must be structured along the lines of the identity/identification continuum. The majority of responsible (civilized) behavior is based on the self restraint imposed by individuals who identify with some socially established principle; some standard of conduct that is promulgated by an esteemed organization.

The establishment of effective identification is apt to be difficult. It may be slow. It is often unsuccessful. As with child rearing, the rules that must be followed are simple; carrying them out (e.g., being consistent) is accomplished by few parents. The holarchic model is based on the following premises:
- Attitudes and behavior will change when:
    a) *the logic of an argument is compelling.*

But individuals with functional defense networks keep threats to their freedom to behave at arms length. They listen but do not hear. They respond but do not understand the significance of their response.
  b) *alternative behaviors seem viable.*
  Individuals must believe that they have the capacity and opportunity to participate in a significant social group. They must see a relationship between the action and the outcome. They must see profit in behavioral change. Need value must be high relative to cost.
  c) *peers manifest disapproval of the offensive behavior.*
  This is often difficult to initiate because of the tendency of group members to protect individuals that may be seen as victims, or who are otherwise not considered fully responsible for their deviant behavior. It has, however, been shown to be effective. Cigarette smoking, often practiced as a mark of urbanity, has become widely disparaged by people of all ages. The result has been a dramatic decrease in its overall practice.
- Consequential learning is not a matter of imprinting data on a "tabula rasa." While memorization can occur passively, the infusion of conviction requires that the learner take an active part in the process. Action may (and often does) take the form of auditory or subliminal speech. Effective teachers involve their audience in such exercises as singing, talking, chanting, etc.. Leader(s) of a drug abuse preven-tion group must require that participants take an active role. They must understand *and defend* arguments that deprecate drug abuse. Potential abusers will come to advocate the position that they support (not one that is promulgated by an authority). Recall that Madeline (Chapter 14) came to change her attitude toward her father when *she* was required to defended his actions.

The process of changing attitudes, where the behavior seems so desirable, takes time. It cannot be accomplished in a workshop, a seminar, or a few group meetings. The individual may be asked, for example, to compare the status of a person who drinks himself into a stupor, with that of one who demonstrates the ability to control his drinking. Ultimately, the behavior that has represented a need will become a cost, as it represents interference with the exercise of a more acceptable behavior. With this approach, however, the cost is not a form of punishment and thus not a threat to positive emotional adjustment.

In each of the types of behavior described above, the remedial process is geared to the rehabilitation of the individual. Obviously, in many instances, abusive behaviors are delinquent or criminal in nature, and social tranquility may demand that the individual be confined or otherwise constrained. The principles applied here do not attend to the legal propriety of their application, but only to the psychological impact. The question of whether socially deviant people would respond positively to such treatment is moot, since its application may be more expensive than a social system can provide. Theoretically, it should be effective under ideal conditions.

Although only a few simple examples have been given, the principles have universal application. Individuals behave in terms of whatever they believe will bring the highest gain in terms of the lowest cost. This does not change because of age, social status, or other variable. Treatment will (and should) vary considerably, but the basis remains the same—every deliberate action can be traced to an attempt to meet desires as efficaciously as possible. In the case of alcohol and other drug abuse, the desire for positive identification is a key to effective ameliorative, as well as preventive, programming.

Summary

In those settings in which behavior and belief are monitored by programs designed to instill efficient and effective practices, manifestations of unsatisfactory performance often provide the opportunity for early intervention. In such cases, the BAP is a useful tool for determining the motivational elements involved and for providing information regarding those beliefs and behaviors most apt to lead to effective resolution. The critical factors are the determination of precisely what behavior is involved, on what beliefs it is based, and what emotions are aroused relative to its performance.

Chapter Notes

1. To attempt to convince an individual that force is not effective in a world that observes it at every political level, is to engage in a hapless task. However, force may be exercised in many ways, from the violent confrontation of an undisciplined aggressor to the persuasive "look" of a caring parent.
2. As has been pointed out, emotions cannot be altered directly, but are modified as relevant beliefs are transformed.
3. Wonderly (1987)
4. The interpretation of a score, or other type of information, as it relates to other data that characterizes an individual, or group, as contrasted with normative information, or that which compares an individual with some reference group.
5. The holarchic model is not a recommendation that failing grades or social promotions should not be employed. It does suggest that such procedures are usually of little or no value as motivating forces. The holarchic approach focuses on a want/cost analysis and the relationship between potential behaviors and their potentiality for developing feelings of power and meaning.
6. This approach is sometimes identified as the PSI approach because it is the model employed by the PSI organization as a counseling technique where the psychologists work with school aged children.
7. This concept must be clearly understood if the holarchic model is to be employed. Anger is an undesirable emotion. One may said to enjoy being angry because it represents a method of manifesting displeasure. However, what is being enjoyed is the display of one's feelings. The test? Provide a solution to the anger provoking situation and observe the ensuing state. One may, of course, be angry because they feel themselves deprived of the opportunity to parade their negative feelings, as when a minor offensive action such as name-calling is eliminated, while many larger issues remain unresolved.
8. Ohio Department of Education, Drug-Free Schools Grant Program Guidelines (1990), p. 1
9. Quest International, 537 Jones Rd., Granville, Ohio 43023, (1989)
10. Children are People Inc., Chemical abuse prevention program, 493 Selby Ave., St. Paul Minnesota 55102, (1977)

Chapter 16
Primary Prevention: A Look to the Future

A primary preventive emotional health program was developed at Kent State University during the 1970s. It proposes an attack on practices that create frustration, dissatisfaction and anger which, over time, result in poor emotional adjustment. It focuses attention on the unique potential of the educational establishment, with an analysis of the roles appropriate to each participant.

The issue of *inalienable rights* is developed as an example of an obstacle to effective interpersonal relationships. It is suggested that the notion of "absolute rights," be discarded in favor of that of *obligation* and respect for the (natural) desires of humans. Similarly, such concepts as *work*, *discipline*, and *responsibility*, should be recast in a form that reveals their proper interpretation, and the potential for improved understanding and emendatory social interaction that such an approach may provide.

This text was born of frustration bordering on despair. Claims and counterclaims regarding the nature of the human personality and the implication of such contentions for emotional health programming have been uniformly disappointing. Programs based on every view, from the occult to the mechanistic have received putative support in a mountain of literature. Concepts have been worried to the finest detail. But their application has made no substantial impact on the level of adjustment of the millions of people they purport to assist. Most importantly, proponents of each major school have deprecated the arguments of opposing theorists, while insisting on the accuracy of their own.

This radicalizing of theories has resulted in defensive networks that make any challenge difficult to sustain. When one aspect is shown to be faulty, a correlative concept is introduced. Positions shift subtly toward a common center. Extreme positions are subject to the leveling phenomenon of gestalt psychology. No tenet of one decade passes uncircumcised into the next.

The common theme that underlies these many psychologies is that *nothing is simple*. Humans must not be viewed as behaving to get what they desire. Such simplistic notions are subjected to re-interpretation to fit the logical postulates of each model. The sophisticated psychologist explains that behavior is directed by demonic forces from within or environmental manipulators from without.[1]

The holarchic personality theory was developed as a response to the vacuum that such shifting allegiances have created. The principal focus of the model is in the area of *primary prevention*, or the application of sound organizational principles to those institutions that have a significant impact on the personality development of those who are affected by their services.[2] The family, schools, churches, and other culture transmitting agencies are considered to be such primary or habilitating institutions.

A variety of secondary and tertiary prevention or intervention points in which the model may also be employed were introduced in Chapters 14 and 15. This approach was taken because most practitioners are interested in techniques that can be applied in cases where distress or behavior anomaly has already occurred, as well as on the observation that it is a far more difficult task to sell an individual, an institution, a community, or a nation on a primary preventive approach to any problem. Bower quoted a psychiatrist's reaction to the suggestion that more effort be put into procedures for even the *early identification* of adjustment problems. "I don't see why you get worked up about this early identification of emotionally disturbed children. We've got more cases than we can handle right now without finding some more."[3] Our own experience in proposing that the majority of the energy of school psychologists go into preventive programming was exemplified by the reaction of a colleague who asked, "Don't you *care* about the children who are already disturbed?"

Hesitancy about focusing on primary prevention is legitimate. Major causes of skepticism must be appreciated. Few models with extensive research data or with compelling logical argument are available. Furthermore, the payoff (if any) on time, energy, and funds invested cannot be expected to occur for long periods of time. Finally, preventive models are difficult to implement. Resistance is encountered at every level of application.

Such arguments, valid as they may be, are subject to re-evaluation as the nature of the problem is more closely considered. Both the extent and the urgency of the incidence of emotional maladjustment cry out for the application of procedures that show a degree of promise. It would have been unfortunate if those who treated poliomyelitis or malaria had shied away from programs that offered preventive

PRIMARY PREVENTION: A LOOK TO THE FUTURE   479

possibilities because the relationship between the disease and the proposed procedures had not been proven beyond the slightest doubt.

In a strong sense, primary prevention is an extension of the practice of *triage* made famous during the first World War by French physicians who gave most of their attention, as well as medical supplies, to those wounded who had the best prognosis for survival. A primary preventive approach is based on the assumption that the best prognosis can be anticipated if individuals are treated before they have contracted the disease! Thus, the Salk vaccine and the draining of mosquito infested swamps and ditches.

Such programming represents, in its early stages, the expenditure of considerable professional time and energy, as well as additional public and private financial support. The long term effect of primary preventive effort should, however, be highly cost/benefit efficient. The evidence can be found in the dramatic revenue-saving that accompanied the implementation of preventive measures for the control of such diseases as tuberculosis and measles.

PSI - Prevention: Systems Intervention

The PSI model was developed in the early 1970s under state and federal grants as a training program for Child Development Specialists and as a specialty in school psychology,[4,5] following which it became the theoretical structure underlying the activities of PSI Associates, Inc., a private human resources consortium (including a mental health agency) operating in northeast Ohio.[6]

The PSI model is based on the contention that schools and other socializing institutions spend a disproportionate amount of time and resources treating the three to five percent of individuals who are identified as experiencing psychological difficulty at the expense of programming in such a way as to improve the lot of all. The LD (learning disabled) program, for example, has become an increasingly expensive socio-political football. Probably fifty times as many children are identified and served as meet sound educational criteria because public interest has been aroused, and because snake oil continues to be a highly salable commodity.

The applicability of holarchic principles to institutional settings is based on the evidence that many ostensibly preventive practices persist in spite of their inefficacy, while others of significant potential value are never attempted. Criticisms of the performance of American schools as documented in such works as *The Closing of the American Mind*[7] are apt to be discussed for a brief period but are ultimately ignored. In spite of this, such significant educators as Albee have suggested that "in the long run...prevention through social change that gives people more security and more power over their lives is our best hope—a faint but persistent hope."[8] In many instances, proposals would be relatively easy to implement and maintain. However, bureaucratic intransigence seems capable of thwarting any effort that calls for even the most minimal change.

Ineffective Practices

In Western societies, an immense network of individuals and institutions has been created whose function is to deal with unacceptable or maladaptive behavior. From the time a child is old enough to be held responsible for mistakes at toilet training to the age at which senility becomes an accepted excuse for deviant behavior, there are established procedures for correction. Standing in a corner, being threatened with suspension or expulsion, and/or being required to meet with a counselor are common techniques employed with school aged children. Encouraging enlistment in the armed services, being admitted to a public or private psychiatric facility, or being jailed as an offender represent some of the more stringent approaches that are used in the attempt to alter behavior in older individuals. In all cases, one purpose in using such techniques is to reshape the personality. It is assumed that the army will "make a man of him," the psychologist will "change his attitude," and prison terms will make offenders penitent—or at least help them to appreciate the folly of their behavior.

If the purpose is to punish or destroy, such approaches may be appropriate. The judge who sentenced the murderer of a policeman to life, with the added condition that each year on the anniversary of the slaying the convict be placed in solitary confinement "to meditate upon his crime," made a foolish decision. The only potential value in such a penalty would be to mollify the family of the victim and perhaps satisfy the community's demand for retribution. The net result insofar as a change in personality is involved will be zero—or worse. If the intention is to cause a change in behavior which will result in a more effective lifestyle (with the gratifying spin-off of improved social conditions), an entirely different approach must be employed. And that approach is essentially preventive.

Let us repeat the paradigm. *Human behavior is a function of desire, as expressed by needs, and an estimate of related cost.* If we wish to change the classroom climate of rigid teachers so that children can be more creative and productive, we are unlikely to succeed by threatening such teachers with the demand that they change their attitude. We must find a way for them to appreciate the rewards associated with active children who love and enjoy their school experience and the teachers who guide them. Any institution or program designed to redirect behavior must be built around principles of human motivation such as those that have been described in previous chapters.

As we consider the factors that contribute to emotional health and the areas in which we might effectively program for improved personality structure, we must keep in mind the motivational sequence, the nature of the self, and the shifting patterns of defense. Beyond this, there are practical constraints which may help to focus attention on the type of desires that ordinarily relate to adjustment as well as the probability of their being thwarted. The desires for meaning, power, and safety tend to be at the root of most adjustment problems, and our emphasis must be placed in these areas.

PRIMARY PREVENTION: A LOOK TO THE FUTURE

Human interaction represents a constant cathectic flow, with allegiances built up and torn down as evidence changes and as desires rise and fall. Identifications are multitudinous in all people with some being strongly joined, as in the relationship between mother and child, while others are so fragile that a careless word may destroy the bond. This characteristic of the affective system is both advantageous and restrictive. The ability of an individual to change an attitude in the light of new information is counterbalanced by the capacity to resist data that threatens integrity or is otherwise unassimilable.

In Chapter 10 we pointed out that the concepts of *identification* and *identity* are best expressed by the terms *who* and *I* respectively. Although it is essential that identity be established—("am I real?")—it is equally necessary that reference groups be available against which the self may be projected and through which meaning may be established. A preventive approach, including the establishment of such targets, offers the greatest hope for success.

It is not enough that I respect myself. It is insufficient to love myself. In fact, such activities are incomprehensible except as the self extends beyond the biological present. This aspect is often misunderstood by psychologists, although political activists, religious leaders, and family members seem to instinctively recognize and act on the intuitive sense which reveals the part/whole relationship. Bloom suggested that: "The young want to make commitments which constitute the meaning of life, because love and nature do not suffice...but they are haunted by the awareness that the talk does not mean very much and that commitments are lighter than air."[9] Thus, the problem of attaining a sense of meaning is compounded by the appalling lack of sincerity so often encountered in social and political environments.

The Role of the School

We have selected the public school as a most appropriate target for primary preventive programming on the basis, first, of the poor track record of other integrating institutions.[10]

> Endless attempts have been made to alter child-rearing practices by offering educational and counseling services to parents. For many reasons, including the fact that home entertainment in the form of television has assumed an inelastic priority and because parents are not obligated to accept such educational opportunities, such efforts have rarely proven successful. Programs provided by mental health agencies, universities, churches, service clubs, and other organizations have usually failed because of poor attendance.[11]

School systems, of course, have not been an unqualified success. They have been regularly criticized on the ground that they do not turn out the effective, productive, well-adjusted, responsible citizens that they are mandated to produce. Furthermore, they are often seen as failing in their responsiveness to community concerns. Thus, there is reason to anticipate some degree of readiness to react to new proposals.[12]

The public school was created for the purpose of reflecting and disseminating the values of the prevailing socio-political group. It performs that function whether it chooses to or not, and in spite of educational philosophies that call for more diverse objectives. The inadequate performance of many schools is due to the political manipulation of both educators and the many power groups that believe they have a mandate to determine what children shouldbe taught.

The school represents, at once, the greatest strength because of its impact on the children it serves, and the greatest weakness in the socialization chain because it develops out of the mixture of ideals of the community, and the desires and limitation of its professional staff. Many problems thus arise. If the community wants children who are "creative" and teachers emphasize conformity—or if the reverse is the case—each is apt to be convinced that the others are ignorant or unconscionable. On the grounds of moral, legal, or intellectual privilege the stage is set for an unproductive program. Each claims the *Unam Sanctum*, and the victim is the next generation— which will prepare its own hellfire for those that follow. In spite of this, the well established role of public education and the commitment that this institution attracts because of the precious nature of its cargo, invests it with far more potential than any other socializing agency.

The approach taken here is to recognize that schools are *open systems*, and to focus attention on several critical characteristics of such organizations. The peculiarity of the open system is that it is characterized by the principle of *equifinality*. "[It] may attain a time-independent state independent of initial conditions and determined only by the system parameters."[13] This critical feature is often overlooked. In principle, it means that, unlike the case of closed systems, the initial state need not determine the outcome. The school, or other social system, is capable of responding to the constantly changing needs of the community it serves. While tradition makes a valuable contribution, it need not stifle progress.

The PSI model deals with three elements of the educational delivery system: *Responsibility*, *coherence*, and *quality*. While many aspects of an institution may be usefully addressed, these three were selected because they are most readily influenced, and should respond most immediately to preventive programming.

Responsibility

The responsibility of a deliberate system, as described in Chapter 4, is always to some entity external to the system itself. School systems are responsible to the communities they serve and the local, state, and federal laws under which they operate. As open systems, they are capable of continual course correction through the use of feedback or information generated by those whose interests the system serves. Effective performance requires that the roles to be played by professional staff members and lay school boards be clearly understood.

The determination of who "owns" the system, who are the clients of the school, where the decision-making prerogative of professionals ends, who should write school philosophies, what requirements should be associated with school board membership, and other critical issues must be dealt with openly if a system is to earn the support of its constituency. Such concerns are rarely debated in open forum. Instead, communities either defer to the power expressed by an assertive superintendent or carry on a running (often subterranean) battle with those who operate the school. Neither approach has been shown to be particularly effective.

Many efforts are made to minimize negative community feelings through such channels as school newsletters, radio broadcasts, and public speeches. However, there is rarely an opportunity for *feedback*. While community members need to know what is happening, they must also have an opportunity to express concerns. This, too, may be accomplished in many ways. The key to the success of the feedback mechanism requires the recognition of the appropriate role of parents, teachers and other professionals, administrators, and school boards.

The Right to Decide

A major issue concerns the problem of who shall make decisions regarding educational goals. Parents claim the right on the basis of their legal status, although they regularly abdicate their responsibility. Children (usually through their advocates) argue that they should take part in determining the nature of the curriculum since their futures are at stake, and that such rights are guaranteed under the same constitutional privilege invoked by parents. Educators, including teachers, counselors, and psychologists, insist that their expertise in the areas of child development and learning is such that they should make the ultimate decisions. Sandwiched between the antagonists are the administrators who are expected to arbitrate the many conflicts. These various claims to decision making priority are based on a misinterpretation or disregarding of the rules and laws which govern American society.

Children's Rights. The rights of children, for many years ignored or misunderstood, have come into focus largely as a result of the activity of adolescents whose dress, manners, and behavior cannot be reconciled with established custom. From the 1921 Supreme Court decision that the school must issue a diploma and transcript in spite of a student's refusal to wear prescribed dress at graduation, to its 1968 decision that personal records of students are to be supplied to them on request, Americans have been moving along a rocky road to confusion about the rights of minors.

One issue of the APGA journal was devoted to situations in which a child's right to privacy is involved.[14] In that issue, Patterson dealt with the problem of the student's right to enter into a continuing relationship with a counselor without parental consent. Patterson argued that to limit the child's confidentiality would be a "mockery of freedom,"[15] and that it would undermine counseling in the schools. He believed that school counselors "should be in the vanguard of those who respect the rights of children to personal privacy."[15] There is considerable ambiguity in such statements regarding whose rights are being promulgated. Asked whether he would expect to be informed if a counselor were seeing *his* child regarding drug use, Patterson responded that he would not, with the qualification "[so long as] the counselor were competent."[15] But who is to determine which counselors are competent?

The rights of children are *civil* rather than *political*. The former refers to those rights that extend to all members of a community by virtue of law, while the latter includes the right to participate in the *establishment* of such laws. The distinction is critical. Child advocates argue that a child should not be forced into a psychiatric hospital by parents without legal counsel. Suppose, however, that a seven year old child who had become emotionally disturbed as a clear result of parental abuse, chose to remain with those parents. Would such a wish be obeyed? And can that child participate in any decision to alter that law? If there is some cloudiness about the answer to the first part of the question, there is surely none about the latter. The welfare of children is a legitimate responsibility of the state, but it is fatuous to assume that their rights are thus elevated to the level of those of the adult community. *Children's rights are bestowed by a community through the actions of its elected representatives. They do not have client status.*

Professional Rights. There is something compelling about the notion that those with superior skill and knowledge should have decision making priority. Plato's *Republic* depended for its vitality on having philosophers serve as kings. "For they know and only they know wherein the public weal consists."[16] However, in a democratic society, wisdom and skill bestow no decision making privilege. In the United States, every decision about permissible behavior is reserved to the people either individually or representatively and *never to a professional of any kind, public or private.* This includes decisions regarding the purpose, or output, of any system such as the school.

Certainly the opinions of professionals are sought and their advice is often followed, However, every recommendation is referred to the citizenry for final decision, either directly or through elected officials. No degree of skill or knowledge is required. (The reference here is to the *rights* of professionals. It is obvious that violations occur in many instances.) Marks on ballot sheets, or holes in computerized voting forms, determine who shall be elected to public office. On the basis of a compromise between what people desire and what is considered morally sound, the law-making bodies so created, establish and implement laws which are, ostensibly, in the interest of the people. But such bodies are the *people* represented and their decisions are not subject to professional approval. The existence of many laws that are based on what is "good" for people does not alter the fact that in theory all legislation is based on what the people desire and the price they are willing to pay. Professional knowledge is limited to providing suggestions on *how to get* what is wanted.

Whether I choose to behave in such a way as to maintain good health is a decision that my physician cannot make. I can be informed, for example, of how I must act in order to lose weight. A diet may be prescribed. However, if I do not follow that diet, the doctor's role is limited to warning me of the dangers of obesity, or threatening to stop seeing me as a patient. Every effort, from cajoling my family, to upbraiding me for my foolishness may be employed. However, in the final analysis the decision is reserved to each citizen, *and the American people want it to remain that way*! Public medicine is no exception. The mandatory vaccination is not performed because of a medical decision, but because on the advice of medical researchers, a congress of (lay) citizens votes to require immunization. The dilemma of fluoridation and the cries over restrictions on the use of marijuana should daily remind us of the power we wish to reserve to ourselves.

Constraint on the behavior of professionals is expressed in the codes that specify those activities that constitute ethical behavior. The distinction between *moral* and *ethical* behavior must be understood. Moral behavior is action based on one's personal conviction regarding propriety. Professional ethics refers to activity of members of a profession (in their professional capacity) as it is prescribed by the tenets of that profession and its obligation to the community it serves. To act unethically would be to violate a professional standard in the interest either of personal gain, or because of some belief which was in conflict with the ethical code.

The deliberate act of choosing a profession and accepting the behavioral code of that profession carries with it responsibilities which are quite different than those based on convictions of a private nature. Physicians whose professional code prohibited the performing of abortions after the twentieth week of gestation would be behaving unethically if they performed such operations. An ethical code represents a *restriction* on one's freedom to act—even though, in some situations, an alternative act may be believed to be morally superior.

The question of whether competence confers privilege is inseparable from the concept of ethical behavior, since it represents the issue of whether professionals may assume rights ordinarily reserved to others. When individuals accept the mantle of a profession they announce to the community their adoption of those standards of conduct with which the profession is identified. Doctor's take the Hippocratic oath; army officers vow to protect their country; judges swear to distribute justice impartially—in each case to act consistently with professional standards *in spite of personal convictions*. Although teachers do not make so solemn a commitment, standards of the profession as they are found in state and national codes are assumed binding on its members.

This restriction obviously creates potential conflict. Some members of a profession may have reservations about certain aspects of the code under which they operate. They are, however, not deprived of any course of action. They have a right, (even a *moral* duty?), to take issue with any part of the code that they find objectionable. This does not, however, relieve them of the obligation to act consistently with the standards involved as long as they hold themselves out to the public as members of that profession.

Some have questioned whether teachers qualify as professionals on the grounds that they have limited decision making power. To the extent that they are identified with a well established professional code, they do. The contention that teachers function *in loco parentis* does not make a case for their freedom to make value judgments. It is, rather, another example of a responsibility which must be accepted. The director of a psychiatric hospital has the same kind of "privilege" in determining whether a particular treatment shall be administered to one considered mentally incompetent. His right is better understood, however, as a *responsibility* spelled out in a law prescribed by representatives of the people. (And how many professionals are willing to accept personal responsibility for the outcomes of their decisions?)

This is by no means an attack on the competence or the virtue of the professional, but is intended to point up the kind of confusion that has developed out of the failure to distinguish between moral behavior and ethical responsibility. The result is seen in the low level of respect and support that teacher groups attract, and the continual harangue regarding their demands. The principle parallels that of the school student. *Professional rights are bestowed by a community through the actions of its elected representatives.. Professionals do not have client status.*

Parent's Rights. Parents often insist that they are the ones who hold decision making authority, but once again the claim is unwarranted, though somewhat less obviously so. The rights of parents can certainly be found expressly stated, or clearly implied in the laws that govern cities, states, and nations. The principle, however, remains the same. The requirement that parental permission be obtained prior to an intellectual or performance evaluation is based on a statute enacted by a legislative body. Although parents, as citizens, may vote to replace members of governing bodies, they hold no mandate to make decisions outside the rules established by such parliaments.

This limitation on rights applies not only to individual parents but to parents as subgroups. Parent teacher associations—whose members certainly have a most intimate concern with the education of children—function appropriately only to study issues and to make recommendations. The 75 year old bachelor who shows no interest in the welfare of children has equal legal status in determining the goals of the public school. The political rights of such individuals have, in many cases, been ignored. Failure to respect the franchise of such groups has been one of the causes for lack of support for school funding and other potentially positive actions.

As with children and professionals, parents are not prohibited from bringing grievances before those who make the laws. One parent exemplified this in her complaint about the employment of behavior management programs in the schools.

> I suggest that you pick up any National Education Association Journal...or attend any school function...and you will be bombarded with the same behavior modification jargon: "We must develop the child emotionally, socially, and psychologically." Who gives the educators that right? What

about educating the minds—which millions of parents believe their children have—and they have every right to believe in the mind; because, the Behaviorist theory has never been proved.[17]

Here we have an example of one class of rights being set against another. It should be obvious that this attack angered and alienated many teachers. Not so transparent, however, is the fact that while the challenge to the practices of professionals in the schools is a legitimate exercise of political privilege, parenthood provides the author of such a tract with no right to effect a change. *Parent's right are bestowed by a community through its elected representatives. They do not have client status.*

The School Board's Role. When we come, finally to the prerogatives of the decision making body we find an equally distressing situation.[18] Charged with the mandate of determining the curriculum and the goals of the school, school boards often abdicate their responsibility, allowing forceful superintendents and interested teachers to make inappropriate decisions. In some instances, school board members debate the relative merit of various approaches to reading, while teachers decide whether the curriculum should focus on preparation for college or industrial employment. Neither is performing a legitimate function.

Within the constraints of state and federal law, school boards are expected to make the critical decisions that bear on the educational program. They should certainly listen to professionals for technical information, parents for the type of curriculum they would like, children for concerns that their age and maturity make appropriate, and to all others in the community who wish to express an opinion. Ultimately, however, they are responsible for making the decisions. And even here there is considerable ambiguity. Should a school board attempt to *convince* its constituency that they should vote higher millage to support the schools or should it present the evidence so that voters can decide for themselves whether to support a tax increase? As long as the confusion regarding the appropriate roles of various segments of the educational community persist, such issues shall continue to create distress, mistrust, and alienation.

Is there a solution? Yes. And it is not particularly difficult. Members of the educational endeavor must learn to appreciate their appropriate role. Professionals, as well as parents and students, should be taught the limitation of their privilege to the providing of recommendations. School board members must realize that their task is to make the final decisions, and to implement the program. Our research revealed that few individuals, including professors of Educational Administration, are clear regarding the role distinctions described here. (Are you?)

Coherence

Coherence refers to the relationship between the functions of a system and its goals or output. In the instance of schools, the question involves the relationship between elements of the curriculum and the objectives of the school as specified in the school philosophy. If a goal is the ability of individuals to make effective decisions, or to develop positive emotional health habits, relevant experiences must be provided at appropriate educational levels.

The same question can be raised regarding each of the many personality characteristics that a school system presumes to instill in its students. And beyond the identification of such factors and the inclusion of relevant experiences in the school program, issue must be taken with how traditional subject matter (the three R's) plays a role. If communication skills are desired, each step from word recognition, through spelling and grammar, to the ability to write an intelligible theme must make a recognizable contribution. It is not enough that students know *how* to write. It is imperative that they have extensive experience at *doing* so.

School philosophies and educational goals are often stated in generalities, which is appropriate to that level of discourse. However, the aims they state must be carried out in specific terms. The "right of every student to have the opportunity to develop intellectually, socially, physically, and emotionally to his fullest potential"[19] may be assured through a wide variety of programs. The prioritization of outcomes will determine the nature of the curriculum. An example may be seen in the stated goals of one school district where the priority of importance is first the development of communication skills and fourth the development of "a feeling of positive self-worth."[19] How is such a prioritization to be translated into a curriculum? Is not one purpose of developing communication skills, to enhance one's feeling of self worth?

Quality

Quality is relevant to the components of a system. In the case of schools, this represents the characteristics of teaching, administrative, and support staffs. How well are they equipped to perform their tasks? How knowledgeable, skillful, cooperative, and creative are they? The PSI model calls for the institution of *perennial* inservice training programs designed to keep teachers, administrators (and interested citizens) aware of both recognized principles of child development and new approaches as they become available. While many schools do offer some such programs from time to time (and a few quite regularly), the impact of such experiences is minimized when it is so limited. Children raised in enlightened environments must live in a world peopled by the vast majority who have not had the benefit of such opportunity.

One example of the content of an inservice series would be the application of the Behavior Adjustment Paradigm as a preventive tool. In its treatment aspect, the clinician observes behavior, infers an emotional state, and proposes a procedure that is designed to alter beliefs and/or behavior while maintaining an optimal level of adjustment. Knowledge of such procedures is, however, based on an understanding of the motivational process that translates directly into a preventive approach. If we are equipped to treat a problem, we can, in many instances identify its causes. The basic principle involved in establishing preventive emotional health programs includes the acceptance of the legitimacy of ineluctable desires while denying the essentiality of many behaviors that represent learned needs.

This approach would seem so obvious as to require no special emphasis. Unfortunately, educators, as well as parents, often persist in denying the essential while accepting that which is trivial, or superfluous. Consider common attitudes toward budding sexuality in young teenagers (many people believe that nice children don't even *think* about sex!) and the acceptance of hooliganism as an indispensable aspect of the need for stimulation. We deny the ineluctable and tolerate the nonessential. Such practices provide the basis for ineffective programming, in spite of the fact that the intelligent application of sound behavioral principles is not particularly difficult.

As to the denial of a procreative urge in the young, there seems no problem with accepting a natural desire for sugar and chocolate while controlling their use. Addictive drugs, which also appeal to a native urge, are in many instances wholly forbidden. Only the most uninformed would deny the innate desires involved. To consider sexual interest as inappropriate at an age that was considered appropriate for marriage only a few centuries ago, and to deny the underlying desires that are related, is to allow a cultural evolutionary step to blind us to a human urge. The intervention strategies involved in modifying school systems and other socializing entities represent the task as it is developed in the PSI model. The implementation of programs based on the model requires considerable commitment and foresight.

The Impact of Schismatic Beliefs

Each chapter of this text provides information that may be translated into both preventive and ameliorative programs through workshops, seminars and other types of presentation. In Chapter 12 a brief sketch of several such issues was presented. Here, a more detailed analysis of a number of beliefs that represents a continuing threat to the development of adequate personalities, as well as to the emotional health of whole societies will be provided. The PSI model calls for the study of these concepts as an integral part of school curricula, beginning at the lowest grades in which students are sufficiently mature to deal with them. Some may be introduced as early as the primary grades, with appropriately adjusted language terms.

Reference shall be made to sections of the text in which relevant concepts have been introduced. In the material that follows, our purpose is only to describe the process that leads from an understanding of a principle to the awareness of alternatives that may be effective. Furthermore, we are dealing with only a few of the multitude of issues that bear on human adjustment. To have a significant impact, programs would require far more general application than could be provided in one school system—one community—perhaps even one nation.

In Chapter 14 the position was developed that emotional health is related to the extent to which individuals believe themselves capable of meeting desires in terms of the price that the behavior extracts. We also indicated that methods of satisfying desires are learned, and that these techniques represent learned *needs*. Certain experiences become needed because of *beliefs* about their desire satisfying potential.

Beliefs, like all mental characteristics, are potentially positive. They are designed to associate need and desire in an effective way. However, when we consider the many types of behavior that persist in spite of the fact that they do not appear to satisfy the desires of individuals or groups, it become obvious that failure must sometimes be due to the persistence of inappropriate beliefs concerning the efficacy of particular behaviors as desire gratifying. The problem is manifested not only at the level of behavior, but in the formation of attitudes which are in themselves debilitating. The conviction that all politicians are dishonest, for example, will cause persistent aggravation if the news media carry reports that attend only to the alleged misdeeds of men in power. (This is totally independent of the legitimacy of news stories, and there is little reason to assume any change in attitude unless evidence of positive or responsible behaviors is also made available.)

We pointed out in Chapter 11 that one's belief about other people may cause continual grief. If the only problem raised by the compulsion of belief was the continued frustration of the believer, it may be considered a relatively minor cause for concern. But the fallout is immense. Contempt for those whose lifestyles differ, especially when they represent potential interference, becomes generalized to prejudicial attitudes toward all of those with identifiable, undesirable characteristics. Because children waste food, they are seen as contemptible by a bachelor uncle. The man with a telephone in his car is considered inexcusably extravagant by another who owns four television sets. But the righteous cannot avoid living among those they deem less worthy, *and there is some righteousness in all of us.*

How do people come to adopt such beliefs? Are we born that way? Is the miser a victim of unavoidable environmental contingency? Are we completely dominated by inexorable forces that limit our ability to change? It is our contention that there is extensive evidence to demonstrate that this is not so, (despite the determinism that we have assumed controls our behavior). By changing our interpretation of the data on which decisions are made, we can effect a considerable modification in human adjustment. To do this, we must recognize the potential for altering the interpretation of beliefs that result in decisions, and behaviors.

To whatever extent beliefs are held, they significantly influence the way in which one behaves, in spite of the fact that their accuracy, as well as their persuasiveness is limited. How satisfactory is it to explain to one's self that shoplifting is an excusable reaction to the immorality of the corporations that own the stores; that cheating and fraud are innate personal weaknesses of a few individuals; that mate swapping and similar behaviors are appropriate expressions of the "new liberation" that a democratic political system provides, and that some of the extreme antics of youth must be excused since they are based on the need for stimulation that is "found in all cultures at all times"? Such rationalizations may be useful defenses, and often possess sufficient surface validity to support almost any view of the causes of human behavior. Unfortunately, they require a variety of interpretations, some of which create more problems than they solve. We have discussed at some length problems associated with inappropriate beliefs regarding political and civil rights. Let us take a closer look at the widely held—and incredibly damaging conviction—that human beings hold certain "inalienable" or "absolute" rights.

The Natural Rights Dilemma
We pointed out in Chapter 3 that a critical characteristic of the holarchy of life is the tendency of parts and instances to develop the attribute of *independence*. The capacity to feel pleasure and pain is of value both to the individual and the species because it provides the impetus to action and reaction that is necessary to survival and growth. While the sense of selfhood continues to represent a valuable asset at the most sophisticated levels of life, it has come to be accompanied, in humans, by a conviction of natural or human *rights* that has had devastating consequences.

The concept is expressed in many ways, and with varying degrees of restriction. At one extreme is the limitation implicit in utilitarian philosophy which proposes that moral behavior is that which provides the "greatest good to the greatest number."[20] Jeremy Bentham, one of the founders of the utilitarian school, was totally opposed to the notion of individual rights, saying that fundamental natural rights are no more than "nonsense on stilts."[21] The reason for the utilitarianist's denial of such rights is that they are in conflict with the principle that the general welfare is of first priority. A number of philosophers have accepted that view, and it is one of the principles on which the PSI model is based.

There are however many thinkers who have taken the opposite view. Spinoza, for example, contended that power and desire give each individual the right to take what is needed "whether by force, cunning, entreaty, or any other means."[22] Locke took the position that individuals are originally in a "state of nature" in which each individual is free to act as he or she pleases. However, he believed that the inherent unfairness of that state—in that some individuals tend to abrogate the rights of others--results in the creation of civil governments, or "social contracts."[23]

Such claims are the basis for the development of what are often termed *inalienable* or *absolute* rights, which refer to privileges that (should) transcend *any* suppressive effort. A variety of arguments have been put forth to demonstrate that inalienable rights exist. Gewirth offered as an example the extreme view that "a mother's right not to be tortured to death by her own son is beyond any compromise. It is absolute."[24] Such a case provides an illustration of the depth of feeling that surrounds the issue.

On a less extreme scale are the claims to such absolute rights as that of free speech, of the right to self protection and many others. The same conviction permeates the thinking of every class of individuals, as well as most political, social, religious, and other groups. It extends from the rights of mothers (that they often deny to their daughters), to the right of peoples to retain the land of their birth—their "birthright."

The potency of the conviction that certain rights are inviolable cannot be overestimated. Where it is not preached as unavoidable fact, it is hinted at by political writers. Buckley stated "I take it as axiomatic that no one has the right to pollute the air I breathe, or the water I drink [and that] the rights of a citizen of the United States to communicate with another citizen...is about as close to an absolute right as exists."[25] If such rights were axiomatic, or absolute, they would not be based on law alone, but would supersede such ordinances, with the implication that whoever was offended in such areas had an inalienable right to take *whatever* action deemed necessary to end the frustration.

The acceptance of the belief that individuals have a natural right to the soil on which they are born has been supported by philosophic treatises for a considerable time. Locke argued that "it is one of the primary ends of the state to preserve the rights of property."[26] International agreements have been based, in most instances, on the acceptance of such a viewpoint. The result has been to create many violent episodes.

Following the period during which advanced nations established industries and educational programs in less developed parts of the world, a burgeoning nationalistic awakening resulted in the demand for ousting foreigners on the grounds that the land should be reserved to the original owners. American Indians, as well as Arab and Irish terrorists, base their claims on the same principle and there is an impressive sentimentality to the idea that the noble savage has more right to the forests of his forefathers than do imperialistic landgrabbers. However, the logic of the argument is not compelling. If we accept the moral principle that individuals have the right to hold and use the property on which they were born, we must face the paradox that the child born on oil producing land has a right to luxury, while the ghetto bastard is appropriately doomed to a life of poverty!

From what source does this conviction spring? Like so many "inalienable" rights, property rights are only a matter of tradition. They are based solely on a legalism. Historically, the practice of respecting the property of others has been considered proper. (Early drafts of the American Constitution called for the right to life, liberty, and the pursuit of property.) The error lies in translating a custom which has been sanctified by law into a moral imperative. A willingness to respect one's birthright as a legal and reasonable matter comes to endow the practice with ultimate propriety.

There are those who would argue that humans possess a "territorial" sense, just as many animals do, and that the desire to protect one's property is thus a natural urge. Our response would be that, (even accepting the accuracy of such a claim), there are any number of human desires—sex for example—whose expression is controlled by civilized communities. Should we allow thousands to die of thirst because one person was born on the only piece of property that produced water?

Unfortunately, those who do not subscribe to what appear to so many to be self evident truths, are seen as insensitive or worse. But the insistence on such principles is flawed at the outset. The inevitable clash between competing rights is as intransigent as the paradox of the irresistible force and the immovable object. Rights, in fact, only become an issue when those of one person, or one group, interfere with those of another. Thus, some support the right of a mother to abort an unwanted fetus, while others claim that the child's right to life should take precedence. In the fracas that ensues, each sees the other as acting from evil motives. While both groups believe in the notion of inalienable rights, they disagree on who holds such privileges.[27] And, here is the point at which an analysis should be useful.

In every instance of a claim of inalienable privilege, the priority of higher holarchic entities is subverted. Instances of life lay claim to a level of significance that belies their subservient role. Human life in *general* becomes hostage to the whim of particular *individuals* and, by extension, to each organization or group of individuals that lays claim to the possession of the highest moral ground. And each such demand sets the stage for carnage, since, as we have indicated, the issue of rights is only involved when one individual, or one group, attempts to express its rights *at cost to another's!*

The Historical Perspective. It is obvious that in many subhuman forms of life behaviors are based solely on the desire/need/cost relationship with little or no attention paid to priorities, except as capacity (i.e., might, or power) plays a role. It has been argued that the reason for this is that animals lack the capacity to recognize the moral aspect. A similar explanation may be offered for the fact that very young children make no such claim. However, there are many examples of baleful adult behavior where no appeal to human rights is made.

The cave man raped and captured a bride because it was accepted as an appropriate procedure. He *wanted* to do so. His right was not at issue. Whole peoples and many subgroups have accepted a lack of freedom without any assumption that their "rights" were being violated. A thousand years ago it was considered normal for a conquering army to rape the females of their defeated enemy, to put the surviving men in chains, or in galleys as oarsmen, and to commit other acts that today would be considered atrocities. As recently as a few hundred years ago, an insult to a woman was considered an affront, not to her, but to her father, husband, or brothers.

In the 1930s, in Russia, Lyons described a group of Kulaks who were being deported by Stalin to Central Asia. Asked why, they responded "because we're Kulaks."[28] "These creatures," Lyons said, "did not even dispute the right of the government to deprive them of everything...its decrees were like the decrees of nature, part of a harsh destiny."[28] In such instances, we can safely assume that those trampled would have *liked* something else. The point to be made here is that in many instances they were not claiming that their rights had been violated, but rather were simply expressing unhappiness about their unfortunate lot.

Ideas regarding the inviolability of human life that were rooted in antiquity have been given a voice both by various religious writings and by moral philosophers especially during the past several centuries. Considerations of liberties that had been in some instances extended by rulers to communities during the Middle Ages "gave way to notions like 'an Englishmen's birthright' or, still more personal and universal, 'natural rights'."[29] The rational consideration was that if God endowed humans with desires, surely they should also be entitled to satisfy those desires. Furthermore such rights must be absolute. Anything less would represent a failing in the omnipotence of the creator. And if the appeal to a superhuman agency is not accepted, humanist principles lead to the same conclusion.

The inconsistency inherent in such a conclusion was recognized by philosophers such as Kant who proposed that individuals should act only in those ways that they would want to see become universal laws, which is a version of the Golden Rule. That obviously entails the relinquishing of at least some of an individual's rights. The utilitarian principle of the obligation to keep a promise is similarly constraining in that in some instances it may limit one's freedom of action. The summary view of such philosophies was captured in the maxim:

Individuals have an inalienable right to do as they wish—so long as they do not infringe on the rights of others.

While such a moral position clearly limited the individual's rights it seemed a workable arrangement and, moreover, it represented both a morally attractive alternative and a prescription for legislative action.

When we review the religious practices of pre-historic people and study documents that define religious orders we discover that in each instance, the focus of the individual's relationship to God was one of *obligation*, rather than privilege. Even today, Hassidic Jews and Christian monks, as well as the devout of many religions, stress their responsibility to serve, to give, to share. The Koran in expressing Islamic thought, describes the duties essential to God's acceptance: "To give of one's substance, however cherished, to kinsman, and orphans, the needy, the traveler, beggars, and to ransom the slave."[30] The life of monks in a Japanese Buddhist monastery is described as "(1) life of humility, (2) life of labor, (3) life of service, (4) life of prayer and gratitude, and (5) life of meditation."[31] In the New Testament of the Christian Bible we find the admonition "the wife does not rule over her own body but the husband does; likewise the husband does not rule over his own body but the wife does."[32] Once again an expression of the *obligation* of each to the other.

It may be argued that we are referring here only to those who accept a religious faith—to those who choose a life of humility—to people who freely give up their "natural" rights to a variety of gods or godheads Such self denial is, however, universally respected as worthy. Humanists, though they exalt the freedom of each individual, see in that freedom, "man's capacity to form his world, to vary it, and to better it absolutely."[33] It would seem absurd to claim inalienable rights for *anyone* under a moral philosophy which calls for self denial and the obligation to "better the world."

How then, do we account for the appeal to human rights that has been reflected in such documents as the Magna Carta, the French and American Constitutions, and other instruments that have been constructed on the assumption of "natural" rights? And how did the notion of natural or human rights come to be defined as *absolute* or *inalienable*? First, we must point out that such documents as those mentioned above provided sovereign privilege to only a limited class of people. The Magna Carta, for example, was a compact between the king of England and British *nobility*.[34] As to the American Constitution, at the time of its ratification only male white freeholders were considered to possess absolute rights. Furthermore, although both the French and the American Constitutions were created to protect individuals from despotic treatment, the power was presumed to reside in the *people*, not in each *person*. Rights in democratic societies are, in fact, held as a legal matter, and are subject to revocation by the governing body.

Despite the fact that civil rights have been extended to only a limited segment of each political entity, two factors must be recognized.[35] First, though freedoms are expressed in the form of laws, or legal instruments, they are assumed to be based on a sense of moral propriety. Second, that priority is predicated on the recognition of the dignity of human life. Laws have been passed to provide individuals with a more secure and satisfying life. From the writ of habeas corpus, to the right to a trial by a jury of one's peers, freedoms based on natural human rights are guaranteed by statute in many countries. The codification of laws designed to implement beliefs regarding the rights of individuals was accomplished as a *reasonable* matter. And when reason began to be applied to moral issues, the step from natural to inalienable rights was a logical consequence. Soon, however, the flaws inherent in any attempt to apply reason to a moral problem revealed themselves.

The Right to Self Indulgence. Being invested with such sovereign control over one's own behavior is assumed by many to include the right to act in ways that may be personally injurious. The right to the use of mind altering drugs, or other potentially destructive substances became a significant social issue as governments increasingly maximized the freedom of its citizenry. In America, as well as in many Western European nations, during the Twentieth Century a significant number of young people took advantage of the legal system to "drop out" of the mainstream— —to exercise their natural rights—as guaranteed by law.

But is their claim to an inviolable right to do whatever they wish, including self injury, reasonable? Consider, first, only the second half of the maxim mentioned earlier (i.e., one should not infringe on the rights of others.) While such a proposition may not be applicable in cases of self defense or retaliatory action it certainly applies to wanton or self aggrandizing behavior. Even those who insist on their own rights appear to accept that reservation. But on what grounds? What is the basis for accepting that constraint while insisting on the right to perform acts that may be injurious to one's self?

Such a belief must be based either on (a) what one has learned from schools and parents, and which is developed from a morally neutral position, (b) on some innate moral sense of what constitutes right behavior, or (c) some combination of the two.

There is considerable ostensible support for the first option which assumes that people can equally easily learn to pillage as to share. There are many situations in which human dignity is not recognized. The degradation and slaughter of Jews, Gypsies, and other minority groups throughout the centuries, the carnal use of women by victorious armies, the extensive abuse of wives and children in many countries, and many examples of pleasure associated with the destruction of life are abundant. Even the vicious destruction of animals and apparent glee at the suffering of others observed in many young children seems to suggest that people must be taught to respect life, and that they can just as easily be taught the opposite. The argument fails, however, on two counts.

First, each of those individuals or groups that visits injury on others holds *some* persons or *some* people inviolate. The rapist soldier demands respect for his own mother, wife, or sister. The "malicious" child cries when another individual is injured. In point of fact, the damage done to one class of individuals is most commonly accomplished *in the interest of the welfare of another.*[36] Second, if people are to be capable of learning a belief, they must have the *capacity* to accept it. Deaf people cannot learn to hear; the psychopathic person cannot learn to feel guilt. People can be taught to be considerate of others as a rule, or law, but if they are to *appreciate* the dignity inherent in life, their must be some innate moral sense. This point, developed in Chapter 8, deserves reiteration.[37]

The second option—innate knowledge of morally appropriate behavior—is equally invalid since, though individuals know intuitively what *right is*, political, social, and cultural idiosyncrasies require that they must learn *what (behavior) is right*. As we have seen, behaviors believed to be morally appropriate by one group are often considered immoral by others.

Since people have the capacity to appreciate the value of gaining control of their environment, it would appear that the same argument can be made for the possibility of learning to destroy, and, as we have pointed out, many learn to be destructive.[38] However, there is once again an error in the interpretation. To learn behaviors which are self oriented and to find such action gratifying—even when others suffer as a consequence—calls for no stretch of the imagination. It is consistent with the *need* to be capable of behavior that enhances survival and growth. But, to appreciate the value of constraining one's self in the interest of the welfare of others is not so easily understood. It is, in fact, a source of great perplexity to sociobiologists and many others of the scientific community.[39]

But *it is just such a sense of propriety* that must underlie the willingness to limit one's freedom where it impinges on others. The acceptance of the latter half of the maxim is based on a belief in the preciousness of life, and on the obligation of each individual to respect it. This raises the obvious question of how individuals can claim a right to destroy themselves. If it is wrong for me to injure you, and for you to injure me, because of the responsibility that we both feel to protect life, on what basis can I argue for the propriety of any behavior of mine *that is injurious to my own life?*

As with all claims to natural rights, the confusion is found in the equation of desire with propriety. The fact that I want to live, and to do as I please, and that such a privilege is often legally supported, leads to a narrow interpretation of fundamental privilege. If I knew my rights innately, they would represent an example of *instinctive* knowledge. But no example of such a case can be produced. Although in many forms of life certain members (e.g., a queen bee) receive what may seem an inordinate degree of subservience from others, that relationship can be shown to be related to species survival, and where conditions demand, the queen will herself be sacrificed. We shall discuss the principle of natural relationships in the following section. However, our concern here is with the continual destruction that is wrought in the name of inalienable human rights.

The Right to Equal Treatment. Returning to the issue of rights as a matter of equality and decent treatment, consider the case of women, Blacks, and other underrepresented minority groups who believe that they are prohibited from gaining access to positions of power and security that should be theirs as a matter of human or natural right. We have taken the position that no such rights exist. However, an understanding of our position should dampen inflammatory reaction. *For neither can those who hold the reins of power appeal to any "natural" right to maintain their monopoly.* Though individuals have no inalienable "natural" right to live, neither do others have such a right to injure them. The issue is fought on inappropriate, as well as ineffectual, grounds.

When any group bases its argument on human or natural rights, they goad their opposition into assuming a defensive posture. The result has been the kind of vitriolic charges and countercharges that have been seen, for example, in the struggle between pro-choice advocates (those who support a woman's right to do as she pleases with her own body), and pro-life (anti-abortion) advocates. It may seem that in view of the fact that most religious groups oppose abortion, morality reside on that side. However, those that champion the woman's right to use her body as she sees fit, are presenting a position that they believe to be morally superior—that a mature woman has rights that supersede those of a fetus whose viability may even be questionable. On both sides proponents appeal to a moral imperative and have amassed evidence in an attempt to prove their point. But such attempts are doomed to failure.

It is simple enough to show that no amount of scientific evidence bears on any moral question. It is perhaps more difficult to show that no "correct" decision could be reached on the basis of any combination of empirical evidence and its impact on the moral sense. Most distressing, however, is the totally ignored fact that in the abortion issue each side is motivated by a respect for the rights of some form of human life, that each group attributes those rights to a different class of individuals, and that as long as they have persisted in this approach, only anger, frustration, pain, and hate have followed.

Consider the elements once again. Inalienable rights is a concept which presumes that individuals can know a correct behavior innately. They cannot. The presentation of evidence presumes that at some point an intellectually sound moral decision can be made. It cannot. The outcome of the struggle will presume to indicate that the winners have won a moral victory. It will not. How tragic that individuals appealing to the same sense of moral propriety should hate those who support a conflicting interpretation of where the priorities should be.

The difference in the positions results from differential learning regarding the supremacy of the individual and the priority of the human species. Individuals are not born Democrats or Republicans, monarchists or Communists, Catholics or Protestants, though some would claim that they are. Neither are *they born with the knowledge of their inalienable rights*. Such convictions are the product of formal and informal learning experiences.

Before describing alternative approaches to the problem, we should point out, once again, that this is not a political but an emotional health text. While social interaction may be altered by adherence to some of the suggested interpretations to be offered, our concern is with personal adjustment. Individuals that believe their rights are being violated, and where there seems little hope of redress, spend much time in states of anger and feelings of hostility. The world often seems against them. Life appears manifestly unfair.

Whether such individuals have a right to expect equity is moot, so far as psychological intervention is concerned. First, as we have indicated, the expression of one's rights often calls forth vituperative responses from those who are believed to be the abusers of such privilege. More importantly, however, there are less abrasive approaches available, as will be developed. As to the political aspect, nothing that is expressed here represents an admonition that civil and women's rights advocates, or those supporting other positions, should not be permitted to express their views. In many instances, insurgency (such as that led by Martin Luther King Jr., in the 1960s), has had long range socially positive outcomes. There is, in fact, an understandable exhilaration associated with fighting to achieve goals—especially those endowed with moral characteristics. However, a distinction must be made between political action, no matter how valid, and the personal adjustment of those involved.

The point we wish to emphasize is that confrontation, *based on inappropriately assumed natural rights*, not only alienates many of those involved, but is an unnecessary approach to an undeniably important issue. The PSI model includes both an analysis of the elements of such situations and recommended alternative approaches. In Chapter 12 six premises that are basic to the PSI model were introduced. Here we shall add several that are germane to the issue of rights.

The Fact/Value Dichotomy

Premise 7: No fact, or collection of facts, can lead to a *true* value, judgment or decision. Facts and values are completely independent forms of knowledge. While both are limited to belief status, they reference separate domains. This is an extremely subtle, and critically important concept. It is the basis for our contention that one can never act reasonably,[40] or morally,[41] nor can responsibility be fixed by any factual test.

In Chapter 8, we pointed out that concepts such as fact, *truth*, and *proof* involve only a communion of agreement regarding what is believed to be the case; how sure one may feel about the validity of an existential claim. Following Hume's dictum, however, we asserted that there is no rational justification for the step from the acceptance of existential veracity to the discovery of a true moral or judgmental conclusion. No path leads from *is* to *ought*; the concepts are unrelated. Value judgments are not subject to truth status, nor to proof of any kind. It is inappropriate to assume any implication of the form "If X is so then Y *should* follow" where X is factual information, and Y is a value statement. While factual data are the basis for the changing of opinions, those altered opinions move no closer to a "true" value.

Consider this example. At what degree of danger should one avoid the use of some form of medication as being "too dangerous"? While some information such as "there have been 25% fatalities among those who have used it" would be recognized as subjective, there is difficulty in appreciating that a figure of 99.99% fatalities would provide no *proof* that the medication should be considered "too dangerous." When pro-life advocates claim to have changed the attitude of some women toward abortion, by showing them photographs of a 10 week old fetus, what they have changed is an *opinion*, which does not take them any closer to the "true" value, as pro-choice advocates who are not so impressed by the evidence will attest.

An Alternative Approach

Suppose two 25 year old women, either both or neither of whom is sexually active, disagree on the propriety of abortion. To what may the difference be credited? Is one of them *innately* more moral than the other? Are all of those on one side of the argument *genetically* morally superior to those on the other? Or can we appreciate that each viewpoint is wholly a product of formal and informal learning experiences. What of a young woman who supports abortionist principles although she has been taught at home, at school, and in her church that abortion is wrong. Which argument is more convincing: That she is inherently immoral (as pro-lifers may insist), or that she has learned somewhere, somehow, that a woman has an inalienable right to do as she wishes with her body? Surely the latter interpretation is more plausible. And this leads to another PSI principle.

Knowledge as Learned

Premise 8: **Almost all human knowledge results from learning experiences.** A principle tenet of the holarchic position is that almost *anything* can be learned.[42] Thus, the acceptance of the killing of infant girls in ancient Rome and reports of similar behavior in developing countries that limit the number of children a family may have; the propriety of killing Jews in Germany as defilers of decent people; and the slaughter of those of different nationalities, races, or religions in so many wars.

In every such instance, people have learned both to defend a position they believe to be morally correct, and to attempt to destroy those that they believe threaten their position. The death threat of the Ayatollah Khomeini, a Muslim Iranian clergyman against the author of a book that he considered sacrilegious is a case in point.

It is chilling to observe films of the tens of millions who shrieked for joy at the massacre of the Ethiopians by Italian war planes, the murder of Jews by Nazi Germans and the genocide practiced by Stalin. Such behavior is often offered as evidence of the inherent depravity of humans. But not only did each group of those fanatics support and defend their own country with their lives when necessary, literally billions of people expend a major effort in caring for and respecting the lives of others in every era. A study of theological and humanistic literature should make that clear. Koestler's contention that humans are possessed of a "paranoid streak," which would make learning to behave in a civilized manner highly improbable, cannot be supported.[43]

Religious people believe in a hereafter, atheists do not. Both commit acts of benevolence as well as violence. Americans will die to protect Americans, while detesting the rich, the poor, lawyers, drug dealers, and many classes of individual of which this country is comprised. Humans are not inherently good or evil; they are rather ignorant of how to develop societies that can provide for some optimal level of personal adjustment. And they are capable of learning.

Applying the principle to the pro-life/pro-choice opposition, how could those who understood that viewpoints are learned, find their opponents morally degenerate? What better intellectual setting in which to deal with such an emotionally charged issue. It is unquestionably easier to learn that which conforms to one's desires (as when a pregnant woman does not want the child she carries, and/or the responsible male does not feel he should have to care for it). However, people also learn to accept that which they recognize as morally worthy even when it means sacrificing some selfish desire.

The principle that "rights" priorities cannot be established in cases where the rights of one person seriously threaten the welfare—perhaps even the life—of another leads to the inevitable conclusion that in such instances, decisions must be recognized as arbitrary. Those with a lifelong commitment to the moral superiority of one side or the other in the abortion argument will see such an interpretation as a shrinking from the responsibility for making the "correct" moral choice. It is because of this dilemma that a preventive approach, through which the vacuousness of such moral claims can be exposed, is essential. This is the basis for the PSI educational program.

The Holarchic Position Restated

The *meaning* of each individual, and the *purpose* that resides in behavior were described in Chapters 2 and 4. Such characteristics are functions of the relationship that obtains between the whole that is life and its instances as represented by individuals. At every level of living existence, parts and instances function to serve the interest of some whole existent from whence they derive their significance, or meaning. No part of my body, for example, has any *right* to exist. Rather, it has an obligation to serve the totality that is, most immediately, my total being. Obligations, however, do not represent negative, but rather positive experiences. The *transcendent* desires were identified as one of the three basic urges which, as do *assertive* and *protective* desires, seeks gratification. To be totally free of obligation represents the basis for one of the most extreme forms of emotional illness.

Moral behavior was defined in Chapter 8 as that activity which has species positive consequences. The only form in which morality is related to the individual without direct reference to the species is in the desirability of self care, which is an *obligation of both self and other,* and which is in no sense a right—except in the negative sense mentioned earlier, that no one holds a right to injure self or other.

The principle to be taught is not that humans have natural *rights*, but that life is a precious thing, and that humans as instances of the totality should be treated with dignity because of an *obligation* to the living principle, and thus to each other, rather than because of the right of each individual to expect it. This in neither a religious pronouncement, nor an appeal to humanist doctrine, although both should find the principle meritorious. It is not based on the contention that the value inherent in human life "makes [humans] the measure of all things,"[44] which sees the transient living being as the focal point of moral behavior. It is rather a recognition of the relationship between the individual and humanity in general, which is most apt to result in the development of satisfying life styles.

The holarchic principle includes a recognition of the universality of *desires* (though not of *needs!*), and the obligation to respect such urges in others. Consider this principle in the context of feminine advocacy—the recognition of the identity of the desires of women with those of men—and the fact that in modern society, "equal pay for equal work" represents a *reasonable* expectation. While the appeal to a woman's *rights* may seem offensive to a chauvinist male, the request for *socially appropriate* treatment need not arouse so vehement a reaction.[45]

The suggestion that such an altered approach be taken immediately would, of course, be absurd. The prejudices of those of us beyond adolescence are fervently maintained, with true motives masked by many layers of justifying veneer. The only sensible approach is to employ a *primary* preventive model[46] which must be built into the educational system when children are at an early, and most impressionable, age.

The initial steps are quite easily applied, since it is common practice to encourage children in pre-school and kindergarten programs to respect the feelings of their classmates (though too often, teachers refer to the right*s* of other children rather than focusing on the nature of obligation). The problem arises with the onset of puberty, and the awakening of sex-linked desires. Because of the natural urge to compete for status, to exercise a developing body, and to probe the many mysteries that adolescence reveals, respect for the dignity of others is commonly obscured. Self interest, understandably a powerful force, tends to dominate the individual's attention. Jealousy, envy, and similar emotions, color reactions to other people. Those favored in appearance, ability, or other assets, are often resented as having an unfair advantage.

Nothing in the PSI model presumes to alter the course of such development, nor to stop the related emotions from occurring. However, this is clearly the period of time during which respect for the dignity and the desires of others needs to be stressed in *curricular* offerings. Recall that the *coherence* of the school's program requires that it offer a consistent, integrated program designed to meet the desired output of the school system. That output is, unfortunately, often couched essentially, in terms of meeting the *assertive* needs of students. Implicit, however, is the need for each student to develop a sense of belonging with its attendant responsibilities, as well as an appreciation of, and respect for the interests of the community at large, which represents the transcendent need.

Because of the fear of impinging on individual rights, considerable unconscionable adolescent behavior is condoned. The sports hero is often excused from responsibility, as is his classmate who traffics in drugs. Old enough to display a self indulgent arrogance, mature enough to terrorize a neighborhood, they are too young to be held accountable. The American promise of maximum freedom, supported by the ludicrous look-out-for-number-one psychology of the sixties, has created an insidious jungle of inadequate personalities—of followers seeking the eternal guru. Much of this inanity is based on the adherence to the principle of natural rights.

The PSI model does not call for the renunciation of behaviors based on assertive and protective desires. It applauds them. What it prescribes is a program that recognizes the many ways in which such desires can be met. The "macho" high school student who intimidates young female teachers can learn that leadership is better demonstrated through behavior that includes the defense of those less physically dominant. In this way both several of the desires of the individual, as well as those of the community may be served. Such an approach must, however, be taught as an integral curricular element. Children do not come to appreciate their social roles as a result of arriving at a certain age. It is not a matter of maturation but experience. In China, during the 1970s it was the ambition of millions of young people to join the Red Guard, an organization that trampled the rights of those who sought individual liberty. A generation later, the young people of that country were clamoring for the creation of a democratic society. The genetic structure of that society has not been altered. The belief structure of many millions has been.

A caution must be exercised in the interpretation of rights that we have presented. In contending that those in authority, no matter how time honored, can claim no "natural" right to constrain the behaviors of others, we may have seemed to make a case for limiting control over children by parents or other adults. What parents bear is the responsibility for training (educating), controlling, providing for the development of self discipline, and otherwise preparing their young for successful adult lives. This

is observed in practically every advanced form of life, and in every human culture—
—with the mother ordinarily carrying most of the burden. However, fathers, need to
learn of their responsibility both for contributing to the family's security, and for
providing a role model for male children. Failure to meet those requirements has
contributed significantly to the many inadequate personalities that are observed in
most Western societies.[47]

Developmental Concepts

Belief has been defined as a potentially positive concept, in that it represents the
capacity to break the bonds of rigid knowledge. Responses are not genotypally fixed,
and decisions can be made that take into account the contingent environment. As in
the case of the belief concerning "inalienable" human rights, however, beliefs are
capable of leading to confrontation and persistent negative emotions, or attitudes.
Many more prosaic issues are subject to the vagaries of belief. The PSI model calls
for a reinterpretation of a number of concepts that influence personality development.
For example, such terms as *discipline, work,* and *responsibility* are regularly construed
in such a way as to lead to ineffective practices.

The Nature of Discipline
Premise 9: **Discipline represents the capacity to perform without the need for
external controls.** With the increasing political freedom that has been experienced
in the Western world, (on the basis of the concept of human rights) an increase in
negative behaviors has been observed among adolescents as they strive to take
advantage of their new found "privileges." Such behavior plagues those who
advocate the desirability of maximizing individual freedom. The reaction has been
a demand from an increasing number of adults, that social institutions take whatever
action is necessary to curb the outbreaks of vandalism, physical violence and other
crimes as well as the less serious, but nonetheless annoying behavior of non-
compliant teen-agers. Unfortunately, the term *discipline* has been used to describe
such activity. That interpretation has resulted in a persistent failure to produce the
kind of young adults that a free society seeks. While effective discipline programs
make use of controls, the appropriate role for such action is to provide protective
barriers as positive behaviors develop.

The PSI program, *(Discipline says "GO!"; Punishment says "NO!"*)[48] identifies
discipline as a *positive* behavioral characteristic that is inculcated through a program
of education, guidance, and support. The goal of the program is the instillation of *self*
discipline, which refers to the ability of individuals to control their own actions with
little or no external constraint. Programming for discipline must begin at a very early
age, and be encouraged at least throughout the educational years. It requires the
cooperative effort of teachers, parents, and other influential agencies.

The PSI model provides a view of discipline that is diametrically opposed to that commonly employed, and demonstrates ways in which "disciplined" young people may be developed in schools and other institutions. Consider some of the common definitions. Funk defined discipline as "to train to obedience, subjection, or effectiveness." and "to punish and chastise."[49] Harriman defined it as "a means of social control."[50] Other dictionaries provide similar descriptions. Such characterizations may be quite accurate for describing programs for the training of animals, but they are wholly inappropriate to the kind of programming that will instill a love of a disciplined life in school children or any other subset of society—even including many incarcerated criminals.

The authors of these negative interpretations of discipline undoubtedly intend, in many cases, that punishment and control under *certain conditions*, may aid in the establishment of discipline. However, the concept is employed as if it referred to sheer control, or as if controlling behavior, in itself, would lead to disciplined living. Parents demand that teachers "discipline" their children by which they mean to achieve compliance. No growth characteristic is even hinted at. And here is the source of the problem.

When we analyze the intention of those that call for disciplining children in a free society, we discover that what they actually seek is not obedience, or subservience, but the development of individuals who realize that well ordered lives are effective and desirable. Such societies seek to produce individuals who do not need rigid, externally imposed, regulations. Discipline is a *preventive* measure; control is a *treatment*. Discipline is *not* what a high school teacher initiates, but what caring parents and effective schools instill. There is a place for control, and even punishment, but such measures are effective only when individuals understand and take pride in working to meet the goals of their program.

There is sufficient natural desire in most individuals for skill development and successful living that controls are acceptable. However, unless constraints are accompanied by *education*, *guidance*, and *recognition* for exemplary performance, the only outcome of rigid barriers will be—and demonstrably has been—resentment, hostility and persistent efforts to undermine the efforts of well intentioned teachers and parents. Individuals also need the opportunity to express natural desires. There is in children for example, a persistent urge to run, to jump, to play. To publish an edict that strictly prohibits children from throwing snowballs, or indulging in "horseplay," and imposing severe penalties for violations begs for transgressions. To provide a *place* and a *time* for such behavior encourages socially approvable activity, and thus, for the development of positive self discipline.

The PSI model calls for an analysis of each situation that includes the potential for self discipline, as well as for potentially deviant behavior. The two ordinarily occur in tandem, since situations that call for self control must include the kind of freedom that may lead to disruptive activity. Any situation that requires restricted movement over extended periods of time is recognized as being difficult for adolescents. However, subject matter that is presented in an uninspired manner, (where the purpose of an assignment is obscure, or where tasks or negative, monotonous, or defined as punitive), also contributes to potentially chaotic conditions. Not only is their little likelihood that self controls will operate, there is every probability that punishment or control—*labeled "discipline"*—will be required.

In Chapter 13 *instrumental* behavior was defined as activity performed in the interest of achieving some goal other than the behavior itself. Although the vast majority of human behavior is instrumental, it is not experienced as odious when the object of the action is believed by the behaver to be worth the effort. Thus, the fisherman spends hours on Saturday evening untangling lines in order to be ready for an outing on Sunday. Many people spend every spare moment planting, feeding, weeding, and watering plots of ground that produce only a few, scrawny flowers. Their persistence is a sign of self discipline.

Adolescents, too, are people. They demonstrate again and again that they can persevere in activity with which they can identify. However, they can rarely cope with goals set decades in their future. Furthermore, they usually have difficulty in relating current activity with those distant rewards. (How does the ability to divide fractions relate to any possible practicality?)

Educators bear responsibility for providing answers to such questions at a level that is within the comprehension of their students. This does not mean that school should be made easier, but rather that under the right conditions students can handle work that is far more difficult. In so doing, they will have the opportunity to learn the kind of work habits that may eventuate in the development of effective self discipline. Figure 16.1 demonstrates the relationship between the application of controls, and the development of self discipline, as well as the role of work and the evolving of responsibility. The instruction point represents an example of the interface between controls and learning experiences. The principle involved is that control—and especially punishment—should always be administered concurrently with instructions as to how such a situation may be properly handled.

Students must have the opportunity to learn that rules, laws, and other constraints are also inherently positive. The rule that establishes the height of a basketball net, or the width of a soccer field, are essential to the enjoyment of the game. Similarly, the rules that call for specified days and hours of school attendance, as well as for student performance of assigned academic tasks, are designed to facilitate growth, rather than to frustrate the individual. It is well worth the effort involved, to assure that this concept is well understood by students at all grade levels.

The Role of Work

Premise 10: **Work is a positive concept. It represents the most potent vehicle for attaining the gratification of desires and for developing a sense of identity.** From the beginning of time humans have faced the task of providing for their sustenance and that has involved, in most instances, some type of *work*. Obviously, such behavior represents a source of power; a technique for gaining access to those needs related to the *assertive* and *protective* desires. Less well understood is the fact that work is also the principle avenue to *meaning*. Simply stated: I am what I *do*. My meaning resides in what I produce.[51] How else describe myself than as a father, a teacher, a carpenter, a mailman? Unless I am a professional, what meaning can be attached to such statements as "I am a golfer; a gardener; a television viewer?" While such descriptions may accurately describe much of my behavior, they provide no clue to what my existence *means*; what my identity *signifies*.

Figure 16.1
Work, Discipline, and Responsibility

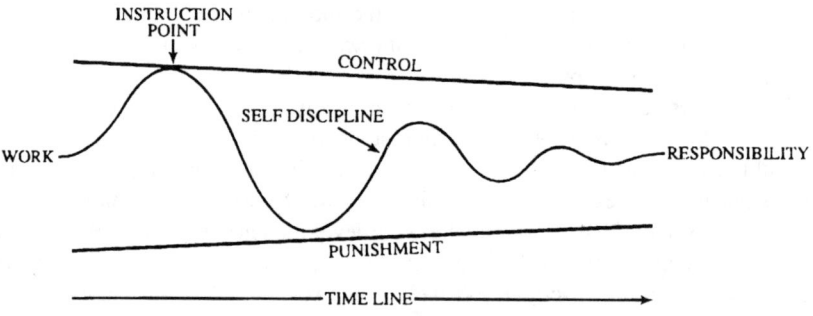

In spite if its significance, work, like discipline, has come to carry a negative connotation. It is assumed by many to represent a necessary evil; an aspect of life to be avoided if possible, tolerated at best. But the perception of work as negative flies in the face of extensive evidence to the contrary. No animal shows a distaste for work, nor is there any evidence that primitive people considered work degrading. Aborigines, even today, look forward with pride to their initiation into adulthood, where they can assist in performing those tasks that support the group. American immigrants of all eras began their lives in this country with delight regarding their opportunity to work— —often for long hours and at relatively low pay. Children are capable of doing extremely arduous work when they can relate it to a desired product. Such efforts have often been defined as "play" by those who decry work. But how many adults would find the requirement that they build airplanes, or bathe and feed dolls for hours on end, a pleasant one? At the other end of the spectrum are the retirees who consistently seek work, regardless of their financial need. And between these extreme age groups are the millions of workers who have indicated to pollsters that they find their jobs satisfying. Can they all be wrong? How did work come to bear such an odious label?

The scholars who wrote the first versions of the Judeo-Christian Bible during the Second Century of the Christian era, described the exodus from the Garden of Eden as including the admonition that individuals would have to work to support themselves, as punishment for their transgressions.[52] That view lent support to the popular notion that to be freed from the necessity of supporting one's self by the performance of menial, daily, tasks was an appropriate ambition. At that time a caste system existed in the Mediterranean world, which was the center of civilized life. Along with that system came a degree of opulence for the privileged class which led to considerable envy of those whose exalted status freed them from drudgery. Little wonder that the scribes of the time presented such a bleak view of work.

Throughout the centuries many other factors have contributed to the negative interpretation of work. The media message in America has been one of extolling the virtue of the pursuit of leisure. To "have nothing to do" is considered a highly desirable state. Many writers have expressed concern about the deterioration of the work ethic in America. Eisenberger speaks of the fact that Monday is an unhappy day for millions of workers.[53] Furthermore, a number of significant people have written about the desirability of increasing leisure time.

Winston Churchill said that one of his greatest hopes was to see a 35-hour work week become the norm for the British people. *His proposal demeaned work.* But Churchill, himself, worked incessantly. And the captains of industry, in their plush offices and private washrooms are, in many cases, workaholics, putting in far more hours each week than do their subordinates. Labor unions also contribute to the problem. Their demand for a greater share of the profits of an organization is based, essentially, on their right to their share, rather than on the *value* of the workers contribution. *This demeans the worker.*

A third source of negativity can be found in the operation of the welfare system. While the plan to assist those in need is admirable, the method in which it is administered also debases work. The message of the advocates of the indigent is that they should not have to perform menial tasks. They contend that federal assistance should make possible educational and business programs that will make it possible for everyone to rise above the "poverty" level. No one should have to work in a low paying service position. No one should have to carry trash. No one should have to clean anyone's home but there own. In view of the fact that tens of millions of Americans hold jobs of a menial nature, and can be expected to do so far into the foreseeable future, *this philosophy demeans both the work and the worker.*

One might hope that the educational system would represent a counterforce in its description of the nature of work. In view of the fact that practically all students will be required to work throughout their lives, would it not make sense to help them to see it as positive? Especially, in view of the fact that it is? Unfortunately, schools consistently play their part in solidifying the negative view.[54] A few of the many common practices follow.

The behavioral approach widely employed in the schools is based on the philosophy that humans act to obtain rewards. The PSI model is based on the same principle. However, in its implementation, the PSI model is significantly different. The BAP shows that the deliberative process includes the weighing of costs against gain. When the school student is rewarded with free time, confections, or other extrinsic recompense, work is identified as a cost—an activity to be dispensed with as was discussed in Chapter 15. The PSI approach eschews such a procedure. Rather work should be pitted against *time*, or *quality standards*. The reward should be pride in performance. Work may, thus, come to be seen as positive. Several of our research projects have demonstrated that work may itself be used as a reward. In one study, students who completed school tasks were *permitted* to perform additional tasks. Quality of work, and school attitudes were maintained.[55] The difference was that students learned the positive feeling associated with performance.

Many other school practices contribute to the problem. The reward for a particular performance is apt to be that the student is excused from doing homework. Disruptive behavior results in the assignment of additional school *work*. At their worst, teachers *model* a negative attitude toward work. In some places they are out of the school building before the children leave. They complain publicly, and constantly, about their job. Where can work, as interpreted by these individuals, *possibly* be located on the BAP?[56]

Disciplined workers are those who have a positive attitude toward their tasks; those who have learned the ability to do their job well enough that they need not drive themselves to persist from day to day. Of course, there are many reasons why a specific job may be unpleasant. One may be overqualified; capable of a more demanding assignment; harassed by an insensitive supervisor. However, the principle involved is that work is not, in itself, a negative concept, since it represents the principle source of access to the gratification of human desires, and to the development of a sense of identity. An effective educational procedure is one that introduces concepts at a level that students can understand, and adds increments that can be successfully handled. In this way, work and self discipline can come to be viewed as positive concepts. The work line in Figure 16.1 refers to the acquisition of skills, and the development of attitudes as discipline is instilled.

The Development of Responsibility

Premise 11. **Responsibility is a morally neutral concept, which refers to one's dependability in a variety of situations.** Unlike work and discipline, responsibility is not a characteristic that can be taught directly. It is a description of behavior that is only possible (though not necessary) for individuals that are disciplined workers. It is, furthermore, not a moral concept. The common misconception that responsible people are *nice* people, leads to teaching practices which can only succeed by accident. The mafia employee who can be depended on to murder the individual to whose demise he is assigned, is just as entitled to be considered responsible as is the man who faithfully supports his family. It is only when this aspect is understood that we may appreciate how to develop responsibility in the school.

Responsibility characterizes behavior that is consistently performed in an expected manner, whether in the interest of the self or others. It may arise from two sources. The first of these is fear; the second is some degree of identification with the individual or institution to whom one may be responsible. As a parent, a teacher, an employer, or a spouse, I can anticipate responsible behavior from those with whom I associate, only if they believe that there is reason to respect my wishes or to fear my wrath.

Fear based responsibility is far more common than may be realized. Employees who resent their employers, or wives who detest their husbands may perform in a dependable manner because they fear the loss of financial security. Children may comply with parents demands because of fear of loss of acceptance, or some form of punishment. In each instance a highly significant factor must be recognized. In Chapter 14 we identified impotence as a cause of poor emotional health. Impotence, however, is not only related to the inability to behave, but also to the inability to cease behaving, because of the high associated cost. Worker's high salaries may have the opposite effect on adjustment than would be anticipated. BAP scores may be at 6/5, with no ameliorative process readily available.

The PSI model calls for the recognition of this peculiarity. Reward systems for school children should be carefully monitored to assure that performance expectations are well within each child's potential, in terms of intellectual ability, energy, capacity, and awareness of the function of the exercise. High level rewards that tax a child excessively can lead to resentment and disinterest. The common practice of competitively rating schools and teachers for levels of student achievement carry the seeds of educational destruction for many.

Since we do not desire to teach people to perform on the basis of fear, we must provide them with opportunities to develop a sense of identification. Children learn very quickly to identify with adults who accept them as fallible people, while encouraging them to do their best. They respect teachers who are knowledgeable, fair, and consistent. For such people they desire to act responsibly. Such behavior––like work—provides for the genesis of a sense of identity.

Responsibility is task and situation specific. Many individuals are consistently responsible—or not. Others, however, are thoroughly dependable in one situation, lax in another. The responsible business man may often be late for appointments with his wife for dinner, or with his partners at the golf course. The child who is admired for dependability by his teachers, may be an entirely irresponsible person at home. The explanation for such unpredictability may be found in the different attitudes that such individuals have toward those to whom responsibility would be anticipated. The business man assumes that he need not be concerned about social interactions. The school child has learned that careless performance bears little cost at home. A BAP rating of the child's "housekeeping" behavior would probably be at 1/1. There is little to be gained if a room is kept clean, and a small price to pay if it isn't.

Recalling the issue with discipline, it is essential that if sanctions are imposed in either of such instances, the offender be advised about how to handle the problem; how to avoid developing a poor reputation for dependability. Adults, as well as children, can learn new behaviors. They are most apt to learn them when they realize that, as with work and self discipline, meaning and power reside in responsible behavior.

A special class of responsibility is the demonstration of social responsibility, which refers to behavior that is not only dependable, but directed in socially appropriate ways. This brings us once again to the concept of obligation that was dealt with under the issue of inalienable rights. Here we are dealing with the same concept, a principle that can be taught, and for which a specific curricular plan can be provided. We have emphasized the fact that the development of cognitive skill has, in humans, resulted in a loss of the power to recognize innate sensibilities. Children must be taught to appreciate the value of socially acceptable activities. They must have the opportunity to give, to share, to sacrifice. Christmas, birthdays, and other holidays should be celebrated not only by the reception of gifts, but by the opportunity to assist others. Programs in the home, as well as in school (on a curricular basis), should include the specification of gifts of service to worthy persons or organizations. Only in this manner can children learn that doing for others is emotionally satisfying, and that one's identity is, in part, a function of the extent to which social responsibility is accepted.

The procedures that we have described make possible the development of a positive attitude toward work, the capacity for self discipline, and a sense of social responsibility. Clearly, such a model is liable to break down in the face of political reality. Individuals from undervalued minorities cannot be expected to identify easily with the greater society, nor to feel an obligation to be responsible to an insensitive totality. Their counterparts among the privileged, who often have little respect for minority groups, face the same problem. However, such prejudicial attitudes are learned, and an effective society must find a way to overcome that stultifying barrier.

Summary

The PSI model is designed to provide a primary preventive approach to problems of human adjustment. Potentially useful in the performance of any social institution, it focuses on the public school as the most significant socializing agency. Emphasis is placed on the concepts of *responsibility*, *coherence* and *quality* as critical elements of the educational establishment. The perennial problem of determining who shall make the critical decisions regarding the goals of the school is reduced to an understanding of the distinction between civil and political rights, and the role of professionals in a democratic society. Neither parents, students, nor professionals can claim any priority of privilege in setting the school's course. That function is reserved to school boards, which operate under state and federal guidelines. Unfortunately, in many instances, decisions are made by unauthorized groups or individuals as school boards fail to carry out their mandate.

Many beliefs which have a negative impact on emotional health may be altered if appropriate curricular steps are taken. The issue of inalienable or absolute rights represent an example of a widely held but unsupportable belief which creates powerful, negative emotions. A program which includes the teaching of the acceptance of human *obligation*, rather than the demand for human *rights*, should reduce some of the undesirable confrontation when major social issues are debated. It should, further, provide the opportunity for the satisfaction of the urge to belong— the desire for meaning and purpose which reside in the relationship between the individual and a more comprehensive whole.

At a more immediate level, concepts such as *work*, *discipline*, and *responsibility*, can be more effectively managed if they are construed in more positive ways. The responsible person must have a reasonable capacity to perform assigned tasks as well as to be self disciplined. The socially responsible individual must have the opportunity to experience the positive feeling associated with morally "appropriate" performance. The school, as well as the home, must accept the challenge of instituting programs designed to provide such opportunity.

Chapter Notes

1. The fact that various schools of psychological thought find their own interpretation of behavior to be uniquely correct was mentioned in Chapter 11. In each instance behavior is construed as being so highly intricate that only the initiate can hope to understand it—and then only in the framework of the leader of the appropriate movement.
2. Wonderly (1979). A more specific approach to the development of a primary preventive emotional health model was addressed by Wonderly & Jessie (1974) in which the public school serves as the principal arena.
3. Bower (1969), p. 482
4. Wonderly (1971)
5. Wonderly (1975)
6. Wonderly (1985)
7. Bloom (1987)
8. Albee, G. (1985), p. 64
9. Bloom (1987), p. 109
10. Bower (1974) coined the acronym KISS (Key Integrative Social Systems) to reference those institutions that are critical to the establishment of positive emotional health in children during the formative years.
11. Wonderly & Jessie (1974), p. 59
12. This, of course, is not to ignore the complaints of teachers that more and more testing and other extra-curricular activities (as well as "new approaches") leave less and less time for teaching!
13. Bertalanffy (1968), p. 18
14. The Personnel and Guidance Journal (1971)
15. Patterson (1971), p. 258
16. Plato cited in Edwards (1967), p. 331
17. Abrig (1971), p. 7
18. Whether school boards are elected or appointed, they are charged with considerable latitude in making decisions regarding the educational process.
19. Glynn County Schools, GA (1987-88), p. 2
20. The utilitarian position retains its potency among many moral philosophers today, though it has been modified and subdivided into a variety of classes, such as "rule" and "act" utilitarianism.
21. Bentham cited in Flew (1979), p. 306
22. Spinoza quoted in Copleston (1963), p. 259. Spinoza did, however, modify his position by making the point that since people desire to live safely, intelligent individuals sacrifice their right to take from others in the interest of self defense. (Note that the desire for safety is recognized as being just as primitive as that for *power*.)
23. Locke in Abrams (1967)
24. Gewirth (1981), p. 8. Gewirth contended that in the event, for example, that terrorists threatened to kill other people unless

he "tortured his mother to death," if he were to acquiesce, responsibility for the crime would rest only with the perpetrators.
25. Buckley (1969), p. 275
26. Locke cited in Edwards (1967), p. 499
27. In many instances, debates are developed in the interest of encouraging *legal* action. However, such appeals are based on the contention that some "right" should be recognized as having *moral* priority.
28. Lyons cited in Kaiser, (1976), p. 297
29. Edwards (1967), p. 195
30. Williams (1961), p. 44
31. Gard (1961), p. 186
32. Corinthians 1 (1952), p. 160
33. Mirandola cited in Edwards (1967), p. 70. The humanists, in fact, according to Edwards "did not have an anti-religious or anti-Christian character" (p. 71). As to human freedom "the freedom of which they spoke is that which man can and should exercise in nature and in society" (p. 71). It is, thus, a bounded freedom most closely related to autonomy, or freedom from oppression.
34. There is some disagreement regarding whose rights the carta protects. "Although some scholars had argued that the carta applied only to a contract between the King and the barons, the puritans...interpreted it to include all freemen" (Dickey, 1986, p. 32).
35. We pointed out earlier that though civil rights are extended to minors in the United States, such rights are not subject to the control of their constituency as are the (political) rights of the electorate.
36. See references to Koestler's (1967) well grounded contention that more murders are committed in the name of a deity than for any other reason.
37. See the section on morality in Chapter 8 for a detailed discussion.
38. The desire for *power* was developed in Chapter 7. However, the fact of such an urge is not *prima facie* proof that there is an inherent urge to destroy other humans, and certainly not in the barbarous manner that many millions have been—and are being—dispatched.
39. We pointed out in Chapter 4 that every biological tract, being based on evolutionist principles, has taken the view that there *must* be some selfish motive underlying generous or self sacrificing behavior.
40. See section on Reason, Chapter 8, pp. 234-235
41. See section on Morality, Chapter 8, pp. 238-249
42. See section on Learning, Chapter 6, pp. 179-184
43. Koestler (1967)
44. Edwards (1967), p. 70
45. The appeal is better based on a request for the recognition that changes in the social structure call for a change in the relative status of the sexes. Women

should not (in the rational sense of the term) base their claim on the concept of timeless inalienable rights, but on cultural conditions. They need not deny that at another time in history, subservience of women may have been appropriate, since role assignment is an arbitrary matter, tempered by what are considered the needs of a group. Civilians are expected to waive their "rights" when under military orders. Similarly, at a time when men carried the responsibility for providing physical protection for the family, it may have made sense to *expect* that their wives would accept a subordinate position.

46. Primary prevention refers to the application of preventive measures to every member of a population at risk. Vaccines, as well as fluoridation and other community health programs, represent common examples. Education is, itself, considered a form of primary prevention in that all children are subject to the process.

47. The notion of "natural" relationships which seems so clearly to describe parent child interaction, has been claimed for many other human roles. Throughout history, philosophers have argued about the right of a man to control the behavior of his wife. Religious tracts have considered the male to be inherently superior, and novelists have described women as creatures to be manipulated. Balzac (1893) said "woman dwells at home: she remains face to face with sorrow.... To feel, to love, to suffer, to devote herself, will always be the text of woman's life" (p. 64). The feminists of the Twentieth Century find such a viewpoint ridiculous. Thus, care must be taken to analyze each aspect of a relationship to determine the extent to which it may be considered natural.

48. The title of a PSI development program.
49. Funk (1963), p. 721
50. Harriman (1974), p. 50
51. Work need not be confined to only that for which one is remunerated—community service and similar behaviors are equally significant.
52. It should be pointed out that the Book of Genesis was written by a *man,* or *men,* attempting to reflect the existing social system. Though it may have been inspired by God, we cannot assume that the particulars were described with any degree of precision.
53. Eisenberger (1989), King (1989) and many others have expressed concern regarding the roles of work and play in current American society, emphasizing the fact that one person's work is often another's pleasure, and that the value of work is usually a matter of social designation.
54. It must be pointed out that teacher's behavior is no worse

than that of others in public service, and that it is often far better. However, their methods, as described here, are based on what they have been taught in teacher training institutions and on school policies that they (in most cases) do not write.
55. Omahen (1984).
56. Teachers are, by and large, underpaid, and many are overworked. This is partly because of an arcane salary system. In a desperate effort to fill classrooms, and under pressure from teacher's unions, school dollars are spent in a suicidally inadequate manner. Novice teachers receive a far greater share of the budget than they should, as compared to that which is allocated to those of demonstrated professional skill

Epilogue

In dealing with the concerns of maladjusted individuals over the years, it became apparent that a common principle was in operation. In every instance, those involved either knew of no behavior that could alleviate their distress, or potential behaviors demanded too great a price. Emotional health seemed, clearly, to be a function of behavior potential. Although past and present factors contribute to malaise, it became obvious that future behavior options *alone* are the key to emotional health status. Emotional adjustment is based on what individual's believe regarding their capacity and opportunity to act. The ubiquitous nature of that seemingly trivial relationship caused us to realize that psychologies that minimize the role of emotion, or interpret emotional health as the consequence of warring unconscious forces, cannot provide an adequate basis for an understanding of human adjustment.

The pursuit of knowledge regarding the nature of behavior and its components led to a study of motivational elements. We discovered the holonic nature of existence––the inevitable part/whole bifurcation of all beings, and the resulting inclusion of the transcendent desires among the basic urges. We discovered further, through the application of the holarchic principle, that assumptions regarding the primacy of the individual account for much of the distress that we encountered.

Beyond this, we came to realize that behavior is based solely on what one believes—in spite of what may be the case in the "real" world—and that most beliefs are learned. We learned that meaning and purpose are characteristics *only* of the individual's relationship with some transcendent existence, and that emotion, which represents the interface between desires and one's perception of the environment, are essential to the deliberative or decision-making process.

On the basis of these principles, and in recognition of the fact that capacity and opportunity must be taken into consideration, we developed a motivation model. From the assumptions of the model, we constructed the BAP, which is designed to evaluate behavior potential in terms of its impact on adjustment. Although it may seem crude by comparison with the elaborate structures of sophisticated theorists, it has been of great value to us in work with our clients.

Our consideration of steps that might be taken to improve adjustment led to the determination that preventive programming offers the most promising approach. We concluded that the appropriate setting for such programming is in social institutions such as the public school that are charged with the task of developing personalities; to inculcate beliefs and practices that will maximize personal adjustment. Since prosocial beliefs are as easily learned as those that focus on the individual's supremacy, and since such beliefs are essential to optimal adjustment, the most desirable curriculum should include the opportunity to learn *how* and *why* to function as a socially responsible person. Furthermore, concepts such as *work* and *discipline* must be redefined and interpreted as the positive characteristics of human behavior that they are. Such a program will require that educational specialists understand the motives that initiate and maintain behavior, as well as the techniques that are most apt to re-establish positive emotional health in those individuals whose quality of life is marginal.

Glossary

AFFECT. Feeling states that represent knowledge as a mental experience. They include such concepts as desire, emotion, conviction, understanding, and belief.

AGENT. An entity in its performance of a function that serves wholes or systems to which it is subordinate.

AGGRESSION. Behavior carried out in order to feel powerful, safe, and/or meaningful.

ANXIETY. An emotional state marked by confusion, based on the inability to properly recognize or assign stimuli.

ASSERTIVE DESIRE. Desire in which gratification is based on the assuaging of physical or psychological deficit, related to the biological or extended self.

BEHAVIOR. Deliberate action based on decisions arrived at through a motivational sequence.

BEHAVIOR INCIDENT. A simple, complete behavioral action.

BEHAVIOR PATTERN. Typical, but not continuous, deliberate activity.

BEHAVIOR SEQUENCE. A series of behavior incidents, including all related activity, such as relevant instrumental behavior.

BELIEF. The limit of mental knowledge. An affective state that represents one's conviction regarding the validity of a proposition or a situation.

COGNITION. The manipulation or processing of information, including conceptualization, abstraction, generalization, etc.

COMMUNICATION. The transmission of information in which either the sender, the receiver, or both performs a function or delivers a message.

COMPLEX PRIMITIVE PERCEPTION. Configuration in which selective responses to stimuli are possible.

CONCEPTS. Mental images; meanings as defined by language terms.

CONCEPTUALIZATION The cognitive act of generalizing from particulars; the creation of concepts.

CONSCIOUSNESS. The state of immediate awareness at which the deliberative process functions.

DECISION. An affective state representing the consequence of weighing the relative merit of competing behavior potentialities.

DEFENSE MECHANISMS. Techniques for providing a state of optimum mental equilibrium; usually homeostatically oriented.

DELIBERATE SYSTEM. System created for use in the interest of living creatures.

DELIBERATION. The weighing of factors that bear on potential action.

DESIRE. The psychological manifestation of a drive.

DETERMINISM. The principle that every comprehensible event has some elements that are fixed by immutable precedents.

DOMINANT EMOTION. The prevailing desire/need complex as weighed against an estimate of anticipated costs that mandates behavior.

DRIVE. Biological alteration that represents the energizing aspect of organic activity.

EMERGENCE. The occurrence in nature of psychological characteristics that cannot be predicted by an analysis of their physical components.

EMOTION. A mediational component of the affective system. The experience resulting from the interaction of desires, needs, and the perceived environment, real or imagined, contemporaneous, anticipated, or recalled. Emotions are private facts. They are essential to, but do not mandate, behavior.

ENTITY. Corporeal existent.

ESSENCE. The attributes of substance which makes possible its revelation as an existent under appropriate conditions.

EVALUATION. The projection of measurement data along a scale of value; originally based on moral considerations, but currently employed in a more general sense. In this text restricted to its original use.

GLOSSARY

EXISTENCE. The product of the interaction of substance and perception.

FACT. Data which are subject to tests of truth and proof.

FREEDOM. That aspect of an event that focuses on potential causal factors by which it is not constrained.

GENE. A phenotype of a plan or pattern of a form of life.

GENE POOL. The totality of potential gene combinations which represents the limiting source of specific phenotypes.

HOLARCHY. An existential chain in which subunits take on characteristics of autonomy and self governance.

HOLON. That characteristic of all entities which describes their simultaneous part/whole nature.

HOPE. Desire plus belief in the possibility of gratification.

HOSTILITY. Behavior based on a reactive emotional state (anger), which includes frustration combined with moral indignation.

IDENTIFICATION. Recognition of the biological self as related to a more inclusive existence.

INDIVIDUAL. A general term used to refer to either a part or an instance.

INFORMATION. The transmission of data which makes possible the translation of substance into existence.

INNATE KNOWLEDGE. The capacity of an entity to respond to information prior to experience.

INSTANCE. One of a collection of similar individuals comprising a common whole.

INSTINCTIVE BEHAVIOR. Behavior which is genetically programmed.

INSTINCTIVE KNOWLEDGE. The capacity to experience an anticipatory emotion on the presentation of stimuli not previously experienced.

INSTRUMENTAL BEHAVIOR. Deliberate action performed in order to facilitate some other action or outcome; not desired for itself.

INTELLIGENCE. The potential for change that is expressible as learning. The docility of a learner to new information.

INTRINSIC BEHAVIOR. Action which is valued for itself.

JUDGMENT. An estimate which is not subject to truth or proof consideration.

KNOWLEDGE. The capacity to experience or respond to information.

LEARNED BEHAVIOR. Deliberate activity based on previously experienced consummatory emotions.

LEARNED KNOWLEDGE. The capacity to experience an anticipatory emotion based on a learning experience.

LEARNING. A change in response potential; the alteration of a knowledge state.

LIFE. The phenotypal expression of genotypal existence as modified by the environment.

MATURATION. Changes in an individual's characteristics that are caused by growth and decay; thus, a form of learning.

MEANING. The impact on an entity of its relationship to some superordinate existent.

MEASUREMENT. Descriptions of entities on an analogic scale; incapable of exact location.

MIND. The locus of the process that involves the cognitive manipulation of perceptual and desire based data and the affective convictions so induced.

MORALITY. An innate sense of propriety against which situations, behaviors, and events are evaluated.

MOTIVATION. A process that flows continually from any emotional state through deliberate activity, which is directed toward the maintaining or optimizing of the affective state.

NATURAL INORGANIC SYSTEM. System in which relationships are defined wholly in terms of chemistry and physics.

GLOSSARY 523

NATURAL ORGANIC SYSTEM. Systems in which the relationship between parts and wholes is directional; where the interests of parts is subordinate.

NEED. A behavior, situation, entity, or event that is believed capable of gratifying a desire.

NETCOST. The summative value of all costs involved in a deliberative sequence.

NETWANT. The summative value of all desires and related needs involved in a deliberative sequence.

PART. Any of dissimilar individuals as they are related to a common whole.

PERCEPTION. Knowledge residing in receptor chains which are sensitive to external stimulation.

POWER. Belief in one's capacity to acquire the needs essential to the gratification of desires. A bridge between desire and need.

PRECONSCIOUS. That aspect of mind, or of mental processing, that includes data not immediately available for deliberation.

PRE-MIND. Forms of life that act and react in terms of immediate response to drive and perceptual information.

PROOF. Truth claims that meet the conditions of public verification.

PROTECTIVE DESIRE. Desire in which gratification is based on order or security.

PURPOSE. The function of parts and instances in which the ultimate existent served is always some living form. No entity is purposive in itself; the term expresses only a directional, functional, relationship between individuals and superordinate existents.

REALITY. Sentient focus along the hierarchy of existence; comprised of holons in their part and/or instance aspect.

REASON. The process of ratiocination and the conviction of the veracity of the conclusions so drawn.

SADISM. Behavior designed to hurt or destroy because of the positive affect associated with such activity.

SIMPLE PRIMITIVE PERCEPTION. Configuration in which the reception of a stimulus mandates an invariant response.

SPECIES. An entity which is comprised of isolated pools of genetic potentiality. More general than a gene pool in its inclusion of many populations of similar, but nonidentical, genotypal components.

SUBSTANCE. Pre-existential being; that which entails existence.

SYSTEM. A collection of interdependent parts and/or instances, and the wholes to which they are related.

TRANSCENDENT DESIRE. Desire in which gratification is based on the experiencing of a relationship with some more comprehensive entity.

TRUTH. The relationship between beliefs about facts, and their existential veracity.

UNCONSCIOUS. The non-dynamic mental realm of memory and instinctive known characteristics of entities, situations, and events.

UNDERSTANDING. The level of knowledge of a complex subject.

WANT. A term used to describe either desire, need, or both, as they bear on a deliberative sequence.

WHOLE. The summative aspect of a holon.

WISH. Desire, where one believes there is no possibility of gratification.

References

Abrig, J. 1971. *An open letter on educational issues.* Available from D. M. Wonderly, 216 Settlers Row North, Ponte Vedra Fl. 32082.
Abrams, P. 1967. *John Locke: Two tracts on government.* London: Cambridge University Press.
Adler, A. 1927. *Understanding human nature.* Garden City, NY: Greenburg.
Albee, G. 1985, February. The answer is prevention. *Psychology Today*, 60-64.
Alexander, S. 1914. The basis of realism. *Proceedings of the British Academy*, 10: 32.
Allee, W. C. 1951. *Cooperation among animals.* New York: Schuman.
Allport, G. 1955. *Becoming: Basic considerations for a psychology of personality.* New Haven: Yale University Press.
Amadon, D. 1966. The superspecies concept. *Systematic zoology*, 15: 245-249.
Ambrose, E. J. 1982. *The biological world.* New York: Wiley.
Anselm, Saint. 1965. *St. Anselm's Proslogian.* Translated by M. J. Charlesworth. Oxford: Clarendon.
Ardrey, R. 1970. *The social contract.* New York: Dell.
Aristotle. 1972. Pleasure and happiness. In J. Randall, Jr., J. Buchler & E. Shirk, *Readings in philosophy.* 423-434. New York: Harper & Row.
Armstrong, R. & King, J. 1970. *Mechanics, waves and thermal physics.* Englewood Cliffs, NJ: Prentice Hall.
Arnold, M. B. & Gasson, J. A. 1968. Feelings and emotions as dynamic factors in personality integration. In *The nature of emotion.* Edited by M. Arnold, 203-221. Baltimore: Penguin.
Ashby, R. 1960. *Design for a brain.* New York: Wiley.
Asimov, I. 1981, June 14. The "threat" of creationism. *The New York Times Magazine.* 90-101.
Attneave, F. 1974. How do you know? *American Psychologist*, 29: 493-499.
Augros, R. M. & Stanciu, G. N. 1986. *The new biology.* Boston: New Science Library.
Augustine, St. 1937. The confessions of St. Augustine. Translated by E. B. Pusey, in *The Harvard classics.* Vol. 7. Edited by C. W. Eliot. New York: Collier.
Aurelius, M. 1937. The meditations of Marcus Aurelius Antoninus. Translated by G. Long, in *The Harvard classics.* Vol. 2. Edited by C. W. Eliot. New York: Collier.
Ayer, A. J. 1946. *Language, truth, and logic.* London: Gollancz.
———. 1956. *The problem of knowledge.* Baltimore: Penguin.
Ayer, A. J. 1979. Replies. In *Perception and identity.* Edited by G. Macdonald, 227-333. London: Macmillan.
———. 1987. Reflections on language truth and logic. In *Logical positivism in perspective.* Edited by B. Gower, 23-34. Totowa, NJ: Barnes & Noble.

Bacca, J. 1945. *Plato: Hipias mayor fedro.* Mexico City: Universidad National Autonoma de Mexico.
Balzac, H. 1893. *The human comedy.* Vol. 2. New York: Fenelon Collier.
Barash, D. 1977. *Sociobiology and behavior.* New York: Elsevier.
Barnes, W. H. F. 1944-1945. The myth of sense-data. In *Proceedings of the Aristotelian society.* Edited by A. A. Kassman, 45: 635-647.
Barnett, L. 1948. *The universe and Dr. Einstein.* New York: Time.
Beach, F. A. 1956. Characteristics of masculine sex drive. In *Nebraska Symposium on Motivation.* Edited by M. R. Jones, 1-32. Lincoln, NE: University of Nebraska Press.
Beck, W. S. 1961. *Modern science and the nature of life.* New York: Doubleday.
Begley, S. 1986, April 8. Science contra Darwin. *Newsweek,* 80-81.
———. 1986, January 20. A fifth force in physics. *Newsweek,* 64.
Beloff, J. 1965. The identity hypothesis: A critique. In *Brain and mind.* Edited by J. R. Smythies, 35-62. London: Routledge & Kegan Paul.
Benner, D. 1985. *Baker encyclopedia of psychology.* Grand Rapids, MI: Baker
Bergquist, E. H. 1972. Role of the hypothalamus in motivation: An examination of Valenstein's re-examination. *Psychological Review,* 79: 542-546.
Berkeley, G. 1938. Three dialogues between Hylas and Philonous in opposition to sceptics and atheists. In *The Harvard classics.* Edited by C. W. Eliot, Vol. 37, 189-285. New York: Collier.
Berrien, F. K. 1968. *General and social systems.* New Brunswick, NJ: Rutgers University Press.
Bertalanffy, L. 1952. *Problems of life: An evaluation of modern biological thought.* New York: Wiley.
———. 1968. *General systems theory.* New York: Braziller.
Bessey, C. E. 1908. The taxonomic aspect of the species question. *American Naturalist,* 42: 218-224.
Binswanger, L. 1958. The existential analysis school of thought. In *Existence: A new dimension in psychiatry and psychology.* Translated by E. Angel, and edited by R. May, E. Angel & H. Ellenberger, 191-213. New York: Basic Books.
Bishop, M. 1936. *Pascal: The life of genius.* New York: Reynal & Hitchcock.
Bitterman, M. E. 1965. The evolution of intelligence. *Scientific American,* 212(1): 92-100.
Blakney, R. 1960. *An Immanuel Kant reader.* New York: Harper.
Bloom, A. 1987. *The closing of the American mind.* New York: Simon & Schuster.
Blum, G. S. 1953. *Psychoanalytic theories of personality.* New York: McGraw-Hill.
Bohm, D. 1969a. Further remarks on order. In *Towards a theoretical biology: 2. Sketches.* Edited by C. H. Waddington, 41-60. Chicago: Aldine.
———. 1969b. Some remarks on the notion of order. In *Towards a theoretical*

biology: 2. Sketches. Edited by C. H. Waddington, 18-40. Chicago: Aldine.
Bohr, N. 1949. Discussion with Einstein on epistemological problems in atomic physics. In *Albert Einstein: Philosopher-scientist.* Edited by P. Schilpp. Evanston, IL: The Library of Living Philosophers.
Bosley, H., ed. 1979. *Webster's new collegiate dictionary.* Springfield MA: Merriam-Webster.
Boulding, K. 1972. Economic and general systems. In *The relevance of general systems theory.* Edited by E. Laszlo, 77-92. New York: Braziller.
Bower, E. M. 1969. Slicing the mystique of prevention with Occam's razor. *American Journal of Public Health,* 59(3): 478-484.
———. 1974. The primacy of primary prevention: The metaphor of screening. *The School Psychology Digest,* 3(4): 4-12.
Brain, L. 1965. Some aspects of the brain-mind relationship. In *Brain and mind.* Edited by J. R. Smythies, 63-79. London: Routledge & Kegan Paul.
Brentano, F. C. 1966. *The true and the evident.* London: Routledge & Kegan Paul.
Bridgman, P. 1961. Determinism and punishment. In *Determinism and freedom.* Edited by S. Hook, 155-156. New York: Collier.
Brill, A. A., ed. 1938. *The basic writings of Sigmund Freud.* New York: Random House.
Broad, C. D. 1914. *Perception, physics, and reality.* Cambridge: Cambridge University Press.
Brown, J. S. 1961. *The motivation of behavior.* New York: McGraw-Hill.
———. 1975. Problems presented in the concept of acquired drives. In *Theoretical readings in motivation.* Edited by F. M. Levine, 36-52. Chicago: Rand McNally.
Bruner, J. S. 1973. The process of concept attainment. In *Beyond the information given.* Edited by J. M. Anglin. New York: Norton.
Bruner, J. S. & Goodman, C. C. 1947. Value and need as organizing factors in perception. *Journal of Abnormal and Social Psychology,* 47: 33-44.
Bruner, J. & Postman L. 1949. Perception, cognition, and behavior. *Journal of Personality,* 18: 14-31.
Buckley, W. 1969. *Inveighing we will go.* New York: Putnam.
Bugelski, B. R. 1973. Human learning. In *Handbook of general psychology.* Edited by B. B. Wolman, 515-529. Englewood Cliffs, NJ: Prentice Hall.
Bugental, J. F. 1967. *Challenges of humanistic psychology.* New York: McGraw-Hill.
Butler, J. & Rice, L. 1963. Adience, self-actualization, and drive theory. In *Concepts of personality.* Edited by J. M. Wepman & R. W. Hein, 79-110. Chicago: Aldine.
Cairns, J., Overbaugh, J. & Miller, S. 1988, September 5. The origin of mutants. *Nature,* 142-145.
Cairns-Smith, A. G. 1968. An approach to a blueprint for a primitive organism. In

Towards a theoretical biology: 1. Prolegomena. Edited by C. H. Waddington, 57-66. Chicago: Aldine.
Cairns-Smith, A. G. 1985. The first organisms. *Scientific American*, 252(6): 90-100.
Calypso log dispatch 1982, July-August, Norfolk, VA: The Cousteau Society
Cannon, W. B. 1927. The James-Lange theory of emotion: A critical examination and an alternative theory. *American Journal of Psychology*, 36: 106-124.
Casti, J. 1989. *Paradigms lost; Images of man in the mirror of science*. New York: Morrow.
Chardin, P. 1965. *The phenomenon of man*. New York: Harper & Row.
Chein, I. 1972. *The science of behavior and the image of man*. New York: Basic Books.
Chisholm, R. 1957. *Perceiving: A philosophical study*. New York: Cornell University Press.
Christian, J. 1958. The roles of endocrine and behavioral factors in the growth of mammalian populations. In *Symposium on comparative endocrinology*. Edited by A. Gorbman, 71-98. New York: Wiley.
Christianson, G. 1984. *In the presence of the creator; Isaac Newton and his times*. New York: The Free Press.
Cofer, C. N. & Appley, M. H. 1967. *Motivation: Theory and research*. New York: Wiley.
Copleston, S. J. 1963. Pascal. *A history of philosophy*. Vol. 4, 161-181. New York: Image.
Corinthians 1. 1952. *Revised standard version of the Holy Bible*. Grands Rapids, MI: Zondervan.
Corsini, R. J. 1977. *Current personality theories*. Itasca, IL: Peacock.
Cowan, P. 1978. *Piaget with feeling*. New York: Holt, Rinehart and Winston.
Coulter, J. 1983. *Rethinking cognitive theory*. New York: St. Martins Press.
Cuffey, R. J. 1984. Paleontologic evidence and organic evolution. In *Science and creationism*. Edited by A. Montague, 255-281. New York: Oxford University Press.
Darrow, C. 1952. The quantum theory. *Scientific American*, 186(3): 47-54.
Darwin, C. 1897. *The origin of species by means of natural selection: or the preservation of favored races in the struggle for life*. 2d ed. Akron: Werner.
———. 1970a. The descent of man. In *Evolution of man*. Edited by L. B. Young, 264-265. New York: Oxford University Press.
———. 1970b. The origin of species. In *Evolution of man*. Edited by L. B. Young, 76-83. New York: Oxford University Press.
Dawkins, R. 1976. *The selfish gene*. New York: Oxford University Press.
DeCharms, R. 1968. *Personal causation*. New York: Academic Press.
Deese, J. 1958. *The psychology of learning*. New York: McGraw-Hill.
DeGreen, K. 1970. *Systems psychology*. New York: McGraw-Hill.
Descartes, R. 1972. *The philosophical works of Descartes*. Translated by E. Haldane

& G. Ross. Vol 1. London: Cambridge University Press.
Deutsch, M., Katz, I. & Jensen, A., eds. 1968. *Social class, race, and psychological development*. New York: Holt, Rinehart & Winston.
DeVore, I. 1977, February. The new science of genetic self-interest. Interview with S. Morris. *Psychology Today*, 42-88.
Dewey, J. 1900. *The school and society*. Chicago: University of Chicago Press.
Diagnostic and statistical manual of mental disorders. 1987. 3d ed., rev. Washington D. C.: American Psychiatric Association.
Dickey, M. 1986. *Funk & Wagnalls New Encyclopedia*. U. S. A.: Rand McNally.
Dobzhansky, T. 1950. The genetic basis of evolution. *Scientific American*, 182(1): 36.
———. 1956. *The biological basis of human freedom*. New York: Columbia University Press.
———. 1970a. Creativity and orientation in evolution. In *Evolution of man*. Edited by L. B. Young, 144-149. New York: Oxford University Press.
———. 1970b. *Genetics of the evolutionary process*. New York: Columbia University Press
———. 1974. *Evolutionary biology*. Vol. 7. New York: Plenum.
Dorland, W. A. 1946. *American Pocket Medical Dictionary*. Philadelphia: Saunders.
Drever, J. 1952. *A dictionary of psychology*. Baltimore: Penguin.
Dreyfus, H. 1965. *Alchemy and artificial intelligence*. Report of the Rand Corporation.
Driesch, H. 1908. *The science and philosophy of the organism*. London: Black.
Ducasse, C. J. 1965. Minds, matter and bodies. In *Brain and mind*. Edited by J. R. Smythies, 81-96. London: Routledge & Kegan Paul.
Ebel, R. L. 1974. And still the dryads linger. *American Psychologist*, 29, 485-492.
Eccles, J. 1967. Evolution and the conscious self. In *The human mind*. Edited by J. Roslansky, 1-28. Amsterdam: North-Holland.
Eddington, A. S. 1933. *The expanding universe*. New York: Macmillan.
Edwards, P. 1965. Introduction. In *A modern introduction to philosophy*. Edited by P. Edwards & A. Pap, 2-9. New York: Collier-Macmillan.
Edwards, P. & Pap, A., eds. 1965. *A modern introduction to philosophy*. New York: Collier-Macmillan.
Edwards, P., ed. 1967. *The encyclopedia of philosophy*. New York: Macmillan.
Einstein, A. 1985, December 22. *Washington Post Insight*. C4.
Eiseley, L. 1946. *The immense journey*. New York: Random House.
Eisenberger, R. 1989. *Blue Monday: The loss of the work ethic in America*. New York: Paragon House.
Eldredge, N. 1985. *Time frames: The rethinking of darwinian evolution and the theory of punctuated equilibria*. New York: Simon & Schuster.
Ellenberger, H. F. 1958. A clinical introduction to psychiatric phenomenology and existential analysis. In *Existence: A new dimension in psychiatry and psychology*. Edited by R. May, E. Angel, & H. F. Ellenberger, 27-34.

New York: Basic Books.
Elliot, H. 1972. Materialism. In *Readings in philosophy*. Edited by Randal, J. Jr., Buchler, J. & Shirk, E., 306-324. New York: Barnes & Noble.
Ellington, J. W. 1983. *Immanuel Kant: Ethical philosophy*. Indianapolis: Hacket.
Emerson, R. W. 1841. *Essays*. Boston: Munroe.
Engel, F. M. 1965. *Life around us*. Translated by J. R. Foster. New York: Cromwell.
Erikson, E. 1963. *Childhood and society*. New York: Norton.
Farris, S. 1985, April 8. An irreverent eye. *Newsweek*, 80-81.
Federn, P. 1952. *Ego psychology and the psychoses*. New York: Basic Books.
Feibleman, J. 1968. *Ontology*. New York: Greenwood.
Feigl, H. 1975. Some crucial issues of mind-body monism. In *Philosophical aspects of the mind-body problem*. Edited by C. Cheng, 20-34. Honolulu: University Press of Hawaii.
Feigl, H. and Brodbeck, M. 1953. *Readings in the philosophy of science*. New York: Appleton Century Crofts.
Feinberg, G. 1977. *What is the world made of?* New York: Anchor Press, Doubleday.
Fernald, L. D. & Fernald, P. S. 1985. *Introduction to psychology*. 5th ed. Dubuque: Brown.
Feynman, R. 1985. *QED*. Princeton: Princeton University Press.
Fichte, J. G. 1848. The vocation of man. In *The popular works of J. G. Fichte*. Translated by W. Smitt. Vol. I, 469-489. London: Trübner.
Flake-Hobson, C., Robinson, B. E. & Skeen, P. 1983. *Child development and relationships*. Reading, PA: Addison Wesley.
Flew, A. 1979. *A dictionary of philosophy*. New York: St. Martin's Press.
Flexner, S., ed. 1987. *Random House Dictionary*. New York: Random House.
Fodor, J. 1981. *Scientific American*, 244(1): 114-123.
Forem, J. 1974. *Transcendental meditation*. New York: Dutton.
Fowler, J. 1883. *Shaftsbury and Hutcheson*. New York: Putnam.
Friedrich, C., ed. 1949. *The philosophy of Kant*. New York: Modern Library.
Freud, A. 1946. *The ego and mechanisms of defense*. New York: International University Press.
———. 1949. Aggression in relation to emotional development: Normal and pathological. In *Psychoanalytic study of the child*. Translated by A. Freud, H., Hartmann & E. Kris. Vols. 3-4, 37-43. New York: International University Press.
Freud, S. 1933. *New introductory lectures on psycho-analysis*. New York: Norton.
———. 1943. *Psychoanalysis*. Translated by J. Riviere. Garden City, NY: Garden City Press.
———. 1949. *An outline of psychoanalysis*. New York: Norton.
———. 1955. From the history of an infantile neurosis. In S*tandard edition of the complete psychological works of Sigmund Freud*. Edited by J. Strachey. Vol. 17, 3-122. London: Hogarth.

Freud, S. 1961. Civilization and its discontents. In *Standard edition of the complete psychological works of Sigmund Freud.* Edited by J. Strachey. Vol. 21, 64-148. London: Hogarth.
Fromm, E. 1947. *Man for himself.* New York: Rinehart.
———. 1973. *The anatomy of human destructiveness.* New York: Holt, Rinehart & Winston.
Fuller, B.A. 1955. *History of Philosophy.* New York: Holt, Rinehart &Winston.
Fuller, R. 1975. *Synergetics.* New York: Macmillan.
Funk, I., ed. 1963. *New standard dictionary of the English language.* New York: Funk & Wagnalls.
Gard, R. 1961. *Budhism.* New York: Braziller.
Gerard, L. W. 1957. Units and concepts of biology. *Science,* 125: 429-433.
Gettier, E. 1963. Is justified true belief knowledge? *Analysis,* 23: 121-123.
Gewirth, A. 1981, January. Are there any absolute rights? *The Philosophic Quarterly,* 31(122): 1-16.
Ghiselin, M. T. 1974. *The economy of nature and the evolution of sex.* Berkeley: University of California Press.
Gibson, J. 1966. *The senses considered as perceptual systems.* Boston: Houghton Mifflin.
Glasser, W. 1968. *Schools without failure.* New York: Harper & Row.
Glynn County school system activity calendar: 1987-88. Brunswick, GA: Glynn County School System.
Goldman, A. 1986. *Epistemology and cognition.* Cambridge: Harvard University Press.
Goldstein, K. 1939. *The organism.* New York: American Book.
———. 1956. The so-called drives. In *The self.* Edited by C. Moustakas, 15-24. New York: Harper.
Gomperz, T. 1901. *Greek thinkers.* Translated by L. Magnus, Vol 1. New York: Scribner.
Gould, S. J. 1984. Evolution as fact and theory. In *Science and creationism.* Edited by A. Montague, 117-125. New York: Oxford University Press.
Gray, W., Duhl, F. & Rizzo, W., eds. 1969. *General systems theory and psychiatry.* Boston: Little, Brown.
Greeley, A. M. 1981. *The cardinal sins.* New York: Warner.
Greene, T. M., ed. 1957. *Kant selections.* New York: Scribner.
Grene, M. 1969. Bohm's metaphysics and biology. In *Towards a theoretical biology: 2. Sketches.* Edited by C. H. Waddington, 61-68. Chicago: Aldine.
Gribbin, J. 1984. *In search of Schrodinger's cat.* New York: Bantam.
Grimsley, R., ed. 1972. *J. J. Rousseau: Du contrat social.* Oxford: Clarendon.
Grobstein, C. 1964. *The strategy of life.* San Francisco: Freeman.
Grusec, J. E. 1981. Socialization processes and development of altruism. In *Altruism and helping behavior: Social, personality and developmental perspectives.*

Edited by J. P. Rushton & S. M. Sorrentino, 65-90. Hillsdale, NJ: Erlbaum.
Guralnik, D. 1966. *Webster's new world dictionary.* New York: World.
Hall, C. 1954. *A primer of Freudian psychology.* New York: The New America Library.
Hall, C. & Lindzey, G. 1970. *Theories of personality.* 3rd ed. New York: Wiley.
Halstead, B. 1984. Evolution—the fossils say yes! In *Science and Creationism.* Edited by A. Montagu, 240-254. New York: Oxford University Press.
Hamilton, W. 1964. The genetical evolution of social behavior. *The Journal of Theoretical Biology,* 7: 1-52.
Handler, P., ed. 1970. *Biology and the future of man.* New York: Oxford University Press.
Harre, R. & Lamb, R. 1983. *The encyclopedic dictionary of psychology.* Cambridge: The Massachusetts Institute of Technology Press.
Harriman, P. L. 1974. *Handbook of psychological terms.* Totowa, NJ: Littlefield, Adams.
Harris, H. 1984. *Stranger on the square.* New York: Random.
Hass, H. 1970. *The human animal.* New York: Delta.
Hatt, H. 1968. *Cybernetics and the image of man.* Nashville: Abingdon Press.
Hawking, S. 1988. *A brief history of time.* New York: Bantam.
Hayes, J. 1978. *Cognitive psychology: Thinking and creating.* Homewood, IL: Dorsey.
Hebb, D. O. 1949. *The organization of behavior: A neuropsychological theory.* New York: Wiley.
———. 1955. Drives and the CNS. *Psychological Review,* 62: 243-254.
Hegel, G. W. 1975. *The philosophy of fine art.* Translated by F. Osmaston. New York: Hacker Art Books.
Heider, F. 1958. *The psychology of interpersonal relationships.* New York: Wiley.
Heisenberg, W. 1958. *Physics and philosophy.* New York: Harper & Row.
Hempel, C. 1965. *Aspects of scientific explanation.* New York: Free Press.
Herbart, J. 1896. *ABC of sense perception.* Translated by W. Eckoff. New York: Appleton.
Hergenbahn, B. R. 1976. *An introduction to theories of learning.* Englewood Cliffs, NJ: Prentice-Hall.
———. 1984. *An introduction to theories of personality.* 2nd Ed. Englewood Cliffs, NJ: Prentice-Hall.
Hesse, M. 1986. Ayer and the philosophy of science. In *Logical positivism in perspective.* Edited by B. Gower, 69-88. Totowa, NJ: Barnes & Noble.
Hibben, J. G. 1911. *The problems of philosophy.* New York: Scribner.
Hicks, G. D. 1938. *Critical realism.* London: Macmillan.
Hilgard, E. 1987. *Psychology in America.* New York: Harcourt Brace.
Hobson, A. 1988. *The dreaming brain.* New York: Harper & Row.
Hoffman, M. L. 1981. The development of empathy. In *Altruism and helping behavior: Social, personality and developmental perspectives.* Edited by J. P. Rushton

& R. M. Sorrentino, 41-63. Hillsdale, NJ: Erlbaum.
Hofstadter, D. 1981. *The minds eye.* New York: Basic Books.
Holton, G. & Roller, D. 1958. *Foundations of modern physical science.* London: Addison Wesley.
Hospers, J. 1953. *An introduction to philosophical analysis.* New York: Prentice Hall.
———. 1965. Free will and psychoanalysis. In *A modern introduction to philosophy.* Edited by P. Edwards and A. Pap, 75-85. New York: The Free Press.
Hoyle, F. & Wickramsinghe, C. 1978. *Lifecloud.* New York: Harper & Row.
Hudson, W. D. 1970. *Modern moral philosophy.* New York: Doubleday.
Hull, C. L. 1943. *Principles of behavior.* New York: Appleton-Century-Crofts.
———. 1952. *A behavior system: An introduction to behavior theory concerning the individual organism.* New Haven: Yale University Press.
Hume, D. 1938. Of liberty and necessity. In *The Harvard classics.* Vol. 37. Edited by C. W. Eliot, 351-370. New York: Collier.
———. 1952. *Locke, Berkeley, Hume.* Chicago: The University of Chicago.
———. 1965. In *A modern introduction to philosophy.* Edited by P. Edwards & A. Pap, 186-195. New York: Collier-Macmillan.
Hunt, J. McV. 1977. Traditional personality theories in light of recent evidence. In *Current trends in psychology.* Edited by I. L. Janis, 218-225. Los Altos, CA: Kaufmann.
Husserl, E. 1931. *Ideas: General introduction to pure phenomenology.* Translated by W. Gibson. New York: Collier.
Hutcheson, F. 1971. *Illustration on the moral sense.* Edited by B. Peach. Cambridge: Belknap.
Huxley, J. S. 1942. *Evolution: The modern synthesis.* New York: Harper
———. 1970. The uniqueness of man. In *Evolution of man.* Edited by L. B. Young, 238-249. New York: Oxford University Press.
James, Saint 1952. The letter of James. *Revised standard version of The Holy Bible.* Grand Rapids: Zondervan.
James, W. 1890). *The principles of psychology.* New York: Holt.
———. 1891. *Principles of psychology.* Vol. 2. New York: Holt.
———. 1892. *Psychology.* New York: Holt.
———. 1965. The dilemma of determinism. In *A modern introduction to philosophy.* Edited by P. Edwards & A. Pap, 25-37. New York: Collier-Macmillan.
Janis, I. et al. eds. 1969. *Personality.* New York: Harcourt, Brace & World.
Jaynes, J. 1986. How old is consciousness? In *Exploring the concept of mind.* Edited by R. Caplan, 51-72. Iowa City: University of Iowa Press.
Jones, D. 1972, April. The death of the Alexandria museum. *Intellectual Digest,* 52-53.
Kagan, J. 1971. *Understanding children.* New York: Harcourt, Brace, Jovanovich.
Kaiser, R. 1976. *Russia: The people and the power.* New York: Athenium.

Kalish, H. 1981. *From behavioral science to behavior modification.* New York: McGraw Hill.
Kamin, L. 1985, October. Genes and behavior: The missing link. *Psychology Today,* 78.
Kegan Paul, C. 1899. *The thoughts of Blaise Pascal.* London: Bell.
Kelly, G. A. 1958. Man's construction of his alternatives. In *The assessment of human motives.* Edited by G. Lindzey, 33-6. New York: Holt, Rinehart & Winston.
Kemp, J. 1968. *The philosophy of Kant.* London: Oxford University Press.
Kierkegaard, S. 1941. *The sickness unto death.* Translated by W. Lowrie. Princeton: Princeton University Press.
———. 1944. *The concept of dread.* Translated by W. Lowrie. Princeton: Princeton University Press.
Kilpatrick, F. P., ed. 1952. *Human behavior from the transactional point of view.* Hanover, NH: Institute for Associated Research.
King, F. 1989, June 5-11. All play and no work. *The Washington Post National Weekly Edition,* 37
Kitcher, P. 1982. *Abusing science: The case against creationism.* Cambridge: The Massachusetts Institute of Technology Press.
Klausmeier, H. 1961. *Learning and human abilities.* New York: Harper.
Koestler, A. 1959. *The sleepwalkers.* New York: Grosset & Dunlap.
———. 1963. *The act of creation.* New York: Dell.
———. 1967. *The ghost in the machine.* New York: Macmillan.
———. 1969. Beyond atomism and holism—the concept of the holon. In *Beyond reductionism.* Edited by A. Koestler & J. Smythies, 192-216. Boston: Beacon.
———. 1972a. Man—one of evolutions mistakes? In *Philosophy now: An introductory reader.* Edited by P. R. Struhl & K. S. Struhl, 8-16. New York: Random House.
———. 1972b. *The roots of coincidence.* New York: Vintage Books.
———. 1978. *Janus.* New York: Random House.
———. 1981. *Kaleidoscope.* London: Hutchinson.
Kohlberg, L. 1958. *The development of modes of moral thinking and choice in the years 10 to 16.* Chicago: University of Chicago Press.
Kohut, H. & Seitz, P. F. D. 1963. Concepts and theories of psychoanalysis. In *Concepts of personality.* Edited by J. M. Wepman, & R. W. Heine, 113-142. Chicago: Aldine.
Krech, D. 1949. Notes toward a psychological theory. *Journal of Personality,* 18: 66-87.
Lachman, R. & Lachman, J. 1979. Science and paradigms. In *Cognitive psychology and information processes.* Edited by R. Lachman, J. Lachman & G. Butterfield, 1-34. Hillsdale, NJ: Erlbaum.
Lacey, A. 1976. *A dictionary of philosophy.* London: Routledge & Kegan Paul.

Lange, O. 1965. *Wholes and parts: A general theory of system behavior*. New York: Pergamon.
Lasch, C. 1979. *The culture of narcissism*. New York: Norton.
Laszlo, E. 1973. *The world system*. New York: Braziller.
Lawrence, D. H. 1932. *Apocalypse*. New York: Viking.
Lazarus, R. 1984. On the primacy of cognition. *American Psychologist*, 39: 124-129.
Leakey, R. & Lewin, R. 1977. Is it is our culture, not our genes, that makes us killers? *Smithsonian*, 88: 56-64.
———. 1978, July. Origins of the mind. *Psychology Today*, 49-59.
Leeper, R. 1963. The motivational theory of emotion. In *Understanding human motivation*. Edited by C. L. Stacey & M. F. DeMartino, 657-664. Cleveland: World.
Lerner, A. 1961. Punishment as justice and as price: On randomness. In *Determinism and freedom*. Edited by S. Hook, 193-195. New York: Collier.
Lewin, K. 1936. *Principles of topological psychology*. New York: McGraw-Hill.
Lewontin, R. 1985. Adaptation. *Scientific American*, 239(3): 212-230.
Locke, J. 1959. *An essay concerning human understanding*. Edited by A. Fraser. New York: Dover.
———. 1969. *Philosophic works*. Edited by J. St. John. London: Bell & Sons.
Lorenz, K. 1963. *On aggression*. New York: Harcourt, Brace & World.
———. 1965. *Evolution and modification of behavior*. Chicago: University of Chicago Press.
MacArthur, R. & Connell, J. 1966. *The biology of populations*. New York: Wiley.
Machiavelli, N. 1952. *The prince*. Translated by L. Ricci. New York: New American Library.
MacKay, D. M. 1952. Mentality in machines. *Proceedings of the Aristotelian Society Supplement*, 26: 61-86.
———. 1965. From mechanism to mind. In *Brain and mind*. Edited by J. R. Smythies, 163-191. London: Routledge & Kegan Paul.
MacLean, P. 1969. *A triune concept of the brain and behavior*. Kingston, Ontario: University of Toronto.
———. 1971. The paranoid streak in man. In *Beyond reductionism*. Edited by A. Koestler & J. Smythies, 258-278. Boston: Beacon.
Madsen, K. B. 1959. *Theories of motivation*. Copenhagen: Munksgaard.
———. 1973. Theories of motivation. In *The handbook of general psychology*. Edited by B. Wolman, 673-706. Englewood Cliffs, NJ: Prentice Hall.
Magill. J. Presidential Address. 1954, July. American Association of Immunologists. Washington D.C..
Malcolm, J. 1984. *In the Freud archives*. New York: Knopf.
Malcolm, N. 1963. *Knowledge and certainty: Essays and lectures*. Englewood Cliffs, NJ: Prentice-Hall.

Mann, T. 1967. *The magic mountain*. Translated by H. T. Lowe-Porter. New York: Knopf.
Margalef, R. 1968. *Perspectives in ecological theory*. Chicago: University of Chicago Press.
Marx, M. & Hillix, W. 1973. *Systems and theories in psychology*. 2d ed. New York: McGraw-Hill.
Maslow, A. 1970. *Motivation and personality*. 2d ed. New York: Harper & Row.
Maslow A. & Mittelmann, B. 1951. *Principles of abnormal psychology*. New York: Harper.
Masson, J. M. 1984. *The assault on truth: Freud's suppression of the seduction theory*. New York: Farrar, Straus, and Giroux.
Matson, F. W. 1966. *The broken image*. Garden City, NY: Doubleday.
Mausner, B. & Mausner, J. 1955. A study of the anti-scientific attitude. *Scientific American*, 192(2): 35-39.
May, R. 1958a. Contributions of existential therapy. In *Existence*. Edited by R. May, E. Angel & H. Ellenberger, 37-91. New York: Simon & Schuster.
———. 1958b. The origins and significance of the existential movement in psychology. In *Existence: A new dimension in psychiatry and psychology*. Edited by R. May, E. Angel & H. Ellenberger, 3-36. New York: Basic Books.
———. 1978. The evolution of ecological systems. *Scientific American*, 239(3): 160-175.
Mayr, E. 1959. Darwin and evolutionary theory in biology. In *Evolution and anthropology: A Centennial appraisal*. 1-10. Washington: Anthropological Society.
———. 1968. Cause and effect in biology. In *Towards a theoretical biology: 1. Prolegomena*. Edited by C. H. Waddington, 42-54. Chicago: Aldine.
———. 1970. *Populations, species, and evolution*. Cambridge, MA: Belknap.
———. 1976. *Evolution and the diversity of life*. Cambridge, MA: Belknap.
———. 1978. Evolution. *Scientific American*, 239(3): 47.
McClelland, D. C. et al. 1953. *The achievement motive*. New York: Appleton-Century-Crofts.
McDougall, W. 1908. *An introduction to social psychology*. London: Methuen.
———. 1930. The hormic psychology. In *Psychologies of 1930*. Edited by C. Murchison, 3-36. Worcester, MA: Clark University Press.
McFarland, D. 1983. Motivation. In *The encyclopedic dictionary of psychology*. Edited by R. Harre & R. Lamb, 329. Cambridge: Massachusetts Institute of Technology Press.
Mead, H. 1959. *Types and problems of philosophy*. New York: Holt.
Menninger, K. 1938. *Man against himself*. New York: Harcourt, Brace & World.
Merleau-Ponty, M. 1966. *Phenomenology of perception*. London: Routledge & Kegan Paul.
Miles, M. B. 1965. Planned change and organizational health: Figure and ground.

In *Change processes in the public schools.* Edited by M. B. Miles, 17-22. Oregon: University of Oregon Press.
Mill, J. S. 1865. *A system of logic.* London: Longmans, Green.
Miller, K. R. 1984. Scientific creationism vs. evolution: The mislabelled debate. In *Science and creationism.* Edited by A. Montagu, 18-63. New York: Oxford University Press.
Miller, N. E. 1941. An experimental investigation of acquired drives. *Psychological Bulletin,* 38: 534-535.
———. 1948. Studies of fear as an acquirable drive. *Journal of Experimental Psychology,* 38: 89-101.
Miller, N. E. & Dollard, J. 1941. *Social learning and imitation.* New Haven: Yale University Press.
Milne, A. J. 1987. Values and ethics: the emotive theory. In *Logical positivism in perspective.* Edited by B. Gower, 89-108. Totowa, NJ: Barnes & Noble.
Montagu, A. 1952. *Darwin: Competition and cooperation.* New York: Schuman.
———. 1976. *The nature of human aggression.* New York: Oxford University Press.
Moore, G. E. 1903. *Principia ethica.* Cambridge, MA: Cambridge University Press.
———. 1918-1919. Some judgments of perception. In *Proceedings of the Aristotelian Society.* Edited by A. A. Kassman, 19: 1-29.
———. 1965. The indefinability of good. In *A modern introduction to philosophy.* Edited by P. Edwards & A. Pap, 321-327. New York: Collier-Macmillan.
Moore, J. N. 1973. Evolution, creation, and the scientific method. *American Biology Teacher,* 35: 23-26.
Morgan, C. T. 1961. *Introduction to psychology.* New York: McGraw-Hill.
Morris, D. 1967. *The naked ape.* New York: McGraw Hill.
Morris, H. M. 1974. *The troubled waters of evolution.* San Diego: Creation-Life Publishers.
Moser, L. 1973. *The struggle for human dignity.* Los Angeles: Nash.
Moustakas, C. 1956. Summary: Exploration in essential being and personal growth. In *The self.* Edited by C. Moustakas, 271-284. New York: Harper & Row.
Mueller, A. 1963. *Psychology and you.* New York: Vintage.
Munroe, R. 1955. *Schools of psychoanalytic thought.* New York: Dryden.
Murphy, G. 1973. Historical review. In *The handbook of general psychology.* Edited by B. Wolman, 3-7. Englewood Cliffs, NJ: Prentice Hall.
Nagel, E. 1961. *The structure of science.* New York: Harcourt, Brace & World.
Nagele, R. 1987. *Reading after Freud.* New York: Columbia University Press.
Nageli, K. von. 1884. *A mechanico-physiological theory of organic evolution.* Translated by V. A. Clark. Chicago: Open Court.
Nietzsche, F. 1955. *Beyond good and evil.* Translated by M. Cowan. Chicago: Regnery.
———. 1960. *Joyful wisdom.* Translated by T. Common. New York: Ungar.

Norman, D. 1980. Twelve issues for cognitive science. *Cognitive Science*, 4: 1-32.
Nowell-Smith, P. 1965. Psychoanalysis and moral language. In *A modern introduction to philosophy*. Edited by P. Edwards & A. Pap, 86-93. New York: The Free Press.
Omahen, S. 1984. An investigation of the use of work as an incentive on the attitude toward work of school children. *Dissertation Abstracts International*.
Oparin, A. I. 1953. *Origin of life*. Translated by S. Morgulis. New York: Dover.
Ouspensky, P. D. 1970. *Tertium organum*. New York: Vintage.
———. 1971. *A new model of the universe*. New York: Vintage.
Pap, A. 1953. Does science have metaphysical presuppositions? In *Readings in the philosophy of science*. Edited by H. Feigl & M. Brodbeck, 21-33. New York: Appleton-Century-Crofts.
Pattee, H. H. 1968. The physical basis of coding and reliability in biological evolution. In *Towards a theoretical biology: 1. Prolegomena*. Edited by C. H. Waddington, 64-93. Chicago: Aldine.
Patterson, C. H. 1971. Are ethics different in different settings? *The Personnel and Guidance Journal*, 50(4): 254-259.
Pauling, L. & Pauling P. 1975. *Chemistry*. San Francisco: Freeman.
Penelhum, T. 1955. Hume on personal identity. *The Philosophical Review*, 64: 571-589.
Perkins, D. 1986. Where is creativity? In *Exploring the concept of mind*. Edited by R. Caplan, 101-120. Iowa City: University of Iowa Press.
Peters, R. 1958. *The concept of motivation*. London: Routledge and Kegan Paul.
Pfaff, D. 1982. *The psychological mechanisms of motivation*. New York: Springer-Verlag.
Piaget, J. 1954. *The construction of reality in the child*. New York: Basic Books.
Polanyi, M. 1968. Life's irreducible structure. *Science*, 160: 1308-1312.
Portmann, A. 1949. *Probleme des lebens*. Basel: Reinhardt.
Prigogine, I. 1980, December. The world according to Ilya Prigogine. *Quest/80*, 15-88.
Putnam, H. 1986. How old is the mind? In *Exploring the concept of mind*. Edited by R. Caplan, 31-50. Iowa City: University of Iowa Press.
Quinton, A. 1965. Mind and matter. In *Brain and mind*. Edited by J. R. Smythies, 201-233. London: Routledge & Kegan Paul.
Rank, O. 1936. *Truth and reality: A life history of the human will*. Translated by G. Taft. New York: Knopf.
Rapaport, A. 1960. On the psychoanalytic theory of motivation. In *Nebraska symposium on motivation*. Edited by M. R. Jones, 173-247. Lincoln, NE: Nebraska University Press.
———. 1968. Foreword. In *Modern systems research for the behavioral sciences*. Edited by W. Buckley, xiii-xxii. Chicago: Aldine.
Rawls, J. 1971. *A theory of justice*. Cambridge: Belknap.

Reid, T. 1965a. The moral faculty and the principles of morals. In *A modern introduction to philosophy*. Edited by P. Edwards & A. Pap, 288-296. New York: Collier-Macmillan.
Reid, T. 1965b. Of the nature and origin of our notion of personal identity. In *A modern introduction to philosophy*. Edited by P. Edwards & A. Pap, 196-202. New York: Collier-Macmillan.
Reiss, B. F. 1950. The isolation of factors of learning and native behavior in field and laboratory studies. *Annals, New York Academy of Science*, 51: 1093-1103.
Restak, R. M. 1979. *The brain: The last frontier.* New York: Warner.
———. 1988. *The mind.* New York: Bantam.
Riesman, D. 1950. *The lonely crowd.* New Haven: Yale University Press.
Riviere, J., ed. & trans. 1959. *Sigmund Freud: Collected papers.* Vol. 4. New York: Basic Books.
Rochlin, G. 1973. *Man's aggression.* Boston: Gambit.
Rogers, C. R. 1951. *Client-centered therapy.* Boston: Houghton Mifflin.
———. 1961. *On becoming a person.* Boston: Houghton Mifflin.
———. 1974. *Toward a science of the person.* New York: Norton.
Root-Bernstein, R. 1984. On defining a scientific theory: Creationism considered. In *Science and creationism*. Edited by A. Montagu, 64-94. New York: Oxford University Press.
Rose, S. 1973. *The conscious brain.* New York: Knopf.
Rosen, C. 1985, April 8. *Newsweek*, 80-81.
Rosenblueth, A. & Wiener, N. 1950. Purposeful and non-purposeful behavior. *Philosophy of Science*, 17: 318-326.
Rosenblueth, A., Wiener, N. & Bigelow, J. 1943. Behavior, purpose, and teleology. *Philosophy of Science*, 10: 18.
Roth, M. D. & Galis, L. 1970. *Knowing: Essays in the analysis of knowledge.* New York: Random House.
Royce, J. 1892. *The spirit of modern philosophy.* Boston: Houghton Mifflin.
Runes, D., ed. 1962. *Dictionary of philosophy.* Totowa, NJ: Littlefield, Adams.
Ruse, M. 1985. *Sociobiology, sense or nonsense?* Boston: Dordrecht.
———. 1984. A philosopher's day in court. In *Science and creationism*. Edited by A. Montagu, 311-342. New York: Oxford University Press.
Russell, B. 1926. *Our knowledge of the external World.* London: Allen & Unwin.
———. 1945. *A history of western philosophy.* New York: Simon & Schuster.
———. 1948. *Human knowledge: Its scope and limits.* New York: Simon & Schuster.
———. 1965. On induction. In *A modern introduction to philosophy*. Edited by P. Edwards & A. Pap, 142-147. New York: Collier-Macmillan.
Ryle, G. 1949. *The concept of mind.* London: Hutchinson.
Salisbury, F. B. 1971. Doubts about the modern synthesis theory of evolution. *American Biology Teacher*, 33: 335-338.
Sartre, J. P. 1947. *Existentialism.* New York: Philosophical Library.

Sartre, J. P. 1955. Existentialism. In *The age of analysis*. Edited by M. White, 116-135. New York: Mentor.

———. 1956. *Being and nothingness: An essay on phenomenological ontology*. Translated by H. Barnes. New York: Citadel.

Sattler, J. 1988. *Assessment of children*. San Diego State University, San Diego: Sattler.

Schachtel, E. G. 1959. *Metamorphosis*. New York: Basic Books.

Schelling, F. W. 1845. *The philosophy of art*. Translated by A. Johnson. London: Chapman.

Schlick, M. 1953. Philosophy of organic life. In *Readings in the philosophy of science*. Edited by H. Feigl & M. Brodbeck, 523-526. New York: Appleton-Century-Crofts.

———. 1962. *Problems of ethics*. New York: Dover.

Schopenhauer, A. 1966. *The world as will and representation*. Vol. I. Translated by E. Payne. New York: Dover.

Schrodinger, E. 1953. What is matter? *Scientific American*, 188(3): 52-57.

———. 1962. *What is life?* Cambridge: Cambridge University Press.

Science and the citizen. 1980. *Scientific American*, 243(3): 90-98.

Scott, J.P. 1973. Hostility and aggression. In *The handbook of general psychology*. Edited by B. Wolman, 707-719. Englewood Cliffs, NJ: Prentice Hall.

Shevrin, H. & Dickman, S. 1980. The psychological unconscious: A necessary assumption for all psychological theory? *American Psychologist*, 35:421-434.

Shostrom, E. L., producer & director. 1965. Three approaches to psychotherapy No. 1 - Dr. Carl Rogers [Film]. Santa Anna: Psychological Films.

Silvern, L. C. 1971. *Systems engineering of education I: The evolution of systems thinking in education*. Los Angeles: Education and Training Consultants.

Simon, M. A. 1971. *The matter of life*. New Haven: Yale University Press.

Simpson, G. G. 1967. *The meaning of evolution*. New Haven: Yale University Press.

Sinnott, E. W. 1958. *Matter, mind, and man*. London: Allen & Unwin.

Skinner, B. F. 1953. *Science and human behavior*. New York: Macmillan.

———. 1961. *Cumulative record*. New York: Appleton-Century-Crofts.

———. 1971. *Beyond freedom and dignity*. New York: Knopf.

———. 1974. *About behaviorism*. New York: Alfred A. Knopf.

Skyrms, B. 1967. The explication of "X knows that P." *The Journal of Philosophy*, 64(12): 373-589.

Smart, J. J. C. 1959. Sensation and brain processes. *Philosophical Review*, 68: 141-156.

Smith, A. 1968. *The body*. New York: Walker.

Smith, J. M. 1969. The status of neo-Darwinism. In *Towards a theoretical biology: 2. Sketches*. Edited by C. H. Waddington, 82-89. Chicago: Aldine.

Smuts, J. C. 1926. *Holism and evolution*. New York: Macmillan.

Smythies, J. R. 1965. The representative theory of perception. In *Brain and mind*. Edited by J. R. Smythies, 241-257. London: Routledge & Kegan Paul.
Soghoian, R. J. 1979. *The ethics of G. E. Moore and David Hume*. Washington, D.C.: University Press of America.
Sperry, R. 1975, August 9. Left-brain, right-brain. *Saturday Review*, 30-33.
Spruch, G. M. 1974. *The ubiquitous atom*. New York: Scribner.
Staats, A. W. 1968. *Learning, language, and cognition*. New York: Holt, Rinehart & Winston.
Stanley, S. 1981. *The new evolutionary timetable: Fossils, genes, and the origin of species*. New York: Basic Books.
Stapp, H. 1971. S matrix interpretation of quantum theory. *Physical Review*, 36: 1303-1320.
Stebbins, G. & Ayala F. 1985. The Evolution of Darwinism. *Scientific American*, 193(1): 77-82.
Stent, G. S. 1984. Scientific creationism: Nemesis of sociobiology. In *Science and creationism*. Edited by A. Montagu, 136-141. New York: Oxford University Press.
Stroud, B. 1977. *Hume*. London: Routledge & Kegan Paul.
Szent-Gyorgyi, A. 1972. *Biology today*. DelMar, CA: Community Research Machines, Painter.
Taylor, I. 1983. Motivation. In *The encyclopedic dictionary of psychology*. Edited by R. Harre & R. Lamb, 403. Cambridge: Massachusetts Institute of Technology Press.
Taylor, R. 1950. Purposeful and non-purposeful behavior: A rejoinder. *Philosophy of Science*, 17: 317-332.
The Personnel & Guidance Journal. 1971. The American Personnel & Guidance Association. 50(4).
Thom, R. 1968. Comments: The basic ideas of biology. In *Towards a theoretical biology: 1. Prolegomena*. Edited by C. H. Waddington, 32-41. Chicago: Aldine.
Thomas, L. 1974. *The lives of a cell*. New York: Viking.
Thomsen, D. 1987, October 3. New clues to the fifth force and its source. *Science News*, 212.
Thorndike, E. L. 1911. *Animal intelligence*. New York: Macmillan.
Thorpe, W. H. 1978. *Purpose in a world of chance*. London: Oxford University Press.
Tinbergen, N. 1951. *The study of instinct*. London: Oxford University Press.
Titchener, E. 1905. *Experimental psychology*. New York: Macmillan.
Toch, H. 1969. *Violent men*. Chicago: Aldine.
Trivers, R. L. 1971. The evolution of reciprocal altruism. *Quarterly Review of Biology*, 46(4): 35-57.
Tryon, E. 1989. Cosmic inflation. In *Encyclopedia of astronomy and astrophysics*.

Edited by R. Meyers, 123-158. San Diego: Academic Press.
Unger, P. 1968. An analysis of factual knowledge. *The Journal of Philosophy*, 65(6): 157-170.
Waddington, C. H. 1968a. The basic ideas of biology. In *Towards a theoretical biology: 1. Prolegomena*. Edited by C. H. Waddington, 1-31. Chicago: Aldine.
———. 1968b. Cause and effect in biology. In *Towards a theoretical biology: 1 Prolegomena*. Edited by C. H. Waddington, 42-56. Chicago: Aldine.
———. 1968c. Preface. In *Towards a theoretical biology: 1. Prolegomena*. Edited by C. H. Waddington, i-ii. Chicago: Aldine.
———. 1968d. Theoretical biology and molecular biology. In *Towards a Theoretical biology: 1. Prolegomena*. Edited by C. H. Waddington, 103-108. Chicago: Aldine.
———. 1969. Sketch of the second Serbelloni symposium. In *Towards a theoretical biology: 2. Sketches*. Edited by C. H. Waddingon, 1-9. Chicago: Aldine.
Wald, G. 1979. The origin of life. *Life: Origin and evolution*. Readings from Scientific American, 47-56. San Francisco: W. H. Freeman.
Wallace, A. R. 1895. *Natural selection and tropical nature: Essays on descriptive and theoretical biology*. London: Macmillan.
Washburn, S. J. 1976. Untitled. *American Psychologist*, 31(5): 353-355.
———. 1978. Human behavior and the behavior of other animals. *American Psychologist*, 33, 405-418.
Watson, J. B. 1930. *Behaviorism*. New York: Norton.
Weinberg, P. 1985. The molecules of Life. *Scientific American*, 253(4): 48-57.
Weiss, E. 1960. *The structure and dynamics of the human mind*. New York: Grune & Stratton.
Weiss, P. 1969. The living system: Determinism stratified. In *Beyond reductionism*. Edited by A. Koestler & J. R. Smythies, 3-55. London: Hutchinson.
Weiss, R. 1988, Jan. 16. Test Tube toxicology. *Science News*, 36-37.
Weisz, P. 1967. *The science of biology*. New York: McGraw-Hill.
Werner, H. & Wapner, S. 1952. Toward a general theory of perception. *Psychological Review*, 59: 324-38.
White, A. 1968. *Nobody Wanted War*. New York: Doubleday.
White, R. W. 1959. Motivation reconsidered: The concept of competence. *Psychological Review*, 66(5): 297-329.
Whitehead, A. L. 1929. *Process and reality*. New York: Macmillan.
Wiener, N. 1948. *Cybernetics*. New York: Wiley.
Wigner, E. ed. 1961. The probability of the existence of a self-reproducing unit. In *The logic of personal knowledge*. 231-238. London: Rutledge & Kegan Paul.
Wild, J. 1966. *The challenge of existentialism*. Bloomington: Indiana University Press.
Williams, J. 1961. *Islam*. New York: Braziller.

Wilson, E. O. 1975. *Sociobiology: The new synthesis*. Cambridge, MA: Belknap.
Wilson, J. R., ed. 1964. *The mind*. New York: Time.
Wolman, B. 1973. Concerning psychology and the psychology of science. In *The handbook of general psychology*. Edited by B. Wolman, 22-48. Englewood Cliffs, NJ: Prentice Hall.
Wonderly, D. M. 1964. The evolution of theories concerning the creative process. *The Gifted Child Quarterly*, 8(1): 77-84.
———. 1971. Training Child Development Specialists. *Experiments in mental health training: Project summaries*, Chevy Chase, 115-117. Maryland: National Institute of Mental Health.
———. 1975. Training Child Development Specialists. In *Explorations in mental health training: Project summaries*. Edited by R. Simon, S. Silverstein & B. Shriver, 96-97. Rockville, MD: National Institute of Mental Health.
———. 1979. Primary prevention in school psychology: Past, present, and proposed future. *The Child Study Journal*, 9: 163-179.
———. 1985. *Prevention: Systems intervention. A model for the 21st century*. Available from PSI Associates, Inc. Twinsburg, Ohio 44087.
———. 1987. The behavior adjustment paradigm. *School Psychology International*, 9: 95-103.
Wonderly, D. M. & Jessie, S. C. 1974. Prevention: Systems Intervention PSI—An alternative model for school psychology. *The School Psychology Digest*, 3(4): 47-61.
Wonderly, D. M. & Kupfersmid, J. 1980. Promoting postconventional morality: The adequacy of Kohlberg's aim. *Adolescence*, 59: 609-631.
———. 1981. Moral maturity as an avenue to mental health: Another blind alley. *Child Study Journal*, 10: 285-296.
———. 1982. Disequilibrium as a hypothetical construct in Kohlbergian theory. *Child Study Journal*, 11: 121-127.
Wonderly, D. M. & Rosenberg, S. 1987. Understanding aggression in treating emotionally disturbed youths. *Child and Youth Services*, 10(1): 29-48.
Woodworth, R. 1918. *Dynamic psychology*. New York: Columbia University Press.
Wundt, W. 1874. *Principles of physiological psychology*. London: Macmillan.
Wynne-Edwards, V. C. 1962. *Animal dispersion in relation to social behavior*. New York: Hafner.
Yarrow, M. R., Scott, P. M. & Waxler, C. Z. 1973. Learning concern for others. *Developmental Psychology*, 8: 240-260.
Young, L. B., ed. 1965. *The mystery of matter*. New York: Oxford University Press.
Young, P. T. ed. 1936. *Motivation of behavior*. New York: Wiley.
———. 1973. Feeling and emotion. In *The handbook of general psychology*. Edited by B. Wolman, 749-771. Englewood Cliffs, NJ: Prentice Hall.
Zajonc, R. B. 1984. On the primacy of affect. *American Psychologist*, 39: 117-123.
Zukav, G. 1979. *The dancing Wu Li masters*. New York: Bantam.

Index

A
Abrig, J., 486, 487
accident, 224
Adler, A., 109, 202
aesthetics, 236–238; defined, 237
affect, 166–168; and belief, 169; and cognition, 167–168; defined, 166; as mental process, 166–168
agency, 87-94
agent, 87; characteristics of, 88; phenotype as, 87
aggression, 366–373, 464–465; as behavioral, 366; defined, 366; and destructiveness, 367–369; as positive, 366, 369; and psychoanalysis, 367
Albee, G., 479
Alexander, S., 143
Allee, W. C., 24
Allport, G., 409
altruism, 92, 94, 246; and hypocrisy, 247; and sociobiology, 247
Ambrose, E. J., 21
analytic dynamism and the self, 303-306
Anaxagoras, 132
anger, 273, 274
Anselm, Saint, 41
anxiety, 263, 269, 296, 423; free floating, 263, 423
apathy, 263
appestats, 208
appetite, 196
Aquinas, T., 4
Ardrey, R., 350
Aristotle, 4, 40, 239, 408
Arnold, M. B., 262
artificial systems, 119
Ashby, R., 43, 44, 157

Asimov, I., 26
assertiveness, 366, 367
attention altering, 413
Augustine, Saint, 4
Aurelius, M., 55
aversion, 271
Ayer, A. J., 29, 155, 169, 170, 176, 177, 178, 189, 229, 251

B
Balzac, H., 515
Barash, D., 244
Barnes, W. H. F., 216
Barnett, L., 17, 43
Beach, F. A., 200
Beck, W. S., 17, 79, 80, 81
being, existential, 50
behavior, 379–401; and anticipatory affect, 327; characteristics, 396–399; classes, 383–384; defined, 382, 480; and deliberative sequence, 381–383; as "good," 351; habituated, 397; incident, 383; instinctive, 386, 388–390; instrumental. 268, 383, 384, 449, 450; intrinsic, 268, 383, 450–452; learned, 393–395; and morality, 350–354; pattern, 383; perverse, 469–471; and rationality, 389; sequence, 383; unmotivated, 326, 396
Behavior Adjustment Paradigm, 448-452
behavior/belief alteration, 445–473; assessing emotional states, 458–460; behavior adjustment paradigm, 448–453; behavior elements, 447, 448; deviant behavior types, 461, 462; diagnosis/treatment examples, 462–473; the diagnostic

process 453–457; and drug abuse, 467–471; emotional elements, 446, 447; employing the BAP, 457, 458
behavioral event, 399, 400
behavioral progression, 400
belief, 153, 168–179; as affect, 168, 172; defined, 168; and facts, 169; and feeling, 169; and knowledge, 169–179; as positive, 490; schismatic, 489–499; and self, 304–306; and truth, 229
Beloff, J., 160
Benner, D., 330
Bergquist, E. H., 141
Bergson, H., 7
Berkeley, G., 41, 44
Berrien, F. K., 62
Bertalanffy, L. von, 15, 21, 62
Bessey, C. E., 53
Binswanger, L., 10
biomass, 55
Bohm, D., 15, 23, 56, 71
Bosley, H., 366, 367, 380
Brain, L., 156
Brentano, F. C., 10, 160
Bridgman, P., 365
Brill, A. A., 328
Broad, C. D., 215
Brown, J. S., 207, 313, 321, 322
Bruner, J. S., 167, 218
Buckley, W. F., 492
Bugelski, B. R., 5
Bugental, J. F., 146
Butler, J., 203-204

C
Cairns-Smith, A. G., 25, 80, 89, 90
Cannon, W. B., 257
caprice, 224, 358
Casti, J., 37
categorical imperative, 240
chagrin, 275

chance, 358
Chardin, P., 5, 12, 72, 109, 143
Chein, I., 256, 327
Chisholm, R., 171
Christian, J., 105
clienthood, 425
clients, 484-487; children as, 484; parents as, 486-487; professionals as, 484-486
Cofer, C. N., 354
cognition, 163–165; and affect, 167, 168; defined, 164; as mental processing, 163–165
communication, 135; and error, 135
conception/conceptualization, 153, 165; of desires, 215; as mental processing, 165; of perception, 215
concepts, 153
conflict, 296–300
conscience, 330
consciousness, 144, 327–328; and the self, 302
contempt, 275–276
Corsini, R. J., 163
costs, 259
counseling, 425–441; the counseling process, 432–434; and counselor characteristics, 431–432; defined, 430; diagnostic principles, 425–426; and eclecticism, 427; and forgiveness, 427; intervention caveats, 426–427; Madeline G, 436–440; and manipulation, 429; and moral alternatives, 435; and personal feelings, 433–434; and reality, 430; setting the stage, 427–430; the therapeutic theater, 434–436; transference, 429, and unconditional positive regard, 428
Coulter, J., 159, 160
creationism, 3, 20, 22, 26
creativity, 58, 186

Cuffey, R. J., 21
cybernetics, 111, 124; and living beings, 134–138; and purpose, 111-112

D
Darwin, C., 21, 23, 24, 243
Dawkins, R., 54, 72, 78, 79, 90, 246
DeCharms, R., 320
decisions, 379–380
Deese, J., 165
defense mechanisms, 412–415; as belief, 415–421; the holarchic interpretation, 414
DeGreen, K., 62
deliberate systems, 119-120
deliberation, 382; and freedom, 357
deliberative sequence, 381-383
Democritus, 13, 72, 132
denial, 412–413
Descartes, R., 155, 179, 327, 357
desires, 193–214; assertive, 198–206; defined, 193; and drives, 194; as emergent, 348; hunger, 199–200; integrity, 207; as limited, 347–350; and mind, 194–197; the negative aspect, 194–197; pleasure, 206; as positive, 194; potency, 202–203; power, 205–206; protective, 206–208; safety, 207–208; self-actualization, 348; sex, 200–202; and sin, 195; stimulation, 203–205; transcendent, 208–209; types, 197–210
deprivation, 324
determination, 380
determinism, 356–363; and freedom, 360; and responsibility, 363–365
Deutsch, M., 185
DeVore, I., 54
Dewey, J., 205
diagnostic principle, 426-427

discipline, 503–505; defined, 503
displacement, 413
DNA, 78, 80, 87; selfish, 247
Dobzhansky, T., 5, 20, 55, 103, 117, 119, 121
dominant emotion, 260; and freedom, 356–363
drapetomania, 305, 411
dreams, 337–339
Dreyfus, H., 187
Driesch, H., 114
drive, 140–142; acquired, 322; defined, 141; and desire, 194, 348–349; as knowledge, 141; learned, 321–322; and motivation, 141, 263; and primitive needs, 142
drug abuse, 467-471
Ducasse, C. J., 160

E
Ebel, R. L., 323
Eccles, J., 26, 27, 328
eclecticism, 427
Eddington, A. S., 121
Edwards, P., 356
effectance, 205
ego, 303, 332–332; and drives, 349; and the self, 295
ego feeling, 291
Einstein, A., 252
Eiseley, L., 8
Eisenberger, R., 507
elan locomotive, 17
elan vital, 17, 134
Eldredge, N., 36
Ellenberger, H. F., 354
Elliot, H., 102, 244
Ellington, J. W., 240
embarrassment, 273
emergence, 16; and desire, 348; and finalism, 73; and life, 73–74; and reductionism, 73; and the self, 348

Emerson, R. W., 234
Empedocles, 13
emotion, 256–285; anger, 273–274; anticipatory, 265, 266, 279, 323, 381, 390; anxiety, 269, 298; apathy, 263; attitudes, 276–283; aversion, 271; and capacity/opportunity, 259; chagrin, 275; and cognition, 256–257; consummatory, 265, 266, 279, 323, 381, 390; contempt, 275–276; as contingent, 262; defined, 262; as disturbed state, 256; dominant, 260, 449; embarrassment, 273; emergency theory, 257; excitation, 283; as facilitative, 257; fear, 271–272; as feeling state, 256–257; frustration, 269–270; guilt, 272–273, 298–299; hate, 263; hope, 279–283; jealousy, 272; love, 263, 276–279; negative, 265; parameters, 276–283; positive, 266–268; as private fact, 256; rage, 274; and satisfaction, 258, 268, 326, 397; and the self, 296–300; shame, 273; surprise, 270–271; will, 262; wish, 280–283
emotional health, 405–421; as becoming, 410; defined, 407; and happiness, 408; the "happy rapist," 410–411; holarchic model, 406–408; and self actualization, 409
emotional maladjustment, 421–425; alienation, 424–425; anxiety, 423; impotence, 423
empathy, 270
Engel, F. M., 9
entity, 52–54
entropy, 30, 41, 57; and systems, 63
epigenetic space, 85–86
epistemics of life, 138–149
epistemology, 42, 129–149
Erikson, E., 332, 366

essence, 40–41
evaluation, 235–249; aesthetics, 236–238; measurement, 230–236; morality, 238–249
evolution, 19–27; falsification, 21; objections, 20–24; odds against, 25; principles, 20
excitation, 283
existence, 40, 42–45, 52; corporeal, 45; emergence of organic, 73–74
existential being, 50
existentialism, 9-13, 161
experience and knowledge, 178
Eysenck, H., 320

F
fact, 225–229; and belief, 169; and emotion, 256; perceptual, 227; private, 230; and value, 498
fallibilist, 176
fantasy formation, 413
Farris, S., 36
fear, 271–272; as drive, 322; as response, 322
Federn, P., 332
feedback, 224
Feibleman, J., 42
Feigl, H., 159, 160, 179
Feinberg, G., 66
Fernald, L. D., 256
Feynman, R., 29
Fichte, J. G., 327
finalism, 3–7
Flake-Hobson, C., 61
Flexner, S., 164, 380
Fodor, J., 160
Forem, J., 408
freedom, 356–363; defined, 358; and deliberation, 357; and determinism, 360; and dominant emotion, 357–363
Friedrich, C., 252

Freud, A., 332, 368
Freud, S., 159, 225, 292, 306, 328–330, 349, 351, 352, 353, 355, 367, 414
Fromm, E., 202, 366, 369, 371
frustration, 269
Fuller, R., 81
Funk, I., 504

G

gene, 54; as blueprint, 54; and gene pools, 91, 92; and ideas, 54; and populations, 54; and purpose, 107; and "rising above," 245–246, 349; selfish, 247
gene pool, 53; and genes, 91, 92; and reality, 64, 69, 90
genotype, 35, 84
Gerard, L. W., 57
gestalt principles, 215, 218
Gettier, E., 171
Gewirth, A., 491
Ghiselin, M. T., 247, 248
Gibson, J., 218
Glasser, W., 428
Goldman, A., 148, 171
Goldstein, K., 203, 409
Gould, S. J., 20, 21, 22
Gray, W., 61
Greeley, A. M., 221
Greene, T. M., 90
Grene, M., 90
Gribbin, J., 67, 68
Grimsley, R., 377
Grobstein, C., 106, 118
Grusec, J. E., 246
guilt, 272–273, 298–299

H

habit, 397
Hall, C., 321, 340, 349
Halstead, B., 26
Hamilton, W., 245
Harriman, P. L., 241, 256, 366, 504
Harris, H., iii
Hass, H., 368
Hatt, H., 104
hate, 263
Hawking, S., 44
Hayes, J., 326
Hebb, D. O., 218, 274, 316, 319, 320, 386
Hegel, G. W., 109, 217, 234
Heisenberg, W., 44
Hempel, C., 97
Herbart, J., 214, 215
Hergenbahn, B. R., 165
Hesse, M., 35
Hicks, G. D., 216
Hilgard, E., 7, 256
Hobson, A., 344
Hoffman, M. L., 246, 247
Hofstadter, D., 16
holarchy 75–78; defined, 76; and motivation, 314–317; the position restated, 500–503
holism, 27
holon, 55–61; defined, 57; and inorganic matter, 58–59; and organic matter, 76; and parts, 56–60; and wholes, 56–60
holonic, 57
Holton, G., 151
homeorhesis, 72
homosexuality, 353, 395
homeostasis, 207
hope, 279–283; defined, 279
Hospers, J., 170, 303
hostility, 373, 466–477; defined, 373
Hoyle, F., 25
Hudson, W. D., 350
Hull, C. L., 141, 319, 321
Hume, D., 169, 308, 356
hunger, 199–200

Hunt, J. McV., 349
Husserl, E., 10, 178
Hutcheson, F., 240
Huxley, J. S., 6, 7, 17, 22, 107
Huxley, T. E., 19

I
id, 303, 328–329
idealism, 44; dogmatic, 44; platonic, 45, 61
ideas, 169; as contingent, 198; as impressions, 169; as perceptions, 169
identification, 293–294
identity, 300–303
impotence, 423
incentive, 213
incest, 352
individual, 60, 120, 136; without species, 83
information, 129–130; and knowledge, 131, 134
instance, 60; and parts, 60; and planets, 63
instinct, 352, 385–391; and emotion, 387–388
instinctive behavior, 391-398
instinctive knowledge, 385-391
intelligence, 148–149; artificial, 187; defined, 148; as innate, 185; as learned, 185; as mental 185–187
integrity, 207; as contingent, 198
interactionism, 309
interiority, 291
introjection, 413
intuition, 395
isolation, 413

J
James, Saint, 195
James, W., 214, 215, 216, 257, 291, 356
Janis, I., 319,

Jaynes, J., 398
jealousy, 272
Jones, D., 19
judgment, 232–234; defined, 232; and freedom, 362; relational, 233–234

K
Kagan, J., 306, 326, 396
Kalish, H., 321
Kant, I., 44, 103, 110, 116, 195, 217, 234, 240, 354, 494
Kelly, G. A., 323
Kierkegaard, S., 11, 30, 269
Kilpatrick, F. P., 221
King, F., 515
Kitcher, P., 245, 349, 350, 351
Klausmeier, H., 165
Klein, M., 368
knowing, 133; and experiencing, 133; and having knowledge, 174
knowledge, 131–134; acquaintance, 160, 228; descriptive, 160, 228; and drive, 141; epistemics of life, 158-149; and information, 131–134; innate, 131; and inorganic matter, 132–134; instinctive, 390–393; as learned, 131, 499–500; and perception, 143; strong and weak, 169
Koestler, A., 13, 17, 28, 57, 74, 76, 103, 110, 284, 359, 360, 372, 500
Kohlberg, L., 186, 241
Kohut, H., 328, 329, 330, 335
Krech, D., 218

L
Lachman, R., 163
Lacey, A., 65
Lange, O., 56
Lasch, C., 241, 277
Laszlo, E., 119
Lawrence, D. H., 291

Lazarus, R., 256, 257
Leakey, R., 245, 371
Leibnitz, 40, 41
learning, 129, 146–148, 386; and belief, 182; conceptual, 183; defined, 146; mental, 179–184; as necessary, 180; and relearning, 182; as a state of being, 179–183
Leeper, R., 257
Lerner, A., 365
Leucippus, 45
Lewin, K., 332
Lewontin, R., 36
libido, 304
life, 69–95; biochemical elements, 78–79; chicken or egg?, 79–84; clay crystals, 80; defined, 70; directionality, 72; earliest manifestations, 79–84; emergence, 73–74; function, 71; genetic process, 71; as holarchic, 75–78; irritability, 71; metabolism, 71; organization, 72; phenotype as agent, 87–95; plan and pattern, 84–87; reproduction, 71; structure, 71; and symmetry, 70
Locke, J., 132, 169, 205, 306, 307, 491
Lorenz, K., 371
Lyons, A., 493
love, 263, 276–279; agape, 276; amour, 276; platonic, 277; and sex, 278

M
Machiavelli, N., 205
MacKay, D. M., 28, 187
MacLean, P., 284
Madeline G., 436-440
Madsen, K. B., 197, 317
Magill, J., 28, 29
Malcolm, J., 353
Malcolm, N., 171
Mann, T., xxi

Margalef, R., 8
Maslow, A., 198, 203, 348, 351, 408, 409
Masson, J. M., 353
Matson, F. W., 29
Mausner, B., 19
May, R., 10, 11, 80
Mayr, E., 19, 21, 23, 53, 54, 72, 73, 107–109
McClelland, D. C., 205–206, 320, 321, 419
McDougall, W., 197, 315, 385
McFarland, D., 326
meaning, 50–55, 64; and analysis, 51; definitional, 51;
measurement, 230–231
mechanism, 13–19; theological, 6
Medewar, R., 21
Menninger, K., 368
mental components, 223–249; aesthetics, 236–238; facts, 225–229; judgments, 231–234; morality, 238–250; reason, 234–235
mental constituents, 163–179; affect, 166–168; belief, 168–179; cognition, 163–165; conception/conceptualization, 165
mental health, 406
mental intelligence, 185–187
mental learning, 179-184
Merleau-Ponty, M., 11, 145
mental processing, 162–163; higher, 188
metascience, 3–13; finalism, 3–7; vitalism, 7–9
mind, 153–192; in action, 158; defined, 153; and desires, 194–197; dualism, 159; existentialism, 9–13, 161; identity hypothesists, 160; as parameter of knowledge state, 158; and perception, 214–219; and philosophies, 155–156; and

psychobiology, 341; unique characteristics, 157
Miles, M., 356–357
Miller, K. R., 26
Miller, N. E., 321, 322
Milne, A. J., 251, 363
Montagu, A., 295
Moore, G. E., 51, 216, 351, 355
morality, 235–239; and behavior, 350–351; defined, 238; and desire, 239; "go" signals, 295; learned aspect, 241; and rational appraisal, 238, 241; and reason, 355; and sociobiology, 243–249; and transcendence, 239
Morgan, C. T., 386
Morris, D., 9
Morris, H. M., 36, 349–350
Moser, L., 277
motivation, 314–375; adient, 204; applied behavioral analysis, 321–327; cognate factors, 347–375; defined, 315; and drive, 263; holarchic model, 314–317, 337–340; psychoanalytic view, 328–334; superego, 333
motive, 317; non-drive based, 349; and wish, 319
Moustakas, C., 203
Mueller, A., 408
multiple personality, 414
Munroe, R., 368

N
Nagel, E., 15, 109, 110, 117
Nagele, R., 344
Nageli, K. von., 114
narcissism, 277
natural rights, 491–498; equal treatment, 497–498; historical perspective, 493–495; self indulgence, 495–497

needs, 142, 210–211; and desires, 211–214; and emotion, 261; instinctive, 210; learned, 210; primitive, 142
negentropy, 30, 48, 57
net want/net cost, 362, 380–381
Nietzsche, F., 7, 24, 25, 110, 205, 328, 409
nominalism, 44
Norman, D., 167
Nowell-Smith, P., 303

O
oedipus complex, 351–354
ontological argument, 4
Omahen, S., 516
Oparin, A. I., 72, 78
org, 57
organicism, 27–28, 31
Ouspensky, P. D., 18, 29, 262

P
pain, 322–323
Pap, A., 157
part, 52; as free of whole, 52, 359; and instance, 60; planet as, 62
particle, as real, 44; as virtual, 44
particularism, 45–46
Pattee, H. H., 71
Patterson, C. H., 483
Pauling, L., 14
Pears, D. F., 49-50
Penelhum, T., 155
perception, 43, 142–146; complex primitive, 145–146; as contingent, 198, 206–207; defined, 142; and ideas, 169; and inorganic matter, 43; as knowledge, 143; and mind, 214–219; multiple relation theory, 216; and quantum theory, 218; representative theory, 218–219; and sensation, 216; simple primitive, 145

perceptual set, 456
peripheral thinking, 433
Perkins, D., 185
personality, 203
Pfaff, D., 140
Peters, R., 326
phenomenology, 9–13
phenotype, 54, 69, 79, 84
philosophy, existential, 9–13; holistic, 27–28; idealist, 44; and mind, 155–156; nominalist, 44; organismic, 55; particularist, 45–46
Piaget, J., 186
Plato, 155, 234
pleasure, 206
Polanyi, K., 27, 28, 31, 32
populations, 53; and genes, 54; and species, 53–54
Portmann, A., 291
positivism, 18
potency, 202–203
power, 205–206; defined, 205; and exhilaration, 263; as spontaneous, 198
pragnanz, 146
preconscious, 158–159; psychoanalytic, 331–332
pre-mind, 139; defined, 139; and information processing, 139
Prigogine, I., 30
primary prevention, 477–510; children's rights, 483–484; coherence, 487–488; parent's rights, 486–487; quality, 488–489; responsibility, 482–483; right to decide, 483–487; rights of professionals, 484–486; schismatic beliefs, 489–503
proof, 229–230; defined, 229; and private facts, 230
projection, 413
propositions, 177; and truth, 177

protective desires, 206–208
protobionts, 78
protoplasm, 51
PSI (prevention/systems intervention), 479
purpose, 101–126; and biology, 105–108; and the church, 108; and cybernetics, 111–112; defined, 114; deliberate systems, 119–121; and deliberation, 115, 124; and desire, 112; and directionality, 115; evidence, 112–114; and genes, 107; and machines, 104; and mechanics, 123–125; as mental, 103–104; and organic forms, 115; and part subservience, 113, 115; and philosophy, 109–110; and science, 102, 109–110; and self interest in children, 125; and sociobiology, 124; the target, 116; the ultimate goal, 121–123
Putnam, H., 189

Q
quantum theory, 29; and perception, 218
Quinton, A., 160

R
races and species, 117
rage, 274
Rank, O., 202
Rapaport, A., 61, 198
rationalization, 413
Rawls, J., 363
reaction formation, 413
realists, 44; strict, 48
reality, 45–50; defined, 50, 54, 430
reason, 234–235; and behavior, 354–355; and desire, 239; and humans, 354; and morality, 355; and rationality, 234

reductionism, 13–19, 58; and emergence, 73
reflex, 85, 387–388
regression, 413, 416
Reid, T., 240, 309
Reiss, B. F., 394
repression, 412, 416
responsibility, 508–510; of schools, 482–487
Restak, R. M., 164, 307, 326, 331
Riesman, D., 409
RNA, 75, 87
Rochlin, G., 371
Rogers, C. R., 351, 409, 410, 428, 429
Root-Bernstein, R., 20
Rose, S., 9, 159
Rosen, C., 21
Rosenblueth, A., 112
Rousseau, J. J., 363
Roth, M. D., 170
Royce, J., 291
Runes, D., 40, 103, 241, 256
Ruse, M., 73
Russell, B., 169, 205, 215, 309
Ryle, G., 155, 159, 170, 177–178, 307, 308

S
sadism, 373–374
safety, 207–208; as contingent, 198
Salisbury, F. B., 25
Sartre, J. P., 10, 45, 110, 202, 292, 327
satiation, 324
satisfaction, 258, 268, 326, 397
Sattler, J., 443
Schachtel, E. G., 348
Schelling, F. W., 234–235
Schiller, F., 235
schismatic beliefs, 489–499, 503
Schlick, M., 102, 356
Schopenhauer, A., 351
Schrodinger, E., 17, 18, 72

Science, 13–19
Scott, J. P., 385
self, 289–310; and belief, 304–306; and consciousness, 302; continuity, 306–307; and ego, 295; and emotion, 296–300; and identity, 300–303; as independent, 307–310; and interactionism, 309; as judge, 294; as object, 292; parameters, 289–296; as part, 292; as result, 290; and species, 291; and the unconscious, 303
self actualization, 203, 348
selfish genes, 247
self sacrifice, 93–94, 203; and consciousness, 302
shame, 273
Shaftsbury, 235
skepticism, 176
sensa, 215
sensation, 143
sex, 200-202
Shevrin, H., 162, 330
Silvern, L. C., 164
Simon, M. A., 17, 79
Sinnott, E. W., 6
Skinner, B. F., 303, 323, 324, 326, 340
Skyrms, B., 171
Smart, J. J. C., 160
Smith, A., 9
Smith, J. M., 93
Smuts, J. C., 27
Smythies, J. R., 176
sociobiology, 25; and altruism, 247; and morality, 243–249; and purpose, 124
species, 55; homo sapiens, 122; and populations, 53–54; and races, 117; and reality, 53, 64; semi-, 242; sibling, 242; super, 242
Sperry, R., 331, 341
Spinoza, B., 40, 491

Spruch, G. M., 65
Staats, A. W., 185
Stanley, S., 36
Stapp, H., 52
Stebbins, G., 80
Stent, G. S., 249
stimulation, 203–205
Storr, A., 350
Stroud, B., 170
sublimation, 413–414
substance, 40–42, 142; and epistemology, 42; and essence, 40; partness, 42; wholeness, 42
superego, (psychoanalytic interpretation); 303, 332; and morality, 333
superluminal speed, 44
surprise, 270–271
symmetry, 70
systems, 61–64; artificial, 119; defined, 62; deliberate, 63, 119; and directionality, 63, 64; and entropy, 63; natural inorganic, 63; natural organic, 63; open, 63
Szent-Gyorgyi, A., 32

T
taxis, 85, 387–388, 391
Taylor, I., 326
Taylor, R., 112
tension, 265
tension reduction theory, 264
therapeutic theater, 434-436
Thom, R., 90
Thomas, L., 247
Thomsen, D., 65
Thorndike, E. L., 141, 185
Thorpe, W. H., 15
Tinbergen, N., 386
Titchener, E., 386
Toch, H., 373
transcendence, 208–209; as contingent, 198

transference, 429
Trivers, R. L., 245
truth, 229; and belief, 229; defined, 229; as existential, 175; and phenomenology, 179; and propositions, 177
Tryon, E., 131

U
unconscious, 328–331; and continuity, 334; as dynamic, 339; holarchic interpretation, 334–340; psychoanalytic interpretation, 328–331; and psychobiology, 331; and the self, 303
Unger, P., 171
universals, 45, 55

V
value, 236; and fact, 498
VanValen, S., 80
vitalism, 7–9, 31–32

W
Waddington, C. H., 20, 71, 72, 93, 102
Wald, G., 25, 78
want, 258; and desire, 258; and need, 258
Washburn, S. J., 248, 249, 325
Watson, J. B., 321
Weinberg, P., 80
Weiss, E., 291, 329, 333, 412
Weiss, P., 71
Weisz, P., 71
Werner, H., 218
White, R. W., 195, 205–206, 367
Whitehead, A. L., 143
whole, 52, 60; as free of parts, 52, 359
Wiener, N., 56, 103, 119
Wigner, E. P., 25
Wild, J., 10, 109
will, 262; Kantian, 354; to live, 300

Wilson, E. O., 25, 54, 90–91, 107, 241, 243–245
Wilson, J. R., 388
wish, 280–283; defined, 280
Wonderly, D. M., 186
Woodworth, R., 140
work, 505–508
Wundt, W., 139
Wynne-Edwards, V. C., 106

X, Y

Yarrow, M. R., 246
Young, L. B., 65–66
Young, P. T., 141, 256

Z

Zajonc, R. B., 256
Zen and sensation, 179
Zukav, G., 40, 71